ROUTLEDGE LIBRARY EDITIONS:
COLONIALISM AND IMPERIALISM

Volume 2

A HISTORY OF
THE GEORGIAN PEOPLE

A HISTORY OF THE GEORGIAN PEOPLE

From the Beginning Down to the Russian Conquest in the Nineteenth Century

W. E. D. ALLEN

Introduction by
SIR DENISON ROSS

LONDON AND NEW YORK

First published in 1932

This edition first published in 2023
by Routledge
4 Park Square, Milton Park, Abingdon, Oxon OX14 4RN

and by Routledge
605 Third Avenue, New York, NY 10158

Routledge is an imprint of the Taylor & Francis Group, an informa business

Reissued in 1971 by Routledge & Kegan Paul Ltd.

All rights reserved. No part of this book may be reprinted or reproduced or utilised in any form or by any electronic, mechanical, or other means, now known or hereafter invented, including photocopying and recording, or in any information storage or retrieval system, without permission in writing from the publishers.

Trademark notice: Product or corporate names may be trademarks or registered trademarks, and are used only for identification and explanation without intent to infringe.

British Library Cataloguing in Publication Data
A catalogue record for this book is available from the British Library

ISBN: 978-1-032-41054-8 (Set)
ISBN: 978-1-032-43688-3 (Volume 2) (hbk)
ISBN: 978-1-032-43689-0 (Volume 2) (pbk)
ISBN: 978-1-003-36843-4 (Volume 2) (ebk)

DOI: 10.4324/9781003368434

Publisher's Note
The publisher has gone to great lengths to ensure the quality of this reprint but points out that some imperfections in the original copies may be apparent.

Disclaimer
The publisher has made every effort to trace copyright holders and would welcome correspondence from those they have been unable to trace.

A HISTORY OF
THE GEORGIAN PEOPLE

"The Hereditary Sovereign and Prince, Irakli II, by the Grace of God King of Kartli, King of Kakheti, Hereditary Prince of Samtzkhé-Saatabago, Ruling Prince of Kazakh, Borchalo, Shamshadilo, Kak, Shaki, Shirvan, Prince and Lord of Ganja and Erivan"

(From the plate published in *Akti Kavkazskago Arkheographicheskago Kommisseyi*)

A HISTORY OF THE GEORGIAN PEOPLE

FROM THE BEGINNING DOWN TO
THE RUSSIAN CONQUEST IN THE
NINETEENTH CENTURY

By

W. E. D. ALLEN

INTRODUCTION BY
SIR DENISON ROSS

LONDON
ROUTLEDGE & KEGAN PAUL

First published in 1932
Reissued 1971
by Routledge & Kegan Paul Ltd.
Broadway House, 68-74 Carter Lane
London, EC4V 5EL
Printed in Great Britain by
Lowe & Brydone (Printers) Ltd., London

ISBN 0 7100 6959 6

To
MY MOTHER

"None from dim ruins, in vast deep abysm of buried ages, Muse, save thou alone, Nurseling of Memory, can revoke again."

C. M. Doughty.

"We must not lose sight of the fact that the wish to write history *scientifically* involves a contradiction. True science reaches just as far as the notions of truth and falsity have validity: this applies to mathematics and it applies also to the science of historical spade-work, viz., the collection, ordering and sifting of material. But historical vision (which only *begins* at this point) belongs to the domain of significances, in which the crucial words are not 'correct' and 'erroneous,' but 'deep' and 'shallow.' The true physicist is not deep, but *keen*: it is only when he leaves the domain of working hypotheses and brushes against the final things that he can be deep, but at this stage he is already a metaphysician. Nature is to be handled scientifically, History poetically."

"Poetry and historical study are akin."

Oswald Spengler, "*The Decline of the West.*"

CONTENTS

	PAGE
INTRODUCTION BY SIR DENISON ROSS	xvii
PREFACE	xxi

BOOK I
THE BACKGROUND

CHAP.
I. THE GEORGIAN LAND AND THE NATURE OF MOUNT CAUCASUS 3
II. BRONZE AND IRON 11
III. THE SWARMING AND THE MINGLING 21
IV. MATRIARCHS, GODS AND EMPERORS . . . 34
V. THE HISTORICAL GEOGRAPHY OF ANCIENT GEORGIA . 46

BOOK II
THE MEDIÆVAL KINGDOM

VI. ORIGINS OF THE MEDIÆVAL KINGDOM . . . 69
VII. KINGS OF THE ABKHAZ: BAGRAT III TO GIORGI II (1008–1089) 85
VIII. HEYDAY OF THE GEORGIAN KINGS: DAVID II TO TAMARA (1089–1212) 95
IX. THE MONARCHY UNDER THE MONGOLS: GIORGI IV TO DAVID VI (1212–1318) 109
X. SPLENDOURS AND MISERIES OF THE LATER GEORGIAN KINGDOM: GIORGI V TO ALEXANDER (1318–1443) 121

BOOK III
REVOLUTIONS OF THE GEORGIAN KINGDOM

XI. WARS OF THE DIVISION AND AFTERMATH (1462–1574) . 131
XII. THE REVIVAL OF ISLAMIC IMPERIALISM (1512–76) . 142
XIII. CLASH OF EMPIRES: THE EPIC OF KING SIMON (1576–1600) 151
XIV. CLASH OF EMPIRES: THE PEREGRINATIONS OF TAYMURAZ I (1586–1663) 161
XV. ABEYANCE OF THE MONARCHY: THE MUKHRANIAN VICEROYS (1656–1722) 174

CONTENTS

CHAP.		PAGE
XVI	EMPERORS ABORTIVE: PETER THE GREAT AND NADIR SHAH (1722–1747)	181
XVII	INDIAN SUMMER OF THE BAGRATIDS: TAYMURAZ II AND IRAKLI II (1747–1798)	196
XVIII	END OF THE GEORGIAN KINGS (1769–1813)	206

BOOK IV
THE PEOPLE AND THE POWER

XIX	FROM THE CLAN TO THE CLASS	221
XX	THE MIDDLE AND LOWER CLASSES IN MEDIÆVAL GEORGIA	228
XXI	THE RULING CLASSES	237
XXII	THE INSTITUTION OF *PATRONQMOBA*	250
XXIII	COURT AND ADMINISTRATION	257
XXIV	RELIGION AND THE GEORGIAN CHURCH	266
XXV	JUSTICE IN GEORGIA	275
XXVI	THE SLAVE TRADE: DECLINE OF THE POPULATION	282

BOOK V
THE LIFE OF GEORGIA

XXVII	THE ART OF MEDIÆVAL GEORGIA	291
XXVIII	GEORGIAN LITERATURE	308
XXIX	THE WEALTH AND STATE OF THE MEDIÆVAL KINGDOM	321
XXX	DOG-DAYS OF THE GEORGIANS	335
	BIBLIOGRAPHICAL AND SUPPLEMENTARY NOTES	359
	ADDENDUM	393
	INDEX	395

PLATES
(Between Pages 208 and 209)

"The Hereditary Sovereign and Prince, Irakli II, by the Grace of God ... King of Kartli, King of Kakheti, Hereditary Prince of Samtzkhé-Saatabago, Ruling Prince of Kazakh, Borchalo, Shamshadilo, Kak, Shaki, Shirvan, Prince and Lord of Ganja and Erivan" . . . . *Frontispiece*

Atskveri (Atskhur)	1
Valley of the Tskhenis-tsqali near the Fort of Laroshi in Dadianis-Svaneti	2
Ardanuchi	3
Bridge over the River Magarauli in Pshaveti	4
The three Villages of the Commune of Ushkuli in Svaneti .	5
The Meskhian Monasteries: Safar and Opisi . . .	6
Mediæval Art: The Icon of St. George of Lagani . . .	7
The Meskhian Monasteries: Khandzti and Shatberdi . . .	8
Mediæval Art: Carved wooden door in the village of Chukhuli	9
Mediæval Art: Icon of the Archangel Gabriel at Lagani . .	10
View from Mount Ugviri in Svaneti—over the valley of the Mulkhra, with the snowclad peak of Mount Mezili in the background	11
View of the Town and Fortress of Gori in the Seventeenth Century	12
King Alexander II of Kakheti	13
King Giorgi X of Kartli, and Giorgi Saakadze—"the great Moʻuravi"	14
King Rustem of Kartli (Khusraw Mirza)	15
King Taymuraz I and his Queen	16
("Taimorasse Kan, once Prince of a great part of Iberia, who, after the depopulation of the country by the Persians, went to Moscow . . . a great Prince and Defender of the Faith."—CASTELLI.)	
King Taymuraz II	17
Khevsur Tribesmen of Gudani, wearing mediæval chain-armour	18

xi

PLATES
(Between Pages 208 and 209)

Shatil: a Stronghold of the Mountaineers 19

A Mingrelian Noble of the Seventeenth Century: Wamek Lipartiani 20
> ("Vomek Lipartiani, the successor to the Prince of Mingrelia (on account of the infirmity of the latter's son), friend and benefactor of our Fathers." After Castelli. "Our Fathers" were the Théatins.)

The Georgian Royal Nuncio, Nicephorus Isbarghi (or Nicholas Erbashi) 21
> ("Nicephorus, surnamed Isbarghi, Nuncio of the King and of the Patriarch of Georgia, who went to Rome, to Urbanus VIII in 1626, to ask him to send to his country apostolic ministers."—CASTELLI.)

Khevsur Women of the Village of Lebaiskari . . . 22

Mediæval Art: Icon of the Christ of Lagani . . . 23

Mediæval Art: Icon of the Mother of God of Chukhuli . . 24

Mediæval Art: Carved wooden door from the village of Dzhakunderi 25

St. Grigol Khandzteli 26
> From the tenth-century MS. of Merchuli, designed by Charles Beazley, after the coloured reproduction of the original, published by N. Marr in *Teksti i Raziskaniya*, Book VII.

Manners and Customs 27
> "Observe the beauty of their horsemanship; how well they master their horses. It is a skill in horsemanship rarely attained. It requires great agility and presence of mind. Beginners frequently fall off the tall running horses."—(CASTELLI.)

King Alexander III of Imereti 28
> "The King of the Georgians (*sic*) is worthy of being loved and exalted by true Christians, for he is a greatly devout Christian, holding in high reverence Christ, Our Blessed Saviour, and the Holy Ghost. He has always hated and fought relentlessly the Turks, the Saracens and the Persians, enemies of Christ.
> Alexander of the dynasty of Bagratiani, otherwise the descendant of the race of David, of consanguinity with Christ, Our Saviour, a great Benefactor to our Fathers, reigning in the year 1649."
> On another drawing Castelli remarks of Alexander—"whose power is on his shoulder, for they say that he has the sign of a small crown and a cross on his shoulder". (Cf. the statement of Marco Polo that all the Kings of Georgia were "in ancient days ... born with the mark of an eagle on their shoulders".

Manners and Customs 29
> "A game the Georgian horsemen call *trocus*, beloved by all classes. (*At side*) The Georgians get used to horse-riding from childhood."
> Castelli further comments on a similar drawing—"Having arrived in Kutais, where resides the King of the Georgians (*sic*), they took me to see a game of ball, played by players mounted on horseback. This game is very popular, being played not only by the nobles, but by the King himself."

Marie-Félicité Brosset, the Historian of Georgia (1802–1880) . 30

TEXT ILLUSTRATIONS

	PAGE
Bronze figurine of beardless man, showing phallic motive—from Timoi	3
(*After Chantre*)	
Bronze figurine of horse *couchant*, with docked tail—from Stepan-tzminda	10
(*After Chantre*)	
Pendant ornament, consisting of rectangle in twisted "ropework", with hanging rings, and a duck at each end; to which are suspended by rings three little beardless men with tails (cf. Pan, Satyrs, Centaurs, etc.)—from Upper Koban, Early Iron Age	11
(*After Chantre*)	
Bronze plaque of deer suckling young—from Diguri	18
(*After Chantre*)	
Early Iron Age pendant of a hermaphroditic (?) figure suspended from a chain, clothed only in a conical helmet, belt and buskins—from Gori	21
(Cf. *C.A.H.*, III, p. 150, for reference to a late Cappadocian representation of the Hattic War-God at Boghaz-keui, and to a bronze figurine now in Berlin, with similarly accentuated breasts.)	
(*From the Komarov Collection, after Chantre*)	
Early Iron Age horse-bit from Gori	32
(Cf. the almost identical Scythian ring-bit from Dévé-Huyuk, published in *C.A.H.*, First Volume of Plates, opposite p. 250—(b).)	
(*After Chantre*)	
Bronze figurine of nude, beardless individual, with exaggeratedly large and malformed hands, the thumbs being pressed against the ears—from Timoi	34
(*After Chantre*)	
Early Iron Age belt-clasp in stamped bronze-leaf, showing pyramidic and swastika decoration—from Stepan-tzminda	45
(*After Chantre*)	
Pitsunda Church in the Seventeenth Century	84
(*After Castelli*)	
Symbolic tail-piece included among Castelli's drawings	126

TEXT ILLUSTRATIONS

	PAGE
A Georgian Noble of the Seventeenth Century, probably a Dadiani (Note the tendency of the Georgian nobility, in this and subsequent illustrations, to adhere to the fashions in costumes and armour of late fifteenth-century Europe.) *(After Castelli)*	134
A Circassian Noble of the Seventeenth Century—" Settemani Prince of the Abaza people—an Illustrious man in the Orient of our time" *(After Castelli)*	136
Georgian Domestic Architecture in the Seventeenth Century: "Another of the houses near Cottatis (Kutais) in which died one of our Fathers" *(After Castelli)*	141
"Benefactor, Simon, the absolute prince of the province of Guria. A great Benefactor to our Fathers. Remember all, how magnificently generous are the Georgian princes and kings who have given to our fathers so many houses and lands. Of the princes, know that in Georgia no one can be crowned a Prince unless he be the absolute master of a province" *(After Castelli)*	144
Georgian Domestic Architecture: "Another of the lodgings placed at our disposal by the King of Georgia" *(After Castelli)*	146
"Datua Biscaia, a Mingrelian noble, born in the mountains of the Caucasus, a man of extraordinary courage, guardian of the fortress of Gorieli; fought against the Abkhazians; was killed in one of the battles against them" *(After Castelli)*	149
A Turkish Archer of the Seventeenth Century *(After Castelli)*	154
A Muscovite Cavalry Soldier of the Seventeenth Century *(After Castelli)*	158
A Muscovite Archer of the Seventeenth Century *(After Castelli)*	163
"The Persian Queen, Elena de Artabac" (daughter of the Atabegi of Samtzkhé and wife of Shah Safi II) *(After Castelli)*	169
Artschillus Bagarationus and Nicholas Davidzsoon (The first is Archili, son of Wakhtang V of Kartli, and sometime King of Imereti; the other is the son of David, eldest adult son of Taymuraz I. Nicholas became King of Kakheti as Irakli I.) *(From Nicholas Witzen's "Noord und Oost Tartarye")*	175
A Turkish Musketeer of the Seventeenth Century *(After Castelli)*	179

TEXT ILLUSTRATIONS

	PAGE
Georgian Peasant Scene *across pages*	222–3
(*After Castelli*)	
Oxen Ploughing	226
(*After Castelli*)	
Rural Scene	236
(*After Castelli*)	
A Baron's Keep	237
(*After Castelli*)	

"Mamia, the Prince of Guria, and his armour; killed by his son Simon" 241
(For a portrait of Simon Gurieli, *see page* 144.)
(*After Castelli*)

A Sheep-Farm of the Théatin Missionaries . . . 256
(*After Castelli*)

"The Georgian princes do not favour solid, stable houses; they prefer portable houses because these are more adapted to the conditions of war; in peacetime they are more serviceable because they love hunting and move about frequently. They bivouac here and there; this provides them also with the pleasure of visiting their subjects and observing and judging them. These houses, of different styles, according to the seasons of the year, are very beautiful and castle-like" 265
(*After Castelli*)

"Papuna Geladze, the priest of the Queen of Colchis" . . 266
There are marginal notes on the original drawing as follows: "They have vases which contain as many phials as there are days in the year. They have good wines which are kept in urns buried in clayey soil. This Georgian nation, they are great drinkers; they esteem much those who can drink much, without either loosing the tongue, or losing reason or legs."
(*After Castelli*)

"Zacharius, Patriarch of Georgia, in his Pontifical Robes; a distinguished man; a great benefactor, very bountiful towards our missionaries" 268
(*After Castelli*)

Priest and Suppliant 273
(*After Castelli*)

Georgian Interlaced Design 291
(*After Dubois, "Voyage"*)

Restoration of the façade of Kutais Cathedral, after the design published by Frédéric Dubois de Montpéreux, in *Voyage autour du Caucase* 298

Georgian Interlaced Design 307
(*After Dubois, "Voyage"*)

TEXT ILLUSTRATIONS

	PAGE
A decorative design of the Georgian letter *gan*, from a contemporary MS. of Saba Sulkhan Orbeliani's Georgian Dictionary, in the possession of the author (copied from the original coloured design by Charles Beazley). An interesting specimen of Georgian book-illumination of the first quarter of the eighteenth century	308
" Camels, of which there are few in Mingrelia; those that are found are brought from Turkey; there are also white camels " *(After Castelli)*	321
" To the Mountains of Treasure. A barque of our Fathers in the town of Arachea, bringing provisions from Constantinople for the Sacred Congregation by order of the Pope Urbano "	337

A note in the top right-hand corner of the original drawing comments: " In time of war the old and unfit flee to the mountains of the Caucasus, taking along with them all their movable possessions, which mountains are under the powerful kings of Mingrelia."
(After Castelli)

" The king sent me his own horse in harness of gold; and amid his noble horsemen I was taken to see the city of Cotatis and the castle, where I was received by the King, who did me great honour to my great confusion. God be praised " *(After Castelli)*	346
" The King invited me several times ... now and then he would put some delicacy into my mouth with his own Fingers, and offered me Wines from his own Glass "	350
" Georgian Pastimes and Gaieties " *(After Castelli)*	357

MAPS

	PAGE
Sketch Map to illustrate Chapter II. The Bronze and Early Iron Ages in the Caucasus	20
Sketch Map to illustrate Chapters II and III. Early Migrations through and about the Caucasus	33
Diagram to show the relation of Georgia to the different Cultures of the Middle East	430
Map to illustrate the Historical Geography of Georgia between the First and Seventh Centuries A.D.	430
Map to illustrate the Historical Geography of the Kingdom of Georgia. From the Tenth to the beginning of the Nineteenth Century A.D.	430

INTRODUCTION

By Sir Denison Ross

OVER three-quarters of a century ago Marie-Félicité Brosset published a monumental work on Georgia entitled *L'Histoire de la Géorgie*. It has never been either re-edited or superseded. It is difficult to borrow and almost impossible to buy. Nearly everything of importance on Georgia that has since been written is in Russian or in Georgian, and mostly buried in learned periodicals. Except for the beautiful translations of Georgian mediæval literature made by the Wardrops, Georgian studies in general have been almost entirely neglected in Europe, although Armenian history and literature—so closely interwoven with that of Georgia—has attracted much attention, including that of a certain number of English scholars. The number of Georgian grammars and dictionaries in any European language is very small, and in English we have none at all.

The last century has produced many notable Georgian scholars, the best known of whom is Prof. Marr, and it is only natural that—Georgia being a part of the Russian Empire—native scholars should have employed Russian for their scientific writings. But what they have written in Russian has not reached a very much wider public than if it had been written in Georgian. Mr. Allen has now made accessible to the English reader the main results of the researches of these scholars, and we may at last learn all about this romantic Christian country in Asia, without the trouble of plodding through the rare and ponderous tomes of Brosset or of learning Russian.

Though still a very young man, Mr. Allen has found time in a singularly varied career—including two years in the House of Commons—to travel extensively in Georgia and to make himself master of the Russian language. The amount of reading that he has done by way of preparation for the present work is self-evident, and I imagine hardly any work or article of importance has escaped his notice. Beyond this, however, Mr. Allen has formed many close friendships among the

INTRODUCTION

Georgian *intelligentsia*, who have been only too ready to lend their expert aid to one who has shown so real an affection for their country.

The ground Mr. Allen has covered in this work is so extensive that matters of interest will be found in it for many besides the student of history : for he has illuminating chapters on the social organization of Mediæval Georgia—a subject hitherto quite inaccessible to the comparative sociologist in Europe ; on the customs and habits of the Georgians between the ninth and the eighteenth centuries ; on their trade relations with neighbouring countries ; and on Georgian mediæval art in which he indicates the interplay of Armenian, Byzantine, and Russian influences.

The historical chapters cover a long period of time : beginning with the rich copper and Early Iron Age cultures of the Caucasus, he passes to the history of the Georgian Kingdom which emerged as an important political entity at the beginning of the tenth century. It is all new history, and very fascinating reading it makes. The Georgian Kingdom of the eleventh–thirteenth centuries emerges as a cultural fact as important in the history of the Middle Ages as the Kingdom of Sicily to which Mr. Allen compares it. We see in the Georgian Bagratids a ruling family as influential in the history of Western Asia as the Angevins were in the Mediterranean, and in the great figure of David the Restorer we see a figure of the type of the early Norman kings. Mr. Allen describes in vivid language the glories of the " Caucasian Kingdom " of Queen Tamara (until now hardly more than a legendary figure to European historians), and the long tragedy of the decline of the Georgian Kingdom during the century of Mongol hegemony.

The succeeding chapters in which Mr. Allen unravels the intricate history of the three contending Georgian Kingdoms during the fifteenth–eighteenth centuries are not only novel and valuable in themselves, but they throw a new light on many aspects of Russian, Persian and Turkish history. The great merit of Mr. Allen as an historian is that he keeps his subject in perspective, and he shows an amazing insight into the contemporary history of neighbouring states.

These historical chapters form the main body of Mr. Allen's book and to none will they be more welcome than to the student of Islamic history, especially in connection with the minor dynasties which ruled in North-Western Persia during the eleventh and twelfth centuries. Particularly interesting

INTRODUCTION

are his researches, for instance, on the influence of Georgian factions at the Persian court during the two crises of the Safavid dynasty.

It is interesting to find a young man of such adventurous and varied interests prepared to devote himself to serious research work in an age which has earned a reputation for frivolity and self-indulgence, and it can only be a source of gratification to his countrymen that Mr. Allen should have filled this important lacuna in our historial literature and that it was left to an Englishman to do for Georgia what H. F. B. Lynch did for Armenia and Mr. Baddeley for the history of Russian relations with Mongolia.

AUTHOR'S PREFACE

SOME ten years ago I was invited by Lord Edward Gleichen to contribute sections on Georgia and Caucasian Azerbaijan to an historical series which he was then engaged in editing. In the course of preparing the brief survey of the modern political history of the Caucasus which was required of me,[1] I was impressed by the lack of any accessible work on Georgian history, either in English or indeed in any West European language. Marie-Félicité Brosset laid the foundation of modern Georgian historical studies, and to him both Georgian and European students must always remain in debt. But Brosset was essentially an editor of materials, and his voluminous publications are scarcely palatable either to the lay reader or to the student of other cultures who may have only a relative interest in Georgia. Baddeley's excellent account of the Russian conquest of the Caucasus covers a particular field, and only incidentally the political history of Georgia contemporary with the conquest. The present work, therefore, has been constructed within very definite limits. It is based on a summary and analysis of the source-materials published by Brosset, supplemented by more recent studies in Georgian and Russian, which—difficult to obtain—have, some of them, become available to me only after the completion of the manuscript of this book. I have taken the period of the suppression of the Georgian Kingdom by the Russians as a suitable point at which to make an end, and Baddeley's *Russian Conquest of the Caucasus* thus becomes supplementary for the earlier part of the nineteenth century. The time has not yet come, nor are the materials available, to attempt the history of Georgia during the last three-quarters of a century.

Within the limits set, there are certain wide *lacunæ*. The chapters on the pre-history of Georgia are really introductory to the body of the book, rather than sufficient in themselves, for I have neither the archæological nor the philological qualifications necessary to the serious study of the earlier

---

[1] Published in a volume entitled *The Baltic and Caucasian States*, in Messrs. Hodder & Stoughton's series, *Nations of Today* (London, 1923).

AUTHOR'S PREFACE

periods. I have, however, included in the bibliographical sections a list of works in Russian and Georgian, which may be of assistance to the student who would proceed further in this field. It is indeed a field which merits exploration, and a student with the requisite qualifications and the necessary leisure should supplement, in the Caucasus, the great work of critical research which Ellis Minns and Rostovtseff have already accomplished for South Russia and the Crimea.

I have also dealt only in the most cursory way with the political history of the Iberian and Albanian Kingdoms during the first six centuries A.D. I have passed thus over this period, because to approach it at all adequately would have necessitated much specialized research. The history of these Kingdoms, and also of the relations of the Roman and Persian Empires in the Caucasus, is a subject which itself calls for prolonged and fundamental study.

In regard to the transliteration of Georgian and other foreign names and words, I have to offer my excuses to the stickler in these matters. I have been engaged in writing this book over a period of nine years, in various places and under varying conditions, and at different times I have come under the influence of different schools of thought in the matter of transliteration. At one moment I went to some expense in engaging the services of a specialist to systematize the spelling of all names in the book on the most approved recent method. Unfortunately, this gentleman, before he could complete the work, accepted an academic appointment abroad, and I found it impracticable to adopt his ideas without his personal assistance. I have therefore attempted, at the last moment, to systematize the spelling, particularly of Georgian names, on a phonetic basis, which I hope will prove comprehensible to the English reader. In the case of Georgian proper names, the laws of euphony in the Georgian language provide that all proper names terminate in a vowel. Where that vowel is an -i, the -i is dropped before a qualifying noun or ordinal numeral, thus :—King Wakhtangi = *Mépé Wakhtangi*, but Wakhtang the King = *Wakhtang Mépé* : Wakhtang the Georgian Lion = *Wakhtang Gurgaslani* ; King David = *Mépé Daviti*, but David II = *Davit Méoré*, David the Restorer = *Davit Aghmashenebeli*. I have followed this rule in transliterating Georgian names into English, as it seems to me to suit the peculiar euphony of the Georgian language, even when the names are read in an English context. In the case of a few names, such as Giorgi and Dmitri, this rule does not apply—for obvious reasons of euphony.

In the case of certain names, such as David, Alexander and Constantine, I have, for no particular reason, adopted the English form—I think generally because it happens to be more pleasing to the eye. There is, of course, a precedent to follow in this matter, as, for instance, the use in English books of the Russian *Ivan* for John, but of Peter and Paul instead of *Petr* and *Pavl*. In regard to Georgian place-names I have always used the Georgian form in preference to the Russianized form—e.g. Kakheti and not Kakhetia (which should, if anything, be Kakhia), Kartli and not Kartalinia. Exception has been made in the case of completely Latinized forms such as Tiflis for Tpilisi, Kutais for Kutaisi, Mingrelia for Samégrelo, Somkheti for Somkhiti. I have also used the Georgian words *mta* (mountain), *tba* (lake) and *tsqali* (river), both in the text and in the maps, in preference to the later Turkish *dagh*, *göl*, and *su* or *chai*.

There are, I suppose, few authors who would not like to rewrite their books, as there can be few men who would not appreciate the opportunity of re-living their lives. I recognize that this book is in certain respects disjointed. This fact arises from the circumstances under which it has been put together. There are a few passages which tend to be repetitive. The treatment of the subject, which is—of intent—horizontal rather than chronological is responsible for this fault, and the obscurity of the subject has induced me to risk, here and there, a certain repetition, in order to attempt greater clarity of exposition.

I am indebted to many friends and to many institutions for their kindness, toleration and help. I shall not, indeed, attempt to mention all those to whom I have placed myself under obligation during the last nine years. I am indebted to the authorities and institutions of the Georgian S.S.R. for many courtesies and favours during my stay in Georgia. In particular I should mention the officials of Tiflis University and of the Centralni Arkhiv Department. I am also indebted to the Turkish authorities for facilities, not usually accorded, during my stay in the eastern vilayets, and I have to record my gratitude for the long and generous hospitality of H.B.M. Consul at Trebizond, Mr. W. D. W. Matthews, and of Ihsan Bey Nemli-zadé, a resident of that city.

To the Biblioteca Communale of Palermo I am indebted for permission to photograph and use a number of Castelli's

AUTHOR'S PREFACE

drawings from his MS. preserved there, and I have to thank Father Stinco, the Librarian, for his great courtesy, while I was working in his mellow sunlit library. I also have to thank my old friends in the Library and Map Room of the Royal Geographical Society and at the London Library for their patience and assistance over many years—particularly the encyclopædic and indefatigable Mr. Cox, who has fathered me now, I suppose, for twenty years.

My greatest sense of obligation is to Mr. André Gugushvili, formerly of the Georgian Legation in London, without whose immeasurable and detailed assistance I could not have completed the work in its present form. Mr Gugushvili's great knowledge of Georgian sources has made accessible to me material which I could not ordinarily have consulted, and I am indebted to him particularly for a complete revision and recasting of the chapters on the social organization of mediæval Georgia.

I am indebted to Mr. Zurab Avalishvili, for his kindness in reading the manuscript of the book and making various valuable suggestions, and to him as also to Professor Marr for providing copies of their works which might otherwise have remained inaccessible.

A man always learns as much—or more—from conversation as he does from books, and I value greatly the many things that I have learned from long talks with Mr. J. F. Baddeley, a veteran in Russian studies, with many years of experience in the Caucasus and rich memories of the country dating back into the last century. To him, and to my many Georgian friends, who have enabled me to soak my mind in the history of Georgia, I owe more than I can say.

KILLYLEAGH,
  Co. Down,
    Ireland.
      September, 1932.

BOOK I

THE BACKGROUND

"And at day-dawn they looked eastward, and midway between the sea and the sky they saw white snow-peaks hanging, glittering sharp and bright above the clouds. And they knew that they were come to Caucasus, at the end of all the earth: Caucasus the highest of all mountains, the father of the rivers of the east. On his peak is chained the Titan, while a vulture tears his heart, and at his feet are piled dark forests round the magic Colchian land."

Kingsley's Heroes: The Argonauts.

"Thou hast been in Eden the garden of God."

Ezekiel xxviii. 13.

CHAPTER I

THE GEORGIAN LAND AND THE NATURE OF MOUNT CAUCASUS

It is a fitting thing, although somewhat in the nature of a pilgrimage, to come upon Georgia from the north. From Vladikavkaz—" Ruler of the Caucasus "—you may follow by motor-bus the track which they say the Cimmerians rode with their ox-carts and their families against Urartu and Sardes. The Russians by an efficient feat of engineering have turned this track into the Georgian Military Road. It is a narrow, trough-like channel over the Caucasus, which at Daryal contracts to a deep gorge, the rock walls of the confining mountains rising sheer to thousands of feet on either side. The pass, even in summer, is cold and wet, and at the summit it had been recently cleared of snow. With the southern decline the road follows the shallow, dashing stream of the Aragvi, and the heavily wooded mountains of Khevsureti drop gradually into the rounded hills and gently sloping valleys of ancient Kartli.

The whole mellow land of Georgia lies before, with its fresh meadows and its lusty uplands, its bright vineyards and its sombre woods, its warm gracious sun and sudden-looming storms. Georgia, like some other countries, has a colour. Ireland is green and grey. Morocco is all red. Georgia is a fine yellow gold like the white wines of Burgundy. The impression of the colour is partly of the sunlight and partly of the tincture of the soil, but also there is some property in the atmosphere, intangible and not easily described, a bouquet, almost imperceptible, which envelops and caresses, fragrant and soft, insidious. The Greeks spoke of the Land of the Golden Fleece, it is supposed because of the scant alluvial gold, filtered in sheepskins from the beds of the westward-flowing streams of Caucasus, But it may be that their fancy thus imaged as a Golden Fleece that aureous hue which lies over all the country like, as it were, to an illumined dew upon the surface of the land.

On the road to Tiflis you pass Mtzkheta, clustered on a tongue of land at the junction of the Aragvi with the Kura. The decrepit balconies of the little tumbling houses are placed on piles above the river and they seem to scramble for a foothold. Forlornly above the village roofs, rise the rugged proportions of the Metropolitan Cathedral of the Georgian kings. Within are marvellous frescoes, chipped and fading badly; but you may still discern—more intriguing than the formal postures of long-forgotten Georgian kings and queens—a curious map of Georgia, of some centuries old, which displays in varied colours the mountains of Caucasus with strange beasts thereon, the rivers Rioni and Kura with cities set about, castles and gigantic trees, and riding in the Euxine two galleys surrounded by monsters of the deep. A coffer of blue stone in the nave of the Cathedral once held the seamless shirt of Christ. The custodian of this royal neglected shrine was a young brown-bearded monk of Khevsureti, with the sallow skin and meek lustreless blue eyes of an undernourished fanatic; and he listlessly lamented the oblivion of God. But for this monk the place was all deserted, and in the courtyard, some drunken picnickers, lolling in the untidy grass, conveyed a piquantly Hogarthian touch. While the sun was sinking I could yet descry upon a neighbouring mountain the ruins of a temple where they say that Armazi was worshipped with fire and human flesh. By the gates a charabanc was waiting for our picnickers, and across the squalid street were festooned scarlet streamers, with the likeness of Karl Marx in black and white, and the hackneyed message calling upon the Proletariat of All Countries to Unite. Two thousand years of history flickered in the evening light.

And thinking on this scene, and on that Georgian land, and on the passing there of history, I now recall to mind the saying of that learned Moor, of ibn-Khaldun the Tunisian in his Muqaddima or Prolegomena. " Know thou ", said he,

> " that the true purpose of history is to make us acquainted with human society, that is with the civilization of the world, and with its natural phenomena, such as savage life, the softening of manners, attachment to the family and the tribe, the various kinds of superiority which one people gains over another, the kingdoms and diverse dynasties which arise in this way, the different trades and laborious occupations to which men devote themselves in order to earn their livelihood, the

sciences and arts; in fine all the manifold conditions which naturally occur in the development of civilization." [1]

Now in the lands of the Caucasus and in the history of them, you may observe all these matters. Not cogitate upon them blinking over books, but relish them with ear and eye and nose—this "*savage life, the softening of manners, attachment to the family and the tribe, the various kinds of superiority which one people gains over another*". For history has been stranded here upon the barren mountains, bottled up in valley-heads, and lost in the dark woods. A tribal name, a trick of speech, a woman's habit, a head's shape, and you will have found forgotten folk of the Bronze Age or Byzantine days, haunting the forest ways.

History has this further purpose, unquoted by the solemn Moor, in that it provides pleasure, by comparison with which I hold its mere instructiveness of small account. For instruction is a means to secret pleasure in this dawdling sunlit world, as so is every sort of effort. For who but the paltry bore of mean delight instructs himself—to feel he is instructed. You or I, if we be honest, for the adventurousness of contemplation, for the ecstasy of understanding. In the history of the Caucasus there is a wide instruction and a mighty pleasure, for it is all instruction born of illustration, rather than of assumption, argument and proof. Here are no serried ranks of causes and effect, no steady march of progress, no smug train of evolution. All the nations of the world have drifted through the Caucasus; all their leavings are to find—but little has been built. Here are the ways of God and men, most horrible and lovely, uncertain and not comprehensible. Such things we may contemplate, learn somewhat, understand a little, and wonder at the colour and the clouding and the sun upon it all.

To cross the Caucasus imposes on the mind a great significance. It is one of the journeys in life which are worth the making—and a certain tribulation. You have left behind that drear Eurasian steppe—the breeding-ground of slaves and conquerors and passivistic thoughts, where the mists and flat forests and the oozing swamps can maudle men. You are among the high shining mountains; the sparkling seas are near; the woods of this uneven country are ever changing —not always the lament birches and mean-visaged pines of the sandy steppe. You are in the lands of Nearer Asia, where man, among the mountains, between the seas, and in

[1] *Les Prolégomènes de Ibn Khaldoun traduits par M. de Slane*, Paris, 1863-8, Vol. I, p. 71.

the pellucid sunlight, early grew to prying intellect; lands of vivid life, of doings and undoings, of risings up and fallings down, of splendours and of shambles, of wisdom and of scattering.

Consider then the mountains of the Caucasus, "the father of the rivers of the East", stretching from sea to sea, from the Black Sea to the Caspian, over six hundred miles.

To the west, three days going now by steamer, to Constantinople and the straits into the Middle Sea; in the older days by sail, maybe from seven to a score of days to Byzantium and earlier to Troy.

To the east, across the Caspian, one day by steamer, two along the railways, to Bukhara and Samarkand; not so far even in the days when Chinghiz ruled at Karakorum, and the unquiet traveller went by sailing-boat and camel-back.

To the south-east by the valley of the Araks, to Tabriz-Tauris of the voyagers—and into the Iranian world.

To the south-west up the valley of the Kura, by Kars, an ancient site of settlement, and the Euphrates valley, to Syria and Egypt, and all the south and west.

So understand the Caucasus, a distant corner of the ancient world, but yet a true part of it, known to the old writers, familiar ground to them. It was the barrier of the ancient world, the end of known lands, the farthest part where travellers went. Here was "Phasis, where ships end their course". Beyond was the land of the Hyperboreans, the Gog and Magog of the Semites.

The mountains stretch north-west to south-east, a dim blue line, capped and flaked with the whiteness of the perpetual snow.

From their middle they throw out, as it were, a lower rib, which curves south-westward, until it is merged into the long high range of the Pontic Alps which bank the southern coast of the Black Sea. This rib is called the Surami (from the high pass which leads over from the western to the eastern plains which lie under Caucasus) or by the Georgians the Mountains of Likhi.

From the region of the Pontic Alps to the east and south are piled the ranges of the peripheral rim of the Armenian plateau. Behind them is the highland country of Armenia—great ranges running west to east and then curving to the north and south. They shelter long extensive river valleys and spread their flanks around wide upland basins—the beds of old lakes. Such is the country where the Kura takes its source; and, eastward, the basins of Kars and Sevan, southward, Urumia and Van.

Between these two mountain masses—the Caucasus and the Ponto-Armenian highlands—lie the two valleys of the Trans-Caucasian Trough; the western crescent-shaped in the elbow of the Black Sea; the eastern sleeve-shaped, draining to the Caspian. The Mountains of Likhi separate the two valleys, and form as it were the spine of the country, so that the Georgians, looking from the mountains, call the western plain Imier, "*that side*" and the eastern plain Amier, "*this side*".

Imier—"that side", the western plain, slopes down to the sea, a fat body nourished by great veins—the Rioni splashing down from the Caucasus, pursued by many tributaries; Tskhenis-tsqali, "*horse's water*", and Qwirila, "*the bawler*".

The long thin tips of the crescent stretch luxuriantly along the coast, north-westwards under Caucasus, south-westward beneath the Pontic bluffs. A multitude of over-generous streams run down to sog the narrow foreshore of this crescent-tip toward the north; the largest are the Kodori and Enguri. The shorter southern tip under the Pontic Alps receives the sluggish waters of many little marshy streams, until, over the pass between the Kertsen Dagh and the great mass of Karchkhali, the Pontic Alps let through the roaring Chorokhi, bearing the pent waters of a dozen mountain rivers fast towards the sea.

Surrounded by mountains, bordering on an inland sea, Imier—"that side"—is a well-favoured land.

"This country", says Wakhushti, "is very wooded and its open places, except for the cultivated ground, are of small extent. In some places the grape and other fruits grow in the woods; the air is excellent—and mild; except outside the woods it is very hot in summer because the wind scarcely blows—but it is bearable except in certain places. In winter it is warm, and for this reason the running waters and the muddy places do not freeze enough for beasts and men to pass over. The snow, nevertheless, is great in height, sometimes an elbow, and worse.

"Except in certain places, the woods hinder a man from seeing the beauty of the country, and, indeed, seen from the height of a mountain—Imereti seems like a vast forest without any kind of habitation.

"All plants and grains grow there in abundance; cotton and rice only are rarely sown, as also corn and barley, but maize, on which the people mostly feed, is found there in abundance. Other grains prosper there; a single man, possessing a coulter or hoe, can grow enough to support himself and his family and pay the tax. There are no orchards but many fruit trees bordering the vineyards, for everything grows in the woods. You find the date-palm, the apple, the chestnut and the peach here more than in any other part; again all kitchen plants and melons of great size grow without cultivation. There are no gardens of flowers, but you find in the plains and in the woods quantities of lilies and of sweet-smelling roses. Mushrooms abound, and there is above all, one sort having a kind of white envelope which later bursts —it is an orange mushroom, and very tasty.

"All animals are found in this country with the exception of the camel, but not in such quantities as in other parts of Georgia; sheep, with and without the fat tail, and always with two and sometimes three or four lambs; they are not kept in flocks. . . . Wild animals abound, excepting the chamois and the hyena. . . . Bees are very profitable through their honey and their wax which is in abundance; the honey is very good, very white in some parts and as hard as sugar; this sort is called 'kripuji'. There are many reptiles and serpents which are not dangerous."[1]

Amier—" this side "—over the mountains of Likhi, is a land of different character. Long and narrow in its shape, not wide and fat, like Imier. To the north the ice-clad mountains of the Caucasus, to the south the formidable plateau of Armenia; to the west the rim of Likhi; and up this valley as up a corridor, the east wind blows from the Himalaya over the Central Asian steppe, and across the Caspian, dry and searing in the summer, loaded with hail and snow through the long winter. So that while men gather oranges " on that side " by the soft sea in the early spring, on " this side " they go with long poles[2] through the snow against the blizzard.

A great river flows through the land, the Cyrus or Kura which comes from the Georgian name *Mtkvari*—a name which the wise derive from the words for " river " of two different tribal stocks; from *mdinaré* = " flowing " or " river " of the Kartlians, and *a-kuara* = " the river " of the Abkhazians; thus bilingually *Mdinaré-a-kuara*—the river-river—" the flowing ", the dominating stream, " the flux " in the life of the primitive tribes who gave the name.

The Mtkvari rises in the lake country south of Ardahani.

"This country is entirely covered by rocks, comparatively high mountains, rough places and forests; it produces reeds and lilies; it contains rivers, springs and lakes, but few plains; cold in winter in certain parts, and with abundant snow. . . . The country produces all kinds of grains, but not everywhere . . . the fruits . . . are good and abounding . . . most of the flowers grow wild in the woods and on the mountains, and in certain localities the scent of the lilies pervades both the mountains and the plains . . . the rivers are many and

---

[1] *Description géographique de la Géorgie par le Tsarévitch Wakhoucht*. Georgian text with French introduction and interleaved translation by M. F. Brosset, Spb. 1842, pp. 339-43 (reference, Wakhushti).
[2] Cf. Strabo, XI, xiv, 4.

THE GEORGIAN LAND

great, and of rapid current; the springs are beautiful, delicious and health-giving; the lakes are good and full of fish."[1]

In these parts the Mtkvari takes its strength; then flows at first from south to north

"now with a strong current . . . through a rocky ravine full of stones"

until below Ardahani its course becomes

"peaceable—and sinuous, because of the plains. It is full of fish—trout above all, big and little, abound up towards the mountains. The water is here better to drink than lower down."[2]

By Akhaltzikhé, the Mtkvari turns west to east, cutting a long gorge through the mountains, overhung on its left bank by the peaks of Likhi and bound on its right by the lesser ranges of Trialeti. The highest peak of Likhi, Makhvilo, "*the Pointed One*", overlooks from some distance this gorge now called Borjomi, this one pass into the valley of Amier.

Through the mountains, the Mtkvari curves eastward and south-eastward, going easily, in leisurely way across its long plain between the Caucasus and the Armenian Mountains. It spreads itself in places now to eighty yards and more across, and forms shallows where it pours past rapidly enough; here again it flows more slowly in a deeper bed.

"In some places steep rocks are found along its bank, but for the most part there are to be seen forests, grassy tracts and reed patches all abounding in wild-fowl and game. The most savoury fishes are caught by nets and other means. . . . Sometimes they fish sturgeon, which spawn below the region of Ganja, but which cannot go higher up because of the current."[3]

Rafts only can make the upper course, bringing the timber of the mountains down to the open plains; but lower, 150 miles before the Caspian, large sailing-boats may ply, drawing up to three feet of water. Low down, 100 miles from the Caspian, the Araks, great river of the Armenians, coming out of the high mountain, Déve Boyun, the Camel's Back, just east of Erzerum (and the Camel's Back forms also the watershed of the western Euphrates) flows in to join the Mtkvari, and the united waters find a double mouth along the sandy foreshore of the Caspian.

Thus the Mtkvari—" the flowing "—the " river " bears down the thawed snows of the lake-country, cuts through the mountains and turns into the long plain to take the streams

[1] Wakhushti, pp. 76–9.   [2] *Ibid.*, pp. 80–1.   [3] *Ibid.*, pp. 135–7.

THE BACKGROUND

that come down from the Caucasus—the Liakhvi, the Ksani and the Aragvi, and lower in a great fork the two considerable rivers which run parallel with the Mtkvari, the Yori, remarkable for the number of pheasants that abound there, and the Alazani, the loveliest valley of the Caucasus.

This is the Caucasian land—between the walls of mountains, a ditch that opens either end on seas—a corridor from the west into the innermost parts of Asia, approachable with no great difficulty from either sea.

And from north to south over the mountains from the northern steppe, there is access through that narrow gorge of Daryal—*Dar-i-Alan*—" the gate of the Alans "; also by the changeful foreshore of the Caspian, along a narrow strip of sandy way under the eastern flanks of Caucasus—*Zghvis-Kari*, " the Sea-Gate " of the Georgians. By this way, mostly, the mounted nomads, Scythians, Alans, Huns, Khazars, were wont to ride through upon the civil countries; and so the vital point upon it where the mountains come down nearest to the sea was called by the Persians Derbend, and by the Arabs *Bab-al-Abwab*, " The Gate of Gates ", and to this day, the Muslims, recalling the Arab terror of the Khazar raids, still call the Caspian, a sea as shifting as the nomads, and washing to their steppe-land parts, *Bahr-ul-Khazar*—" The Khazar Sea ".

From the south and east access was easy, across the Araks fords and up the open valley of the Mtkvari. From the west, unless by sea, more difficult; for an invader must go through the mountains up the feeders of the Araks to the sources of the Mtkvari, and penetrate the long Borjomi defile, or follow down the rocky valleys of the Trialetian and Somkhetian mountains, that fall to the Mtkvari from the west.

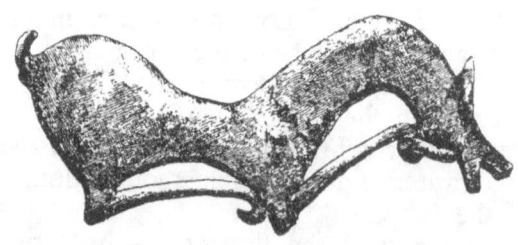

CHAPTER II

BRONZE AND IRON

" A land whose stones are iron, and out of whose hills thou mayest dig brass."
Deuteronomy viii. **9.**

" Javan, Tubal and Meshech, they were thy merchants: they traded the persons of men and vessels of brass in thy markets. They of the house of Togarmah traded in thy fairs with horses and horsemen and mules."
Ezekiel xxvii. 13 *and* 14.

THE first traditions of the Georgian Annals about the coming up into the valleys of the Mtkvari and the Rioni of Kartlos and his brothers, giants issue of the loins of Japhet —refer to the latter end of these unruly centuries, when the Bronze Age had passed and a new age was coming in on the iron swords of nomad looters. New people were swarming into Western Asia, through the Balkan passes, and across the Thracian plain—Dardanians and Phrygians, Mysians and Bithynians. All the Eastern Mediterranean and Western Asia shuddered before the onslaught. The " Peoples of the Sea "—uprooted remnants of the old Ægean trading cities mixed with the new incoming pirates from the north—were threatening Egypt, about 1190 B.C. In a generation Western Asia was all changed; Troy was thrown down. In 1175 B.C. the Hittite records come abruptly to an end. The strength of the young Assyrian monarchy was strained. Babylon fell into anarchy and the Kassite dynasty, themselves descendants of nomad raiders, were exterminated. Five centuries passed before the old world finally succumbed, before the later swarms of nomads, Cimmerians and Scythians, Medians and Persians, coming out of the north and east. Through all this period the elements of the older civilization were held together in some extent by the Assyrians, who, with all their ugly name for ruthlessness, were the efficient wardens of the marches to the north; by the new barbarian states of Phrygia, Lydia and Bithynia, grown upon the wreckage of the Hittite empire; and by the kingdom of Urartu, around Lake Van, whose people assimilating something of the civil ways and notions of the Babylonians and the Hittites, carried these things as far as the Araks. At the end of the seventh century B.C., Urartu and Asshur, Nineveh and Babylon, went down in the turbulence and devastations of new wars. The old world was fading out; the Classic world was drifting into written light.

That the Caucasus lay within the area of the old Bronze Age civilization—which was spread, a series of connected cultures, from Northern Africa to North-western India and Turkestan—is certain, although in the present state of knowledge conclusions can be little more than reasonable hypotheses based upon the application of the slender evidence of myths and isolated archæological discoveries to the probabilities of history.

Vague knowledge of the abundance of copper in the Caucasus, associated with the Promethian myth and with the identification of the Biblical Tubal and Meshech with Uplos and Mtzkhetos, two of the eponymous heroes of the Georgians, induced earlier students of the origins of the Bronze Age to locate in the Caucasus the invention of the metallurgical arts. Dufréné went so far as to derive the Egyptian word *khespet* (tin) from Mount Kazbek,[1] while Lenormant, having scoured the whole of the prehistoric world for tin-mines accessible to the ancients, concluded that "*restent les gisements de l'Ibérie Caucasienne et ceux du Paropamisus*".[2]

The explorations of competent geologists, such as Abich, Bayern and others, having convinced historical science that tin was not found in the Caucasus, there followed a tendency rather to underestimate the significance of the Bronze Age in that region. Chantre considered that "*l'âge de bronze ne parait pas avoir atteint un grand développement au Caucase*",[3] and in this opinion Jacques de Morgan concurred.[4] But Rostovtseff, the most recent authority on the archæology of the Caucasus, now insists upon the existence in the valley of the Kuban, and probably in Trans-Caucasia, of a highly-developed Copper (and later Bronze) Age. He makes comparisons between the art of things found in the Kuban and at Koban, with the antiquities of Anau, of Sumer, of Susa and Elam, of Astarabad and of pre- and proto-dynastic Egypt. He places the full development of this Caucasian Copper civilization in

[1] Dufréné, *Etude sur l'histoire de la production et du commerce de l'étain*, Paris, 1881, p. 22.
[2] Fr. Lenormant, *Les Premières Civilizations*, Tome I, p. 128.
[3] Chantre, *Recherches Anthropologiques au Caucase*, Tome I, p. 93.
[4] De Morgan, *Mission Scientifique au Caucase*, Tome I, pp. 33 *et seq.*

BRONZE AND IRON

the Third Millennium B.C. while admitting the possibility of the later date of the Second Millennium B.C. suggested by other authorities. Rostovtseff sees this Caucasian culture as original and native, influenced only slightly by, and not derived from, other contemporary cultures of the Near and Middle East.[1]

The Argonautic legend, which really embodies the form of an early " Black Sea Pilot " handed down by word of mouth from generation to generation, and modified and embroidered according to the fluctuations of geographical knowledge and the fertile imagination of all sailors, relates to the history of a maritime commerce in the Black Sea, dating back to round about the fifteenth century B.C., eight hundred years before the great days of the Hellenic mercantile marine, and several hundred years before the Aryan nomads and pirates overturned the flourishing monarchies and the great sea-trading cities of the Bronze Age. The buried bones and wealth of metal things found in the Kuban, and the carved stones set along the cliffs of the Abkhazian coast illuminate this epic monument of Orpheus, and the maritime smack of all the scattered evidence seems to indicate that the prehistoric civilization of the Caucasus, if indeed native and original, was in familiar and enduring contact with one or the other, or all, of the succeeding thalassocracies of the Bronze Age. The Kingdom of Æa—whose riches amazed the rough crew of Jason's ship, as in a later age the treasures of Mexico astonished Cortez' sailors—may indeed have been very similar in character to the Bosporan kingdom which, twelve centuries later, rose to great prosperity on the north-east coasts of the Black Sea; that is, a country of farming and mining, ruled by a native dynasty in regular contact with sea-traders who had opened up the navigation of the Black Sea. And in the way that the Bosporan kingdom grew to wealth and political importance as the warden of the ways to Central Asia by the Don and Ural and as the garnerer of all the products round about, so the kingdom of Æa, master of the mines and natural products of the Trans-Caucasian Trough, straddled the through-route to the Caspian and Iran and the ways that went south-east to Lake Van and the Mesopotamian Plain.

---

[1] For Rostovtseff's views on the relation of the Caucasus to the civilizations of the Bronze Age, see particularly R.A. (1920), *L'Âge de cuivre dans le Caucase Septentrional et les civilizations de Soumer et de l'Egypt protodynastique*; his book, *Iranians and Greeks in South Russia*, Introduction and Chap. I, " The Prehistoric Civilizations "; J.E.A. (1920), *The Treasure of Asterabad*; see also his recent book *Animal Style in South Russia and China* (1929) for qualification of his earlier views. See also Note A, p. 366.

THE BACKGROUND

The identity of the maritime nations who traded with the Caucasus during the Bronze Age remains obscure. The existence of the megaliths along the Cherkess and Abkhaz coasts brings the Caucasus within the sphere of all those elaborate theories which have been constructed to explain the setting up of the stone monuments, everywhere so curiously similar.[1] The theory that these monuments were built always under Egyptian influence may find confirmation in the story of Herodotus about the Egyptian origin and customs of the Colchians.[2] Mr. Peake, however, contends that

> "several lines of evidence point to the Sumerians, or certain groups of them, as being the traders who travelled the Mediterranean and the Atlantic coast of Europe in search of precious metals, and who are somehow responsible for the spread of the megalithic culture.... Dolmens and other megalithic structures are found all round Sumer, in Syria and Palestine to the west, in the Crimea and in the Caucasus."[3]

On the other hand it may be suggested that the Minoans, rather than the Egyptians or the Sumerians, were the first of the sea-going nations to set about the navigation of the Black Sea. Certainly the Mycenæans, the immediate heirs to the maritime supremacy and to the civilization of Cnossus, appear to have extended their adventuring to the eastern coast of the Black Sea, and the traces of their trading may be followed to the valleys of the Mtkvari and the Alazani, and even by the southern shore of the Caspian.[4]

Knowledge of the relations of the early Asiatic land-powers with the tribes and principalities of the Trans-Caucasian Trough is confined to deductions such as those made by Rostovtseff, based on a comparison of the artistic technique of scattered archæological finds. The inscriptions of Sumer, of Susa and Elam, and of Babylon, give no indication that the commercial and political influence of the people of these sites extended even as far as the Araks. We cannot indeed doubt that the fertile Trans-Caucasian Trough was, during the Bronze Age, as it was during the early Classic period, more easily accessible by sea than by the difficult land-routes from Southern Asia. It is, however, not unreasonable to assume that there

---

[1] For review of the megalith problem see *C.A.H.*, II, 597–600.
[2] See V. de St. Martin, *Mémoire Historique sur la Géographie Ancienne du Caucase*, pp. 49–54; Uslar, in *Zap. Kav. Ot. I.R.G.O.*, Tome XIV, Part 2, pp. 391–403, Zametka o Kolkakh.
[3] H. Peake, *The Bronze Age and the Celtic World*, p. 59; see also Rostovtseff, *Animal Style in South Russia and China*, pp. 17–20.
[4] See Salomon Reinach, *La Représentation du Galop dans l'Art Ancien et Moderne*, Paris, 1925, pp. 55–59; for "Ægean" activities on the Pontine coast in the thirteenth century B.C., cf. J. L. Myres in *C.A.H.*, III, 661–2.

existed in the ancient Mesopotamian cities some knowledge of, and some irregular and indirect intercourse with, the valleys of the Rioni and the Mtkvari.

At a later date there is a probability that the Hittites were in regular contact with Trans-Caucasia, but here again their inscriptions, which have so far been deciphered, give no indication of the fact, and a vast tract of archæologically unexplored country, of whose history in the pre-Classic period we are entirely ignorant, separates the region of Ætes' kingdom from the seats of the Hittites on the Halys.

It is first in Assyrian records that mention frequently occurs of names of tribes who are, later, in the early Classic period, found settled in the Mtkvari valley. But in the period of the Assyrian wars, from the eleventh century B.C. to the seventh century B.C., these tribes were cantoned much farther south and west, in the neighbourhood of the Middle Taurus and the upper valley of the Euphrates, and there is no inscriptional evidence to indicate that the Assyrians had any knowledge of, or any intercourse with, the country beyond Mount Ararat.

It would seem that the kingdom of Urartu, called also Khaldi—which covered all the country round Lake Van, and stretched north-eastwards as far as the Araks, and possibly northward to the valley of the Chorokhi—was the only land-state of the older civilizations which had a close intercourse with the Ponto-Caspian Isthmus, and which had extended its commercial and, maybe, its political influence into those parts. The Urartians used a language which has been found to have some affinity with Georgian,[1] and although it is probable that their dynasty and aristocracy was Aryan, there seems little reason to doubt that the people of the Vannic kingdom were racially connected with, if indeed their descendants did not form part of, those tribes who, about the time of the fall of the kingdoms of Van and Assyria, were beginning to settle along the Mtkvari valley.[2] The Urartians developed a culture which was borrowed directly from the Assyrians, and the historical roots of which drew nurture from Babylon. Planted across the

---

[1] Sayce, A. H., *The Cuneiform Inscriptions of Van*, in J.R.A.S., Vols. XIV *et seq*; cf. also Marr, *K'izucheniyu sovremennego gruzinskogo yazika*, Leningrad, 1922.

[2] The kingdom of Urartu was called also Nairi or Khaldi and the chief god of the Urartians was Khaldis. During the Middle Ages the Trebizond country formed the Byzantine "theme" of Chaldia; the name also occurs in Kalnis-mta (Georgian for the Sughanli-dagh) and in the Kaldi-kara Mountains (north of the river Khrami). Between Gumush-khané and Baiburt on the road to Erzerum, there are villages inhabited by people called Khalt, who speak a dialect which I was told had no resemblance to Turkish, Armenian or Georgian. The local explanation of the name is that it means simply a "mixed people". For further on this question see Lynch, II, 68, and Lehmann-Haupt, in *Zeitschrift für Ethnologie*, 1892, p. 131.

routes which led from the treasure-bearing mountains of the north to the cities of the ancient world, the Urartians, in the very nature of their quickly accumulated power and prosperity, must indeed have been the energetic pioneers of the exploitation, by the land-routes, of the mineral resources of the Pontic and Caucasian lands.[1]

The authors of the Georgian Annals derive the peoples of the Caucasus from Targamos, a descendant of Japhet. Targamos is the Torgom of Armenian tradition, the Togarmah of Genesis. Of the sons of Targamos, Haos was the ancestor of the Armenians (HA'IQ), his seven brothers of the various peoples of the main chain of the Caucasus and its southern valleys. The Annalists wrote under the influence of the historical ethnology of the Old Testament, and they sought to combine the "mappa mundi" of the tenth chapter of Genesis with local vague traditions of the Swarming Time. The names given to the sons and grandsons of Targamos represent a late attempt to explain geographical names in use during the first centuries of the Christian Era. The Annals preserve, however, several authentic tribal names mixed with these primitive attempts at geographical ethnology. They preserve, also, in the genealogy of the sons and grandsons of Kartlos, the tradition of the expansion and of the extension of the political power of the tribes who settled in the middle basin of the Mtkvari. Kartlos, the second of the eight sons of Targamos, is the ancestor of the Kartlians—of the eastern branch of the Georgians, as his brother Egros is of the Mingrelians or western Georgians. Of the second generation, of the five sons of Kartlos, the eldest, Mtzkhetos, represents a tribal name, and of his three grandsons Uplos may again be identified as a tribal as distinct from a geographical name. The principalities allotted to the sons of these two latter generations seem to indicate two successive waves of expansion by which the territory of the Kartlians was extended from the middle valley of the Mtkvari to the Alazani and the Yori on the east, and to the Chorokhi on the west.

Of all the relations of Haos, these three, Kartlos, Mtzkhetos and Uplos, may in different degrees be identified in tribal names, known to the early historic peoples of Asia in forms derivative from the roots K-D, M-S, and B-L.

The root K-D is at once the most important and the most

---

[1] *C.A.H.*, III, 185. "In metallurgy the people of Van were very expert, as might be expected from the proximity of the mineral wealth. Gold, silver, bronze, copper and iron were all in requisition."

obscure. It is represented in Kartli, a Georgian provincial toponym. It has survived in the contemporary name KURD, which covers a number of tribes of primitive and mingled stock in the Armenian mountains. These tribes certainly include in their composition the descendants of fugitive elements from the period of the Scythian and Cimmerian invasions.[1] And the name Kardukhoi applied by Xenophon to the tribes in the upper valleys of the Euphrates and the Araks, constitutes an historical indication of the connection between the various forms of this name-root.[2]

The roots M-S and B-L are common in the geographical nomenclature of Asia Minor and the Caucasus. Mtzkh-eta, "the place of Mtzkh", and Uplis-tzikhé, "the castle of Uplos", perpetuate in familiar way the names of the mythical forefathers of the Georgians. The root M-S appears again in the names of the town of Mush and of the district of Mughan, and in the form Masis, the old Armenian name for Mount Ararat. The inhabitants of south-western Georgia called their province Samtzkhé and themselves Meskhians until the end of the eighteenth century.[3] In the early Hebrew, Assyrian, Vannic and Greek records the forms of these two roots M-S and B-L frequently occur as the names of peoples who, in the period between the first Assyrian references and the later Greek descriptions, had shifted from the Taurus region to the neighbourhood of the Pontic mountains. Thus in Assyrian inscriptions the Mushki and Tabal appear, in the Old Testament Tubal and Meshech, and in Herodotus and later writers the Meskhoi and Tibarenoi.

The racial affinities of these M-S and B-L peoples are obscure. The Mushki first appear in history in the twelfth century B.C. when they were settled in the anti-Taurus region. This location would appear to confirm the tradition of the Georgian Annals of the coming of Targamos and his sons from Babylon.[4] It is probable, however, that the basis of this tradition was the desire of the chroniclers to co-ordinate their

[1] It is noteworthy that the term "Meshkin" is at the present time applied among certain Kurdish tribes, to the lowest and poorest section of the population.
[2] Kardukhoi = root KARDU or KARTU + nominal suffix -KH + Greek nominal suffix -OI.
[3] Cf. *The Man in the Panther's Skin*, by Shota Rusthaveli (late twelfth century), ed. Wardrop, R.A.S., 1912, quatrain 1572: "I, a certain Meskhian bard of the borough of Rusthavi, I write this." In Samtzkhé, sa- is a Georgian territorial prefix, which is accompanied by the suffix -e or -o (e.g. Sa-KARTVEL-O, *the land Kartvel* = Georgia). The infix Kh- in Samtzkhé is common as a nominal suffix to names in Armenian; we have therefore Sa-MTZ-KH-E, the land of the MTZKH; i.e. Meskhians, Mosokh or Mushki. See also Note B, p. 367.
[4] Brosset, *Histoire de la Géorgie*, 1ière partie, p. 16.

THE BACKGROUND

origins in accordance with the conventions of Holy Writ, rather than that it is the reflection of a real tradition of the early Georgians. If, as is suggested, the Mushki had before the twelfth century B.C. a common history with the Mitanni and Phrygians, they must have come originally from the north-west.[1]

The frequent association of the names Tubal and Meshech with the origin of the use of metals, and the fact that the Mushki first appear in history at the beginning of the period when iron was coming into use, would appear to confirm the idea that the Mushki came in with the iron-using nomads who were threatening the Bronze Age civilization at the beginning of the twelfth century B.C. There is evidence that the first effective use of iron was made by nomad peoples in the region

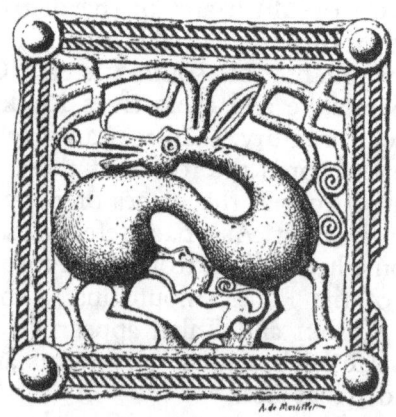

to the north of the Caucasus. A recently published papyrus from Oxyrhynchus, containing fragments from Hellanicus, records that the use of iron weapons was first introduced by one Saneunos, a Scythian king.[2] Peake, further, has shown that it was possible for groups of the horse-riding nomads of eastern Europe to have learned the use of iron from the tribes of the Caucasus. On the other hand de Morgan has suggested that the discovery of the use of iron was an accidental result of the efforts of bronze-using folk to find a substitute for tin in a country where only copper was available. He finds these conditions in Trans-Caucasia, and he would postulate the

---

[1] *C.A.H.*, II, 274; III, 137 *et seq.*; cf. also Dr. Hogarth, *Ibid.*, III, 503—" we must credit the Mitanni and the Mushki, as well as the makers of historic monarchy in Phyrgia, with belonging to an immigrant element from Europe, and include them among the invaders who came from the same Balkanic region at different epochs ".

[2] Rostovtseff, *Iranians and Greeks*, p. 18. For name Saneunos, cf. pp. 28-29.

discovery of iron-smelting in the Caucasus, and the propagation of the idea southward and westward from that region. The Khalybes of the Pontine coast, identical probably with the Halizones of the Alazani and lower Mtkvari valleys, and with the Albanians of the Classical period—all of which names may be correlated to the B-L root—were associated in the minds of the Greeks with the discovery and production of iron.[1] The actual trade in iron with the Greeks cannot be dated before the seventh century B.C., but it is likely that the country had for many generations before this date been known as rich in iron.

[1] Chantre, I, 68; St. Martin, *Géog. Anc.*, pp. 82 *et seq.*; cf. also Dubois, IV, 138, who connects the iron-mines of Kulp twenty *versts* from Akhtala with the name Khalyb.

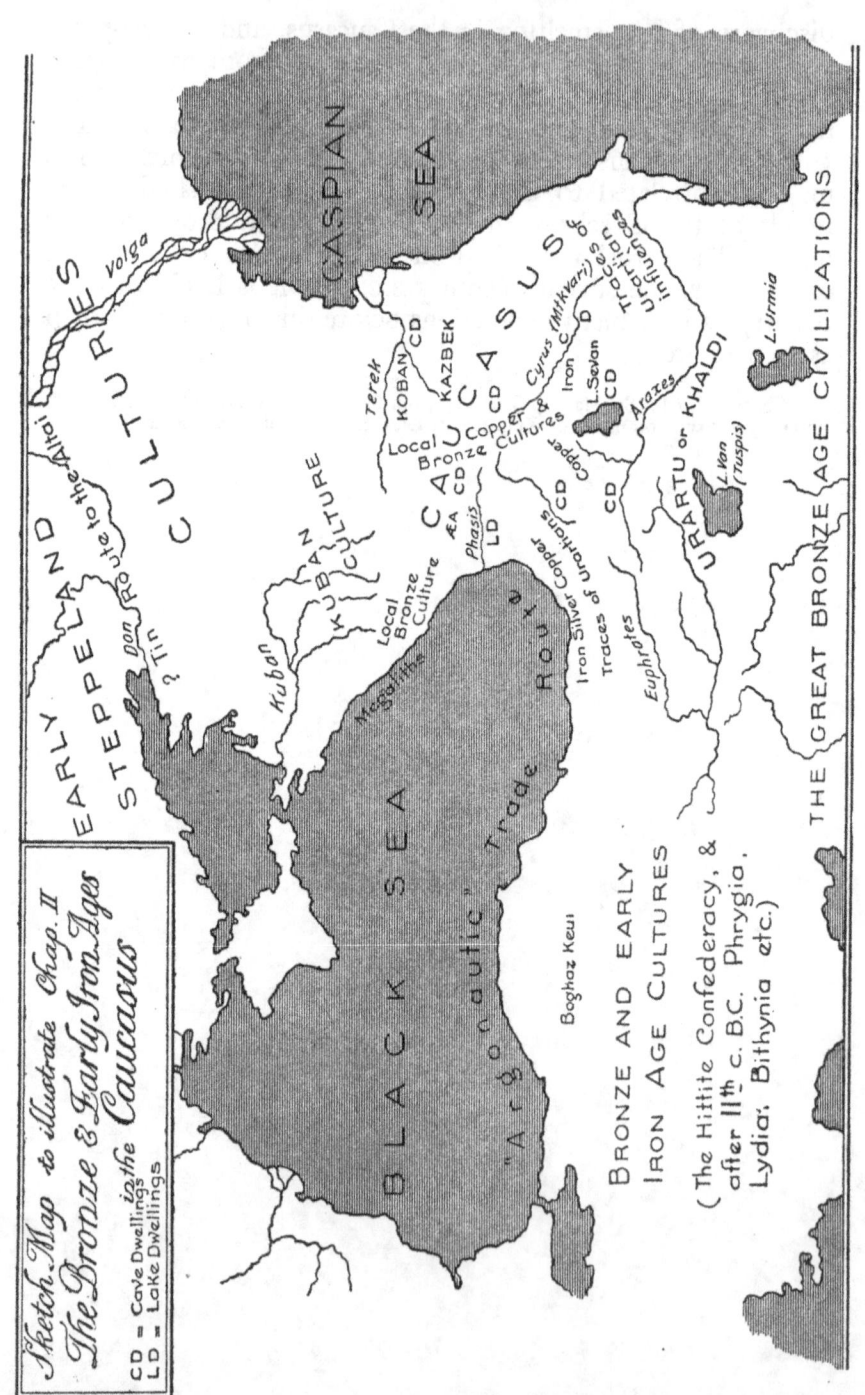

CHAPTER III

THE SWARMING AND THE MINGLING

"Thus saith the Lord God; Behold, I am against thee, O Gog, the chief prince of Meshech and Tubal; And I will turn thee back, and put hooks into thy jaws, and I will bring thee forth, and all thine army, horses and horsemen, all of them clothed with all sorts of armour, even a great company with bucklers and shields, all of them handling swords. . . . Gomer, and all his bands; the house of Togarmah of the north quarters, and all his bands, and many people with thee."

Ezekiel xxxviii. 3, 4, 6.

IN Western Asia, the process of the mixing of different stocks dates back to remote periods, long before the Swarming Time of the eleventh to seventh centuries B.C. That peculiar type which is native to these parts, so-called autochthonous—out of the ground—is quite permanent, always resurgent, mastering the bodies of new masters. The strong-boned physique, the broad " square " head with its strong growth of wavy hair and beard, the wide dark eyes, the sallow skin, are bred to these mountain countries from the Ice Age. This type is called " Armenoid ", or more appropriately " Alpine ", and it has spread to Europe in prehistoric times along the mountain belt as far as the Pyrenees, and over Iran to the Pamirs; and it has filtered down through Palestine to Egypt, surviving, as all types, mostly in those parts which were likest in condition to its homeland.[1] The peasantry of Western Asia, whether they be called Georgian, Armenian or Turkish, are of this autochthonous stock—out of the ground. The two longheaded stocks—" Mediterranean " man from the south-western quarters of Asia and from North Africa, and " Nordic " man out of the northern steppes—are foreign to these parts, remnants of old pressures, invasions and intrusions. Men of the " Mediterranean " stock pressed up the valleys of the Tigris and the Euphrates; they made their own the lands south of the Taurus. Men of the " Nordic " stock—whose movements

[1] See Note C, p. 368.

swept the old world from the Atlantic to the Himalayas—mastered Western Asia, but as in North Africa, their type did not survive in any great degree. They were the lords of the old Hittite and Urartian kingdoms, and later of Armenia; but the physical type survives to these times only among the upper classes of the Kurds; here and there in Turkish villages, and among the Ossetians about the Daryal Pass.

All origins—of physical types, of styles in art, of languages—must always remain relative rather than definifive. One group, one family, one stock or style, when followed logically and dug into, is found to merge with others, and so on to imponderable depths. Languages, and for that matter styles in art, and men in their bodies and their minds, are like to rocks—here petrified and stratified, here crumbling, mingling with other crumblings, here growing all unnoticed, and receiving to themselves minute unnoted particles of what is crumbling and being blown about.

The languages of the Caucasus have been compared and in turn related to the various groups already classified: to the Aryan or Indo-European, to the Finno-Ugrian and Altaic—and to the Semitic. But it would seem that they have no connection with these families, except maybe the obscure affinities which fundamentally each group must have with all.

It would appear that the languages of the Caucasus may be regarded as a distinct and integral family of languages.

Professor Nikolai Marr, the greatest living student of the languages of the Caucasus, has appropriated the label " Japhetic " as applying, first, to the north and south Caucasian groups and further to various other languages with which he suggests they have affinity. These Japhetic languages, as do the Bantu languages in Africa and the Finno-Ugrian and Altaic languages over Asia, represent the human speech in a certain stage of development. They have become stratified in the agglutinative stage; that is, the languages have not developed beyond the running together of primitive words into compounds, in which the form and meaning of the constituent parts undergo little or no change. Marr finds elements of the Japhetic stratum in many of the languages of Europe, particularly in Basque, which he has compared with Georgian; and to a lesser degree in German. Further, he has by the evidence of tribal and place-names attempted to correlate many of the dead languages of the Mediterranean. Etruscan has certainly some points of affinity with the south Caucasian languages. Sayce, many years ago, established a connection between the languages of the Urartian inscriptions and Kartvelian. And of the Hittite languages there are certain elements in Kanesian, which indicate that this principal language of Boghaz-Keui, which has been recognized to be Aryan, was, like the later Armenian, a mixed language, having a substratum of the older language forms of Asia Minor.

The languages of the Caucasus represent the surviving remnants of this once widespread family of languages. The primitive ways of life of the mountain tribes, the continuity of a fixed social state, imply no change in thought, and hence little modification in the manner of expressing it. In Georgia, in the plains, foreign words by hundreds have intruded into the speech of the people—Persian words, Greek and Armenian, Arabic, Turkish, some few Russian words. But the structure of the language has been in no way modified; thus while to the English the Saxon Chronicle is in an unknown language and Chaucer difficult to mouth, the literary Georgian language has changed little since the days of the twelfth-century troubadours, and the first manuscripts, in Georgian, of the Bible.

For the study of Georgian and the elucidation of the character of the early historic languages of Western Asia, Armenian is important. The Japhetic substratum is protruding everywhere. Armenian is classified as an Indo-European language "*which appears to be a half-way dialect between the Aryan branch and the Slavo-keltic*".[1] Armenian contains a large number of Persian loan-words, and Semitic influences in the language are also noticeable. Yet

> "when the Persian and other loan-words are removed, a stock remains of native words and forms governed by other phonetic laws than those which govern the Aryan, i.e. Indian and Iranic, branch of the Indo-European tongues."[2]

As contrasted with Georgian the clear Japhetic type-language—Armenian represents a hybrid language, in the development of which the Aryan speech of an intruding element has failed to submerge altogether the primitive language-forms of the autochthonous people among whom they came.

We may then consider the wave of Aryan conquest sweeping into Asia Minor in the centuries of the Swarming Time.

---

[1] F. C. Conybeare, *Armenian Language and Literature*, in *Encyclopædia Britannica*, eleventh edition. Cf. also Note D, pp. 368-9.
[2] F. C. Conybeare, supra.

THE BACKGROUND

The conquerors came with their new language, and as the wave of conquest dribbled through to the remoter valleys, so the language dribbled through, growing thinner and less staying on its way. The conquerors, as soldiers and overlords, mixed with the uprooted population, and dragged them on—as did the Turks and Mongols of the Middle Ages with the Georgian and Armenian barons and their burnt-out tenantry—to shift and fight in further nomad conquests. Thus were formed great tribes, potential peoples, who settled or stayed half-nomadic like the Kurds and Tatars of the present day. And when the Swarming Time was over, and men began to rule in cities, and others to write again, these shifting peoples emerge into the light of history; with changed names, moulding languages and old traditions, borrowed from the word-of-mouth anthologies of conquerors and conquered, woven to the doubtful fabric of a common history.

In this way the Armenians, sons of Haos (HA'IQ) spoke a language of which the predominant elements are recognized as Aryan. And the remains of the Aryan swarming are to be traced in some place-names of the parts bordering on the Caucasian lands.[1] The Georgians, speaking a language which is quite alien to those of the Aryan group, retain the clear tradition of close kinship with the sons of Haos (HA'IQ); and the records of their tribal foundings, of Mtzkhetos (MESH-(E)-K) and of Uplos (TUBAL), affirm great movements into the Mtkvari valley, about the time of this same Aryan swarming. Marr, who has attempted to deduce some elements of the Mushki (MOSOKH) language, finds in it certain indications implying Aryan influence, and we may, indeed, consider the Mushki as a mixed people akin with the Armenian tribes who were then founding principalities along the valleys of the Euphrates and the Araks—a people compounded of some conquering Aryan elements mixed with the drifting native folk of all these parts, who had been disturbed and dispersed in these anarchic times.[2]

Marr places the shifting of the Mushki (Mosokh) northwards and eastwards towards the Mtkvari plains in the fifth

---

[1] e.g. Georgian Tao, Armenian Daikh, the land of the Dakæ; Sakasene of the Sakæ; Gumri (now Leninakan) and Ghimri in Daghestan seem to retain the memory of Cimmerian settlements. Cf. Marr in *Iz. Gos. AK. I.M.K.*, IV, pp. 299-310.

[2] Hogarth, *C.A.H.*, III, 503, has suggested that before the twelfth century B.C. the Mushki had a common history with the Mitannians and Phrygians; i.e. there were definite Indo-European elements in the composition of the Mushki people. With regard to the other ethnic elements—autochthonous or Japhetic—it should be noted that G. Huisyng finds an affinity between Phrygian and Georgian; Börk between Mitannian and Georgian.

century B.C. In the following hundred years they must have been in continuous conflict and contact with the local tribes settled in this quarter; nomadizing from the river valleys in the winter to the mountains in the summer, now fighting, now in friendly cognizance—as in the Georgian Annals we read in later centuries of the Kipchak and the Seljuk doing in like manner.

The indigenous tribes hereabouts were, it would seem, covered by the name CHAN (↔SON↔SVAN); and a memory of the period of the mingling of the two peoples may be suspected in the composite name SOMKH-eti (So↔MEKH↔SON↔MESKH) which is still applied to the mountains along the left bank of the Borchalo river—the border march between the Georgians and the Armenians.[1]

The Swarming Time became a vague memory in the legend of the sons of Targamos. The migrant tribes had settled, had displaced the tribes they found there, or had mingled with them; the mingling tribes had grown to peoples or had scattered, left their fragments, disappeared. Name-forms and their locations change in every written account from Ezekiel to Strabo and Pliny, and the historians of the first centuries of the Christian era. Feudal kingdoms had arisen and these again had changing names.

By the first century B.C. when the campaigns of Lucullus and Pompey had made the lands of the Transcaucasian Trough accessible to Roman travellers, the ethnic complexion of the peoples inhabiting the valleys of the Rioni and the Mtkvari was constant, to the extent that the flux which is race can be said to establish constant traits. The historical division of the Georgian peoples—the western Georgians, the Imierni "*on that side*", and the eastern Georgians, the Amierni "*on this side*"—had appeared. In the western basin, along the Rioni, and its tributaries were the people of Colchis, Egrissi of the Georgian Annals, Lazica of the later classical writers. In the eastern basin over the middle valley of the Mtkvari and the upland country north and south, was established the Kingdom of Iberia. These were the lands where the Georgian language in its kindred forms—Kartlian, Mingrelian and Svanian—was current.[2] And to the west and south-west between the rivers

---

[1] Compare also the composite names Celtiberia and, now, Czechoslovakia. The name Svan had originally wider implication than at present, as applied to the people of the upper valleys of the Enguri and the Tskhenis-tsqali. It was applied to all the country as far as the Aragvi and the mountains inhabited by the Kists and Khevsurs. As late as the sixteenth century, Russian diplomatic documents use the name SONI in this sense. Cf. Brosset, *Histoire de la Géorgie*, 1^{ière} Part, p. 44. The Georgians call the Armenians *Somekh-ni*. [2] See Note E, p. 369.

feeding the Mtkvari was the country marching to the Armenians—Somkheti or the land of the Armenochalybes—" the Moschic territory " of Strabo—a borderland of mongrel stocks. The memory of the Swarming Time had dwindled to the vague legends of the hero-gods of tribes which were themselves merging their group-identities into the kingdoms of the Caucasus. Nevertheless the memory of the Mingling Time remained and with it the tradition of the common origin of the sons of Targamos, and some notion of the prevalence and decline of Aryan blood and speech which had flowed in on the troubled currents of the swarming.[1]

The ethnography of the main chain of the Caucasus is less clear. The western mountains were not well known to the ancient geographers; of the eastern mountains between the Daryal and the Caspian they only give us fabulous tales.

The western mountains of the Caucasus run in a south-easterly direction from the neighbourhood of the stagnant Sea of Azov—the Palus Mæotis of the Greeks—and they constitute the forearm of the easterly elbow of the Black Sea. They are precipitous forest-clad mountains which overhang the sea, and until the Russians built a coastal road at the beginning of the present century, there was no way past by land; all passage was made in the long flat-bottomed boats of the people of the country. Innumerable torrents find their way down from the short narrow valleys between the mountains into the sea, and in this way the coast is divided into mountain bluffs, which are cut off, each from the other, by these fast and furious unnavigable streams. Many of the streams make, at their mouths, among the woods, wide marshy tracks of ground. After Pitsunda point, the mountains turn inland, leaving a widening stretch of flat alluvial country. As the mountains turn inward and eastward, and the lowland strip widens to the Colchian plain, the rivers grow in length and size. All this country is favoured by the protection of the mountains; it is warm in winter, nor, unlike the Colchian plain, is it here too hot in summer. The moisture of the sea nourishes a rich vegetation. The orange, lemon, peach, pear, apple and grape flourish here, and the country has always been particularly noted for the growth of its cherries, chestnuts and plums.

Inland and eastward, the mountains are the most formid-

---

[1] Cf. the tradition embodied in the early apocryphal Annals. Brosset, *Histoire de la Géorgie*, 1ère Part, p. 31 and notes 3 and 4; cf. also p. 32, note 5.

THE SWARMING AND THE MINGLING

able of all the parts of Caucasus. From the Black Sea coast to the Daryal Gorge there is no pass under nine thousand feet and here Elbruz, Adai Khokh and Kazbek raise their splendid heads. Under Elbruz and Shkara is a high alpine region. The streams run down from here into the middle course of the river Rioni, the greatest of the westward-flowing waters of south Caucasus. The land is poor and snowbound, craggy and periculous. From the Colchian plain there is access only during the months of July and August, when with difficulty the traveller can ascend the valley of the Rioni, and, crossing to the upper valley of the Tskhenis-tsqali, enter this bleak land of untutored hunters and shepherds of mean flocks.

The northern slopes of Caucasus are easier than the southern. In the west the grassy uplands are watered by many streams of a middle size, running down to join the great Kuban which finds its mouth round about the Taman peninsula—dividing spit between the Black Sea and the Sea of Azov. Over all this back-side country, the upper valleys, of their nature, are sparse in the raw mountain atmosphere. Here the rare orochs —the European bison—survived until the beginning of the present century in one or two thin herds. The lower valleys and all the line of the Kuban are rich grainlands. This country, which suffered much during the centuries of horse-riding nomad power, was, in the Classic period, well inhabited by people trading with the Greeks—Scythian tribes who rose to passing kingdoms; and in the Bronze Age, before the time of written history, a great culture flourished here. Over the watershed of the western Caucasus, from the uplands of the Kuban to the steep forest-coast of the Black Sea, passage was rare and difficult; the best by the now-called Klukhor Pass, by the high tarn Teberdá.

Here to the north and west of the open Colchian plain, lay this great mountain country, closed to newcomers by cliffs and precipices and snow, by forests and the sea; a good haven for remnants in flight from the coursing of the fairer lands, and where, once set, they might hold their peace against the conquerors of the open south; and scrape a meagre life, fall to a great obscurity among the nations, and cause some idle men to wonder on their ancient coming. And so there are in all this country tribes of some affinity with the people living in the southward open country, yet of a forgotten history, and with obscurely differing idioms. Of these tribes the Svans—Georgian *Svanni*—who inhabit the alpine country under the great peaks of Elbruz and Shkara—may be a remnant of the old indigenous stock which had the rich lowlands before the Swarming Time. The name root SVAN-SON was widespread through the Caucasus in the Classic period. The Lazes are still called *Channi* by the Georgians, and the Mingrelians in the Rioni basin are called *Zanar* by the Svans. The Svans are the Soanes of Strabo, and he is cognizant of their connection with the Mingrelo-Colchians when he remarks that—

> "some say they are called the same name as the western Iberians from the gold-mines found in both countries".[1]

Ptolemy speaks of the Suannokolkhoi. In Suannokolkhoi we have a composite name as in Son-Meskh (for Somkheti) and in Mos-San (for Mos-syn-oekh-oi, i.e. the native nominal synthesis with the native and the Greek terminations). The name-root SVAN↔SON crops out again in that of the Sineli, a tribe which Scylax of Caryander, writing in the sixth century B.C., places in the neighbourhood of the Taman peninsula, in the Heniokhes of Strabo and Appian,[2] the Sanighes of Arrian,[3] and in Sanna, the name given by mediæval Italian geographers to the ruins of Nikopsia.

The Abkhaz people who inhabit the country to the west of Svaneti and to the north-west of the Colchian plain, speak a language which is distinct both from the Svanian and the Mingrelian dialects of Georgian and from the idioms of the Circassian tribes, occupying the coastal valleys to the north-west and the Caucasian uplands to the north of Abkhazeti. The Abkhaz were known to the classical geographers as Apsilai, and later as Abasgoi. They call themselves *Apsua* and their country *Apsu*. A is the Abkhazian definitive article, and the root of the name is P-S. The sound-change P-B-M is in accordance with Georgian phonetics, and the name of the Abkhaz is undoubtedly identical with those tribal and place-names in the Caucasus which have their root in M-S (i.e. a-BAS-goi = (a) MAS-khoi. Again the various forms of the name PHASIS may be connected with the root M-S ↔ B-S. Varied forms of Phasis are widespread throughout the Caucasian lands. By the classical writers the name was applied with much confusion both to the Rioni and the Chorokhi. In the Georgian province of Samtzkhé at the sources of the Araks was the country of Basiani,[4] Byzantine *Phaziané*, Armenian *Pasean*, Turkish *Pasin*. It was the district of the

---
[1] Strabo, XI, ii, 19.   [2] Cf. Dubois, I, 56-8.   [3] *Idem.*, I, 69.
[4] Wakhushti, p. 121.

Phasianoi of Xenophon.[1] The name Basiani occurs again in that of a valley situated to the west of the source of the Digori and to the north-east of Svaneti. Janashvili has correlated the words meaning "*water*" in Georgian, Abkhazian and Circassian with the root P-S, and it seems likely that this, as many other tribal name-forms, derives from a common element of nature.

Along the seaward mountains the names and the languages are obscure in their affinities to those of the Transcaucasian plains. Among the ancient geographers names recur in different forms from Scylax of Caryander in the sixth century B.C. down to the Middle Ages; yet we can see that the relative position of tribes bearing those names did not greatly change. Thus the small tribe Kerketes of the classical writers are the Cherkess of the Turks, the Circassians of the mediæval Italian travellers, and gave their name to all the people of the coast. These tribes may well have affinity with the Georgians, but the degree of their affinity and the origin of their tribal names and languages remain obscure. All the so-called Circassian tribes had some sense of common relationship; and they called themselves collectively ADIGHÉ, which the Georgians rendered JIKHI, the Arabs KECHEK or KASHAK, the Byzantines ZEKHI, the Venetians ZICHI. The name of the Akhæans of Strabo and Pliny, which some have thought to have indicated the existence of a colony of Akhæan Greeks, appears to be a mismouther of this native name. The Circassian (Adighé) people extended, in the early historic period, over the watershed along the valley of the Kuban and round the Sea of Azov and into the Crimea,[2] but they were submerged by the nomad peoples and pressed towards the upland valleys. Whether there was more than one ethnic element among the tribes who inhabited the coastal mountains in the historic period remains questionable. The existence among them of a strict caste system seems to indicate an imposed foreign element, but this caste system may have originated among them in the necessity of regulating the social status of the large number of slaves whom they captured in their raids against the peoples both of the Colchian plain and of the Crimea. The traveller, Dubois, records that when the Circassian princes and their familiars gathered in council to discuss the plans for a raid, they made use of a special

---

[1] Xenophon, IV, vi.
[2] There was a Circassian settlement in the Crimea as late as the beginning of the fifteenth century. See Dubois, I, 78 *et seq.*

language called "*chakobza*" which had no resemblance to Circassian. The people were not allowed to speak this language. Dubois suggests that this may be

> "an original language which might prove that there are several elements in the population of the Cherkess nation and that the princes and the nobility are intruders".[1]

The general name given by the Georgian Annalists to the tribes of the central mountain region—and in fact to any peoples entering Georgia from the north—is Alan. The Alans were, of course, well—and equally vaguely—known to the ancients. Minns is of the opinion that

> "Ammianus meant by the Alans all the nomadic tribes about the Tanais";[2]

and he suggests that

> "on the coming of the Huns, part of the Alans were forced westward, joined the Germans, against whom they were thrown, and ended as the inseparable companions of the Vandals in North Africa. Part of them were pressed up against the Caucasus ... and about them are the Tatar tribes that penned them in".[3]

It is only at a later period that the Georgian and Armenian sources distinguish between the nomads from the steppe to the north of the Caucasus (Tatars or Turks, generally referred to as Kipchaks or Khazars), the mountaineers of Daghestan (Lazghi or Leki), and the Alans of the Central Caucasus (Os, As, or Iron,[4] Georgian Osni, Russian Ossetini). The distinctly Aryan character of the language of the Ossetians gave currency to the popular tradition that they were the descendants of Persian prisoners carried north after one of the many nomad incursions south of the Caucasus. And although it is possible that such settlements of Persians did become established in the valleys of the middle Caucasus, this story is not necessary to explain the existence of Aryan elements in the mountain country. Furthermore, Marr has established the Japhetic substratum of the language spoken by the present-day Ossetians, and it would seem likely that the Alans

---

[1] Dubois, I, 141 and 142. He states that Reineggs, II, 248, is the only one who has preserved "a few examples of this jargon". For the study of the Circassian language and its various idioms see works of Uslar and others. The best recent study is by A. Dirr in *Caucasica*, Fasc. IV, pp. 65-144, and Fasc. V, pp. 1-54—*Die sprache der Ubychen*. (The author pursued his studies among the remnants of the Ubych (Ubukh) Circassians scattered through Asia Minor.) For a contemporary survey of the remnants of the Circassians in the Northern Caucasus see *Sovyetskaya Adigeya*, Krasnodar, 1925.
[2] Minns, *Scythians and Greeks*, p. 37.   [3] *Ibid.*, p. 41.
[4] The name of the Sea of Azov (classical Palus Mæotis) is a mediæval Russian nomenclature meaning literally "Sea of the Az" or Os; compare the Arab name for the Caspian—Bahr-ul-Khazar—"Sea of the Khazar".

—and their textual descendants the Ossetians—were a people composed of mixed racial stocks.[1] The Cimmerians, and the Scythians after them, were, in all probability, of predominantly Aryan stock. And the Sarmatians, who followed the Scythians as the lords of the land round the north-east of the Black Sea, were a third and new Aryan element. These Aryan peoples—Cimmerians, Scythians and Sarmatians—each in their turn disturbed and displaced or absorbed the older inhabitants of the country north the Caucasus. Later the Turkish conquerors who succeeded the Aryan peoples—Huns, Avars, Khazars, Pechenegs, Polovtzi and Kipchaks—did the same in like manner. The indigenous natives of the Euxine coasts were of a different stock to the conquering Aryan peoples who replaced them as the masters of the land, and they were presumably Caucasian, that is related to the Circassian tribes, who in historical times have inhabited only the narrow coastal valleys between Tuapse and the Kodori and inland as far as the Kuban. And the ruling tribe of the Scythian period, between the seventh and second centuries B.C., must have "*dominated many tribes of various origin, some Iranian and some Caucasian*".[2]

The Alans are, in fact, a people of mixed origin—the leavings of the migrations and disturbances which swept the plains to the north of the Caucasus, in the latter centuries of the pre-Christian era. Reclus, reflecting on their predominantly Aryan character, states at the same time that the Ossetians are "very mixed, including Georgian, Armenian and Kabard and other elements".[3] The country occupied by the Ossetians straddles the Daryal Pass—to which they give the Persian name "Dar-i-alan" or "gate of the Alans". In modern times they have always occupied the valleys of the Ardon and the Digor and smaller streams flowing north to the Kuban; and south of the watershed, the upper valleys of the Liakhvi and the Aragvi, draining to the Mtkvari. Along the Daryal Pass itself, they are mixed with mountain Georgians—who speak a curiously mediæval dialect and claim to be descended from old garrisons of the Georgian kings. The date of the establishment of Ossetian settlements south of the main chain is uncertain. Their incursions into the valley of the Mtkvari were frequent during the first thousand years A.D., and they were certainly settled in large numbers between Dusheti and Gori in the thirteenth century.[4]

[1] Marr, in *Iz. R.A.N.*, 1918 and onward, *Ossetica-Japhetica*.
[2] Minns, p. 127.
[3] Reclus, *Universal Geography*, VI, 72.
[4] Brosset, *Additions et Éclairissements à l'Histoire de la Géorgie*, p. 377.

THE BACKGROUND

Of the ethnography of the east Caucasus, the ancients were entirely ignorant. The Amazons occupied the blank upon the map, and Strabo records only two names which may be recognizable: the Ghelæ, possibly the Galgai of Russian writers; and the Legæ, the Leki of the Georgians —Lazgis,[1] a generic name sometimes applied to all the tribes of Daghestan. It is not until the Arab conquest in the seventh century A.D. that the names of the many tribes of Daghestan find their way into the works of Arab travellers.

[1] Strabo, XI, v; cf. Marr in *Iz. R.A.N.* (1917, No. 5), who derives the name-root LESK from words meaning "side".

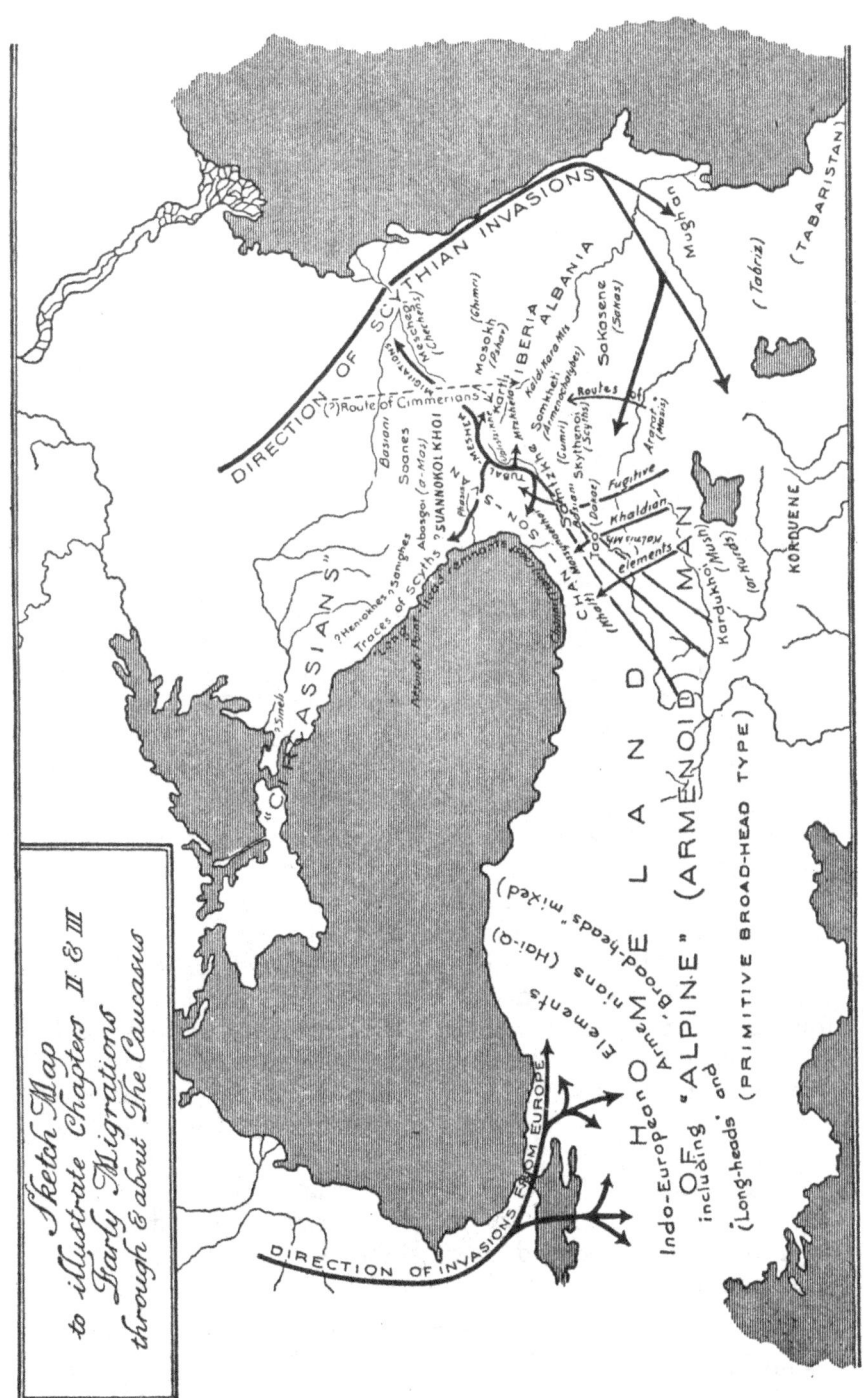

CHAPTER IV

MATRIARCHS, GODS AND EMPERORS

"They are born of the wells, and of the woods and of the holy rivers that flow forward into the salt sea."
Odyssey, X. 352.

"And they said, Nay; but we will have a king over us; That we also may be like all the nations; and that our king may judge us, and go out before us, and fight our battles."
1 *Samuel viii.* 19, 20.

THE life of the early Georgians was patriarchal. All authority was vested in the head of the family group—the *mamasakhlisi*, literally "the father of the house". Gradually the *mamasakhlisi*—the autocrat of the large family clan (*gwari*) grown into the tribe (*temi*)—became the ruler of the peasant principality (*tomi*). The ruler of Mtzkheta continued to call himself *mamasakhlisi* until the third century B.C. and it was only later that the title of king, *mépé* or *méupe*, came into use.[1] The whole basis of the early social organization of the Georgian tribes, as depicted in the Georgian Annals, was patriarchy, the rule of the fathers or the elders, and the historical tradition and the religion of the early Georgians derived from the reverence for the hero-father-founder of the tribal group. This conception goes back obviously to the Swarming Time when the migrant tribes—composed most often of heterogeneous elements, owed each their vague cohesion to the personal authority of some nomad soldier.

There are not, however, wanting many signs of an older form of social organization, which at a remote period appears to have been widespread over all the lands of Western Asia. The basis of this organization was the woman rather than the

---

[1] In the word *méupe* (←→ *méupali* ←→ *mé upali*) *mé* denotes the noun of "agent", *upali* "lord", *upli* = *upléba* "the right", hence *méupali*, *méupé*, "the holder of the right, the highest". *Upali* is also a religious term meaning "Lord". Cf. the term *ipani* used by the Urartian King Rusas in the Gökcheh inscription (*C.A.H.*, vol. III, page 178).

MATRIARCHS, GODS AND EMPERORS

man, the mother rather than the father. The woman was the stable unit of the community; the man the drifting element. Descent passed through the woman, by so-called Mother-Right. Frazer has shown that this Mother-Right existed in ancient Latium, where the rulership passed in the female line, and the husband of the ruler was merely the father of the children, and himself of no account.[1] Peake notes traces of this Mother-Right in the succession to the rulership in Minoan Crete.[2] Mother-Right was, in fact, a phase of social development, not only in Western Asia but throughout the ancient world. It has been called Matriarchy —"the rule of Mothers", but the extent to which women were the ruling influence in the primitive community—as well as forming the stable unit of such ordered life as was— must remain a doubtful question. The origin of Mother-Right derives from the days when hunting was the basis of the economic life of the community, when the women held the camp, to which the men were fleeting visitors between their expeditions; when mortality was high among the men, and there was no stability or permanence in the life of a man. And the continuance of much of this Mother-Right among the mountain tribes of the Caucasus is explained in that until the nineteenth century the basis of their economic life was only a development of the hunting stage. The tribes along the Circassian coast were concerned little in agriculture and fishing. Their principal occupation was in piratical expeditions and slave-raiding into the settled countries. The tribes of the eastern Caucasus again—while their secondary occupations were lumbering, gardening and herding—were first of all fierce rievers, incendiaries and thieves, who descended each year northwards across the Terek, and southwards and eastwards into the Mtkvari valley.

Thus in the lowland country the people fell long ago to a settled life, and took from their conquering forefathers the patriarchal ways of remote hero-fathers; but in the sparse mountains the loose-living habit of the early hunting, later raiding, communities was carried on.

Nature in all her manifestations could cower and trouble, delight and excite, the wondering pagan mind. The worship of the elements of Nature, the sky, the sun, the moon and the stars, was common to all primitive religions, and these

---

[1] Frazer, *The Golden Bough*, abridged edition, London 1924, pp. 152 *et seq.*
[2] Harold Peake, *The Bronze Age and the Celtic World*, pp. 119 *et seq.*

elements came to be personified in deities, around whom elaborate cults were built up. The sanctity of vegetation was a primitive conception, which had deep roots through the whole area of Western Asia. In the old Mazdaistic religion, plants were considered sacred, and in Asia Minor, and among the Abkhaz, Ossetians and Khevsurs of the Caucasus the sanctity of trees and woods continues to survive down to the present day.[1] Fire, in its relation to the sun, became the central theme of more than one advanced religion of the ancient world, and the cult of fire received a wide propagation in the Caucasus with the impulse of early Iranian Imperialism. Among the Japhetic peoples of the Caucasian region, the divine force of water was widely recognized and deeply reverenced. With the worship of water sanctity came to be attributed to aquatic creatures such as fish, otters and —by a process of association—snakes, dragons, dogs and wolves. An elaborate art, common to the area in which the Japhetic peoples were in movement, was developed in the stylization of these creatures, and their representation ranged from the giant stone-fishes of the Meskhian mountains to the intricate decorative snake-belts of the Kuban and the South Russian steppe. These religious symbols also came to have a totemic significance, and the fish, the wolf-dog,[2] the deer, the horse, the panther and the stork were adopted as tribal insignia by the peoples of both sides of the Caucasus mountains.[3]

The conceptions of the primitive tribal deities became confused and finally merged with the entities of the foreign gods of neighbouring peoples. The Hittite weather-god, Teshub, was reverenced by the Khaldians after their own hero-god Khaldis; and through the changing forms of Tarku the Thunder-god, the Sun-god and the War-god, he appears at last as the Roman Zeus Dolichenus in the West, and as Armazi (Ormuzd) in the Georgian-Iranian pantheon. In the

[1] For tree-worship, see Veidenbaum in *Iz. Kav. Ot. I.R.G.O.*, Vols. V and VII; Janashvili in *Khrist. Vos*, No. IV; and other sources given by Wesendonk in *Caucasica*, I, 85-6. Wesendonk quotes Markwart as thinking that "the tree-cult against which the Slav apostle, Constantine, fought in the Crimea, is aboriginal among the natives of the Caucasus, especially among the Circassians and Abkhazians. It is supposed that it spread from these nations to the Alans (Ossetians) and the Huns of the Caucasus".

[2] Myrsilus, the last Lydian king of the Heraclid dynasty, had the cognomen Candaules—"the Strangler of the Dog or Wolf"—possibly a title like Bulgaroktonos, conferred on him for his wars against the "wolf-totem" tribes of Eastern Anatolia (cf. *C.A.H.*, vol. III, page 506). The wolf has recently been adopted as the official symbol of the Turkish Republic.

[3] I. Meshchaninov, *Zmeya i Sobaka* . . . in *Zap. Koll.*, I (1925), 241 *et seq.* and *idem. Kamennye statui ryb-vishapi, ibid.*, I (1925), 401 *et seq.*

opinion of Wesendonk, Armazi was the Iranian name transposed to some old home-god of the Georgians. The worship of Armazi was closely connected with that of Kartlos, the hero-founder patriarch of the Kartlians. According to the *Life of St. Nino*, the image of the god Armazi—Ormuzd —in the city of Armazi was in the form of a man made of copper, wearing a gold cuirass, with a gold helmet and gold shoulder-pieces. He had one eye of onyx and one of beryl, and he held a sharp sword which shone and turned in his hand, foreboding death to whomsoever approached him. In this, the Georgian-Iranian Armazi corresponds to the Hittite Teshub, who sometimes carried a curved sword, and his worship may be connected with the sword-cult of the Scythians and Alans, and with the axe-cult the indications of which are found in the remains at Koban and Kazbek.

In association with Armazi were the gods Ga and Gatsi, whom the Annalists accept as the old native gods of the Georgians in contradistinction to Armazi, Zadeni and other gods of foreign origin.[1] Zadeni is a puzzling figure. He seems to have become eventually identical with the Iranian Mithra, but Tsereteli is inclined to see in him the Hittite god of vegetation, Sandon.[2]

An interesting problem of Georgian palæontology, which has its origin probably in matriarchal psychology, is the confusion between male and female. This is illustrated in the transposition of the primitive words for "father" and "mother" which have a common form in so many languages. *Mama* in Georgian means "father", *déda* "mother". As gender is not used in Georgia, it is only as a convention that a word is considered to be masculine and feminine. The sun is called in Georgian *mzé*, and it is an interesting fact that the Georgian considers the sun as female. The moon, *m'tvaré*, is male, and the name means probably "the ruler" (of the sky or night). Sandon, the old vegetation-god of the Hittites, may well be Zadeni, whose shrine by Mtzkheta was held among the Iberians as only second in honour to that of Armazi, and who, in the time of Strabo, was the Moon-god worshipped by the Albanians, taking precedence even of the Sun-god.[3]

---

[1] Marr, *Bogi Yazicheskoi*, is inclined to attribute to Ga and Gatsi a Semitic origin, and finds a possible correspondence with the Palmyran god Kat'é.
[2] For discussion, see Wesendonk, *Caucasica*, I, 85.
[3] Strabo, XI, v, 1.

THE BACKGROUND

The seven principal deities of the Georgian pantheon were associated with the cult of the Sun, the Moon and the five planets and the worship of Kartlos-Teshub-Armazi, the national god in his various transformations, continued to hold the subconscious religious mind of the Georgians throughout the whole period of Christianity. St. George was the Cappadocian successor of the Hittite Teshub, and in Georgia the Christian Saints George and Elias retained many of the attributes accorded in pagan times to the solar-lunar deities Kartlos-Armazi and Zadeni. Wesendonk has noted that on the Georgian representations of St. George are the Sun, the Moon and the five stars, which nowhere else occur, while Javakhishvili has pointed out that in the worship of St. George pagan features exist, and that St. George is in reality a Moon-god. Seven was a significant and often sacred figure in Georgia, and in the Middle Ages the Seven Heavenly Bodies symbolized the seven parts of the Georgian Kingdom. But while sun- and moon-worship may be native to Georgia, it is probable that the worship of the five planets and the sanctity of the number seven indicate early Mesopotamian influences upon the native cults.

Wesendonk has suggested that the Cappadocian St. George became identified with the Georgian solar-lunar deity at the period of the introduction of Christianity into Georgia under influences from Syria. He continued to be associated with the Seven Heavenly Bodies and he was worshipped as the older gods Armazi and Zadeni had been, most often on mountain-tops and heights.

St. George holds the supreme place in the devout heart of the Georgian peasant, and he is reckoned even before Christ. Javakhishvili has observed that in the folk-lore of the people, St. George, and not Christ, is considered as the more important being, and he is regarded as the first in rank and the greater god. He is the protector of the human hearth, and of shepherds, and he guards man and beast and crops against the destructive forces of nature, even against the caprices and the evil humour of God. Only a second place is accorded to Christ. The Khevsurs address St. George in the words " *Oh God, thou Holy George.*" The Svanians respect St. George more than the Creator and consider him as more powerful than God. The *Khatoba*, the great feast of St. George, in August, is made to fall on the night of the full moon, and the ceremonies connected witht his nocturnal celebration are none other than the pagan rites of moon-worship. Finally, the association of St. George with the dragon, so common on the religious objects surviving from the Caucasian Bronze Age and with the horse which recalls the Scythian totem or indeed the white horse of Mithra, affirms that mediæval Georgian Christianity was compounded of a mass of obscure pagan traditions derived from the remotest spiritual experiences of the people.[1]

Beside the two great deities, Armazi and Zadeni, and the lesser Ga and Gatsi, there reigned in Georgia three goddesses, whose worship was definitely associated with the cult of the Great Mother. The Georgian lowlands lay open to many foreign influences, and as Teshub was identified through the centuries with Kartlos, Armazi and St. George, so the Great Mother was worshipped in Georgia in the names of Itrujani, of Ainina and Danana, and of Aphrodite. Itrujani was Ishtar or Astarte of the Semites. Ainina was Anaitis of the Armenians, Anahit of the Semites; with her name it always conjoined that of Danana, the Nana of the Semites.[2] Aphrodite, the Greek goddess, was introduced after the Roman conquest, as a Mediterranean adjunct to the native cult of the Great Goddess.[3]

The personifications of the Mother Goddess, Astarte, Nana, Anahit and even the Hellenic Aphrodite, were essentially native to Asia and their cult derives from the centuries before the Aryan swarming. Astarte was the wife of the Moon-god and the goddess of fertility and child-birth. Aphrodite, although she came to Georgia from Greece, was the love-goddess of Cyprus and Anatolia and the consort of the Phrygian-Armenian Ares. In the cult of Anahit, ritualistic prostitution occurs and E. Meyer considers the customs associated therewith, which occur also in the Lydian cult, as being non-Semitic. They belong perhaps to the oldest layer of population in Asia Minor.[4]

The memories of a matriarchal way of life which survived into the classic period, and the persistence of the Mother-Goddess cults with their emphasis on the physical and sexual theme of life, proclaim the existence in pre-Aryan Asia of a

---

[1] " The Bible is full not so much of religious as of racial culture; Christianity itself has taken over these survivals to such an extent that the division of culture into Christian and pre-Christian is scarcely permissible ".—Meschaninov, *Zmeya i Sobaka*.

[2] Danana used always with the name Ainina, appears to be formed of the Georgian conjunctive particple *da* + Nana.

[3] Aphrodite had her idol at Mtzkheta in the second century A.D., Brosset, *Hist.*, I, i, 77.

[4] Ritualistic prostitution of boys whose gains go to the shrines of Muslim saints, is still practised among the non-Semitic—and only nominally Muslim—Berbers of the Wadi Sûs.

cultural background which emerges in vivid contrast to the civilizations of the Greek and Roman world, which parented our own. Among the Lydians and Carians and other peoples who retained the elements of the matriarchal culture, the position of women was one of freedom and independence, sexual life was promiscuous in character, and the social structure was communal. Certain elements of the matriarchal system persisted in Georgia, and more definitely among the mountain-tribes down to modern times. And the Mother Goddess in her different incarnations held sway over the minds of the Georgians down to the first centuries of the Christian era. Indeed, the love of the Mother Goddess endured throughout the Middle Ages, nor is it now altogether dead. For as the Moon-god became transformed into the Saints of the Christian Church, so the wild and hungry goddesses who had been adored at the love feasts of the pagan past assumed the forms of the Holy Virgin Mary, of the chaste evangelist St. Nino, and of the austere Queen Tamara. A hundred years ago the Circassians still worshipped Merissa, protectress of bees. They say that once all the bees were destroyed but one which took refuge in the sleeve of Merissa, and that this bee was the ancestor of all the bees that followed after. Merissa had also the second name Mareime, and was said to be the Mother of God.[1] Similarly there are other legends round the name of the Virgin Mary and rites due to her which are not of Christian provenance, as the peculiar sanctity which surrounded in the Middle Ages the worship of the Virgin of Atskveri (Atskhur). Again, the fame throughout Georgian lands of the great Queen Tamara, can be associated with the older reverence in the confused mind of the peasants from the Great Mother, and the legends which attach in many places to Tamara's name are to be derived sometimes from earlier legends of the Woman-god.[2]

The Aryan Empire of the Persians rose out of the chaos of the Swarming Time, and in the fifth century B.C. when Herodotus was describing the newly-ordered lands of Western Asia, he included the tribes settled in the Trans-Caucasian Trough within the XVIIIth Satrapy of the Achæmenian Monarchy.[3] And however loose and sporadic the control of the Achæmenians may have been, it is in great part to this

---

[1] Dubois de Montpèreux, *Voyage autour du Caucase*, I, 136.
[2] Lermontov, who misrepresents so grossly the character of the authentic Queen Tamara, has associated with the name of the great queen some vague legends of the orgiastic rites which corresponded to those practised in honour of Astarte.
[3] Herodotus, VII, 76–9.

extraneous "world" influence that must be attributed the evolution of the mixed tribal elements of the Swarming Time into the comparatively civilized Kingdom of Iberia, which Strabo knew and Pompey conquered.

During the fourth century B.C. the Empire of the Achæmenians collapsed, but the civilization of Iran was still young, and the political habits and religious beliefs of the Persians continued to penetrate to the eastern parts of Trans-Caucasia.[1]

In the half-legendary figure of the first Georgian dynast, Farnavazi or Parnabazus, who is credited with a reign lasting for sixty-five years, the Annalists have embodied the tradition not only of the setting-up of a military monarchy in the Mtkvari valley during those eventful generations which followed the overthrow of the Achæmenian Empire by the Macedonians, but of the gradual development, under Iranian influence, of a feudal society.

Farnavazi, descended from Uplos and born of a Persian mother, liberated the Iberians from the yoke of Azon, a legendary Macedonian governor. Kuji, the ruler of Egrisi, the classical Colchis, came under his suzerainty and his authority appears to have extended from the Alazani to the sources of the Mtkvari and the middle reaches of the Chorokhi.[2] The beginnings of a feudal system undoubtedly date from this time. Farnavazi appointed eight governors (*eristavni*) to the different divisions of his kingdom, who represented the power of the central authority over the heads of the old local *mamasakhlisi*. Farnavazi, further, appears to have been supported by a large body of Greek mercenaries, upon whose shoulders his military control reposed, and we read that—

> "they were, in recompense for their bravery during the war . . . distributed in the valleys and in different districts, and well treated by Farnavazi, who called them *aznaurni*."[3]

That the rule of Farnavazi represented the imposed control of a foreign element—partly Iranian and partly Hellenistic in character—is again indicated in the fact that his death was signalized by a sanguinary revolt against his heir, Saurmagi, who, in suppressing it, seems to have relied altogether on the support of these same *aznaurni*, of the Dzurdzuks, his

---

[1] Cf. Kovalevski, *Zakon i Obichai na Kavkaze*, I, 83–122.
[2] Brosset, *H. de la G.*, pp. 40–1.   [3] *Ibid.*, pp. 42–43.

mother's tribe, and of the Ossetians. And the Annals state that Saurmagi—

"having crushed the Kartlosids, raised the *aznaurni* in honour and secured to the Dzurdzuks a great prósperity." [1]

The spread throughout Georgia during this period of the religion of Ahura-Mazda is a further indication of the definitely Iranian character of the early feudal culture of the Mtkvari valley. The eastern part of Trans-Caucasia—the region of the mysterious natural fires of the Apsheron peninsula, was always a country sacred to the imagination of the worshippers of fire.[2] In the days of Farnavazi the new religion swept the Georgian land and Mtzkheta with the neighbouring great temples of Zedazadeni and Armazi became a principal centre of the cult which, for the next nine hundred years, constituted the intellectual background of half the peoples of the Caucasus, and whose devotees, later, for so long contested for supremacy with the followers of Christ.

Mirvani, another Magian, the successor of Saurmagi, and Farnajomi, his son, furthered the religion of Ahura-Mazda.[3] But the new cult was not accepted with contentment in many parts of the country. The older animistic cults had a strong hold upon the affectionate imagination of the primitive Georgians and the struggle between the royal evangelists of the Iranian religion and the priestly devotees of the gods and goddesses of the natural world was long, bloody and indeterminate.

The fourth king after Farnavazi, Farnajomi, Mirvani's son, who reigned from 112 to 93 B.C. was driven from the throne as a "blasphemer against the idols" as one who had transgressed the religion of the fathers of his people, and abandoned the cults of the gods, protectors of the Georgians. A representative of the Armenian Arsakids secured the Iberian throne, and it would appear that this rising against the Magians in Georgia was contemporary with a reaction in favour of the older gods throughout Armenia. It is likely also that in the earlier rising during Saurmagi's reign, feeling in favour of the national gods was combined with a dislike of the new half-foreign aristocracy, and it is recorded by the Annalists that Saurmagi in later years restored the idols of the goddess Ainina-

---

[1] Brosset, *H. de la G.*, p. 44.
[2] Cf. Wesendonk, *Caucasica*, I, 4-5; *ibid.*, pp. 73 and 76, for traces of the remains of fire-temples in Georgia, at Muget', " place of the Magi ", and elsewhere.
[3] Cf. Marr, *Bogi Yazicheskoi*, in *Zap. Vost. Ot. I.R.A.O.*, Vol. XIV, Parts 2-3, pp. 1-30. See particularly pp. 1-11 for the Iranian derivations of the names of the early Georgian kings.

MATRIARCHS, GODS AND EMPERORS

Anahit [1]—presumably with the object of allaying the idolatrous misgivings of the common people.

In the third century B.C., with the establishment of the half-legendary dynasty of Farnavazi in Iberia, a kingdom had been established, a house ruled, which had about it at least a strong touch of foreign manner, be it Iranian or Armenian or Greek, and the life-spoke of the country swung to change in the wheel of the surrounding world. The commune was passing into the feudal barony; the great tribal regions were becoming principalities; kings, sitting at the junctions of the rivers, were building roads and castles, walled towns and cities, known to the traders and soldiers of the lands beyond the mountains.

The usurpation of the Iberian throne by a cadet branch of the Armenian line of the Parthian Arsakids occurred in the first decade of the last century B.C. About the same time Colchis was included within the dominions of the Arsakids of Pontus. A struggle was already imminent between these half-Hellenized dynasts of Western Asia and the growing power of Rome, and in 86 B.C. began the first of the long campaigns of the Romans against Mithradates, King of Pontus. In the winter of 65 B.C. the resources of the Pontic king were at last exhausted and from Colchis he fled by boat along the Circassian coast to his last possessions on the Cimmerian Bosporos. The Georgian kings in Iberia and Albania, clients of Mithradates, were involved in his disaster. Pompey, in command of the Roman army in eastern Armenia, wintered on the banks of the Mtkvari, intending, with the spring, to pursue the Pontian to extremity. He found it urgent, however, to conduct a serious campaign against the Albanian and Iberian kings. Having defeated the Albanians, Pompey advanced to Harmozika (Armazis-tzikhe), the city of Armazi in the bend of the Mtkvari below Mtzkheta, and after heavy fighting, received the submission of the Iberian king, the Otokos of Appian, Artagi of the Annals.

In the Copenhagen Museum there is a bust of Pompeius Magnus, conqueror of the East. Competent and supercilious, understanding but not kindly, his stone mask stares upon the ages—the unseeing eyes and the clever mouth of the man of action. Thus may Pompey well have looked, so intelligent and quick and soaring in his plans, upon the barbaric Georgian kings, as they brought to him a "*bedstead, table and a chair of state, all of gold*".[2]

[1] Brosset, *H. de la G.*, I, 47.   [2] Plutarch's *Lives, Pompey*, p. 97.

THE BACKGROUND

Pompey caused a pillar to be raised commemorating his victories,[1] and the tribes that he had beaten, and went his way well satisfied, with victorious troops, a heightened name and looted wealth to pursue his contest with other men as great.

In the first century B.C. the lands of the Caucasus lay in the road of Imperial politics. The military power of the Roman Republic, growing from the hardy militia who came together to defend their homesteads in the Punic Wars, had won the mastery of the Mediterranean world. The figure of Coriolanus, the father of his people, remained a quaint and somewhat rustic memory; dictatorships, dynasty-building, the Imperial purple, intoxicated the intelligences of able men, the leaders of the Roman people—Marius, Sulla, Pompey, Cæsar, Mark Antony. The mean field of the thrifty Roman blossomed into the tropic garden of the Empire. Egypt and all Africa, Spain and Gaul and Britain, Greece and Macedon, the Islands, the ancient cities of Syria and Anatolia, fell to these clever soldiers. Men might well become intoxicated, plotting, bullying and murdering, as they grasped the riches of the ancient world. Great armies marched and counter-marched, great navies sailed the seas, the spoil of cities, slaves and vast taxes gorged the children of lean conquerors. And men grew rich and wise—and disillusioned. As the soldiers brawled and murdered like their masters; the middling classes lost all power and groaned beneath their taxes; the proletariat grew to be a dangerous and untended mingling of all the nations of the West and East; and civic rights fell into a desuetude when men were Roman citizens who had no drop of Roman blood.

Meanwhile the mills of empire ground. The Roman Empire in the east was the political heir of Macedon, and Macedon itself had been but the political and military expression of the economic and cultural expansion of the Greeks over the lands of Nearer Asia. Hellenistic Asia had fallen naturally to the new power which dominated the Greek and Latin world, and the Romans might indeed have marched in the track of Alexander and carried their eagles to the Indus, but that over the Iranian plateau was established the empire of the Parthian Arsakids, a dynasty more virile than that of the Persian Achaemenians who had confronted Alexander.

The Arsakids were nomad soldiers whose origin is doubtful; as Parthians they may have been either of Turkish or

[1] Pliny, VII, xxvii. The late Prince Iverico Mickeladze told me that there is still a bridge known as Bombais-Khidi—Pompey's Bridge.

Aryan stock. They had imposed their rule over the feudal satrapies of the Iranian plateau. They made their capital at Ctesiphon on the Tigris, and thus controlled not only the Iranian plateau, but the ways up into Armenia and Syria, by the valley of the Euphrates. The Romans had broken the power of the Arsakids in Pontus, Colchis, Armenia and Iberia, but Pompey's campaigns were the beginning only of a protracted struggle between the empires of the West and East. For nearly three centuries the two empires ruling Hellenic and Iranian Asia were to contend for mastery, until with the overthrow of the Parthian Arsakids by the native Iranian family of Sasan (A.D. 226) and with the foundation of the Eastern Roman Empire (A.D. 312) the struggle was to assume almost a national form as the old antagonism between Persian and Greek.

CHAPTER V

THE HISTORICAL GEOGRAPHY OF ANCIENT GEORGIA

" For the cities which were formerly great, have most of them become insignificant ; and such as are at present powerful were weak in the olden time. I shall therefore discourse equally of both, convinced that human happiness never continues long in one stay."

Herodotus, I, 5.

" There are very few Cities in all Georgia . . . though there has been more formerly . . . but now they lie all in ruins . . . and I heard say, while I stay'd at Tefflis, that these Cities were very large and sumptuously Built, as may be well enough conjectur'd, as well by that which is not as yet altogether destroy'd, as by the ruins themselves."

Chardin, 1686 ed. (*p.* 187).

THE " influence of geographical conditions " on the history of a country is a favourite motive of writers of history—particularly in these later days. This " influence of geographical conditions " is, I think, professed too much. In the writing of history, as in other writings, the most of us get certain current notions which we elaborate to the current intelligence —itself aware of some part of them already. And thus we give some satisfaction in confirming with much detail that which is already current, and find agreement and our due approval. But this labouring of " geographical influence " should be a line and not the theme of him who is concerned with the past life of his fellows. For the theme of history is the woof and web of man's intelligence (the theme of natural life may be this " influence of geographical conditions "). The history of man is his amazing fight, most darkly, humbly and almost without consciousness, to control all natural life in its manifold and various forms, his own natural self therein. This reverential mouching of " geographical influence " and " economic forces " is but the iterative incantation of man's past weakly fears of the vast power and menace of the natural things he could not comprehend. In our vain and soaring minds we build up natural certainties to rule our puny lives, and supernatural certainties before us, our aching for finality. And our history is so wonderful; a brave riding through the mists, a fine shouting in the sun, a weeping in the darkness, a snarling over meats—a flukish combination of electrical atoms or a War of Good and Evil, the fulfilment of the soul.

Discerning, then, the limitations of this conception of "geographical influence" in relation to the history of man, we consider the influence of geographical conditions on the development of history in the Caucasus. The Mountains of Likhi, which divide the Transcaucasian Trough into two separate basins, have had their blind effect upon the life of man in the lands to the south of the Caucasus. Imier, "that side," facing to the open sea, has lain open to the Mediterranean world; Amier, "this side," draining to the shut Asiatic Sea, the Caspian, has always been a continental region, a shelf of the Iranian world. The folk living in these two basins, on "that side" and on "this side", have used the wall of the mountains as a bridge, and since they have for so long been one nation, speaking if not one tongue, at least in tongues intelligible to each other, of the two lands they have made one country. There have always been differences in the culture, as in the political history of "that side" and "this side". In the Roman days, Colchis, the western country, was more civil. Iberia, over the mountains of Likhi, was more rusticated. Strabo notes a harder, rougher way of life, as he goes eastward, from the busy ports of Colchis over the mountains into the agricultural plain of Iberia, and further towards the Caspian into the parts of the half-nomadic Albanians.

Colchis was, then, in the first centuries A.D. the most civil part of the Caucasus; a part, in fact, of the Græco-Roman civilization which was spread round the shores of the Black Sea from the mouths of the Danube to the Caucasian Mountains. The country was, indeed, for some decades during the first century A.D. included in the Bosporan kingdom of the Roman clients, Polemon and Pythodoris. Iberia remained the rougher land over the mountains, the up-country parts; its kings, cadets of the Persian royal houses and veering in their politics between the Roman Emperors and the Court of Ctesiphon; their capital was rather ruder, more remote than those of the Armenian kings in the cities on the Araks; their weight in politics much less significant.

When Strabo knew it, Colchis, the civil part, the country

by the sea, already had a long tradition of urban life and foreign trading. The days of its commercial history go back to the centuries certainly when the cities of Greece were opening up the Euxine business; the legends of it to much earlier time. It is likely that in the Colchian towns was preserved some remnant and memory of the old Bronze Age culture that covered all the Caucasus before the Swarming Time. The Greeks, in spreading round the Euxine in the seventh century B.C. were only resurrecting the cities, the sea-ways and land-routes of this former vivid age. The great Hellenic cities of the Cimmerian Bosporus grew up on the foundations of an earlier and forgotten building. Phanagoria and Hermonassa had been founded before the Milesians came, and Panticapæum was, in the words of Rostovtseff—

" Active probably hundreds of years before the Greeks settled there. ... The Barbarian name of the town, and the legend preserved by Stephanos of Byzantium that it was founded by a son of Aietes, King of those Colchians who appear in the story of the Argonauts, testify to the great antiquity of the town, to its ancient intercourse with the Caucasus, and to its existence as a seaport long before the arrival of the Milesians." [1]

It does not seem fantastic to believe, perhaps, that the Greeks came into the Black Sea rather as in a later age the Normans and the Saracens broke upon the cities of the Mediterranean, and that they suppressed, imposed themselves upon, supplanted an older Euxine thalassocracy, built up maybe by the natives of the litoral lands, or by some earlier Ægean power.[2] They may have come upon, disrupted and chaotic after the ruin of Cimmerian and Scythian invasions, some older state of things, in which Colchis had had the part which later the Bosporan kingdom had during the period of the Hellenic thalassocracy.

At the time of the Roman conquest Colchis was a rich and prosperous land. Its decline during the subsequent six centuries of Roman-Persian hegemony in Trans-Caucasia was progressive and catastrophic. This decline, as was that of Græco-Scythian cities of the Tauric Chersonese and the Cimmerian Bosporos, was due obviously to the unsettled political conditions occasioned by the great movements of barbarian hordes over the Eurasian steppe to the north of the Caucasus, and round all the shores of the Black Sea. But it was occa-

---

[1] Rostovtseff, *Iranians and Greeks*, pp. 18 and 19.
[2] The story of the rape of Medea seems rather to indicate the piratical character of early Mediterranean adventurings in the Black Sea. Cf. also my paper in *J.R.G.S.*, July, 1929, " The March-Lands of Georgia ".

sioned also in part by the recurrent Roman-Persian wars, and the consequent interruption of normal commercial goings along the great trade route up the valley of the Rioni over the mountains of Likhi and along the valley of the Mtkvari and its tributaries into Armenia.

At the time when Strabo wrote, and Polemoń ruled, the territory of Colchis occupied the whole of the great alluvial plain between the main chain of the Caucasus, the mountains of Likhi and the massif of Shavsheti, which divides the Rioni plain from the narrow valley of the Chorokhi.

The Classic writers have left a picture which conveys at once the prosperous state of Colchis and its old tradition of civility.[1]

The basin of the Rioni was spread with thriving towns. The site of Kutais of later days, seat of the Imerian kings, and the capital of western Georgia—Kutatisi of Wakhushti[2]—was covered by the two towns of Cytaia or Kotatissium and Oukhimerion,[3] which are described in fullest detail by Procopius, who wrote, in the sixth century, of the Lazic War. The twin emplacements lay in a curve of the Rioni, a few miles above its confluence with the Qwirila. Oukhimerion was situated to the north on the right bank of the loop of the Rioni; Kotatissium was to the south, in the angle of the left bank. Oukhimerion, the fortress, was situated on a hill at a height of about 250 feet above the level of the river and it was formed of an acropolis on the summit of the hill, an upper town with battlements and a lower town opening over steep rocky slopes to the waters of the Rioni. Across the river, extended the open streets, the markets and the scattered suburbs of Kotatissium. Kutais to-day gives to the traveller this impression of a scattered, loose disjointedness. The few streets, the churches, the houses, the gardens and the orchards of this casual town are spread out around the great rock of the ruined citadel and they are littered along the two banks of the river. In the last foothills of the Caucasus fineing to the Colchian plain, in the sparkling sunshine, the river gleaming past down from the mountains to the sea, the lovely city stretches lazy

---

[1] Strabo, XI. ii., 17-18: "The country is fertile and its produce is good, except the honey, which has generally a bitter taste. It furnishes all the materials for shipbuilding. It produces them in great abundance, and they are conveyed by the rivers. ... It was from this country that the king (Mithradates) derived the greatest part of his supplies for the equipment of his naval armament. ... It supplies flax, hemp, wax and pitch in great abundance. Its linen manufacture is celebrated, for it was exported to foreign parts."

[2] Wakhushti, p. 371, who attributes the construction of the mediæval Georgian town to Levan II, King of the Abkhaz (744-89).

[3] Cf. Dubois, I, 398-400; II, 72.

brave and laughing, like as it were to some free woman who has known so many grasping dirty masters, and remains fresh in all her shame.

Farther down the river below the conflux of the Rioni and the Qwirila, lay in the Classic time Rhodopolis [1]; it is Vardistzikhe of the Georgians, in literal translation "the castle of the rose". Situated on low ground among the woods, it became a favourite winter residence of the Lazic and Imerian kings. Men dealt badly by it; the natives razed their rose castle in the Lazic War (A.D. 549) to prevent its seizure by the Persians; about twelve centuries later the Russians smashed the ageing walls of the Imerian foundation, "*afin d'empêcher les Turcs d'y prendre position*".[2] And thus when Dubois visited the site, about a hundred years back, he found that nothing rested but a strong wall of seven or eight feet in thickness, of which a part dated, perhaps, from the time of the Lazes, for it was in their style of architecture.[3] Lower down, again, in the angle of the conflux of the Tskhenistsqali with the Rioni, was the "plain of oaks" Mukherisi,[4] dominated by a fortress of the name, a hold much contested in the Lazic War. And higher up the Tskhenis-tsqali was Onurgurisi, Khoni[5] of later days, commanding the way up into the mountains to the Svanian country. Many more were the sea-ports, towns and castles of the Colchian-Lazic basin, from Bathys, "the deep anchorage",[6] near the mouth of the Chorokhi and Phasis at the mouth of the Rioni,[7] round the crescent up to Dioscurias; inland to Petra,[8] a Roman stronghold under the Gurian hills, and to Alexandria,[9] which twin-marcher fort with Sarapana [10] guarded the way over the mountains from Iberia.

But there was one place in all this country so much older than the others in tradition that the Greeks distinguished it as Archæopolis—"the ancient city"—and the Georgians, through the long years to this present day, have named the site of it Nakalakevi, which has the meaning of "where there was once a town". In Wakhushti's time, Nakalakevi was an obscure Mingrelian borough, a residence of the Dadianis,

---

[1] Procopius, VIII, xiii. 22.   [2] Dubois, II, 221.   [3] *Ibid.*
[4] Mocheris of Procopius, who calls it and Rhodopolis "two cities of the greatest importance".
[5] Dubois, I, 405.
[6] Now Batum (Georgian—Batomi).
[7] Phasis—the mediæval Fasso—now Poti. The lower course of the Rioni was called also Phasis by the Classic writers.
[8] Dubois, III, 86, located the site of Petra by the village of Ujenar.
[9] Dubois, II, 72, and Wakhushti, p. 363, use the mediæval Georgian name Skanda.
[10] Shoropani.

situated on the right bank of the Tekhuri, a small stream which falls into the Rioni, some miles below the Tskhenistsqali. Wakhushti describes it as "a town and fortress built by Kuji in the time of the first King Farnavazi". Kuji was the ruler of Egrissi, the old Georgian name for all the western plain. Wakhushti adds that Nakalakevi was destroyed during the Arab wars, "became a town again and was ravaged".[1] Dubois, who visited the ruins of Nakalakevi, decided that in great detail they answered to the description of Archæopolis of the Lazes, written by Procopius. He found the ruins of a bridge over the Tekhuri, a castle or acropolis, and a great walled area inside which were the ruins of a palace, a bazaar, and a small Christian church, in the earliest style of East Christian art.[2] Brosset also visited the site and accepted the identity of Nakalakevi with Archæopolis.[3]

The special antiquity of the town is patent in both the Georgian and the Greek nomenclature. In the Georgian Annals, the legend of its foundation dates to the first days of the Georgian monarchy. And it may well be that "the old city" of Procopius was the successor of Æa, the capital of the mythical kingdom of Aietes, where the Argonauts came. In fact the sparse indications as to the whereabouts of Æa given by Strabo, by Pliny and by Stephanos of Byzantium, all indicate that Archæopolis, the Lazian capital, and Nakalakevi, the obscure Mingrelian borough of the Middle Ages, rose the one upon the other, upon the site of Æa.[4]

We have already observed that the country eastward of the mountains of Likhi lay, generally, beyond the borderland of Greek knowledge. The mountains which encircled and frowned down upon the enchanted land of Colchis gave no inspiration to the mythological fantasies of the early Greeks. Even to the later geographers, the up-country valleys were remote lands ruled by bucolic heathen kings.

It is not until we come to the great work of the Emperor Constantine Porphyrogenitus,[5] in the tenth century A.D., that we find a western geographer really familiar with the topography of hither Georgia. Nevertheless, the culture of these parts was venerable. Urartian place-names may be traced along the valley of the Araks,[6] and north to the Chorokhi

---

[1] Wakhushti, pp. 396–7. Nakalakevi was called also Tzikhé-Godja (? "Kuji's castle").
[2] Dubois, III, 51 *et seq.*
[3] Brosset, *Voyage Archéologique*, 7ᵉ Rapp., p. 60; 9ᵉ Rapp., pp. 22 *et seq.*
[4] For discussion of this question see Dubois, *ibid.*
[5] Constantine Porphyrogenitus, *De Administrando Imperii.*
[6] Meshchaninov, *Iz. Gos. AK. I.M.K., Geographicheskiya nazvaniya verkhovev Araksa po Khaldskim nadpisvam*, IV (1925), 43–64.

THE BACKGROUND

valley. Carved lions, as yet unstudied, among the boulders of the Chorokhi and the Tortomis-tsqali confirm the declaration of the place-names. Some kind of not uncultured life went on continuing from the Bronze Age right through the centuries which saw Trebizond and Phasis grow to rich emporia for the trade of all these parts. The Georgian Annals embody the tradition of the most ancient foundation of many settled sites; in describing the legendary invasion of Georgia by Alexander, the Annalists give a picture of the country still suffering from the devastation of the Swarming Time, and they adjoin a list of the settled sites which were then flourishing.

> "He saw horribly barbarous nations, established on the Mtkvari and along its tributaries, nations which we call Bunturki ('primitive Turks') and Kipchaks; he was astonished for no people acted as they did. He found also in the middle of Georgia, the strong towns of Tsunda; of Khertvisi on the Mtkvari, of Odzrakhé perched on a rock of Ghado; of Tukharisi, on the river of Sper or Chorokhi; of Urbnisi, of Kaspi, of Uplistzikhé; great Mtzkheta and its suburbs; Sarkiné, Tzikhé-didi; Zanavi where the Jews lived; Rustavi; Dédatzikhé, Samshwildé, Mtkvaris-tzikhé or Khunani, and the towns of Kakheti; all towns and citadels defended by a population of intrepid warriors." [1]

The character of these settled sites must have been varied. We are familiar with Strabo's account of the towns of the Mtkvari plain—

> "where the houses have roofs covered with tiles and display skill in building; there are market-places in these and various kinds of public edifices".

Such were the towns in the open plain of the Mtkvari. But the most characteristic and original features of Georgian domestic architecture had always been the use which the people have made of the innumerable natural caves along the banks of the narrow river-valleys of upland Georgia. These sites have been occupied from time immemorial, and mention is made of them, almost from page to page, in the Georgian Annals. Wakhushti, in his *Geographical Description of Georgia*, mentions by name over one hundred and twenty sites of such cave-dwelling communities, which in his day in the middle of the eighteenth century were still either continuously inhabited, or resorted to as places of refuge by the people during the frequent slave-raiding expeditions of the Turks of

---

[1] Brosset, *H. de la G.*, I, 33. Ghado is an ancient name for a part of the Mountains of Likhi.

Akhaltzikhé.[1] To this present day, many villages, particularly in the mountainous country of the upper Mtkvari, consist of hovels, hollowed partly out of the rocks and made habitable by a wall of stone and plaster on one or two sides. To so great an extent was the use of rock-dwellings a part of the domestic economy of the Georgians, that more than one of these trogoldytic sites grew to the dimensions of a town, and to the significance of a royal residence. Uplistzikhé you may see soon after the train leaves Gori for Tiflis. " The castle of Uplos " is carved out of a long low ridge of rock, which overlooks the wide valley of the Mtkvari. Here, cut out of the natural caves of the ancient mountain, is a great hall of audience, baths and reservoirs, a church, and numerous lesser dwellings, covered passage ways, and a secret way down to the water of the river. The style of architecture of the great hall of audience and the church indicate that certainly as late as the twelfth century it was restored and prepared for the reception of a new master. More inaccessible and less ancient is the cave-town of Vardzia which lies up in the mountains, a few miles west of Khertvisi on the main road from Akhaltzikhé to Akhalkalaki. Vardzia—the rose-fortress—was a town of unascertained antiquity. Its royal palace and its church were, according to the Annals and to Wakhushti, begun by King Giorgi III and completed by Queen Tamara.

The settled sites of early Georgia consisted, therefore, of towns and villages of wood-tiled houses in the open Mtkvari plain, and—where the mountain side offered a worn flank—of rough troglodytic dwellings, which, as at Uplistzikhé and Vardzia, grew to the rank of royal towns.

In the upper valley of the Mtkvari and in the valley of the Chorokhi, the people have for the most part lived always a half-nomadic life, packed in the winter into troglodytic hovels among the boulders along the narrow valleys of the rivers; moving in summer to camp over the lush highland pastures. Such to-day is the habit of the Tatars of the eastern Caucasus, nomads by race, who move their quarters from the Mughan plain in winter to the mountains of Karabagh in the summer

---

[1] In the summer of 1926, I found many of the inhabitants of Gori, a comparatively large town on the Trans-Caucasian Railway, living in troglodytic conditions, as the result of the destruction of their houses by an earthquake. Xenophon, IV, v., 25, has left a description of life in these troglodytic dwellings. " Their houses were underground, the entrance like the mouth of a well, but spacious below: there were passages dug into them for the cattle, but the people descended by ladders. In the houses were goats, sheep, cows and fowls with their young; all the cattle were kept on fodder within the walls. There was also wheat, barley, leguminous vegetables and barley-wine in large bowls."

months; and of the Kurds all over the upland country from Van to Ardahani. Such also is the habit of the Georgian-speaking Ajars, who in the summer move up from the hot valleys to the alpine meadows of Karchkhali and Shavsheti;[1] and of the people of the right bank of the Mtkvari in its upper course, and of its smaller tributaries, which fall north from the Trialetian mountains into the middle valley. And the people of the valleys of the Ktzia-Khrami and Berduji move their herds in summer to the highland lakes, to Panavari—"the lake of butterflies", and to Saghamo—"the evening lake", called Tuman Göl, "the mist lake", by the Turks.[2]

This half-migratory habit of the people of the upland country can explain the lack of topographical detail of the early Greek geographers, and their exaggerated ideas of the barbarous character of the inhabitants thereabouts.[3]

The westward limits of the Georgian-speaking country, and the limit also of that country which is regarded as Georgian by the authors of the Georgian Annals, is indicated roughly by the line of the great trunk-road from Trebizond to Erzerum. The southern limit of the Georgian country on this side were the mountains overhanging the valley of the Araks from the north. This country is in the shape of a foreshortened arm, extending westward from the twin-body of the Rioni-Mtkvari basin. The long narrow valley of the Chorokhi, running west to east, divides the mountain country into two. The mountains to the north of the Chorokhi are the country of the Lazes or Chans (La-zan), Chaneti of the Georgian Annals.[4] The Laz communes cling to the narrow foreshore of the sea, and are scattered along the sides of the short narrow valleys falling steeply from the high mountains. Their settlements are communes rather than villages, as in the Ajar country,

---

[1] See *Zap. Kav. Ot. I.R.G.O.*, X, Part I, D. Kazbegi, *Tri mesvatz v' Turetskoi Gruzii*, for an account of the nomadizing of the Ajars.

[2] Wakhushti remarks curiously about Lake Parnavari to this effect, about the summer migration of the kine: "Lake Parnavari is very large and full of fish which are not very savoury. Since in summer, great numbers of sheep, of horses, of cattle and beasts from Kartli and Kakheti are stationed round about, and since their excrement is washed down to the lake by the melting of the snows, they say that this is the cause of the bad taste of the fish."—Wakhushti, *D.G.*, p. 163.

[3] Procopius, in the sixth century A.D., says: "The mountains of the Meskhoi are not rough or unproductive of crops, but they abound in all good things, since the Meskhoi, for their part, are skilful farmers, and there are actually vineyards in their country. However, this land is hemmed in by mountains which are very lofty and covered by forests, so that they are exceedingly difficult to pass through."—*History of the Wars*, VIII, ii., 25, 26.

[4] The name Lazistan is Turkish. The Greeks called the country Lazica, including under this form also Mingrelia. La- is a Svanian territorial prefix, and the Svanians call Mingrelia, as well as Lazistan—Lazan—the land of the Zan←→Chan←→Son←→Svan (cf. Procopius, I, xv, 21, who speaks of the Tzani or Sani).

in Abkhazeti and Cherkezeti—in fact, as it is all along the mountain parts of the eastern coast of the Black Sea. The houses in these communes are wooden chalets—one-floor shanties standing above the ground on piles and scattered at a fair distance from each other, and each among its own grove of trees. Dubois has explained how the Abkhaz and the Circassian sought always a solitary emplacement for his dwelling, and chose his situation near a wood into which, at any sign of danger, his family might flee. The way of life of the Laz is similar, as Strabo exemplified in his account of the Mossynoeci, "*who attack travellers, leaping down from the floors of their dwellings among the trees*".[1] The Lazes were always clever wood-workers and boat-builders,[2] lumbermen, fishermen[3] and pirates; their mountains were impassable, and their allegiance went to the master of the sea-coast between Trebizond and Phasis, in the degree to which repression could be brought to bear upon their coastal communes.[4]

Along the coast of the Channi or Laz, where the fertile river valleys come down to the sea between the mountain bluffs covered with rhododendron and azalea, there have been from remote antiquity sites which were at once roadsteads and beach-markets rather than towns. The classic writers call these places Greek foundations, but the names are Laz; and it would seem that the Greeks in developing their Euxine trade, settled here, along the Lazian coast on older native sites, as Rostovtseff has shown they did in Colchis and round the north-east shore of the Euxine to the Cimmerian Bosporus. The place-names of the greater classic ports along the southern littoral of the Euxine are not indeed of Greek origin; they are rather Greek mouthings of older native names, which later received a definitely Hellenic form, and had attached to them some legendary explanation of the word. In the time of Xenophon the Greek population of the Pontine littoral was more sparsely scattered than in later times when Strabo, Pliny and Ptolemy wrote of it. From Samsun, eastward by Sinope and Kerasund, Greek influence thinned to its ultimate bulkhead at Trebizond. Immediately east of Trebizond there were Greek depots established at Susurmena (Surmena) and

[1] Strabo, XII, iii., 18.
[2] Xenophon, *Anabasis*, V, iv, 11; Wakhushti, pp. 110–11.
[3] Strabo, *ibid*.
[4] The Lazes were as dangerous to the troops of the Byzantine emperors and the Georgian kings as they were to the cohorts of Pompey (cf. Strabo, *ibid*.). The Turkish Government by savage measures suppressed, during the forties of the last century, the virtual independence which they had always enjoyed. (See Kazbegi, *Tri mesyatza v' Turetskoi Gruzii*, for an account of this campaign.)

Rhizæum (Riza), but they were only trading centres and the people of the district were actually of Laz stock. Even in Trebizond in the Middle Ages, the Laz element in the population appears to have been numerous and powerful. Abu'l-Fida, who says that "Trebizond is a celebrated port", quotes ibn-Said as authority that "the greater part of its inhabitants are Lazgis".[1] And the feud between the "town-party" and the "country-party" which vitiated the politics of the Comnenian "empire" appears to have been a continuing contrariety between Greek and Laz.[2]

During all the classic period down to the Middle Ages, there was a flourishing trade driven along the Lazic coast. Eastward from Susurmena and Rhizæum were Athenæ, Archabis and Apsarus, in the land of "the Romans who are called Pontic".[3] Speaking of these places Procopius mentions that the Tzani (Laz) who had been fighting the Byzantine army at Petra, after passing through Rhizæum and Athenæ, "betook themselves to their homes through the territory of the Trapezuntines". Athenæ is Atina of the Laz, Archabis is Arkhave, and Apsarus appears to be Khopa.[4] Most of the names of the Greek settlements between Trebizond and the mouth of the Chorokhi may be derived from the Laz tongue: Riza is Erizeni, "the place where people (or soldiers) meet": Atina is "the place where there is shade"; Mapavri means "leafy".

The valley of the Chorokhi in its upper and middle course has always been thinly populated, for it is a lean and narrow part, hedged by bleak mountains and nourished by this fast and shallow river. The Georgians call this region Klarjeti. Only where the main trade routes run over it from the sea to the Araks valley have the settled sites risen to some small importance. Such is Baiburt on the road from Trebizond to Erzerum, and Ispir farther down the Chorokhi, which lies on the shorter but more perilous way over the mountains from Riza on the sea, to Erzerum. Baiburt has been identified doubtfully with the Gymnias, a town described by Xenophon;[5] it cannot well be a town of lesser age than Trebizond. Ispir may be the Saparda of the Cuneiform inscriptions,[6] and

[1] Abu'l-Fida, II, ii, 146.
[2] See my paper "The March-Lands of Georgia" in *J.R.G.S.*, July, 1929. Cf. also William Miller, *Trebizond: The Last Greek Empire*, in which a family bearing the clearly Laz patronymic of Tsanichites is frequently mentioned as playing an active part in Trapezuntine politics.
[3] Procopius, II, xxx, 14.
[4] Dewing in his excellent text and translation of Procopius from which I quote, identifies Apsarus, I think, incorrectly with Makriali (Makryalos).
[5] Xenophon's *Anabasis* (Hamilton's ed.), p. 326.
[6] St. Martin, *Pop. prim. du Caucase*, p. 44.

GEOGRAPHY OF ANCIENT GEORGIA

its district is the Hysperitis of Strabo. From the south many small streams fall into the Chorokhi; chief are the Tortomis-tsqali and the river of Olti. Here is the Georgian borderland, and the high pass which leads up from Erzerum to Tortomi is called in Georgian *Kartlis-Qeli*, in Turkish *Gurgi-Bughaz*—" the Georgian throat ". The Georgians call this region Tao; the Armenians, Daikh. Here Xenophon's troops found themselves *"in the country of the Taokhoi, where provisions began to fail them; for the Taokhoi inhabited strong fortresses in which they had laid up all their supplies"*.[1] It was in these parts towards the end of the sixth century that the family of Bagrationi, shrewd marcher-lords—playing their prospects between the kings of Armenia and Iberia, the Byzantines and the Persians—began to build the power which was to bring them later to the Armenian and Georgian thrones.

The Chorokhi, twenty-five miles above its mouth, turns north-east to the sea. At this point it receives the turbulent stream of Imer-Khevi, coming out of the mountains of Shavsheti, and a little before it has been joined by the smaller " river of Ardanuchi ". The traveller might ascend the Chorokhi along its high banks to the neighbourhood of Artvini, and then ride up the precipitous valley of Ardanuchi, past the town of that name, and by Ardahani and its river to Akhaltzikhe and the Mtkvari highway into Georgia; alternately from Ardahani south to Kars and the valley of the Araks. This way by Artvini and Ardahani was only less important than the more familiar route by Trebizond and Erzerum. From the Georgian Annals the antique user of it is apparent; and if the identity of Ardahani (old Georgian Artaani) with Irdaniunis of the Urartian inscriptions be accepted, it would seem that the Khaldians and the sea-traders who had business with them, went by these mountains in the remotest times. Such, indeed, seems beyond dispute; for all the lower valley of the Chorokhi and of the Oltis-tsqali is rich in copper and lead. There are iron deposits on the left bank of the Chorokhi and gold is found near Artvini.[2] The narrow valley-ways are fertile too, and the most delicious grapes in all the Caucasus come from the little district of Ligani, between Artvini and the sea. The earlier geographers are vague about this stretch of country. Ptolemy refers to Artanisa;[3] the Georgian Annals indicate

---
[1] Xenophon's *Anabasis*, IV, lxxi.
[2] See *Carte Economique de la Géorgie* (Labrot, Paris), also Ghambashidze, *Mineral Resources of Trans-Caucasia*.
[3] Ptolemy, V, 10.

the considerable antiquity of Ardahani and Artvini. Tukharisi, whose ruins Wakhushti locates near Artvini,[1] was one of the towns which by tradition, Alexander found in Georgia. During the fifth century and onwards, the Iberian kings looked with favour on this region; they began to build castles, monasteries and churches in abundance. In the seventh century, when the Muslims were in occupation of all eastern Georgia, the lower Chorokhi became the refuge and the centre of Georgian life. The monasteries of Khandzti and Opisi, near Artvini, were built during the ninth century; the fine church of Tbeti in Shavsheti and Kakhuli, near Tortomi, a few years later. The rising Georgian dynasts, the Bagrationi, Kuropalatês of Tao and Basiani, established their seat at Ardanuchi, and in the ninth century Constantine Porphyrogenitus could write that

> "The citadel of Ardanutzion is very strong, and has ramparts suitable to the capital of a district; it is the centre of all the business of Trebizond, of Iberia, of Abkhazia, of all Armenia and Syria, and it does an immense commerce with all these countries. The country or 'arzen' of Ardanutzion is large and fertile; it is the key to Iberia, Abkhazia and Meskhia."[2]

In the beginning we were quoting Wakhushti's account of the fine country where the Mtkvari takes its source. By this way we have said went the roads from the Chorokhi country into Georgia, and to the Armenian lands along the Araks. It was in the early classical days, a borderland, the "Moschic territory" of Strabo, divided between the Colchians, the Iberians and the Armenians. The Georgians called this country Zemo-Kartli, "Upper Georgia", or Samtzkhé, "the Meskhian land"; the Armenians called it Kukar; in the classical writers it is Gogarene.[3] Upper Kartli remained, until the consolidation of the Georgian monarchy in the eleventh century, a wild borderland filled with the din and skirmish of Armenian and Georgian forays. The villages were most of them troglodytic; the names of places mark only strongholds on the hills: such were the three famous fortresses of Lomsia,[4] "the lion"; Odzrakhé[5] and Juaristzikhé[6] guarding the way into Georgia by the Mtkvari defile

---

[1] Wakhushti, p. 113.
[2] Brosset, quoting C. P., H. de la G., Add. et Eclair., p. 149.
[3] Cf. St. Martin., Mém. sur l'Arménie, 1, 81 et sqq.
[4] "Lomsia", Wakhushti, p. 83, mentioned in the first century A.D.
[5] "Odzrakhé", Wakhushti, p. 87. The Annals attribute its foundation to the period of the Georgian patriarchs.
[6] Juaris-tzikhé ("the castle of the cross"), Wakhushti, p. 85.

and the high passes of the Likhi. Khertvisi, at the junction of the river of Akhalkalaki with the Mtkvari, guarded the way up from Kars; Tsunda, an ancient hold, held the way by the small lakes over the Trialetian mountains. The very names of the large settled sites in Upper Kartli—Akhaltzikhé (the new castle) and Akhalkalaki (the new town)—indicate that the foundation of them was comparatively late. Akhaltzikhé town it seems rose round the site of Lomsia [1]; Akhalkalaki became a walled town in the eleventh century, but the foundation of a town upon the site is attributed in the Annals to the first King Farnavazi, and the name of the hill of Amiran above the town serves to confirm the tradition of the building by the Magian king.

Along the right bank of the Mtkvari lies a stretch of mountain country shaped like a mutton leg. The north-eastern part called Trialeti faces the mountains of Likhi; the curve south-westward is called Somkheti. North-eastwards the mountains decline to the wide plains of the middle reaches of the Mtkvari in which Tiflis lies; southward they face to the lake country, round the sources of the Mtkvari. These mountains are in fact a section of the peripheral rim of the Armenian plateau, linking the mountains of Likhi with the range of Shah Dagh which overhangs the lake basin of Sevan. From these mountains of Trialeti and Somkheti, a number of rivers of middle size flow eastward into the plain of the Mtkvari. The principal are the Algeti, the Ktzia, lower down called Khrami, and the Débéda (or Borchalo). The course of the last is rather north-north-east than east and it joins its waters with the Khrami a few miles before the two fall into the Mtkvari. All this country is rough and rather bare; the rivers fast and shallow, and falling to the valley of the Débéda is the hottest patch in all Georgia. Trialeti and Somkheti formed always an extension of the borderland between Armenia and Georgia. The shortest way to Tiflis, up from the Araks and the Arpa Chai lay along the Débéda, and by this way, by contrary, the Georgians might strike quickest at Kars and Ani, and the cities on the Araks. And so Trialeti and Somkheti became a land of strongholds and marcher-lords, ready to change allegiance, and they at the same time made their houses rich from the copper-mines and lead-mines, the gold [2] and porphyry and lapis-lazuli [3] of the valley of the Débéda. Here

---

[1] Wakhushti, p. 85: "I think that this is Lomsia, because from the time that the name of Akhaltzikhe is met with in history, Lomsia does not appear."
[2] Cf. Dubois, IV, 133-4, and 141 *et sqq.*   [3] Wakhushti, p. 145.

there rose up in the first days of the Iberian patriarch kings Mtkvaris-tzikhé or Khunani[1] at the confluence of the Débéda with the Mtkvari; Gachiani and Arkvani[2] below the great ravine of the Khrami; and, higher up the river, Orbeti or Samshwildé,[3] the patrimony of the celebrated family of Orbeliani.

It was only along the middle valley of the Mtkvari from Tashis-kari,[4] "the rock-gate", along to the confluence of the Aragvi, that Iberia equalled the Rioni basin in density of population. In contrast to the sparsely peopled mountains all around, the wide stretch of the middle Mtkvari teemed with towns and villages. Here were the oldest towns of the eastern country. Zanavi, near Tashis-kari, "where the Jews lived", caught the caravans as they emerged from the mountains. Lower down the river was Urbnisi, or *Uriat Ubani*, "the Jew's town", where St. Nino, the Evangelist, found welcome owing to her familiarity with Hebrew.[5] Farther east, below the junction of the Liakhvi with the Mtkvari was Uplistzikhé which we have described; and below the point where the small river of Rekhula falls into the Mtkvari, was the old site of Kaspi, a great town once where now only an inconsidered village bears the pregnant name. At the place where the Aragvi joins the Mtkvari was the city of Mtzkheta, and on the southern bank of the Mtkvari, in the loop of the river within a triangle formed by the small stream of Kartlis-khevi was the city of Kartli or Armazi. These two places were the most important sites in ancient Iberia. The Georgian Annalists and Wakhushti—writing in the eighteenth century—were aware of this ancient fame, but, as in the case of Caspi and Nakalakevi, no substantial attempt has ever been made to explore them by excavation and to arrive at an appreciation of the extent to which civilized life was developed there. The name of the three sites—Caspi, Kartli and Mtzkheta—imply their foundation by the tribes who settled in Georgia after the

---

[1] Wakhushti, p. 169.   [2] *Idem*, p. 145.
[3] *Idem*, p. 167; cf. also *Sbor. Mat.*, XIII, i, pp. 3-13, S. Majnikov, *Pamyatniki drevnosti goroda Samshvilde*.
[4] The name is a Turko-Georgian combination. It is applied in the Annals to the head or the whole of the Mtkvari defile, now generally called "the defile of Borjomi" after the town of that name. Cf. Brosset, *H. de la G.*, II, 22 and note.
[5] See Brosset, *V.A.*, 6ᵉ Rapp., p. 19. The Georgian Annals record a curious tradition as to the settlement of the Jews in Georgia; that after the taking of Jerusalem by Vespasian, Jewish fugitives came from there to Mtzkheta and established themselves with their compatriots who had settled there formerly. Among the fugitives was the son of Barabbas. For an account of Urbnissi, Uplistzikhe and of Gori—a town whose foundation dates only from the eleventh century—see *Sbor. Mat.* I, Part I, pp. 59-108; Javakhishvili, *Gorod Gori*; also XXXIV, i, pp. 163-200, M. G. Janashvili, *Gori i eya okrestnostei*.

seventh century B.C., but it is possible, as in the case of Nakalakevi that the cities of Tubal and Meshech were founded on or near the sites of earlier settled centres dating to the Bronze Age. Kartli or Armazi, its later name when it had become the shrine of the Magian cult, was known to the Romans as Harmozika, while Mtzkheta is the Mestika of Pliny and—apparently—the Seusamora of Strabo.[1] Mtzkheta seems to have replaced Armazi as the capital some time during the first century A.D., possibly in view of its greater strategic convenience, opposite the Daryal Pass, during the war with the Alans. Kartli-Armazi was, according to Wakhushti, finally ruined by the Arabs in the seventh century A.D. Place-names in the immediate neighbourhood of the site still seem to retain some fragmentary memory of departed grandeur; to the west, across the Kartlis-khevi, are the ruins of Tzikhédidi—" the great castle "; to the east is a spot called Nakulbakevi—" where there was once a bazaar ".

Mtzkheta, eventually, was replaced by Tiflis—Georgian Tpilisi.[2] Tiflis, if it existed at all during the Classic period, can have been only a small village. Tiflis first received some importance during the fourth century when a Persian military governor with a view to maintaining surveillance over the Iberian king in Mtzkheta, built a fortress—*Kalah*—on the famous hill of Tiflis. In the following century, according to tradition, that somewhat shadowy paladin of the Georgian Annals, King Wakhtang Gurgaslani abandoned Mtzkheta and established his capital in Tiflis. Certainly at the beginning of the sixth century Tiflis had become a walled city and the seat of the Iberian dynasty—at that time a cadet branch of the Persian Sasanids. The original foundation of the Cathedral of Sioni dates from the same century. At the time of the Arab conquest in the seventh century, Tiflis was a very thriving place and with Barda'a and Derbend it remained for three centuries a stronghold of Mussulman power and a

[1] Strabo, XI, iii. "They have on their banks strong cities, set upon rocks, at the distance from each other of about 18 stadia, as Harmozica on the Cyrus, and on the other (Aragus) Seusamora." Hamilton, entirely at random, identifies Harmozika as Akhaltzikhé, but his identifications of Caucasian place-names are worthless. It is of course Armazi. Dubois identifies Seusamora as Samtavro (the place of the *Mtavari*), but Strabo's distance, a little over two miles from Armazi, leaves little doubt in my mind that his Seusamora was Mtzkheta.

[2] For the history of Tiflis see D. Bakradze and N. Berzenov, *Tiflis v'istoricheskom i ethnographicheskom othnosheniyakh*, Spb, 1870. Bakradze, a competent archæologist, states that the Arabs built an observatory in the Kalah of Tiflis. Both Chardin (end of seventeenth century) and Pitton de Tournefort (beginning eighteenth century) give interesting descriptions of Tiflis. Of later European travellers Dubois de Montpéreux (Vols. II and III) is the best. For a scientific summary of the historical topography see the excellent and learned article by V. Minorski in *E.I.*

THE BACKGROUND

centre of the flourishing trade which grew up under the realist government of the Arabs.

In the uplands of the middle Caucasus, eastward of the Daryal gorge, two rivers find their sources—the Yori and the Alazani. They run with the same direction as the Aragvi, and when the latter falls to the Mtkvari, these partner rivers take still the same direction, running parallel with the greater stream, until after a course of some two hundred and fifty miles, the two of them curl round to join the Mtkvari, first the Yori and then the Alazani entering it at points about two miles apart. The country of these two tributaries form two long sleeve-like valleys, converging gradually to the south-east. The upper part where the rivers take their source is high alpine country, the immemorial settlement of crude clans of Georgian mountaineers—the Khevsurs, who border on the Ossetians, the Pshavs and Tushes, who beyond the watershed have for neighbours to the north the Chechens, a forest-folk, and to eastward the highland-tribes of Daghestan. These Georgian clans from antique times were subject to the Georgian kings, who, in the first centuries of the Iberian kingdom, were making expeditions against the Phkhoels or Pshavs.

Lower, where the Aragvi, the Yori and the Alazani run through wide and gently sloping valleys, flanked by wooded bluffs, is the old settled land of Kakheti, rectangular between high Caucasus, the bleak escarpment of Daghestan and the Mtkvari—broad about one hundred miles and long close on two hundred. It is a fertile land, but wilder than Imereti and Kartli. It is mostly wooded and, above all, oaks abound. Pigs are more plentiful than in any part of the Caucasus; sheep and buffaloes particularly grow strong and plentiful. The people, as in all the serried valleys of the Caucasus, have their own character—and differ somewhat from the other Georgians. Strong they are and lithe, their limbs well hung, with daring eyes, alert, keen, animal. Proud they are and arrogant, great talkers, lovers of compliment, makers of faction; reckless and loyal they are ever without reason, with gallant laughter, honourable without thought, faithful and generous; these peasants are great noblemen.

In early history the country of Kakheti was divided into three; between the Yori and the Daghestan mountains was Kakheti, which in the eighteenth century still retained the name particularly as Inner Kakheti; the land between the Yori and the Mtkvari was Kukheti and the lower region, above the confluence of the three rivers was Hereti. According to

Wakhushti the name Kukheti went out of use, during the period of Arab hegemony, when a local dynasty became established in Kakheti; and the name Hereti was abandoned in 1466, when the kingdom of Kakheti was set up.[1] The country, particularly Kukheti between the Aragvi and the Yori, was under the political influence of the *mamasakhlisi* of Mtzkheta from the earliest period of the Annals, and it had part in the relatively civilized life of the Iberian plain from Mtzkheta and Kartli to Urbnisi. Zedazadeni, on the left bank of the Aragvi, a few miles north-east of the Iberian metropolis, was a principal centre of the cult of Zadeni,[2] and there were considerable settlements at Rustavi, on the left bank of the Mtkvari twenty miles below Mtzkheta; at Cheleti; at Déda-tzikhé or Bodchorma on the Yori; and at the troglodytic site of Nekresi at the foot of the mountains to the east of the Alazani. Lower down the Yori was the fortified place of Ujarma, which in the fifth century A.D. had become a large town;[3] and on the farthest border of Kakheti, in the triangular corner of the Yori and the Alazani was the ancient town of Hereti or Khoranta which had already seen its great days when it was destroyed during the Arab invasions.[4] Telavi did not become a town until the ninth century, and Signakhi, Gremi and Zaghani did not rise to importance until after the establishment of the independent kingdom in the latter part of the fifteenth century, at which time the strength of the Kakhian dynasts seems to have laid in the inaccessible eastern district of Inner Kakheti. In this region in the fifth century, besides Nekresi, both Iqalto and Alaverdi became of some importance, as noted shrines of the new religion.

Kakheti lay off the main trade-routes, which are also the routes of invasion. There are, however, records of early infiltrations of foreign elements. In the fourth century B.C. the Annals refer to a settlement of "Turks"—refugees from Persia who were granted the stronghold of Sarkine,[5] "the

---

[1] Wakhushti, pp. 284–5. That there was originally real distinction between KAKH and KUKH is clear both from Wakhushti and from the Annals. The root KAKH-KUKH is common in Ponto-Mediterranean place-names. It may have some relation to the form KOLKH, although it should be noted that Colchis was a Greek name and is never applied in Georgian sources to the land of Imier. We may compare such Mediterranean place-names as Kalkhis, Kalkedon and the Caucasian tribal-names Koraxi (Strabo, III, ii, 6) and Kerketes (Scylax, ref. Dubois, I, 64). Hereti means the "land of Her" and from the context of the Annals, it seems to be a name older than any Georgian tradition. It is possible that it indicates some survival of the Harri or Hurri of the Boghaz-keui inscriptions among the early Georgians. The name-root is widespread. There was an Armenian canton of Her to the north of Lake Urmia, and a fortress of the same name in the province of Udi.

[2] Wakhushti, p. 301.   [3] *Idem*, p. 293.   [4] *Idem*, p. 289.
[5] Brosset, I, 30 and 33.

place of iron ", and there was an ancient coming of Jews to Kherk in Kukheti.[1] The Iberian kings were masters of all the fertile parts of Kakheti as far as the lower reaches of the Alazani. Here was the border of the Albanian country— Aghovanq of the Georgian and Armenian chroniclers. The border country between the Yori and the Mtkvari were the cane-brakes and marshes of the classical Cambysene, in Georgian Kambechovani—" the plain of buffaloes ".

The classical Albania stretched eastward from the Alazani as far as the Caspian, about two hundred miles; and from the " Albanian Gates " to the swampy embouchure of the Cyrus-Araxes, over two hundred miles from north to south. The Albanian territory extended along the southern bank of the Mtkvari, where it had an undefined and changing boundary with the Armenian province of Otene (Udi) and Sakasene (Siuniq) and with Median Atropatene.[2] It was a fertile land of wide grassy plains and wooded hills. The people, herdsmen mostly, and tillers of the soil led a life that was more than half-nomadic. Here, there was nothing of the civil life, which the Roman travellers remarked in Colchis and Iberia. In the first century A.D. there seem to have been no settled places unless it were Kabalaka near the site of Shamakha of later days.

The Albanians in manner and way of life were not very different from the nomads of the north;[3] they were great huntsmen and horse-breeders;[4] people unfamiliar with weights and measures, who used no coined money and who transacted their exchanges by loads. Yet when Pompey invaded the country, they put a more powerful army into the field than the Iberians, and while they fought in the hide breast-plates and helmets in use in Iberia, their leaders wore Armenian armour.[5]

Albania was under the cultural influence always of the Armenians and Persians rather than of the Iberians. In the *History of the Aghovanians* of Moses of Kaghankaituk, the author states that a cadet of the Armenian Arsakids was imposed as

[1] Wakhushti, p. 285: " It was called Kherk, because the Jews, flying from Nabukhodonvsor, were established in this place by the Mamasakhlisi of Mtzkheta, as tributaries, *Mékharké.*"

[2] For these two provinces see St. Martin, *Mém. sur l'Arménie*, I, 86–91 and 142–56. The northern part of Siuniq along the Mtkvari to its junction with the Araks became later the provinces of Artsakh and Paidaragan.

[3] Pliny, V, i, 10.

[4] Strabo, XI, xiii, 7: " The country is peculiarly adapted, as well as Armenia, for breeding horses. There is a meadow-tract called Hippobotus (' horse-pasture ') which is traversed by travellers on their way from Persia and Babylonia to the Caspian gates. Here, it is said, fifty thousand mares were pastured in the time of the Persians and were the King's stud."

[5] Strabo, *ibid.*

king on the Albanians in 152 B.C. This Arsakid line, like the Iberian branch, did not survive the fall of the Persian Arsakids (fourth century A.D.); and a cadet branch of the Sassanids gained sovereignty over the Albanians. Moses of Kaghankaituk, who writes, like some of the Georgian Annalists, under Armenian influence, attributes the conversion to Christianity of the Albanians to Gregory the Illuminator, the princely Armenian evangelist. Similarly the Armenian Mesrop, to whom is attributed the invention of the Armenian alphabet—and more doubtfully of the Georgian—is credited by Moses of Kaghankaituk with the invention of an Aghovanian alphabet. This detail is particularly interesting, since it indicates the existence in the historian's knowledge of a distinct Aghovanian literary language. No less interesting is the history of the Aghovanian Catholicosate, which carried to a successful conclusion a bitter struggle against particularly bloody survivals of paganism in Aghovanq; and which as late as the seventh century—a few years before the kingdom succumbed to the attacks of the Arabs and Khazars—sent two missions to the Huns. Most of the geographical names in Albania, mentioned by Moses of Khoren cannot be identified; and many of the places referred to in the manuscript of Moses of Kaghankaituk have disappeared altogether or have been replaced by later Tatar settlements. The towns which can be identified were situated either along the line of the Mtkvari or on the land-route north from Media Atropatene to the Albanian Gates; and they seem to have developed along the Mtkvari under Armenian influence—almost as Armenian towns and along the route to the north as Persian trading stations. South-eastwards of the Mtkvari was a line of towns on the borders of Albania and Armenia, which were all of them thriving by the end of the fourth century A.D.; they were Gandsag (Ganja), Pertav (Barda'a) and Paidaragan (Bailakan). Pertav, the newest of these towns, which was in the fifth century the capital of Albania-Aghovanq, was fortified by an Albanian dynast under the authority of Perozes (Firuz), a son of the Persian King Yazdagird I. Named in honour of Perozes—Perozabad, it came to be called Pertav by the Armenians, Barda'a by the Arabs. As a stronghold under Persian control it was particularly well-placed, for it commanded the way up into the plain of the middle Mtkvari and it oversaw, at once, the borders of Armenia and of Iberia. After Pertav and Koght, a town whose site is unknown, the most important place in Albania was Kabaghak, the Kabalaka of Pliny, and the Kabalah of the later Muslim writers. Kabaghak was not far distant from the mediæval Shamakha; it was the seat of a bishopric, the capital of the northern part of the country and a fortress well-emplaced to watch against the barbarian highlands of Daghestan.

From the fourth century onwards, the Sasanid kings of Persia gave a particular attention to the north-eastern districts of Albania, with the object of protecting the rich province of Atropatene [1] from the inroads of the nomads. Yazdagird I built a strong fortress at the Albanian Gates—Derbend—and Khusraw Anushirvan strengthened it with a land-wall to cover the narrow littoral gap and a sea-wall to protect the port. To the reign of Khusraw Anushirvan, ibn Khurdabdih also attributes the foundation of Shaberan (Shirvan) and Maskrat (Muskur).[2] Such was Aghovanq, the eastern part of the Caucasus, during the first six centuries A.D.; a wild, half-nomad people taming gradually to feudal ways; with kings but little more than Persian governors, with fortresses set here and there, and some few walled market towns, a people only coming out of paganism, gross and simple, credulous and warring, ruled by hard bucolic princelings and tough missionaries of bishops.

[1] Adiabene-Azerbaijan.
[2] ibn Khordabdih (de Goeje ed., p. 200); see also the admirable articles on Derbend and Shirvan in *E. I.* Baku is not mentioned in the same context by ibn Khordabdih. St. Martin (*Mem. sur l'Arménie*, I, 153) suggests that the Pakavan mentioned by Moses of Khoren may have been Albanian Baku. Pakavan means in Armenian " town of statues " or " idols ", and this may be a memory of the religious practices of the Magians.

BOOK II

THE MEDIÆVAL KINGDOM

"They poured down mercy like snow on all alike, they enriched orphans and widows and the poor did not beg, they terrified evil-doers.... Their tale is ended like a dream of the night. They are passed away, gone beyond the world."
Shota Rusthaveli, "The Man in the Panther's Skin", quatrains
1571–2.

"That mayden and unconquered Kyngdom of the Georgians."
Sir Jerome Horsey in a "Memorial to Sir Francis Walsingham."

CHAPTER VI

ORIGINS OF THE MEDIÆVAL KINGDOM

THE essential of Classic history lies in form; the essential of Mediæval history in colour. And in this truth we see contrasted the contravailing spirit of the West and of the East.

The Classic period represented the triumph of the West—the consummation of the wide raid of the iron-using Aryans. Old Greek civilization was clear form—a thing in architecture of eclectic grace; in sculpture of a fine and delicate illusion; in literature and thought of clean lucidity, of purity and nakedness. The Romans carried on this spirit in heavier and an already degenerating manner. That new-born spirit of the Greeks—a mingling of something wild and fresh out of the West and of no little of the lovely ancient and primitive life of the Ægean Bronze Age—had passed into the middle-aged body of Roman œcumenicity. It happens and is inevitable—as each one of us must lose the golden wonder and the lucent mystery of our youth. The Romans carried on the Grecian form. But they marched in column—they did not leap alone. Their architecture was bulky and pretentious; their sculpture had character, not inspiration; their literature had lost the fay and lilting genius of the Greek, as ours, in this day, has of the Elizabethan. The Romans trod the road to Empire and did not sail for adventure; laws they made and ideas were not born.

Life passed to change. And over the lumber of the Roman world, the Middle Ages came roaring in through tumult and through fire. The chaos was like that at the end of the Bronze Age must have been. Asia and Africa rose upon the West. Alexander had marched to the Indus; Attila rode to the Marne: the Romans destroyed Carthage; the Arabs streaked up through France. In the eighth century it was as though the historical processes of the preceding two thousand years had been obliterated. The old Bronze Age peoples resumed their former preponderant rulership in the world. The Semitic and Hamitic peoples in Babylon and Egypt—submerged and pushed under for two thousand years by the successive emplacements of Aryan mastery—came up in the all-consuming fire of the spirit of Islam. Baghdad and Samarra, the Syrian cities and Cairo were built in the places of the world-capitals of the Bronze Age. In this new time Semitic arms won far beyond the reaches of Babylon and Assyria. Islam spread out over all Iran and Turan; mastered half India and stretched to China. The Caspian countries and three parts of Asia Minor prayed for the Caliph; and Semites and Hamites—Arabs and Berbers—like the Carthaginians once before, overran Spain, half Italy and the great islands of the Mediterranean.

The Byzantine Empire alone remained to represent the form of Roman Empire and a little the spirit of the West. Byzantium retained the laws and much of the social system of the Roman Empire, and it retained the language and the rags of the intellectual being of the Greeks. But Byzantium with its god-Emperors, its Bulgarian and Armenian soldiers, its ornate and formal, royal and priestly edifices, its cantankerous stifled thought, and the colour-passion of its marvellous mosaics, its frescoes, paintings and illuminations, its gorgeous stuffs—Byzantium, how much of it was Eastern? Was not the rivalry between Byzantium and the Caliphate a reborn contrariety between the old Hittite-Anatolian power and Babylon and Egypt rather than the assumed conflict between West and East. Byzantium was a social phenomenon intrinsic in itself. It assumed the forms of Rome, but later Rome in its form and in its spirit had digested much that was Oriental. Byzantium was the expression of the Oriental tendencies in the life of later Rome. In Byzantium the Orient was crescent, and in the Ottoman Empire, the territorial heir of Byzantium, the Orient was fulfilled.

Byzantium and the Ottoman Empire and Imperial Russia —which again took over and appropriated to itself so much that was Byzantine in thought and art and forms—all these three have represented in their time, and in differing degrees, curious syncretisms of Western and of Eastern ways of life and ways of thought. Equally they have been, in their turns, mistrusted by the West and hated by the East. Each of them have stood for the most antique conception of the body politic—the concentration of the highest administrative and priestly functions in the person of an autocrat—the Basileus, the Sultan-Caliph, " the Little Father ". They stood for something stately, dominant, fixed and permanent —something static, unchanging, inorganic. Of the three,

Byzantium alone fulfilled, in its time, a vital need in the social economics of world-history. For in the centuries of barbarism, turmoil, incessant petty carnage, Byzantium was a fortress, a preserve of cultured settled life. But already when the Ottoman and Romanov Empires were rising up, fortresses were becoming out of date.

And so the achievement of the Byzantines was to perpetuate the essentials of urban civilization—through the long centuries between the end of the Classic world and the first birth-pains of the modern world. That stately city straddles history. For Byzantium was founded less than fifteen hundred years after the Dardanians and Phrygians, Mysians and Bithynians rode against the kingdoms of the Bronze Age; and when at last it fell, the Cabots and Caxton had been born and the Paston boys were at Eton.

The Georgians emerge clearly into the light of the new Oriental world of the eighth century, and their history is henceforward well-documented—if not, even now, adequately edited.

Some early sources of the Georgian Annals date back to this period; Armenian chroniclers from the eighth century onwards are numerous and overlapping; and Byzantine historians and Arab travellers concern themselves considerably with the Caucasus. The Georgians bordered on the two contending Imperial powers of the early Middle Ages. The Arabs held Iran and eastern Trans-Caucasia and dominated the sea-ways of the Caspian eastward to Central Asia and northward to the half-civilized Turkish kingdoms on the Volga. The Byzantines held the Black Sea coastal regions, and their colony of Kherson—successor to the old Hellenic cities on the north-eastern coast of the Black Sea—controlled the trade between Asia and the rising Slavonic principalities in South Russia.

The survival of the Georgians, not only as a people but as an individual cultural and political whole during these centuries of aggressive Imperial intervention from west and east and of formidable sporadic attack from nomads—Khazars, Turks and Mongols—is remarkable.

There is a curious element in the character of the Georgian people, a kind of irresponsible individuality of the nation as a unit, which is comparable to a somewhat similar individuality which may be observed in the national characters of both the Spaniards and the Irish.

This characteristic of the Georgian people may be described as an æsthetic irresponsibility. Thus the Georgians, like the Spaniards and the Irish, have come under many forms of alien political and cultural coercion. They accept this domination, but they do not take it seriously, and when the domination passes the people that have suffered it remain in character much the same as formerly. It would be untrue to say that they do not resist such domination; they frequently resist it savagely, but they resist as a nation, as a living animal, and their resistance is not for a principle. Thus we find throughout the history of Georgia, as of Spain and of Ireland, that it is the nation that is held sacred and not this or that principle. And if one people or the other has fought with ostensibly religious aims, it will be found that it is because the religious cause represented the national cause. The Georgians are not a religious people, neither are they a political people, but they have a very strong and abiding sense of their community as a nation, and their individuality as a nation. This sense of national individuality is very old—far older than the clamant sense of nationhood which is voiced by so many of the comparatively young European nations. The Georgian sense of themselves as a nation certainly dates from the time of the mediæval Georgian kingdom, and it is voiced by Rusthaveli and others of their mediæval poets.

The sense of nation is in itself a kind of æstheticism—a form of sensual taste—a preference for one's kind in contrast to other kind.

On the other hand no man—or no people—of essential æstheticism, of taste, can conceive a fixed preference for a certain religious or political conception. Martyrdom is essentially a breach of æsthetics, while heroism on the other hand is an orgasm of individualistic artistry. Thus we find that the Georgians are often, indeed always, heroes and never, or very seldom, martyrs.

In this "*æsthetic irresponsibility*" of the Georgians lies the secret both of their charm as a nation and of their survival as a strongly individualistic national unit. The Georgians retain in a remarkable degree, both individually and as a people, the clear and gentle outlook, the free and inquiring intelligence and the high amoral and untrammelled mind of primitive man. The generosity, the loving simplicity and the humanity, the animal love of life which characterizes the Homeric poems and the ancient literature of the Celts and Scandinavians lights the pages of the mediæval Georgian epics and declares indeed the mind of the Georgian of these days.

ORIGINS OF THE MEDIÆVAL KINGDOM

It is this "*æsthetic irresponsibility*" which has secured the integrity of the Georgians through the vicissitudes of their history. Many political systems and many creeds have lain heavy on the country. They have passed away, and the Georgian has remained, laughing, easy, unchanged and untroubled.

The remoteness of the geographical position of the country has been one of the fundamental causes of the strong sense of kind—of national individuality—of the Georgians. This remoteness has at once isolated them and caused them to develop a sentiment of long and ancient and independent communion among themselves.

At the same time the climate is a mellow joyous climate and the wine is good, so that neither the air nor the diet are conducive to the worrying over principles and the gnawing over grievances.

The unfortunate Armenians, on the other hand, nursing hard dogma upon their icy uplands, made material in their bleak economic want, have as a nation come very near at times to that physical extinction which usually awaits the martyr, and to that cultural extinction which falls to the lot of a community composed of individual materialists. For during the early Middle Ages the Armenians fought doggedly against the Muhammadan invaders as the enemies of the Christian religion and they entered with enthusiastic heat into the interminable theological disputes that rent the East Christian world. But the individual materialism which is inherent in men born in a sterile unfriendly land always drew off the most vigorous spirits of each succeeding generation into the services of rich masters—Byzantine, Arab, Mongol and Turk. Thus we may view upon a very broad and general background of the history of these peoples—the Georgians in their broad and mellow land, with their troubadours and light philosophies, their joistings, their drinking-bouts, their heroes and their games; and the Armenians, a dour and dogged yet self-pitying people, with their dogmas and their rites, their monkish chroniclers, their hard soldiers, their merchants and their martyrs.

The mediæval Kingdom of Georgia struck the imagination of Western travellers, Marco Polo, Ruy Gonzalez de Clavijo and others, as an isolated community of Western culture and Christian religion surviving in the midst of powerful Mussulman tyrannies and half barbarous tribes and peoples. And we now may marvel less at the military prowess which maintained the independence of this culture than at the tenacity of those Classic traditions of life and at the vigour of that East-Christian civilization which after every devastating storm could sprout new twigs of life upon the ancient soil of Colchis.

The last segment of the great Classic world which stayed when the Armenian kingdoms had crumbled, when the hiving cities of Hellenic Asia lay in utter ruin, when the young Kievian state and the proud merchant-centres of the Cimmerian Bosporus had been swept away, was the kingdom of the Georgians. And the strength of Georgian Classicism, though little understood, though buried in the debris of great legendary conflicts, must be apprehended if we are to arrive at an appreciation of the character of the kingdom of the Middle Ages.

Centuries before the Roman Conquest intercourse between the Georgian lands and the Classic world was very considerable. There were the comings and goings of merchants, of drovers of caravans and sailors.[1] Later the Iberian and Armenian kings were accustomed to visit Rome, where a policy was pursued with consistency of pampering and seducing the outland potentates with the luxury and splendours of the metropolis.

Strabo in his own person is an example of the extent to which the Pontic aristocracy was attracted to the Roman world, for he was essentially a citizen of the Empire, while his mother's paternal uncle, Moaphernes, in the days before the Roman conquest had been Mithradates' governor in Colchis.[2] The Iberian king, Rev *Martali* ("the truthful"), who reigned between A.D. 182 and 190, had a Greek queen;[3] and Gubazes, the Colchian leader during the wars of the sixth century, is said to have been of Roman stock on his mother's side. Procopius, commenting on this fact, states that

"the kings of the Lazi from ancient times had been sending to Byzantium, and, with the consent of the Emperor, arranging marriages with some of the senators, and taking home their wives from there".[4]

During the first and second centuries A.D. Roman political influence was dominant through the Georgian country, and

---

[1] Cf. Xenophon, speaking of the Macrones, a tribe in the region of the Chorokhi: "At this juncture one of the peltasts came up to Xenophon, saying that he had been a slave at Athens, and adding that he knew the language of these men. 'I think indeed', said he, 'that this is my country and if there is nothing to prevent, I should like to speak to the people.'" *Anabasis*, IV, viii, 3–4; cf. also Phasmer, in *Iz. Gos. Ak. I.M.K.*, II, 282–5 and 287–8, for a list of the finds of numerous Greek and Roman coins in different districts of Georgia.
[2] Strabo, XI, ii, 18.   [3] Brosset, H. *de la G.*, I, 79; cf. also *ibid.*, p. 145.
[4] Procopius, *De bello persico*, VIII, ix, 8–9.

ORIGINS OF THE MEDIÆVAL KINGDOM

while the Western provinces lay within the immediate control of the military masters of the whole Pontic littoral, the Iberian kingdom accepted an Imperial protection which enabled the rulers in Harmozica both to strengthen royalty within their frontiers and to withstand the pretensions of the powerful Armenian kings in the valley of the Araks.

The Roman historians are the only reliable authorities for this obscure period of Georgian history, and it is through their scattered references to Iberian affairs that we are able to confirm the names and dates of the early Iberian kings—names which emerge from a confusion of legends and transpositions collated by the Annalists who attempted, in later centuries, to bring together the beginnings of a national history.[1]

A stone with a Greek inscription discovered at Mtzkheta in 1867 and now in the Tiflis Museum proclaims a king Mithradates (Mihrdati) as "the friend of the Cæsars", and as the King "of the Roman-loving Iberians".[2]

Farsman II (116–140), called *Kweli*—"the good", who was in many respects the founder of the Georgian state and the most significant king of the pre-Christian period, was the friend of the Emperor Hadrian who did him the signal honour of erecting his equestrian statue on the Martian Fields, and who permitted him, in the words of Dio Cassius, "the unusual honour" of making offerings in the Capitol.[3]

During the first half of the third century A.D. the Iberian and Armenian rulers were involved in the strife which followed the overthrow of the Parthian Arsakid dynasty in Persia and the usurpation of the throne by the native line of the Sasanids. This period of Georgian history is obscured in the difficult problem of the Khusrawid succession.[4]

The Roman political interest and the influence of the Classic world continued strong in Georgia, and with the opening of the fourth century the establishment of the capital of the Empire of the East at Byzantium and the impulse of a young and vigorous Christianity gave renewed strength to

[1] For a provisional list of the early Iberian kings, see Note F, p. 376.
[2] I. Pomyalevski, *Sbornik grecheskikh i latinskikh nadpisei Kavkaza* (Tiflis, 1881), p. 68. The Cæsars were Vespasian (70–79), Titus (79–81) and Domitius (81–96).
[3] Tacitus in his *Annales*, Dio Cassius in his *Historia Romana* and Ælius Spartianus in his *Scriptores Historiæ Augustæ* furnish noteworthy material for Georgian history of this period.
[4] Professor Javakhishvili suspends judgment on this obscure question which he proposes to examine in a promised new edition of his *Kartveli Eris Istoria*. The statement in *Kartlis Tzkhovreba* that the Iberian King Miriani and his successors belonged to a junior (Khusrawid) branch of the Persian house of Sasan is confuted by the evidence of the older Georgian document *Moktsevai Kartlisai* (cf. Th. Jordania, *Kronikebi*, I, 18–19), and for a full statement of the arguments against "the Khusrawid tradition" see S. Gorgadze in the journal *Moambé* of Tiflis, Nos. III, IV, 1905.

THE MEDIÆVAL KINGDOM

Mediterranean cultural tendencies throughout the Middle East. During the long reign of the Iberian King Miriani, the Christian religion spread through the Georgian lands and the flow of intercourse between Georgia, Armenia, Syria and the Hellenic Mediterranean was running strong and free.

The third quarter of the century saw the revival of the conflict between the Imperial powers set in Anatolia and Iran. And when in 390 the Roman and Persian emperors proceeded to the first partition of Armenia, the Iberian kingdom, also, was riven by their great pretensions. Between 368 and 393, there were two kings in Iberia, Saurmag II, the rightful king ruling in Mtzkheta as the client of the Romans, while Aspagur II sat in Armazi under the protection of Shah Shapur.[1]

Throughout the greater part of the first half of the fifth century A.D. Iberia passed under effective Persian control, although during the reign of the enlightened and unpopular Yazdagird I in Persia,[2] the Iberian King Archil I (428–438) was able to resume some measure of independence.

The period was one of the greatest expansion of Iranian influences in Iberia.[2] Persian proper names, Persian titles and usages became increasingly common, and although the nobility continued to favour the Christian religion, the Magian cult was spreading rapidly among the common people.[3]

During the latter part of the fifth century the period of anarchy in Persia which covered the reigns of Yazdagird II, Perozes (Firuz) and Balash corresponds to that period in Georgian history which is occupied by the half-legendary career of King Wakhtang Gurgaslani.

The Gurgaslani legend has the same relation to Georgian

---

[1] According to Ammianus Marcellinus (Gan. *Sbor. Mat.*, IX, p. 188) the Mtkvari was the boundary between the domains of the two kings. Professor Javakhishvili is of opinion that the Aragvi continued the boundary towards the north. The Annalists transpose this period of the divided kingdom to the end of the first and the beginning of the second century A.D. (see Brosset, I, 70–4).

[2] Brosset, *H. de la G.*, I, 148. For the archæological history of Persian relations with Georgia and Daghestan during the Sasanian period, see *Iz. Kav. I.-A. I.*, III, 83–6, G. Chubinashvili, *Der Fund von Sargweschi*, and *Novie Vostok*, V, N. Baklanov, *Iskusstvennaya Kultura Dagestana* (with a photograph of a fine Sasanian capital found in the Avar country).

[3] Cf. Brosset, *H. de la G.*, I, 149. According to *Kartlis-Tzkhovreba* an agreement between Archili and the Persian governor of Ran and Movakan secured toleration for the Christians in Persian territory and for the Magians in Iberia. The Shatberdi version of *Moktsevai Kartlisai* indicates the same. The Magians of Mtzkheta, with their priests called Mogui, lived in a suburb of their own called Mogueta. Their chief priest was called Mogpeti or Mogbedan-Mogbedi (cf. Eristavt-Eristavi). In the Georgian sources this high priest, whose rank equalled that of a Christian bishop, was called Mobidan-Episkoposi, in which construction Mobidan came to be taken as a Christian name, hence the confusion of Brosset and other historians. (See D. Karichashvili, *Who was Mobidan-Episkoposi?*, Tiflis, 1901.)

history as the Arthurian legend has to English, and while Wakhtang Gurgaslani emerges as the shining figure of the Georgian heroic period there is little contemporary evidence which can confirm the native record of his exploits.

The reign of Wakhtang Gurgaslani [1] in Iberia (450–503) was posterior by more than half a century to that of Bahram Gur in Persia (420–39), and if it be allowed that the emergence of a strong king in Georgia during a time of trouble in Persia is a historical probability, it must be admitted also that the legendary deeds attributed to Wakhtangi by the Georgian Annalists bear a strong resemblance to those of the hero of Persian epic literature. Wakhtangi was probably an historical figure of the type of Taymuraz II in Georgian history of the eighteenth century, and his exploits in Sind were doubtless based on some historical tradition of his fighting for the Persian kings against the Hephthalites or White Huns on the eastern frontiers of the Empire.

Whatever may have been the degree of independence secured by the Georgians during the latter half of the fifth century, the sixth century was to see the destruction both of their political and their cultural life.

The disastrous series of wars between the Romans and the Persians, which endured with intervals into the second quarter of the seventh century, broke out in 502, with the seizure of Theodosiopolis (Garin) by the Persians.

From 524 the full strength of the two contending Empires was concentrated in the Caucasus, and while the Byzantines sought to control the Caucasian passes that they might at all times call in their nomad allies from the north to devastate the provinces of Persia, the Persians aimed to conquer Lazica

> "that starting from there they might overrun with no trouble, both by land and by sea the countries along the Euxine Sea, as it is called, and thus win over the Cappadocians and the Galatians and Bithynians, who adjoin them, and capture Byzantium by a sudden assault with no one opposing them".[2]

During the period of the first Lazic War (527–33) the Byzantines pursued a political policy of consolidating their position in the coastal regions. In Abkhazeti they were particularly active and their missionaries engaged in the con-

---

[1] "Lion-Wolf" is the traditional interpretation of *Gurgaslani* by Georgians. The name would appear to me to be a combination of the Turkish words *gurgi arslan*, the "Georgian lion". The Annalist gives the original form of Wakhtangi as Waran-Khusraw-Tang.

[2] Procopius, II, 28, 23.

THE MEDIÆVAL KINGDOM

version of the Abkhaz, and penetrated even into Cherkezeti and Kabarda.[1] In 541 and 550 the Byzantines had to suppress formidable revolts among the Imerians and Abkhaz and they proceeded to raise fortresses at Sevastopolis (Sukhum), Pitiunt (Pitsunda), and at Petra in Guria.

Hostilities were renewed with Persia in 549 and continued until 562. The Persian armies penetrated as far as the remote coastal district of Apsilia (Samurzaqano), and during the first five years of obstinate and desperate marches and ambushes, battles and sieges throughout the Lazic country, the ancient sites of Colchian culture, Kotatissium (Kutais), Rhodopolis (Vardis-tzikhé), Archæopolis (Nakalakevi) Sarapana and Skanda were ruined and destroyed. The sparkling lowlands of the Rioni were devastated and depopulated, and the fury of these emperors' wars was carried even into the fastnesses of Svaneti.[2]

Following the peace of 562, Persian preoccupations on the Oxus frontier allowed the Byzantines to set on the Iberian throne Guaram, a Meskhian noble who commanded for the Emperor in Klarjeti and Javakheti and who was descended through his mother from Wakhtang Gurgaslani.[3] Guaram, with the Byzantine title of *Kuropalatês*, made his capital at Tiflis and from his reign dates the decline of Mtzkheta, while the *Kalah* of Tiflis replaced Armazi as the principal stronghold on the Mtkvari.[4]

During the period of internecine strife in Persia which closed the sixth century, Guaram Kuropalatês enjoyed his years in peace and in 600 was succeeded by his son Stephanos. Stephanos, "fearing alike the Persians and the Greeks, dared not take the title of king but called himself *Eristavt Mtavari*".[5]

In 602 the Emperor Maurice was murdered by the usurper Phokas, and Khusraw II Parwiz, who himself had owed his throne to Maurice, invaded the Byzantine dominions. The slender stem of the Iberian dynasty leaned to the stronger power, and in *The Life of Saint Ewstaté of Mtzkheta* it is written that a Persian commandant was set in the citadel of that place and a Persian *marzpan* administered the affairs of Tiflis,

---

[1] Brosset, *H. de la G.*, I, 213.
[2] For details of the first two Lazic Wars see Procopius; also Brosset, *Add. et Ec.*, Add. IV, for summary and commentary.
[3] Brosset, *H. de la G.*, I, 215–16. The Annalists state that Guaram was a Bagratid, but recent Georgian authorities fail to agree. For discussion see Note G on the Origin of the Bagratids in Appendix to Book III, page 377.
[4] *Ibid.* 219. "Mtzkheta thinned and Tiflis thickened."
[5] *Ibid.* 224. For the significance of this, and other Georgian administrative titles, see Chapters XIX–XXIII.

while the Persian artisans living in Mtzkheta were able to procure the death of the Saint as the apostate son of a Magian.

But Stephanos I, like so many of his successors, was mistaken in the choice which he had made between the two Imperial aggressors.

In 623–5, when the Persians were in possession of three parts of Asia Minor, the new Byzantine Emperor Heraklius with brilliant daring landed in Lazica and, in two years' campaigning, marched across Armenia into Cilicia, defeating the Persians in three pitched battles. In the following year Heraklius appeared before Tiflis supported by an army of Khazars. Stephanos was flayed alive after the capture of the citadel by the Khazar general, Thong Yabghu Khakan, and his skin was sent to the Emperor who was then in Gardaban on the estates of Waraz-Gageli.[1] Aternerseh (Adarnasé), Eristavi of Kakheti, a descendant of Dachi son of Wakhtang Gurgaslani and a cadet therefore of the old Iberian line, was named *Eristavt Mtavari* by Heraklius, while the Khazar Thong Yabghu was appointed *Eristavi*. The Byzantine troops at the same time remained in occupation of Ispiri, part of Klarjeti and all the Black Sea coast.[2]

Stephanos II succeeded his father Aternerseh as *Eristavt-Mtavari* in 639, and during the first years of his reign began the Arab invasions of Georgia. After the capture of Tiflis in 645, the two sons of Stephanos, Miri and Archili, sought refuge in Egrisi (Mingrelia) with Leon " the Imperial Eristavi ".[3]

The Georgian lands conquered by the Arabs were regarded by Arab writers as forming part of Armenia, and to the Armenians the Caliph accorded a wide autonomy. The government of Armenia was customarily delegated to a high Armenian noble, and if he were replaced by a Muhammadan, it was usually the temporary consequence of some veering in the intricate policy of the Caliph's court. And while his policy naturally favoured the Muslim supremacy, the Caliph did not hesitate to make use of the militant truculence of the Armenian nobles in order to check the seditions and the ambitions of Muhammadan governors in Azerbaijan and Kurdistan.

For the Caliph, Armenia and Iberia were frontier provinces where it was necessary to consider at once the continuing menace of Khazar invasions along the Caspian littoral, and the local implications of Byzantine policy which remained at grips with Islam over the breadth of the long inland seas,

[1] Brosset, *H. de la G.*, I, 227. [2] *Ibid.*, p. 229. [3] *Ibid.*, p. 240.

from the Pillars of Hercules to the Bosporan Chersonese. The culture of the Caliphate was urban, founded upon walled merchant-towns, fed by their trade-routes and frequented by the unceasing caravans which were the life-stream of Semitic Islam.

In the Transcaucasian lands the Arabs held the cities at the junction of the traders' ways: Tiflis—Shamakha—Derbend; Kars—Dabil—Barda'a to Tabriz. By their control of the Armenian cities they were the masters of Armenian politics, but otherwise they let alone the mountain lords, using them as military auxiliaries, deposing them or killing them as fitted polity, beating down the older prouder houses, setting one against the other, favouring small and upstart men. So, for two centuries, the Caliphs held the country from Daryal to Van; in the north they fought against the mountain clans whom they might buy sometimes to serve against the Khazars; in the more civil Armenian feudal lands they pulled down the princely might of the older houses of Sasanian times and raised the newer families of Bagratuni and Artzruni.

In Imereti, Abkhazeti and the Chorokhi uplands beyond the reach of Arab politics, the agents of the Byzantine emperors on this distant frontier played with the little Georgian princes a game of the same sort.[1] Byzantine power had been firmly set in Abkhazeti and in Tao and Klarjeti during the period which passed between the reigns of Justinian and Heraklius. The Emperors had built fortresses along the Black Sea coast; their garrisons were posted in all the mountain holds along the Chorokhi valley; their missionaries had worked manfully among the pagan clans of Cherkezeti, Kabardá and Osseti; the towns of the Abkhaz and the Imerians had been endowed with churches, and gifts of plate and icons, and their unimportant princelings were honoured by the high-flown but servile household titles of the Imperial court.

Towards the end of the eighth century, direct Byzantine control over the Georgian Westlands began to weaken and their fortresses in the mountains were abandoned. But the influence of the Imperial court remained strong, and interference in the affairs of the Georgian princes was not infrequent. Power in the west passed to the Eristavi of Abkhazeti. The remote position of the Abkhaz had enabled them to escape both the domination of the Arabs and the ravages of the Khazars; their dense forests protected them

---

[1] In 713, Leo the Isaurian, later Emperor, was sent on a diplomatic mission to the Abkhaz and Ossetians, and underwent many perilous adventures (cf. Brosset, *Histoire*, I, 251).

ORIGINS OF THE MEDIÆVAL KINGDOM

from the dangers of effective Byzantine control over the interior of the country, while their proximity to the sea enabled them to receive through their coastal towns the benefits of trade and cultural contact with Byzantium and Kherson. The ruling family, which claimed descent from a former Greek governor of the country,[1] is believed, in fact, to have been of Kabardan extraction and it was closely allied with the Khazar royal house.[2] During the third quarter of the eighth century, the Eristavi Levan II Anchabadze took possession of all Imereti and, even before the death of the last Iberian prince Juansheri, assumed the title of king (*Mépé*).

Meanwhile, the scions of the prolific house of Bagratuni or Bagrationi [3] were pushing their interest towards the north, a brave and cunning, greedy clan, who played against the older princely houses and foraged for profit in the middle of the changing polities of the Caliphs and the Emperors. The Byzantine patronage had once given them a passing hold on the Iberian throne; it still sustained them in Tao and Klarjeti, where at the beginning of the ninth century, Ashot *Kuropalatês*, built himself a fine baron's capital at Ardanuchi commanding the Chorokhi gorges and the way from Ani and Kars to the Black Sea. The Caliphs allowed other sprigs of the Bagrationi stem to enclose those two great trading fortress-cities. And yet some others carved themselves principalities north of Lake Sevan, Siuniq—part of old Aghovanq —and Lori. One more was lord of Kartli, without Tiflis, and had his seat at Uplistzikhé. Only in Kakheti, the native family of Donauri grew up to independence in the hereditary office of *Khorepiskoposi*; Mussulman emirs held Tiflis; and to the south the Artzrunis, rivals to the Bagratunis, made themselves masters of Van with the province of Vaspurakan. The massacre of the Georgian and Armenian insurgent nobles by the Arabs at Bagrevan in 772, cleared the older houses from the path of the Bagratunis.

With the opening of the ninth century the Imperial structure of the Caliphate in the Caucasus showed signs of early cracking. The formidable revolt of the Emir of Tiflis, Ismail-bn-Shuaib, during the reign of the Caliph Harun-al-Rashid, was only crushed with the help of the Armenian princes. In 813, there were serious revolts at Dabil (Dwin)

---

[1] Brosset, *H. de la G.*, I, 249; cf. Guliya, *Istoria Abkhazii*, Tome I, pp. 181 *et seq.*
[2] *Ibid.*, p. 259.
[3] Bagratuni is the Armenian and Bagrationi the Georgian form of the name of this family, whose possessions were widely scattered throughout Armenian and Georgian territory.

and Barda'a, and in 829 the Muslims of Tiflis were again insurgent in support of their emir, Muhammad-bn-Hattab. The Caliph's forces were defeated in Kakheti in 840 and 842; and in 843, Ishak-bn-Ismail, Emir of Tiflis, broke out only to allow the armies of the Caliph under the Turk, Bugha-al-Kabir-al-Sharabi, to destroy for ever the chance of Tiflis becoming the centre of an Islamic state in the Caucasus.

The Imperial power of the Byzantines, shaken by the Iconoclastic conflict, was weakening at the same time as that of the Caliphs, and in 842 a Byzantine intervention in Abkhazeti ended in disaster.

In 858 the Emperor Michael III was defeated by the allied forces of the Paulician sectaries, the Armenians and the Emir of Malatia, and two years later took place the first Russian expedition against Byzantium.

With the continued crumbling of the outer walls of the two Empires, the House of Bagrationi emerged as the expression of a mutinous reaching-out of the raw rough mountain-lords of the border marches. In the south in Van, Ashot Artsruni made himself King of Vaspurakan. The rest of the Armenian lands and most of Georgia was divided between the hungry scions of the House of Bagrationi. The toughest of them all, brave and shrewd but elderly for the fierce days of the ninth century, was Ashot Bagratuni of Shirak. Victorious against the Arabs and the recognized leader of his turbulent cousins and contemporaries, Ashot Bagratuni was, in the years 886 and 887, recognized as King of the Kings of the Armenians by each of the harassed autocrats in Baghdad and Byzantium.[1]

Ashot died in 890, but under his successors Smbat I (890–914) and Ashot II (914–28) the hegemony of the Shirakian branch of the Bagratunis was maintained over all the Armenian lands and the neighbouring parts of Georgia and Kurdistan. The character of the Armenian high-kingship was peculiar. The capital of the Shirakian Bagratunis was Ani, which was in fact a rich mercantile city-state having authority over a ring of satellite cities and towns as Kars, Mush and lesser places. The great "*nakharars*" or feudal lords of the surrounding uplands were nominally dependent on the kings of Ani, but their fidelity was to be measured in terms of the force which their overlord could bring to bear upon them. The Artzrunian kings of Vaspurakan were rivals rather than feudatories of the Shirakian kings; and the

---

[1] Shahin-Shah-i-Armen / Arkhôn Arkhontôn tôn Armenôn.

cadets of the stem of Bagrationi, who ruled in Tao and Basiani and in Kartli, in Siuniq and Lori, were almost independent. The Anchabadzes of Abkhazeti and the Donauris of Kakheti were sometimes dependent on the kings of Ani and allied with them and at other times were antagonistic. And the powerful Muslim city-state of Tiflis, with the feudal dynasties of the Sajids at Tabriz, and the Shabanids at Amida, were fierce and sometimes dangerous enemies of the new Christian kingdom.

Conditions geographical, social and political prevented the Armenian kings from building up the powerful autocratic state of the type which in those same days was being constructed by the Varangian kings in Kiev. Already, into the third quarter of the tenth century, the Shirakian patrimony had been divided into the two kingdoms of Ani and Kars. No ruler of the type of the first Ashot rose up to consolidate and weld the half-dozen thriving principalities of the Armenians. And when towards the middle of the eleventh century, the last reglow of Byzantine aggression threatened feudal regionalism, while the nomad Seljuks were beginning to batter down the urban cultures of the Iranian marches, the numerous kings of the Armenians were able to make no real resistance.

In Georgia the development of an independent feudal monarchy during the first decades of the tenth century was conditioned by these four external events; the temporary suspension of Byzantine Imperialism and the collapse of Muslim power in the Caucasus during the last half of the ninth century; the rise of the Armenian national-feudal monarchy, and its quickly following decline at the beginning of the tenth century. For it was the removal of Byzantine control from the Black Sea littoral which enabled the Anchabadzes of Abkhazeti and the Bagrationis of Tao and of Basiani to stretch out their hands for kingship and the weakness of the Arabs put a kingdom in their reach. It was the prosperity of the Armenian kings of Ani which brought strength and confidence to the outlying Christian dynasts in the north; and finally it was the pressure of the Byzantines from the west and of the Seljuk Turks from the east and south which impelled the eager, needy Bagratids to seek towards the Caucasus the security and the royalty which they were losing along the Euphrates. For two generations or more there were difficult manœuvres, obscure dynastic skirmishes, ferocious little wars between the pushful princelings of young mediæval Georgia. The Abkhazian Anchabadzes seemed likely to absorb all Kartli and they broke the power of the Donauris in Kakheti; then events favoured rather the Bagrationis of Tao who successfully sustained their cousins in Kartli against the aggression of the Anchabadzes, while the power of the kings of Ani weighted the scales towards an Armenian rather than an Abkhazian hegemony in the valley of the Mtkvari.

But finally a series of dynastic accidents and the skill of the Eristavi Ioanné Marushidze served to unite the princely patrimonies of Abkhazeti, Kartli and Basiani to the good fortune of one Bagrat Bagrationi. Bagrati was the son of Gurgeni, Kuropalatês of Kartli, by Gurandukht Anchabadze, daughter of Thewdos II, King of Abkhazeti, and he inherited Abkhazeti through his mother (989) and Kartli through his father (1008). By the diplomacy of Ioanné Marushidze the Kuropalatês of Basiani, another Bagrat Bagrationi, called " the Sot ", made Bagrati of Kartli his heir (994). The Kuropalatês David Bagrationi of Tao had been persuaded to follow the same course, but when he died in 1001, he bequeathed his estates to his titular overlord, the Emperor Basil II. The *aznaurni* of Tao delivered the fortresses of the mountain principality to the Greeks, and Bagrati and his father Gurgeni received from the Emperor the splendid honorifics of *kuropalatês* and *magistros* to solace their chagrin.

PITSUNDA CHURCH IN THE SEVENTEENTH CENTURY, AFTER CASTELLI.

CHAPTER VII

THE KINGS OF THE ABKHAZ: BAGRAT III TO GIORGI II

BAGRAT III ruled for six years over his united patrimony and died in 1014. His son, Giorgi I, a rash and violent youth of eighteen, succeeded to the uncertain kingship of the lands so carefully put together by his father and his grandfather. And although the Kingdom of Abkhazeti was the most powerful political structure in the Caucasian lands, the young king was only one among a dozen rival despots between the Black Sea and Lake Van.

In his walled capital of Kutais Giorgi had some importance and his writ went over the Mountains of Likhi, eastward of Uplistzikhé; but within his own frontiers the dangerous rising house of Orbeliani had influence as nearly royal as his, for they were lords of half the Meskhian uplands and the wide lands of Argueti in Imereti. In Trialeti, the estates of the Orbelianis bordered the independent principality of the Bagratids of Lori; and north-eastward they adjoined the ancient Kingdom of Kakheti and Hereti, where the house of Donauri had ruled in Bodchorma for more than two centuries. Westward the lands of the Orbelianis ran with the Imperial frontier in Tao, and beyond the principality of Lori lay the Armenian city-states of Kars and Ani. Tiflis remained the metropolis of the Muslims and its citizens could muster a force which was not incompetent to confront the levies of allied Georgian and Armenian princes. To the north of Tiflis lay the mountain Kingdom of Alaneti, which included not only the Ossetian clans but the tribes of Kabardá and Cherkezeti. And to the south-east, sure allies to the emirs of Tiflis, were the Muslim cities in Shirvan and Aran, which, under the leadership of the emirs of Ganja and Dabil, could prove as strong a combination as any confederation of the Christians.

In the first quarter of the eleventh century, the petty potentates of all the Caucasus began to group themselves in hazardous and temporary alliances according to the needs of every year. The Mussulman group—Tiflis, Ganja and Dabil —remained distinct, always hostile to the rest and dependent for an ultimate survival upon the course of history in the great world of Iran of which it formed a cultural and political appanage. The northern kingdoms of Abkhazeti and Alaneti tended to keep together in hostility towards the older Armenian principalities and there developed a distinct contrariety between the Georgian and mountain group, whose centre was the court of Kutais, and the agglomeration of Bagratid Armenian principalities, which looked for political leadership towards the already declining dynasty of Ani. The Bagratid Armenian tradition and Armenian cultural influences were strong in all Samtzkhé and in Trialeti and Lori, and the political orientation of Kakheti was towards the Armenians rather than to the Abkhaz.

And so when the ambition to expand which inspired the Abkhazian Bagratids threatened the Donauris of Kakheti, they turned naturally to the Bagratids of Lori and the south. At the same time the powerful Orbelianis, Armenian by tradition and sympathy, showed no loyalty to their Abkhazian overlords, and their hostility to the kings in Kutais delayed the unification of a Georgian kingdom for a hundred years, and proved more than once a dangerous menace to the Abkhazian dynasty. King Giorgi could only counter, ineffectually, the alignment of the Orbelianis with the Armenians by an alliance with that distant rival of the Bagratids, Senakerim Artsruni, King of Vaspurakan, whose daughter, Mariam, he received in marriage. But both the Armenian and Abkhazian dynasts who were playing for supremacy throughout the Caucasus were now menaced, and presently broken by the reviving Byzantine Imperialism of the Macedonian emperors.

The conflicting policies of Byzantium and of the Caliphate had for three centuries allowed the paltry independencies of the Armenian highlands to eke out a tenuous continuity. When the Caliphate collapsed and while Byzantium was weak, the Armenians under Ashot I and his successors had for some years the chance of an eventual unity. But with the elevation of Basil II Bulgaroktonos to the Imperial purple, the days of the small highland royalties were numbered. With ruthless force and farseeing capable diplomacy, Basil II, both in the Balkans and on his eastern frontier, set himself to restore the military and political splendours of Byzantium. But although he succeeded in snatching at the Armenian lands, he smashed the very strength of those marchland wardens, who, tiresome often to Byzantine statesmanship, had at the same time always been an uncertain, but on the whole effective barrier between the Imperial Themes of Asia and aggressions from the east.

These aggressions were already threatening, as the captains of freebooters out of Turkistan, who had for two centuries served the Caliphs and successive Muslim dynasts as mercenaries, now lifted themselves to power throughout the breadth of Iran. Turkish overlords had begun to rule in the Persian and Iraqi cities, and every year they were reinforced by bands of hungry horsemen from beyond the Oxus. The pastoral tribes of the lean uplands that stretch from the Jungarian Gap to the Chinese Wall spurred their speedy ponies and rode west to the glittering cities whose gates had been prised open by their earlier adventuring fellows. The age-old course began again as the steppe-land nomads fell upon the meadows and the gardens, broke into the palaces and rifled the bazaars of all the antique settled lands, and the cohorts of the rude and needy rose with them to pillage the masters who now were proving that they could not hold their mastery.

Between the years 1018 and 1021, the first bands of Turks, augmented by a trash of Turkomans and Kurds, came on to the edge of the Armenian country. David Artsruni was defeated by the Seljuk chief Er-Toghrul; and his father Senakerim—the ally of Giorgi of Abkhazeti—quailing before the terror, ceded the 4,000 villages, the 70 castles and the 8 cities of Vaspurakan to the Emperor Basil, receiving in exchange the territory of Sivas as a personal appanage. Basil thus advanced his eastern frontier. Farther north he was watching Ani and Kars where the two brothers, Ashot IV and Hovannes Smbat, were wrecking the Armenian kingdom in a mean ferocious civil war On the north-east frontier the Abkhaz were more formidable, and the young King Giorgi was waiting the chance to go into Tao, which his father had so nearly inherited.

In the summer of 1021, the Emperor Basil was at Theodosiopolis negotiating with the Abkhaz to satisfy the frontier question and to receive some acknowledgments of suzerainty from Giorgi. Mischief-makers raised misunderstandings and the splendid army of the Emperor was set in motion, marching up through the remote alpine passes of Samtzkhé to bring the young king to order. The Emperor found the Abkhaz stronger than he might have anticipated from the previous Byzantine experiences against the Armenians. A great battle was fought by Lake Palakatsio and ended with the exhaustion of both armies. Giorgi retired into Trialeti where he received reinforcements from Kakheti and even from the Muslim city of Shaki, while Basil, after burning Ardahani and cruelly devastating all the country, retired to winter in Trebizond. There followed the formidable revolt of Nikephoros Phokas and Ziphias against the Emperor. The leaders were in correspondence with the Abkhazian and Armenian kings and for some weeks the whole authority of Byzantium in the eastern provinces was seriously threatened. But the insurgents were defeated and the leaders betrayed each other, so that in the spring of 1022 Basil could once more take the field against Giorgi. The Georgian army was surprised in the mountains of Basiani, and the vanguard of Giorgi was routed by the Varangian corps of the Emperor.[1] The royal treasury was taken and the King was in flight. But Basil had to turn to confront other looming dangers, and he made a peace with Giorgi which exacted only the evacuation of the estates of the late Kuropalatês David in Tao and in Basiani, in Shavsheti and Javakheti, and round Ardahani and Kola.

The devastations and losses of this costly war had gravely affected the stability of the Abkhazian monarchy and when in 1027, Giorgi died at the age of thirty-one, leaving the kingdom to his nine-years-old son, Bagrati, the country slid towards disorder. Giorgi's widow, Mariam Artsruni, ruled for the infant Bagrati; and throughout his long reign this magnificent and clever woman continued to influence, if not to govern, her son who grew to be a frustrated, hesitating man.

After the death of Giorgi, Liparit Orbeliani, called "the Great", became the most powerful man within the Abkhazian kingdom and in the politics of all the Caucasus. At first he reined his long ambitions and had no part in the intrigues of the Meskhian nobles with Byzantium, which were running during the short reign of Constantine VIII.[2]

The aggressive Imperial policy of Byzantium had really come to an end with the death of Basil, and when Romanos Argyros was elevated to the purple in 1028, relations between Byzantium and Abkhazeti were smoothed by the visit of the Catholicos Melkisidek to the Emperor. Queen Mariam followed the prelate to Byzantium and a marriage was arranged

---

[1] Brosset, *H. de la G.*, I, 309.   [2] *Idem*, 311-12.

between the youthful Bagrati and Elena, daughter of Michael Argyros, the Emperor's brother.[1] In 1032, the girl was brought in state to Kutais, carrying as her marriage portion "one of the nails of Jesus Christ, the icon of Okona and great riches". But her death next year ended the brief approach of the Abkhazian Bagratids to Byzantium and relations soon became embittered by the revolt of Bagrati's half-brother Dmitri Giorgishvili, who delivered the fortress of Anakopia to the Greeks and fled, himself, to the Imperial capital.[2]

Bagrati ignored all prospect of a further Byzantine alliance by his marriage with Borena, an Ossetian princess; and between 1034 and 1039 set himself towards a policy of expansion in the eastern Caucasus. His great barons, Liparit Orbeliani, *Eristavt-Eristavi*, and Ioanné Abazadze, Eristavi of Kartli, in combination with the Kings Kwiriké of Kakheti and David of Siuniq, inflicted a severe defeat on the army of the banu-Shaddad of Aran in 1034, and in the following year the Emir Jafar of Tiflis was treacherously surprised by the Orbelianis and Abazadze. In 1038 the Georgian kings, Bagrati and Gagik of Kakheti, were strong enough to lay siege to Tiflis. The blockade endured into the following year, and the inhabitants were reduced to such extremities that "the flesh of an ass was sold for five hundred drachmas".[3] Liparit Orbeliani was the genius of the combination, and, at last, the erratic Bagrati and the Kakhian nobles, fearing the enhancement of his power if the city fell, compounded, without his knowledge, with the Emir Jafar.

The reaction of Lipariti to the betrayal of his work and plans was immediate and of a character disastrous to the Abkhazian kingdom. For nearly twenty years with varying fortune, the King and his powerful vassal carried on a deadly feud, which weakened fatally the internal and external position of the Kingdom and ended only with the ruin of the house of Orbeliani. In 1039, the pretender, Dmitri Giorgishvili, came into Samtzkhé with Greek support, and Lipariti sided with him. The movement was unsuccessful, and next year Bagrati laid siege to the Greek garrison of Anakopia. Tiflis in the same year fell into his hands without a fight; for, on the death of the Emir Jafar, the inhabitants invited him to come, and he was received with acclamation in the streets,

---

[1] Brosset, *H. de la G.*, I, 314, and note 2.
[2] Dmitri was the son of Giorgi, by Alda, an "Alanian" princess.
[3] Brosset, *H. de la G.*, I, 317.

although the Muslim soldiers in the *kalah* resisted all attempts to take possession of it.

But the luck of Bagrati was not in for long. In 1041, Dmitri Giorgishvili again took the field supported by Lipariti and the Greeks, and Bagrati, with his Varangian auxiliaries and the levies of Shida-Kartli, was heavily defeated.[1] Dmitri died in the same year, but in 1042, while Bagrati was supporting a revolt of the Meskhian *aznauri* against Lipariti, he was again beaten in the field.

The Greeks now began to revive their pretensions to authority on the Armenian and Georgian marches, and Lipariti became the principal agent of their policy. In 1045, Ani was delivered to the Emperor and Greek ambitions reached out to Kars, to Dwin and even to Ganja. But meanwhile the inroads of the Seljuk Turks into Armenia and Asia Minor were accumulating force, and Alp-Arslan, the son of the old freebooter Er-Toghrul, was assuming the pretensions of a conqueror of empires. In 1048, the combined forces of the Greeks and of Liparit Orbeliani were routed by the Turks in Samtzkhé and Lipariti was sent a prisoner into Khurasan. In the following year the Seljuks pillaged Ani and Theodosiopolis, and they sent Lipariti, their prisoner, to ravage Javakheti. Fear of the nomad riders drew together the more civil rulers, and while Lipariti deserted Alp-Arslan for the Emperor, Bagrati himself went to Byzantium to seek the Imperial support. He stayed there for three years from 1050, and in his absence Lipariti caused Giorgi, Bagrati's son, to be crowned at Ruisi, and assumed all power in the Kingdom.

When Bagrati in 1053 landed at Khopi and rode in state to Kutais, the Turks were in Kars, and in the following year they burned Theodosiopolis and ravaged Tao as far as the Parkhali mountains. But the feudal masters of the mediæval Christian Orient continued to ignore these grim realities. In 1056, Bagrati was engaged in the reduction of the petty independency of Lori, and three years later, while the Turks were sacking Mush and Sivas and wrecking the Christian culture of half Anatolia, Bagrati at last pulled down his stiff old foe, Lipariti. In the following year, 1060, he was bringing to obedience the fortresses of Kakheti and Hereti when the full force of the Turkish storm broke upon his western provinces. Alp-Arslan ravaged all Klarjeti and Tao as far as Panaskert; his riders passed even through the highland gorges of Shavsheti and penetrated the ravine of the Mtkvari

---

[1] Brosset, *H. de la G.*, I, 321.

as far as Tori, scoured the populous valleys of Trialeti and Javakheti and burned Akhalkalaki. The Turkish raids were organized and disciplined, efficient devastation. Alp-Arslan and his commanders were tacticians who evolved a new methodology in mediæval Asiatic war. There are Tatar dances in the Caucasus which still preserve the actual pattern of the plan pursued by the Turkish captains in those cavalry campaigns which in the space of fifty years altered the whole face of human culture from the Oxus to the Mediterranean. When the Turks invaded a country it was customary for the whole army to advance in a solid body to some central point. From this point as a base, four corps of equal strength were despatched to the four points of the compass. After these corps had covered a certain distance, each would divide again into three small sections, which would then spread rapidly fanwise. These smaller sections having reached their appointed distances, would then disperse in smaller bands to pillage the surrounding country. Each band, with its loot and prisoners, would then return by an appointed day to its sub-divisional camp; the sub-divisions would proceed to concentrate on the divisional bases, and finally the four divisions would reassemble at the central headquarters from which the expedition had been organized. The whole army would then return whence it had come, carrying with it its mass of booty and slaves, or it would move on to untouched country.[1]

The Turkish menace encouraged a closer relation between the harassed Christian monarchs of the Pontus, and in 1065 the alliance of the Abkhazian and Byzantine courts was cemented by the marriage of Bagrati's daughter Martha to Michael, son of the Emperor Constantine X Dukas.[2] But in 1064, Ani—metropolis of the Armenians and object of Byzantine diplomacy and war during the preceding half century —had fallen to Alp-Arslan. In 1068, the Turks were ravaging Kakheti, and Gagik's son, the Bagratid Aghsartani I, was compelled to apostasize and to pay the *kharaj* to Alp-Arslan, who had now succeeded his uncle, Er-Toghrul, as " King of the East and West ".

From Kakheti, Alp-Arslan rode into Kartli dragging in his train King Aghsartani and a horde of Kakhian, Persian and Armenian auxiliaries.

---

[1] See Brosset, *H. de la G.*, I, 347, note 4 ; he gives a diagram to illustrate these tactics.
[2] Brosset, *H. de la G.*, I, 330, and note 2. The Byzantine writers call Martha of Abasgia (Abkhazeti), Maria of Alania.

"In the morning", wrote the Annalist, "he launched his bands and by the evening the whole of Kartli was covered with them; it was Tuesday, the 10th December of the year 1068. Kartli being at that time gorged with corn and wine, the Sultan remained there six weeks, putting all to fire and blood. His bands passed into Argueti and drove their raids as far as the citadel of Sweri, and an infinite number of Christians were killed and made prisoners: Kartli presented a hideous spectacle to the eye. All the churches were ruined, and the sight of the land covered with corpses horrified all men. . . . It was a hard winter, and those who got away to the mountains, died there from excess of cold." [1]

From Kartli, the Sultan with his army passed up to Kars, where he received Ioanné Orbeliani, the ambassador of Bagrati, who secured peace for his master on the condition of paying the *kharaj*. The city of Tiflis was granted by Alp-Arslan to Fadlun the Kurdish Emir of Ganja, and over the ruined land hostilities at once broke out between the rising Muslim ruler and the Kings Bagrati and Aghsartani.

In the summer of 1071 Alp-Arslan, at the head of a picked force of 15,000 Turkish cavalry, defeated at Malaskert the Emperor Romanos Diogenes with his miscellaneous host of 200,000 Byzantines, Georgians, Russians, Bulgarians, Franks and Armenians. The battle marked the end not only of Byzantine political and military power in Anatolia, but of the whole cultural life of the Christian Orient between the Mediterranean and the Caspian. The Persians had fought for six centuries, the Arabs for three more, to win the Armenian passes which could give them the mastery of Asia Minor. The Turks, after four decades of cavalry fighting and one pitched battle, had overthrown the proud Empire of the East and won the richest provinces of the ancient world.

It was the lack of political vitality, the decay of organic life within the Byzantine Empire, which gave the Turks their triumph. Their strong barbarian arms had thrown down the rotten walls of the Classic Greek and Christian culture of the Middle East. Henceforth the fresh uplands of Anatolia were to become a Turkish homeland, as congenial to Turks and indeed more habitable than the bare pastures of Inner Asia which they had so lately left. And the Turks became masters of Anatolia and peopled it, which the earlier Asiatic powers, Persian and Arabian, could never do, really because they liked the land; it suited their dour northland nature, and they wanted to inhabit it. They brought with them the beliefs and ways of Islam, civil clothes but lately borrowed by spiritually naked

[1] Brosset, *H. de la G.*, I, 331–2.

pastoralists, and they found and used and lived upon, rather than built upon, the debris of the feudal culture of the East Christian world. These needy reivers, fierce destroyers, now settled over their wide provinces as comfortable and unprogressive, but still warlike barons; they built their feudal states and pressed against the broken towers, left standing, of Eastern Christianity in the Mediterranean coastlands, along the Pontus and in Georgia.

In 1072, the year following the battle of Malaskert, Alp-Arslan was murdered at the early age of thirty-four. About the same time, during November of that year, King Bagrat IV, now an elderly man, died of an affection of the stomach. "I suffer for you", he told his mother, the fine old Queen Mariam Artsruni, "for we, your children, have gone before you, and now death awaits you all alone." [1]

The new king, Giorgi II, gallant, generous, without experience, was confronted with immediate crisis. The brothers Ioanné and Niania Orbeliani rose against him and were joined by Wardani, Eristavi of the Svans. Giorgi had scarcely got the better of the insurgent nobles, when the new Turkish Sultan, Malik-Shah, came up into the Caucasian lands to assert his new authority over both the Christian and the Mussulman rulers of those parts. The Orbelianis played for his favour, but he nevertheless seized Ioanné's stronghold of Samshwilde, then repressed the Mussulmans of Ganja and sent raiding parties into Kartli. In the following year, however, Giorgi, supported by Aghsartani of Kakheti, inflicted a severe defeat on the local Turkish forces at Fartzkhisi on the Algeti. At the same time, with the complete collapse of the Byzantine military machine in the region of the Eastern Pontus, Giorgi recovered Anakopia and occupied other Byzantine ports along the coast, sent his troops to take over the Greek territories in Shavsheti, Klarjeti and Javakheti and seized possession of the ruined city of Kars and its district.

His luck was not of long duration. By Kweli on the Jagis-tsgali the army of the Abkhazian king was surprised and routed by the Turks, and while Giorgi fled into the forests of Achara, the Turkish mounted corps proceeded to wreck and ravage all the kingdom.

"Why go to Greece", they said, "when here is Georgia without inhabitants and stuffed with treasure." [2]

---

[1] Brosset, *H. de la G.*, I, 336.   [2] *Idem*, 346.

THE MEDIÆVAL KINGDOM

The whole of Shavsheti and Achara, Klarjeti down to the sea-coast, all Kartli and inner Samtzkhé, Argueti and the country round Kutais, were raked and harried and driven over through to the early snows. On one and the same day, the all-destroying bands of plundering cavalry burnt Kutais the capital, the noble town of Ardanuchi and the ancient monasteries along the Chorokhi.

With the opening of the year 1080 Giorgi in desperation journeyed in person to Isfahan and made complete submission to Malik-Shah. The policy of the Turkish Sultan was to maintain the native rulers in the remote Caucasian north, and he exacted no more than subjection and due payment of the *kharaj*. At the same time the Turks pursued the object of still further affirming their authority by favouring first Giorgi, then Aghsartani and playing the one against the other. And so the Georgian lands in the last quarter of the century were falling into an anarchy of petty wars, and the people, ruined, driven and oppressed, suffered in plague, rapine and famine the crumbling of the Abkhazian kingdom which had as yet endured no more than eighty years.

CHAPTER VIII

HEYDAY OF THE GEORGIAN KINGS: DAVID II
TO TAMARA

THE twelfth century was an age of ferment throughout the Eurasiatic world. It produced the spiritual and social phenomenon of the Crusades; it saw the rise of national feudal states—Latin-Norman powers with big dynastic appetites; a short-lived Kievian Russia: a flowering of Turkish power on Classic Anatolian soil; the Kingdom of the Georgians. For the most part the new political structures, whether in the West or in the East, were the creations of tough military bands, the Normans over Europe and the Turks in Asia. And the clash of the Crusades was the far-flung conflict of these freebooters, coming out of Scandinavia and Turkistan and making their battle-field all the old world round the Mediterranean. With the closing decade of the eleventh century the full impetus of the Turkish aggressions was expended, but the Viking wanderlust, the Norman land-lust, was still raw and palpitating, and it was directed by the old man's sapience of the Roman Church into a great counter-drive against the Infidel, into a war of the Cross which could offer all to all, salvation to the simple and the fervent, prey for the men of blood, potential royalty for landless princelings, new markets for the Italian cities, world-power for the mastering Church. The storm piled slowly to its sudden cataclysm. The Seljuk Turks had taken Jerusalem in 1071, the same year as their victory over the Byzantines at Malaskert. In the following year the Emperor Michael VII made a first appeal to Rome, but twenty years passed before the genius of Urban II swung in motion the lumbering war-horses of Western chivalry and the knights of Burgundy and the Rhine, of Provence and Sicily took their long ways to Byzantium.

In 1072, Malik-Shah, the third and last of the conquering Seljuk captains, had died, and in Konia and Sivas, in the cities of the Euphrates and Syria, over Iraq and Iran, princes of the Seljuks and their mutinous lieutenants were each and all grasping out for separate power in the lands which had been so recently subjugated. The first drive then of the confederate fanatics, freebooters and merchants of the West met with a wide success. Between the years 1096 and 1099 the Seljuks were hammered in Asia Minor and Syria, and by the year 1100 Norman princes were setting up their little courts and their assizes in Jerusalem, in Tripoli and Antioch, and in Edessa.

This sudden political revolution in the Levant occasioned during the twelfth century a temporary revival of Oriental Christianity, a strong commingling of Greek and Norman, of Armenian and Latin. And while the Byzantine Empire suffered politically from the bullying patronage of the Western Church, of the Italian cities and the Norman baronage, the Armenians in their new kingdom of Sis—a unique product of the amalgam of Latin and East Christian elements—and the Georgians in the Caucasus were enabled to mount once more to vigorous expression of their nationhood.

The Georgian kingdom of the twelfth century was in many ways a direct product of the Crusades, for it was the campaign of the Norman French against the western provinces of the Seljuks which enabled David II in Georgia to scour the desolated valleys under the Caucasus of the nomad invaders who had come there during the preceding quarter of a century. David II, surnamed *Aghmashenebeli*—" The Restorer ", succeeded his father, Giorgi II, in 1089, at the age of sixteen. When he died in 1125 he had not only restored the former suzerainty of the Abkhazian kings over a part of the Georgian lands, but he had set up a new Caucasian monarchy with a capital at Tiflis, a state which straddled the Caucasian isthmus and owned a hegemony alike over Georgians, Armenians and Muslims. The causes of this development of a strong feudal state in the valley of the Mtkvari are not far to seek. The collapse of Byzantine military power, the decline of the Seljuk despotism, and the attacks made on it by the Crusaders from the West, left the Caucasian provinces ready to the sword of any master who had the power to take them. That power lay with the rulers of Abkhazeti, whose lands had suffered less than those of neighbouring kingdoms during the period of Seljuk aggression. Furthermore, the desolation of the greater part of Georgia and Armenia had weakened the little feudal principalities which hitherto had been everywhere so strong. The half-independent feudal lords had not now the strength to oppose the institution of a superior national authority, and so the Seljuk invasions prepared the way for the autocracy of David and his successors.

David, then, had to meet no threat to restore the historical Byzantine hegemony in the eastern Pontus; the Islamic lands were wrung by dynastic wars and harassed on their flank; and the age-old petty independencies of the Georgian lords were ripe for a kingly hand. David's hand was very kingly. This "woodland king", as the Muslims contemptuously called him, was the greatest native figure of Little Asia since Mithradates Eupator and, obscure as he remained, he was without doubt the most distinguished soldier and statesman of the contemporary world. He succeeded as a boy to a desolated kingdom and he built up a strong administration which secured prosperity to his successors for a century and a half. A master of guerrilla warfare, he yet could organize a mercenary field-army and carry difficult sieges to success. A vigorous and grasping conqueror, he quickly showed that he could consolidate his winnings, and gain over the affection of his Muslim subjects.[1]

> "There was no one his equal", wrote the Annalists, "in weighing the actions of men, and discerning their qualities. . . . His friendliness, his kindness, his wisdom, caused men to come together from the corners of the earth, urged by the desire to attach themselves to him. He was gracious in his intercourse, gentle in his words, stimulating in his silence; of a charming countenance, but more charming still in his carriage; with an attractive smile which was even more pleasing in moments of sadness; of a gracious but sometimes terrible aspect; wise in his knowledge, but still wiser in his discernment: simple in his manner but sensitive in his relations; he was gentle in his anger, gave praise in giving reprimand and he never embarrassed a man of good intent. He was haughty towards the proud and humble with the poor, and he was loved and cherished even by his enemies for his modesty and his virtues." [2]

And the old Annalist continues with intimate affection, that

> "without speaking of some actions in his youth, which God himself has forgotten, I know with certainty that during the entire space of ten years, he received the incorruptible mysteries of Jesus Christ with a pure mouth, a soul without stain, a conscience tranquil and without remorse".[3]

---

[1] Muhammad-el-Hameki (1233): "he possessed a great knowledge of the Muslim religion and would often dispute with the Kadi of Ganja whether the Koran were inspired or of man". El-Aini (1460): "He rejoiced the hearts of the inhabitants . . . David and his son, Dmitri, visited the principal mosque each day, listened to the prayer and the lesson for the Koran; gave much money to the Khatib for the soothsayers, Sufis and poets, and allowed them pensions."
[2] Brosset, *H. de la G.*, I, 378.   [3] *Ibid.*, p. 375.

THE MEDIÆVAL KINGDOM

The death of Malik-Shah in 1092, and the progress of the First Crusade from 1096 to 1101, enabled David to pass the first twelve years of his reign in the steady extension and stabilization of his power within the Georgian lands. The imprisonment and exile of Liparit Orbeliani in 1097 and the death of his son, Rati, five years later, deprived the feudal lords of leadership in their resistance to the monarchy. In the same year, 1101, David attacked Kwiriké IV of Kakheti and took from him the important stronghold of Zedazadeni. The noble Kwiriké died in 1102 and was succeeded by his nephew, Aghsartan II,

> " a man without any of the qualities of royalty . . . malevolent, impious and as ignorant as he was unjust ".[1]

The ancient independence of Kakheti was terminated in the person of Aghsartani, who was delivered to David by his own nobles in 1104-1105.

One king at last ruled Georgia from the Black Sea to the foothills of Daghestan, but all the south and west still lay open to the annual inroads of half-nomadic Turkish hordes, and Tiflis remained an advance stronghold of Mussulman power. It was the custom of the Turks each year in October to overrun the whole valley of the Mtkvari from below Tiflis to Barda'a, so that their kine might enjoy the rich herbage of the surrounding country. With the coming of spring the shepherd armies would withdraw to the mountains of Somkheti and the region of Ararat. David, therefore, undertook a long and continuous series of operations lasting from 1110 to 1122 with the object of clearing the nomads from the reaches of the middle Mtkvari, and as he made progress in the south-east he also extended his operations to the depopulated districts round the Meskhian lakes.

In 1110 the Turks were harried out of Somkheti and an army sent to their assistance by the Seljuk rulers of Persia was defeated in the field; but it was not until 1115 that David finally checked the annual incursions of the nomads by the capture of Rusthavi, a fortress which had protected them in the enjoyment of the pastures of the middle Mtkvari and the Yori. In 1116 David's cavalry cleared the Turks out of Tao and Klarjeti; in 1117 Shirvan was successfully invaded, and in 1118 the fortress of Lori, which gave the Turks access into Somkheti, was taken and a Turkish army was defeated on the Araks.[2]

---

[1] Brosset, *H. de la G.*, I, 354.   [2] *Ibid.*, 359.

HEYDAY OF THE GEORGIAN KINGS

David was now attaining to a position of no mean importance in the politics of contemporary Asia, and he proceeded to strengthen his dynasty by foreign marriages. One of his daughters, Tamara, was married to the Shirvanshah, who, although a Muslim, showed a preference always for a Georgian rather than a Seljuk alliance. Another daughter, Kata, was sent to Byzantium to be the bride of Alexios the son of Nikephoros IV Bryennios.

David's ambitions were growing also with his fortunes, and he now began seriously to recruit a mercenary standing army from among the Ossetians and Kipchaks. His connection with the Kipchaks was close, for his wife was a Kipchak princess, and David deliberately consolidated this connection by the construction of fortresses in the Daryal, which gave him direct and continued access to his allies in the north. About 1118, he formed a special guard of 5,000 Kipchak slaves, all converts to Christianity, and he introduced by the Daryal Pass a multitude of Kipchak families whom he settled in the depopulated districts of Georgia and Armenia, which had recently been reconquered. The Kipchak settlers are stated by the Annalist to have been able to provide him with 40,000 trained warriors, and although he was troubled with recurrent plots and mutinies on the part of these half-savage mercenaries, the addition of their strength provided him with a force which gave him the mastery over both the Seljuk Turks and his own baronage.

David passed the seasons of 1119 and 1120 in a series of minor operations against the Seljuks on his south-eastern and south-western borders, in Shirvan and in the country between the Chorokhi and Erzerum, and so disturbing did his successes become to the Seljuk rulers that in 1121 something approaching a *jihad* was proclaimed against the Georgians. A levy was made of all the Mussulman emirates between Ganja and Aleppo, and Ilghazi-bin-Ortok, the ruler of Aleppo, fresh from his victory over Roger of Antioch, commanded the great host which in August of that year invaded Trialeti. But the confederate emirs were utterly routed by David near Manglisi, and the victory gave the Georgians Tiflis, which capitulated in the following year.

David had recovered the ancient Georgian capital which had been a city of Islam for nearly four hundred years. He was soon challenged by a Persian Seljuk army which took Shamakha, the capital of his son-in-law, the Shirvanshah. But the field armies of the Sultan and King David, when they met, both withdrew without a fight,[1] and David was left free to pursue his favourite strategy of widespread minor operations—in Shirvan, Aran and Tao, during the years 1123 and 1124. In the latter year his long career of victories was crowned by the capture of Ispir on the Chorokhi and of Ani, the ancient Armenian capital; and in Shirvan he was able to appoint his own governor in the person of Bishop Simon of Dchqondidi.

The third decade of the twelfth century saw the high-water mark of the East Christian revival in Lesser Asia. The whole coast of the Levant from the Gulf of Alexandretta to the Sinai peninsula was in Armenian or Latin-Norman hands. The reign of the wise and brave Alexios Comnenos at Byzantium had helped to a constricted restoration of Greek power along the Anatolian littoral. But most conspicuous and least ephemeral were the successes of David the Restorer throughout the Caucasian lands. For David had brought under his control all the Georgian country from Daryal to Ispir, from Pitsunda to the Caspian shore; he had incorporated within his dominions wide districts of the ancient Armenian kingdom; and he had established the hegemony of a Christian feudal monarchy in the important Mussulman province of Shirvan. But while his victories were the most impressive, his methods of government were more enlightened than those of the majority of his Western contemporaries. He promised, had he lived, to weld the stranger nations and the contending creeds of the Caucasian lands within the framework of a tolerant state, and it is possible that a strong continuing monarchy, backed by the standing army which he had formed, might have achieved a balance between the Muslim and Armenian towns and the Georgian military nobility and have attained a lasting stability based upon a natural unity of geographical background. The problem which offered itself to coming Georgian kings was, in its elements, no more formidable than that which confronted the Spanish monarchs in the fourteenth and fifteenth centuries.

But the thirty years which followed the death of David II in 1125 were years of stagnation in the political life of the Caucasian lands by contrast with the epic period of the first quarter of the century. Both in the west and in the east there was check to the East Christian revival. The reign of Muham-

---

[1] Al-Aini says that the Muslims "feared the Georgians terribly" and hesitated to fight, but a mutiny among the Kipchak mercenaries prevented David from attacking the Persian army. (Quoted by Brosset, *Add. et Ec.*, Add. XIII.)

mad Sanjar—a son of Malik Shah—in Persia gave strength to the Mussulman dynasts who ruled in Diarbekr, Mardin, Mawsil, Aleppo and Damascus. Neither the energy of John Comnenos at Byzantium nor the fair ability of the new King Dmitri I in Georgia were sufficient to meet the mounting reaction of the Muslim powers, while the Latin states in Syria and Palestine were failing because they had not in them the elements of a continuing stability. In 1143, John Comnenos died; in 1144 Edessa was lost to the Muslims; and in 1148 all the Crusading fervour of the West was stricken by the utter failure of the great effort made by the Emperor Conrad and the French King Louis VII to restore the Norman-Latin power in the Levant.

The reign of Dmitri in Georgia from 1125 to 1154 or 1156 is treated briefly in the Annals, and it is apparent that the Annalists writing under the reign of his son, Giorgi III, are responsible for the omission of facts which would doubtless have been unpalatable to that truculent usurper. Between the years 1154 and 1156, Dmitri took the monk's cowl and died, while his elder son David III who succeeded him only reigned six months and actually predeceased his father. Giorgi, the younger son, ruled in the stead of David's heir, an infant Dmitri or Demna. Such are the bare facts which serve to disguise the first of the sanguinary family conflicts which were to recur so frequently over the succession to the Georgian kingship. The pretensions of younger brothers to the succession, which, in fact, began in Georgia with the attempts of Dmitri Giorgishvili against his half-brother Bagrat IV are no unusual phenomenon in mediæval dynastic history, and in the great days of the Georgian kingdom they were only rare because of the tendency of the Bagratid men to breed daughters rather than sons.[1]

During the thirty years of the reign of Dmitri II the country enjoyed a term of prosperity and relative peace. It was in fact a period of recovery from the desolation of the Seljuk wars and from the mighty effort put forward by the people under David Aghmashenebeli.[2] But on the whole David's successor failed to maintain the position of political predominance in the Caucasus which had been attained by the

---

[1] During the two hundred years between Bagrat IV and Giorgi IV, the succession depended upon one male life on no less than three occasions.
[2] Brosset, *H. de la G.*, I, 381: "When the great King David took Tiflis and swallowed Hereti and Kakheti, there were no inhabitants to be found anywhere, unless it were in the citadels and towns of Hereti, of Somkheti, of Tashiri, of Javakheti, and of lower Ardahani and Artvini. In the reign of Dmitri the lands of Tao were repeopled."

year 1125. Ani, the last conquest of the great king, was restored to the banu-Shaddad in 1126, and although two years later Dmitri took Dmanisi and Khunani, the two keys of Trialeti, and beat the Turks in the plain of Gagi, his success was not lasting. Between the years 1132 and 1139 the Georgian forces engaged on the borders of Armenia and Azerbaijan suffered several serious reverses at the hands of the Atabeg Ildeguz, who had established himself in independent power in Tabriz. The opening years of Giorgi's reign were coincident with the defeat of Muhammad Sanjar by the Ghur Turks, an event which marked the definite collapse of effective Seljuk power in Persia. But the result was to strengthen rather than to weaken the influence of the Atabeg Ildiguz in the north-western provinces, and when Giorgi undertook a protracted war against him between the years 1161 and 1166, he found that the new Mussulman power in Azerbaijan was the equal of the Georgian kingdom. Giorgi's possession of Ani and his capture of Dwin proved only temporary advantages, and both these cities had been recovered by Ildeguz before the end of 1165.

Impetuous, violent and unscrupulous, extravagant and cruel, Giorgi was not without certain coarse qualities of kingship. He strengthened the hold which his father and his grandfather had already gained over the insolent and quarrelsome nobility, and, like his contemporaries in mediæval Europe, he sought to check their power and humiliate their spirit by the elevation of his own creatures to the seats of power. Thus he made a certain priest, Mikela Mirionisdze, first, Bishop of Dchqondidi and Atskveri and Grand Secretary, and later preferred him to the See of Mtzkheta. Aphridon, a simple *aznauri*, became Chief of the *Msakhurni* and was accorded the Commandancy of Tmogvi and other fortresses, while Qubazar, brave and shrewd, but a man of lowly origin, was given the magnificent posts of *Amir-Spasalari* and Chief of the *Mandaturni*.

The resentment of the great nobles against the arbitrary favouritism and growing power of the King found expression in 1174, when Demna, the youthful and attractive son of David III, attempted to establish his right to the throne. The older princely houses were behind the pretender—the Orbelianis, Gamrekeli, and the baronage of Kakheti and Hereti, and the strength of the movement lay in the districts bordering on Armenia, where the Orbeliani interest had always been strongest. The insurgents were defeated in

Hereti. Demna sent emissaries to Persia to solicit assistance, but he was cornered by Giorgi in the citadel of Lori and escaped from his own supporters to surrender himself to the king. With a calculating ruthlessness Giorgi settled the dynastic issue and extirpated the oldest houses of the Georgian nobility with blinding iron and knife. Demna was relegated to prison, a sightless eunuch, and the whole seed of the Orbeliani were visited with forfeiture and mutilation. Only two or three cadets of this overbearing brood made good their escape to Persia, and Giorgi sealed the record of their two centuries' rivalry with the Bagratids, by ordering that even the name of Orbeliani should be removed from the annals of the kingdom. The royal ferocity is execrated by Stephen Orbeliani, the episcopal biographer of his family, but if later kings had used the blinding iron and knife with the same cold brutality against the Jaqelis and the Imerian Bagratids, the history of the Georgian people might have been less bloody and more fortunate.

When Giorgi III died in 1184, he was succeeded by his daughter, Tamara, the only representative in the direct line of the royal stem of Bagrationi. Tamara had already been associated in the government by her father in 1178, and after her proclamation as "King of Kartli" by the assembly of the bishops and nobles, she began to rule with the advice and under the influence of her strong-minded aunt Rusudani. Tamara's mother had been a princess of Osseti who had been married to Giorgi during the lifetime of his father, and it is probable therefore that the new monarch was little less than thirty years of age at the time of her accession and nearly forty at the period when her children were born. The legend of her beauty is the theme of the Annalists and of contemporary poets, and although queenly beauty is not infrequently a courtier's convention, it is likely that she was endowed with the attractions of her handsome house. But her marriages were conveniences and, despite the poetic licence of Lermontov, there is no evidence to show that she was subject to those erotic failings to which her son and daughter were addicted in their time and tasted to the full. Rather Tamara was the matriarch, the sage and puritan administrator, the careful, anxious diplomat, the steady soldier, pious, gentle and humane. The curiously maternal influence which a good woman ruler exercises over the minds of men was forceful throughout her reign, when civil life was thriving, religious thought was active, and the nation expressed its unbounding energies in vigorous building throughout the country, and continuous victories beyond the frontiers.

The accession of Tamara was marked by a conservative reaction of the nobles against the upstart favourites of King Giorgi. But such was the prestige of the Catholicosate that Mikela Mirionisdze, unpopular though he was, was able to defy the desire of the court to depose him. Qubazar, who had profited most from the confiscations following the attempt of Demna and who had since become a paralytic, was deprived of his wealth and emoluments, and Aphridon, Chief of the *Msakhurni*, was thrown from power. But Tamara seems to have held the balance fairly between the avenging aristocrats and the new-rich of Giorgi's reign, for while she gave high honours to two former supporters of Demna, Gamrekeli and Dchiaberi, and favoured the noble houses of Wardanisdze, Dadiani and Marushidze, she retained and leant upon the numerous relatives of Sargis Mkhargrdzeli, an *aznauri* of Kurdish origin and ancient stock whom Giorgi had raised up.

In 1185, Tamara, on the insistence of the nobles and of her aunt Rusudani, was married, with reluctance, to George Bogolyubskoi, a son of the Great Prince Andrew of Suzdal and at that time a fugitive in the Kipchak country. The Russian was a truculent and overbearing adventurer, a drunkard, violent, cruel and vicious, and from the first affairs went badly between the lucky fortune-hunter and the chaste and serious queen.

The military successes of George Bogolyubskoi during the annual forays against the Muslims, which were undertaken into Shirvan, Aran and Armenia, gained him a certain degree of popularity which he was later to turn to effective account; but in 1187–8 Tamara obtained the consent of an assembly of bishops and nobles to her divorce and the Russian prince was exiled to Byzantium. The fact that the Queen was still childless was doubtless an inducement to the clergy to condone the divorce, and steps were immediately undertaken to find a father for an heir to the Georgian crown. In 1189, Tamara was married once more, to David Soslan, an Ossetian prince, who was descended in the female line from Dmitri Giorgishvili, the half-brother of Bagrat IV; and her second marriage was blessed in 1194 by the birth of an heir, Giorgi, and in 1195 of a daughter, Rusudani.

Meanwhile, in 1190–1 took place the formidable attempt of George Bogolyubskoi to seize the kingdom. From Erzinjan he came into Samtzkhé, probably with the active support of the Seljuk Sultan of Erzerum. George immediately met with a welcome, the character of which serves to indicate the underlying dangers of the political state of Tamara's kingdom. He was supported by all the representatives of the powerful reactionary faction which had become so menacing after the death of Giorgi III. Only the Amir-Spasalari Gamrekeli, Dchiaberi of Hereti and one of the Wardanisdzes, remained faithful to the Queen. Secondly, all Samtzkhé and Imereti, Abkhazeti and Svaneti rose in his favour, and the eastern provinces alone, the newest part of the kingdom, gave their support to Tamara. This important rising therefore had a triple character: for George Bogolyubskoi it represented a freebooting attempt to seize a kingdom; for the old aristocratic houses who aided him, it meant a revolt of the once half-independent feudal princes against the enveloping power of the monarchy; and the regional aspect of the movement, as a rising of Imier against Amier, proclaims the existence of those fundamental differences in sympathy between the western and eastern parts of the kingdom which later were to develop with such disastrous results for the life of the Georgian nation and which were to prove fatal to the possibility—envisaged in the policy of the Bagratids—of building a great Caucasian state.

For a few weeks in the summer of 1191 the position of Tamara was seriously threatened. The insurgent nobles came against Tiflis in three separate armies. Bogolyubskoi was proclaimed king at the palace of Geguti (called also Tzikhé-Darbassé) in Imereti; and while the Imerians advanced to Gori and Nadcharmagevi, the Meskhians came up from the south over the passes of Trialeti. The three invading forces were, however, met and defeated in two pitched battles by Gamrekeli and the four Mkhargrdzelis, and finally George Bogolyubskoi, "king for a day", was delivered to Tamara by the Svans. The Queen used her victory with tact and moderation and even allowed Bogolyubskoi "to take once more the way of his ill fortune" by retiring to Byzantium. But neither her military triumph nor her humanity could altogether stay the crude forces of insurrection, which were fermenting always, for that matter, within the social bodies of the Middle Ages. The tough mountain lords of Samtzkhé were scarcely cowed, and in 1193 they broke out into a dangerous revolt which was put down only after serious fighting. Seven years later, in 1200, Bogolyubskoi, who had meanwhile been banished from Byzantium and who had become a pensioner of the Atabeg of Azerbaijan, rode with a horde of Turks into Kambechovani in one last futile attempt to seize the throne.

During the two decades following the insurrection of 1191, Tamara embarked upon a policy of aggressions against the neighbouring Mussulman rulers. In undertaking this policy she seems to have been following the shrewd advice of the Amir-Spasalari Zakharia Mkhargrdzeli, who advocated the continuous engagement of the Georgian armed forces in active operations—a course which at one and the same time could rally the Christian feudality against the Infidel and afford to the restless fighting men, particularly of the Meskhian highlands, full opportunities to satisfy their lust for war.[1]

The last two decades of the twelfth century had seen a period of vigorous activity in Islam; in Palestine and Egypt the Kurd Saladin was confronting and defeating the embattled kings of Western Europe; beyond the Oxus the Khwarazmshahs were building an empire which, although short-lived, was to recover for Islamic Persia a brief return of the glories of the earlier Seljuks. But while in the far west and the far east of the mid-Asiatic world Islam was crescent, the provinces of Persia and the emirates of Anatolia were feeble and disordered. Mamluk atabegs, often men of Caucasian servile origin, ruled as "mayors of the palace" in the seats of the Seljuk Sultans; and in northern and central Persia, the sinister sect of the Ismailis, built upon a curious syncretism of ideas which partook at once of religious mysticism, advanced radicalism and murderous magic, were establishing a tyranny over the cities, the country, and the princes of Iran.

So within a decade after the kings of France and England had gone with contumely out of Palestine, the royal army of Georgia could carry terror and rapine through all the Muslim lands which lay between the Black Sea and the south-eastern corner of the Caspian.

In Azerbaijan the three decadent grandsons of the Atabeg Ildiguz were contending for the succession, and the first campaign of Tamara was undertaken to assist her relative the Shirvanshah Aghsartani, who had become involved in the unsuccessful hostilities which one of the brothers, Usbeg, was pressing against the reigning Abu-Bekr. In June, 1203, the Atabeg, who had invaded Aran with a considerable army, was defeated at Dzagam near Shamkhor by an army of Georgians and Kipchaks under David Soslan and Bishop Antoni of Dchqondidi. Shamkhor, Ganja and Dwin fell

[1] Brosset, *H. de la G.*, I, 470.

HEYDAY OF THE GEORGIAN KINGS

into Georgian hands, and with the restoration of the Shirvanshah Aghsartani the suzerain authority of the Georgian kings—which had lapsed since the days of David II—was restored over the Muslim districts north of the Araks.

Between 1205 and 1206 there was serious war between the Georgians and the troops of the Seljuk Sultan Rukn-ed-din, who had established himself as the successor of the Saldukid dynasts in Erzerum. The blockade of Kars had been carried on intermittently for some years by local Meskhian forces under Sargis Tmogveli and Shalva Torveli, and in 1208 or 1209 formal siege was laid by the Army of Upper Kartli under the command of David Soslan and the brothers Zakharia and Ioanné Mkhargrdzeli. With the capitulation of Kars, to the government of which her fourteen-year-old son Giorgi was appointed, Tamara had acquired possession of the fortress which down to modern times has properly been regarded as the key to the Caucasian provinces.

Now, during the last years of Tamara, a Caucasian state was in actual being. This state was ruled by a Georgian royal house and dominated by a military aristocracy in the composition of which not only Georgian, but strong Armenian and lesser Mussulman elements were included. The royal control was effective and could remain effective so long as it rested in efficient hands. The boast that the House of Bagrationi ruled from Nikopsia to Derbend was no fantastic reclamation. It is true that a wide autonomy was allowed to the Muslim feudatories, to the Shirvanshah, to the chiefs of the powerful Kipchak settlements along the middle Mtkvari and to great cities of mixed Armenian and Muslim population, like Dwin, Ganja and Ani. But this autonomy was in effect no more than that enjoyed by the great Georgian territorial princes, as Sharvashidze in Abkhazeti, Dadiani in Mingrelia, or to the lords of more scattered domains as the Gamrekelis, the Wardanidzes, and the rising house of the Mkhargrdzelis. This loose autonomy was essentially the most practical method of government in the economic and social conditions of the early thirteenth century. For so long as the royal power was strong and competent at the centre, that power could make itself felt as a master and protector throughout the lands over which it claimed authority, whether it were in the repression of the Meskhian revolt of 1196, or in the defence of the Araks frontier in 1208–9, or in the taming of the Georgian mountain tribes, the Tush, Pshav and Mtiul in 1211. Beyond the frontiers, in foreign politics, Tamara made her authority equally felt, and when, after the capture of Byzantium by the Latins in 1204, she sent Georgian troops to Trebizond and Kerasund in the interest of her relation Alexios Comnenos,[1] she established her kingdom as a power on the Black Sea. But it was in Persia that the power of Georgia at the beginning of the thirteenth century achieved its most dramatic demonstration. In the summer of 1208, the Emir of Ardabil had crossed the Araks and taken and sacked the frontier city of Ani. Twelve thousand Christians were massacred in the churches alone.

In the following year a Georgian punitive expedition was secretly organized under the orders of Zakharia and Ioanné Mkhargrdzeli. It crossed the Araks to the east of Urdubad and rode straight through to Ardabil, which was taken by surprise. The Emir was killed; the town was gutted; twelve thousand people were massacred as a reprisal for the slaughter at Ani, and the remainder were carried away into slavery.

The facility with which this success had been achieved against one of the most important cities of Persia, provoked in the following year a great raid on a wide and daring scale. In October, 1210, large forces were concentrated at Tiflis and then moved down to Nakhchevan under the orders of the Mkhargrdzelis. The Georgians crossed the Araks at Julfa and moving down the valley of Daraduz, they took Marand by surprise. A large, but ill-organized Persian force was routed by a picked cavalry corps of five hundred nobles under Thaqiadin Tmogveli; and, without further resistance the terrorized inhabitants of Tabriz and Miana hastened to purchase the immunity of their cities at the cost of heavy contributions.

The Georgian cavalry then rode through Ghilan, took the town of Zinjan by storm and received the submission of Kazvin without a fight. After capturing Romgor in the district of Nishapur, the Georgians set about to return, loaded with the booty of half northern Persia. The slaughter by the inhabitants of the Georgian garrison of Miana caused Zakharia to visit it with fire and massacre, and as he moved northwards towards the Araks he exacted further contributions from the towns of Azerbaijan.

[1] The connection of the Comnenoi with the Georgian royal house had always been close, and goes to explain their peculiar interest with the remaining eastern provinces of the empire. Andronikos, the witty and evil grandfather of Alexios, had taken refuge at the court of Giorgi III and left descendants in Georgia who, as Andronikashvilis, still bear his name.

CHAPTER IX

THE MONARCHY UNDER THE MONGOLS: GIORGI IV TO DAVID VI

IN 1212, Giorgi IV, called *Lasha*, which has the meaning in the Abkhaz tongue of "light of the world", succeeded his mother, at the age of eighteen. A man, brave and vigorous, ready to quick decisions, rash and changeable, presumptuous and arrogant towards the great, splendid and fantastic in his ways, charming and affectionate, easy and licentious, he alarmed the ageing counsellors of the late Queen Tamara, and scandalized and infuriated the princes of the Church.[1] The ten years of his reign represented a period of reaction against the militant puritanism of the Tamaran epoch, and while the court of Tiflis gave itself over to a life of magnificent debauchery and Giorgi surrounded himself with dissolute and low-born favourites—the groundlings of his cups, the noble veterans of the Persian wars withdrew to their estates growling that they might soon cease to recognize the King.[2] But the monarchy in its strength was now a century and a quarter old and it is eloquent of its stability as an institution that the forces of revolt took the form of an effort to coerce the King in the interests of the country, rather than of attempts by the territorial princes to revive their old independencies. The one attempted revolt—on the part of the Muslim Atabeg of Ganja—was crushed, and the all-powerful Mkhargrdzelis set themselves to rule the Kingdom rather than to partition it. The *Amir-Spasalari* Zakharia had died in 1211, and political leadership had passed to his brother Ioanné who had the title of *Atabegi* and to his son Waram (Bahram) of Gagi the *Msakhurt-Ukhutsesi*. The Mkhargrdzelis, working with the bishops, were strong enough to force Giorgi to part with his mistress, a Kakhian peasant woman who had already given him a son, David, but they were not able to compel him to a suitable marriage.

The personal struggle between the King and the great nobles never reached an ultimate issue, for the Georgian land

---
[1] Brosset, *H. de la G.*, I, 481 and 485.   [2] *Ibid.*, p. 484.

was now licked by a mighty wave, which in the next two decades was to wipe away many of the proud despotisms of Dar-ul-Islam, and not a few of the most ancient monarchies of mediæval Europe. In the early autumn of 1220, a courier came to King Giorgi from the Atabegi Ioanné and Waram of Gagi on the frontiers of Georgia and told " of the arrival of a strange people, speaking a strange tongue, who were devastating Armenia ".[1]

This was the first news of the Mongols, who in a brief decade had conquered half China, who had overthrown the powerful Muslim-Turkish Empire of the Khwarazm-shahs in Persia and Turkistan, and who had carried their victories into India. The army commanded by the *no'ins* Subutai and Chébé, after pursuing the fugitive Khwarazm-shah Ala-ul-din Muhammad to the Caspian, had devastated all northern Persia. Usbeg, the bibulous old Atabeg of Azerbaijan, purchased the immunity of Tabriz with a heavy contribution; and the Mongols rode north into the grassy steppe-lands of Mughan, where the rich grazing might have tempted them to winter. But Giorgi Lasha, after a hasty levy of the Kingdom, moved through Somkheti, with ninety thousand horse. The Mongols met him near Khunani and the Georgian feudality were utterly routed. After the victory, the Mongol army turned south to Hamadan. Three years later, the new Queen Rusudani, in her letter to Pope Honorius III, could refer to their invasion as an unimportant episode. But the contemporary Annalist appreciated the significance of Giorgi's defeat and regarded it as the turning-point in the history of Georgian arms. The sacred standard of David and of Gurgaslani, under which the Georgians had never known defeat since the days of the Restorer, had been carried in flight.[2]

When the Mongol army returned in 1222, the Georgians did not venture to meet them in the field, and as the conquering horsemen rode north against the Russian dukedoms all Somkheti and Shirvan were ravaged, and the nomad Kipchaks upon whom the Georgian kings had so frequently relied were decimated and subdued.

Giorgi died in January, 1223, leaving only the infant bastard, David, the promise of whose ultimate succession he endeavoured to secure from the nobles. The dead king's sister, Rusudani, was proclaimed after the style of her mother " King of Kartli ". The *kiz-malik*, the " maiden-king " of the Muslim writers, was twenty-nine and without a husband.

[1] Brosset, *H. de la G.*, I, 492.   [2] *Ibid.*, 493.

THE MONARCHY UNDER THE MONGOLS

The adored sister of the splendid Lasha, she shared his carnal tastes, but lacked his swash-buckling courage. She was fearless only in her lusts,[1] and her polity was confined within the cruel and lurid meannesses of an erotic woman.

When Rusudani succeeded in 1223, the Mongol invasions had already seriously shaken the political and social fabrics of both the Caucasian and Iranian lands. But the Georgian Queen and the neighbouring Muslim rulers, alike, ignored the imminence of disaster. While Rusudani was contemplating participation in the Crusade of the Emperor Frederick II[2] and intervening in the affairs of Shirvan and Azerbaijan,[3] the new Khwarazm-shah, Jalal-ul-din, in the middle of a desperate effort to restore the power of his house was preparing to attack the Georgians.

"This brave and reckless Turkoman chief . . . laughing only at the tips of his lips,"

defeated the Georgians at Garnhi in Siuniq during August 1225. The jealousy of the old Atabegi Ioanné against his relative Shalva Mkhargrdzeli of Akhaltzikhé is alleged by the Annalists to have been the cause of the demoralization of the Georgian strength. Jalal-ul-din devastated all the eastern districts up to Ganja, and after a fruitless conference with Ioanné's son, Awagi, at Bedshni, he marched against Tiflis. The capital was betrayed by some of the Persian inhabitants, and while the Queen fled to Kutais, the wealthy city which had now enjoyed a hundred years of peace was submitted to the horrors of pillage and massacre by the wild troops of the Khwarazm-shah.[4]

For six years all Kartli and Samtzkhé lay open to the ravages of the Khwarazmian army—itself an army without a country whose captains lived by roaming and fighting over all the lands between Iraq and the Black Sea. In 1228, a great effort was made to rally the forces of the Kingdom, and a heterogeneous army, composed largely of Lazghi, Kipchak, Svan and Armenian mercenaries, was gathered under the command of Awag Mkhargrdzeli, Waram of Gagi and Tzotné Dadiani; but they were routed by Jalal-ul-din at

---

[1] Brosset, H. de la G., I, note 2, quoting Abu'l Fida.
[2] V. Langlois, *Numismatique de la Géorgie*, p. 28, note 2, quoting Raynaldi, *Ann. eccl.*, Tome XIII, pp. 339–40, No. 17, and Alberic des Trois-Fontaines in *Rec. des Hist. de Fr.*, Tome XXI, ed. Nat. de Nailly, p. 603, and other sources.
[3] Brosset, H. de la G., I, 497, note 2, quoting Defrémery; *Extraits d'Ibn-al-Athyr*, in *J.A.*, IVième sér., Tome XIV, pp. 477–80.
[4] For details see Brosset, H. de la G., I, 504–5; Nasawi (ed. Houdas, p. 122), who confirms the extent of the massacre of the Christians.

Bolnisi.[1] From that date the writ of the Georgian crown ceased to run east of the mountains of Likhi, and only in the forests of Imereti were the people protected from the anarchy which was maintained by the wandering bands of Muslim soldiery.

The final invasion of the Caucasian provinces by the Mongol armies in 1236 served to alleviate rather than to intensify the misery into which the people had been plunged. For the Mongols were distinguished from earlier nomadic conquerors of Western Asia, in that they were authoritarian rather than crudely predatory, a fact which has been emphasized recently by D. S. Mirsky in his short but brilliant study of Mongol rule in Russia.[2] The Mongols combined with their own native military genius the administrative capacity and methodical discipline of the Chinese whom they had so recently conquered, and they came upon the west as a trained and scientific fighting and governing machine, innocent of all the inhibitions which castrated the strength of the feudal and superstitious societies of the contemporary world of Islam and of Christendom. They established themselves from the Dniepr to the Yellow Sea, from the Dwina to the Persian Gulf, as a master nation, a ruling army; and it was only later, when their leaders became impregnated with the subjective ambitions of feudal tyrants that they failed and fell. Even their devastations which horrified the mediæval world—bloody-minded as it was—were methodical rather than emotional. They annihilated all resistance, but where they met with submission they treated their subjects with greater consideration than was usual in the contemporary world, and with a scrupulous respect for their pledged word which amazed the princes of the forswearing chivalry with whom they came into contact.

The Georgians, who suffered so hardly at the hands of the Mongols, had nothing but admiration for them:

> "There is truly reason to be astonished", wrote the Annalists, "to see them you would have thought that they were destitute of sense, but their wisdom and their ability was without bounds. They talked little and never said that which was not true. Incapable of partiality under any circumstances, above all in anything which concerned the decisions of justice, they observed the excellent laws established by Chingiz Khan." [3]

In 1235, the Mongols under Charmaghan having reduced the Muslims of Khlat and Tabriz, devastated the eastern

---

[1] Brosset, *H. de la G.*, I, 310; cf. also Djuwaini, II, 170.
[2] D. S. Mirski, *Russia: a Social History*.   [3] Brosset, *H. de la G.*, I, 486.

THE MONARCHY UNDER THE MONGOLS

provinces of the Caucasus as far as Derbend. In the following year on their approach to Ganja, Rusudani, who had only recently reoccupied Tiflis, fled to Kutais, while her governor burnt the city to prevent its falling into the hands of the invaders. All Kartli and Samtzkhé as far as Ardahani were devastated, and the principal nobles, ignoring their allegiance to the queen, fortified themselves in their own strongholds and began to negotiate their submission to the Mongol *no'ins*. The Amir-Spasalari Awag Mkhargrdzeli was the first to make his peace with the conquerors; his example was quickly followed by his cousin Shanshé, the Mandaturt Ukhutsesi, by Waram of Gagi the son of Tamara's counsellor Zakharia Mkhargrdzeli, by the head of the ancient house of Gamrekeli, by Sargis Tmogveli the philosopher and poet who owned wide lands in Javakheti, by Ioanné Jaqeli, and the principal nobles of Kartli, Hereti and Kakheti. The whole of the Georgian kingdom east of the Mountains of Likhi was divided among the four Mongol *no'ins*, who commanded the armies in Western Asia, and the Georgian nobles became their direct feudatories. In the west in Imereti, Queen Rusudani at Kutais still retained her independence; but in 1243, Awag Mkhargrdzeli, who showed no mean skill as a diplomat, arranged her submission to the Mongols. It was further agreed that her son, David, then about nineteen years old, should receive the royalty over Kartli with Tiflis, and in the same year, in company with Mkhargrdzeli, he was sent as a hostage to the camp of Batu, at the great centre of the Northern Mongols at Saray on the Volga. The fate of the Georgian royal family now became involved in the complicated rivalries of the sons and grandsons of Chingiz, which arose after the death of the Great Khan Ogotai in July, 1241.

About the time of the departure of David son of Rusudani to the camp of Batu, the Mongols had defeated the Seljuk Sultan of Konia, Ghaiath-al-din Kai Khusraw II,[1] who had married Rusudani's daughter Tamara. The Turkish Sultan had held for some years as a prisoner in most sordid circumstances King Giorgi's bastard, David, who had first resided at his court, and had later fallen into disfavour as a result of the intrigues and insinuations of Rusudani.[2] Bichui, the

[1] The Seljuks were defeated in a pitched battle between Erzerum and Erzinjan. The Mkhargrdzelis commanded the Georgian corps in the Mongol army, while the Seljuk army fought under the command of Dardan Sharvashidze of the princely house of Abkhazeti. As a result of the victory, Sivas and Kaisariah were taken by the Mongols; Erzinjan and Konia submitted to contributions. See Brosset, *H. de la G.*, I, 518–21, and notes.

[2] For the remarkable adventures of David Giorgishvili, see Brosset, *H. de la G.*, I, 523–7.

THE MEDIÆVAL KINGDOM

successor of Charmaghan in the West and a rival of Batu, took David Giorgishvili from the noisome pit in which he had been incarcerated for nearly seven years and had him brought to Mtzkheta, where he was crowned king as David V. He was then despatched to Karakorum, where he arrived soon after David, son of Rusudani, who had been sent there by Batu some time in 1244.[1] The two princes, who were present at the investiture of Kuyuk as Great Khan, in 1246, remained for five years at Karakorum, and while the grandsons of Chingiz played their great game for power over Asia, the petty destinies of the Bagratid cousins were bandied around between their Mongol protectors and their own Georgian suites. But the two pretenders, although opposite in character, were sympathetic one to the other, and they formed a friendship which endured in a quaint continuity throughout the following three decades of troubled time. David IV, the son of Rusudani, whom the Mongols called *Narin*, " the clever ", was some years younger than his cousin. Slight and supple, silken-haired, soft-voiced and eloquent, he had yet a name for courage in the field; yielding, equable and open-handed, he could never conceal the itch of a live ambition. The Mongols preferred his rival whom they called *Ulu*— " Big "—David. The son of Giorgi Lasha was strong and fat and simple. He delighted in the chase, gave his confidence to all men, was subject sometimes to fits of surly depression, which could make him cruel and obstinate. The long misery of his imprisonment had left him with a painful stutter.[2] Such were the two kings who in 1249 returned to Georgia, as David IV and David V to rule jointly in Tiflis,[3] under the protection of Hulagu, who had received from his brother, Mangu Khakan, dominion over all the Mongol Empire between the Oxus and the Mediterranean.

The fifteen years which had passed since the establishment of the Mongols in Georgia had seen the progressive decline of monarchical authority throughout the country. The death of Rusudani in 1247, the prolonged absence of the two Davids at Karakorum, and the irregular privileges exercised by the Mongol *no'ins* over individual Georgian magnates, were productive of a sequence of circumstances in which the Georgian

---

[1] Brosset, *H. de la G.*, I, p. 356, note 3, quoting Armenian sources.
[2] Cf. Brosset, *H. de la G.*, I, 545, 556, 564.
[3] " The two King Davids were so united, one with the other, that there are to be found, and I have myself seen, charters which are headed David and David, Bagratids, Kings by the Will of God; with their double signatures ' On behalf of me, David, that is authentic, that is authentic, on behalf of me, David '."

THE MONARCHY UNDER THE MONGOLS

territorial princes were in fact impelled to accept a status of partial independence conditioned only by the sporadic interference of their Mongol overlords and by their tradition—which died slowly—of loyalty to the House of Bagrationi. The first abortive revolt against the Mongols which followed the death of Rusudani had a royalist character, and it proclaimed the developing sense of nationhood with which the country had become impregnated before the reign of Giorgi Lasha. In spite of the circumstances, external and internal, which were conducive to disintegration, the Georgian nobles, particularly those of lower rank, made a conscious effort to maintain the unity of the country. Nor were the Mongols concerned to divide the country. They rather favoured the maintenance of a coherent authority, and during the period of interregnum they buttressed the power of the impecunious Kakhian *aznauri* Egarslan Bakurtzikheli, who had become at once an unofficial governor-general for the Mongols and the representative of the centralist aspirations of the lesser nobility.[1]

It was only after the return of the two Davids that the unity of the Kingdom was finally subverted by the example of the members of the House of Bagrationi themselves and by the actions of the greater territorial princes, who shared with their kings those subjective ambitions which in a feudal society characterized so frequently those whose fortunes were so nearly royal. The three princes of the House of Mkhargrdzeli whose wealth had been accumulated during the triumphs of Tamara's reign—Awagi the Amir-Spasalari, Shanshé the Mandaturt-Ukhutsesi, and Waram of Gagi the Msakhurt-Ukhutsesi—had been the first to make conditions with the Mongols, and over their vast estates which stretched from Ani to Somkheti they now conducted themselves as powerful feudatories of Hulagu and patronizing protectors of the Bagratid kings in Tiflis. In Siuniq and the Armenian districts on the borders of the Georgian kingdom the Orbelianis, at first protected by the Atabegs of Tabriz, had begun to restore their ancient power, and the two brothers Smbat and Elikum allied by marriage with the Mkhargrdzelis played no humble part in Mongol and Georgian politics. In fact, the pretensions of the Mkhargrdzelis and the Orbelianis, both families which were Armenian in religion and not Geor-

[1] Brosset, *H. de la G.*, I, 532: "At that time, Egarslani, of whom I have spoken, an estimable man and very versed in the science of war, had such consideration that he only lacked the name of king. All the Georgians obeyed him as a monarch; even the great Shanshé, *Mandaturt-Ukhutsesi*, full of honours as he was, as well as Waram Jaqeli and the other *mtavarni*." Cf. also p. 540.

gian by origin, represented a definite revival and assertion of Armenian influence throughout the eastern provinces of the Kingdom.

In the west, Imereti did not long remain fast in the united Kingdom. In 1258, David Narin, in fear of the ill-will of Hulagu, fled into the Mountains of Likhi. He was brought to Kutais by Liparit Thoreli and proclaimed King of the Imerians [1] by the assembled lords of Abkhazeti, Svaneti and Mingrelia. The Mongols had never penetrated the forests of the western country, and Hulagu, who was preparing his attack on Baghdad, appeared satisfied with the formal submission of the recalcitrant King.[2]

The elder David, son of Lasha, set in Tiflis, lazy, middle-aged and fumbling, bore the brunt of Mongol tyranny; and the heavy military levies imposed by the Ilkhan on all the subject nations, fell with full force upon Ulu David and the men of Kartli and Kakheti. In 1256, David had attended with a Georgian contingent the long and difficult campaign in the forests of Ghilan which Hulagu conducted against the Ismailis of Alamut. In 1258, David commanded the Georgian levies which took part in the siege and sack of Baghdad by the Mongols, and in the following year he was present at the battle of Ain-Jalut when the Mongols suffered their first serious defeat at the hands of the Mamluks of Egypt.

The continual conscription for the Mongol armies, the onerous requisitions, the unjust exactions of the tax-gatherers and the menacing census taken by the Mongols at last drove the King to follow the example of his cousin, David Narin. It was characteristic that the offensive conduct of a Persian tax-farmer in Tiflis, Hajji Aziz, should at last have harassed the poor slow-witted giant to action. David raised the standard of revolt during the autumn of 1260, but his principal nobles made their own composition with the Mongols, and the King fled into the mountains of Samtzkhé where Sargis Jaqeli raised 8,000 men in his support. In December, the Mongol advance-guard was defeated at Akhaldaba; but the forces of Sargisi were later routed through the resource of Kakha Thoreli, who was commanding the Georgian contingent in the Mongol punitive expedition. Ulu David fled to Kutais where he was kindly received by his cousin. Dissensions, however, arose between their supporters, for, while Sargisi wished that Ulu David should be proclaimed king in Imereti, the Dadiani supported the sole pretension of David

---

[1] Brosset, *H. de la G.*, I, 546; cf. II, i, 245, *Hist. d'Imeréthi*.   [2] *Ibid*.

Narin, the man in possession. Even the Svans became divided into two factions, and, while the Mongols carried fire and sword through the Meskhian uplands, an internecine war was threatened in the western provinces. But the personal goodwill of the two kings towards each other enabled a compromise to be effected. David Narin was recognized as sole king in Imereti, and Ulu David in all the lost territories east of the mountains of Likhi. And the royal treasury of the Bagratids, which, concealed in the caves of Khomli in Mingrelia, had remained under the hand of David Narin, was now divided equally between the two cousins.

In 1261, hostilities had broken out between the Northern and Western Mongols and the Khan of the Golden Horde, Béréké the son of Batu, was preparing to attack Hulagu. The friendship of the fugitive Ulu David became therefore a matter of interest to Hulagu and a reconciliation was effected, upon terms which restored all Kartli and Kakheti to David, while he was allowed to satisfy his outraged dignity by the decapitation of the tax-assessor Hajji-Aziz, whose oppressions had been the occasion of his revolt.

The war between the Golden Horde and the Il-Khans endured until 1266, and Ulu David took a part in the campaigns of Hulagu and his successor Abagha in Shirvan. But David was ailing, and, with his furtive stupid ways, the Kingdom was falling into deeper misery. He intrigued ineffectually with Béréké and even with the Mamluk Sultan Bibars.[1] He was fortunate in his advisers, but he could turn sullenly upon them and he executed two, Jikuri, his clever low-born secretary, and the Dchqondideli Basil. The brave and faithful Sargis Jaqeli he estranged, and the last of them, Sadun Mankaberdeli, outlived him. When Big David died of an affection of the bowels in the spring of 1269, he had fallen to nothing more than the administrator of Upper Kartli and parts of Kakheti; great vassals like the Jaqelis had become the direct feudatories of the Il-Khan and accorded scarcely a nominal recognition to the King in Tiflis. Shortly before his death, David, like some paltry baron, had received Ateni and its dependent territories, in fee from the new Il-Khan Abagha.

In Imereti, the situation of David Narin was little better, for Abagha had reversed the traditional policy of the earlier Mongol rulers which was to sustain established authority in tributary lands and he had abetted Kakhaberi, Eristavi of

---

[1] Brosset, *H. de la G.*, I, 563, note 2, quoting Makrisi, *Hist. des Mamel.*, trad. fr., livraison II, pp. 18 and 51.

Radsha, in attempts to overthrow the rule of the King in Kutais. In 1269, David Narin, surprised at the baths in Kutais by Mongol cavalry, narrowly escaped with his life by flying almost naked on horseback.[1]

During the long minority of Ulu David's son, Dmitri, from 1269 to 1278, Sadun Mankaberdeli, high in favour with Abagha, ruled not only Georgia east of the Likhi, but wide territories for which he owed direct allegiance to the Mongols. He was administrator of the vast estates of Awag Mkhargrdzeli, whose daughter he had married; Kars was his, Telavi and Belakani and the rich lands dependent on the town of Akhaltzikhé.[2] The Il-Khan Abagha, in fact, depended upon Sadun and upon the Jaqelis for the maintenance of Mongol authority in the Caucasian lands during the difficult period of the Egyptian war, between the years 1276 and 1281.[3]

Abagha died in April of 1282 and Sadun Mankaberdeli in the same year. The young King Dmitri was now of age and he began to rule, himself, with moderation and sagacity. He was the most lovable and sympathetic king of all the House of Bagrationi.

> "He was a man of great height, of grace, and of good mien, fair-haired and bearded, full of life, with dark brown eyes and a straight back, a capable soldier, a perfect horseman and a first-class archer; he was generous, merciful and modest, full of pity for the poor, for widows and unfortunates, more than any other descendant of the kings, more than any man who had ever existed. It was his practice to get up in the night and go about the town, well provided with money; he visited the poor, the unhappy and the orphans, and distributed alms with his own hands. And the poor, knowing his humour, went into the streets at night, to await his appearance."[4]

The regency of Sadun and the active reign of Dmitri II covering the two decades between 1269 and 1289, was a period of relative prosperity for Georgia. The Church, which had secured from the heathen Mongols, impartial always in matters of religion, the protection of their privileges and immunity even from taxation, had been assailed by Ulu David, desperate for money with which to satisfy the Mongol requisitions in the last days of his reign. Under Dmitri, it increased its power and recovered some part of the sources of its wealth.

---

[1] Brosset, *H. de la G.*, I, 585. [2] *Ibid.*, pp. 586, 589, 590.
[3] The Mongols suffered a severe defeat at the hands of the Mamluks near Sivas, on the 16th April 1277; a corps of 3,000 Georgians was cut to pieces. In 1280, the army of Mangu Timur, in which the young King Dmitri was serving with a Georgian contingent, was defeated on the frontiers of Syria. In the autumn of 1281, Mangu Timur, who was supported by a corps of 5,000 Georgians, was defeated near Hamah.
[4] Brosset, *H. de la G.*, I, 589.

THE MONARCHY UNDER THE MONGOLS

At the same time there was a revival of religious activity, unprecedented since the days of David Aghmashenebeli, and the monks of the famous hermitage of Garesja in Kakheti began to undertake the conversion of the Lazghis.

But the morals of the court were increasingly influenced through the continuous contact of the Georgian kings and nobles with the cosmopolitan entourage of the Mongol Il-Khans. Muslim and Mongol titles and names were appreciated by the Georgian aristocracy, while the drunkenness to which the Mongol *no'ins* were habitually addicted and the polygamous habits of the Muslims became fashionable at the court of Tiflis. The gay and gallant Dmitri enjoyed no less than three wives, of whom the first was a princess of the House of Palaiologos, the second a Tatar, and the third a daughter of Béka Jaqeli.

After twenty years the prosperity of the country and the power of the Georgian King were recovering when Dmitri met with misfortune through his confusion in the domestic enmities of the Mongol Il-Khans. In 1284, Tekudar, afterwards called Ahmad, the first Muslim Il-Khan and the son of Abagha, had been overthrown by his uncle, Arghun. Dmitri, who had supported Ahmad as a loyal vassal, had survived the fall of Ahmad's supporters and, in 1288, had marched with Arghun against the revolted inhabitants of Derbend. But in the spring of the following year, the disgrace and execution of Arghun's vizier, Bukai, the friend and protector of Dmitri, involved the fate of the Georgian King. He was betrayed by Kutlu-Shah Mankaberdeli, the son of Sadun, and brought to the camp of Arghun in Mughan where, after suffering the barbarous punishment of the bastinado, he was decapitated. Dmitri had surrendered to Arghun in order to save the country from devastation and his devotion was remembered by the people who called him Tav-dadébuli—" he who sacrificed his head ", or " the devoted ".

But his sacrifice was in vain. The Georgian kingdom was derelict without an effective head. Wakhtang II, a son of old David Narin, was made King in Tiflis, but he died two years later. The death of David Narin, himself, in the following year threw Imereti also into anarchy, for his three surviving sons, Michael, Constantine and Alexander were each contending for the throne. The power even of the new Il-Khan Ghazan was threatened by the irruption of the Northern Mongols through the Gap of Derbend.

In the western provinces all the nobles—the Sharvashidze,

the Gurieli, the Dadiani and the Eristavni of Radsha and Svaneti asserted their independence against the sons of David Narin; in the east, the Jaqelis refused to recognize David VI, a son of Dmitri set up in Tiflis by Ghazan, and the wild Ossetians came down the valleys of the Ksani and the Liakhvi to pillage the Kartlian countryside.

The short reign of the reformer Ghazan (1295–1304), who had his capital at Tabriz, was the last period of effective Mongol power in north-western Persia and the Caucasian provinces. It presaged also the adoption by the decadent Il-Khans of a fanatical Muslim policy. The heirs of the Imperial sons of the great Chingiz were becoming no more than petty Muslim despots. The new policy was first marked during the reign of Ghazan by the savage attacks on the Christian subjects of the Il-Khan carried out by the Emir Nawruz, a fanatic who was in the end suppressed by Ghazan. The revival of Muslim aggression scared the Georgian nobles. David VI, who as a boy had been present at Arghun's camp when his father was tortured and executed, took refuge in Hereti and later in Mtiuleti. He fortified himself in the remote fastnesses of the Khevi, and supported by only a few hundred mountain soldiers, he continued to refuse for ten years to put himself at the mercy of Ghazan or of the Il-Khan Uljaitu who reigned in Tabriz between 1304 and 1317. David VI, while negotiating year by year with the representatives of the Il-Khan, continued to pursue constant intrigues with the Kipchak Khans, and he maintained, until his death in 1310, a frightened furtive but not unsuccessful resistance to all the expeditions sent against him.

"He was a man with neither faith nor fear of God"

is the comment of the Annalists.[1] Meanwhile, from year to year, the Ossetians ravaged the Kartlian lands, the Jaqelis strengthened their power, and the Il-Khans tried other shadow kings in Tiflis. These were Wakhtang III, a brother of David VI, who fought in the Mongol armies in Syria and Ghilan, and died at last at Nakhchevan; Giorgi V, a younger son of Dmitri II by the daughter of Béka Jaqeli, who reigned nominally (1299–1301) and who was carefully protected by his maternal relatives; and Giorgi VI, called *Mtsiré*, or "the Little", the young son of David VI, who reigned also only in name (1310–18).

[1] Cf. Brosset, *H. de la G.*, I, 617.

CHAPTER X

SPLENDOURS AND MISERIES OF THE LATER GEORGIAN KINGDOM: GIORGI V TO ALEXANDER, 1318–1443

THE collapse of the Imperial strength of the Mongol Il-Khans in Persia during the first quarter of the fourteenth century was the occasion of the rise or recovery of regional independencies throughout the lands which lay between the Mediterranean and Mount Caucasus. In Western Asia Minor the Turkish tribe of the Osmanli was already building on the ruins of the Byzantine Empire and of the kingdoms of the Seljuks a power which towards the end of the fifteenth century was to grow into a reincarnation of the ancient Hellespontic Imperialism of the Byzantines. But for the two middle quarters of the fourteenth century, the lesser potentates of Western Asia and the Caucasus—Armenian in the Taurus, Georgian and Greek along the Pontus, and Muslim Kurd and Turkish throughout the mountain hinterland—were able to restore those regional cultures which had been so rudely overthrown by the invasions of the Mongols.

For Georgia the whole period from the decline of the Il-Khans to the disruption of the Bagratid kingdom in the third quarter of the fifteenth century is badly documented, in contrast to the rich mass of materials which exists for the history of the preceding century. Only the wars of Timur in the Caucasus are described in some detail, but the informed descriptions and the shrewd and sometimes witty characterizations of the thirteenth-century Annalists give place to the pompous rhetoric and vague generalizations and the want both of accuracy and of humanity which is typical of decadent phases of Oriental histriography.

In 1318 when the politics of Persia were falling into utter anarchy following the death of the Il-Khan Uljaitu, Giorgi V, who had been for two decades a shadow king in Tiflis, began to secure an effective authority. Giorgi was a younger son of Dmitri II, and he was strongly supported by his maternal relatives, the Jaqelis. The death of Giorgi VI, the Little, the heir of David VI, and the internecine feud which was being

THE MEDIÆVAL KINGDOM

pursued in Imereti between the sons of David Narin, left the grandson of the skilful old king-maker Béka Jaqeli without a rival. Giorgi was under thirty, strong-minded, unscrupulous and prudent, and his administrative abilities even more than his military successes earned for him the soubriquet of *Brtsqinwalé*—" the Brilliant ". His close friendship with his uncle Sargis Jaqeli gave him the mastery of all Kartli, Somkheti and Samtzkhé. He laid the foundations of a restoration of the royal authority over the great nobility by summoning an assembly at Tzivi in Kakheti, where he caused the massacre of all those vassals who might be suspected of recalcitrancy. He carried out extensive operations against the mountaineers of the Khevi, Mtiuleti and Osseti, and he proceeded to codify the customary laws and reform the whole administration of the mountain cantons.[1] In 1330 he marched into Imereti and after capturing the person of Bagrati, the young grandson of David Narin, he received the submissions of the Gurieli, the Sharvashidze and the Eristavi of the Svans. The death of Sargis Jaqeli in 1334 enabled the King to establish real control throughout the whole of Samtzkhé, and he made a triumphal progress through the mountains as far as Ispir— the first Bagratid who had shown himself as a master in Samtzkhé since the days of Giorgi Lasha.

Under the successors of Giorgi V, David VII (1346–1360) and Bagrat V (1360–1395) the condition of the Georgian kingdom remained relatively stable. The raids of the Turks along the borders of Samtzkhé were generally held in check and the political influence of the Bagratid kings in Shirvan and Aran, restored by Giorgi V, was on the whole maintained, while the close alliance with the Comnenian emperors of Trebizond, which had endured since the reign of Tamara and which had been soldered by matrimonial alliances between the Comnenians and both the Houses of Bagrationi and Jaqeli, was continued as a fixed policy which formed the basis of a close defensive understanding between the Georgians and the Greeks.[2]

In 1361, soon after the accession of Bagrat V, the Svans had risen—maybe in support of the pretensions of Bagrat Mikelishvili, the grandson of David Narin—but the Georgian

[1] Brosset, *H. de la G.*, I, 646-8 and note 3 of p. 644.
[2] David Narin and Béka Jaqeli had married Comnenian princesses; Dmitri II, a Palaiologa. Bagrat V married in 1367, Anna, daughter of the Emperor Manuel III Comnenos. The Emperor Constantine Dragosès was negotiating for a Georgian marriage the year before the fall of Constantinople. Apart from the Georgian Annals, there are many interesting details of the relations between the Georgian kings and the Trapezuntine emperors in *The Chronicle of Trebizond* of Michael Panaretes.

THE LATER GEORGIAN KINGDOM

King had defeated the insurgents and had pressed a successful punitive campaign into the Svanian valleys.[1] In 1366, the country was visited by the Black Death, which was then ravaging Constantinople and the cities of the eastern Mediterranean. The defection of the Atabegi Béka and other Georgian magnates which preceded, and the revolts in Imereti which followed the invasions of Timur in 1386, indicate that the strength of the monarchy was not so effective under Bagrat V as it had been under Giorgi Brtsqinwalé, but if Timur had not revived with sudden violence the power of the Mongols in Western Asia it is likely that the Georgian kingdom would have achieved a normal recovery from the period of political and economic weakness, which resulted immediately from the ravages of the Black Death.

The resurgence of Mongol power under Timur, the grave and simple, laborious and ferocious soldier who carried his arms in forty years from the borders of China to the pillage of Russia, India and Anatolia, was politically no more than an episode which served to demonstrate the lack of organic coherence in the social bodies of the mediæval east. In the winter of 1386–7 Timur came north to Tabriz to pursue his war against the Kipchak Khan Toktamish. At the same time a Mongol army was set in motion against the provinces of Georgia. Tiflis was taken by assault and Bagrat V with his Queen Anna Comnena were made prisoners. But his son Giorgi remained in the field and continued master of most of the country. The zeal of Timur for the Muslim faith caused him to direct against the Georgians a policy of peculiar bitterness, and in 1393, before his final campaign against Toktamish,[2] he undertook an invasion which was a fanatical outburst against the Christians rather than a political conquest of the country. Bagrati had apostasized and had been liberated by the Mongols, but on his return to Georgia as the vassal of Timur he had conspired with Giorgi to such effect that the latter had been able to ambush and defeat a considerable force

---

[1] Brosset, *H. de la G.*, I, 662–3.
[2] Timur defeated Toktamish on the Terek (14th April, 1395); he subsequently advanced through the Kipchak territory into Russia and reached the Yeletz (26th August 1395). Later in the year the Kipchak cities of Azac (Azov), Hajji-Tarkhan (Astrakhan) and Saray were sacked. In the spring of 1396, Timur returned by Derbend into Azerbaijan (Bartold, *Toktamish in E.I.*). During this march he carried out operations against the Lazghis (Brosset, *Add. et Ec.*, Add. XXII, p. 389, particularly note 3). Sir T. W. Arnold, in *Bihzad and his Paintings in the Zafar-Namah MS.*, reproduces two beautiful paintings representing the defeat of the Kipchaks by Timur. Bihzad illustrates a Mongol tactic in mountain warfare to combat the use of caves for defence, to which reference is frequently made in the Georgian Annals. The artist shows archers being lowered in baskets from the top of a precipice to dislodge the enemy who had taken refuge in caves in the side of the mountains below.

of Mongols. The avenging army of Timur again took and sacked Tiflis, and carried utter devastation through all Kartli and Kakheti. The monuments and servants of the Christian religion were assailed with unusual barbarity. The Cathedral of Mtzkheta and the Church of Sweti-Tzkhoveli were plundered and ruined; a horrible massacre took place at Kavtis-khevi where large numbers of refugees of all classes had sought the protection of the monks; the historic pile of the Ghtaeba at Ruisi was levelled to the ground and, while the Mongols camped there, the terrors of pillage and massacre were carried through all the valleys of Upper Kartli.[1]

In 1395, while Timur was fighting in Kipchak, Giorgi, who had succeeded his father as king, took the field against Miran-shah, Timur's son, who had been left as governor in Azerbaijan. Combining his forces with those of Sidi Ali of Shaki, Giorgi defeated the Mongols who were besieging in the fortress of Alinjak, near Nakhchevan, Tahir-Sultan the son of Ahmad Jalayar, a Mussulman dynast who had proved an inveterate opponent of Timur. Timur was pursuing his Indian conquests during the two following years, and it was not until the winter of 1397 that he could set about the repression of the Caucasian potentates. After sacking Shaki and devastating Shirvan, he marched in the spring of 1400 on Tiflis and demanded that Giorgi should surrender the person of Tahir-Sultan. On the receipt of an evasive answer, Timur went into camp at Mukhrani and from this base he proceeded to organize the systematic devastation of all Kartli. Tiflis received a garrison of Khurasani troops, and when Giorgi fled into Svaneti, Timur, who had caused maps to be made of the difficult routes into those formerly unconquered fastnesses,[2] sent an expedition against him and laid waste the highland valleys. Giorgi went into Abkhazeti and sent Tahir to the court of the Ottoman Sultan in Anatolia. Through the intermediary of a Muslim he now offered to pay the *kharaj* and Timur accepted his submission. Timur, after resting two months in his summer quarters at Min-göl (" thousand lakes ") west of Kars, sent an expedition against the new Atabegi Ioanné of Samtzkhé, who by supporting Giorgi had redeemed the treachery of his father Beká towards Bagrati V.

At the end of 1401, Timur came to Tabriz from Sivas, and

[1] According to Sharaf-al-din, Timur also conquered " certain Georgians called Karakalkanlik ", or " Black Coats ", by which name he designates the Pshavs, Tushes and Khevsurs living in the mountains to the north-east of the Aragvi.
[2] Brosset, *Add. et Ec.*, Add. XXII, p. 392, quoting Sharaf-al-din.

his delegates were sent to collect the *kharaj* from Giorgi, who sent his brother Constantine with the contributions. In the early summer of 1402, before his campaign against the Ottoman Sultan Bayazid, the conqueror was still hovering on the borders of Georgia, and from his summer quarters at Min-göl he sent a force to capture the ancient hold of Tortomi in the country between Kartlis-Qeli and the Chorokhi.

When in the spring of 1403 Timur came to Erzerum after his great victory over Bayazid at Ankarah, he had decided to punish Giorgi for not having come to offer his congratulations on the Mongol triumph. At Min-göl, Ioanné Jaqeli and the King's brother, Constantine, who was then on bad terms with Giorgi, arrived with rich gifts; and from there Shaikh Ibrahim of Shirvan was sent to estimate the revenues and charges of the Georgian kingdom. Giorgi sent new presents, but Timur refused them and summoned the King in person. Giorgi tried to stay Timur by negotiations in order to allow time for the gathering of the harvest, but Timur, determined to catch the people in the fields, suddenly rode through Somkheti, devastating all the country. The King withdrew without offering resistance, and the hitherto impregnable fortress of Bintvisi (Kurtin) on the Algeti, gallantly defended by Zaal Orbeliani, was taken after a siege of ten days.

The Mongols proceeded to lay waste all the Georgian lands as far as the borders of Abkhazeti " which is the end of this country ". According to the historian of Timur, seven hundred towns and villages were destroyed before Giorgi offered his submission. The Georgian King sent as gifts 1,000 *tangas* of gold struck in the name of Timur, 1,000 horses, a ruby weighing 18 *mithkals*, and quantities of plate and rich stuffs.

The satisfied conqueror accepted the allegiance of the King and retired to Baylakan, from whence he rode east to Samarkand to prepare an invasion of China which he did not live to achieve.

The widespread disruption and disaster caused by the campaigns of Timur were reflected not only in the parlous state of Georgia during the first quarter of the fifteenth century, but in the inability of the successors to the Empire of Timur to build upon the ruins of the countries which he had conquered even states with that capacity for a brief survival which the heirs of earlier Asiatic conquerors had erected. Timur himself was a man of foresight, intelligence and constructive will, but the ruthless violence of his warring had destroyed such natural force as was left to the declining feudal societies of Eastern Christianity and of Islam, and had deprived his grandsons of the economic bases upon which they might have endeavoured to perpetuate his Empire.

The recovery of the Georgian kingdom from the horrors of the Timurid wars was slow and weakly. The gallant Giorgi was killed in 1407 at a fight by Nakhiduri against the Tatar nomads of Somkheti. The rise of the Turkoman dynasty of Kara-Koyunlu at Tabriz threatened the south-eastern frontier; and in 1414 Shaikh-Ibrahim of Shirvan and Giorgi's brother

Constantine were defeated by the Turkomans on the Araks and the Georgian prince was killed. The Turkoman aggressions continued, and between 1414 and 1444 their raids into Samtzkhé became a chronic danger.

Giorgi's son, Alexander (1413–1443) was the last member of the House of Bagrationi to enjoy a long reign as King of all Georgia. He proved that he had some military capacity, and in the first year of his reign he defeated the Atabegi Ioanné at Kokhta. But he was a young man greatly under the influence of his grandmother, and he spent his time and resources in the repair of Sweti-Tzkhoveli and other shrines which had been destroyed during the Timurid wars.

THE LATER GEORGIAN KINGDOM

If his reign is remembered as a period during which " the Georgians reconquered their independence and tasted the sweets of peace ", it was due to the anarchy which then reigned among the aspirants to power in Persia, rather than to the abilities of the King, whose character found expression in a religiosity which could impose a special tax upon an exhausted peasantry to provide for the restoration and embellishment of churches and convents.[1]

[1] Brosset, *H. de la G.*, I, 681.

BOOK III

REVOLUTIONS OF THE GEORGIAN KINGDOM

" Bloodthirsty and deceitful men shall not live out half their days."

Psalm lv.

" Wilde Irish are as civil as the Russies in they're kinde,
   Hard choice which is the best of both, ech bloudie, rude and blinde."
From Certaine letters in Verse written by Master George Turbervile out of Moscovia, 1568.

CHAPTER XI

WARS OF THE DIVISION AND AFTERMATH
(1462–1574)

In the middle of the fourteenth century, during the reign of King Giorgi Brtsqinwalé, Georgia held promise of that development into a strong centralized national state to which the feudal monarchies of contemporary Christendom were, all of them, tending.

The vaunt that the House of Bagrationi held sway " from Nikopsia to Derbend " was no empty reclamation, and the difficulties which impeded the consolidation of a strong Caucasian State were no greater than those which had stood in the way of the rising Houses of France and Castile in the West. Set against Persian influence in the eastern Caucasus the predominance of the English in Anjou, Gascony and Guienne or of the Muslims in Andalusia; set against the disintegrant local lordships in Imereti and Samtzkhé the dukedoms of Brittany and Burgundy or the powerful independencies of Aragon and Navarre; you have the same picture. And the problem presented to the Bagratids by the mountaineers of Circassia, Osseti and Daghestan was no greater than to the Plantagenets and Tudors was the problem of " the Celtic fringe " in Ireland, Wales and Scotland. For the Georgian Kingdom of the Bagratids, the possibilities of power, of nascent nationhood, the chances of history, were much the same as those of Aragon and Castile, little less than those of Valois France and of Plantagenet England. And therefore we may inquire why at the end of the eighteenth century, when France and Spain and England had grown to be the proud world-empires of the West, Georgia was no more than a string of paltry principalities ready to the maw of the Russian Emperors. In history we speak much of economic forces, of geographical conditions, of universal political tendencies. Yet so much of it is man-made and chance-made. Character and luck are the fundaments of Empire. The characters of individual men and the luck of not infrequently a loaded dice it was that gave England power in the five continents, and left Germany emerging tardily from mediæval divisions to impotent resentful unity; that made the Castilians rise to Empire, while ancient cultured Italy remained a congeries of senile principalities; that thrust down Sweden with the feckless Vasas and reared up the Dutch, so careful, obstinate and grasping; that sank derelict the jabbering liberties of Poland, and founded the sombre rigidity of the Muscovian Monarchy.

In Georgia history went askew. In the fifteenth century the period of decentric spontaneities of kingships was passing; but between the invasions of Timur and the swing of the Osmanli power towards the Caucasus, the Georgians had an ample time, one hundred years, in which to consolidate a stable kingdom based on a common nationhood, which no less than sprawling, disjointed Poland might have resisted the onset of the Turks.

Through most of the fifteenth century, neither the Turks nor the Persians were strong enough, nor themselves sufficiently well-set and ordered, to turn to the conquest of the Caucasian provinces. Yet in that century the political battle of the Georgian people was lost, and the nation passed to a perpetual minimality.

Throughout Christendom the feudal order was writhing in extremity. In England they took their blood-bath in the Wars of the Roses; and each country that mastered the feudals sprang forward on to Empire—England and France and Spain and Russia. In Germany and Italy and Poland, some great magnates fended without decision and to an ultimate retardation of the political life of those three nations.

In Georgia the great territorial princes won, as they lost in Spain. The position in these two countries, each at the extremity of the great inland sea, is rather parallel. The Castilian-Aragonese Monarchy, masters within, mastered the powerful Mussulman element in Spain. In Georgia, the shattered and dissected monarchy forgot even its vain pretension to rule " from Nikopsia to Derbend "; " the Mussulman third " of the Caucasus which in the twelfth and even in the fourteenth century had been partly won and might have been consolidated, was lost for ever.

Events in Spain and Georgia, to the west winning, to the east losing, proceeded parallel. Constantine III, the man who lost in Georgia, sent greetings and gifts to Isabella, the woman who won in Spain. Success and failure were cumulative. Each country faced a common danger which

WARS OF THE DIVISION

was age-long—the revival of Imperial power on the narrow straits; as in the old Byzantine days, the new masters of a terrific military and bureaucratic machine faced west to the Mediterranean and the Spanish western nation, faced east to the Euxine and the Georgian eastern nation. In 1571, the western confederates defeated the Turks at Lepanto, and broke the menace of a revival of Constantinopolitan control over the Inner Sea. Twenty-five years before the Georgian confederate dynasts had been routed at Sokhoista in Basiani by the army of Sultan Sulaiman; the battle laid open the way to Turkish military predominance as far as the Caucasian mountains and it was the last effective attempt of the Georgians to fight as a nation.

The battle of Georgian monarchy was lost in the fifteenth century. The battle against the military imperialism of the Turkish Osmanlis and the Persian Safavids was lost in the sixteenth century; but the first struggle for national unity and monarchic mastery having been lost, the struggle against foreign aggression could have only one conclusion.

The battle of Georgian monarchy was a matter of individual character and luck. Giorgi VIII and his son Constantine III were ineffectual men, neither strong nor very weak, neither good nor bad. Their luck was indifferent. Giorgi VIII lost the battle of Chikhori in 1462 and all the western provinces. In the following year he was defeated and captured by the Atabegi of Samtzkhé. For the nation, the legitimate Bagratids did not matter. But the pretenders were no more effective and no more fortunate. The Imerian pretender Bagrati might have overthrown the Kartlian line and established unity if the chance of intervention by the Turkoman dynast Usun Hassan had not restored the fortunes of Giorgi's son Constantine III. Av Giorgi—Bad George —of Kakheti was bad enough to found a state, ruthless violent and ambitious, but his luck was out, for he fell into an ambush.

The Georgian rivals fought like chivalrous boys; they did not kill like kings. The House of Bagrationi spawned far and wide its handsome knightly claimants, but not one of them grew cunning, mean and watchful—to scotch the rest. Here were no cold, wary Tudors whetting the axe for their distant cousins, but a pack of Christian gentlemen wasting the land in chivalrous fracas. In this period the gallantry of one claimant towards another is as amazing as the futility of their plots and combinations. From which let us remember that it is not Black Princes that have built the nations,

A Georgian Noble of the Seventeenth Century (after Castelli).

WARS OF THE DIVISION

but black livers. And the man who can throw his conscience into the hotpot of the nation's life may show a greater love than he who casts away his glamorous life. Salute to the base men who disdain to be understood, remembering in themselves what their fellows do not think on, that nations, like tunnels, roads and bridges, are not built by gentle men.

The seventh decade of the fifteenth century was an uneasy moment for the Georgian monarchy. The Turks were in Constantinople: they were encroaching on the borders of Samtzkhé. A savage naval raid by the Turks had some years before swept the coast of Abkhazeti (1451); Trebizond, whose house was allied with the Bagratids, had fallen; the Turkoman rulers of Persia, with their capital in Tabriz on the very borders of Georgia, presented a chronic threat of aggression. The moment was the occasion of a formidable rising of the great feudatories of the southern and western lands. These perennial cracks appeared in the crust of the ancient monarchy; they passed, but now a dozen rents appeared. For over two centuries the genial kings in Tiflis had suffered the mutinous stock of David Narin to thrive in Imereti. More than once they had almost rooted it out, but Alexander, who had married a daughter of the rival house, had made her brother Dmitri, the last male of the breed, *eristavt-eristavi* of Imereti. In 1455 Dmitri died and his son Bagrati, who was confirmed in the succession to his father by Giorgi VIII, immediately began to plot. The rising began in 1462. Contarini, who saw Bagrati fifteen years later, says that

"the King was tall and about forty years of age; he had a brown complexion, and a Tartar expression of countenance, but was nevertheless a handsome man".[1]

Of tougher build was his ally, the Meskhian Atabeg Qwarqwaré Jaqeli, the second of his name.

"He was a man, haughty and ambitious, quarrelsome and turbulent, but full of energy and daring."[2]

So were all the Jaqelis, lords of the Chorokhi defiles and the lake country round the sources of the Mtkvari; a thousand years before the Bagratids had been breeding to this type as masters of these same highlands. Each strong, audacious, selfish—eight of the Jaqeli brood had served or betrayed successive Georgian kings; a dangerous nest of

[1] Contarini, *V. in P.*, p. 139.
[2] Wakhushti, *Histoire de Samtzkhé*, in Brosset, *H. de la G.*, 2ième partie, 1ère livraison, p. 207.

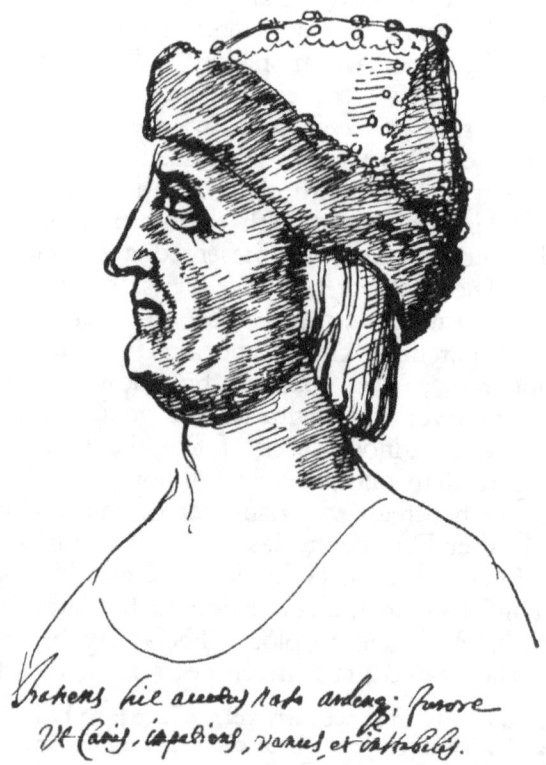

A Circassian Noble of the Seventeenth Century. "Settemani Prince of the Abaza people—an Illustrious Man in the Orient of our time" (Castelli).

WARS OF THE DIVISION

mountain-birds, like Douglases or early Bourbons, meet to be exterminated or to hatch a king. They held all the gates to Georgia from Kartlis-Qeli—" the throat of Kartli "—to Tashis-Kari—" the rock-gate ". They sold the gates time and again to make their house secure and lost themselves and more, as all men do who are clever only for themselves.

With Bagrati were joined Gelovani, Eristavi of the Svans; Kakhaberi Wardanidze, Eristavi of Guria: the Dadian Lipariti, lord of all the rich pastures and woodland-country of Mingrelia or Odishi; and the ancient half-royal house of Sharvashidze, who held the King's writ over Abkhazeti and Jiketi.[1]

The Imerian feudality met the Georgian king at Chikhori in the summer of 1462, and the royal army was routed. Bagrati—" the handsome man "—was crowned King of Imereti in Kutais, and he fulfilled his obligations to the confederate nobles by relieving them from all obligations except military aid and a formal suzerainty. Four " mtavarates " were recognized which left the Dadiani virtually independent in Mingrelia, Gelovani in Svaneti, Sharvashidze in Abkhazeti and Wardanidze in all the country between the mouth of the Rioni and the Chorokhi.

Qwarqwaré of Samtzkhé was less fortunate. Without declaring himself, he had awaited the result of the battle of Chikhori, holding ready his levies in the Persati mountains. King Giorgi, although defeated by Bagrati, was still strong enough to enter Samtzkhé, where many of his *eristavni* remained loyal, and to drive Qwarqwaré over the mountains into Imereti.

In the following year, however, a Turkoman advance on Tiflis so weakened the position of Giorgi that Qwarqwaré was able to make himself master of Samtzkhé in spite of the vigorous opposition of the King's *eristavni* in Tao and Klarjeti; and—as between little kings—Qwarqwaré ceded to the Gurieli Kakhaberi his rights over Achara and Chaneti (Lazistan).

Two years later in 1465, the King again entered Samtzkhé, but he was taken prisoner by the Atabegi in a sudden attack by Lake Panavari. This disaster emboldened Bagrati to in-

---

[1] Jiketi = Circassia; the Sharvashidzes, sometimes, were accorded the title of Cherkez-batoni, prince of the Cherkess, but their authority over the Cherkess tribes, established by the mediæval kings, was after 1445 merely nominal, and the rule of the Sharvashidzes was confined to Abkhazeti, where they maintained themselves until the time of the Crimean War. The Sharvashidzes claimed descent from the ancient Shirvanshahs.

vade and occupy Kartli, but if he hoped to establish his succession to the whole of the derelict Kingdom, he counted without his fellows. In Kakheti, the nobles, aware of Giorgi's disaster and fearful of Bagrati, elected as King, David, a grandson of Alexander, late King of all Georgia, and a nephew therefore of Giorgi. In Samtzkhé the Atabeg Qwarqwaré II died in January 1466 and his son Bahadur, a boy of twelve, uneasy at the success of Bagrati and frightened by the Turks' occupation of Trebizond and their encroachments in Klarjeti and Chaneti, set himself to restore Giorgi VIII.

Giorgi's son, who succeeded as Constantine III in 1469, found himself master only of part of Kartli and some districts of Kakheti. His attempt in 1474 to secure the defeat of Bagrati by concerting the rebellion of Wamek Dadiani failed. Bagrati seriously threatened Constantine's position in Kartli, and four years later it was only the fortuitous invasion of the Turkoman Uzun-Hassan, to whom Constantine attached himself, that prevented the probable usurpation of the Georgian throne by the Imerian line.

The death of Bagrati at this juncture offered a turn of luck to Constantine. Acting with Wamek Dadiani he occupied Imereti (1479) and two years later invaded Samtzkhé, where the young Atabeg Manuchar had succeeded his brother Bahadur. All the country east of the Arsiani mountains was reincorporated in the Kingdom. But in 1483 the King was defeated by the Meskhians, and in the following year Bagrati's son, Alexander, was proclaimed at Kutais. During the year 1485 Constantine again subdued Imereti, but in 1489 Alexander with the support of the Svans retook Kutais. Meantime the country was seriously threatened by the attacks of the Turkomans of Tabriz. In 1486 Yakub Khan, the son and successor of Uzun-Hassan, ravaged Samtzkhé, and four years later he laid siege to Tiflis. But the Turkomans were defeated before Tiflis through the valour of the powerful clan of Baratiani, and were finally expelled from the country.

Twenty-seven years had passed since the rebellion of Bagrati and all Georgia was devastated and exhausted. The contending factions could fight no further, and a council of bishops and nobles under the presidency of the Catholicos urged Constantine to make peace. At the cost of perpetuating the Division, it was made. In 1493 Constantine III made treaties by which he recognized Bagrati's son, Alexander, as King of Imereti; another Alexander, grandson of that David elected in 1465, as King of Kakheti;

and Qwarqwaré III, a cousin of Manuchar, as Atabegi of Samtzkhé.

David VIII, who succeeded his father Constantine in 1505, had abandoned all idea of the restoration of the former kingdom. He was a peaceable, easy man, not without a certain naïve assurance. "He who likes trouble, meets trouble", he told his more militant brothers when they urged him to expel the Imerians from Gori. His intervention in Kakheti was forced upon him by the truculent reclamations of the usurping parricide, Av Giorgi; and he soon let that ancient province of the Georgian crown slip back into the hands of Giorgi's son, Levani. David, however, was not without capacity, for although the Persians captured Tiflis in 1522, he recaptured it in the following year. After this exertion he retired into a monastery (1525) and was succeeded by his brother, Giorgi IX. Giorgi, after a reign of ten years, followed his brother's example.[1]

Luarsabi, David's son, was of a different calibre,

"brave and strong and daring to attack, faithful and God-fearing."[2]

But his luck was out. While Georgia had been in the extremities of civil war, Persia had emerged from similar conditions under the new dynasty of the Safavids, Iranian by birth, with all the popularity of a Persian national revival, with the dignity of religious inspiration, and with the prestige of an Empire reborn. In spite of the disastrous defeat of Shah Ismail Safi by the Ottomans at Chaldiran in 1514, the new Safavid house, under his son Shah Tahmasp, was able to dispute with Sulaiman, the most magnificent of the Ottoman Sultans, the mastery of the Armenian highlands and of the long Iraqi river valleys; and in Georgia they were raising their old pretensions to a suzerainty which since the eleventh century had been enjoyed only for some hundred years by the Mongol Il-Khans. In 1536 a Persian army, secretly concentrated at Ganja, captured Tiflis by surprise attack, while King Luarsabi was burying an infant child at Mtzkheta. Luarsabi recovered Tiflis in 1538. But his luck was never lasting. In 1545 he shared in the defeat of the Imerian King,

---

[1] Giorgi IX is remarkable only for his participation with the Kings Levani of Kakheti and Bagrat III of Imereti and the Atabeg Qwarqwaré III in a "crusade" against Jerusalem, at the invitation of Sultan Sulaiman the Magnificent. The account of Wakhushti is very circumstantial, and Brosset is inclined to believe that the Georgian kings participated in the Turkish campaign against Janberdi-Ghazali, the rebel *vali* of Syria, in 1524. See Brosset, *H. de la G.*, II, i, 25, and note 2.

[2] Brosset, *H. de la G.*, II, i, 27.

Bagrat III, by the Turks at Sokhoista, and three years later he again lost Tiflis to the Persians. During the ten following years he was maintaining a harassed fight against the Turks and Persians in Samtzkhé and Somkheti, for the Georgian kings could still fight as kings, and not yet as the clients of rival aggressors, and "*this prince would never submit either to the Sultan or the Qaen*". Luarsabi was killed in 1558 at the fight by Garisi, after his son, Simon, had already routed the Persian horse.

Most interesting during the half-century following the Division was the history of Kakheti. Giorgi I, the second King (1471–92), was in his small field something of a kingdom-maker. Wary of the conditions in the greater Kingdom which had conduced to his own elevation, he would have no grand nobility. Constantine of Kartli was working on the Kakhian nobles, as he had done also in Samtzkhé, to secure the reunion of the Kingdom. Giorgi, after his village coronation at Bodbé, cunning in his own back-land, fell upon his *eristavni* and set up in their place *mo'uravni* or prefects, removable at will.[1] He copied from the old Kingdom, the military-territorial organization into four banners, but the commands went to bishops, so that they should not become hereditary. Giorgi, and later his son and successor, Alexander I, kept clear as they could of the interminable hostilities in the old Kingdom, and the latter maintained cautious diplomatic relations with Shah Ismail and with Tsar Ivan III.

The occupation of Kakheti by David VIII during the minority of Levan I was an unimportant interlude, and during Levani's reign of over half a century (1520–74) Kakheti flourished and was quiet. King Levani, intelligent, debauched and cynical, played for his own hand, and steered a careful course for Persian favour. He served with his troops for Shah Tahmasp against the rebellious Mussulman emirs in Shirvan, yet astutely could send a detachment to help the Kartlian King, Luarsabi. He kept his son, Yésé, near the person of the Shah and married a daughter to Simon of Kartli. He maintained relations with the Russians, but held and loved the Shamkhal's daughter as his mistress, and by diplomacy and a vigorous border policy, kept the land clean of Lazghi raids. That bad old man, so sprightly, so careful

---

[1] The "mouravates" were Kisiqi, Tsuketi, Eliseni, Didoeti, Tianeti, Dshauri, Shilda, Quareli, Martqopi, Gremi, Pankisi " and other places ". Cf. *Hist de Kakheth*, H. de la G., II, i, 148.

and so lecherous, who had begun his reign disguised as a page serving wine at the table of those who hunted him, died—intriguing for his bastards—after having given to his kingdom fifty years of peace. And that was no mean achievement in the Caucasus in the sixteenth century.

CHAPTER XII

THE REVIVAL OF ISLAMIC IMPERIALISM
(1512–76)

THE phenomenon of the expansion of Turkish power during the fifteenth and sixteenth centuries is not difficult to explain. The Sultans inherited the Turkish-Mongol tradition of military efficiency and nomadic aggression and they inherited the administrative machine and some part of the experience in state-craft of the Byzantine emperors. An empire may have character; it has never, like a nation, soul. And that age-old soulless tradition of Imperial Rome in union with the gruesome power-hunger of the steppe-land nomads, tinctured with the sombreness of Islam—the sated soldier's creed, irrupted up a Mongol tyranny, which, squat upon the Bosporus, loomed to the terror of the three old continents for close upon four centuries.

Into the fifteenth-century world where emperor-power was trampled amongst a plethora of kings, the Turk pushed suddenly and heavily the new model of an old machine—the great Imperial army. And half-way up through Europe it scattered princes' levies, as in another age the legions of other emperors had driven the old tribes before them like chaff before the wind.

The Turks had the best cannon and all the new-fangled engines that were coming in with powder; the best ships; great corps of trained professional soldiers drawn by conscription from the raw young peoples of the Empire; and big pay went to renegades from Spain, Italy and Germany, who gave them the newest science in fortification, navigation, shipbuilding and engineering. The loose-knit feudalities of eastern Europe went down before the shock of armies that proved able to exterminate the proud chivalry of France and Burgundy, crusading down the Danube. The Serbian kings, the rulers in Bulgaria and Bosnia, the Wallachian princes and the manly kings of Hungary were no more able to withstand them than were the squabbling potentates in Georgia.

When Byzantium was finished the Georgian state indeed was parlous. The considerable maritime power of the Latins in the Euxine was severed at the roots. The Greek communities along the Pontic coast were rapidly submerged; and it was these communities, who, although harassed, had remained vigorous and had linked the East Christian Caucasus with the culture and the commerce of the Balkans and the Mediterranean. Georgia certainly until the Timurid wars—had a state comparable with Hungary. In 1453 the monarchy, although weak, was still united, and for another three-quarters of a century the Turks did not seriously threaten the Georgian borders. Turkey and Persia were never for long strong at the same time; their politics were perpetually opposed; and even when Georgia lay in weak and divided little royalties the Sultan and the Shah each sought, often with anxiety, the alliance of the different Bagratid kings. And so, if Georgian unity had been maintained during the fifteenth century, it is possible that the kings in Tiflis, by playing a policy between the two Muslim empires, might have upheld continuingly the unity and the independence of the Kingdom. For Georgia was only a secondary field of interest to the Sultans, gaming always in the rich and varied pool of western politics. The Turkish troops hated the damp woods and the hot low pasture lands of Mingrelia, the indeterminate skirmishes in the passes of Trialeti, the continual warrings which the Georgians—so weak —could still maintain endlessly. The Persians, as against the Turks, were generally the losing fighters and engaged long and desperately, each generation, to hold Erivan, Tabriz and Baghdad.

But the Georgians after the wars of the Division did not maintain the semblance of a national polity. The standing army of the Bagratids, swelled by the feudal levies, had been in the reign of Giorgi Brtsqinwalé an army good enough in the conditions of the fourteenth century. At the end of the fifteenth century, this fourteenth-century army was no more, and against the trained Janissary regiments, with their cannon, their engines and their supply trains, the kings of Imereti could only oppose their peasant companies reinforced by the untrustworthy bands of the Gurieli and the Dadiani. The strategy of the earlier kings—quick to meet sudden attack with mobile detachments along the marches, backed by a main force which was fed by a comprehensive system for the mobilization of feudal reserves—gave place to the furtive, flying fight of puny lords, who garrisoned their strongholds with men who sold them to the invaders; who withdrew themselves into the mountains, leaving open to be raked and harried the lands of their poor people. And so the Turks gave

"Benefactor, Simon, the Absolute Prince of the Province of Guria" (Castelli).

tongue, their nomad blood a-tingling, and when high politics even were not in question they would often take a ride in spring through Imereti.

The Imerian Bagratids and the Atabegni of Samtzkhé had riven the kingdom, and they were the first to suffer for the riving. Already in 1466, when Trebizond had fallen, the bruit of Turks had scared the boy, Bahadur. By the first decade of the next century, the Turks were encroaching in Basiani and Chaneti, without taking any account of the rights of the Atabegni. These operations on the eastern frontier were connected with the impending trial of strength between Sultan Selim Yavuz and the new Safavi Shah Ismail. The Atabegi Mzedchabuki the Great was, unlike his line, a quiet and peaceful man who won his soubriquet as a just ruler, for in his days they said "*justice was such that not a cock was stolen throughout his domains*".[1] He had an unwholesome

[1] Brosset, *Hist. de Samtzkhé, H. de la G.*, II, i, 214.

REVIVAL OF ISLAMIC IMPERIALISM

fear of the Turks, and in 1512 allowed, without a blow, the occupation of the whole of Samtzkhé by the Seraskier of Erzerum.[1]

Bagrat III (1510-48) had in Imereti recently succeeded his father Alexander I, who had repressed the more truculent among the *mtavarni* and had left the country in a state of peace and order. The Turks, after the occupation of Samtzkhé, crossed the Persati mountains under the conduct of the Atabegi Mzedchabuki and, as Bagrati retired before them, they burnt Kutais, Gelati and other places.

Sultan Sulaiman and Sh'ah Tahmasp—lords of an age when emperors took their wars like tourneys—went at it again in 1535; and until 1548, when they took their third and greatest bout, they or their governors on the marches were watching for movement, shifting grip and using the little marchland kings to try the ground. So it fell out that in 1535, Bagrati of Imereti, in favour with Shah Tahmasp and seeking vengeance on the son of Mzedchabuki the Great for having led the Turks to Kutais, made an invasion into Samtzkhé. The Atabegi Qwarqwaré IV was beaten and taken at Murjakheti Fight and died shortly afterwards in Kutais. Bagrati occupied all the fortresses of Samtzkhé and gave over to the Gurieli the lordship of Achara and Chaneti. Meantime Otar Shalikashvili, the friend and councillor of the dead Atabegi, had fled to Stambul with Qwarqwaré's son, Kai Khusraw. He secured the promise of support from the Sultan, but a Turkish force which invaded Samtzkhé in 1541 was routed by Bagrati and the Gurieli. The Sultan was touched, and in 1545 a levy was made of all the vilayets east from Sivas, and the Seraskier of Erzerum with the Pasha of Diarbekr—Otar Shalikashvili and Kai Khusraw in their train—came up into Samtzkhé by the passes through Basiani. A Georgian army met them— Bagrati with the Imerian levies and Luarsabi with a Kartlian force, the Meskhians also—the first national hosting since a hundred years. The Meskhian soldiers mutinied on a point of feudal honour—for they had been refused their historic right to constitute the vanguard. And so a hundred years after the feudal ways were withered everywhere, a hundred years after the Kingdom had really been already lost, the last army of the Georgians broke and fled upon a point of feudal honour. Sokhoista was not a decisive battle, for the real issues were never in doubt; these had been sealed by the partition treaties in 1493. But it marked an end,

[1] Brosset, *Hist. de Samtzkhé, H. de la G.*, II, i, 214; cf. von Hammer, IV, 190-206.

like Culloden, of the futility of men who keep their minds romantic.

"The conquered kings returned each to their own"; Kai Khusraw II was Atabegi in his father's place and the Turks at the instigation of Shalikashvili installed themselves in all the fortresses, for, they were told by this romantic partisan of feudal independence that "*if you make yourselves masters of the citadels, the country will henceforth obey you*".[1]

Between 1548 and 1554, Sulaiman and Tahmasp fought their last big round. These two spoilt lions were past their early vigour and the war was ding-dong, long and indecisive, staleing rather. But the pashas could win loot, an extra horse-tail, or risk the bow-string; and the soldiers, uprooted peasants from far lands, thinned by the winds, scoriated by the storms, baked by the long suns, had got the taste for uprooting other peasants. And so they stormed Erivan; slaked their parching in the wicked lanes of Tabriz; wrecked the shrines of Echmiadzin.

Tahmasp was the weaker, but Sulaiman had better game to play elsewhere; away in the West the Emperor Charles, that other ageing lion—for each Imperial paladin was getting rather worn—the Emperor Charles was there to engage him on a vaster field.

Meanwhile, the reviving Empire game went on—here in the East more clumsily, not with the neat efficiency, the legal forms, the moral overwash, which they were perfecting in the West. And here they had no elbow-room, in these old lands, as had the Russians in the Ukraine and Siberia, the English, the Spanish and the French in the Americas; where men, finding little to destroy, might start to build, working and thinking, get away. And in the East, the leaders of the passive-thinking soldier-stuff were on the top for good—Turks, Tatars, Turkomans, thick men from the steppe, like rocks hardened by millennia of the inclement elements; small-eyed, broad-faced men with short necks, big eaters, of a crude and simple humour, incurious, slow in the uptake. And the sprightly men, of that old, inquisitive, restless, creative, sparkling, high-pitched way of mind—Greeks, Georgians, the real Persians, Arabs—were gotten under, smashed and trampled on.

Here in the East, the social body, bruised to death, had ceased to heal itself. It had no organic being. Men were being slaughtered in the East as in the West, but they were being slaughtered because they were men, and for their goods;

[1] Brosset, *Hist. de Samtzkhé*, H. de la G., II, i, 216.

not because they were heretics and for their ideas. Men died for petty things, personal treasons, harîm whims; not as they were now dying in the West, because they saw the light and laughed, because the old men hated them.

The clumsy lumbering mechanisms of the two Mussulman Empires went slowly grinding on, chipping off and granulating one by one, the little easy-going, anarchical feudalities along the Caucasian borderlands. The business was rough, chaotic, on no settled plan. Cannon were in it, weight of numbers; the continuing force of autocratic polity, which could play so easily as each generation changed, with the subjective emotions, the wee personal schemes of all the pack of feudal princes, their littering sons and their " in-laws ".

Samtzkhé-Saatabago, "the Atabegi's country"—proud, upland breeding-ground of Georgia's poets and kings, core of the power of the mediæval monarchy—was first, but slowly morcelated. In 1550 the Turks had Tao, the earliest domain of the Bagratids; and two years later the Janissaries were put in Ardanuchi [1]—the oldest Georgian capital set above imponderable ravines upon a table-rock, its stone walls and towers so curiously carved, looking out towards the bleak Arsiani mountains which the Turks now came to call Yalanuz-cham—" The Lone Pine Mountains ". At the same time the Turks were encroaching into Guria, and while King Bagrati was intriguing to weaken the Gurieli, the Turks set themselves down in Batum and Gonia.[2]

While the Turks came through from the west, the Persians were pressing into the districts of the eastern Caucasus. The minor Mussulman rulers in Shirvan and Aran, who had accepted, as occasion led, sometimes a Persian and sometimes a Georgian suzerainty, were brought under the direct control of the Shah, who either assured them as his own governors or replaced them by his own men. Thus the new Iranian Safavids were reclaiming the antique inheritance of the old Iranian Sasanids. Hassan Beg of Shaki and his son Dervish Muhammad fought the Shah for some years and, as has been mentioned, Levani of Kakheti served against them (1548).[3]

Persian reclamations in the eastern Caucasus, given impulse by the Division of the Kingdom, had for long been extended to the two easterly kingdoms of Kartli and Kakheti. The Kings Luarsabi and Levani had pursued directly contrary

---

[1] Wakhushti, *Hist. de Samtzkhé*, in Brosset, *H. de la G.*, II, i, 217.
[2] Wakhushti, *Hist. de l'Imereth*, in Brosset, *H. de la G.*, II, i, 259-60.
[3] Cf. p. 140.

"Datua Biscaia, a Mingrelian Noble, born in the Mountains of the Caucasus —a Man of Extraordinary Courage" (Castelli).

policies, for while the Kartlians fought continuously, the wily Kakhian rulers fended dexterously with fealties, presents and contingents. His alliance with the Shamkhal family, one of quite personal ties, had given old Levani always Muslim sympathies, and his court at Gremi reflected the new influence.

> "As a result of mixing with the Persians, the Kakhians", comments Wakhushti, "had taken them for a model in eating and drinking and in giving themselves to a soft life and an improper affectation in dressing after the Persian manner. In this way they gradually abandoned their Georgian customs and introduced those of the Persians."[1]

Nevertheless, the careful, unromantic policy of the Kakhian Bagratids—particularly of Levan II (1520–1574) and of his son Alexander II (1574–1605)—fatal as it was to any conception of a united Georgian resistance, gave to Kakheti nearly a hundred years of relative peace, free of the devastations which were afflicting Kartli and Samtzkhé, and broken only by an occasional feudal fracas. Wakhushti draws a pleasing picture of the peace of Kakheti towards the end of Alexander's reign and before the disastrous conflict between Taymurazi and Shah Abbas I.

> "Kakheti", he says, "was so thickly peopled, that a wild animal was scarcely to be found, so that Alexander, who had a passion for the chase, would say 'Would to God that Kakheti were devastated in my time. I should then have game in plenty'. That was what happened", comments Wakhushti, "under his grandson Taymurazi, who had never, poor devil, the time to hunt."

Wakhushti adds of the fortunate king that

> "having learnt from his falconers that they had seen strange birds in the plain of Aloni, he went off in haste and found that they were peacocks. He wanted to take them alive, but not a single falcon would take any notice of them; there was only a red hawk which took as many as there were; they were brought to Gremi, where they called incessantly, which made Kakheti seem like the fabulous land of the Qapuzuna where the sheep go to."[2]

---

[1] *Hist. de Kakheth*, in Brosset, *H. de la G.*, II, i, 153.

[2] See Wakhushti's *Hist. de Kakheth*, in Brosset, *H. de la G.*, II, i, 154–5. The Qapuzuna, says Brosset, are monkeys, and the allusion is to a passage in the Book of Kalila and Dimna. Those who believe in the superstition that peacocks bring bad luck will notice that the arrival of these birds at Gremi was followed by the murder of Alexander by his son Constantine (1605) and the devastation of the country by Shah Abbas from 1616. For the ancient Persian Book of Kalila and Dimna, see E. G. Browne, *Literary History of Persia*, I, 76 etc.; II, 18, etc.

CHAPTER XIII

CLASH OF EMPIRES: THE EPIC OF KING SIMON
(1576-1600)

IN 1576 Shah Tahmasp died.[1] Politics in Kazvin spluttered into instant excitation, for the number of his sons, some middle-aged, some youths, all noodles, weak and crapulous, offered an infinite variety of chance to the great company of eunuchs, to king-making captains of the guard, and to crimping nobles with women in the royal harîms. Shahs were made and unmade, murdered, blinded, thrown away. Persia once more dropped into pungent anarchy. And all the thieves and lords and bullies, adventuring brood of Asia, Turkomans and Afghans, Lazghis, Georgians, Kurds, gathered from the four quarters of the land, and bared their knives; with gleaming teeth and sombre eyes, stepped down into the pit.

In Turkey, old Sulaiman had died ten years before, and a Grand Vizier ruled for the half-Jewish Sultan, Murad III. The Vizier, Muhammad Sökölli, a Herzgovinian Janissary, a long, cold, studious man, played a deep game; living in splendid quietude upon the Bosporus, he steered his bulky galleon through changing seas. Feeding his obstreperous rivals with the lure of distant glory, he thought all kinds of mighty schemes—a canal across the Suez isthmus to rule in the Indian Ocean and fight the Portuguese; a canal from the Don to the Volga and power in the Turkish east. Alone of all the rulers on the Bosporus, who wasted their great soldiering force bombarding up the Danube, the thoughtful Slav had dreamed perhaps of a real Turkish state, mastering the Muslim world. Meanwhile, he cared for his own family on the "polye" away back from Ragusa, and endowed some caravanserais; soon, of course, he petered out and was forgotten in the barrack tumults and the palace brawls of Stambul.[2]

[1] Shah Tahmasp died on the 11th May according to Don Juan. Other authorities state that he was murdered in his bath (cf. von Hammer, French ed., VII, 71).
[2] Sökölli, "le plus grand des viziers ottomans", occupied the Grand Vizierate for fifteen years, from 1564, two years before the death of Sulaiman, throughout the reign of Selim II and through the first years of Murad III, to 1579.

REVOLUTIONS OF THE GEORGIAN KINGDOM

In 1577, although his greater Asiatic plans had already failed, Sökölli threw the Turkish armies against the disordered western frontiers of Persia; and at the same time neatly rid the capital, for a year or two at least, of its most dangerous pashas, staving off his own fall. By the end of the year Kars, Erivan, Nakhchevan and Tabriz had fallen to the Turks.

In the churning pool of Persian politics, two Georgian marriages, intruding strangely, made their own cross-currents of jealousies, resentments and ambitions. Thirty years before, in 1548, Shah Tahmasp had added to his wives a Meskhian girl, the daughter of Otar Shalikashvili,[1] who, as the councillor of Qwarqwaré IV and protector of Kai Khusraw II, had always played a high and risky game. The special favourite of the passé paladin in his later years, Shalikashvili's daughter had borne a son to Tahmasp.[2] And in the sultry atmosphere of Kazvin, surrounded by her brigandly countrymen, the brisk audacious dowager, herself the daughter of a master of intrigue, took a vigorous and artful hand in all the intrigues for the succession.[3]

The other current crossing had its origins in the now old amours of King Levan of Kakheti, who himself had wheezed out as recently as 1574. By his first marriage with Tinatin Gurieli, Levani had had two sons, Alexander and Yésé. By his later and unhallowed union with the Shamkhal's daughter he had had four sons and a daughter, Nestan-Darejani, who had been given in marriage to the young King Simon of Kartli (1559). Levani, although so old and calculating, favoured devotedly his children by the second marriage, and he had set his heart on securing their succession. But when the old man died Alexander fought a battle with his half-brothers. They were defeated and killed by Alexander's troops, but the feud continued. Simon of Kartli had been friendly with his four brothers-in-law—the Shamkhal's grandsons. A warlike, rash and vital man, he kept on harrying the Persians, who since his father Luarsabi's time had had a garrison in the citadel of Tiflis but had left the town itself and the surrounding country to the Kartlian king. In 1569, Simon had been made an outlaw by the Persians and Shah Tahmasp had set in his place David, a worthless wastrel son of Luarsabi, who had become a Muslim and, as Da'ud Khan,

---
[1] Wakhushti, *Hist. de Samtzkhé*, in Brosset, *H. de la G.*, II, i, 217.
[2] Wakhushti, *Hist. de Kartli*, in Brosset, *H. de la G.*, II, i, 37.
[3] See Note H in Appendix to Chap. XIII, p. 381.

had curried favour in Kazvin. At the end of 1569, Simon was taken and sent as a prisoner to the fortress of Qahqahah (Alamut) in Mazanderan and later to Shiraz (1573). And in the following year it had been Daʻud Khan who had helped Alexander to overcome the Shamkhal's grandsons in Kakheti. Together Daʻud and Alexander had their way throughout all Kartli and Kakheti. Daʻud married a near relative of Alexander, and Alexander himself had already a wife, Tinatini, daughter of Bardzim Amilakhori, the most powerful and ambitious of the Kartlian vassals, who with his close ally Elisbari, Eristavi of the Ksani, lorded over great part of the northern districts. Simon's queen, Nestan-Darejani, of the hated Shamkhal line, was pillaged by those two almost to penury, and word went through the country " Down with King Simon and all that is his ".[1]

Alexander's name continued high with Shah Tahmasp, and his full brother Yésé, who had become a Muslim under the name of Isa Khan, had for years been a favourite at the Persian court.[2] Only on the other side the Meskhian interest, strong through the Shalikashvilis, rather hung towards Simon, since the dowager of Kai-Khusraw II, Dédis-Imédi, was the daughter of Wakhtangi, Prince of Mukhrani, who had been very close to Simon; and Dédis-Imédi ruled in Samtzkhé with her favourite, Waraza Shalikashvili, brother to Shah Tahmasp's wife.

In 1574 old Shah Tahmasp had come to Ganja suspecting Alexander of playing with the Turks; he seemed about to ravage Kakheti, when Otar Choloqashvili, who stood always at the elbow of King Alexander, threw down a desperate very dirty trump. He sent express to Dédis-Imédi, informing her that Waraza Shalikashvili was plotting against her; meant to kill her and her three young sons, and make himself Atabegi.[3] Dédis-Imédi was "*a woman haughty, violent and as hot as she was stupid*".[4] She took no thought of any trap. Waraza was seized and cut down out of hand—" *the brother of the wife of Shah Tahmasp* ".[5] And Tahmasp, at Ganja with an army, forgot his plans on Kakheti and raked all the Meskhian country with fire and sword. Then, on a passing understanding with the Turks, he suddenly withdrew. Dédis-Imédi and her sons had taken refuge in the forests of

---

[1] Wakhushti, *Hist. de Kartli*, in Brosset, *H. de la G.*, II, i, 34.
[2] See Appendix to Chap. XIII.
[3] For the naïve account of this ruse see Wakhushti, *Hist. de Kakheth*, in Brosset, *H. de la G.*, II, i, 134-5.
[4] Wakhushti, *Hist. de Samtzkhé*, in Brosset, *H. de la G.*, II, i, 219.   [5] *Ibid.*

A Turkish Archer of the Seventeenth Century (after Castelli).

Achara and, since with the new turn Waraza's son, Kokola, had got in before them in the Turkish favour, the young Atabegi Qwarqwaré V and his brother Manuchar appealed despairingly to Tahmasp. In 1576 events moved to a crisis of confusion. In Samtzkhé Kokola Shalikashvili and the young Jaqelis were loosing a desperate civil carnage. Every little baron in the upland country took a hand for one side or the other, and the peasants paid in a most dreadful spoliation. In that war the last strength of the marchland principality—for long so turbulent and free—was altogether wasted.

In Kazvin when Tahmasp died, the Shalikashvili dowager, working with Yésé, Alexander's brother,[1] had made Shah a weakly, high-strung boy, Haydar. But the Georgian adventurers in Kazvin, nominal Muslims whom the easy Shi'ah men about the court regarded with no animosity, were glowered upon by the strong Sunni faction, who on the death of Shah Tahmasp began to raise their heads. The leader of the Sunni nobles was a member of the Shamkhal family, cousin to Alexander's rivals; and when his faction, acting quickly against the Shalikashvilis, murdered Haydar and set up their own puppet Ismail, Simon, the declared enemy of Alexander in Kakheti and of Da'ud in Kartli, was set at liberty. The pappy Da'ud sent frightened appeals to the Turks,[2] but the Turks, without attending to him, were already swarming over Persian territory. In the summer of 1578, they prepared a heavy drive which was to add all Georgia and Shirvan to their conquests of the previous year. At the beginning of August, Lala Mustafa Pasha—the conqueror of Cyprus—defeated the weak and only Persian army of Tokmak Khan by Lake Chaldir and the road into Georgia lay open. In Samtzkhé, the Jaqelis at first resisted him, then fawned for his favour, while Kokola Shalikashvili—grandson of Otari—tried to hold a fort or two in the Persian interest. Over the Trialetian passes the Turks poured into Kartli and all the much-fought Kingdom was theirs almost without a shot. Da'ud, the creature of Shah Tahmasp, went cringing to Stambul, and after him were sent as prisoners the Atabegi Qwarqwaré and his brother Manuchar. That line of rather boyish traitors had run their wrecking course and now the Jaqelis were not even dangerous; in Stambul a German diplomat gave Qwarqwaré a watch, of which he could not understand the works, so he asked for another present; later the Sultan was pleased at his prowess as a wrestler.

[1] *Don Juan of Persia*, p. 129; cf. also Note A.   [2] Cf. *Chronique Géorgienne*, p. 12.

From Tiflis Lala Mustafa Pasha advanced to the borders of Kakheti, but neither he nor Alexander desired to fight. They came to an understanding, and Lala Mustafa, after defeating a Persian force at the junction of the Alazani and the Kanak, overran Shirvan with his troops.

In Kazvin, during the last week of November 1577, Shah Ismail was murdered. The new Shah was the weakly Khudabanda who from his birth had been almost blind. In the heat of plots and counterplots, revolts and war, the brave Meskhian dowager, back in power in the harim, ruled for the wretched invalid. After the loss of Shirvan she was desperate and she thought of King Simon. Recalling an ancient Georgian custom, she wrapped a sabre in a woman's veil and sent it to him with the message, " Take which you will of the two and go into your country to make war on the Turks ".[1] Simon, the young fighter, was a man of over forty now. He called himself Mahmud Khan and lived in Shiraz as a Muslim. Yellow with malaria, ill and venomous, an opium addict and a drinker, he still had a flame that leapt.[2] They gave him 9,000 tumans, all the Georgian prisoners, and the insignia of royalty. And while the Turks with an imperial vigour were organizing Kartli into " sanjaks ", dismantling the Cathedral of Sioni, and fortifying Gori, Samshwildé and Dmanisi as if they thought to stay, *Kheli Swimoni*—" mad Simon "[3]—came upon them, a sick man[4] riding hard.

The winter months were on; the Turkish troops were tired, unpaid and mutinous,[5] and in that much-plundered country had had but little plunder. Lala Mustafa, with a new change in Stambul threatening his gambler's throat, had already gone through Samtzkhé, leaving men of fewer tails to hold the conquests in Azerbaijan, Georgia and Shirvan. Sullen movement flickered through the rifled valleys, and the pillaged peasants, as they faced the hungry frosts, gathered, bony blue and angry, to pillage the convoys.[6]

The war began to change. While another woman, the wife of Khudabanda,[7] drove the Turks through Shirvan up as far as Derbend and scattered their Tatar auxiliaries who had come round overland from the Crimea, Simon won in Georgia.

---

[1] Wakhushti, *Hist. de Kartli*, in Brosset, *H. de la G.*, p. 35; cf. *Don Juan*, p. 155, who dates the intervention of Simon to the beginning of 1579.
[2] *Ibid.*, p. 41.   [3] *Ibid.*, p. 42.   [4] *Ibid.*, p. 36.
[5] *Don Juan*, pp. 144 and 147.
[6] Wakhushti, *Hist. de Kartli*, in Brosset, *H. de la G.*, II, i, 34–5; cf. also *Don Juan*, p. 148.
[7] Identified by E. G. Browne (*Literary Hist. of Persia*, IV, 102) as a lady of the family of the Marashi Sayyids of Mazanderan, and the mother of Khuda-banda's four sons.

CLASH OF EMPIRES

With small forces badly armed, without cannon, he drove keen and fast, a master in the horseman's genius of quick and sudden mobile war. He cut off garrisons, provoking sorties, turned on them, surprised and captured isolated posts, slaughtered convoys, hung upon retreats. By February 1579 he had cleared the Turks from everywhere in Kartli except the citadel of Tiflis. Then the victor turned for an account on all the lewd and treacherous vassals who had cried " Down with King Simon and all that is his ". He carried the long feud of Levani's rival heirs against the Kakhian king and his creatures, Bardzim Amilakhori and Elisbari of the Ksani. And when Alexander raided the castle of Queen Nestan-Darejani and rode off bearing his half-sister's drawers high upon a lance,[1] Simon met and beat him at Jotori (1581).

But the hard-bitten, winning King had longer views than his mean fellow-potentates and vassals who fought their little tourney wars—on sex and personalities. While the bigger ding-dong war went on, and Turks and Crim Tatars and the Persians rode and marched and raged, and pest and famine crept the land, Simon closed the feud with Alexander, condoned the knavish vassals, and, a little of a statesman through all the insensate muck, he turned to confront those greater issues which the time had passed to solve.

Mahmud Pasha in 1582, the beggarly Manuchar in his train, pressed a new invasion into Kartli. While he engaged the Imerians to ravage Inner Kartli, the Turkish general captured Gori, Lori and other strong places and advanced to Mukhrani. Simon roundly beat him in two fights and drove him into Tiflis citadel. The havering Jaqelis, spotting a new winner, went over to the King, and in 1583 Simon defeated Hassan Pasha at Tabakhméla; and later took the citadel of Tiflis, so that the Georgians could breathe in their own capital for the first time in thirty years. Then Simon took Samshwildé, beat the Turks at Katis-Sopheli and captured their new stronghold which they had built at Dmanisi.[2]

By 1586 the war in its wider action was whittling down. In Persia that year the blind crock Khuda-banda died; his son, Abbas, was made Shah by the factions, and in the coming years he ate them.

---

[1] Wakhushti, *Hist. de Kartli*, in Brosset, H. de la G., II, i, 37.
[2] In the account of these somewhat confused operations, I follow Wakhushti in *Hist. de Kartli* (Brosset, H. de la G., II, i, 37–8) and *Suite des Annales* (Ibid, pp. 365–7). Cf. also *Don Juan of Persia*, pp. 156–75, which, in outline, confirms the Georgian versions, but which is obscured as a narrative by the omission of many Georgian place-names; and von Hammer, Vol. VII, pp. 101–15.

A MUSCOVITE CAVALRY SOLDIER OF THE SEVENTEENTH CENTURY (AFTER CASTELLI).

Simon was stronger in his kingdom; watched Persia—to whose ruler he owed a vague but dangerous allegiance—becoming gradually more ordered; awaited the perennial spluttering irruptions from along the Turkish border. Throughout the Georgian country Simon was now the most powerful man, and scenting it the Kakhian and Imerian kings slightly drew together to bar what plans he might construct. The King was vital, brave, intelligent, beloved of the people, and although of a quick temerity, when not in heat he knew his strength or weakness and was careful, reckoning, objective. He had chewed experience, suffered all the basest things, trod the stones of hopelessness, bathed miseries in vice. Alert and restless, always ill, he salvaged for a year or two the wreckage of a kingdom, where if there had been others like him he might have ruled as a great king.

In 1588, he put back Manuchar who had become his son-in-law, as Atabegi in Samtzkhé—in spite of the Turks. He intervened in Imereti in the same year. For forty years ever since the death of Bagrat III, the weak King Giorgi II, the Gurieli and the Dadiani, the Liparitianis, the Chiladzes and the Sharvashidzes had been engaged in squalid, interminable, internecinal hostilities. When King Giorgi died in 1585 leaving as heir a boy of twelve, Levani, the tiresome tumults, mangy plots, low murders, all renewed themselves. Simon invaded the country and defeated the Imerians in a battle at Gophanto. But in the following year the young Levani came back and, during fighting in 1590, the boy was defeated and captured by Mamia Dadiani. He died in prison in the fort of Shketi in Odishi. The Mingrelian faction then raised to the throne the late King's cousin Rustem, while the Gurieli brought forward another cousin, Bagrati.

Simon came in again. With a considerable force and a train of cannon, he crossed the Mountains of Likhi. He captured all the principal Imerian strongholds and entered Kutais. The pretender Bagrati was his prisoner and he marched against the Dadiani—to lay his hands on Rustem, the last legitimate heir of the Imerian line. Simon ruled in Kartli; his word went in Samtzkhé; Imereti was nearly his. Persia was quiet, the Turks engaged elsewhere. The feverish man, after his battered life, seemed to be going to have all Georgia. His troops followed the Dadiani up through the wet woods and soggy paths of Mingrelia. It was not the Kartlians' fighting country and the cannon were of no great use. But Simon thought he had the last King of Imereti run to ground and he refused an offered compromise. Then the Mingrelians on their own ground, out of the surrounding woods, surprised his camp at dawn. Simon saw his troops in flight and he called for his horse Shurdani; for in retreat he always rode Shurdani and in victory Palawani.[1] He lost all his cannon and the scattered Kartlians went back over the Mountains of Likhi. "What had happened?" a peasant woman asked the King as he stopped unrecognized at Kavtiskhevi—"was the King saved?" "Thanks be to God," she cried, "for if the King be safe and sound God can have all the others in his stead."[2]

Simon reigned nine more years. He was ageing then, at sixty-two, but he continued wiry, active, apprehending, always on horseback, a burned-out man still quick and masterful. He was fighting the Turks again—preparing to attack at Nakhiduri, when he was taken in a rather rash reconnaissance. So pleased was Jafar Pasha that he immediately retired, holding his prisoner to be sufficient prize for the campaign. Simon was sent to Stambul and held in the Seven Towers, that look out, unhappily, over the Thracian plain. Eleven years passed before the old man died.[3]

[1] Wakhushti, *Hist. de Kartli*, in Brosset, *H. de la G.*, II, i, 41.
[2] *Ibid.*
[3] Cf. Wakhushti, *Hist. de Kartli*, in Brosset, *H. de la G.*, II, i, 42-3, who states that Simon died in 1600. Brosset from further evidence considers that he lived until 1611.

CHAPTER XIV

CLASH OF EMPIRES: THE PEREGRINATIONS OF TAYMURAZ I (1586–1663)

In Europe during the latter part of the sixteenth century the leisured pomp of Emperors' wars was giving place to the hard-knuckled grind of conflicts which in their bitterness of social hates and their raw economic greed we recognize to be our own, so sane and unromantic. The merchants hardly hid their power behind the skirts of marriageable princesses; and the youth of an enlightened West no longer rode to battle for the royal dowry of an epileptic, but for trade-routes and Capitulations, silver-mines, Monopolies, pepper, cloves and negro slaves.

Slowly the new realities of these mighty forces began to vibrate through—without yet shaking—the senescent social fabrics of the East. The English and the Spaniards, the French, the Portuguese, the Dutch were groping, stumbling, grabbing into the Turkish Empire, into Persia, India, China, fighting remote and bloody little battles in their wooden ships, carronading coasts that they had not known before, intriguing in exotic courts, dying awful deaths and gaining glorious fortunes.

Out of the wrack great changes came. The capacious majesty of the eastern world, seeming imponderable to the small mediæval West, crumbled before ordered intelligence and bullying method; but in the same time while men scarcely realized, there grew up to overbear the little western lands, two mighty centres of new power—the Russian Empire and America. The "Land of the Hyperboreans"—the vast plains and forests beyond the cold north wind, unknown to the ancients—grew potent suddenly in human force, in towns and ships and men.

The unfolding of an oceanic, a trans-Atlantic, background to the conflict of the nations, and the emergence of a modern steppe-land state, of a trans-Asiatic power, were the two great revolutionary facts of the seventeenth century, and in the following centuries the whole aspect of world politics was utterly transformed.

REVOLUTIONS OF THE GEORGIAN KINGDOM

The origins of the new power of the Muscovian monarchy lay in a strange amalgam of those antique elements in Asiatic history, which, in the middle of the fifteenth century, had been already dead or dying. The administrative system, the religious and intellectual life, and the artistic tradition of Byzantium were combined with the military methods of the Tatars, so that the Asiatic cavalryman carried the portable icons and the rigid ideas of Roman autocracy from the Vistula to the Pacific. The commercial and military adventurers of Europe, who mined and then mastered the aged rulerships of the East, were not strong enough nor coherent enough to seize upon and dominate nor yet to morcelate the cumbrous body of the Muscovian monarchy. Neither the Teutonic Knights nor the Poles nor the Hanse cities nor the Swedes, nor the last grand gesture of Napoleon's French, could pull down that mighty buck. The most westerly of eastern states was sufficiently the most easterly of western states to acquire and to absorb much of the strength which the West had to give, while it was strong enough to reject that which the West had to impose. Baltic Germans, Swedes and Poles, Scots soldiers of fortune, the Wild Geese of Ireland, organized the army and served in the administration; English, French and Dutch merchants and engineers took a building hand in the trade and industry of the country. And that strange mediæval body emerged, dressed in a modern accoutrement, with its German brain, its Byzantine mind, its Tatar hands and Slavic soul.

The rise of the Russian monarchy was remarkably quick. At the end of the fifteenth century Ivan III of Moscow had got the better of his rivals who stood in the way of Russian unity, and had assumed by his marriage with Sophia Palaiologa those vast pretensions to Imperial power which in future centuries were to swell the breasts of his successors from the petty courts of Germany. Half a century later Ivan IV overthrew the Tatar dynasty of Kazan (1552). By the capture of Astrakhan (1555) he made the Volga a Russian river and Muscovy became a potential aggressor against the heart of the Muslim east.

In twenty years under that portentous man Russia grew to be the strongest Asiatic power. While the Stroganovs were developing the trade across the Pechora and into Siberia, Cossack bands were pressing through four thousand miles of wilderness towards the Chinese marches. And in the south other bands of these useful outlaws were establishing themselves under the northern slopes of the Caucasus in the

A MUSCOVITE ARCHER OF THE SEVENTEENTH CENTURY (AFTER CASTELLI).

valleys of the Kuban and the Terek. In 1579, the year of Yermak's expedition to Siberia, the forts of Terki and Andreyevo were built on the Terek by the outlaw Andrei Shadrin. In the period covered by the following twenty-five years the modern period of Caucasian political history may be said to have begun. The new Russian political machine was rumbling southwards to the Black Sea and the Caspian and the fruitful lands of Western Asia. The Cossacks appeared—an excellent political weapon, mobile cavalry—restless, warlike and adventurous—at once bandits and colonists, who could be repudiated or who could be brought to obey. The diplomats followed, and much later, the regiments and the ships. The volatile intriguing minds of the Georgian dynasts and their nobles saw in the Russian interest a new element, which could vary the incessant play of wits and plots which they wound between Stambul and Kazvin. The Turks and Persians were not slow to apprehend the significance of the proximity of an aggression new in method to their own, and were stirred through uneasiness to fear and fearful action. The game of plots, incitements and solicitations, of counter-plots and massacres, began in the damp huts of Terki in 1586 when the envoys of Tsar Feodor Ivanovich and of Alexander of Kakheti came together, and it went down through the generations in logical and morbid sequence to the slaughter and obliteration of a great part of the Armenian nation between the years 1914 and 1921.

The first big round, from 1586 to 1615, with its penalties dragged out to 1629, moved with the horrid quick fatality which we have learnt to know in the present generation for the Greeks, the Kurds, the Armenians and the Assyrians.

Between 1586 and 1594, three embassies, exchanged between Moscow and Kakheti, took the long way over the mountains and by Terki, Astrakhan, Kazan and Saratov. King Alexander II was pursuing his feud with the Shamkhal, and engaged the Russians in military operations in Daghestan. He at the same time accepted the protection of Feodor Ivanovich, who proceeded to assume—somewhat prematurely—the style of "*Lord of the Iberian Land, of the Tsars of Georgia, of Kabardá, of the Cherkess and Mountain Princes.*"[1] In Daghestan the Boyar Khvorostin had some small successes, but in 1594 a Russian expedition of 7,000 men was cut to pieces by the Shamkhal's sons on the Sulak. Another Russian force was destroyed in 1599.

[1] Baddeley, *Russian Conquest of the Caucasus*, p. 9.

CLASH OF EMPIRES

The intervention of the Russians in the affairs of Kakheti had already caused uneasiness at Kasvin during the reign of Shah Khuda-banda, and the issue had been raised by a Persian envoy to the court of Moscow.[1]

Shah Abbas I, at the height of his prestige and in the vigour of his youth, now undertook a comprehensive policy which was directed towards restoring the position of Persia in all the region of the north-west frontier. In 1603, in a first campaign to expel the Turks from the territories which they had gained in the war of 1578–86, he laid siege to Erivan, and summoned the two Georgian kings, Alexander of Kakheti and Simon's son, Giorgi X of Kartli, to assist him. He reasserted Persian suzerainty over Kartli and deprived Giorgi of the fortress and district of Lori. The Russians meanwhile continued their military operations in Daghestan, and in March 1604, the Russian envoy in Kakheti, Tatishchev, was insisting that Alexander and his sons should declare themselves vassals of Tsar Boris Godunov. But Constantine, a younger son of Alexander and a creature of Shah Abbas, arrived at *Zaghani (Zagem)* while the Russians were there and murdered both his father and his elder brother, so near to Tatishchev's tent that the envoy could hear the cries of the wretched royalties.[2]

Tatishchev was no more fortunate in Kartli, where he went to arrange a dual marriage between the children of Boris Godunov and two offsprings of the Kartlian Bagratids.[3] Giorgi X died soon afterwards as a result of biting a cake in which was a bee which stung his tongue.[4] When Tatishchev returned to Moscow he found that Tsar Boris Godunov was dead and "the Time of Troubles" was upon Russia.

Shah Abbas the Great was now able to consolidate Persian power in the north-western frontier region without conflict with a major power. The vigorous Caucasian policy of Boris Godunov was at an end; Turkey, particularly since the Hungarian campaigns at the close of the century, was becoming, as Sir Thomas Roe reported in 1622, "like an old body, crazed through many vices, which remains when youth and strength is decayed". The Georgian kingdoms—by a series of accidents in which the shrewd Abbas had had his hand—were each ruled by young and untried boys. In Kartli, Luarsab II, a youth gallant, passionate and feckless, had succeeded his father. In Kakheti a revolt of the nobles against the parricide

---

[1] Byelokurov, *Snosheniya*, p. 563. [2] Brosset, *H. de la G.*, II, i (Add. X), p. 339.
[3] *Ibid.*, pp. 339–40. [4] Brosset, *Chronique Géorgienne*, p. 31.

Constantine, had placed on the throne Taymuraz I—a boy of sixteen who had been reared at the Persian court. In Imereti, a bastard cousin, Giorgi III, had in the same year succeeded the bastard Rustem. And in each kingdom the nobles loomed big, jostling to pluck at the new pigeons. In Imereti, Levan Dadiani, the most powerful of his line, presumptuous, lewd and violent, bullied the unsure King, and with his creature Paata, called Tsutska, a witty evil invalid, gathered all the riches of the kingdom to himself. In middle Georgia, the Amilakhoris and the Eristavni of the Ksani and the Aragvi played high in Kartlian and Kakhian politics, as once the Atabegni of Samtzkhé had done within the greater Georgian kingdom. They were in touch with the Russians and the mountain tribes and they could sell themselves to either king for lands and marriages; bar the envoys going between the Georgian courts and Terki; hold out for gifts and office from the Shah. Close to Luarsabi, and jealous rather than loyal, stood the powerful *gwari* of Baratashvili, whose lands covered a great part of Kartli south of the Mtkvari. But most formidable of all in that small contending world of Georgian politics was Giorgi Saakadze, the upstart prefect of Tiflis, Krtzkhilvani and Dvaleti, "the great *Mo'uravi*",

> "a man, brave and strong, who united tremendous energy with audacious courage, but who was cunning, cavilling, distrustful, whispering always and ceaselessly interfering in the affairs of his neighbours."[1]

Giorgi Saakadze gained a great name for his defeat of an inroad of Crim Tatars who had been landed at Trebizond and had ravaged the valley of the Mtkvari in 1609. He skilfully brought about the marriage of his sister to the King and was the real master of Georgia, when the noise of a plot against him caused him to flee to the Persian court. Shah Abbas, meanwhile, was planning, as he had leisure, the complete subjugation of the two Georgian kingdoms, and Saakadze, "the great *Mo'uravi*", became his most useful instrument. In 1614, the Shah's plans were ripe and with that combination of ferocity and subtility which characterized all his actions, he proceeded by treachery and overwhelming force to the destruction of the two young kings. The Persians advanced from Ganja in the middle of winter because "the great *Mo'uravi*"

---

[1] Wakhushti, *Hist. de Kartli*, in Brosset, *H. de la G.*, II, i, 45; for an account of "the great *Mo'uravi*" by a contemporary and apparent familiar, see also Brosset, *Chronique Géorgienne*, pp. 34 *et sqq.*

had shown that "*it was better to enter Kartli in winter so that the inhabitants could not flee to the mountains and they would have them under their hands*".[1] Saakadze had worked well; some of the principal nobles went over to the Persians, the Kartlian and Kakhian troops refused to fight, and Luarsabi and Taymurazi fled into Imereti.

Luarsabi subsequently surrendered to the Shah who took him as a prisoner into Persia after having set up as King in Tiflis, Bagrati a son of Simon's brother Da'aud Khan.

In Kakheti during the summer of 1615, Taymurazi reappeared and inflicted several defeats on the Persians at Areshi, Aloni and Alaverdi. The vengeance of Abbas was terrible. If his policy in the previous year had been to weaken the two kingdoms and to appoint his own puppets as rulers, he now was set upon the deliberate extermination of the Christian population.

> "He made this proclamation to the Lazghis: 'I want to exterminate Kakheti. Kill or make prisoners all those Kakhians who pass into the mountains on your side and I will enrich you with gifts.' . . . From Tiflis, Shah Abbas sent numerous bands against Kherk, to Ertso and to Tianeti and he, himself, entered Kakheti which he submitted by force, took prisoners and carried off the population, devastated, pillaged the churches, broke the icons and the crosses, and gave their ornaments for the toilets of his concubines. Nevertheless some saved themselves in the strong places, among the peaks, in the woods and in the mountains of the Pshavs and Khevsurs and in Tusheti. For their part the Lazghis carried out the promises which they had made to Shah Abbas."[2]

The country was left in Persian military occupation, and masses of the population were deported into Mazandaran, Khurasan and the islands of the Caspian.

In 1623, Shah Abbas attempted to carry out the same policy of wholesale massacre and deportation in Kartli, but "the great *Mo'uravi*" Giorgi Saakadze, who meanwhile had distinguished himself in the Shah's Afghan campaigns, discovered that his master intended to have him executed, and he therefore anticipated events by putting himself at the head of a general rising. For the six last years of Shah Abbas's reign a savage war was fought throughout Georgia, during

---

[1] Wakhushti, in *Hist. de Kartli*, in Brosset, *H. de la G.*, II, i, 49.
[2] Wakhushti, *Hist. de Kakheti* in Brosset, *H. de la G.*, II, i, 164. Cf. also *Chronique Géorgienne*, pp. 49–50. In his learned article "*Tiflis*" in E.I., V. Minorski quotes *Alam ara*, the official history of Shah Abbas, p. 615, that—the number of those he put to death was 60/70,000 and the number of young prisoners of both sexes 100,000 to 130,000; "since the beginning of Islam no such events have taken place under any king". The same source gives the number of those massacred by Karchikai-Khan at 10,000—"as if at a battue" (shikari-wār).

which even the remote northern districts—Mtiuleti, the valleys of the Ksani and the Aragvi and Osseti—were ravaged, while the insurgents under Giorgi Saakadze inflicted many bloody defeats on the Persians. That restless bitter spirit, "the great Moʻuravi" was at last beaten and fled to Turkey. He was executed while with the Turkish army at Konia, for some disturbances created by his followers.

> "He was an old man of an extraordinary stature", says Iskander Munji, "and so full of strength that they called him the Bull. Without regard for his past services, he was given over to the executioner."[1]

Shah Abbas died in 1629 and with him passed the full vigour of the Persian frontier policy. Under his successors, Shah Safi II and Shah Abbas II, the Persian control slid into the sporadic tyranny and slipshod tolerances which characterized the bureaucracies of Persia and Turkey during the seventeenth and eighteenth centuries.

The wars of Shah Abbas during the first quarter of the seventeenth century had thoroughly restored the military and political power of Persia in the eastern Caucasus. The Turks had been driven from all Shirvan, and from Tabriz, Erivan, and Nakhchevan, and Persian control in Georgia—which had never been effectively exercised since the time of the Il-Khans in the thirteenth century—had been re-established. Persian garrisons were in Tiflis, Gori, Surami and other Kartlian fortresses, and although Mussulman Bagratids were allowed to reign as kings in Tiflis and, at intervals in Kakheti, real political authority derived from the new court of the Safavids at Isfahan.

The sudden revival of the military power of Persia under Shah Abbas happened to correspond with a period of stagnation in Turkey and with the "Time of Troubles" in Russia, and that the recovery of the lost hegemony in the eastern Caucasus should be an object of Persian policy is easy to understand. But the ferocity of Shah Abbas's methods contrast with the relatively amiable, but sometimes cruel, although always cautious methods pursued by the Persian courts during the preceding two hundred years. The policy of the Persians towards the Georgian kings had always been to persuade, cajole and threaten, rather than to destroy. Chardin has noted that the principal object of Turkish and Persian diplomats was to win the Georgian dynasts from the other

---

[1] Brosset, *H. de la G.*, II, i, 61, quoting Iskander Munji. The execution took place at the end of July, 1629.

"The Persian Queen, Elena de Artabac," (daughter of the Atabegi of Samtzkhé, wife of Shah Safi II, after Castelli).

side, and Georgian kings and nobles with sufficient cunning and deficient scruples could always make their price. The ferocity of Shah Abbas was without precedent. He caused King Luarsabi to be drowned in 1622. He caused the two young sons of Taymurazi to be castrated, and he had the King's mother Katevani tortured to death. His slaughters in Kakheti and Kartli recalled the manner of war of the Mongols, and were without parallel until the present generation. It would seem that the Shah was seriously disturbed at the advance of the Russians to the Terek and their subsequent intervention in Kakheti, and that he became exasperated at the intrigues which their envoys conducted with Alexander II and Giorgi X and later with Taymuraz II and with Giorgi III of Imereti. The reaction of Persian policy to Russian intervention in Georgia at the beginning of the seventeenth century was very similar to that of Abdul-Hamid to the intervention of the European powers in Armenian affairs during the latter part of the nineteenth century.

The second quarter of the seventeenth century was a period of relative calm throughout the Georgian kingdoms. Bagrat VI, the nominee of Shah Abbas, dying in 1619, his son had succeeded as Simon II—an ineffectual young man who was bandied about between the fierce *mtavarni* during the long insurrection against the Persians. Simon was killed in 1629, and Taymurazi of Kakheti for five harried years attempted to rule in Kartli. Finally in 1634, a Persian force installed as king in Tiflis, Khusraw Mirza, another son of Da'ud Khan. Khusraw Mirza, who assumed the style of Rustem I, was a Muslim who had lived all his life in Persia. He had held high rank as *darugha* of Isfahan and it had been rather through his influence that Shah Safi had secured the succession on the death of Shah Abbas. A gracious hedonist of sixty-seven, worldly, rich and tactful, Rustem was able to clear the charred ruins and heal the seared wounds of the preceding twenty years. Rustem got himself married to Katevan Abashidze according to both the Muslim and the Christian rites; built himself the airy palace overlooking the river where Chardin, half a century later, supped with Shah Nawaz I; and restored the Cathedral of Mtzkheta. But the amiable and dexterous septuagenarian was still a good man to horse, and he took the field a dozen times against the restless *mtavarni*, and to keep out Taymurazi who was always flitting from Imereti to Kakheti, raising sudden risings against the Persian governors there and furtively intriguing with the Turks, the Vatican, the Russians and even with the Shah.[1]

Taymurazi was a character very different from the poised and courtly Rustem. A strange fatality dogged him to his death, of the loss of all his nearest kin and of his dearest friends. Castelli has left a portrait of him, with his mournful eyes, his haggard jowl, his look so hung with tragedy. A fevered hopeful plotter, he had no luck in arms; a pretender on the run for forty years, he rode and tramped and sailed the seas with a sick heart and a soaring head. A Persian scholar and a poet, he has left a Georgian translation of " *Yusuf and Zuleika* " and he wrote two pieces " *The Rose and the Nightingale* " and " *Conversation of the Butterfly with the Candle* ".[2] Yet venom gnaws the hunted, and he could, on occasion, mutilate his prisoners.[3] Taymurazi pursued the weary way of the pretender in the corridors of other potentates, all careless, bored or prepossessed. Between 1618 and 1625, he sent envoys several times to Moscow and Stambul to seek intervention against Shah Abbas, but when the Sultan granted him an appanage in Samtzkhé the effect was to disturb the Gurieli and to antagonize the Tsar. The mission of Nicholas Erbashi to the Vatican and the courts of Europe was no more fruitful. The monk spent several years in Rome compiling an Italian-Georgian dictionary and returned a Roman Catholic. The reservation of two seats for Georgians at the International College of Propaganda was the only gesture made by the Vatican to Georgia since the unfruitful peregrinations of Ludovico of Bologna two hundred years before.

After his expulsion from Kartli in 1634, Taymurazi again attempted to renew relations with Moscow, and Nicholas Erbashi[4] arrived in Moscow in 1636, after a difficult journey occupying over a year. In May 1637, Erbashi, in company with the Russian envoys, Prince Volkonski and the deacon Khvatov, set out on the return journey, but it was not until August 1638 that they arrived at the camp of Taymurazi in Kakheti. On 23rd April 1639, Taymurazi, who had only

---

[1] In 1638 Taymurazi was pardoned by the Shah and installed in the governorship of Kakheti. He immediately embarked on operations in Didoeti with the object of clearing the route for the arrival at Zagem of a Russian Embassy from Terki. He carried on a sporadic warfare against Rustem of Kartli and was finally driven into exile in 1648. (cf. Brosset, *H. de la G.*, II, i, 169-171, and 169, note 3).

[2] *Ibid.*, p. 167, note 3.   [3] *Ibid.*, p. 167.

[4] Nicholas Erbashi (Isbarghi or Irbakhi) was a member of the distinguished Kakhian family of Choloqashvili. As a religious, he assumed the name of Niciphoros, and he was known to contemporary Russian travellers as the Metropolitan Nikiphor or Mikiphor.

recently received the confirmation of his occupation of Kakheti from the Shah, took the oath of allegiance to the Tsar. It was at the same time agreed by Volkonski that on his return Taymurazi should receive an Imperial Rescript whereby the Tsar would undertake to guarantee Georgia against the Lazghis and would cause to be built in the mountains a city of refuge for the people of Kakheti. On the 28th April 1639, Volkonski's mission left for Russia accompanied by Nicholas Erbashi, but they did not reach Astrakhan until the 10th July.

Erbashi again left Moscow in 1641, returning with the mission of Prince Mishetski and the deacon Kliucharev, bearing rich gifts of money and sables, and the Imperial Rescript which Taymurazi had required.

Between the years 1641 and 1648, two further missions were exchanged, the object of the first of which was to arrange the marriage of a grandson of Taymurazi with the sister of Tsar Alexei Mikhailovich.[1] The Russian envoy, Babarikin, was drowned in the Caspian and nothing came of the proposition. In 1648 Taymurazi took refuge in Imereti and it was at his manor in Radsha, the gift of his son-in-law, King Alexander, that the mission of Tolochanov and Yevlev found him.

The elderly pretender was losing heart and he had had his fill of misfortune. He sent his grandson, Nicholas, to be educated in the safety of the Muscovite court. In 1655 he was asking for an escort to meet him at the sources of the Malka that he might journey there himself. He spent the long winter of 1657–8 in Astrakhan and in the following June he was received by Alexei Mikhailovich in Moscow. In May of 1659, Taymurazi was again in Astrakhan on his way back to Imereti, when he had the news of the death of his favourite grandson Luarsabi. He took the way over the mountains to Imereti and when he came there he found that his wife was dead. Shortly afterwards his protector Alexander also died and civil wars broke out in Imereti. The old man was in extremity. He was hiding his penury in the fortress of Skanda which lies over against the Mountains

---

[1] The equanimity with which Boris Godunov and Alexei Mikhailovich considered matrimonial alliances with the uncertain dynasties of Georgia is explained by the fact that the Russian princesses were not allowed to marry subjects, and it was exceedingly difficult in view of religious sentiment to arrange their marriages in the European courts. Many of the princesses in the seventeenth century in fact died in convents. Further to the parvenu houses of Godunov and Romanov an alliance with the Bagratids, of the most ancient lineage in Christendom and collaterally descended from the Comnenoi, was not without attraction.

of Likhi and he threw in his hand—surrendered himself to the Kartlian viceroy Shah-Nawaz. He was sent to Isfahan. Abbas II, a puckish drunkard, first flattered him, feasted him, then flung a wine cup in his face, then fawned upon him and next day sent him to imprisonment at Astarabad.

Taymurazi died there in the winter of 1663 after taking the monk's frock. The Kakhians living in Astarabad were given permission to take his body to Alaverdi where it was buried. Already his young grandson, Nicholas, taking the name of Irakli (Hercules) had gone into Tusheti and raised an insurrection that had failed.

CHAPTER XV

ABEYANCE OF THE MONARCHY: THE MUKHRANIAN VICEROYS (1656–1722)

THE period of fifty-nine years which intervened between the death of Taymuraz I in 1663 and the rise of his great-grandson Taymuraz II in 1722, corresponds to a distinct phase in Georgian history. Taymuraz I may be regarded as the last of the heroic but ineffectual series of soldier-kings, including the two Luarsabis and Simon I, who endeavoured to resist the aggressions of the Mussulman powers and who in political thought still hove back to the glories of the national kingdom. Taymuraz II and his remarkable son Irakli II, pursued, as we shall have occasion to observe, a different policy, directed not so much to the revival of the ancient kingdom, as to the erection of a Caucasian state based indeed on a Georgian nucleus and on a Bagratid hegemony, but a state integrally Caucasian, centred on Tiflis and drawing its strength from an army by no means predominantly Georgian and from political combinations which implied the acquiescence of both Armenians and Mussulmans.

The directive causes of the policy of the Kakhian Bagratids during the eighteenth century are to be found in the political and economic tendencies which were developing during the preceding seventy years.

The period between the active lives of Taymuraz I and Taymuraz II (1663–1722) roughly corresponds with that during which the cadet branch of the Bagratids, whose seat was Mukhrani on the Aragvi, ruled in Tiflis as hereditary viceroys of the Shah (1665–1724).[1] The Mukhranian Bagratids were descended from Bagrati a younger son of Constantine III and since the death of Luarsab II they had loomed nearer to the throne. Finally the favour of old King Rustem, the last of the senior line, and the concordance of the Shah, had, without a fight, brought the remains of Kartlian kingship to Wakhtangi, Prince of Mukhrani, in 1656.

[1] " He had the title of vice-roy (*janisin*) but passed for king " ; according to Sekhnia Chkheidze, see Brosset, *H. de la G.*, II, ii, 28 : *Chronique de S. Ch.*

ARTSCHILLUS BAGARATIONUS (ARCHILI OF MUKHRANI, SON OF WAKHTANG V OF KARTLI, AND SOMETIME KING OF IMERETI). NICHOLAS DAVIDZSOON (NICHOLAS, SON OF DAVID, ELDEST SON OF TAYMURAZ I. NICHOLAS BECAME KING OF KAKHETI AS IRAKLI I).

(From Nicholas Witzen's Noord und Oost Tartarye.)

Distinguished, cultured and intelligent, soldierly and very rich, Wakhtang V, called also Shah-Nawaz I, was the greatest figure in contemporary politics, not only in the Caucasus, but throughout the Persian Empire.[1] He was a new type among the royal nobility of Georgia, a type to which his sons and grandsons nearly all conformed. In them an apprehending pliable intelligence replaced the erratic heroism of earlier kings in Tiflis. Viceroys in the Caucasus, the Mukhranians were also great nobles at the court of Persia. Patrons of the Georgian Church, who reserved its sees for their cadets, they were at the same time leisurely Shias who assumed Muslim names, and took their part in the religious controversies and sectarian intrigues of the Muslim factions in Isfahan. They numbered among them two Catholicoses, and one of them, Antoni, became a great reformer of the Church. They translated Persian works into Georgian, and carried icons and Psalters with them when they led Persian armies into Afghanistan.[2] They married the Shah's daughters and dabbled in Roman Catholicism. Wakhtang VI (called also Hussain-Quli-Khan) lost his uncle and his brother in the Persian campaigns in Afghanistan and while he prepared to conquer Daghestan, his envoy, Saba Sulkhan Orbeliani, was visiting the court of Louis XIV. The military prowess of Giorgi XI (Shah-Nawaz II) and of his sons and brothers buttressed the last decade of the Safavi dynasty in Persia and on the Afghan border; and while some of the family intrigued and fought for the Shah at Mashhad and Herat, others, or the same at other times, were playing for their own independent rule in Georgia. Only the tragic farce of Persian politics in the first quarter of the eighteenth century could have produced such contrary circumstances; only the Georgian nobility could have bred such brilliant and bewildering adventurers. And all the fifty years of bravery and courtly skill which had gone to build the fortunes of the Mukhranian Bagratids were lost in a few months when the Turkish and Russian invasions of 1722 intruded the cold force of reality. But if the Mukhranians were Isfahani grandees first and Kings of Kartli afterwards, it was because they were the dwellers in, and not the architects of, the political and economic fabric which had been erected as a result of the successful Empire-building of Shah Abbas the Great.

---

[1] For Wakhushti's description of the character of Wakhtang V, see Brosset, *H. de la G.*, II, i, 79.
[2] *Ibid.*, p. 103.

ABEYANCE OF THE MONARCHY

With the establishment of permanent Persian military control in Kartli and Kakheti, these two provinces became an integral part of the Perso-Caspian economic region. Georgia was partitioned. There was now no belt of unified territory stretching across the Trans-Caucasian Trough from the Black Sea to the eastward. Georgia was split into two. Kartli and Kakheti—in administration and in economics—formed a part of north-west Iran, and the Mukhranian viceroy in Tiflis—an hereditary Mussulman grandee—was also, generally either governor of Aran, or, even greater, General of Azerbaijan.[1] Western Georgia—Imier, " that side " of the Mountains of Likhi was entirely separate both in administration and in economics.

This separation was confirmed in political fact by the Turko-Persian Treaty of 1636, which defined Kartli and Kakheti as Persian dependencies and included Saatabago (Samtzkhé) and Imereti within the Turkish sphere of influence.[2] This partition which assumed the Mountains of Likhi as the border between the Turkish and Persian zones was accepted and accorded a rigid adherence in both Stambul and Isfahan. And while defining beyond further dispute the areas subject to the two Empires, it was the more acceptable to both in that it limited the potential ambitions of strongminded Georgian dynasts within each area. In the fifteenth century Bagrat II of Imereti had aspired to conquer Kartli; in the sixteenth century Simon I of Kartli had come near to achieving a reunion. Taymuraz I had had similar ambitions and it was to the interest of both Sultan and Shah to perpetuate that division which the Bagratids by their ineptitude had originally brought about. When Wakhtang V (Shah-Nawaz I) taking advantage of the civil war in Imereti, fought a successful campaign in the west and, after occupying all Mingrelia, and even Abkhazeti, attempted to set up his son Archili as king in Kutais, a Turkish army intervened to enforce the Treaty of 1636, and the Shah under pressure of an ultimatum from Stambul, set an immediate check to the ambitions of his viceroy.[3]

Wakhtangi continued to play with the idea of Archili's candidacy to the Imerian throne, and between 1663 and 1698 Archili made no less than five attempts to sit upon the slippery seat of royalty in Kutais. He left behind him the best epic poem in Georgian of the seventeenth century[4] and a record

[1] Brosset, *H. de la G.*, II, i, 117.
[3] *Ibid.*, p. 77.
[2] *Ibid.*, p. 68.
[4] *Archiliani*.

of vicissitudes and adventures even more varied than those of Taymuraz I. Archili's life of erratic pretensions and gallant failures marked the last attempt to revive a national kingdom of Georgia. The Mountains of Likhi were becoming a boundary between the purely Georgian western lands and the rich and cosmopolitan half-Muslim principality which the Mukhranians were holding in the basin of the Mtkvari and which, under Taymuraz II and Irakli II, gave promise of becoming a hybrid Georgian-Armenian-Perso-Tatar, Christian-Muslim, east Caucasian state.

For sixty years from 1661 to 1721 Imereti and the western lands were prey to the most dreadful civil war which has ever devastated a country of small area and sparse population. When at last the factions were exhausted and Alexander V—put in by the Turks and propped by the Dadiani—began his long uncertain reign, the country had become a depopulated wilderness—a lovely wilderness of woods where a bucolic feudal life struggled to survive its own sultry feuds, the incursions of the Turks and the slave raids of the Abkhaz and the Cherkess.[1]

The Mukhranian princes quarrelled and intrigued among themselves. They had a dangerous rival in Taymurazi's grandson, Irakli, the representative of the Kakhian Bagratids. And they had to cope with the pretensions of the powerful *mtavarni*, the Eristavni of the Ksani and the Aragvi, the Amilakhoris, the Tzitzishvilis, the Baratashvilis, and the Choloqashvilis of Kakheti. The period is well documented, for Wakhushti, Sekhnia Chkheidze and other Georgian writers were contemporary with the events recorded, and Chardin, Peyssonnel, Pitton de Tournefort, Krusinski and Hanway were travelling in Georgia or met the Georgian princes in the palaces of Isfahan. The detailed events of this period are, however, relatively unimportant. Wakhtang V (Shah-Nawaz I) died in 1676. The Persian court was uneasy at the growing influence of the house of Mukhrani and against Wakhtang's son Giorgi XI (Shah-Nawaz II or Gurgin-Khan)

[1] The beginnings of the civil war in Imereti are vividly described in the pages of Chardin. Its confusing detail is such that it is impossible to summarize it in a book of the general character of the present work. If, as I hope, one day I am able to edit the Georgian sections of Chardin, I propose to collate the various sources. In the fifty years 1661-1711, no less than sixteen claimants seized, for short periods, the throne of Imereti. They included Bagrat IV, son of Alexander III, Alexander IV, bastard of Bagrati, and Simon his son, Archili of Mukhrani, Dmitri Gurieli, Wakhtang Jujuniashvili, Giorgi III Gurieli, Mamia Gurieli, Giorgi Abashidze and Giorgi VI, another son of Alexander IV. Alexander V, who eventually secured the succession, was a son of Alexander IV and a bastard descendant, therefore, of the royal line. His succession marked the passage of the crown for the third time to illegitimate offspring.

A Turkish Musketeer of the Seventeenth Century (after Castelli).

they played off Irakli of Kakheti (called also Nazar-Ali-Khan). Giorgi ruled in Tiflis from 1675 to 1688 and from 1691 to 1695[1]; Irakli in the interval and again from 1695 to 1703.[2] Three nephews of Giorgi XI, reigned intermittently between 1703 and 1724, namely Wakhtang VI (Hussain-Quli-Khan),[3] Kai Khusraw[4] and Yésé (Ali-Quli-Khan)[5]; and Wakhtang's son Bakari (Shah-Nawaz III) ruled as deputy for his father from 1716–18. In Kakheti a series of Persian governors, subject to the authority of the vice-roy in Tiflis, were appointed between 1657 and 1703. Of these only the adventurous Archili (called also Shah-Nazar-Khan, 1664–1775) was a royal Georgian; but in 1703, David III (Imam-Quli-Khan), a son of Irakli, received the governorship and proceeded to satisfy the intention of the Persian court by continuing his father's conflict with the House of Mukhrani.[6]

[1] For character of Giorgi XI, see Brosset, *H. de la G.*, II, i, 82. He was killed near Kandahar in 1709.

[2] For Irakli of Kakheti, see Wakhushti's description, Brosset, *H. de la G.*, II, i, 87-8: " He did not know Kartli, nor was he familiar with Georgian customs and he had no experience of government. He was foul-mouthed and was addicted to drink, feasting and dissipation, but he was brave, tall and with a fine air about him, kindly and ready to listen to lowly people and to set a check to the great, a thing which he could not always do without the support of the Qæn; he was of a fiery temper, but not to the point of spilling blood." Wakhushti had no friendly feeling towards the Kakhian line, but his description of Irakli is more generous than that of Tournefort (*Voyage*, I, 61).

[3] For Wakhtangi's character, see Wakhushti's description, Brosset, *H. de la G.*, II, i, 100-1, and Sekhnia Chkheidze's, Brosset, *H. de la G.*, II, ii, 28-9.

[4] Kai-Khusraw, who gained distinction in the Afghan campaigns and who administered Kartli for two years (1709-1711), died in Moscow in 1711.

[5] For character of Yésé see Brosset, *H. de la G.*, II, i, 118 and 125.

[6] For the peculiar character of David III of Kakheti, see Brosset, *H. de la G.*, II, i, 181-2.

CHAPTER XVI

EMPERORS ABORTIVE: PETER THE GREAT AND NADIR SHAH (1722-47)

THE first quarter of the eighteenth century was remarkable for the number of paladins who "o'er reached themselves". Louis XIV, now senescent amid the debris of his might, had set the fashion. Charles XII at Pultava had ruptured finally the military and political power of Sweden. Peter the Great in 1711, rode into a dangerous trap by the river Pruth, and only narrowly slipped out. The fashion was maintained into the second quarter. Alberoni did not put his lofty dreams to a blood test, but monarchs so prosaic as Charles VI of Austria and the Empress Anne got their armies badly mauled by the Turks in 1739. It was as though the wind of the South Sea Bubble, wafted through the courts of Europe, had carried the heads of rulers into the clouds of glory which drift in rarefied facility over the mud, the marshes, and the seas of flat reality.

In the East, in Persia, through the spring months of 1722, the decrepit House of Safavi went stumbling to its sordid end. Not again, as after Tahmasp's death, a century and a half before, did the harîms, though full of mountain girls from Georgia and Daghestan, of desert-princes' daughters and women of Turkish blood, not again did they throw out a strong cadet into the light. The one battle of Gulnabad, fought in March of 1722, gave the wealthy cities of central Persia into the hands of a pack of Afghan rievers.

> "The sun had just appeared on the horizon, when the armies began to observe each other with that curiosity so natural on these dreadful occasions. The Persian army just come out of the capital, being composed of whatever was most brilliant at court, seemed as if it had been formed rather to make a show than to fight. The riches and variety of their arms and vestments; the beauty of their horses; the gold and precious stones with which some of their harnesses were covered; and the richness of their tents, contributed to render the Persian camp very pompous and magnificent.
>
> "On the other side there was a much smaller body of soldiers, disfigured with fatigue and the scorching heat of the sun. Their cloathes were so ragged and torn, in so long a march, that they were scarce

sufficient to cover them from the weather: and their horses being adorned with only leather and brass, there was nothing glittering among them but their spears and sabres." [1]

The provinces of Persia slipped into the anarchy which attends upon a state where the few who rule the people forget that they at least must rule. From Mashhad to Baghdad, from Derbend to the Gulf, the day was for the bold men, all power to the hard and rude. Afghans, Kurds, Turkomans, Lazghis and Arabs butchered the patricians, looted all the cities, ravaged the harîms, spilt the caravans, burned out and tortured all the merchants, cut in pieces the Armenians. And bigger men reached out further for the mastery of the racked land, Afghan chiefs, Persian pretenders stepping nearer to the throne over heaps of headless cousins, Khurasani freebooters, brigand khans of Daghestan. The two most tough, most bloody men of the eighteenth century were looming in the moil; Peter, the Russian Emperor, ten years after the Pruth, over-reaching once again; and later Nadir, the obscure Turkoman soldier, who for a decade bestrode Asia from Erzerum to Delhi, in the authentic Mongolian tradition.

Since the death of Taymuraz I, the Russian court had continued to follow with a detached interest the course of events in the Caucasus. Besides the merely military aspects of Russian policy in the neighbourhood of the Northern Caucasus, the Sea of Azov and the Crimea, the trade across the Caspian was, at the end of the seventeenth century, beginning to assume an international importance. The English, the Dutch and the Holsteiners were concerned in the import trade to Persia through Russia and over the Caspian, and the export trade, particularly in silk, by the same route, was accumulating rivalries which, before Hanway died, were to go very far to ruin it.

Between 1678 and 1710, the adventurous Archili of Mukhrani—a king in passage—had taken the place of Taymurazi in earlier days as the principal agent, dupe and provocator of the Russian court in the Georgian lands. His activities aroused the anxiety of his brother, Giorgi XI (Shah-Nawaz II), who, wiser than some of his successors, adhered more or less consistently to the Persian connection.[2] But while Boris Godunov more than a century before had been attracted by the romantic

---

[1] Hanway, *Account of British Trade across the Caspian Sea*, III, 104-5.
[2] Cf. Brosset, *H. de la G.*, II, ii, 350. See also *ibid.*, p. 83, note 1; and p. 91, note 1. Archili lived for many years in Moscow, and at one time conducted a correspondence with the noted savant and traveller, Nicholas Witsen (see *Nord en Oost Tartarye*, Amsterdam, 1785, pp. 504-554). Archili's eldest son, Alexander, was an officer of artillery in the Russian army, and was taken prisoner at the Battle of Narva (1700).

possibilities of Georgian dynastic politics, it was with the Caspian and the Caspian trade that Peter concerned himself. An outrage committed by the Lazghis on the Russian merchants at Shamakha in 1712, was the occasion of Russian intervention in 1722, and it was southward that Peter struck; he sent his armies into Shirvan, Ghilan and Mazandaran. His was not a Caucasian but a Caspian policy; he reached out to the far hot waters of the Gulf; he did not pad through the Georgian passes to plant his garrisons in the dried-out lake-basins of Armenia. The uncouth bully had more genius than all his successors—pompous or crazy or well-meaning—who for the next two centuries gloomed upon his Will.

Peter's intervention was made professedly in the interest of the harassed Shah Hussain, and he met his opposition in the eastern Caucasus, neither from the ruined Persians, nor from the usurping Afghans, but from a powerful confederation of the tribes of Daghestan. In the mountains during the past two decades the reforming propaganda of the Sunni Mudarris Hajji Da'ud Effendi had aroused one of those waves of evangelical hysteria, which sometimes move the needy of the mountains and the desert. The fanatics, released by the collapse of the Persian frontier system, set themselves to pillage the wicked cities of the Shiâhs of Shirvan and they turned also to the ravishing of the fat valleys of Christian Kakheti.[1] The movement out of Daghestan, which gained in impetus and ferocity throughout the eighteenth century until it shook and threatened to disrupt the whole settled life of Georgia and Shirvan, was in character at once, political, economic and religious. The collapse of strong and relatively ordered government in Georgia and north-west Persia, and the grave depopulation which was proceeding particularly in Georgia, was an invitation both to the cupidity and the aggressiveness of the mountain tribes. The poverty and the multiplication of the population in the mountains impelled the hungry tribesmen to go as raiders and conquerors into the provinces where they had formerly sought their livelihood as soldiers, cameleers and labourers. And, indifferent Muslims though they were,[2] the puritanism which is natural to mountaineers, and the intrigues of Turkish agents who had been attracted to the

[1] As early as the period of Bejan-Khan's governorship of Kakheti (1677-83) the Lazghi raids, formerly a nuisance, were becoming a recurrent danger (see Wakhushti, *Hist. de Kakheth* in Brosset, *H. de la G.*, II, i, 178-9).

[2] The Lazghis did not impress Evliya Chelebi as pious Muslims, and Hanway says of them that "they talk very lightly of the pretended miracles of Mahommed; adding that he was a very artful man and whether he has any particular interest with the Almighty, will be best known hereafter" (I, 374).

country since the wars of the late sixteenth century,[1] aroused in the Lazghis that fanaticism, fed upon rapacity, which incited them to perpetual attacks upon the unorthodox Shiâhs and the infidel Georgians. The political heads of the Lazghi confederation were Chulak-Surkhai-Khan of the Ghazi-Ghumukh, and Sultan-Ahmad-Khan, Usmi of Kara-Kaituk. Chulak-Surkhai, Sulkhavi in the pages of Wakhushti, was the particular scourge of the Georgians, until, towards the middle of the century, he was succeeded in the leadership of the tribes by Omar Khan of the Avars.[2]

By August of 1722, operating from Astrakhan, Peter had concentrated at the mouth of the Sulak, an army numbering 82,000 regular infantry—all veterans of the Swedish War, 9,000 dragoons and about 70,000 Cossacks, Kalmucks and Tatars—the first European army of the modern type which had entered upon a campaign in Asia. Tarku, the Shamkhal's capital, was occupied without fighting ; and, after defeating a horde of 16,000 Lazghis under the Usmi Sultan-Ahmad-Khan at Utemish, Peter entered Derbend. "Lo," cried he, when an earthquake shock alarmed his army, "*Nature herself gives me a solemn welcome and makes the very walls to tremble at my power.*"[3] But welcoming Nature failed further to accommodate the Emperor Peter. His flotilla on the Caspian Sea was seriously damaged and almost incapacitated by violent storms and the consequent shortage of supplies made further operations impossible. And so, while Colonel Shipov invaded Ghilan with only two battalions of regular infantry, Peter returned to make a triumphal entry into Moscow (13th December, 1722).

The Russian adventure already had in it the elements of abortive failure. The newest arms and uniforms did not make an efficient army even in the eighteenth century. And the Russian army then—as often since it has—lacked that amalgam of qualities, not easily defined, which go to make

---

[1] The Turks provided by the Treaty of 1612, that the Shamkhal and others of their protégés should not be interfered with by Shah Abbas. In 1638 the Usmi Rustem Khan supported the Turks in hostilities against Persia, and in 1712, after the capture of Shamakha, the first step taken by the Lazghi confederates was the despatch of an embassy to Stambul (see Bartold, article in *E.I.*). The history of Turkish frontier policy with regard to Persia is a neglected subject, full of interest. Beside the Lazghis the Porte maintained constant relations with the Usbeg rulers on the eastern frontier of Persia (see von Hammer, French ed., tome XIV, pp. 77 *et sqq.*).

[2] For an excellent survey of the history of Daghestan, see the article under this head in *E.I.* by Professor Bartold. The political leadership gradually passed from the magnates into the hands of popular religious leaders, such as the four Imams of the early nineteenth century. For this late period and for general history, see Baddeley, *Russian Conquest of the Caucasus.*

[3] Baddeley, p. 27.

success in the business of war. Courage, daring and endurance the Russians always have had, but the sense of teamwork—co-ordination, honourable efficiency, awareness and adaptability, the genius of improvization, they have been without. In the following year, 1723, General Matiushkin took Baku, but the Russian invasion petered gradually over several years to a dreary failure without defeat. The same deficiencies in organization, in supply, transport, and, above all, sanitation, which during the next two decades were to cause the dreadful Russian losses at Okzakov and in the Crimea, ruined their offensive struggle in Shirvan, Ghilan and Mazandaran during the years from 1724 to 1732.

Nevertheless, this first Russian invasion of the Caucasus was for all the local potentates both a portend and a snare.

Peter had sent envoys to King Wakhtangi in Tiflis [1]; had even played to the hopes of the petty Armenian meliks in the mountains of Karabagh.[2] In Persia it was believed that Wakhtangi might yet save the house of Safavi, and the Shah-zadé Tahmasp, who, in Tabriz, was organizing an army to fight the Afghans, sent him " a crown, an aigrette and a jewelled dagger ",[3] and invested him with the title of General of Azerbaijan. Wakhtangi had very considerable forces at his disposal; in 1720 he had been credited with the ability to raise an army of 60,000 for the reduction of Daghestan. The intrigues of the Persian court had compelled him to abandon this expedition under orders from the Shah, and Krusinski suggests that it was his chagrin at this interference which caused him to refrain from intervening to support the Shah against the Afghans.[4]

In Stambul there was alarm at this new aggression of the Russians. The Porte was not unconcerned in Caspian policy, and, in the Black Sea, they had no wish that the favourable position created by Peter's surrender of Azov in 1713, should in any way be modified. And so while a Turkish envoy visited the camp of Peter at Derbend and protracted negoti-

[1] Brosset, *H. de la G.*, II, i, 117, and note 4.
[2] The five Armenian " melikates " in Karabagh were, with their reigning families: Gulistan or Thalish (Beglarian), Chrapiert'h (Israelian), Khachin (Hassan-Jalalian), Varranda (Shahnazarian) and Thizak (Avanian). See *Life of J. Emin*, pp. 332–59, " Note on the Five Meliks of Karabagh " (based on Raffi's Five Meliks, Vienna, 1906). For an account of fighting between the Meliks and the Turks in September 1726, see von Hammer, XIV, 150 (based on Chelebi-zadé).
[3] Brosset, *H. de la G.*, II, i, 117, and note 3; cf. also Hanway, III, 133, and Krusinski, II, 76.
[4] Krusinski, I, 267–8. The fear that Wakhtangi would become himself too strong and that the subjection of the Lazghis would facilitate a Russian invasion, caused the Shah to interrupt the expedition. See also Hanway, III, 86–8.

ations were conducted in Stambul under the ægis of the French ambassador, the Seraskier at Kars received orders to prepare for the invasion of Georgia, and emissaries were despatched to sound the politics of Tiflis.[1]

Wakhtang VI for a few weeks found his favour sought by the agents of three Empires. As a man Wakhtangi was the most pleasing of all the gifted house of Mukhrani. Gentle and studious, of a mind devout and equable, he was yet a gallant soldier, a fine horseman, a courtier of grace and wit. But he was rash and sentimental, without judgment or dexterity, or the peculiar *flair* which jealous men call luck.

In September he cast in his lot with Peter [2]—who was then at Derbend—and moved on Ganja by Kazakh. The Shahzadé Tahmasp, playing on the rivalry between the Mukhranian and Kakhian Bagratids, fended by engaging the support of the Kakhian princes Constantine (Mahmad-Quli-Khan) and Taymurazi, and near Kazakh the two Georgian forces fought an indecisive action. Then, while Constantine, reinforced by the Jari Lazghis, ravaged the villages of Lilo, Wakhtangi sent his son Bakari to ride through the Kakhian district of Saguramo. Sekhnia Chkheidze, the Kartlian envoy in Tabriz, betrayed Wakhtangi's plans to Tahmasp,[3] who responded by according to Constantine of Kakheti the reversion of the Kartlian viceroyalty.

Through the winter months of 1722-3 there was heavy fighting round Tiflis; the Kakhian princes were supported by Mussulman contingents from Erivan and Ganja and by the Lazghis; Wakhtangi by mercenaries from Imereti led by his relative, Simon Abashidze.

With the spring of 1723 the Turks proceeded to intervene. A Turkish envoy informed Wakhtangi that he was taken under the protection of the Grand Signior and warned him to give no aid to the Persians. The King, in answer, sent Edisher Rodshikashvili to Kars with a cheerful message to the effect that he had no intention of sustaining the Persians and that he was awaiting the arrival of the Emperor of Russia.[4] Meanwhile, on May 8th, Constantine suddenly attacked Tiflis with a corps of 7,000 Lazghis; and Wakhtangi and Bakari

---

[1] For the Turkish-Russian negotiations during the summer and autumn of 1722, see von Hammer (French ed.), tome XIV, pp. 90-107; cf. also Brosset, *H. de la G.*, II, i, 116-17; Hanway, III, 173-81.

[2] Brosset, *H. de la G.*, II, i, 118, " hoping thus to free the churches and to strengthen Christianity ".

[3] Tahmasp styled himself Shah from the date of the abdication of his father, Shah-Sultan-Hussain in favour of the Afghan, Mir-Mahmud (21st October, 1722).

[4] Brosset, *H. de la G.*, II, i, 121.

narrowly escaping with their lives fled to Mtzkheta and thence to Gori.

The triumph of the Persian interest was short. On the 12th June a Turkish army, supported by Wakhtangi, Bakari and Simon Abashidze, was under the walls of Tiflis.[1] Constantine surrendered without a fight, and the Persian garrison of the city was massacred by the Janissaries. The political ineptitude of the Georgian princes was characteristic. Having played every card wrong they now all went broke together. Constantine was imprisoned,[2] but Bakari, having been set up in Tiflis by the Turks,[3] connived at his escape, and by the spring of 1724, both Bakari and Constantine had taken to the woods and, with Taymurazi, the three were engaged in a guerrilla warfare against the Turks. Wakhtang VI, a fugitive in Radsha, went to Russia, and at Tsaritsin heard of the death of the Emperor Peter (28th January 1725)

The Turkish commander Ishak Pasha, a Mussulman Jaqeli of Samtzkhé, set up as prince in Tiflis, Yésé, a disreputable brother of Wakhtangi,[4] and, while the Pasha proceeded to levy taxes on men, goats, oxen, buffaloes, horses, vegetables and fruit-trees, the last Mukhranian ruler, who was remarkable only for his cupidity, set about confiscating lands *en bloc* by which means he soon became " extremely rich ".[5]

The death of the Emperor Peter with the consequent abandonment of his plans, and the continuing anarchy in Persia, allowed the Turks to pursue a rather incoherent policy of aggrandisement over a wide area from which all the elements of stable government had disappeared.[6] They grasped far and wide. In 1725, along the Black Sea, they installed a garrison in Poti and occupied the province of Odishi, the better part of Mingrelia.[7] The Imerians, enervated by half a century of civil war and dominated by a Turkish garrison in

---

[1] Brosset, *H. de la G.*, II, i, 123; Hanway, III, 178; von Hammer from Turkish sources gives the date as July 10th.
[2] Thus confirming a Georgian proverb " To trust an Ottoman is to lean upon a wave " (Hanway, III, 178).
[3] Bakari, who had ruled in Tiflis from 1716 to 1718 under the Persian style of Shah-Nawaz III, was now dubbed by the Turks Ibrahim Pasha.
[4] Yésé assumed consecutively the Persian style of Ali-Quli-Khan and the Turkish style of Mustafa Pasha.
[5] Brosset, *H. de la G.*, II, i, 125.
[6] By a treaty concluded 2nd October, 1723, the Shah-zadé Tahmasp, in Tabriz, had ceded to the Russians Derbend, Baku and the Caspian littoral provinces of Ghilan, Mazandaran and Astarabad. Peter in return had undertaken to establish Tahmasp on the throne of Persia (von Hammer, XIV, 98–9). After protracted negotiations with the Russians lasting until June 1724, the Turks accepted the implications of this treaty, but received themselves a " free hand " in Persian Iraq, Azerbaijan, Mughan and Karabagh, Ganja, Erivan and all Georgia (von Hammer, XIV, 106–7).
[7] Brosset, *H. de la G.*, II, i, 315.

the citadel of Kutais,[1] were incapable of any resistance. In Persia, during the same year, the Turks took Tabriz and advanced to within three days' march of Isfahan. In 1726 they occupied Kazvin and Maragha. Next year a treaty which proved very temporary, signed at Hamadan with the Afghan usurper Ashraf Khan, confirmed the Turkish hegemony over all those parts of the Caucasus which they might choose to hold.[2]

Yésé died in 1728 and Ishak Pasha proceeded to divide Georgia into a number of districts which seemed destined, like Samtzkhé, to become hereditary pashaliks of the Ottoman Empire: Erast Qaplanis-shvili received Somkheti and Sabaratiano; Bagrat Tzitzishvili, all the country below Mtzkheta; Giv Amilakhori had Zemo-Kartli, the Eristavi Shanshé was confirmed in the *khéoba* of the Ksani; and the Eristavi Taymurazi of the Aragvi had the place of his cousin Otari who had fled to Russia.[3]

Nevertheless, the country after five years of tyranny began to stir. Between 1728 and 1731 there were bloody risings and internecine fighting in Upper Georgia. As only the Georgians know, they made war in the wooded country—Taymuraz Machabeli, the Eristavi Shanshé, Taymurazi of the Aragvi and his brother Rewazi. Anarchy was rampant; the swoop and cut of little fights, the grilling enfilading of convoys in the mountains, the bitter sieges of castles and tall towers. Constantine of Kakheti first made common cause with the Turks against his enemy, Shanshé of the Ksani, then turned against them and was killed (1731).

Meanwhile, the Lazghis burned and ravaged all Kakheti, raided into Kartli, and raked even into Javakheti where they routed a considerable Turkish force.[4]

All this time with ponderous incompetence, a dull persistence, the Porte pursued new schemes of expanding power. A pasha arrived at Poti with orders to bring into submission all the littoral as far as Azov (1733). He summoned Alexander V of Imereti to assist him; and Alexander marched up through Odishi with his levies, in spite of the protestation of the

---

[1] Brosset, *H. de la G.*, II, i, 284. A Turkish garrison had been established in Kutais since 1669—the earlier period of the Imerian civil war.

[2] For details see von Hammer, XIV, 155–6; cf. Hanway, III, 254–5. During the same period a Russo-Turkish commission was engaged in delimiting the frontiers of the territories acquired by the two powers from Persia in the Caucasus. A French diplomat, M. Allion, was attached to this commission, but was unable to accompany it (von Hammer, XIV, 156–8).

[3] Cf. Brosset, *H. de la G.*, II, i, 127, and genealogical trees.

[4] Brosset, *H. de la G.*, II, i, 128. The Lazghis on this occasion adopted a most peculiar method of insulting the enemy corpses.

EMPERORS ABORTIVE

Dadiani Otia that "*it is not good for us that they should be masters of the littoral*".[1] They burned the fine old church at Ilori, spoiling the frescoes. Sharvashidze in Abkhazeti submitted without a fight and consented to become a Muslim. But when the allies crossed the Kodori, and the Pasha proposed to march through the coastal forests of Jiketi, Alexander and the Imerians leaving all their baggage-train retreated in the night. Fighting then broke out between the Abkhaz and the Turks, and the Pasha after a running battle was forced to escape by sea, with the loss of all his baggage and the greater part of his force.[2]

Events in Persia were now beginning to take a remarkable turn and within a decade the whole political situation in Middle Asia was entirely transformed by the activities of one man. The Turkoman bandit, Nadir-Quli-Khan, was already forty-six years old when after a series of coups and murders he succeeded in restoring the Safavi prince Tahmasp to the blood-stained throne of Persia. Violent, bold and brutal, alert and cynical, Nadir was the ultimate expression of an age of dreadful anarchy. He laughed at peril and religion, was immune to chivalry or pity, believed supremely in himself—the ruthless steppe-land rider, unlettered empire-builder.

In February 1732, the new Shah Tahmasp signed a peace with Turkey, which, with few advantages to Persia, in effect confirmed the terms of the Treaty of Hamadan made by the usurper Ashraf in 1727. One clause, however, provided for joint action to compel the evacuation by the Russians of Shirvan, Ghilan and Mazandaran.[3]

Nadir, taking advantage of popular opinion which was discontented with the Treaty,[4] seized and imprisoned Tahmasp and renewed the war with the Turks. The position of the Turks was really very weak. The capital was disorganized as a result of the recent revolt of the Janissaries under the Albanian Patrona, and the new Sultan Mahmud I was expecting war on his European frontiers. In the autumn of 1733, the only competent Turkish general, Topal Osman Pasha, was defeated at Kerkud and Daylem.[5] The whole Turkish defence collapsed; Nadir occupied Tabriz and the other Turkish conquests of the past ten years and proceeded to invade Georgia and Shirvan (spring of 1734).

In the Caucasian provinces there was all confusion; the

[1] Brosset, *H. de la G.*, II, i, 317.   [2] *Ibid.*, p. 317.
[3] Hanway, IV, 64.   [4] *Idem.*, pp. 65–6.
[5] For the interesting biography of Topal Osman and for an account of his romantic friendship with the Frenchman, Vincent Arnaud, see Hanway, IV, 100–8.

Russians sent Wakhtangi to Derbend, intending him to seize Shamakha and invade Kartli.¹ In Kartli Giv Amilakhori seized the citadel of Gori; then rode to join Nadir before Ganja. In June 1735 Nadir inflicted a severe defeat near Erivan on another Turkish army under Abdulla Kuprulu Pasha. Erivan, Lori, Ganja and Tiflis fell into his hands. He ravaged Kartli, destroyed Shamakha and defeated the forces of the Usmi of Kara-Kaituk.² On the Persian Navruz (New Year's Day—8th March, 1736) Nadir was proclaimed Shah, before his assembled army in the plains of Mughan.

The circumstances of international politics beyond the Danube now served his vast ambitions. A combination of the Russians and the Austrians was preparing against the Turks in Europe,³ and both the Sultan and the Empress Anne were concerned to secure themselves against the hostility of Nadir on their Caucasian frontiers. In 1735 Nadir's Ambassador in St. Petersburg had already negotiated a treaty by which the Russians withdrew to the line of the Sulak, thus abandoning all the conquests of Peter in Shirvan, Ghilan and Mazandaran.⁴ In the following year (1736) a month after the proclamation of Nadir as Shah, Ahmad Pasha of Baghdad signed the Treaty of Ganja, by which the frontiers existing between the two empires previous to 1732 were in substance, restored.⁵

Nadir proceeded to carry out his cherished project for the conquest of India, and in December 1736, his army left Isfahan for Kandahar. Before undertaking this new expedition, Nadir had, however, provided for the government of the north-western provinces, which, so recently conquered, represented a problem of great importance since they bordered on those two empires, from either one of which he might

---

¹ Brosset, *H. de la G.*, II, i, 129.
² *Ibid.*, p. 132; cf. also Chkeidze in Brosset, *H. de la G.*, II, ii, 47–9.
³ The pending war broke out in 1737 and was terminated in 1739 by the Treaty of Belgrad, under the terms of which the Porte recovered from Austria all those parts of Bosnia and Serbia ceded under the Treaty of Passarovich in 1718. So far as Russia was concerned the results of the war were negative. The Russian conquests in Moldavia and the Crimea, and the city of Okzakov were abandoned. The city of Azov was to be demolished and its neighbourhood neutralized and the Russians were prohibited from maintaining armed ships in the Black Sea and the Caspian. On the death of the Empress Anne (next year, 1740) the German party in Russia, who had promoted this disastrous war, were driven from power.
⁴ Hanway, IV, 116–18. For an account of the shrewd diplomacy by which Nadir managed to exploit the implications of the pending war in Europe, see also *idem.*, pp. 121–2, 132.
⁵ Hanway, IV, 133–5. The fact that Nadir was a Sunni formed the basis for provisions in the Treaty whereby " the Shah, as a pure effect of the greatness of his soul, will cause the differences in religion to cease by abolishing the sect of the Schias, and for the future tolerating only the Sunnis ". Cf. *Papouna Orbeliani*, in Brosset, *H. de la G.*, II, ii, 63.

expect an immediate aggression in the event of the miscarriage of his Indian schemes.

His brother Ibrahim Khan, who was left as generalissimo of the forces in Persia, was particularly entrusted with the governorship of Azerbaijan and the surveillance of the north-western frontier.[1] The more dangerous of the Georgian nobles were seized and forced to accompany Nadir as honoured volunteers on the road to Kandahar. The most distinguished of these prisoners was Taymurazi of Kakheti who had succeeded his brother Constantine in 1731; his son, Irakli, later followed him to Kandahar. The formidable Kilij-Ali-Khan (or Khanjal) was appointed to overlook Kartli, while Alexander (called also Ali-Mirza) an insignificant son of David III of Kakheti, was made Vali of Tiflis, with the Persian Safi-Khan to watch by him.[2]

All throughout the Persian Empire heavy taxes were levied for the costs of the Indian expedition, and Kilij-Ali, after the manner of his Turkish predecessors, set about squeezing taxes out of trees, stock, farming-land and vines.[3] The people began to growl; soldiers were conscripted; hostages taken in great numbers,[4] and sent along the road to Kandahar. The Eristavi Shanshé revolted in Zemo-Kartli and brought in hordes of Lazghis to pillage the country. Even Ali-Mirza stirred, and Tamara, Taymurazi's queen, fearful for her husband and her son as hostages, narrowly averted a general rising in Kakheti.

Taymurazi returned from Kandahar in 1738[5] and next year took part in an expedition against the Jari Lazghis, during which Nadir's brother Ibrahim was killed.

In the autumn of 1741 after his return from the Indian expedition, Nadir came up into Daghestan with the object of avenging the death of his brother. But, Hanway observes,

"there is a proverbial saying among the Persians, 'If any Persian king is a fool, let him march against the Lesgees'".[6]

---

[1] Brosset, *H. de la G.*, II, i, 196.
[2] *Ibid.*, p. 132; cf. also Chkheidze in Brosset, *H. de la G.*, II, ii, 96.
[3] *Ibid.*, p. 132. *Ibid.*, p. 49.
[4] The hostages arrested in 1735 included Abel, *mo'uravi* of Kisiqi, Giv Amilakhori and Kai-Khusraw Avalishvili, and Mamuka, Prince of Mukhrani (of the junior branch descended from Constantine, a brother of Wakhtang V). Amilakhori and Avalishvili subsequently took to the hills; Mamuka escaped to Russia (Chkeidze in Brosset, *H. de la G.*, II, ii, 49). In 1736 Otar Amilakhori, Kai-Khusraw Qaplanishvili, the Archbishop Kirilé Tzitzishvili, Avtandil Javakhishvili, Peshang Palavandishvili, Farsadan, Melik of Lori, Bahadur, Melik of Somkheti, and Ali-Quli-Beg, the *Amir-Ejibi*, were all sent to Persia (*idem.*, p. 53).
[5] Irakli remained with Nadir in India and was present at the Battle of Karnal and the sack of Delhi; see *Vie du Roi Érécli II* par Oman Kherkhéulidze, published by Brosset in *H. de la G.*, II, ii, 203–27; also Add. XII to same volume, *Lettres du Roi Érécli II*, i, *Campagne de l'Inde*, pp. 354–69.
[6] Hanway, IV, 223.

Nadir received a serious setback in the mountains of the Ghazi-Ghumukh,[1] and a few days later, a force of 8,000 men which was covering his rear, was badly mauled. His army of 35,000, the pick of his Indian veterans, was reduced to a bare 20,000 and he withdrew to Derbend, where he found himself for some time dependent for provisions on supplies from Russia, which were sold at enormous profit by the merchants of Astrakhan, despite the strict prohibition of the Russian Government.[2] The Russians, suspicious of Nadir's intentions, began to concentrate troops at Kislyar; they sent Bakari to Astrakhan[3] and negotiated with the Lazghi leaders who had demanded the protection of the Empress Elizabeth, at the same time offering to put 66,000 men into the field to co-operate against Nadir.[4] Nadir while he engaged the English Captain Elton to organize Persian shipping on the Caspian,[5] turned his attention to Georgia and Turkey where the position was equally threatening to his interests. The onerous taxes and requisitions which he was imposing on the whole of his dominions to finance his military undertakings, produced among the Georgians a state of savage desperation. Corn had become so dear that the peasants were living on boiled nuts and giving their children into slavery in default of finding the corn tax; and slaves were so cheap that men were sold for four shillings each. In order to escape the taxes on vines and fruit-trees, the people destroyed them wholesale, and great numbers emigrated so that "Turkey was full of Kartlians".[6] In Tiflis, thousands of wild Indian and Afghan troops terrified the population,[7] and the revolt of the Eristavi Shanshé was suppressed in the bloody desolation of the valleys of the Liakhvi, the Ksani and the Aragvi.[8] Nadir summoned the principal Georgian nobles to Derbend and covered them with gifts and honours. But while the cautious Taymurazi endeavoured to persuade his master to relax the rigidity of his tyranny, Giv Amilakhori, who had been appointed *wakil* of Kartli, fled suddenly from Tiflis and lit an insurrection more formidable than that of Shanshé.

In 1742 the outbreak of war between Russia and Sweden,

---

[1] Hanway, IV, 224, "they came down during the night and put his rearguard into the utmost confusion. They even attacked the royal tent, took away some of Nadir's treasures and several of his women".
[2] *Idem.*, p. 225.   [3] Brosset, *H. de la G.*, II, i, 135.
[4] Hanway, IV, 227, "we are determined to hold the golden border of her imperial robes".   [5] *Idem.*, p. 225.
[6] *Chronique de Papouna Orbeliani*, in Brosset, *H. de la G.*, II, ii, 57–61.   [7] *Ibid.*, p. 58.
[8] *Ibid.*, p. 59. Shanshé escaped to Akhaltzikhé where he was surrendered to Nadir by the Turks, who were at that time engaged with the Persians in the protracted negotiations at Erzerum which preceded the war of 1743-7.

averted from Nadir the danger of hostilities from the north. His position, however, was still precarious. His defeats in Daghestan had tarnished the legend of his invincibility, while the revolts in Georgia were but a local manifestation of the state of feeling throughout all the Mussulman provinces of his Empire. The big sanguine man was elderly, and had become rather heavy; he was getting rattled and knowing that he could not afford to lose another battle,[1] he went into another war with Turkey (June 1743).

Giv Amilakhori, who ten years before had led the insurrection against the Turks, now joined forces with them against Nadir. Sudden, bold and popular, he was the reverse of the calculating Taymurazi who for these long years had ground his axe with Nadir. The Turks, with Amilakhori, met Taymurazi and the Persians at Thédo-tzminda near Gori and the latter were beaten; but soon after Irakli redeemed his father's defeat by the rout of Yusuf Pasha at Ruisi on the Liakvi, and in the following year a Safavi pretender whom the Turks had sent into Daghestan and Shirvan was defeated and, during his flight, captured by Irakli.[2] The two Kakhian princes now received the reward of their perpetual patience. Nadir was fighting a difficult war in the Armenian and Kurdish mountains, and to ensure his interest in Georgia he appointed Taymurazi to rule over Kartli and Irakli over Kakheti.[3]

The war lasted for nearly three more years. In spite of the appalling state of Georgia when it began,[4] shrewd old Taymurazi strengthened his position and at the same time effected some amelioration of general conditions.[5] Nadir was dependent on the Kakhian princes, father and son, to secure his north-western flank and to prevent the junction of the Turks with the Lazghis and the rebellious khans of Shirvan. And Taymurazi could draw on Persian resources to enable him in his own interest to frustrate the Turks, to get the better of Giv Amilakhori,[6] and to clear out the Lazghi bands whose raids had now for so long been a curse upon the country. In July of 1744, Taymurazi was crowned with many celebrations and some pomp in Tiflis and he later attended similar ceremonies for his son in Kakheti.[7]

[1] Hanway, IV, 238-9.
[2] *Papouna Orbeliani* in Brosset, H. de la G., II, ii, 77-80; cf. Hanway, IV, 242.
[3] Brosset, H. de la G., II, i, 136, and P.O. in Brosset, H. de la G., II, ii, 83 and 86; in July 1744, according to *Papouna Orbeliani*.
[4] P.O. in Brosset, H. de la G., II, ii, 73.   [5] *Ibid.*, p. 83.
[6] Amilakhori eventually surrendered during the summer of 1746, and was treated by Taymurazi with much consideration (P.O. in Brosset, H. de la G., II, ii, 97 *et sqq.*).
[7] *Ibid.*, pp. 86-7 and 100-1.

REVOLUTIONS OF THE GEORGIAN KINGDOM

The war dragged on and while Nadir laid siege without success to Kars, Taymurazi's cavalry raided into Javakheti,[1] and even as far as Ardahani.[2] Taymurazi reorganized his army with the historic four banners of the mediæval kingdom,[3] and so excellent were his methods that later in 1746, Nadir was sending to borrow 170 Georgian gunners for special services in Azerbaijan,[4] while Hanway avers that Taymurazi "had formed a regiment of infantry after the European manner".[5]

In the summer of 1745, Nadir at last, after a hard and weary war, won the spectacular victory which he was seeking and which was so necessary to restore both his own self-esteem and the prestige of his régime. The army of the Seraskier, Damat Muhammad Pasha, was routed near Erivan, and although the fighting continued through another year, the war was staleing to its end.[6]

In the first months of 1747, Nadir, triumphant, avid and suspicious,[7] proceeded to rack new taxes from all the sullen provinces and he assessed Kartli and Kakheti at 300,000 *tumans*, a sum calculated at once to relieve the Persian treasury and to crush the aspirations of Taymurazi and his son.[8]

Taymurazi, confident in the new building of his power, prepared to resist; evacuated his army and the principal inhabitants of Tiflis to Ananuri; set the castles in a state of defence; and in Kakheti began to withdraw the peasants into four strong places.[9] Nadir, to pacify the dangers of a formidable revolt, sent a courier with the offer of some slight reductions in the assessment. Meanwhile, the months dragged on and, while there were divided counsels among Taymurazi's nobles, some of the mountain levies at Ananuri, growing restless, showed signs of impending mutiny. Finally Taymurazi decided to go to Persia himself to intercede with the Shah, who was then in Khurasan. The Georgian king found

---

[1] P.O. in Brosset, *H. de la G.*, II, ii, 89–90.   [2] *Ibid.*, p. 109.
[3] *Ibid.*, p. 101.   [4] *Ibid.*, p. 108.   [5] Hanway, IV, 259, note.
[6] *Idem.*, p. 252. Peace was signed on the 11th January, 1747. Cf. Brosset, *H. de la G.*, II, ii, 113 and note 2.
[7] Hanway, IV, 258. "From an incessant fatigue and labour of mind, attended with some infirmities of body, he had contracted a disposition, which in the generality of Mankind is called by the name of peevishness, but in him was a diabolical fierceness.... His avidity, as common to sickly minds, increased with his years."
[8] Brosset, *H. de la G.*, II, ii, 114, note 4, estimates the sum to be levied on Georgia as the equivalent of £337,500—" somme véritablement fabuleuse pour la Géorgie ". Hanway commenting on the character of Nadir says (IV, 267) " He had studied the state of the finances and knew the particular revenue of every province; but he was so great a master of the art of ways and means that he overshot his mark ". *Papouna Orbeliani* (Brosset, *H. de la G.*, II, ii, 73, 114, etc.) gives interesting details as to the financial methods of Nadir, which included an enquiry into the standard of living of the nobles of Kartli.
[9] P.O. in Brosset, *H. de la G.*, II, ii, 115–17.

Persia in a ferment and while he entered into relations with the Shah's nephew, Ali-Quli-Khan who was his own son-in-law, Nadir alternately cajoled and threatened both of them. But the old bandit's end was near. Some of his officers decided after the Persian saying "*to breakfast off him ere he should sup off them*",[1] and he was murdered in his camp near Mashhad towards the end of May 1747. With the stern grip of tyranny removed, all the provinces of Persia plunged once more into anarchy and internecine war.

[1] Cf. E. G. Browne, *Literary History of Persia*, IV, 137.

CHAPTER XVII

INDIAN SUMMER OF THE BAGRATIDS: TAYMURAZ II AND IRAKLI II
(1747–1798)

"In Asiatic camps, pitched in the night time in their irregular way, a person when wanted is not easily found, especially the Georgians among whom no sort of regularity or order is kept; but from eight to twelve at night, there is as much hallooing and noise, as if they were already beaten by the enemy; servants hunting for masters, and masters for servants till they find one another exactly like cows and calves in a dispersed herd: then they directly spread the table-cloths, set down the skinful of wine, eat and drink till they are full, and then sleep as sound as a rock, without watch or sentry; so that if the beasts of the field were to come and prey on their bodies, they would hardly be sensible of pain till sunrise. The only watchful man Emin ever saw among them was the prince himself, who sat up sometimes till one, sometimes till two in the morning, with his household servants, whom one might see often half-asleep standing upon their legs before the prince, till they dropped down upon the ground, and afforded him great amusement." [1]

THUS wrote the traveller, Joseph Emin, of the Georgians and their king, Irakli II, in the year 1763.

During the second half of the eighteenth century, the Georgian kingdom was revived under that brave and cunning king, and, for a few decades, the shadow of antique pretensions was illumined by the bright flare of one of the most gallant gestures in history. The renewed Georgian kingdom was, all through its brief and turgid heyday, a "one-man show", and the one man was Irakli, who, in 1747 at the age of thirty-one was already the veteran of fifteen years of Asiatic diplomacy and war. The kingdom which he and his elderly and failing father began to build was essentially a personal state rather than a restored Kingdom of the Georgians, and it seemed to be assuming, if it had continued, a Caucasian rather than a Georgian character. Circumstances favoured this development. The Persian Empire, after the death of Nadir Shah, lay for many years in a state of impotent anarchy and when some degree of order emerged, the new power of Karim-

[1] Emin, pp. 247-8.

INDIAN SUMMER OF THE BAGRATIDS

Khan-i-Zand at Shiraz did not extend beyond the Araks. The north-western provinces of Persia invited the rule of any master, and while the incompetent pretenders in Tabriz, Muhammad-Hassan-Khan-Kajar and later Asad-Khan, threatened to perpetuate the miseries of civil war, the petty Mussulman rulers of the eastern Caucasus regarded with respect and little animosity the sage Taymurazi and his able son, Irakli. And Irakli and his father turned naturally, and of necessity, to the pursuit of a vigorous and aggressive policy on their eastern frontier.

In 1747-8, during the absence of Taymurazi in Persia, Irakli had confronted and defeated the dangerous insurrection of the Mussulman elements in Georgia who had rallied round Abdulla-beg the son of the apostate Yésé brother of Wakhtang VI. The movement which had at once sought to restore the Mukhranian line and to re-establish their influence in the Mussulman tradition had combined interests so antagonistic as those of the great *gwari* of Baratashvili and the Tatar nomads of Baidar and Kaikul.

In 1749, after the return of Taymurazi from Persia, the two kings undertook a series of operations beyond their southeastern frontier which were as urgent as they were ambitious. Irakli occupied Erivan at the request of the inhabitants and defeated the marauding forces of Muhammad-Hassan-Khan-Kajar. In the following year Taymurazi took Shahverdi-Khan of Ganja under his protection; and defeated the truculent Sharji-Panah, a town-crier fugitive from Persia, who had put himself at the head of the Jevanshir Turkomans and who was tyrannizing the Armenian *meliks* of Karabagh.[1]

In 1752 the two kings sustained a severe defeat at the hands of Hajji-Chelebi, Khan of Shaki, who had been successful in negotiating the defection of their Mussulman allies, the Khans of Ganja and Erivan. In July of the same year Irakli beat Asad-Khan, the usurper of authority in Azerbaijan. But in the following spring a second victory of Hajji-Chelebi over the Georgian levies was followed by the sanguinary incursion of his son, Agha-Kish, into Kartli.

In spite of changing fortunes in the field the supremacy of Georgian arms in the eastern Caucasus was maintained and extended. The petty Mussulman rulers lacked cohesion and although their policies were veering, they accepted the hegemony of Irakli in the interval of Persian weakness.

---

[1] For an account of Sharji Panah, see Notes on the Meliks of Karabagh, in Emin, pp. 341 *et seq.*

In 1760 Irakli, who was acting with Karim-Khan-i-Zand, defeated and captured Muhammad-Hassan-Khan-Kajar, whom he delivered to the Persians.[1] In 1767 and 1769, the Georgians conducted operations against the Kurds round Ararat who had refused tribute [2]; in 1780 after suppressing an insurrection of the people of Erivan, Irakli led a punitive expedition against the Kurds into the district of Bayazid [3]; and, in 1786, Ioanné, Prince of Mukhrani, intervened with Georgian troops and artillery to restore Kalb-Ali to the khanate of Nakhchevan. A Georgian *mo'uravi* supervised the administration of Erivan until 1795, and, while the Khan of Shusha was "bound by friendship" to the Georgian crown, Ganja was administered jointly by representatives of the King and of the Khan.[4] But while Irakli revived a Georgian political supremacy in Shirvan and north-eastern Armenia which recalled the glories of the twelfth century, a formidable scourge devastated the lands of both the Christian and the Muslim peasantry. The Lazghi raids into the settled lands of Georgia and Shirvan had increased in force and frequency since the time of Shah Abbas I, and after the death of Shah Nadir they became endemic. In fact the insurgence of the Kurdish tribes in the south-east and the terror imposed by the Lazghis in the north-east, were alike symptomatic of the dissolution of effective government and with it of all settled cultured life throughout the Caucasian isthmus. This life was so hard crippled, so long bled, that of itself it could not recover. Only Irakli, subtle, brave and desperate, growing old, more cunning, and less strong, like a driven fox, was making the fine futile gesture of the last king of a broken people.

While Irakli, king of a city, pursued his tortuous diplomacy and short campaigns against the princes of the smaller cities of Armenia and Shirvan, the Lazghi hordes girt up themselves to ravage all the pastures and the valleys of the land. Nur'Ali-Khan, the Avar *nutzal*, and his son, Omar, were the political chieftains of the loose confederation of the tribes of Daghestan, and they captained the biggest expeditions. Irakli was able always to beat the larger forces in the field, but the smaller more frequent raids of bands up to 400 or 500 strong under their *bélads* or guides, plundering, kidnapping and burning, were more difficult to fend. In 1752, the Lazghis were

---

[1] Brosset, H. de la G., II, ii, 218.   [2] Ibid., p. 219.   [3] Ibid., p. 224.
[4] Ibid., p. Br. 226. The Georgian representatives were high nobles; at Erivan, Ioanné, Prince of Mukhrani, a son-in-law of Irakli, and at Ganja Kai-Khusraw Andronikashvili. Zaza Tarkhanashvili was the first to be appointed *mahmandar* of Erivan, in 1749 (P.O., in Brosset, H. de la G., II, ii, 147).

defeated at Damghisi, and in 1754 and 1755, Irakli routed Omar Khan. But in 1757, during a period of incessant raids, the noted *bélad* Chonchol-Musa-Htarisa surprised and nearly succeeded in destroying the two kings at Krtzkhilowani. Two years later the *bélads* Chonchol-Musa and Kokhta ravaged all Upper Kartli, and in 1760 other bands were devastating Karaia and the district of Javakheti bordering on Samtzkhé.

So serious was the threat to the stability of the kingdom that in 1760 the aged Taymurazi [1] passed into Russia to seek the help of the court of St. Petersburg. The Lazghi attacks increased in intensity until the year 1767 when they penetrated even as far as Radsha.[2] At the same time the tribal restlessness had spread to the north and the Kabardáns were attacking the Russians round Mozdok.[3]

Emin the enterprising little Armenian soldier-of-fortune, who was in Daghestan in 1765, gives a remarkably circumstantial account of events at that time, and while his descriptions of the raids are sometimes appalling, he has some good to say of the Lazghis.

Emin attributes the worst violence of the Lazghis not to the natives of the mountains themselves but to those of Persian, Georgian and Armenian blood who had grown up as prisoners amongst them, and he says that before foreigners became common in the ranks of the Lazghis,

> "their abstinence in regard to slaves had been remarkable.... It was death to anyone who offered to meddle with a slave woman, unless he chose to marry her".[4]

Emin maintains that the leaders of the raids were in many cases Georgians

> "from the highest degree to the meanest of subjects; who, being oppressed by tyrannical princes or masters, went over to them (the Lazghis) and being chosen by them as their guides, marching at the head of thousands, carried fire and sword through the country; while the Georgians were sitting in banquet-houses, eating and drinking like beasts".[5]

The Armenian traveller is not a friendly critic of Irakli and his subjects; his statement is, however, confirmed by Georgian records. In 1789, we find the Jari Lazghis making a raid on Kisiqi under the leadership of a native of Kazakh; in the same year the three sons of the Eristavi of the Ksani, with Zakharia Tzitzishvili, ravaged the valley of the Mtkvari at the

---

[1] Brosset, *H. de la G.*, II, ii, 218; cf. Emin, p. 175. [2] *Ibid.*, 219.
[3] Baddeley, p. 33.   [4] Emin, p. 284.   [5] *Idem.*, 264.

head of Lazghi bands, while Mikéla Argutashvili, a fugitive from Irakli's court, raided Somkheti and carried off two hundred prisoners.¹

Emin admits and indeed boasts that Armenians had an equal or greater part in the leadership of these raids and devastations, and he expresses a great admiration for Michael, an Armenian *bélad* of Lazghi bands, who was killed by Irakli.²

The Lazghi devastations had a real social and economic significance. As the slave trade in Western Georgia constituted, in effect, a forced emigration of the people from a land where political conditions had made all settled life intolerable, so in the eastern Caucasus the movement of the Lazghis, recruited and led by the uprooted elements of the settled population, represented the subversion by the dispossessed of the authority of those elements—both feudal Georgian and imperial Persian—who by their demoralization and their ineptitude had failed to maintain that order and security which is the least required of masters. The Georgian Annals of the eighteenth century and Emin give a picture sufficiently instructive of the dissolution of a feudal, agrarian and mercantile society, and of the emergence through anarchy of new incoherent elements compounded of invaders and of the dispossessed. Such were the conditions in all probability of earlier and greater changes in Asiatic history, of which there has been left no circumstantial picture; and such, maybe, were the social and psychological conditions of the lands of Western Europe after the collapse of the authority and fixed institutions of the Roman Empire.

In the eighteenth century the Middle Eastern cultures, incapable of reproducing the elements of an organic continuing social life, were in process of disintegration. Fresh raw peoples were ready to repeat the traditional processes of Asiatic history —Cossacks and Turkomans, Afghans, Kurds and Lazghis. But now a new force which does not even yet know itself— dynamic and incomprehensible—the young mechanistic culture of the West, was preparing to crush, morcelate and remould, all the elements decrepit or primitive of the eastern world.

¹ Brosset, *H. de la G.*, II, ii, 256-7.
² " When his firelock was broken, he drew his sword, and with his dagger in his left hand, defended himself, fighting and calling Heraclius by all manner of bad names . . . Michael received nine balls through his body before he fell . . . his heart was amazingly large and his liver was as black as jet; which puts me in mind of an expression of the sailors, as a rebuke to a cowardly man, 'Go your way, you white-livered fellow!' The appelation signifies that a black liver belongs to a brave man. When his son was taken, he said that his father was seventy-two years of age " (Emin, p. 391).

INDIAN SUMMER OF THE BAGRATIDS

Irakli, nervous, brittle and intelligent in his small tumbling world, felt out this way and that for the bricks of some stability. He cast artillery,[1] he set about to organize regular troops, a regiment of guards on the model of European courts,[2] and attempted to impose conscription.[3] He brought in Greek miners from the Levant to work the gold and silver deposits of Akhtala,[4] and he sacrificed his plate to lay the foundations of a stable currency.[5] He built forts in Kakheti and with his weak resources attempted to set up a block-house system against the Lazghis.[6] He recalled the Catholicos Antoni, a Mukhranian prince suspected of Romanism, from Russia, and helped him to restore the ancient universities of Tiflis and Telavi where they began to teach Bachmeister, then fashionable in Russia.[7] He surrounded himself with competent Armenians; Joseph Emin, a former favourite of London society and veteran of the German wars,[8] Ter Philipé Qaitmazian the philosopher and scholar,[9] and the accomplished Mirza-Gurgina Enikolophian who became his principal diplomatic agent.[10]

A redoubtable soldier and a master of all the tricks, quick turns and subtleties that went by the name of statesmanship in contemporary politics, Irakli held a solitary place in the Caucasus and he had no little renown in Persia, in Turkey and in Russia. His name was spoken in the West, and to Frederick the Great is attributed the remark: " *Moi en Europe, et en Asie l'invincible Hercule* ".[11]

---

[1] Brosset, *H. de la G.*, II, ii, 246, under the supervision of Paata Andronikashvili, who had gained a wide experience in the Russian artillery.
[2] *Ibid.*, p. 223 ; cf. *ibid.*, pp. 142 and 189.
[3] *Ibid.*, pp. 223, 246–7. The conscription was on the basis of one month's service in every year. The King himself, and his sons, were trained with the regular troops, and malingering conscripts were flogged. Cf. also Emin, p. 207.
[4] *Ibid.*, p. 222 ; cf. Dubois, IV, 142–5. In 1785 the miners were slaughtered by the Lazghis. Brosset, *H. de la G.*, II, ii, 252.
[5] *Ibid.*, p. 169.   [6] *Ibid.*, p. 142.
[7] *Ibid.*, pp. 234, 237.
[8] Joseph Emin was born at Hamadan in 1726, was taken by his father to India, and found his way to England as a sailor (1751). He lived for some time in London in great poverty, but eventually through the influence of Edmund Burke, Lord Northumberland and other highly placed friends, he was able to obtain the military training which it was his ambition to receive. He took part in the expedition to St. Malo (1758) and saw some fighting in Germany. In 1759–61 he visited the Armenian districts of Turkey to study the situation with a view to promoting insurrection. Between 1762 and 1769 he was in Russia and the Caucasus, but he finally despaired of his patriotic plans and went to India where he saw service as an ensign in the E.I.C.'s forces. He died in Calcutta in 1809.
[9] Brosset, *H. de la G.*, II, ii, 237 ; cf. Emin, p. 226.
[10] Mirza Gurgina, a native of Karabagh and a competent linguist, was sent on a mission to Stambul in 1774 (Brosset, *H. de la G.*, II, ii, 223) ; and was employed to intervene in the affairs of Erivan in 1783 (*Ibid.*, p. 249). His son Karaman acted as intermediary between Irakli and Agha-Muhammad-Khan in 1795 (*Ibid.*, p. 262).
[11] *Ibid.*, p. 266, note 2.

Of Irakli Emin writes in his curious English,

> "his common complexion was black, mixed with green; his stature was short, half an inch taller than Emin's; but he was well made and strong in bones and nerves. Heraclius had been one of the greatest men living if his mind could have been turned into the path of truth. In regard to the character of the people ... he was in every respect the first man among them, which enabled him to have the command over all. He was without the least pride, stiffness or domineering deportment which are so common to Asiatic princes; and with such a quickness of apprehension, that at the opening of any subject, he understood the whole extent of it. His voice in pronouncing words, conversing, or treating any topic, was so melodiously sweet that the hearer, without seeing his greenish brown complexion mentioned before, would have thought an angel was haranguing. Of pride he had not the least particle, he never perhaps boasted in his life." [1]

In domestic politics Irakli was extremely conservative, and he failed to display the enlightened toleration of his predecessors of the Mukhranian line. Both he, and his father before him were fond of pomp and circumstance, and their biographers, Papuna Orbeliani and Oman Kherkéulidze, stress their attempts to restore the traditions and ceremonies of the ancient monarchy. The subject Muslim cities, such as Ganja and Erivan, were oppressed with heavy taxes rather than attracted by leniency, and the Tatar nomad tribes of Borchalo whose allegiance could be so important during periods of war were alienated by oppressive impositions.

On the other hand, Irakli failed signally to discipline his nobles, although their arrogant privilege and continuing immunities constituted an anachronism in the social body which threatened and eventually occasioned the destruction of the monarchy and of the state.

> "With all my care and pains, I cannot make anything of them, nor find a single soul who has sense enough to incline his mind or bend his thoughts towards meaning well; but, on the other hand they are wicked to the soul, false to the very bone: in a word they were born twenty-four hours before the devil. As for fighting, they do not want courage; but what of that. The wild beasts of the field have as much. ... But what shall we do", Irakli asked Emin, "to make men of them?" Emin said, "Break them into small pieces like glass, to be cast afresh." [2]

Irakli's difficulties with his nobles were frequent in the middle of the Lazghi wars. The Mukhranian branch, who had never abandoned their hopes of restoration, intrigued against Irakli at the Russian court and maintained relations with all the discontented elements in Georgia. In 1755

---
[1] Emin, pp. 209 and 227.   [2] *Idem.*, p. 207.

Rustem-mirza, son of Abdulla-beg, was plotting with the Baratashvilis [1] and ten years later occurred the more formidable conspiracy supported by members of the families of Amilakhori, Tzitzishvili and Diasamidze, to murder Irakli and set up as king Paata, a worthless brother of the historian Wakhushti.[2] The popularity of the Mukhranian branch was long in dying and as late as 1779 Irakli was disturbed by the rumours of the plots of Alexander, the son of Bakari and heir to the claims of Wakhtang VI.[3] In 1779 the Eristavi of the Ksani revolted,[4] and in 1789 the powerful *gwari* of Tzitzishvili broke into protracted and troublesome rebellion.[5]

The economic state of the country was equally precarious. The Lazghi wars caused frequent famines particularly in Tiflis,[6] and recurrent epidemics of the plague increased the toll of war and slave-driving among the poor people of the country.[7]

The ravages upon the population, the continuing danger of attacks by the Lazghis, and the unwillingness of the peasants to submit to conscription, imposed upon Irakli even during the early part of his reign the necessity of recruiting mercenary troops among the Cherkess clans. These people, at once more civil than the Lazghis and of a close sympathy with the Georgians, came to constitute an important part of Irakli's army. In 1749, a large proportion of the troops which Irakli was raising to fight Sharji-Panah were Cherkesses and also Ossetians, Pshavs, Khevsurs and Tushes.[8] Two years later Irakli was sending agents all over Cherkezeti to recruit further contingents,[9] and in 1752 he secured also the support of a Lazghi contingent under the Shamkhal's son for the campaign against Hajji-Chelebi.[10] After the defeat of the Georgians by Hajji-Chelebi, Irakli himself went up to the Khevi and was anxiously concerned to attract bands from Cherkezeti and Osseti,[11] and when Agha Kish retired the Cherkess leaders were treated to five days feasting at Dighomi.[12] Papouna Orbeliani has left a curious description of the impression created by these alpine mercenaries on the minds of the urbane Georgians.

---

[1] P.O., in Brosset, *H. de la G.*, II, ii, 195.
[2] Brosset, *H. de la G.*, II, ii, 238–9; cf. also P.O., *ibid.*, p. 165; and Emin, pp. 276–8; and also P.O., in Brosset, *H. de la G.*, II, ii, 186, for the intrigues of the Mukhranian faction at the Russian court.
[3] Brosset, *H. de la G.*, II, ii, 225 and 247–8. [4] *Ibid.*, p. 246. [5] *Ibid.*, p. 256.
[6] e.g. P.O., in Brosset, *H. de la G.*, II, ii, 194; cf. also *ibid.*, p. 264.
[7] In 1770 in the middle of the Turkish war, 8,000 people died of the plague in Tiflis "without counting the dead in the villages" (*Ibid.*, p. 241).
[8] Brosset (P.O.), II, i, 148; cf. also p. 153. [9] *Ibid.*, pp. 160–1.
[10] *Ibid.*, p. 165.   [11] *Ibid.*, pp. 170–1; cf. also p. 172.   [12] *Ibid.*

REVOLUTIONS OF THE GEORGIAN KINGDOM

"The auxiliary troops required by the kings arrived at Ananuri. There were Cherkez, Kalmuks, Jiks, Kists, Ghlighwis, Nogais and Ossetians; each nation commanded by its chiefs and professing a particular religion, Islam or more generally idolatry; some uncouth men feeding on foul and unclean food, some of a superb appearance, others of a hideous ugliness, hairless and beardless, with excessively coarse noses; all, in battle, fine horsemen and intrepid archers." [1]

Thus Irakli, with his Georgian nobles, his Armenian diplomats and agents, and his Cherkess, Ossetian and Kalmuk mercenaries, held together for over half a century a strange kingdom of his own creation, which, founded on the nucleus of the derelict appanage of the Mukhranian Bagratids, had become in fact a Caucasian state. Irakli's kingdom stretched from the Daryal to Nakhchevan, from the Mountains of Likhi to the foothills of Daghestan and the sandy plains of Shirvan. Not more than half the people living under the authority of the king in Tiflis were Georgian. In the capital and at Gori, Ali and Surami, a large part of the inhabitants were Armenian. The valleys of the Ksani and the Liakhvi were occupied by an Ossetian peasantry owing allegiance to a Georgian feudality. To the south-east of Tiflis in the valleys of the Borchalo and the Akstafa the nomad pastoral tribes were Tatar, and the people of Ganja, Erivan and Nakhchevan were Tatar and Armenian.

The oldest historic lands of the Georgians lay beyond the border of Irakli's kingdom; Samtzkhé was in Turkish hands; Imereti, Mingrelia, Guria, Svaneti and Abkhazeti endured the reign of Solomon I in a state of intermittent civil war and although Irakli intervened from time to time and made his influence felt there, Imier—"that side"—formed no part of his dominion. The Georgian Kingdom of the eighteenth century, was, in fact, a Caucasian, not a Georgian state. And while the mediæval kingdom had constituted an agrarian community stretching across the isthmus, Irakli's kingdom was rather mercantile. So long as Irakli controlled the string of towns between the Mtkvari and the Araks—Tiflis, Nakhchevan, Erivan and Ganja—it represented a loose federation of city-principalities, depending economically upon the Persian Caspian lands and extending in a belt of fortified and relatively civil centres between Iran and the approaching power of Russia north of the Caucasian mountains.

---

[1] Brosset (P.O.), II, ii, 184; cf. also p. 185. Jiketi is a local name for that part of Cherkezeti which adjoins Abkhazeti; the Kists are a sub-tribe of the Chechens; the Ghlighwis are the Galgais of Russian writers.

INDIAN SUMMER OF THE BAGRATIDS

Psychologically, Irakli's kingdom was an interesting experiment in Middle Eastern politics, for it demonstrated the capacity of Georgian, Tatar and Armenian elements to beat out a common political life, so long as they had a breathing period free of foreign interference. The three peoples had a natural centre in Tiflis, a town more Armenian and as nearly Tatar as it was Georgian. In point of numbers throughout the kingdom, the three peoples were nearly balanced and each formed a nucleus that might later have attracted their fellow-people and co-religionists beyond the established borders.

Politically at the end of the eighteenth century, the new Caucasian state had little chance to stand, for in the sudden grind of young and vigorous Imperial organisms arming with the new mechanics, older bodies like Poland—in some ways similar to Georgia—went down. But Irakli's experiment was interesting, more interesting than would have been that of a reconstituted Georgian national kingdom. For natural conditions had tended to throw up—without the conscious direction of Irakli—not a new Georgian Kingdom as Irakli may have thought that he was building, but an experimental federation of the Caucasian peoples.

CHAPTER XVIII

END OF THE GEORGIAN KINGS
(1769–1813)

WHEN Taymuraz II came to St. Petersburg in 1760, a quarter of a century had elapsed since the termination of the last Russian adventure in the Caucasus. The Seven Years' War had occupied the energies and resources of Russia in the West, but with the accession of Catherine II in 1762, and the unfolding of the ambitions of that mighty woman, attention was once more directed to the pursuit of long-reaching Asiatic plans. The first Russo-Turkish war of 1768–74 was forced on Catherine by clever French diplomacy in Stambul and the Turks were pushed into an expensive defeat in order to create a diversion in favour of the tottering kingdom of Poland. Catherine conducted the war in most modern fashion. Wallachs and Moldavs, Greeks and Montenegrins were encouraged to participate; and to supplement the Russian armies on the Danube and in the Crimea, a Russian fleet with some English officers aboard appeared in the Ægean. Catherine with her fine taste in gallant men had put Alexei Orlov in command, and he won at Chesmé the first Russian naval victory in the Mediterranean (1771).

In the Caucasus the Turks had the advantage of surprise, and their allies, the Kists, took the important post of Kizlyar on the Cossack Line (1769). The Russians, whose interest in the appeals of Taymurazi and Irakli had until then been lukewarm, proceeded to use the Georgians as they were using the Rumanians and Greeks, and they undertook to assist Irakli and the Imerian King, Solomon I, in operations against the Turks.

Solomon, who was called the Great—maybe in contrast to his numerous predecessors during the last century—had succeeded his father Alexander V in 1752, at the age of twenty-two. Fiery, violent and intrepid, a man of charm and of a fanciful wit,[1] unquiet and volatile, he had spent nearly two

---

[1] Emin, pp. 399–405, gives an entertaining account of the "valiant Solomon" in 1768. He found Solomon's court in the open country composed of "about 300 aznavurs or knights all from twenty-five to thirty years of age. So many handsome, well-made men he had never seen before, except the English Oxford Blues, the king's horse grenadiers, and the Leib company (or the company of lions) the bodyguard of her Imperial majesty, Catherina".

END OF THE GEORGIAN KINGS

decades in the sordid muddle of the civil strife in which the Dadiani and the Gurieli, the Eristavni of Radsha and Lechkhumi, the Gelovanis, Sharvashidzes, Tseretelis, Abashidzes, Tzulukidzes, all contended for passing power within the dissolving western kingdom. In 1765 the Turks had intervened at the invitation of the Abashidzes and of the Eristavi Rustem of Radsha, and Solomon was only enjoying a fragile tenure with the support of Lazghi mercenaries, when, on the outbreak of the Russian war, he appealed for troops to the Empress Catherine. In 1770 General Todleben, the erratic conqueror of Berlin, was sent into Georgia with four regiments and some guns, and, after achieving the not inconsiderable feat of the passage of the Daryal defile, he was joined by Irakli at Kobi. The jealous Solomon united his forces with those of Todleben and Irakli before the Turkish fortress of Atskveri (Atskhur) in the Tashis-Kari defile and dissensions immediately broke out between the commanders of the three armies. While Irakli fought a desperate action with the Turks, the Russians retired into the Khéoba and then marched, in conjunction with Solomon, to attack the Turkish garrisons at Bagdati, Shorapani and Kutais. The original objective of the allied armies had been Akhaltzikhé [1] and Irakli now proceeded on his own initiative to invade Samtzkhé. He defeated a combined force of Turks and Lazghis at the bridge of Aspindza [2] and in the following year captured Khertvisi, an important point between Akhaltzikhé and Akhalkalaki.[3] Meanwhile, Todleben, who had failed to capture Poti, had been recalled, and before the same strong place, his successor, General Sukhotin, proved equally unfortunate.[4]

In 1772 the Russians, disturbed by the revolt of Pugachev in the Volga, abandoned their active intervention in Georgia and withdrew their troops to the Cossack Line; but Catherine's envoy, Ivan Lavrentivich Lvov, continued to urge an aggressive policy on Irakli. The two kings in the summer of 1772 united their forces to besiege Akhalkalaki; but Solomon was laid low of a sweating fever and the Imerian troops withdrew. The Turkish commander, Sulaiman Pasha, then took the offensive and invaded Kartli, where he was defeated by Irakli at Uplistzikhé. At the same time Irakli, uneasy at the withdrawal of the Russians and aware of the Congress of Foksani, sent his son Levani and the Catholicos Antoni on a mission to St. Petersburg.[5]

---

[1] Brosset, *H. de la G.*, II, ii, 240. [2] *Ibid.* [3] *Ibid.*, p. 221.
[4] *Ibid.*, p. 241; cf. Baddeley, pp. 25–6. [5] *Ibid.*, p. 241, and cf. note 3.

REVOLUTIONS OF THE GEORGIAN KINGDOM

Solomon in this year gained a resounding victory over the Turks at Khresili, and the debris of their army was cut to pieces in the Gurian forests. Solomon was able to occupy the rebellious *saeristo* of Radsha, and a few months later he defeated the other rebel in the field, Kai Khusraw Abashidze, at Chikhori.

In 1774 the Russians concluded with the Porte the Treaty of Kuchuk-Kainarji. Following the abortive Congresses of Foksani and Bucuresti in the two preceding years, the new treaty was hastily agreed under the threat of intervention by Austria and France. Russia was confirmed in the possession of the two fortresses of Azov and Kilburun and the two Kabardas, while the interests of King Irakli and King Solomon were entirely ignored under the condition which provided for the evacuation by the Russians of all conquests in Georgia and Mingrelia.[1] Irakli, however, found little difficulty in coming to an accommodation with the Porte through the good offices of his faithful servitor, the Armenian Mirza-Gurgina Enikolophian.[2]

That Catherine had betrayed the interests of her two small allies is obvious, but such betrayals in relation to the wide policies of Empires were, and remain, no new thing. From the standpoint of Russian imperial strategy it was impracticable to maintain responsibilities beyond the Caucasian mountains, until the whole vast front between the Danube and the Caspian had been consolidated. The Treaty of Kuchuk-Kainarji was merely an armistice in the mighty conflict which was continued between Russia and Turkey during the six decades between 1768 and 1829, and in this conflict the fate of Georgia was no more than a minor incident.

The magnificent power of the new Romanov Empire straddled the old world from the frontiers of Sweden to beyond the Caspian, and its capacity to wreck, then build upon the tottering structures of the Polish kingdom and the Turkish and the Persian empires, appalled the courts of London, Paris and Berlin.[3] All eyes were turned upon the brawny bastard of old fashions and corruptions, banging the weapons of new science—while in the farmsteads of America and the squalid tenements of French provincial towns things new, rabid and incredible, took time to germinate.

---

[1] von Hammer, XVI, 393.   [2] Brosset, *H. de la G.*, II, ii, 244.
[3] "Could anyone imagine that the aggrandisement of Russia would not naturally affect the disposition of other powers.... The safety of all Europe might afterwards be endangered."—William Pitt, House of Commons, March 28th, 1791.

Atskveri (Atskhur)

(From a photograph published in *Materiali po Arkheologii Kavkaza*, Vol. VI)

Valley of the Tskhenis-tsqali near the fort of Laroshi in Dadianis-Svaneti
(From a photograph published in *Materialï po Arkheologii Kavkaza*, Vol. X)

Ardanuchi

(From a photograph by Marr published in *Teksti i Raziskaniya*, Vol. VII)

Plate 3

Bridge over the River Magarauli in Pshaveti

(From a photograph published in *Materiali po Arkheologii Kavkaza*, Vol. X)

Plate 4

The three villages of the Commune of Ushkuli in Svaneti

(From a photograph published in *Materiali po Arkheologii Kavkaza*, Vol. X)

Plate 5

The Meskhian Monasteries : Safar and Opisi
(From a photograph of Safar published in *Materiali po Arkheologii Kavkaza*, Vol. VI ; of Opisi from a photograph by Marr, published in *Teksti i Raziskaniya*, Vol. VII)

Mediaeval Art: The Icon of St. Theodore of Lagani
(From a photograph published in *Materiali po Arkheologii Kavkaza*, Vol. X)

The Meskhian Monasteries : Khandzti and Shatberdi
(From a photograph by Marr published in *Teksti i Razīskaniya*, Vol. VII)

Mediaeval Art: Carved wooden door in the village of Chukhuli
(From a photograph published in *Materiali po Arkheologii Kavkaza*, Vol. X)

Plate 9

Mediaeval Art: Icon of the Archangel Gabriel at Lagani
(From a photograph published in *Materiali po Arkheologii Kavkaza*, Vol. X)

View from Mount Ugviri in Svaneti—over the Valley of the Mulkhra, with the snowclad peak of Mount Mezili in the background

(From a photograph published in *Materiali po Arkheologii Kavkaza*, Vol. X)

Plate 11

View of the town and fortress of
(From the drawing by Castelli in the possession

Gori in the seventeenth century
of the Biblioteca Communale in Palermo)

Plate 12

King Alexander II of Kakheti

(From the photograph of a Persian miniature—probably contemporary—published in Z. Chichinadze's *Sakartvelos Tzkhovreba*, Tiflis, 1913)

Plate 13

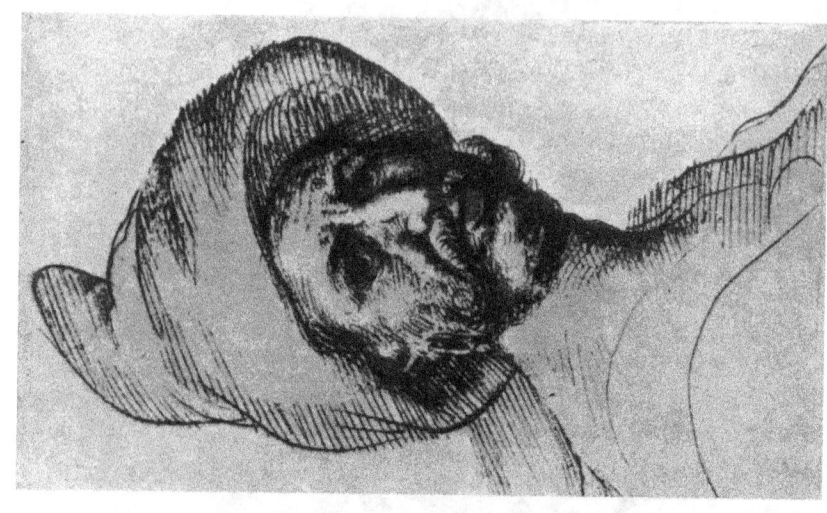
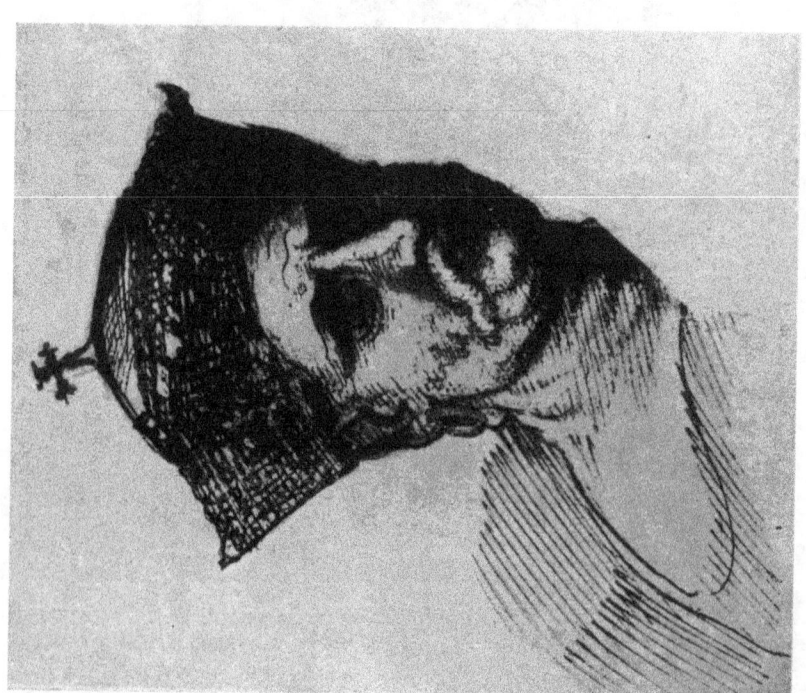

King Giorgi II of Imereti, and Giorgi Saakadze—"the great Mo'uravi" (after Castelli)

King Rustem of Kartli (Khusraw Mirza)

(From a picture—probably contemporary—reproduced by Chichinadze)

Plate 15

King Taymuraz I and his Queen

"Taimorasse Kan, once Prince of a great part of Iberia, who, after the depopulation of the country by the Persians, went to Moscow .   .   .   a great Prince and Defender of the Faith." Castelli

King Taymuraz II
(From a Georgian miniature reproduced by Chichinadze)

Khevsur tribesmen of Gudani, wearing mediaeval chain-armour

(From a photograph published in *Materiali po Arkheologii Kavkaza*, Vol. X)

Plate 18

Shatil: a stronghold of the mountaineers

(From a photograph published in *Materiali po Arkheologii Kavkaza*, Vol. X)

Plate 19

A Mingrelian Noble of the Seventeenth Century: Wamek Liparitiani

"Vomek Lipartiani, the successor to the Prince of Mingrelia (on account of the infirmity of the latter's son) friend and benefactor of our Fathers." After Castelli. "Our Fathers" were the Théatins

The Georgian Royal Nuncio, Nicephorus Isbarghi (or Nicholas Erbashi)

"Nicephorus, surnamed Isbarghi, Nuncio of the King and of the Patriarch of Georgia, who went to Rome, to Urbanus VIII in 1626, to ask him to send to his country apostolic ministers." Castelli

Khevsur Women of the Village of Lebaiskari

(From a photograph published in *Materiali po Arkheologii Kavkaza*, Vol. X)

Plate 22

Mediaeval Art: Icon of the Christ of Lagani
(From a photograph published in *Materiali po Arkheologii Kavkaza*, Vol. X)

Mediaeval Art: Icon of the Mother of God of Chukhuli
(From a photograph published in *Materiali po Arkheologii Kavkaza*, Vol. X)

Mediaeval Art: Carved wooden door from the Village of Dzhakunderi

(From a photograph published in *Materiali po Arkheologii Kavkaza*, Vol. X)

St. Grigol Khandzteli, from the tenth century MS of Merchuli, designed by Charles Beazley, after the coloured reproduction of the original published by N. Marr in *Teksti i Raziskaniya*, Book VII

Manners and Customs

"Observe the beauty of their horsemanship; how well they master their horses. It is a skill in horsemanship rarely attained. It requires great agility and presence of mind. Beginners frequently fall off the tall running horses." Castelli

King Alexander III of Imereti

" The King of the Georgians (sic) is worthy of being loved and exalted by true Christians, for he is a greatly devout Christian, holding in high reverence Christ, Our Blessed Saviour, and the Holy Ghost. He has always hated and fought relentlessly the Turks, the Saracens and the Persians, enemies of Christ

Alexander of the dynasty of Bagratiani, otherwise the descendant of the race of David, of consanguinity with Christ, our Saviour, a great Benefactor to our Fathers, reigning in the year 1649 "

On another drawing Castelli remarks of Alexander: " whose power is on his shoulder, for they say that he has the sign of a small crown and a cross on his shoulder." (Cf. the statement of Marco Polo that all the Kings of Georgia were " in ancient days . . . born with the mark of an eagle on their shoulder "

Plate 28

Manners and Customs

" A game the Georgian horsemen call *trocus*, beloved by all classes. (At side) The Georgians get used to horse-riding from childhood "

Castelli further comments on a similar drawing—" Having arrived in Kutais, where resides the King of the Georgians (sic), they took me to see a game of ball, played by players mounted on horseback. This game is very popular, being played not only by the nobles, but by the King himself "

Marie-Félicité Brosset, the Historian of Georgia (1802–1880)
(From Laurent Brosset's *Bibliographie Analytique de M. F. Brosset*)

END OE THE GEORGIAN KINGS

The imposing Catherine and her court of brilliant grasping men pursued the fantastic "Oriental Project". In 1779, Catherine was provided with a second grandson who received the name of Constantine as the destined ruler of a resuscitated Byzantine Empire. In 1784, the Crimea was annexed and the Tatar house of Ghirey was deposed in violation of the Treaty of Kuchuk-Kainarji; but the Turks hesitated to resume the war.

Catherine made a triumphal march through Southern Russia and at Kherson—the antique Byzantine metropolis of the Tauric Chersonese—she received the Emperor Joseph of Austria travelling incognito as Count Falkenstein. The two sovereigns passed through an arch which bore the inscription "This is the road that leads to Byzantium." A partition of the European dominions of the Sultan was arranged under the terms of which Russia was to receive Bessarabia, Moldavia, Wallachia and Bulgaria; Austria was to obtain Bosnia and Serbia; and a "Greek Empire" for the Grand Duke Constantine was to be formed out of the Morea, Thessaly, Macedonia, Thrace and Constantinople. Meanwhile, large numbers of agitators, disguised as priests, were sent to stir up insurrection in the Rumanian principalities, in Montenegro and Greece.

In the Caucasus continuous preparations were made both by the Russians and the Turks for a renewal of war. In 1775 the Russians carried out a successful expedition against Kara-kaituk and Derbend; and two years later the strengthening of the Cossack Line was entrusted to two of the most distinguished of Catherine's generals, Jakobi and Suvorov. The fortresses of Ekaterinograd, Georgievsk and Stavropol were founded and the systematic colonization of the Kuban province by crown serfs was undertaken. The Turks in the meantime were busily engaged along the Cherkess coast. With the help of French engineers they built the strong fortress of Anapa to offset the loss of Azov; and while they fortified Anakalia, Sukhum-Kalé and Poti, their agents among the mountain tribes were active in carrying on a fierce religious propaganda against the Russians.[1]

The first savage preliminaries of the coming struggle in the Northern Caucasus were the slaughter of the nomad Nogai

---

[1] For Turkish propaganda during this period see Klaproth, *Travels in the Caucasus and Georgia*, pp. 316-17, " Ever since the peace of Kutschuk Kanardshi in 1774, the Porte has endeavoured to spread the religion of Mohammed by means of ecclesiastical emissaries in the Caucasus and especially among the Tscherkessians; and in regard to the latter it has attained its aim."

Tatars by Suvorov in 1782. And in reply the Turks set fire to all the mountains when, in 1785, Shaikh Mansur lit a *jihad* from Anapa to Kizlyar.[1]

With the initiation by the Russians of a " forward policy " in the Northern Caucasus, Irakli's time had come; and while the mountains rose to carnage, Paul Potemkin, first Viceroy of the Caucasus, played with the Georgian King a neat and rapid game.[2]

Both the political condition of Transcaucasia and the psychological state of Irakli were favourable to the diplomacy of Paul Potemkin. Erivan was in revolt against Irakli's man Qulamani-Khan; and in Imereti Solomon the Great, after a disastrous defeat at the hands of the Turks and Gurians, had died recently in Kutais (23rd April, 1782).[3] Irakli himself, now well into the sixties, was beginning to fail and the death of his favourite son Levani (7th February, 1781) had hit him very hard.[4]

By a Treaty signed at Georgievsk on the 24th July, 1783, under the hands of Paul Potemkin and the *Mtavarni* Ioanné of Mukhrani and Garsevan Chavchavadze, the united Kingdoms of Kartli and Kakheti were placed under the protection of the Russian Empress; Irakli acknowledged her suzerainty; and while the succession to the Georgian throne remained within the Bagratid family, the control of foreign relations passed to Russia. A voluminous and controversial literature has accumulated round the interpretation of this Treaty. Its implications are obvious enough. The harassed House of Bagrationi had made a voluntary capitulation of their sovereign rights to the Russian Crown, and the fact that the Empress Catherine and her successors failed signally and repeatedly to carry out their protective obligations under the treaty could scarcely modify the blank reality of the position into which Irakli, by force of circumstances, had been impelled.[5]

The Treaty was a triumph for Russian policy and, with the annexation of the Crimea in the following year, it filled

---

[1] Shaikh Mansur is said to have been a renegade, Giovanni Battista Boetti, son of an Italian notary of Montferrat. See Baddeley, pp. 47–56, who regards with caution the evidence of Professor Otteno, published in *Curiosità e richerche di Storia Subalpina* (Torino, 1876), No. IV.

[2] Paul Potemkin was a cousin of Catherine's favourite, Gregory. His actual appointment as a Viceroy was made in May 1785, after the Georgian Treaty (Baddeley, p. 46).

[3] Brosset, *H. de la G.*, II, ii, 249.

[4] *Ibid.*, pp. 249 and 225. " Sulaiman Pasha said ' During the old age of King Irakli, Georgia had a curtain which covered it on all four sides; now the king has lost his strongest support.' . . . As for the king, plunged in grief at the death of his son, he ceased to fight; he was unwilling to take any part in expeditions."

[5] Avalov, pp. 133 *et sqq.*; Tsagareli, Tsereteli, Nippold, etc.

END OF THE GEORGIAN KINGS

the Turks with fury and alarm. Potemkin was quick to follow his advantage. He built a fort in a few months at the northern embouchure of the Daryal defile and called it Vladikavkaz—" Ruler of the Caucasus ". And while he proceeded to connect it by a string of blockhouses with Mozdok, 800 soldiers were employed to convert the bridle-path across the mountains—followed by Todleben in 1770—into something in the nature of a road. To such effect did the soldiers labour, that in October 1783, Potemkin was able to drive into Tiflis in a carriage drawn by eight horses.[1] He was followed on November 3rd by two Jäger battalions with four guns.[2]

On 24th January, 1784 the Treaty of Georgievsk was ratified by

> "the Hereditary Sovereign and Prince, Irakli II, by the Grace of God and the Benevolence of Her Imperial Majesty, King of Kartli, King of Kakheti, Hereditary Prince of Samtzkhé-Saatabago, Ruling Prince of Kazakh, Borchalo, Shamshadilo, Kak, Shaki, Shirvan, Prince and Lord of Ganja and Erivan".

David Orbeliani and Kai Khusraw Choloqashvili endorsed the signature of Irakli.[3] On the following day Catherine's Proclamation establishing her suzerainty over Georgia was published in Tiflis.[4] The uneasiness of the Turks was reflected in the invasion of Georgia in 1785 by their ally Omar Khan of the Avars, and Irakli supported by the meagre Russian forces at his disposal became involved in heavy fighting in the Jaro country and Borchalo.[5] The simultaneous *jihad* of Shaikh Mansur in the northern Caucasus seriously strained the resources of the Russians.

When the Russo-Turkish war broke out again in 1787, the Russians suffered disaster in two attacks on Anapa (1788-9) and the small garrison in Georgia was recalled to the Cossack Line.[6] Following the second Russian defeat before Anapa, a Turkish army of 50,000 men invaded the Kuban, but it was routed by the corps of Generals Hermann and Rosen. In 1790 the Russians, after fighting of amazing ferocity, captured Anapa in their third attempt. In Georgia, meantime, the period of the war passed without event, for neither the Turks nor the Russians were capable of effective action on yet another front.[7]

---

[1] Baddeley, p. 20.   [2] *Idem.*, p. 21 ; Brosset, H. de la G., II, ii, 250.
[3] Avalov, pp. 140-1, for discussion of the immediate political implications of the treaty, see *idem.*, 134-48. Brosset, Wakhushti, *Géographie*, pp. 463 and 487-93, publishes the names of a large number of *mtavarni* and *aznaurni* who are reputed to have endorsed the treaty.
[4] Baddeley, p. 21.   [5] Brosset, H. de la G., II, ii, 251-2.
[6] Baddeley, p. 51.   [7] Brosset, H. de la G., II, ii, 227 ; Avalov, pp. 146-7.

REVOLUTIONS OF THE GEORGIAN KINGDOM

In Europe, royal and imperial courts were alarmed at the progress of the French Revolution; and both Pitt and the Prussians were disturbed by the victories of the Russians in the Balkans. The Poles had risen under Thadeus Kosciusko, and the Empress was anxious for a peace with Turkey in order to carry out the final Partition. Accordingly in 1791, the Treaty of Jassy was concluded without any advantage to Russia substantial enough to excuse the fearful four years' carnage into which Catherine had been led by the mirage of the "Oriental Project".

Potemkin was dead and Platon Zubov reigned in his stead. Catherine renewed her energies as she renewed her men. Russia was mighty under that mighty woman. While Catherine fought her wars she founded nearly two hundred new towns.[1] She was interested in inoculation as well as in "Oriental Projects". Having won in Poland,[2] grasped the Taurida, failed in the Balkans, in the last years of her reign she turned to cut away some portions of the amorphous Persian Empire. The peace-loving Karim-Khan-i-Zand, modestly ruling Persia as *wakil* in Shiraz, had died in 1779 and the land was once more in anarchy. Potemkin had played with the idea of founding a "Melossopol" in eastern Persia which should become the emporium for all the merchants of India, Kashmir and Tibet, and in 1781 had gone so far as to send a flotilla to Astarabad.[3] The Russians, with Irakli, had intervened in 1787 to sustain the Armenian *meliks* of Karabagh,[4] and both the courts of St. Petersburg and Tiflis had tested and intrigued with the rival pretenders of the House of Zand.

Again Persia threw up one of those dynamic tyrants such as that uncertain land had produced before to suddenly frustrate the imminent politics of predatory neighbours. Agha-Muhammad-Khan-Kajar was the son of that Muhammad-Hasan-Khan who in Tabriz had contested with Karim-Khan-i-Zand the succession to Nadir's power in the early years of Irakli's reign. Agha-Muhammad, who had been made a eunuch in his youth, had waited for his day and won it by qualities of cold patience, cunning and ferocity.[5] "The

---

[1] Rambaud, II, 145. [2] *Idem.*, p. 147.
[3] Avalov, pp. 130-1. [4] Brosset, *H. de la G.*, II, ii, 226-7.
[5] "The person of that monarch was so slender that at a distance he appeared like a youth of fourteen or fifteen. His beardless and shrivelled face resembled that of an old woman; and the expression of his countenance, at no times pleasant, was horrible when clouded, as it very often was, with indignation. . . . His knowledge of the character and the feelings of others was wonderful; and it is to this knowledge and his talent for concealing from all the secret purposes of his soul, that we must refer his extra-

END OF THE GEORGIAN KINGS

Monarch's head", it was said of him, "never left work for his hand."[1]

While the Russians, giving no weight to the new tyrant, made their preparations for aggrandisement across the Caspian, Agha-Muhammad, who

> "used to observe that he had no title even to the name of king till he was obeyed throughout the whole of the ancient limits of the Empire of Persia",

undertook to resume the ancient suzerainty of Persia in Shirvan and Georgia, without account to the new conditions which had arisen since the death of Nadir Shah.[2] In Georgia Irakli had been intervening in the affairs of Imereti. In 1789 he had set upon the throne of Solomon the Great his own grandson David, a son of the dead King's brother, Archili. David, who had assumed the style of Solomon II, was maintained only by Irakli's help, and in 1791 Kartlian troops were employed to suppress the dangerous rising of Wakléman Dalakishvili. Irakli had turned to the affairs of Ganja when, in 1792, he received a conciliatory proposal from Agha-Muhammad who offered to allow him the suzerainty of Ganja, Erivan, Karabagh, Shaki and Shirvan and the government of Azerbaijan, conditional on Irakli's agreement to resume the former relationship of Georgia to the Persian crown.[3]

Irakli was not prepared to break his Russian engagements. Agha Muhammad was occupied in other fields and it was not until the spring of 1795 that he suddenly surprised the Russians by his enterprise and the Georgians by his vengeance.

In May 1795, Agha-Muhammad appeared before Shusha with an army of 60,000 men. The siege of Shusha dragged on until Agha-Muhammad, leaving the city blocked, suddenly marched on Tiflis by Borchalo, a surprise movement in the hottest time of the year through the hottest valley of all Georgia.[4] Old King Irakli was unprepared. The Imerian auxiliaries of King Solomon began to pillage the terrified inhabitants of Tiflis, fleeing from the town. At Signakhi, the Batonishvili Giorgi, timorous and fat, failed to move

---

ordinary success in subduing his enemies. Against these he never employed force till art failed; and even in war his policy effected more than his sword."—Malcolm, *History of Persia*, II, 300–2.

[1] *Ibid.*, p. 302.
[2] Like Nadir, Aga Muhammad was proclaimed Shah by acclamation in the Plain of Mughan in the spring of 1796, also like Nadir after his re-conquest of Georgia for the Persians.
[3] Brosset, *H. de la G.*, II, ii, 258–9.
[4] For an account of Agha-Muhammad's invasion of Georgia, see Brosset, II, ii, 260–6.

with the Kakhian troops.¹ With a muster only of 2,500 men, the octogenarian Irakli and his grandson of Imereti met the Persian invaders, 35,000, strong, at Krtsanisi. The Georgians were routed. And on Tuesday, 11th September, the Persians entered Tiflis. All the King's artillery was taken and the town was submitted to a dreadful sack.²

Irakli, deserted by all his sons, fled up the Aragvi into Mtiuleti. His former protégé Kalb-Ali-Khan of Nakhchevan was sent to track him down with a force of 8,000 Persians guided by the King's musician, Aghajan Qulamanishvili. But a band of only 500 local men, some Pshavs and Khevsurs, were successful in ambushing a part of the Persian force at Bulachauri; and the Persians suffered two further defeats at Gori and on the Ksani.

Agha-Muhammad, threatened by Russian intervention, now opened negotiations with Irakli, but the old King, in spite of the objections of his entourage, refused to treat. In the spring of 1796, the Russians took the field. The gallant and popular Valerian Zubov, then only twenty-four, was in supreme command.³ In May the Russians occupied Derbend, and by the end of the summer Zubov had taken Baku, Kuba, Shaki and all the country as far as Karabagh. In the meantime the Batonishvili Giorgi had reoccupied Tiflis where he was reinforced by Russian artillery and Jäger and Grenadier battalions under Colonel Sirikhnev. Ganja fell to the Russians in the autumn, but in November the death of Catherine and the accession of the eccentric Emperor Paul occasioned the sudden recall of all Russian troops to the line of the Terek.

Agha-Muhammad was at that time involved in the affairs of Khurasan, but in the spring of 1797 he came again to Shusha. Bands were sent to ravage Kakheti and he was preparing to take a fearful vengeance on the two Georgian kingdoms, when on the night of the 12th June, 1797, he was killed by his servants while he slept in the citadel of Shusha.

Six months later, on the 12th January, 1798, old Irakli died of dropsy at Telavi. The new King, Giorgi XII, slothful, weak and gluttonous, devout and middle-aged—himself already dropsical—was not the man to confront those difficulties, through which his splendid father had persisted to the last.⁴

¹ Wardrop, *The Kingdom of Georgia*, p. 127.
² For contemporary accounts of the sack of Tiflis, see Brosset, *H. de la G.*, II, ii, 261, note 2.
³ Valerian was a brother of Catherine's favourite, Platon Zubov.
⁴ Brosset, *H. de la G.*, II, ii, 265.

END OF THE GEORGIAN KINGS

Irakli had attempted to modify the right of succession in favour of his younger sons,[1] and while Giorgi sent envoys to St. Petersburg to secure confirmation of his own succession with remainder to his son David, his brother Farnavazi seized the citadel of Surami.[2]

Meanwhile, Fath'Ali Shah, the nephew and successor of Agha-Muhammad, was trying to detach Giorgi from the Russian alliance,[3] and in July 1799 Alexander, another son of Irakli, fled to Omar Khan.[4]

The Emperor Paul was forced to intervene, and in view of the imminent Persian attack ordered General Knorring, commanding the troops in the northern Caucasus, to prepare an expeditionary force for intervention in Georgia. Alexander and the Avars were defeated at Niakhuri on the Alazani by the troops of Giorgi's sons, Ioanné and Bagrati. In the following year two Russian battalions under the orders of General Lazarev arrived in Tiflis; and, while the Persian Sardar at Nakhchevan still hesitated to commit overt acts of war, Alexander, who had been joined by his brothers Yuloni and Wakhtangi, descended into Kakheti at the head of a great horde of Lazghis.

Giorgi lay ill to death of dropsy at Tiflis, and was more concerned with the careful reparation of the miraculous icon of St. George of Bodchorma by the jeweller Gabriel, than with the things of this world.[5] While panic reigned in Tiflis, Lazarev with a miscellaneous force of 2,000 Russians, Kakhians, Pshavs, Khevsurs and Tushes met the army of Omar Khan and Alexander, again, at Niakhuri (7th November, 1800).[6] The invaders were routed; the Avar prince was severely wounded; and Alexander fled to Karabagh. On 28th December Giorgi died in Tiflis,[7] and his son David supported by the Russian General Gulakov suppressed the attempted revolt of Irakli's sons, Yuloni and Wakhtangi. David hesitated to have himself proclaimed king, and on 18th January, 1801, was published the Manifesto of the Emperor Paul, by which the territories of the two Georgian kingdoms were incorporated in the Russian Empire.[8] General Knorring

---

[1] Brosset, *H. de la G.*, II, ii, 269, and cf. p. 260. [2] *Ibid.*, p. 267. [3] *Ibid.*, p. 267.
[4] *Ibid.*, p. 269; Baddeley, p. 61. For an account of Alexander's character and subsequent adventures see Monteith, pp. 72–8.
[5] Brosset, *H. de la G.*, II, ii, 270. [6] *Ibid.*, p. 271.
[7] *Ibid.*, p. 273 and note 4; Monteith, p. 31, "Despised and detested by his subjects and having been for a considerable time quite incapable of moving from excessive corpulence and dropsy."
[8] Baddeley, p. 61, dates the Manifesto to the 18th December, 1800, ten days before Giorgi XII died. Paul met his death in March 1801, and the annexation was confirmed by the Manifesto of the Emperor Alexander I, 15th September, 1801.

proceeded to occupy the country with a corps of 10,000 men, and to set up a civil administration under which the two ancient kingdoms were divided into the five *okrugi* ("circles") of Gori, Lori, Telavi, Signakhi, and Dusheti with the Aragvi.¹ The princes of the blood-royal were deported to Russia, an action complicated by the tragic assassination of General Lazarev by Giorgi's dowager Queen Maria. Only Alexander remained dangerous—a fugitive to fight the last bitter skirmishes of the sequestered House of Bagrationi.²

On the 6th February, 1803, Paul Dmitriivich Tzitzianov arrived in Tiflis as successor to General Knorring. The grandson of a Tzitzishvili who had followed Wakhtang VI into exile, he combined the discipline of a European education with the reckless intrepidity of a Georgian aristocrat. Hard and bold, of a biting wit, gifted with energy and penetration, he was at once a fine soldier and an able administrator. He served the purposes of political evolution rather than his ancestral country, and if in the three years of his rule he did more than any other single man to reduce the Transcaucasian lands to the position of a Russian province, he deserved well of the people when he wiped away the princes and stamped upon the khans.

"Yours is the soul of a dog and the understanding of an ass," he wrote to the Sultan of Elisu.³ "Fear and greed are the two mainsprings of everything that takes place here," he informed the Emperor Alexander. "These people's only policy is force and their rulers' mainstay valour, together with the money requisite to hire Daghestanis. For this reason I adopt a system of rule contrary to that hitherto prevailing, and instead of paying, as it were, tribute in the shape of subsidies and gifts intended to mitigate mountain manners, I myself demand tribute of them." ⁴

Tzitzianov proceeded rapidly to liquidate the remnants of resistance and independence within the Georgian kingdom. On 13th March, 1803, Alexander, his nephew Taymurazi, and the old rebel Mikéla Argutashvili, were defeated in the Jaro country. In the same year Grigol Dadiani, harassed by the troops of Solomon in Odishi and Lechkhumi, submitted to the Russians, and Tzitzianov began the construction of the fortress of Redut-Kalé (Qulevi).⁵ Solomon himself did not

---

¹ Brosset, *H. de la G.*, II, ii, 274.
² Popular tradition attributes to Alexander the paternity of the celebrated Shamil, a legend for which there appears to be no confirmation beyond surmise based upon the prolonged sojourn of Alexander in Daghestan and a certain physical resemblance of Shamil to the Bagratid family type.
³ Baddeley, p. 68.   ⁴ *Idem.*, p. 65.
⁵ Brosset, *H. de la G.*, II, ii, 278.

END OF THE GEORGIAN KINGS

hesitate to follow the example of his enemy and while General Litvinov was sent to occupy Imereti the veteran Solomon Leonidze, an old servitor of Irakli at his grandson's court, was sent to St. Petersburg as the envoy of the new vassal.[1]

In the eastern country in 1803, Tzitzianov was engaged in occupying the Tatar Khanates—Ganja, Shusha and Nukha. In the following year Fath'Ali Shah having secured his throne after a number of troublesome insurrections, intervened. Alexander, Farnavazi, and others of the sons and grandsons of Irakli, joined his forces. Tzitzianov was repulsed before Erivan and next year was assassinated during a parley under the walls of Baku.

The Persian war endured until 1813. Russia was involved in the throes of the Napoleonic Wars, and as the conditions of that gigantic struggle varied, first the French and then the British attempted to maintain the interest of the Shah in the recovery of his Caucasian provinces. Further, in 1807 the diplomacy of Napoleon in Stambul was effective in involving the Turks, also, in a conflict with Russia which was continued until 1812. It was through the efforts of the British representatives in Stambul and Tihran that the difficulties of the Russians on their two Caucasian fronts were finally liquidated by the Treaties of Bucuresti and Gulistan. By the former the Turks recovered Anapa, Poti and Akhalkalaki, which places had been taken by the Russians during the preceding years. By the latter Treaty, negotiated through the good offices of W. Sir Gore Ouseley, the British Minister in Tihran, Persia ceded to Russia all rights over the Khanates of Shirvan, Ganja, Shaki, Karabagh, Derbend, Kuba and Baku, and recognized the position of Russia in the Georgian kingdoms.

While the mighty conflagration of the Napoleonic Wars raged across all Europe, the Americas, and the adjoining parts of Asia, the poor embers of Georgian independence had been trodden out unnoticed. In 1810, during the Turkish war, Solomon II of Imereti, whose vacillating equivocations had been the occasion of his deposition and incarceration at Tiflis, made good his escape to Akhaltzikhé, and then went into his old kingdom.[2] The Russian general Suimonovich was blockaded in the citadel of Kutais; and Melkisedek Andronikashvili with Rustem Tsereteli inflicted severe losses on the Russians at Kortokhti. But Solomon wasted time in

---
[1] Brosset, H. de la G., II, ii, 285.
[2] For the Imerian rising of 1810, see Brosset, H. de la G., II, ii, 293-7.

the pursuit of his personal feud against the Dadiani; when Russian reinforcements arrived the Imerians were twice defeated in the field and Solomon fled back to Akhaltzikhé.

In the same year Levani, son of Irakli's son Yuloni, raised an insurrection among the Ossetian peasantry of the valley of the Liakhvi.[1]

In January 1812, the year of Napoleon's invasion of Russia, the people of Kakheti, driven desperate by the exactions of the military authorities and by the severity of the prevailing famine,[2] broke into a more formidable revolt. The Russian position was serious, for all the country, Muslim and Christian, had been excited by the recent Persian victory at Sultan-Budá. Russian detachments were massacred at Akhmeti and Tianeti; Telavi was besieged; Signakhi was taken and the garrison slaughtered with horrible cruelties. Numerous detachments coming to the relief of the beleaguered places were attacked and cut to pieces; a battalion of the famous Kabardá Regiment was badly mauled at Bodbis-Khevi; and while the revolt spread to the Aragvi and into Osseti, the Governor of Tiflis, Orbeliani, warned the Russian authorities that he could not answer for the safety of the city.

But the failure of a considerable Turkish offensive at Akhalkalaki enabled the Russians to concentrate heavy reinforcements in Eastern Georgia; the rebels were defeated in actions at Dusheti and Ananuri; and the force of the insurrection was broken in a pitched battle near Telavi.[3] On the 14th October of the same year that persistent pretender, Alexander—the only survivor among Irakli's sons who displayed something of his father's character—was defeated near Signakhi and fled into Daghestan.[4] Six days later the Persians were defeated in the last battle of that long war, at Aslanduz. Two British officers took part in the battle contrary to the instructions of the British Minister in Tihran, who was at that moment concerned to secure the Russian interest. One of them, Major Christie, was killed in circumstances of heroic folly[5]—a gesture we may measure with the greater follies of diplomacy, a profession which, among fatuities, is innocent of chivalry alone.

[1] Brosset, *H. de la G.*, II, ii, 299. [2] *Ibid.*, p. 301.
[3] Baddeley, pp. 84–5; Akti, V, 67–81. Brosset in his materials for *L'Histoire Moderne de la Géorgie* omits all reference to the rising in Kakheti.
[4] Baddeley, p. 88; cf. Brosset, *H. de la G.*, II, ii, 302.
[5] Monteith, *Kars and Erzerum, with the Campaigns of Prince Paskizwitch in 1828 and 1829.* (London, 1856.)

BOOK FOUR

THE PEOPLE AND THE POWER

" Moabad that day sent so many gifts that nobody can mention them one by one : many a coffer full of gold, jewels and pearls ; many a garment of great price, withal numberless brocades, broidered at the edges ; many a cup of crystal, trays and golden vessels, all inlaid with jewels ; and scents of many kinds, and withal furs ; and many slaves and handmaidens—Greeks, Chinese and Balkhians, all pretty and untamed as wild goats and yet as fair as peacocks in womanliness and beauty."
Visramiani, p. 63.

" I stand here in the snow and frost, and thou art comfortable in a warm house scented with musk and hast begun to talk of a thousand vain things.

" This is not a time for comfort and luxury ! Thy conversation and thy beauty are equally inexhaustible ; while as for me, death is thirsting for me through the keenness of the air."
Visramiani, p. 386.

CHAPTER XIX

FROM THE CLAN TO THE CLASS

STRABO was the first foreign writer who attempted to describe the social system of Georgia. His reference to the way of life in Georgia in his time is very brief indeed—only fourteen lines in all. But it is precious in that it lends support to the native sources embodied in *Kartlis Tzkhovreba*, which thus secure confirmation for the first time from foreign sources.

The references in the Georgian sources and the study of Georgian social terminology indicate that life in ancient Georgia was based on the communal or *sagwareulo* system. The word *sagwareulo* is derived from *gwari*, and denotes "that which is of *gwari*". *Gwari* was made up of an aggregate of families having common descent and forming a community of its own; it was called also *sakhli*.[1] The conception of a collective unit of the inhabitants born of the same stock was denoted by the word *tomi*. Each *tomi* was divided into a number of *temni*, and each *temi* into *gwarni* or *sakhlni*. The holdings of a *gwari* constituted *sagwareulo*. Each *sagwareulo* was administered by a *mamasakhlisi* or "father of the house"; in other words, by the oldest member of *gwari* or *sakhli*.

Gwarni naturally differed in size and wealth. A *gwari* with a great number of members wielded greater power and influence over other *gwarni*. The *mamasakhlisi* of such a *gwari* became at the same time the *mamasakhlisi* of the *temi*—*temis-mamasakhlisi*. In like manner the most influential among the *temis-mamasakhlisni* became the *mamasakhlisi* of the *tomi* (*tomis-mamasakhlisi*). The *tomis-mamasakhlisi* was thus an over-*mamasakhlisi*, or an over-lord of all other *mamasakhlisni* —whether of *temi* or *gwari*. He was called *meupé-mamasakhlisi*.

The *meupé-mamasakhlisi* retained of course as his direct appanage the chieftainship of his *temi* and the *mamasakhlisate* of his *sagwareulo*. At the same time the dignity and importance of his own *gwari* was enhanced and it

[1] The present-day common meaning of *gwari* is surname, and of *sakhli*, house.

became *sameupé gwari* or *sakhli*. Of this type was the *meupé-mamasakhlisi* of Mtzkheta whose power according to *Kartlis Tzkhovreba* had become established in eastern Georgia as early as the fourth century B.C.

The abolition of the office of the ordinary *mamasakhlisi* is ascribed by *Kartlis Tzkhovreba* to the hypothetical first King Farnavazi at the end of the fourth century B.C. But the only historically authentic Farnavazi of whom we know reigned in the first century B.C. and his rule was not distinguished by such a reform. It is, however, quite possible that some ambitious *meupé mamasakhlisi* may have thought it desirable to reform the administration of the country by centralizing it in his own hands; he would naturally abolish the positions of *mamasakhlisi* over *tomi* and *temi*, and dividing the country into administrative units appoint over them governors directly responsible to himself.

In whatever manner this may have happened there can be no doubt that kingship arose in Georgia out of the *sagwareulo-mamasakhliso* system, the essential characteristics of which continued to survive down to the Christian era, as is testified by Strabo.

Writing of the division of the inhabitants into four classes, the Greek geographer states that " the first and chief is that from which the kings are appointed ".[1] The " first and chief class " is nothing more or less than the *gwari* of the *meupé-mamasakhlisi* of the earlier centuries, the *sameupé gwari* or *sakhli*, the royal clan. Further, Strabo states, " the King is the oldest and the nearest of his predecessor's relations ".

---

[1] Strabo, XI, iii, 36.

Here too we can perceive an essential element of the old system, according to which the eldest member of the *gwari* administered the *sagwareulo*, succession passing from the eldest to the eldest of *gwari*, i.e. to the brother or uncle, and not from father to son.

In Strabo's time then the highest power belonged to one *sagwareulo*, the eldest member of which, or, using the old term, the *mamasakhlisi* of which, was King of the whole of Iberia.

In the actual administration of justice and of military affairs the King was assisted by the second eldest member of his *gwari*, who after the King held the first place in the country. In time of peace he administered justice, while in time of war he led the King's army.

Next to the *samepo* or royal *gwari* the place of honour was held by the *samghudelo gwari* or "priestly clan," which besides administering religious affairs provided also the executive elements in the primitive state.

No person except a member of the royal *gwari* had the right to possess bondsmen. The numbers of the royal *gwari* as well as of the priestly *gwari* were small. The number of *gwarni* in bondage was also limited. The *gwarni* in bondage were the property of the royal *gwari* in whose *sagwareulo* they lived and to whom they paid their dues in service and in kind.

The rest of the population was entirely free and consisted of free *gwarni* which in time of peace followed an agricultural life and in time of war armed themselves and fought the enemy. This free population was divided into *gwarni* or *sakhlni*, who lived each on their respective *sagwareulo*. Private ownership of land was unknown. Immovable properties belonged to the *gwari* as a whole and the oldest member of it, the *mamasakhlisi*, was its sole regulator and manager. *Gwari* or *sakhli* then represented a basic social group welded by common descent, common ownership and communal production; in other words ancient Georgia did not know a social economic unit smaller than the *gwari*. This however, does not mean that there were no family households. The household or family as a biological and moral union did of course exist, but juridically and economically it formed an inseparable part of the *gwari*. Families could and did naturally live in separate homes, but socially they were very closely bound to their respective *gwarni* outside of which they had no legal existence. The *gwari* and *sagwareulo* system was the keystone of all social life. Hamlets, villages and towns were organized in accordance with this system, for in the majority of cases the whole village was held in a single *sagwareulo*. This system lasted until the seventh century A.D., and in some cases survived until the thirteenth century; while among the mountaineers of the Aragvi and the Ksani valleys, it persisted till as recently as the eighteenth century.

With the invasion of the Romans in 65 B.C. and the subsequent imposition of a " treaty of friendship " on Iberia, this native system of state and social organization became increasingly subject to external influences. The Romans interfered frequently, for instance, with the succession rights with a view to placing their own creatures on the Iberian throne; but the older practices proved strong enough to persist until the end of the second century A.D. when succession by primogeniture became the rule.

Other modifications began to take place. Differences in social status gradually developed within the *gwarni* and by the middle of the second century A.D. social inequalities had become already, at least partially, established.

The first foreign writer to allude to the existence of social inequality in Georgia was Dio Cassius who lived in the second half of the second century A.D. In giving an account of the arrival in Rome of Farsman II (A.D. 116-40) King of Iberia, and of the reception accorded him by the Emperor Hadrian, Dio Cassius states that

" the Emperor watched Farsman and the sons of other *illustrious* Iberians perform tournaments ".[1]

---

[1] Dio Cassius, *Hist. Romana*, III, 69.

FROM THE CLAN TO THE CLASS

In the Greek text Cassius uses the word *protos*; now *protos*, which means literally " the first ", " the illustrious ", is rendered by the Georgian translators of the Greek by the word *aznauri*.[1] It was *aznaurni* then who composed the suite of Farsman II. The word *aznauri*, of which *aznaurni* is the plural form, comes from the Perso-Armenian root *azn* formed with the suffix *ur* = *ver*, that is *azna-uri* = *azna-veri*, wherein *azn*, according to Prof. Marr, denotes birth, origin, descent, and *ur* = *ver* = son.[2] *Aznauri* thus means " son of birth "— in other words, " son of illustrious birth or origin ". The Georgian equivalent of *aznauri* is *gwarishvili* = son of *gwari*; also *gwarovani* or *gwariani*, of illustrious *gwari* or clan. The *Protoi Iberôn* of Cassius and the *aznaurni* or *gwarianni*, *gwarishvilni*, of the Georgians all have then one and the same meaning, the only difference between the two Georgian words *aznauri* and *gwariani* being in this, that the first is formed from a foreign and the second from a purely Georgian root.

If *aznauri* denoted the person or the rank of persons, of high, illustrious birth, there can be no doubt that there must have been some denomination of the persons or rank of persons of lower, less illustrious birth. We can find no indication of this in Dio Cassius' work, since he makes reference only to the *aznaurni* in Farsman's suite. There are no Georgian sources for the same period. But in later Georgian monuments, the earliest of which belongs to the fifth century, namely, *The Martyrdom of St. Shushaniki the Queen*, we are provided with valuable retrospective light; in it we find that the population of Georgia was divided in the fifth century into *aznaurni* and *uaznoni*.[3]

Uazno, of which *uaznoni* is the plural form, is the negative form of *aznauri* and consequently means of non-illustrious or of low birth, literally birthless, without birth. The *uaznoni* or *ugwaroni*, that is the people who were without *gwari*, who did not belong to a *gwari*, were of no consequence at all, since they possessed no *gwari* to uphold them. An *aznauri* or *gwariani*, a *gwarishvili*, on the contrary, because he belonged to a *gwari* could feel himself assured of his personal independence. The social state is, as Professor Javakhishvili has correctly observed, " perfectly reflected " in the term itself used to designate the " members of privileged *gwarni* "—in the word

---

[1] Translation of St. Mark's Gospel, VI, 21. That *protoi* must designate *aznaurni* was first suggested by the Georgian Professor Javakhishvili; see his *Gosudarstvennie stroi drevniei Gruzii i drevniei Armenii* (Spb. 1905).
[2] N. Marr, *Tek. Raz. A-G*, Book IV.
[3] Cf. J. M. Sabinini, *Sakartvelos Samotkhé* (*The Paradise of Georgia*), Spb. 1882, p. 191.

THE PEOPLE AND THE POWER

aznauri which etymologically has the meaning of "son of *gwari*", *gwarishvili*, but was also used in the sense of "the free".

Aznauri, then, meant also free or *tavisupali* in Georgian, and in this sense it was used in ancient Georgian literature, particularly in the translations of the Scriptures. Etymologically *tavisupali* means "lord" or "master of self"; consequently *tavisupali* was he who was his own master; who had no overlord; and was independent.

In like manner *uazno* was he who was not his own master; and was not independent.

From the earliest Georgian literary document mentioned above we learn that in the fifth century there existed in Georgia *aznaurni-did-didni*, that is the "great *aznaurni*".[1] Though it is not mentioned in our source, there can be no doubt that in contradistinction to the "great *aznaurni*" there existed also the "small *aznaurni*" or *aznaurni mtsireni*, otherwise the qualification of *aznaurni* as *did-didni*, the great, would have no sense whatever. *Aznaurni* then were already differentiated in

the fifth century. A better definition and a more complicated gradation of the *aznaurni* may have existed in the fifth century itself, but we possess no definite information on this point. From the same above-mentioned document we learn also that in the fifth century differentiation was not only shown in the *aznaurni* but also in the *uaznoni*. Thus while in the first century A.D. social inequality was almost unknown in Georgia, no one except the royal *gwari* having the right to possess bondsmen, in the fifth century A.D. inequality had become the very essence of social life, and the population was divided

[1] Sabinini, *Sakartvelos Samotkhé*.

into distinct social groups or ranks. The population had become at this period divided into two main groups:
aznaurni who were *tavisupalni* and
uaznoni who were *utavisuploni*.
The *aznaurni* as a group or class were divided into two ranks:
aznaurni-did-didni, "the great *aznaurni*", and
aznaurni mtsireni, "the small or common *aznaurni*".
The *uaznoni* in their turn were divided in the following groups: *Msakhurni*, *Qrmani* and *Mona-mkhevalni*.

CHAPTER XX

THE MIDDLE AND LOWER CLASSES IN MEDIÆVAL GEORGIA

Msakhurni constituted a distinct social group, although the different categories within the group did not enjoy equal rights and an equal social position; they also, like the *aznaurni*, were differentiated. According to *The Life of St. Abo*,[1] an eighth-century document, a *msakhuri* was a person attached to another, his master, for whom he performed certain duties. It follows then that *msakhurni*, of which *msakhuri* is the singular form, and the etymological meaning of which is "the servant", were attached to the kings and to the *mtavarni* and *aznaurni*. St. Abo, for instance, was in the service of Nersé, the *eristavt-eristavi*, in the capacity of "a skilled blender of face-creams, powders and scents". Another particular and special duty of a *msakhuri* is preserved in *The Life of Serapion Zarzmeli*—namely, that of a courier or messenger.[2] The *msakhurni* of the kings and of the *mtavarni* constituted a group of higher social standing than the *msakhurni* of the *aznaurni*. In like manner the *msakhurni* of the great *aznaurni* enjoyed a higher social status than those of the small or common *aznaurni*. Unfortunately the Georgian historical sources do not contain detailed information about the grades of *msakhurni*. Two grades, however, are mentioned casually, namely, *mtavris dsinashe mdgomelni*[3] and *tadzreulni*.[4] Although it is difficult to glean the nature of the offices held by these *msakhurni*, it is clear, judging from the meaning of the qualifying terms, that their duties put them in close contact with the *mtavarni* and the palace, for the first term strictly signifies "the before mtavari standing", and the second "of the palace".

---

[1] It was written by Ioanné Sabinisdze. See German translation by K. Schultze, *Das Martyrium des heiligen Abo von Tiflis*, in *Texte und Untersuchungen*, XIII, 4, 315, 27–8. Abo was martyred in 785. See also *Sakartvelos Samotkhé*, p. 338.

[2] *Tzkhovrebai da Mokhmedebai*. . . . *Serapionisi* (*Life and Activities of Serapion*), published by M. Janashvili in his *Georgian Literature*, Book II.

[3] See *Tzkhovrebai Grigol Khandztelisai* (*Life of St. Grigol of Khandzti*), by Merchuli, published by N. Marr in *Tek. Raz. A-G.*, Book VII, page 16, Cap. XI.

[4] See *Tzkhovrebai Mepisa Wakhtang Gurgasalisai* (*Life of the King Wakhtang Gurgaslan*), by Juansheri, published by E. Takaishvili, p. 209.

THE MIDDLE AND LOWER CLASSES

With the growth of a strong central power and the development of the mediæval administrative machine people began to be distinguished not only by their birth, but also by the service they rendered to the state. *Gwarishvilni* so distinguished became known as *msakhureulni*, which is not to be confused with *msakhurni* mentioned above. A *msakhureuli* (singular) was he who possessed a record of long service to the state. *Msakhureulni gwarishvilni* were thus doubly illustrious by birth and by service.

For a *gwarishvili*, backed by the worth and influence of his *gwari*, it was comparatively easy to enter the administrative service. It was not, however, so easy for the *ugwaroni* or *uaznoni*, who entered upon their career without the advantage of the influence of their *gwari* and all which that implied. The advancement and promotion of an *ugwaro* naturally would not be free of prejudice and unopposed by the *aznaurni*. In such a position undoubtedly were the *msakhurni* of the higher grades. In course of time, however, their personal worth and merit began to be recognized and rewarded. In the work of Juansheri quoted above, it is stated that King Archili " presented Kakheti to his *tadzreulni* and made *aznaurni* of them ".[1]

The promotion and elevation of the *msakhurni* became a frequent occurrence in the tenth and the following centuries, and strong kings such as Bagrat III, David Aghmashenebeli and Giorgi III pursued a policy of favouring poor and capable *msakhurni* at the expense of the proud and turbulent *aznaurni*. The preferment of *msakhurni* to *aznaurni* became increasingly common, and in the time of David Aghmashenebeli there was a whole class of *aznaurni* called *aghzeebulni* (" the raised "). Of this type of *aznaurni* may have been the *mosakargaveni* whose duty was the collection of taxes [2] and the *aznaurni sazuerelni* [3] who were in charge of the Customs Houses.

The elevation of *uaznoni* to *aznauroba* led to a new distinction among the *aznaurni*; henceforward the *aznaurni* who were such by the right of birth, *aznauroba* having been handed down to them by their ancestors, began to be known as *aznaurni memamuleni* or *natesavit aznaurni* in contrast to the *aghzeebulni aznaurni*, i.e. " the raised ", those who had acquired their *aznauroba* by bestowment.

[1] Juansheri, pp. 209-10.
[2] *Shio Mghvimis Sami Sigeli (Three Sigels of Shio Mghvime)*, published by S. Kakabadze, p. 5.
[3] *Matiane Kartlisai*, published by E. Taqaishvili, p. 230.

THE PEOPLE AND THE POWER

Notwithstanding the fact that *aznauri* originally meant "the free", social changes had not spared even the *aznaurni*, and in Merchuli's work we read of *aznaurni mepisai*, that is "king's *aznaurni*"[1]; later monuments show that there were not only the King's *aznaurni* but those of the *eristavt-eristavni* and of other high state officials.

The free *gwariani aznaurni* constituted the influential social class of Georgia. Their material wealth was enormous and some of them possessed even considerable military power; in this respect the *aznaurni*, according to the historian Sumbat Davitisdze, were divided into two groups, namely—to use Sumbat's own words—"some with castle-fortresses and some without".[2] The lords of the castle-fortresses or "the great", as they were called, were those who possessed their own fortresses and were supreme in their respective domains. Each such great *aznauri* also possessed his own *sagwareulo* cemetery, monastery, church and castle-chapel.

Social differentiation in Georgia had by the eleventh and twelfth centuries become very marked, but social ranks were not divided by insurmountable barriers. A man could be ennobled, he could lose rank through adverse circumstances, or he could be degraded. Descent and social status remained all-important, but individual qualities such as courage, talent and loyal service could raise a man above the class into which he had been born. A person who had distinguished himself by his individual qualities was held in great respect and was, in the words of Merchuli, "an eminent man" (*satchinoi-katsi*). Loyal service was duly rewarded irrespective of birth; persons of long distinguished service received the rank of *msakhureulni*. The fame accruing from this rank reflected not only on him, but also on his whole family. Thus there arose the *msakhureuli sakhli*, analogous to *gwariani sakhli* (the noble house). The *gwariani sakhlni* were very often *msakhureulni-sakhlni* as well. If the dependent *aznaurni* of the great distinguished themselves by service they enhanced their reputation and prestige, and in the eyes of their lords and of their neighbours they became "highly estimable and respected" *aznaurshvilni*. Even the slave-peasants had full scope for improving their lot, and those who showed ability and gifts were not merely common slaves, but *vargi da satsnauri*, that is "good and noteworthy". It is significant in this connection that *varg* in the Svan dialect denotes *aznauri*.

[1] *Tzkhov. Gr. Khandztelisai*, p. 13, Cap. IX.
[2] *Tzkhovreba da Udsqeba Bagratonianta tchven Kartuelta Mepetasa*, p. 359.

THE MIDDLE AND LOWER CLASSES

Vadcharni—the merchants—constituted a separate social class, as is evident from the *sigelni* (charters) of the Catholicos Melkisedeki,[1] dating from the year 1020, wherein they are mentioned for the first time. The earlier literary sources preserve very little information about them, from which it is to be deduced that in the remoter times the merchants commanded little or no influence in the political life of the country. From the eleventh century they are, however, comparatively frequently mentioned.

The merchants were divided into two main groups—*did-vadcharni*, the great merchants, and *vadcharni*, the merchants. The great merchants participated in the affairs of state; the King not infrequently appointed ambassadors from among them, and they were sometimes accorded civil appointments. Some public prosecutors, for instance, were from the merchant class.

The group of *vadcharni* was of course more numerous, and their position differed greatly from that of the " great merchants ". While the latter were free and participated in the political life of the country, the former included many who were not free, being the slaves of others, and they could be bought and sold like the ordinary serfs.[2]

The merchants possessed their own organizations and associations and were under a *Vadchart-Ukhutsesi*[3]—the Chief of the Merchants. Unfortunately, however, no indication has been preserved as to whether he was elected by the merchants themselves or was appointed by the King. *The Man in the Panther's Skin* indicates the fact that the merchants wore a distinctive dress or uniform of their own.[4]

The Georgian literary sources give very little information about the position of the artisans, and it is rather difficult to state whether socially they formed a social group such as the *msakhurni* or the peasant class. From the work of Abuseridze Tbeli we can glean that in the twelfth century —and it may be inferred that even earlier—there existed in Georgia artisans who maintained themselves and their families by their labour and that they were free; for they seem to have been able to move freely about the country and even to go abroad to gain their livelihood.

The word *qma* or *qrma* in the sense of serf or slave is first

---

[1] See Th. Jordania, *Kronikebi da Skhva Masalebi Sakartvelos Istoriisa (The Chronicles and other Materials of Georgian History)*, II, 33.
[2] See Jordania, *Ibid.*, II, 33.
[3] See *The Man in the Panther's Skin*, by Sh. Rusthaveli, English Edition by M. Wardrop.
[4] *Ibid.* See Quatrain 1058.

used in *The Life of St. Shushaniki the Queen*. In the translations of the Bible, however, with a very few exceptions, it is invariably used in the sense of "the child". The word used in the early literary sources to denote slave is *mona*. It must therefore be deduced that the original Georgian word designating slave was *mona* and not *qma*. Later however *qma* supersedes *mona* and in this new sense of "slave" or "serf" it was frequently used in the documents dating from the eighth and ninth centuries so that it must have come into general use in the eighth century at least, if not before. In the documents dating from the eleventh century very often *glekhi* is used instead of *qma*. Writers such as Grigol Merchuli and Basil Zarzmeli do not use the term *glekhi* nor is it used by any other earlier writers. It is used for the first time in the *sigelni* of the Catholicos Melkisedeki in the year 1020. In the earlier sources different words are used in place of *glekhi*, namely *mdabioi*, "the low", by Merchuli; *dsurilni erni*, "the small people", in the *Matiane Kartlisai*; and *erni msoplioni*, "the people of the villages", by Sumbat Davitisdze.

All *qmani* did not enjoy the same rights; their position differed in accordance with the conditions on which their *qmoba* was based. Thus there were,

Nebierni qmani,
Nasqidni qmani,
Shedsirulni qmani,
Shedsqalebulni qmani,
Nadsqalobevi qmani,
Sheudzlebelni movaleni.

Among these *qmani* some were *siglosani*, that is holders of *sigelni* or charters, whose rights and duties were defined in writing; and some *ara-siglosani*, that is they held no charters and their rights and duties were defined verbally and according to the rule of custom.

A *nebieri qma* was one who entered into a patron-and-client relationship of his own free-will, in pursuance of his own wishes, and as such he had it entered in his contract that under certain circumstances he could resume his freedom.

The *nasqidi qma* or *glekhi*—the bought serf or peasant—occupied a much lower status. The fact that he had become a serf not of his own free-will but as a result of purchase would naturally alter his condition; and he had none of the rights possessed by the *nebierni qmani*. Some of the bought peasants possessed their own lands, but the majority were landless and they received grants of land or other provision for maintenance from their patrons. At the time of buying, often, a special agreement was drawn showing the purpose for which a peasant was bought. If a patron required a man for some particular job he would naturally buy one skilled in that job. For instance, when Grigol Surameli the *Msakhurt-Ukhutsesi* built mills for the monastery of Shio-Mghvimé, he bought for these mills a "peasant-miller" and donated him to the monastery. This particular peasant then was bought as a professional, he was a miller skilled in the art of milling, besides which special duty he had no other duties to perform. From his descendants one member always had to be trained as a miller to serve in the mills.[1]

Shedsirulni qmani or dedicated serfs were serfs consecrated to the churches and monasteries. The rights and duties of such serfs were always put down in writing and clearly defined and limited in the dedicatory *sigelni* or charters. Their status was therefore permanent and unchangeable. A dedicated *qma* or peasant was consequently always a *siglosani qma*. It, however, must not be understood that every *siglosanni* serf was a dedicated serf. As the dedicated serfs were meant for the redemption and repose of the souls of the dead, their duty was to provide food, wine and other provisions for the dedicator's *aghapi* and to assist in every way in the annual memorial services. The dedicators when consecrating their serfs took special care that the *shedsirulni* were placed in good circumstances in order that they on their part might retain good memories of their late patrons and might pray for the blessing of their souls. The patrons, therefore, freed such serfs from all services and tributes due from them. Moreover, they endeavoured to obtain for them exemption or even complete immunity from taxation. The dedicator himself defined the rights and duties of the dedicated serf who usually was enjoined, as already stated, to provide the monastery with a certain quantity of bread and wine and once or twice a year with anything else that might be necessary for the service of a requiem mass and the preparation of *aghapi* for the brotherhood of the monastery and the destitute. The duties once defined by the dedicator were not subject to alteration either by the monastery or by anyone else. In a *sigeli*, dated 1202, it is stated that Anton Dchqon-

[1] *Book of Donations of the Year 1250 of Grigol Surameli*, edited by S. Kakabadze, p. 7.

dideli, the *Mdsignobart-Ukhutsesi*, built an aqueduct for the monastery of Shio-Mghvimé, dedicating at the same time Giorgi and Yaberi with their respective households, whose duties, specified by Antoni himself, were to look after the aqueduct. Except this, in the words of the dedicator himself—

> "No other service of any kind whatsoever is to be imposed upon them".
>
> "I fixed", says he, "as their duty the service of the aqueduct. From each of the two households one of the sons must be trained as an aqueduct fitter and thus maintain it in good working condition." [1]

Looking after the aqueduct was not then the duty of every member of the two households, but only of two, one from each, and each generation of each household was to provide one trained fitter to the monastery. The other members, while they were required to help in maintaining the aqueduct in good condition, could choose whatever profession they liked and do generally as it pleased them, the monastery having no other rights over them.

It is obvious that the owners of *shedsirulni qmani* could only have been the churches, the monasteries and charitable institutions. As the *shedsirulni qmani* were dedicated to secure the "redemption of the soul" and for the *aghapi* of their donors the monasteries and churches more particularly favoured were those that were renowned for their miracle-working icons or for the purity of their monastic life. For this reason the more renowned a monastery or a church was the more donations and dedications it received in the shape of lands and *qmani*. As a result of these customary dedications the Georgian Church early became the most powerful individual "patron" of serfs within the Kingdom.

Shedsqalebulni qmani constituted a particular group of *qmani*. The duty of all *qmani* towards their patrons was a loyal service. *Qmani* were important not only economically, but also from a military point of view. The power of a patron depended on the number of *qmani* he possessed and on the loyalty and devotion they showed. During a war *qmani* fought alongside their respective patrons. In recognition of devoted service, a patron would grant a gift of land, elevation in his service, immunity or some other favour, and *qmani* so rewarded were called *shedsqalebulni*. The act of conferring

---

[1] See *Istoriuli Sabutebi Shio-Mghvimis Monastrisa (The Historical Documents of the Monastery of Shio-Mghvime)*, by Th. Jordania, p. 28.

such favours was called *shedsqaleba* and the *sigeli* granting it—*dsqalobis-sigeli*. *Shedsqaleba* was practised widely in Georgia as well by the kings as by patrons, great and small. *Shedsqaleba* indeed became a powerful political factor as we shall presently see in the hands of the kings and was used to the advantage of the *msakhuri* class as against the *aznaurni*.

A separate group of *qmani* was constituted by the so-called *Nadsqalobevi qmani*. In the Code of Laws of Wakhtang VI (1703–24) these *qmani* were called *dsqalobis qmani*. Whether the same term was used in ancient times is not yet definitely known. A *nadsqalobevi qma* was one given away as a gift by way of *shedsqaleba*; such a *qma* was given by a patron to another loyal and *shedsqalebuli qma*.

Insolvency was one of the primary causes of the enserfment of free men. An insolvent debtor "*is slave of his creditor and a slave bought whose service is never-ending*" states one of the documents. This occurred often when money was borrowed at compound interest. Compound interest has this peculiarity that it "*early begins to accumulate and infinitely multiplies the original*". Thus because of the rapid increase by successive additions of the interest to the original loan, the debtor was in the end confronted with the payment of so great a sum that often he was unable to settle it and in consequence either he was compelled to become his creditor's slave or he died before he could effect a settlement of any kind. Then, to quote our source, "before the eyes unfolded the sight pitiable, the free sons for the debts of their fathers were taken for sale".[1]

A landowner would place a *qma* on his land only when it was vacant. The act of so placing a *qma* was called "placing or settling upon the land".[2]

Tributes or taxes paid by the peasants for holding lands for cultivation were called *begara*. *Begara* was of different kinds. A *begara* levied for holding vineyards was called *kalukhi* and for holding ordinary fields *ghala*.

The holding of lands subject to the payment of *begara* called in Georgian *sabegrod gatsema* did not necessarily entail the relation of serf to patron. The patron-client relationship demanded service or to use the Georgian expression "the slavish service" of a *qma*, and of a patron the placing or settlement of such a peasant on his land. *Sabegrod gatsema*

---
[1] See the eleventh-century *sigelni* of Nicortzminda in Jordania's *Kronikebi*, II, 47.
[2] *Ibid.*, p. 135.

THE PEOPLE AND THE POWER

does not seem, so far as can be deduced from the eleventh-century *sigelni* of Nicortzminda,[1] to have involved either of these conditions.

[1] See the eleventh-century *sigelni* of Nicortzminda in Jordania's *Kronikebi*, II, 48.

CHAPTER XXI

THE RULING CLASSES

ACCORDING to *Kartlis-Tzkhovreba*, the office of *eristavi* was first introduced by Farnavazi, the hypothetical first King of Georgia. Having united the country, King Farnavazi, to quote the Annals,

" created eight *eristavni* and one *spaspeti*. This *spaspeti* was second in power after the King; he ruled over the *eristavni*; under these *eristavni* in various districts he appointed *spasalarni* and heads of a thousand, and through them all taxes, royal as well as eristavian, were collected. Thus was all this created by Farnavazi after the manner of the Persian State ".[1]

The titles mentioned in this quotation are all, with the exception of *eristavi*, of Persian origin; *spaspeti* is the Persian *spahpat*: *spasalari*—*sipahsalar*: *atassistavi*, head of a thousand, is the translation of the Persian *hasarapat*. *Eristavi*, however, is of purely Georgian origin and, as we shall see presently, denoted " commander of the army ".

In the ancient literary sources the word *eri* implies two different conceptions, " the people " and " the army ". Which of the two meanings of the word *eri* is the earlier it is difficult to say at the present stage of research, but it is a fact that *eri* was the only native word which the early translators of the Gospels used to convey the conception of the army.

Eristavi is a compound word consisting of *eris*, which is the genitive case of *eri*, and of *tavi* meaning the head; the whole therefore etymologically means " the head of *eri* ", i.e. the head of the army. *Eristavi* is thus the equivalent of the

[1] See *Kartlis-Tzkhovreba* version of Queen Mary, pp. 20 and 21.

Greek word *strategos*, in which sense it is indeed used by the ancient Georgian translators.

In the historical period the *eristavni* appear as rulers or governors of provinces and as the most important pillars of the early Georgian monarchy. Within their competence came not only military, but civil matters. When the royal power was abolished in Georgia in the sixth century A.D., the control of affairs devolved upon the *eristavni* or the *eristavt-eristavni*, invested, as it were, with interim sovereign authority. The dominating character of the position of the *eristavni* at this period is revealed in the *Lives* of St. Eustasius of Mtzkheta and St. Abo of Tiflis and also in the Chronicles of Sumbat. It was from the ranks of the *eristavni* that the renovators of the royal power eventually emerged.

The Georgian historical sources frequently refer to *eristavni* and *eristavt-eristavni*, but the information preserved about them is of a casual nature and incomplete. Among the early authorities only Mroveli [1] and the anonymous historian of Queen Tamara [2] have preserved for us a comparatively full list of *eristavni*. According to Mroveli, in the time of Farnavazi there were eight *eristavni* in all:

"*Eristavni* of Margueti, of Kakheti, of Khunani, of Samshwildé, of Tsunda, of Odzrkhé, of Klarjeti, of Kujo and of Egrisi."

The enumeration of provinces shows that this list does not include all the *saeristoni* of Western Georgia; nor does it include, strangely enough, the *eristavi* of Kartli.

In *Matiane Kartlisai* the following *eristavni* are mentioned:

"In Kakheti—*Eristavt-Eristavi* of Kakheti, Gordedzi, *Eristavi* of Pankisi, of Khornebuji, of Shtori, of Makeli and of Vezhini.
In Meskheti—*Eristavni* of Shavsheti, of Ardanuchi, of Tukharisi, of Kalmakhi, of Kweli, of Samtzkhé and of Tao. [3]
In Svaneti—*Eristavi* of the Svans."

The historian of Queen Tamara mentions one *eristavi*, namely the *Eristavi* of Hereti and eight *eristavt-eristavni* of the time of Giorgi III (1155–84) and of Queen Tamara (1184–1212), namely,

"*Eristavt-Eristavni* of the Svans, of Radsha, of Tskhumi, of Odishi, of Kartli, of Kakheti, of Hereti and of Samtzkhé." [4]

---

[1] *Tzkhovreba Mepeta* (*Life of the Kings*), by Leonti Mroveli, pp. 20–1.
[2] *Istoriani da Azmani* (*The Histories*, etc.).
[3] An *Eristavi* of Tao is mentioned by the Georgian Chronographer, p. 767.
[4] *Istoriani da Azmani*, p. 410.

THE RULING CLASSES

The ancient Georgian historians Juansheri and Mroveli state that originally *eristavoba* was a personal office and that it was only later that it became *sagwareulo* or hereditary. This change, according to Juansheri, must have taken place during the domination in Georgia of the Sasanian kings of Persia —to be exact, during the time of Hormuzd IV (579–90).[1] Brosset has, however, proved that no such reform took place under Hormuzd IV.[2] Whether Hormuzd had any connection with this change or not, there can be no doubt that as the power of the Iberian monarchy declined, the importance of the *eristavni* must have tended to increase, and it is quite probable that the ascendant Persians would have been inclined to strengthen the position of the *eristavni* and to weaken that of the royal *gwari* in the same way as the Mongol Il-Khans favoured the pretensions of the nobility against the two Davids during the latter half of the fourteenth century.

It is only from the *Life of St. Abo of Tiflis* by John Sabinisdze, who lived in the eighth century, that we definitely learn that in his time the office of *eristavi* had become hereditary. As the power of the monarchy renewed itself the hereditary character of the office was naturally challenged by the kings, and a struggle between the kings and the *eristavni* ensued. We have as yet little information as to the vicissitudes of this struggle during the ninth and tenth centuries, but in the eleventh century, during the reign of Bagrat III (989–1014), the hereditary rights of the *eristavni* were seriously shaken, and Bagrati more than once removed unruly and insubordinate *eristavni* and replaced them by " loyal and devoted men ".

In some of the earliest Georgian documents *erismtavari* is used in place of *eristavi*.[3] It was later used also in the abbreviated form of *mtavari*.[4] At first it was a mere variation of the term denoting the same rank, but later, when differences of gradation developed in the ranks of the *eristavni*, *mtavarni* are found to have acquired precedence over the *eristavni*, and *eristavi* and *mtavari* had come to denote two distinctly different offices, the term *mtavari* being accepted as the equivalent of the Greek *arkhôn*.

Besides *mtavarni* there were in Georgia, as it will have already been noticed, the *eristavt-eristavni*, i.e. *eristavni* of the *eristavni*. In what relationship an *eristavt-eristavi* stood to a

---

[1] *Tzkhov. Mepisa Wakhtang Gurgasalisa*, p. 190.
[2] Brosset, *H. de la G.*, I, 216, note 1.   [3] See *Sakart. Samotkhé*, p. 338.
[4] *Tzkhov. Serap. Zarzmelisai*.

mtavari it is difficult to discern; some provinces were governed by *eristavt-eristavni* and some by *mtavarni*. The office of *eristavt-eristavni* is first mentioned in Georgian documents of the ninth century. A province governed by an *eristavi* was called *saeristavo*, by a *mtavari-samtavro*, and by an *eristavt-eristavi—saeristavt-eristao*.

In the earliest Georgian documents "the country" is called *sopeli*;[1] from the eighth century, however, it is called *kueqana*, in which sense the word is still in use.[2] But anciently *kueqana* denoted not only the whole of the country, and each principal component province of Georgia, such as formed separate kingdoms before the union under the mediæval kings, was called also *kueqana*. Furthermore, the same word was used to designate even the smaller units, the provinces which had never been independent, such as Trialeti, Shavsheti and the like. *Kueqana* could thus mean an administrative unit. At the head of the administration of a large *kueqana* stood an *eristavt-eristavi* and at the head of that of a smaller *kueqana* an *eristavi*.

Eristavt-eristavni did not enjoy complete equality. Their greatness depended on the importance of the provinces which they administered. Those who governed provinces that had been independent kingdoms before the unification of Georgia were held in greater honour and respect. Such *eristavt-eristavni* were known in the words of the mediæval Georgian historians as "holders of kings' seats". The historian of Queen Tamara mentions two such "holders of kings' seats" one of whom was Guzani, Lord of Klarjeti and Shavsheti, "whom the King had elevated to the seat of the Tao(khi)an kings".[3] The "holders of kings' seats" were in all probability more than two, since Georgia before the unification had consisted of a number of separate kingdoms.

According to the author of *The Life of Serapion Zarzmeli*, an *eristavi* was "lord and master of the places and holder of everything therein".[4] According to another document called *Dzegli Eristavta—The Monument of the Eristavni* (of the Ksani) the duties of an *eristavi* included the "administration of churches, service to the King and government of the province".[5] "Largweli when appointed *Eristavi*, received these seven *Khevni* for administration, the churches and every *aznauri* domiciled therein."[6] From these extracts it is

---

[1] The present-day meaning of *sopeli* is "the village", which formerly was called *daba*; the present-day meaning of the latter is "the small town".
[2] *Kueqana* = *Kua qana* = stone field. [3] See *Istoriani da Azmani*, p. 434
[4] *Tzkhov. Serap. Zarzmelisai*, pp. 10–11. [5] *Kronikebi*, II, 4. [6] *Ibid.*

240

"Mamia, the Prince of Guria and his armour; killed by his Son, Simon" (Castelli).

clear that an *eristavi* was the ruler and master of the land and the inhabitants of his *saeristao*; to him were subject not only the peasants but also the *aznaurni* and even the churches—the latter, however, only in so far as their relationship with the civil government was concerned.

The *eristavi* wore a particular dress which was exactly like that worn by Justinian, the Byzantine Emperor; by way of distinction he also wore " a ring and a belt "; besides " he had a banner, a horse (of particular breed) and a spear ".

The *eristavt-eristavi* had authority over all *didebulni* and *aznaurni* domiciled in his *saeristavt-eristao*. Thus there was this difference between the *eristavt-eristavi* and the *eristavi*, that *didebulni*, " the great ", were subject to the former and not to the latter; after the King, the *didebulni* obeyed the *eristavt-eristavi*.

In military matters, and especially during war, the *eristavt-eristavi* held supreme authority; every *didebuli* and *aznauri* and all the other inhabitants of his province had to follow his banner. *Mtavarni* and *eristavt-eristavni* wielded great power and influence; materially also they were very wealthy. Some of them were so powerful that they vied with the King and often openly opposed themselves to the royal power. At the royal receptions an *eristavt-eristavi* had this privilege, that his personal Grand Treasurer stood behind his seat with a shield and sword.

One of the functions of an *eristavt-eristavi* was the supervision of justice at the peasants' court of law; the actual dispensation of justice was entrusted to his *saeristavt-eristao mamasakhlisi*. Ecclesiastical peasants, however, were excluded from his jurisdiction.

For the benefit of an *eristavi* a special tax called *saeristavoi gamosavali* (" the eristavi's due ") was collected annually. In addition to these usual and permanent dues he also received a tribute which was collected periodically. For the supervision of the peasants' court of justice he received a fixed portion of the fines imposed by the courts, which was called *kerdzi saeristavoi* (" the eristavi's portion "). When these concerned thefts this eristavi's portion appears to have amounted to one-seventh.

An *eristavt-eristavi* had a great many subordinate officials, including *temis-eristavni* (eristavni of districts); his own *mdsignobart-ukhutsesi* (" grand secretary ") and *molaret-ukhutsesi* (" grand treasurer ") and numerous *msakhurni*. He also had his *dsinashe-mdgomelni*, and his *sakutarni* (own), "fleet-footed runners and daring riders", the special messengers.

In their respective provinces, the *eristavt-eristavni* and *eristavni* had the following executive officials,

Tsikistavni, Khevisupalni, Mamasakhlisni and *Gzirni*.[1]

Tsikistavni—"heads of fortresses"[2]—were not only commanders of fortresses, but also heads or mayors of small towns. The eleventh-century inscription at the Cathedral of Ateni mentions the *tsikhistavi* of Ateni.[3] The *tsikhistavi* of Mtzkheta and the *tsikhistavi* of Mukhrani[4] were particularly notable men. We know very little of the rights and duties of *tsikhistavni* during the eleventh or the twelfth and thirteenth centuries. The only thing we can glean from the *sigelni* of this period is that the *tsikhistavni* received *satsikhistao* dues in the same manner as the *eristavni* received their *saeristao* dues.[5]

Khevisupali,[6] as the etymology of the word indicates, must have been the lord or chief of a *Khevi*. In ancient Georgian literature, *khevi*, the literal meaning of which is "the valley", was used to designate an administrative unit smaller than *kueqana*. Just as at the head of the administration of a large *kueqana* stood the *eristavt-eristavi* and at that of a small one an *eristavi*, so at the head of the administration of a *khevi* stood a *khevisupali*. Of the functions of a *khevisupali* we know very little. It is clear, however, that he too received *sakhevisupalo* dues.[7]

Gziri is a term generally derived from the Persian *gizir*. In Persian it was the title of a police official. We do not, however, know what was the function in Georgia of a *gziri* at the time it is first mentioned in the documents. According to Professor Javakhishvili, this word usually has a meaning indicating that a *gziri* was the deputy of the village *mamasakhlisi* and a special messenger to the officials generally. If it had this meaning in ancient times then it is quite possible, according to Javakhishvili, that it may be a purely Georgian word derived from *gza* = road.

The Georgian historical monuments very frequently refer to *didebulni, dsartchinebulni, mkvidrni* and *tavadni*, who appear to have exercised great influence on the affairs of the state.

[1] See *Kronikebi*, by Jordania, pp. 98, 15-19.
[2] Ibid., II, 73-4.
[3] See Prof. Javakhishvili's *K'voprosu o vremeni postroeniya gruzinskago khrama v' Ateni*, in *Khrist. Vos.* I, III, 2862.
[4] See *Kronikebi*, II, ii, 14-15.   [5] Ibid.   [6] Ibid.   [7] Ibid.

Etymologically *didebuli*, of which *didebulni* is the plural, represents the past participle of the verb *dideba*, "to make great", "to greaten". From its literal meaning, therefore, it is evident that *didebuli* originally meant promoted, elevated, honoured, distinguished, exalted, great, glorious.

In ancient times *dideba* denoted a high state office or the honour resulting from holding such an office. *Didebulni aznaurni* are frequently referred to in Georgian historical documents, namely, in *The Life of Grigol Khandzteli* (pp. 63, 33); in *Matiane Kartlisai* (pp. 252, 260), and in *The Histories* by the Historian of Queen Tamara. In the first-named source is mentioned an *aznauri didebuli* whose name was Gabriel Dapanchuli (pp. 12, 14), but from another page (13) we learn that he was a *mtavari* (Greek, *arkhôn*). It is evident that he was called *didebuli* because he was a *mtavari*. His *didebuleba* then depended on the high office he held.

Didebuleba, which is the abstract form of *didebuli*, was thus also connected with *aznauroba*, but no *aznauri* is ever called *didebuli* just because he was an *aznauri*. *Didebuli* was a term denoting a member of a particular group distinct from the *aznaurni*. The relative positions of the *didebulni* and the *aznaurni* are perfectly reflected in the following sentence of the Historian of Queen Tamara, who states that, under that Queen, Georgia " was so prosperous that the land-tillers lived like the *aznaurni*, the *aznaurni* like the *didebulni*, and the *didebulni* like the kings " (p. 41).

Didebulni at the same time did not, like the *aznaurni*, constitute a social rank or class. The characteristic feature of *aznauroba* was that every son of the *aznauri gwari* was an *aznauri* by right of birth. *Didebuleba* did not have this same feature. A *didebuli* was *didebuli* personally, and no other members of his *gwari* or family had any right to the title, nor did it necessarily pass after his death to any of his descendants.

The privileges of *didebuleba* were accorded to the group of great state officials who stood in the immediate circle of the King, and the word *didebuli* in the documents is often qualified with such words as *Kartuelni, Sameposani* or *Sakartvelosani*. If there existed any difference—which is very difficult to discern—then it may have consisted in this, that *didebulni sameposani*, which means " of the Kingdom ", may have been the *didebulni* at the head of the central institutions of the Kingdom and the *didebulni sakartvelosani*, meaning " of Georgia ", those at the head of the administration of the provinces ; while the *Kartuelni didebulni*, that is the Kartlian *didebulni*, may have meant simply what it denotes, the national regional origin.

Kartuelni didebulni constituted an extremely influential circle and played a prominent rôle in the councils of the state, taking precedence over other ranks of the officials and the nobility. Thus according to the Historian of Queen Tamara, Giorgi III (1155–84) declared his daughter, Tamara, "King of Georgia" with the consent of all the patriarchs and bishops, of the *didebulni* of Amier and Imier, of the *vazirni* and of the *spasalarni* and *spaspetni*.[1]

Dsarchinebuli was a term employed in a much wider sense, although it is used sometimes in place of *didebuli*, and more than once it appears as its equivalent. In the will of David Aghmashenebeli, however, they are mentioned separately, viz. "the King commands you all, every *didebuli* and *dsarchinebuli* of his Kingdom",[2] which suggests that there was also some difference between these two terms.

The Historian of Queen Tamara clearly reveals that the *dsarchinebulni*, like the *didebulni*, took a great part in the affairs of the state.[3] He, for instance, relates that Queen Tamara, when approached by the commander of her armies to sanction the invasion of Persia, "summoned the Council of all the *dsarchinebulni* of her Kingdom, of Amier and Imier, for consultation" (p. 516). It is evident that under *dsarchinebulni* here are understood *didebulni* also.

It is difficult to discern as to who or what were these *dsarchinebulni*. From a passage in the *Georgian Chronographer* this much is, however, clear, that *mtavarni* were sometimes at least styled as *dsarchinebulni*, thus "Béka the *Spasalari* of Samtzkhé summoned the *dsarchinebulni* of Samtzkhé and addressed them thus: Listen, *mtavarni* of Georgia, brothers and compatriots" (p. 767). This passage proves not only that *mtavarni* were sometimes styled *dsarchinebulni* but also that there were *dsarchinebulni* in every province of Georgia. *Dsarchinebulni*, like the *didebulni*, were *Sameposani*, *Sakartulosani* and *Kueqnisani* (of the country).

Mkvidrni, of which *mkvidri* is the singular, originally meant an inhabitant, a native. Besides this general meaning, in civil-legal literature it was used in the sense of "heir", the modern form of which is *memkvidré*. The Historian of David Aghmashenebeli states, for instance: "Thus died Rati son of Liparti, a man disloyal, and thus ended his house, no heir

[1] *Istoriani da Azmani*, p. 390. [2] *Kronikebi*, II, 514–15.
[3] *Istoriani da Azmani*, pp. 481, 492, 516.

(*mkvidri*) remaining and his estates taken over by the King ". *Mkvidri* at the same time meant also the heir to the throne.¹ But the term *mkvidrni* is also used in a different and particular sense. For instance, it is stated by the Historian of Queen Tamara that when the expelled Prince George Bogolyubskoi invaded Georgia, and Samtzkhé and Imereti rose in his favour, Queen Tamara " inquired of the reasons from her *mkvidrni* ".² In this sense the term can mean neither the inhabitants nor the heir to the throne. In *Matiane Kartlisai* it is stated that after the death of Dmitri of Abkhazeti, who died childless, " the *mkvidrni* of the country brought Thewdosi and crowned him King " (p. 237). Thewdosi was blind, and yet they had to crown him, for according to *Matiane* no one else was there of the royal *gwari* or house (p. 236). It is apparent from the context of this sentence that *mkvidrni* implies here, not the inhabitants of Abkhazeti, but in general the notables of the land, who had the right and power to choose the successor to the throne.

The extraordinary position held by the *mkvidrni* has led Professor Javakhishvili to the conclusion that, in Georgia, the Royal House was not the sole master of the Kingdom, but that there existed a circle whose members, known as *mkvidrni kueqnisani* (of the country) or *mkvidrni sameposani* (of the Kingdom), also had a substantial share in the government.

The scarcity of the information at our disposal makes it as yet impossible to deduce as to who were these *mkvidrni* " of the country " or " of the Kingdom " ; it is evident only, that they included the *didebulni* and *vazirni*. The Historian of Queen Tamara mentions as one of the *mkvidrni* of Tiflis " Abulasan *tavadi* and *amira* of Kartli and Tpilisi ". He also mentions " one of the *mkvidrni*, the great merchant Zankan Zorobabeli ".

Etymologically *tavadi* is derived from *tavi*, meaning " the head ". *Tavi* at the same time is the formative of " self ". It is thus the Reflexive Pronoun ; with this meaning *tavadi* represents the instrumental case and denotes " by himself' ; *tavadi* then means " one who stands by himself " ; who stands out ; who is conspicuous. From *tavi* is also formed the verb *tavoba*, meaning " to head ", " to lead ", " to undertake ", the future past participle of which is *tavadi*. *Tavadi* thus originally meant " a headman ", " a leader " or " a chief ". And indeed in this sense it is used in *Matiane*

---

¹ *Tskhovreba Mepet-Mepista Davitisi* (*Life of David King of Kings*), p. 290.
² *Istoriani da Azmani*, p. 437.

Kartlisai, wherein (p. 264) it is said of Liparit Orbeliani, the *eristavt-eristavi*, who had rebelled against his King, Bagrat IV (1027–72), that he approached "the upper fortresses and secured the help of the *tavadni katsni*", that is of the head-men or chief men.

In course of time, however, the *tavadni* had acquired considerable importance in the affairs of the state and had become *motaulni sameposani*; *motauli* (singular), which is another derivative of *tavi*, the head, denotes even more clearly than *tavadi*—one who stands at the head. *Tavadni* then were *motaulni* or men who stood at the head of the state. The term itself has been more or less in common use in the documents dating from the eleventh century, but it is also clear that, between the eleventh and thirteenth centuries, it did not denote, like *aznaurni*, a social class.

The Georgian Chronographer mentions *tavadni* very frequently in his work; from him it is clear that they exercised a great influence on the affairs of the state; no problem of great importance could be decided "outside of their consideration".

Who then were the *tavadni*? Many passages in the ancient documents indicate that the term was yet another classification of the great officials of the state. For instance, *Matiane Kartlisai* mentions Kakhaberis-dze Kakhaberi, the Eristavi of Radsha, Kuabulis-dzeni, Sargis Parnajaniani and Jonsheris-dze Dadian-Bediani as *tavadni*. In the *Life of Giorgi Mtadsmindeli*, the King of Antioch, called in one place *mtavari (arkhôn)*, is mentioned as another *tavadi*.[1] In *The Histories* there is a passage which induces one to think that the commanders of the armies also were called *tavadni*. This kind of definition of the term *tavadi* is, however, short of precision. *Tavadni* could, of course, have been the holders of high state offices, but on the other hand not every great state official, be he *mtavari* or *eristavi*, was considered a *tavadi*. Many passages in the historical documents wherein *tavadni* and *eristavni* are mentioned separately convey the idea that *tavadi*, *mtavari* and *eristavi* were terms expressing different notions. Moreover, there are even passages in the ancient documents which clearly show that a man could be *tavadi* without holding a high state office; such a personage, for instance, was Abulasan whom we have mentioned above.

Tavadni, like *didebulni* and *dsarchinebulni*, were *Sameposani*,

---

[1] *Tskhovrebai . . . Giorgi Mtadsmindelisa*, published by the Ecclesiastical Museum of Georgia, p. 308.

Sakartuelosani and *Kartuelni*. *Tavadni* were found not only at the head of state institutions but also at the head of cities and towns; Abulasan mentioned above was one such *tavadi* of Tpilisi (Tiflis). In *The Life of David Aghmashenebeli* we read that "there arrived the learned from among the Anelian *tavadni* (of Ani) and informed King David of their decision to hand over to him the town and the fortresses" (*ibid.*, p. 311). It should be noted that the term is used in the plural, which shows that there was more than one *tavadi* at the head of the town of Ani.

We have inquired above who and what were *mkvidrni*. Compared with *tavadni* there existed, according to Professor Javakhishvili, this difference, that *mkvidri* was a term expressing a wider notion and denoting a comparatively numerous and variegated circle, while *tavadi* was the appellation of a member of a narrower and more particular group. To the *mkvidri* group belonged not only *didebulni* and *vazirni* as stated above, but also *tavadni* and even the great *vadcharni*—merchants. But the *tavadni* were not numerous.

The terms *tavadi* and *didebuli* also were not expressive of an equivalent notion. It may have been, of course, that a *tavadi* was invested with a high office and bore the title of *didebuli*. In such a case he would not be *tavadi* only but *tavadi didebuli*. And indeed *Matiane Kartlisai* mentions "*tavadni didebulni* of this kingdom". But that these two terms did not denote the same thing is proved by the fact that the Georgian Chronographer mentions them separately—" the *tavadni* Kartuelni and *didebulni* gathered together ".

From all that has been said it is clear that *tavadi* was not like *aznauri* a term denoting a social class but a term implying personal worth. A *tavadi* was *tavadi* personally during his lifetime; none of his relations had any right to his title nor could any of them inherit it after his death. The exclusive quality of the rank was preserved long after it had become an hereditary social title, for in the eighteenth century in the list of *didebulni tavadni* in the Code of Laws of Wakhtang VI, we find a definition quoted below, from which it is clear that there could be only one *didebuli tavadi* in any one *gwari*. According to the Code, the following were the *didebulni tavadni*,

> "One head of the undivided (*gwari*) the *Eristavi* of Aragvi himself; one head of the undivided (*gwari*) Amilakhori himself; undivided one head Orbelishvili; and when his (*gwari*) was undivided Tzitzishvili also, and though not with these, has also been the *Meliki* of Somkheti."

THE RULING CLASSES

Thus in the Kingdom of Kartli there had only been six *didebulni tavadni*, or " great lords ", and they were entitled to the honour in respect of their chieftainship of the six great *gwarni*, and the honour was only due if each could claim to represent an undivided *gwari*. Thus Tzitzishvili ceased to be *didebuli tavadi* when his *gwari* became divided.

The terms *tavadi* and *didebuli* did not express exactly equivalent notions. A *didebuli*, it is true, was like a *tavadi* the son of a great *gwari*, but his *didebuleba* depended essentially on his holding a high office, without which, in spite of his being of great *gwari*, he could not have become a *didebuli*. The case was, however, different with a *tavadi*; his *tavadoba* did not depend in any way upon any state duty; to be a *tavadi* he need not have held a high office; for a *tavadi* it was enough that he was head and chief of a great *gwari*. But if he, at the same time, held a high office, he then became as already stated a *didebuli tavadi*.

CHAPTER XXII

THE INSTITUTION OF PATRONQMOBA

THE term "feudalism" is rendered in Georgian by *patronqmoba*, which is a compound word consisting of *patroni* and *qmoba*. *Qmoba* is the abstract form of *qma*, the serf or slave, and means serfdom or slavery. The word *patroni* is the Georgian variant of the Roman *patronus* and is first met with in Georgian documents dating from the eleventh century.

As the etymological meaning of the word indicates *patronqmoba* denoted an organization or society based on the relationship between master and slave. The word *patroni* had several meanings. It denoted:—

1. A private owner or possessor, as for instance *tsikhis patroni*—owner of a fortress: *midsis patroni*—owner of land.
2. A tutor, protector or guardian: *Matiane Kartlisai*, for instance, relating the way in which Giorgi, the minor heir-apparent of Bagrat IV, was brought up, says, " They chose the sister of Bagrati as his *patroni* or tutoress ".[1]
3. A king or sovereign: the historian of King David Aghmashenebeli, speaking of the service rendered to the King by Giorgi Dchqondideli, the *Mdsignobart-Ukhutsesi*, says that " he was from boyhood in the service of the *patroni* ", i.e. of the King.[2] The Historian of Queen Tamara (1184–1212) uses *patroni* particularly frequently in the sense of " king " or " queen ".[3]

Patroni thus denoted not only an owner, protector and guardian, but also even the supreme ruler of the country, the King himself. The *didebulni* officials and the powerful *gwarishvilni* (" sons of *gwarni* ") were also, like the kings, called *patroni*.

Just as *patroni* denoted owner, protector, guardian, lord and king, so the term *qma* also in its turn was used to denote " a subject ", even though he were a *didebuli aznauri* or a *didebuli* official. The Historian of Queen Tamara speaks, for instance, of the Queen's *didebulni*, namely of Zakharia Panaskerteli and Daniel Kalmakheli as " the good *qmani*, the favoured of the *patroni* ", that is as of good subjects of the sovereign. The Historian of Queen Tamara calls the Shirvanshah, whose

[1] *Matiane Kartlisai*, p. 226. [2] *Tzkhovrebai Mepet-Mepisa Davitisa*, p. 301.
[3] *Istoriani da Azmani*, p. 418.

250

domains were under the Queen's protection, "the *qma* of Tamara the King", while he describes his condition as *qmad qola*—holding as *qma*.

Just as the King was *patroni* of his *didebuli* subjects, so the latter, the *qmani didebulni*, were in their turn *patronni* (plural) of their subordinates, who also were called *qmani*. The *qmani* too had their own *qmani* and were consequently *patronni* in their turn.

Patronqmoba was the mainspring of the public life of the country. It characterized not only the social and economic life but also the political and state order of the Kingdom. *Patroni* denoted, as it has already been seen, the king, the lord, the guardian, the protector and the owner-proprietor, while *qma* meant the subject as well as the one under the protection of another or owing obedience to another.

The characteristic features of *patronqmoba* in Georgia, as of feudalism in Western Europe, were twofold, namely the personal relation and the land relation; to the personal aspect of the institution of *patronqmoba*, as affecting the individual, reference has already been made. The other aspect of the institution relating to the holding of land was called in Georgian *shedsqaleba* which in meaning and substance is equivalent to the early Western European *beneficium* or the later *feudum*.

Shedsqaleba was particularly important to the high and influential officials of the state. As "the loyal and faithful service" of the great officials was of great value to the King he would naturally bestow *shedsqaleba*, or benefices, mostly on these high officials, and the King's *shedsqalebulni—beneficiarii*—were generally the great state officials and members of the aristocracy to whom fell the greater part of benefices.

Shedsqaleba was the very essence of *patronqmoba*, and it is necessary to examine the working of it in order to arrive at a correct understanding of the character of feudal institutions in Georgia. The Historian of Queen Tamara, for instance, states that the Queen *sheidsqala* Guzani, "*Patroni* of Shavsheti and Klarjeti to the seat of the ancient Tao(khi)an kings".[1] *Sheidsqala*, which is the past perfect tense of *shedsqaleba*, is herein used in the sense of "elevated". Guzani was appointed the *eristavt-eristavi* of the province of Tao. *Shedsqaleba* thus meant the conferring by the King of a high office.

Another passage from the same source shows that *sheds-*

[1] *Istoriani da Azmani*, p. 434.

qaleba or *dsqaloba* was followed by blessing. Of Zakharia Mkhargrdzeli the Annalists write that the Queen "conferred *dsqaloba* by blessing upon his son, Zakharia, also"; elsewhere again it is stated that she "*sheidsqalnes* and blessed many other *didebulni* also".[1] Blessing or *dalotsva* on occasion formed part of the ceremony of conferring of every high office.

Those of the lesser *qmani* who showed great zeal, loyalty and devotion were, of course, correspondingly *shedsqalebulni*. If a *qma* who had distinguished himself received such a favour for the first time, he was *shedsqalebuli* by being newly blessed, or if he already held some office, or was entrusted with another duty he was *shedsqalebuli momatebita*, that is "additionally".

At the time of blessing the beneficiary or *shedsqalebuli* received from his lord ceremonial investiture; for instance, the *Mandaturt-Ukhutsesi* was presented with a gold ferule; the *Amir-Spasalari* received a golden sword. The *eristavni* and *eristavt-eristavni* had a banner each as an ensign which distinguished their office and, although direct information is not available, it is probable that they received this symbol from the King at the time of investiture.

It is not known whether the *shedsqalebuli* took the oath of fealty, but it is certain that at the time of blessing *taqvaneba*—adoration—was laid down as a rule.

The holding of lands and provinces was directly connected with the holding of office. The lands or provinces so connected with or dependent upon the office held by the *shedsqalebuli* were called *sapatio*, i.e. held in honour.

Besides these *sapatio* provinces and lands, the King's "loyal and devoted" state officers also received by way of *shedsqaleba* the so-called *sakharajoni*. *Sakharajo* is derived from *kharaji*, meaning "the tax", and denotes "for *kharaji*"; *sakharajo* towns therefore constituted grants, the taxes from which the beneficiary could divert to his own benefit.

Sakharajo towns, fortresses and villages were granted to *shedsqalebulni* on different conditions, some as *sakutari*, meaning "own", and some as *sanakhevrot*, meaning "for half". *Sakutari*—own—should not be understood as if the grantee received the towns as his own possessions. The term has no relation to the actual ownership of the places granted; it implies only that the whole of the taxes collected from them were given to the recipient as his own for his own use, while in the case of *sanakhevrot* (for half)—granted towns the grantee

[1] *Istoriani da Azmani*, p. 442.

was given the benefit of only half the amount of the taxes collected.

Shedsqaleba thus meant the bestowing of favour by the King or some other *patroni* upon a *qma* by conferring an office or some other exclusive privilege and granting or conceding *sapatio* or *sakharajo* (*sakutarit* or *sanakhevrot*) towns, fortresses, villages and lands.

On occasions a *shedsqalebuli qma* received a heritable grant *mamulobit* or *samamulot*; grants *mamulobit* were conferred both upon the grantee and his descendants.

The terms of *sapatio* and *nadsqalobevi* grants were subject to variation. When a state official was removed from his office, the *sapatio* property, which he held as a perquisite of that office, reverted to the crown, but the King did not always strictly enforce his reversionary rights and occasionally left some of the properties in the family of the former beneficiary. Thus, for instance, when Queen Tamara deprived Qubasar of the office of *Amir-Spasalari*, she took into consideration his " slavish service " to her father, Giorgi III, and " deprived him of nothing except the office and of Lori ".[1] Lori constituted, among other places, the *sapatio* property of the *Amir-Spasalari*, and once Qubasar was deprived of the office of *Amir-Spasalari*, Lori also was taken from him, but the remainder of his property—his *didebuli koneba*—the Queen left to him. In like manner when Gamrekeli, the *Amir-Spasalari*, died, because of the services he had rendered, " except Tmogvi, of nothing else were his sons deprived " by command of Tamara.[2]

Sapatio and *nadsqalobevi* property thus tended to become hereditary; the former rarely, but the latter more often. But it is noteworthy, as is evident from later *sigelni*, that neither the property granted *mamulobit* nor that which became in course of time hereditary, was ever considered to be fully and completely the private property of the *shedsqalebuli* or of his descendants. The holders of such properties, although called owners, were not in fact in a position to sell, exchange or donate them without the express permission of the King; only by " consulting " and by " permission " of the *patroni* could they deal in these properties. It follows therefore that the supreme owner of the *mamulobit* (heritable) and *nadsqalobevi* property remained after all the donor-*patroni* himself and not the *shedsqalebuli* or grantee.

According to the degree of *dsqaloba* bestowed, a *qma*

[1] *Istoriani da Azmani*, p. 406. [2] *Ibid.*, p. 444.

might be either simply *shedsqalebuli* or " superlatively " (*aghmatebit*) *shedsqalebuli*.

In time of war *qmani* fought alongside and under the leadership of their respective *patronni*. From the Historian of Queen Tamara, we learn that during military operations *qmani* closely surrounded their *patronni*; after a stiff hand-to-hand fight " rejoiced ", says the Historian, " as finders . . . *patroni* of his *qma* and *qma* of his *patroni* ";[1] and, as he states elsewhere, during a battle "*patroni* forged ahead of his *qma* and *qma* ahead of his *patroni* ".[2]

Not only in war, but also in daily life when a *patroni* travelled, he was accompanied by his *qmani*. The suites of the great *didebulni* included *aznaurni*; such *aznaurni* were called *aznaurni tanamqolni* or accompanying, that is *aznaurni* companions; their duty was to defend their patrons. *Qmani* who lived on the estates of their patrons were called *mamulis katsni* or " men of the estates ".[3]

Whether all the *mamulis katsni* were, irrespective of their status, obliged to accompany their patrons in war it is difficult to say, but it is certain that the bounden duty of *shedsqalebulni qmani* was " faithful service ". This obligation of a *shedsqalebuli qma* was definitely stated in the *dsqalobis dsigni*.

As yet only one *dsgalobis dsigi* or " book " has been discovered which is of the first half of the thirteenth century. This document, which was granted by the Church, gives an incomplete, but fairly approximate idea as to the manner in which *dsqaloba* was bestowed. Only on exceptional occasions after great wars and expeditions, or particular and extraordinary service, was *dsqaloba* conferred by the *patroni* himself on his own initiative; on all other occasions of everyday life *dsqaloba* had to be solicited by the loyal and *msakhureuli qma* himself; his supplication and petition had to proceed by way of a reminder that the *patroni* might reward the *msakhureuli*, or deserving, *qma*. The Catholicos Mikel speaks thus, for instance, in his *dsaqolobis dzigi*:

" When first the invasion of the Khorazmians and then that of the Tatars devastated this kingdom and laid waste some countries (i.e. provinces) and villages, and thou and thy brothers were overtaken by misfortune, and as a result had lost whatever lands and properties you possessed, and were unable in consequence to subsist . . . hast submitted to us thy supplication so that we might confer *dsqaloba* upon

---

[1] *Istoriani da Azmani*, p. 373.
[3] Abuseridze Tbeli, in *Kronikebi*, II, 120-7.
[2] *Ibid.*, p. 421.

THE INSTITUTION OF PATRONQMOBA

thee, Vaché Guaramisdze, and grant thee subsistence . . . *samamulot* to serve the Church. . . . We have listened to thy supplication and grant *samamulot* to thee Vaché Guaramisdze, our *Msakhurt-Ukhutsesi* and thy sons and descendants, the village of Oromasheni in return for services (*samsakhurod*) to the Church." [1]

It has already been stated that *shedsqaleba* proved particularly beneficial to the high state officials and to the great *gwarishvilni* and that to them fell the greater part of the benefices. *Shedsqaleba* enriched the " loyal and obedient " *gwariani* officials. From the works of the Historians of David Aghmashenebeli and Queen Tamara we learn that in the twelfth century, especially during the reigns of Giorgi III and his daughter, the over-generous use of *shedsqaleba* on the part of the kings, made it possible for an enormous amount of wealth both movable and immovable to accumulate in the hands of the *didebulni* and *shedsqalebulni*, rendering them owners of immense estates and of numerous *qmani*.

In order to curb the power of the grasping and unruly *didgwarianni* the kings began to follow a policy of replacing them by persons of *ugwaro* or *uazno* descent who were personally dependent on the goodwill of the Court. By means of *shedsqaleba* the King made strong his " loyal and faithful servant ", enriched him materially and increased the number of his *qmani*. Thus by the side of the *didgwariani* officials there came into existence in each generation a group of *msakhureuli shedsqalebulni* who, although they lacked the distinction of birth and the influence of class, were at the same time very strong, since they had been raised to the patronage of numerous towns, fortresses and villages. But the over-generous character of the beneficence shown towards the promoted *ugwaro* officials and administrators in the end defeated its own purpose; and the system of *shedsqaleba* served to perpetuate those evils to eradicate which the kings had directed all their energies and their favours. *Shedsqaleba* gradually raised the new favourites, these *ugwaro* officials, to a position of influence and power; in course of time it concentrated in their hands new accumulations of wealth; the administrative positions which they held gained them a steadily increasing political influence, and their descendants, finding themselves in the position of great hereditary land-owners, easily forgot their *uazno* or *ugwaro* origins and their indebtedness to the Crown. In these circumstances their ambitions proved as matchless and their

[1] S. Kakabadze, *XIII Saukunis pirveli nakhevris Sakartvolas Katolikosebi* (*The Georgian Catholicoses of the first half of Thirteenth Century*).

THE PEOPLE AND THE POWER

lust for power as arrogant as that of any of the older houses whom they aspired to overshadow, and the thirteenth century saw the renewal and continuance of the struggle between the kings and their clamant feudatories, the former to assert their rule and the latter to resist it.

CHAPTER XXIII
COURT AND ADMINISTRATION

THE officials of the state were called in Georgian *mokheleni* or *khelosanni*. Both words *mokhele* and *khelosani* (singular) are derived from the word *kheli*, which in its meaning is the equivalent of the Latin *manus*—hand. *Kheli* in ancient Georgian was used as a juridical term conveying the notion of "right", "authority", "power"; also of "function", "office". From *kheli* is formed *khelmdsipé*, the literal meaning of which is "hand-ripe", i.e. ripe of hand, in other words a person invested with full power or authority.[1] From the same word *kheli* is also formed *khelisupali* meaning master of *kheli* or office, that is a holder of office or authority. *Kheli* thus meant both "power", "authority" and "office", while *mokhele*, *khelosani* or *khelisupali* denoted the officials or the holders of offices. Thus in a *sigeli* granted by Queen Tamara to the Shio-Mghvimé Monastery, we read:

"Neither over the waters, nor over the peasants shall our *khelisupalni* (i.e. officials) have any *kheli* (i.e. power or authority)"[2].

The office or authority with which a *khelisupali* or official was entrusted was called *khelisupleba*; while his department of administration was called *sakheloi*.

Mokheleni of the state were divided into two groups, namely into *khelisupalni* and *sakmis mokmedni*; *mokhele* thus was a general term, while *khelisupali* was a term of a particular group of officials. A *khelisupali* was an official entrusted with high authority, the responsible head of his *kheli* or department of state affairs; the *khelisupalni* thus were the principal departmental officials while the *sakmis mokmedni* (literally the "business doers") constituted the junior executive officials.

Khelisupalni holding great offices were called *didebulni khelisupalni*. *Didebulni khelisupalni* were also called *ganmgebelni*, *zedamkhedvelni sakmeta*, that is directors, controllers of state affairs. They were therefore also entitled *tanaziarni mepobisa*, i.e. "sharers of kingship".

---
[1] Later, however, it was used to denote "The King".
[2] See *Sami Sigeli*, published by S. Kakabadze, p. 7.

THE PEOPLE AND THE POWER

Sakmis mokmedni were of two grades, namely *didni* and *mtsireni*, that is " great and small ". *Mokheleni* were divided in accordance with the arena of their activity; thus the officials serving in the principal central institutions of the state, called *Darbazi* (Persian *Dar-bar*) constituted the group of *Darbazis kars Mdgomni mokheleni*, i.e. " the officials of the court ", *Darbazi*, while those of the provincial institutions constituted the group of *sakueqnod gamrigeni*, that is the provincial officials.

THE APPROXIMATE LIST OF DARBAZI OFFICIALS AND THEIR SUBORDINATES.

1. *Mdsignobart-Ukhutsesi* [1] the Chief of the Secretaries, resembling in some ways the Pehlevi *Dabribed*, in others the Byzantine *Protoascrit*.
    Mdsignobarni [2]—secretaries. This word literally means " bookers ", i.e. book-learned men.
    Sadsolis Mdsignobari—Secretary of the Royal Bedchamber.
    Zardakhnis Mdsignobari—Secretary of the Royal Arsenal.
    Sadchurdchlis Mdsignobari—Secretary of the Royal Treasury.
    A document entitled the " Court Regulations " reveals that there were in all 26 departmental *mdsignobarni*, their titles, however, excepting the three given above, are not mentioned.
    Mdseralta Mtavari—the Chief of the Scribes.
    Mdseralni—the Scribes.
2. *Amir-Spasalari*—War Minister and Commander-in-Chief corresponding to the West European Grand Constable.
    Amirakhori—Grand Equerry; assistant War Minister.
    Meabjret-Ukhutsesi—the Chief of the Armourers.
    Meabjre—Armourer.
    Abjris Mtvirtveli—Armour-Bearer.
    Mejinibet-Ukhutsesi—the Chief of the Grooms.
    Mejinibeni—the Grooms.
    Atchukji (a Turkish word, equivalent to the preceding).
    Amirtchkari—the Chief of the Messengers.
    Meremet-Ukhutsesi—Chief of the Stud-Grooms (*Mereme*—literally, *horse-herd*).
    Saremos-Ukhutsesi—Chief of the Stud (*Saremos*—literally, *place where the horse-herd is kept*).
    Saremos-Natsvali—Assistant Chief of the Stud.
    Meremeni—Stud-Grooms.
    Zardakhnis-Ukhutsesi—the Chief of the Arsenal.
    Zardakhnis-molare—the Treasurer of the Arsenal.
    Zardakhnis-mejinibe—the Equerry of the Arsenal.
    Zardakhnis-mdsignobari—the Secretary of the Arsenal.
    Misratult-Ukhutsesi—Chief Clerk of the Stables Department.
    Megodreni—Cofferers (? Treasurers, Accountants).
3. *Mandaturt-Ukhutsesi*—the Chief of the Mandators, resembling in some ways the High-Marshal of Ceremonies, in others the Byzantine *Proto-Mandator* or *Dromos-Logothete*, the Grand Domestic.

---

[1] *Ukhutsesi*, chief, means literally " eldest man ", " elder ".
[2] The term *Mdsignobari* gave place during the fourteenth century to the Persian form *mdivani*.

COURT AND ADMINISTRATION

Mandaturni—the Mandators.
Amir-Ejibi—the Grand Chamberlain.[1]
Ganmget-Ukhutsesi—the Chief of the Stewards.
Ganmgeni—the Stewards.
Ejibni—the Chamberlains.
Mestumret-Ukhutsesi—Chief Receiver of Guests.
Mestumré—Receiver of Guests.
Mejamet-Ukhutsesi—the Chief of the Butlers.
Mejameni—the Butlers.
Merige—the Arranger.
Sagamgeos-Mukipi—Administrator of the Office of Gifts.
4. *Medchurdchlet-Ukhutsesi*, the Chancellor of the Exchequer.
Natsvali Medchurdchlet-Ukhutsesisa—the Vice-Chancellor of the Exchequer.
Kalakis-amirani—the Amirs of the Towns.
Mushribi—the Commissioner of the Exchequer.
Medchurdchleni-Kalakisani—the Treasurers of the Towns.
Darbazis Medchurdchleni—the Treasurers of Darbazi.
Sadchurdchlis-Mukipi—Administrator (" Receiver ") of the Treasury.
Medchurdchleni—the Treasurers.
Mokharajeni—the Tax Collectors.
5. *Atabagi* (a military-administrative title of Persian origin; literally, *ata-beg* = father-lord).
6. *Msakhurt-Ukhutsesi*—the Chief of the *Msakhurni* (Privy Purse).
Molaret-Ukhutsesi—the Chief of the Royal Treasury.
Molareni—the Treasurers.
Mesadsolet-Ukhutsesi—the Chief of the Royal Bedchamber.
Mesadsoleni—Gentlemen of the Bedchamber.
Dsina Mdsolni—Gentlemen of the Bedchamber (literally, *in front sleepers*).
Sadsolis Mekare—Officer of the Guard of the Bedchamber.
Paresht-Ukhutsesi—the Chief of the Valets or Lackeys of the Court.
Pareshni—the Valets or Lackeys.
Mkervalt-Ukhutsesi—the Chief of Tailors.
Mkervalni—the Tailors.
Mekhilet-Ukhutsesi—the Chief of the Fruit Servers.
Tsitskhvt-Ukhutsesi—the Chief of the Ladle Bearers.
7. *Meghvinet-Ukhutsesi*—the Chief of the Wine Servers.
Saghvinis-Mukipi—Receiver or Administrator of Gifts in the Wines Department.
Saghvinis Molare—the Treasurer of the Wine Cellar.
Meghvineni—Those who serve or look after the wine.
Piris Meghvine—Personal Wine Server of the King.
Melupeni—Wine Tax-collectors.
Mdsdeni—the Cup-bearers.
8. *Monadiret-Ukhutsesi*—the Chief of the Hunters.
Monadireni—the Hunters.
9. *Tqismtsvelt-Ukhutsesi*—the Chief of the Foresters.

---

[1] According to Wakhushti, the *Amir-Ejibi* had a general authority over all the Palace. At banquets he replied in the name of the King; the King's relations with courtesans were arranged through him, and no one might approach the King except through his mediation.

THE PEOPLE AND THE POWER

THE APPROXIMATE LIST OF *Saqueqhod Gamrigeni* AND THEIR SUBORDINATES

1. *Eristavt-Eristavni*, the Eristavis of Eristavis.
2. *Eristavni*—the Eristavis.
   Temis-Eristavni—the Eristavis of Temi (districts).
   Mdsignobarni—the Secretaries.
   Molaret-Ukhutsesi—the Chief of the Treasury.
   Molareni—the Treasurers.
   Tsikhis-tavni—the Captains of Fortresses.
   Khevisupalni-Mamasakhlisni; *gzirni*.
3. *Amirt-amirani*—the Amirs of Amirs.
4. *Tanuterni*—the Mamasakhlisni.
5. *Otkhmisdurni*—[1]
6. *Marzpanni*—the Frontier Officials. (A word of Persian origin.)
7. *Monapireni*—the Frontier Officials.

The first place among the *khelisupalni* was held by the *vazirni*—the viziers. The term *vaziri* (singular) is an Arabic-Persian word. In Arabic *Vaz-irum* meant assistant, collaborator and minister. The vazirate among the Arabs was first introduced by the Ummayyad Caliphs; in course of time and especially since the time of the Abbasid Caliphate the *vazirs* acquired great power and influence. Usually there was only one *vazir* under the Caliphate and he was the principal and the most powerful of all the ministers of the state. In the early Muslim despotats in Persia the title of *vazir* was given to only one of the ministers.

In Georgia, however, the term *vaziri* had been adopted as a general term for the ministers of the state. It seems to have been first introduced into Georgia during the reign of King Giorgi III (1156–84). At first, in Georgia, as in the Arab states, the term *vaziri* denoted assistant. For instance, in the *Court Regulations* it is stated that " Amirakhori is *vaziri* to the *Amir-Spasalari* ".[2] As early as the reign of Queen Tamara, however, the term *vaziri*, as already stated, had become a general title denoting a minister.

At first there were only four *vazirni* at the Georgian Court, namely:

Mdsignobart-Ukhutsesi
Amir-Spasalari
Mandaturt-Ukhutsesi
Medchurdchlet-Ukhutsesi.

This number was increased to five by Queen Tamara who in 1212 created the office of *Atabagi* (*atabagoba*).

[1] This title is only mentioned in two *sigelni*, dated 1027 and 1189. Georgian historians, some of whom think it to have been a title in use only in Imereti, do not seem to have been able to interpret its meaning.

[2] *Khelmdsipis Karis Garigeba* (*Court Regulations*), published by Prof. E. Taqaishvili, p. 9, par. 18.

COURT AND ADMINISTRATION

Queen Rusudani further increased the number to six by elevating the *Msakhurt-Ukhutsesi* to the rank of a *vaziri* or minister. There was a seventh *vaziri*, namely, the *Amirakhori*, who, however, did not enjoy full Cabinet rank; he was the assistant *vaziri* to the *Amir-Spasalari*, and as such he attended the Cabinet meetings or *vaziroba*, but only in a consultative and not in a deliberative capacity; that is, he could not participate in the deliberations of the cabinet ministers or *vazirni* or express his opinion unless he were invited to do so. "He hears debates and deliberations, but he says nothing," according to the *Court Regulations*.

The *Mdsignobart-Ukhutsesi* was the first and principal *vaziri*, in other words he was the Prime Minister. The other *vazirni* were divided into two groups, namely the Three *Vazirni* Group and the Two *Vazirni* Group.[1] The first group enjoyed a slightly greater prominence both at great banquets and at *vaziroba*. The Three *Vazirni* group consisted of:
Atabagi
Amir-Spasalari and
Mandaturt-Ukhutsesi.[2]
and the Two *Vazirni* group of:
Medchurdchlet-Ukhutsesi, and
Msakhurt-Ukhutsesi.[3]

Another document, namely the *Regulations for the Coronation of the Kings* reveals that this grouping of the *vazirni* represents a division into a military group and a civil group. In this document it is stated that in the procession of the Royal Coronation to the Cathedral the "*Amir-Spasalari* . . . rides on the right side (of the King) . . . likewise also *Amirakhori* and *Meabjret-Ukhutsesi* ride on the side of *Amir-Spasalari*, while the Dchqondideli (*Mdsignobart-Ukhutsesi*) and *Atabagi* are on the left side . . . and also other *mtavarni*."

The same document reveals the seniority of the *vazirni*. After the coronation the ceremony of congratulation was to be carried out in the following manner; first the Queen made her bow and offered her congratulations; then the Catholicos, the Dchqondideli, the *Atabagi*, the *Mandaturt-Ukhutsesi*, the *Amir-Spasalari*, the *Medchurdlet-Ukhutsesi* and the *Msakhurt-Ukhutsesi*.

Wakhushti in his *Geographical Description* gives the title of a number of minor court officials in addition to those enumerated above. These were:

The *Baziert-Ukhutsesi*, or Chief of the Falconers, who had

---
[1] *Karis-Garigeba*, p. 12, par. 22. [2] *Ibid*. [3] *Ibid*., p. 14, par. 25.

charge of all the King's Falconers and dogs and was over all the keepers of the royal woods.

The *Ezos-Modzghvari*, or Master of the Courtyard who had under his inspection all the workshops of the palace.

The *Mzareult-Ukhutsesi*, or Chief of the Cooks, who was over all the table-servants, the kitcheners, the bakers, water-carriers, musicians and dancers. He was later called by the Persian title of *Chunchirakhi*.

The *Momgheralt-Ukhutsesi*, or Chief of the Singers, and the *Juaris-Mtvirtveli* or Cross-Bearer who was the King's messenger to the Catholicos and the Bishops; he also made public pronouncement of all penalties inflicted by royal command.

The royal revenues were derived from various sources. First, there were the feudal dues from the estates of the royal house which were paid in large part in kind, but also partly in money.

Secondly, the Kings of Georgia and the earlier rulers of Iberia coined money for circulation in the realm. Gold and silver was never found in any but negligible quantities within the country, and therefore the rarer metals used for coining and for the manufacture of objects of luxury came at all times from abroad. Large quantities of foreign coins were always in circulation in the country. Money was, however, minted in Georgia with intervals from the second century A.D. down even to the times of the paltry sovereignties of Mingrelia and Imereti, who according to Chardin, had their own mints.[1]

Again, the Kings of Georgia and the later rulers of the divided Kingdom imposed customs dues on goods entering the country and on goods in transit. In Chardin's time there were customs levied at Iskaur (Dioscurias-Sukhum), in Abkhazeti and Fasso (Poti) in Mingrelia, and the insolence which he met from the Pasha of Akhaltzikhé's customs officers at Gonia was in the true tradition of the *douane*. There were also provincial and municipal customs where levies were made not only by the King, but by other authorities such as the Catholicos of Mtzkheta or the chieftains of Osseti. Boat traffic on the Mtkvari and ferries over this and other rivers were subject to levy, and also caravans entering and leaving Tiflis and Gori.

Further, the Kings levied a miscellaneous collection of taxes of all kinds and descriptions. The *Dastulamali* gives a list of taxes paid to the later Kings of Kartli, together with the shares of these taxes to which certain court officials were

---

[1] Chardin (1686 ed.), pp. 91 and 106.

entitled. The King controlled the farming of the famous mineral springs at Tiflis and he farmed the monopoly of the sale of brandy. He and his *Mdivan-begi* or Chief Judge had a share of all judicial fines imposed and of damages gained by plaintiff parties. The King drew rents from the irrigation canals and revenue from taxes on wine, on flocks and on the tents of nomads; the shopkeepers of Tiflis bore the cost of the lighting of the royal palace; one district was under the obligation to supply beaters for the King's hunt; another to cart snow for the ice storage of his larders. In a third district we learn that the King having originally distributed geese to the inhabitants, there was an annual tax of two goslings on every goose. Further examples of ingenious but unscientific extraction were taxes on married men, ploughs, furnaces, beasts of burden and falcons and their nests.

Another—and a principal—source of revenue, particularly in times of emergency, were the special poll-taxes which were levied sometimes on the individual or on families, at other times on houses, cattle, horses, trees or agricultural produce. Such taxes were generally levied in the emergency of war, but from the sixteenth century onwards they were more often extracted to meet the demands of the commanders of invading armies of Persians and Turks. We have already referred to the taxes imposed during the days of the Mongol hegemony and to the special levies in human kind made by the Shah and the Sultan, to meet which the Georgian Kings on occasion made levies with the object of purchasing substitute slaves from the mountaineers.

The invaders from time to time also made direct capital impositions. In 1724, the Turks imposed a poll-tax on the whole male population and levied also on cattle, horses and agricultural produce; and in 1736 the Persians imposed such an onerous tax on cattle and trees that five years later the army of Nadir Shah was beset by famine. The Persian exactions continued until in 1747, when King Taymuraz II effected a kind of general strike by moving all the peasantry of the open country into the hills and strong places. As a result, Nadir reduced his imposition from 200,000 to 25,000 *tumans*.

Lastly, throughout the Middle Ages the Kings not infrequently levied special poll-taxes enduring over a period of years, the proceeds of which were spent in the repair of churches and royal castles, and of towns which had been devastated during foreign invasions.

It was the practice of the Georgian kings and of the earlier

THE PEOPLE AND THE POWER

Iberian rulers to maintain a force of regular paid troops in garrison at Tiflis and in the provincial fortresses. David Aghmashenebeli in the twelfth century is reputed to have kept 60,000 paid troops always under arms.[1] A proportion of these regular troops appear generally to have been foreign mercenaries. David Aghmashenebeli certainly had large numbers of Kipchaks and Ossetians in his pay; his grandfather Bagrat IV in the eleventh century had three thousand Warangs—Russians or possibly Saxon and Norse freebooters like those who served the Byzantine Emperors—fighting for him in his difficult wars against the feudality [2]: Giorgi Lasha according to the Annals, lost an eye in a brawl with his mercenary horsemen in the streets of Tiflis, when he visited their barracks drunk and they did not recognize him [3]: and it was the Persian mercenaries of Rusudani who betrayed the gates of Tiflis to Jalal-ul-din, and who together with the Persians living in the city attacked the Georgian defenders from inside.[4]

The regular troops were apparently responsible for providing their own arms, but they received a fixed pay. The *Amir-Spasalari* exercised the functions of command under the King, and the *Msakhurt-Ukhutsesi* was responsible for the practical and technical organization of the army. During the great days of the mediæval Kingdom, the *Mdsignobart-Ukhutsesi*, Chief of the Secretaries of the King, who was by custom the occupant of the important Imerian see of Dchqondidi, occupied a special relation to the army. He was responsible for the issue of writs of mobilization, he bore the Holy Cross before the army on the march and, during action, he carried out the duties of *Chakhtauli* or commander of the rearguard. In time of war, the body of the army was, of course, composed of feudal levies, who were summoned by writ and messenger on the approach of hostilities.

The feudal army of the Georgian Kings was organized in four banners: the advance guard was made up of the Meskhians; on the right wing were the men of Imereti and Mingrelia, with the Abkhazian and Circassian contingents; on the left were the men of Kakheti and Hereti. The King's bodyguard with the royal standard was composed of Kartlian troops.

It was not always the case that a general mobilization was made, and on the occasions of outbreak of a frontier conflict

---

[1] Wakhushti, *Dés. Géo.*, pp. 35 *et seq.*   [2] *Annals*, Brosset, *H. de la G.*, I, 321.
[3] *Ibid.*, p. 321.   [4] *Ibid.*, p. 503.

COURT AND ADMINISTRATION

sometimes only the men of Samtzkhé or of Imier might be called out.

After the Division of the Kingdom, the Kings of Kartli and the lesser rulers ceased to maintain any effective bodies of troops; in the seventeenth century the Shahs established Persian garrisons in Tiflis and Gori and the Turks had a garrison at Kutais to overlook the Imerian kings. The military strength of the Georgian rulers was then little more than that of powerful feudatories, and when they went to war they had to rely, not upon the armouries, castles and trained mercenaries of the mediæval Kingdom, but upon untrained, unpaid and ill-armed tenants' levies.

CHAPTER XXIV

RELIGION AND THE GEORGIAN CHURCH

THE vastness of the influence enjoyed by the Churches during the Middle Ages, both in the Christian West and the Christian East, is a monument to the credulity, to the intellectual laziness and to the pathetic kindliness of the human mind.

The credulity of the mediæval mind might seem almost incomprehensible to the modern mind were it not that we see in our own day large numbers of people of no mean intelligence engaged in the sterile devotions and the sterile controversies, both of modern religion, and of its derivative, modern social philosophy. And the schisms of the Byzantine Church can scarcely seem ridiculous to the modern man who contemplates around him the heated feuds over the English Prayer Book, or the bloodthirsty vendetta between the rival interpreters of the real thoughts of Lenin.

The teaching of Christ—that lean and gentle Cynic, that humanistic Lover of men and of nature, that outspoken Paladin of the deceived, that Hater of the mean and hypocritical, bears as little relation to the body of the Church, as an oak tree, gleaming in the sun and freshened for ever by the winds, bears to an oak coffin, covered with homilies inscribed in silver and having inside the emptiness of death. And it is no exaggeration to say that had Christ been born during any one of the twenty centuries during which controversies have roared around the simplicity of His kindly Faith and Nature, He would have been burned at the stake as a blasphemer or put into prison for sedition.

The Church—organized religion—is, like any other corporate institution, a product of the human mind. It is within the parasitical—or, more euphemistically, the self-supporting —character of Nature—that everything lives upon something else and gives birth to something that lives upon it. And long before the Christian era, the human mind, a credulous

RELIGION

mind, had already created the wherewithal to satisfy its credulity—priesthoods which at once lived upon and satisfied " the believer ". For the human mind in its pathetic aching for finality, for an attainable perfection, always sets up fetishes, the idealization of hopes and the contrary embodiment of fears—religions and social systems—that encumber it. And this will go on, in religion and in politics, until men realize, as they have been taught by experience, that there is no foreseeable finality; that all will change and that change is the salt of life; that faith rests in themselves; that divinity, untouchable and not to be imagined, rests here around ourselves and lies forward in the spaceless spaces of eternity. And so out of credulity, we have that great corporate body catering for credulity; and like a gigantic and fraudulent insurance upon the divinity of men, it sprawls across the ages —the community of priests. Therefore in approaching the history of Christianity in Georgia we do not seek to inquire when the Georgians became Christians, but when the priesthood in Georgia took over the forms of Christianity.

The Christian religion was introduced into Georgia in the fourth century A.D. under the influence of the Græco-Roman world. The Christian faith, in the pure elements of its early form certainly produced a revolution in the minds of the Georgians of the following centuries. The essential stem of early Christian faith is self-discipline, and in studying the psychology of the Georgians during different epochs, we can appreciate the real values of Christianity in its conversion of the human mind from the irresponsible ingenuousness of the pagan which is exemplified in Xenophon's account of the Mossynoekhoi, to the courageous self-discipline, the conscientious charity and the intellectual poise of the mediæval mind, of which in Georgia Queen Tamara, Sargisi of Tmogvi and King Dmitri II, are the best representative types.

Christianity in Georgia produced its many strong thinkers and its single-minded protagonists of faith. In the sixth century there were the remarkable missions to the Huns undertaken by Aghovanian monks to which reference has already been made. In the seventh century we read of the saintly life and martyrdom of Neophyte, Bishop of Urbnissi, and in the ninth century we find St. Grigoli of Khandzti fulminating from his monastery on the Chorokhi against the matrimonial aberrations of the Kuropalatês Adarnasé.

The Georgian Church went the way of all other churches. The bleak strong spirits built it—and passed into a memory

"Zacharius, Patriarch of Georgia in his Pontifical Robes" (Castelli).

RELIGION

revered and neglected by their sanctimonious successors. The priest-mind took the rough clean spirit of the Founder and the rugged sacrifices of these old and dim-remembered men who found in it a divine message for humanity; and violent and abortive, cunning and obsequious, the priest-mind turned it into the sour wine of the Mediæval church.

It is difficult to appreciate the extent to which the Church checked the development of human knowledge during the Middle Ages. Education was the preserve of the Church in Georgia, as in other countries of the Christian East and West. The wealth and the intellectual monopoly of the Church attracted to it much of the best human material of each successive century. This material was physically sterilized in the monasteries and mentally sterilized in the copying and illumination of sacred books and in the development of bleak theses upon futile religious controversies. Georgian ecclesiastical literature produced nothing of intellectual value with the exception of certain parts of the Annals and some historical manuscripts, and through the pages of these works there runs the endless thread of priestly perversion of the truth to suit the moral reclamations—or more frequently the purely material designs on property—of the Church. It was left to the wild growth of the troubadour literature—evolved under the freethinking influence of the Persian poets and the Classic philosophers—to express the natural art and creative genius of the Georgian spirit.

The Georgian Church remained always in close alliance with the Greek. At an early period Greek ecclesiasts were active in Georgia, and Georgian monks were numerous in Syria and Greece. The Georgian Church was originally subordinate to the Patriarchs of Antioch, but the Armenian Church exercised a closer influence on Georgian ritual and dogma, until, in the beginning of the seventh century, the decisions of the Council of Chalchedon produced the Schism which led to the separation of the Armenian from the Greek Church. Thenceforward the Georgians, following in the train of Greek religious thought, carried on a long and often politically disastrous feud with the Armenians, although both David the Restorer and Tamara called Councils in an attempt to reconcile the dogmatic scruples of the contending priests. At the same time the Churches of Byzantium and Georgia were closely associated. The Byzantine Emperors endowed churches in Georgia, and made donations for the restoration of others including the Cathedral of Mtzkheta, while the Georgian kings assisted the considerable colonies of Georgian monks who settled in the Byzantine territories by the foundation and endowment of churches and monasteries on Mount Athos, at Antioch, Jerusalem, and on Mount Sinai.

The Georgian Church in two respects bears an important relation to the political history of the country. First Christianity, both in Zoroastrian and Mussulman days, represented the influence of Byzantium and the Christian West as opposed to that of Persia and the East. And the prosperity and power of the Church fluctuated according to the respective strength of Christendom and Islam. Secondly Georgia did not experience the struggle between Church and State which was taking place in other parts of Christendom. This fact must be attributed directly to the menace of Islam. The influence of the Church over the peasantry was too valuable to the King, and the armed protection of the King was too important to the Church, to allow either of them to attempt to weaken or dispense with the other. Thus when the Arab invasion drove the Iberian rulers over the Mountains of Likhi, the Catholicos of Mtzkheta followed them, while during the abeyance of the Bagratids, between the seventh and tenth centuries, the Catholicosate apparently lapsed. The revival of the Georgian monarchy saw the reappearance of a Catholicos at Mtzkheta and the rich endowment of churches and monasteries. While Henry II in England was wrangling with Thomas à-Becket, the Georgian kings were showering favours and privileges on their clergy.

During the great days of the Bagratid monarchy, the Georgian Church flourished and grew rich under the protection of and in alliance with the Crown.[1] And it is but rarely that that friction between the two dominant bodies in the state, which was troubling the politics of contemporary England and of the Western Empire, and which, under the Iconoclastic Emperors had arisen in Byzantium, is to be noted in the history of mediæval Georgia. David Aghmashenebeli indeed, carried out a drastic cleansing of the Church, but his conduct is approved by the monkish Annalists. Tamara supported by the nobles tried without success to remove the unpopular Catholicos Mikélo Mirionisdze, who "was generally detested,"[2] and both Giorgi IV Lasha and Dmitri II incurred

---

[1] See particularly Brosset, *H. de la G.*, I, 315–16, for the great acquisitions of property by the Church during the reign of Bagrat IV.
[2] *Ibid.*, p. 423.

the anger of the Catholicos of their time on account of their way of living.

The two powers of the Church and the Crown seem to have been virtually interdependent. The Catholicos and his bishops held wide lands and owned great numbers of serfs—"the sons of Mtzkheta". The Church property was free from taxation except in events of emergency, and the Catholicos enjoyed a share of state dues and in addition such perquisites as the takings of the toll-house at Gori and a tax on dye-houses. Many *mtavarni* and *aznaurni* were his vassals; and the levies from the estates of the Church went on campaign under their own commander, who was, in principle, independent of the royal surveillance. Together the Crown and the Church monopolized all the power and the greater part of the wealth of the country, and on terms of amity and confidence, the one supported the other. The King nominated a new Catholicos, and the Catholicos presided over the assembly of lords, spiritual and temporal, at the coronation of a new king.

> "An affront", says the Code of Wakhtangi, "of whatever nature it may be, made against the King or the Catholicos, is of equal gravity; for if the first is master of the body, the second is of the soul, and they have both received the consecration of God and men." [1]

Much of the wealth that poured into the country as a result of the consolidation of the monarchy and the successful wars against the Muslims, found its way into the hands of the ecclesiasts. Triumphant kings endowed the Church with new lands and further numbers of serfs, and successful soldiers minted their loot into richly bejewelled icons and the spoils of Muslim harîms into sacerdotal plate.

Hundreds of churches and monasteries sprang up, constructed at great cost by architects, stone-masons and wood-carvers, many of whom were brought from Byzantium. The churches were full of gorgeous vestments, of rare illuminated holy books, of miraculous relics presented by noble devotees returned from the Holy Land,[2] of costly gold and silver vessels. At the boards of the Catholicos and of his bishops, holy men and their lay guests feasted to their full on the first fruits of the land. And the Church was chosen by the cadets of the aristocracy as a career more lucrative and more pleasing than service at the court, or in the trains of the great *didebulni*.

---

[1] Brosset, *H. de la G.*, Intro. et Add., p. cx. In the reign of Bagrat IV the Annalists refer to the Catholicos as "the Holy King Melkizideki" (I, 315).

[2] For an account of the curious relics in the possession of the Dadiani see Chardin, 1686 ed., p. 99.

THE PEOPLE AND THE POWER

With the fall of the national monarchy and the predominance of the Mussulman powers began the decline of the Georgian Church. The Turkish capture of Constantinople severed all connection with the Greeks, who had so profoundly influenced every aspect of Georgian religious life, its doctrines, its rites and its architecture. Finally when the Georgian Kingdom was divided, the authority of the Church became divided too.

The writ of the Catholicos of Mtzkheta ceased to extend beyond Kartli. The King of Imereti revived the Catholicosate of Abkhazeti which henceforward exercised a shadowy authority over the Western Caucasus and the Rioni valley; and in Kakheti the Bishop of Alaverdi, in Mingrelia the Metropolitan of Bedia, in Guria the Bishop of Shemokhmedi, followed the separatist tendencies of the local rulers. The influence and efficiency of the clergy speedily declined. All the European travellers in Georgia during the seventeenth century unite in condemning their ignorance, their drunkenness, their immorality and their levity. The bishops were hardly to be distinguished from the ordinary feudal proprietors, and their seats were bought and sold by or conferred as rewards upon the relatives of the different ruling princes. The nobles, demoralized by the humiliating political conditions, which often compelled them to embrace Islam, to send their sons in hostage to be educated by the mullahs of Isfahan, or to give their daughters into Persian or Turkish harîms, had assumed a cynical indifference towards their religion. They combined Mussulman polygamy with Christian drunkenness and interested themselves in either religion only to the extent of celebrating with admirable impartiality the feast-days of both.

The Kartlian kings were frequently required by the Shahs to profess an outward devotion to Islam, and Pitton de Tournefort gives us an amusing picture of the religious exercises of the ruler, contemporary with his visit.

> " Le Prince de Tiflis ", he says, " étoit du Rite Grec, mais on l'obligea de se faire circoncire. On dit que ce malhereux professoit les deux religions, car il alloit à la Mosquée et venoit à la Messe chez les Capucins, öu il beuvoit à la santé de la Saintête." [1]

Only among the peasantry and the artisan class did any true religious sentiment survive, and this, in reality, took the form of national feeling against the Persians and Turks.

---
[1] Pitton de Tournefort, *Relation d'un Voyage du Levant* (Paris, 1717), tome II, p. 310.

RELIGION

At the end of the seventeenth century, in Tiflis, Persian preparations to build a mosque could still arouse enough resentment to provoke a riot.[1]

A few of the rulers, particularly in Kartli and Kakheti, made some efforts to maintain their spiritual integrity in spite of adverse political conditions. The heroic Queen Katevani of Kakheti, an elderly woman, suffered torture and execution in the Shah's prisons rather than abandon her faith, and King Wakhtang VI of Kartli preferred to relinquish his throne rather than conform outwardly—as many of his predecessors had done and his successors would do—to the Islamic creed. But amid the inconsequent but sturdy adherence of the peasantry to the faith of their fathers and their nation, and the courageous fidelity of an occasional ruler in the Georgian Kingdoms, the generality of the nobles and the priests led a spiritual life of irresponsible depravity.

Chardin, who bases his account upon personal observation and upon the manuscript made for him by Brother Zampi, a Théatin of Mantua who had lived for twenty years in Georgia, gives a lamentable account of the state of the Christian religion in Mingrelia.

> "The priests of Mingrelia", he says, "are very numerous; and a sort of miserable creature that live upon whatever they can get.... There needs no more than to be able to read and say a Mass by Heart, to be admitted into the Priesthood.... Nor is it to be imagined how the Priests are contemn'd and scorn'd.... Now that which

> causes this contempt is their ignorance their Gluttony and their Poverty. Their Poverty is so great that they go Barefoot, and in Tatters that hardly cover their Tails.... There are but few churches which have any Bells, but they call the people together by knocking with a good big Stick upon a Board.... The Parish Churches are more

---

[1] Chardin (1686), pp. 209-10.

Nasty than Stables; the Images mangl'd and brok'n and cover'd with Dust and Spiders.

". . . The Ornaments of the Altar are nothing but a few Nasty Tatter'd Clouts, torn and stain'd with Wine. . . . But the Cathedrals are very clean and well-adorn'd. And I could wish, that every Bishop had as much care of the Education and Instruction of his Flock, as he has of the Cleansing and Adorning of his Church. There are six Bishops in Mingrelia, but those Prelates take no care of the Souls of their Flocks, nor do they ever visit their Churches in their Dioceses. . . . The chief Imployment of the Bishops is continued Feasting and Banqueting, where they are Drunk almost every day: they are Rich and go Sumptuously Habited; their Principal Revenue arising from what they Spunge from Their Vassals, and the price of the Women and Children which they sell to the Turks." [1]

---

[1] Chardin, pp. 95 *et seq.*; for the state of religion in Kartli see Chardin further, and Pitton de Tournefort, Vol. II, pp. 301 *et seq.*

CHAPTER XXV
JUSTICE IN GEORGIA

JUSTICE in the mediæval Kingdom of Georgia was based on certain primitive customary laws, combined with later accretions borrowed from the legislative principles of Byzantium and the Islamic world. The right to take personal vengeance for a grievance suffered at the hands of another is the basic principle of justice in most primitive societies. From the conception of this right has arisen the devastating system of blood-feud which persists not only in many parts of Asia, but in Europe, at any rate in Sicily and Albania. In the Black Sea countries neither the Russian nor the Turkish Governments with all their elaborate methods of bureaucratic interference have succeeded in mastering or even controlling the tendency which still persists strongly among the mountaineers of the Caucasus and of Lazistan to resort to blood as the final test of justice between man and man. Philosophically there is much to be said for the solution of injustice by blood, and for blood reprisals for personal injuries; and civilized countries, by legislating against the duel, have certainly gone too far in the reduction of all justice to a matter of hair-splitting arguments and mean damages in the law courts. For certain injuries which one man can inflict upon another are of so intimate a nature that sentiment—and it is in cases where sentiment and not property has suffered—can only be satisfied by blood. Blood satisfaction has, however, in all primitive communities for long generations been reduced to the farce of the blood-feud; whereby if one man kills another, for however good a reason, the relations of the dead man are bound to avenge the death on the killer or on one of his relations, and so indefinitely, until as happens sometimes, in Albania and Lazistan, the males of two contending family groups are almost exterminated; and, moreover, the principle of blood vengeance has reached such a pitch, that if one man kills another by accident the relations of the dead man must still exact retribution for the death. The custom of the blood-feud is still, as we have said, widespread in the mountainous districts of the Caucasus and in Lazistan. But in the relatively ordered state of feudal

Georgia, the principle of blood vengeance with its resulting feuds, had at an early date been replaced by an elaborate code of " blood-price " (still called *siskhli*—blood) whereby degrees of compensation were provided for almost every injury which one man in a feudal state of society could inflict upon another.[1] In feudal times there was a strict class basis to the code; so that if a man killed his equal he paid the fixed blood-price, if he killed his superior he paid the superior's blood-price which was higher than that of his own class and in addition might suffer expropriation for a number of years, imprisonment, mutilation or even execution.[2] The system of " blood-price " was certainly fully established in Georgia in the eighth century A.D., since *sigelni* or charters defining the scale of " blood-prices " and granted by the kings to different families, are in existence from that date. Gradually the granting of these charters, with especially drastic " blood-prices " for injury to person or property, appear to have evolved into a method whereby the Crown could reward individual families for services which they had rendered.

The character of the *sigelni* is interesting, and their scope may be indicated by quoting a typical *sigeli* of the twelfth century. King David the Restorer had taken a bad fall from the top of the scaffolding of the church which he was building at Gelati, and his recovery was attributed solely to the baths of bitches' milk which had been provided for him by a nobleman named Avshandadze. In recognition of his timely service Avshandadze was appointed *Baziert-Ukhutsesi* or Grand Falconer,[3] and the King renewed in his favour a *sigel* of " blood-price " originally accorded to the family of Avshandadze by King Levan II of Abkhazeti at the end of the eighth century and confirmed by Bagrat III in the eleventh century. The *sigeli* runs as follows,—

> "Whosoever as a result of the Divine wrath or at the suggestion of the Devil, renders himself culpable of the murder of a member of your family, or causes such murder to be committed by another, shall pay thee 200,000 *botinauris* of ancient money as *sanakhshiré* (preliminary payment) and as *shesamqrelo* (reconciliation) 400,000 *botinauris* as the complete blood-price; he who carries off a woman of your family, shall pay the half of this blood-price;

---

[1] In the reign of Bagrat IV in the eleventh century we find an interesting instance of blood-feud. Kwiriké III, King of Kakheti, had killed the King of Osseti in battle. Some time afterwards Kwiriké was murdered, while hunting, by an Ossetian slave, who thus, say the Annalists, " accomplished blood-vengeance ". See Brosset, H. de la G., I, 317.
[2] Wakhushti, *Dés. Géo.*, pp. 15–16.
[3] Brosset (*Introduction à l' Histoire de la Géorgie*, p. xliii) calls Avshandadze " guardian of the royal forests ", by which he apparently implies that he held the office of Grand Falconer.

JUSTICE IN GEORGIA

"For an attack on the place where you are resting at peace with your family, the same price:

"He, who on your pasturages, on your arable fields or in the vineyards included within your borders, shall carry off, under any pretext whatsoever, any animal belonging to your house, be it horse, ox or other beast, shall pay a quarter of the blood-price;

"He who shall wound a member of your family shall pay according to the ancient rulings, which to-day have the force of Law."

Later on in the document the blood-price of an Avshandadze is fixed at 200,000 *tzkhumuris*, to which are added as *sanakhshiré* 12 peasants, 12 white mules, 12 white falcons, 12 running dogs, 12 stone-falcons, and some satin legs of boots.[1]

A *botinauri* was a Byzantine coin which took its name from the Emperor Nikephoros III Botiniates (1078–81), and a *tzkhumuri* was assumedly a coin minted by the Abkhazian Bagratids who had their capital at Sukhum (Tzkhumi). Brosset estimates the value of a *botinauri* and a *tzkhumuri* as approximately the same[2]; that is equal to two of the common Georgian coin, a *tetri* or "white". A *tetri* was approximately the equivalent in gold value of an English penny, so that the price of blood of an Avshandadze in the eleventh century was about five thousand pounds sterling. That the blood-price was punitive rather than compensatory is borne out by the comparative heaviness of the fines for a theft of stock in comparison to that imposed for the actual killing of an Avshandadze and by the fact that it was an established practice that substantial portions of the penalty went to the judge concerned and to the Crown.[3]

The Georgians had also established other legal methods which correspond very closely to those in use in other feudal countries during the Middle Ages; these included "trial by combat" and "trial by ordeal". Trial by combat was imposed in the event of one noble accusing the other of conspiracy against the Crown, or of sacrilege, and Wakhushti indicates that this method of justice dated back to pagan times.[4]

According to Wakhushti the accuser and the accused would pass forty days in prayer. At the end of that period they would enter the lists, each of them mounted and fully armed, and each accompanied by a second armed only with a whip.[5] Then at a signal from "the whips" the two antagonists would

[1] Brosset, *Introduction*, pp. xciii and iv.   [2] *Ibid.*, p. clxxvii.
[3] Cf. *Ibid.*, clxvi and vii.
[4] Wakhushti, pp. 16–17; for an instance of "trial by combat" in Tiflis in the seventeenth century, see *Chardin*, p. 207.
[5] Whip—in Georgian *matrakhi*—hence the second was called *mematrakhé*, or "the whip".

set to. He who was unseated was considered to have been convicted; he had his head cut off and his goods and houses were confiscated, or " by an act of grace " his eyes, only, were put out. Trial by ordeal was employed generally in cases concerning the lower classes. For instance, a ploughshare was made red-hot and raised in the air. The accused man had to take hold of it, with his hand covered only by a thin rag, carry it three paces and drop it. His hands were kept covered for three days; if at the end of that time they were not burnt he was acquitted; if they were burnt he was convicted. A similar test was carried out with boiling water.

In disputes over property the oath was resorted to, a practice similar to that of old Muhammadan Law, under which an oath is considered as superior to documentary evidence.

Legislation for the protection of property was relatively mild by comparison with that in use in contemporary Europe. A thief, a brigand or one caught in the act of pillage, had to pay seven times the value of his loot. For the third offence the penalty was blinding, or for petty theft amputation of the feet.[1]

Blinding and amputation were abominable features of penal legislation not only in the East but in the West down to the eighteenth century; but during the great days of the Bagratid Kingdom these universal methods of applying justice seem to have been exercised with a certain degree of mildness in Georgia. Executions, blinding and mutilation were not always resorted to by the Georgian kings even after the capture of rebellious nobles; and neither the burnings which were the ready resort of the Christian penal code, particularly where the interests of the Church were concerned, nor the impalements which were so commonly practised in Muhammadan countries, appear in Georgia to have attracted the minds—in some countries so fanciful—of the executors of justice. The Annalists, indeed, record of Tamara at the beginning of the thirteenth century, that " she had a horror of blood, of blinding and of mutilation ".[2]

Deliberate legal cruelty is the product sometimes of fear and sometimes of moral fervour, and it must be distinguished from the half-animal and inconsequent cruelty of children and of savages. When we consider the hideous record of deliberate, delighted and intentionally prolonged cruelty in the history of

---

[1] For examples of the execution of justice in Tiflis at the beginning of the eighteenth century, see Pitton de Tournefort, pp. 310-11.
[2] *Annals*, Brosset, H. de la G., I, 407.

the Middle Ages, we discover that the abominations are usually perpetrated by the agents of religious corporations or by groups inspired by those fixed ideas known as ideals. The psychology of cruelty is exceedingly obscure; there are the terrible records of the animal cruelty of half-savage hordes like the Mongol invaders of Persia and Russia; there are the defensive cruelties of those resorting to political repression through fear; and there are the administrative cruelties carried out by judges and agents of the law, and, more especially during the Middle Ages, by the agents of the Church. A combination of moral fervour and an insane sensualism seems to inspire the latter kind of cruelty, and when we consider the unnatural environment in which the agents both of the law and of the Church lived, particularly during the Middle Ages, it seems probable that both the moral fervour and the strain of deliberate cruelty which characterizes the historical psychologies of judges and priests may be attributed to a combination of mental and physical repression. From those dried sterile brains the cruelty seemed to ooze like some filthy distillation of the once clean and natural juices of their aborted bodies.

Now the Georgians were not men full of fears, and they did not repress themselves. The fine bright spirit of the mediæval knight, King Dmitri Tavdadébuli, a soldier loved by his people for his justice, his kindness and his charity, a lover of song and of women and a deep philosopher, who at the end could give himself, all naturally, to execution that he might save the people from invasion—that spirit type of the Georgian, laughs down the ages at the men of moral fervour, of repressions and oppressions, with their pincers, their thumbscrews and their racks; and if in the later age of Georgian history, after the Division of the Kingdom, we see cruelties everywhere through the pages of the histories of Kartli, Imereti and Kakheti, we must remember that the demoralization of the long Turkish and Persian wars had eaten deep into the spirit of the Georgians. And even during this period, their cruelties are the cruelties of animals in triumph and animals in fear, quick mutilations with sword and knife, comparatively clean; while over the Latin West in those three centuries there hung the shadow of the torturing Inquisition.

The bulk of cases in mediæval Georgia, apart from those of a criminal nature, were concerned with disputes over the boundaries of property. In such cases, a settlement was arrived at by ordeal of oath and by arbitration. Under Georgian law, as under Islamic law, the oaths of the plaintiff and defendant, and those of witnesses, were considered of much greater weight than written evidence. In Georgia, documentary titles to property were, in the unsettled state of the country, frequently non-existent, while forgeries of charters—in cases where documentary evidence was forthcoming—were not uncommon. The sacred oath, on the other hand, both for Georgians and Muslims, was held particularly binding, and claimants who were aware that their reclamations were not valid, would, when put to the test of the oath, hesitate to commit blasphemy.[1]

The usual procedure in the case of disputed boundaries was for the claimants to walk over or round the ground in question, the two of them carrying between them a particularly revered icon. And it was rarely that either would forswear the truth known to him, in the presence of the sacred image.[2]

Confiscations of property by the Crown were not uncommon and restitution was sometimes made. Further in times of war the appropriation of the property of a neighbouring noble, or even of Church property, by some adventurous spirit often occurred.

The Code of Giorgi the Brilliant offers numerous examples of the procedure of confiscation, and refers also to cases in which nobles had occupied Church property, and others in which the Church had appropriated private property. In the settlement of such cases the aggrieved owner received a fine or indemnity from the occupier more often than the restoration of the property.[3]

Local justice was administered by itinerant judges known in Georgia as *msajulni* and later by the Georgianized Persian title of *mdivan-begni*. The *Dastulamali* contains a lengthy disquisition on the functions of the *mdivan-begni* appointed by the King. There were others appointed by some of the great territorial princes; and the *Dastulamali* contains a provision for the division of the judge's share of the fine in the event of a case in which both the *mdivan-begni* of the King and of the *tavadi* Amilakhori might be concerned.[4] The interest of the agents of justice in the fine imposed or the damages given might appear to have acted as an incentive to litigants to make private settlement of their disputes. But even in more highly-

---

[1] Cf. Brosset, *Introduction*, p. cxlii.
[2] For the great sanctity in which icons were held see *Chardin*, p. 98. "They are horribly afraid to swear by these rever'd images, and when they do there is no gainsaying such an oath. For they believe whatever is sworn by these Images. Some there be that will not call these Images to witness the most certain truths, for fear of being kill'd by 'em."
[3] For examples see Brosset, *Introduction*, p. cxl.   [4] *Ibid.*, p. clxvii.

developed communities, where the judges have no direct interest in the losses imposed on a litigant, the ancillary agents of the processes of the Law certainly have every inducement to prolong the course of the dispute from which their legitimate profits are derived; and yet that odd being the litigant still chooses "to have it out in court". And so we must suppose that the Georgians took full advantage of the facilities offered by the courts of the *mdivan-begni*.

CHAPTER XXVI

THE SLAVE TRADE: DECLINE OF THE POPULATION

It has already been stated that, as under the mediæval feudal laws of Europe, a peasant in Georgia could be transferred with an estate, given away by his master, sold, or could sell himself into slavery. He could also purchase his freedom, or he might be given his freedom, either in perpetuity or for the life of his master. There are frequent records for the seventeenth century, of the sale of peasants and their families. Thus a document of 1689 records the sale of eight peasants "for a handful of gold"; according to another document, the *tavadi* Amilakhori takes a peasant in settlement of a debt of ten *tumani*[1]; a certain Bejan manumits his *glekhi* Papia in consideration of four head of cattle, a well-harnessed horse and a copper pot.[2] From the end of the fifteenth century, when intercourse with the Persians and Turks became very close, the seignorial right to sell serfs—which had its parallel under most feudal systems—was abused and abased by the wholesale exportation of serfs of both sexes to the slave-markets of Tabriz, Akhaltzikhé, Trebizond and Constantinople. The iniquitous commerce was particularly brisk in Mingrelia, Guria and Imereti. During the seventeenth century we find King Taymuraz I of Kakheti accusing the Dadiani of selling ten to fifteen thousand Christian boys every year to the Turks, and the Gurieli of disposing of at least twelve thousand. The practice of selling the young people into slavery was not always confined to the serfs, and Papuna Orbeliani records that in 1747, one hundred sons of *tavadni* and *aznaurni* were sent to Persia on the demand of Shah Ibrahim, while in 1741 Nadir Shah, who was then fighting in Daghestan, demanded delivery to him of three hundred young widows, an equal number of boys and girls, five hundred peasants' families, and twenty thousand measures of wheat.[3]

---

[1] Then equivalent to about £10 sterling.
[2] For full references, see Brosset, *Introduction*, p. lxxii. [3] *Ibid.*, p. cii.

THE SLAVE TRADE

Sir John Chardin, who was in Mingrelia and Georgia during the last quarter of the seventeenth century, wrote that:

> "Mingrelia is at present very much dispeopl'd; there not being in it above twenty thousand inhabitants. Though it is not above thirty years ago there was no less than fourscore thousand. The cause of which decrease proceeds from their Wars with their neighbours and the vast number of people of both sexes, which the Nobility have sold of late years. For a long time there has been drain'd out of Mingrelia every year, either by Purchase or Barter, above twelve thousand persons; all of which are sold to the Mahometans, Persians and Turks, there being none but they that deal in that sort of Traffic in those parts. They carry three thousand every year directly to Constantinople, which they have in Exchange for Cloth, Arms and other things which they carry, as I have said, into Mingrelia." [1]

Chardin adds that "I have been shew'd several Gentlemen who have been so prodigiously unnatural" as to sell their own children, wives and mothers. And he proceeds to give an account of an impecunious but enterprising nobleman, who, in order to find the wherewithal to marry his mistress, had recently sold his own wife and twelve kidnapped priests to a Turkish sea captain.

The Caucasian slave-trade was, of course, no new phenomenon,[2] although during the period of Turkish and Persian intervention in the country from the fifteenth to the eighteenth century, the exportation of human flesh attained unprecedented dimensions.

The trade in human flesh was even more rife among the mountaineers—Abkhaz and Cherkess—than it was among the Georgians; and for a period as late as that of the Crimean War, the archives of the British Consulate at Trebizond contain interesting references to the illicit commerce in slaves carried on by Turkish vessels trading from Trebizond along the Circassian coast—which at that date was under more or less effective Russian control.

Repulsive and abhorrent as the trade is to the modern mind, it must be remembered that the evil has—as have so many of the evils of the world—a way of righting itself. The mass deportation of slaves amounted in fact to a popular

---

[1] Chardin (1686 ed.), pp. 90–1.
[2] From the earliest historic times Caucasian slaves were celebrated. Ezekiel records that Tubal and Meshech " traded the persons of men " in the cities of Syria, and Herodotus notes the tribute of boys and girls sent by the Colchians to the Persians. In the fifth and sixth centuries of the Christian era, the Byzantines resorted to the Abkhazians for their most fashionable breed of eunuch. Procopius, VIII, iii, 16–21, "*for each one of them* (the Abasgi) *had to dread that at some time he would become the father of a comely child.*"

emigration from countries which, although rich enough to support a thriving population, were so disorganized by existing political conditions that life had become in fact intolerable for the lower social elements. The miserable Georgian boy dragged away from the sordid poverty of his father's feudal holding, found his way, through the Turkish slave-market, into the Janissary corps—where at least the life of a soldier, and not of a slave, awaited him. The highest posts in the Turkish and Persian Empires were filled many times by the unfortunate deportees, and the Mamluk corps, for so long the masters of Egypt, was recruited from the Black Sea slavers. Again, wretched girls from the mountains, whose future at home would have been to have been sold by a peasant father to a peasant husband for the price of a few sheep, was passed on from the slave-ships to the comparative comfort, and sometimes to the luxury of Muslim harîms, where they would find, more often than not, a husband more kindly and more desirable than their own bucolic kinsfolk.

The effect on the ethnography of the Middle East of this forcible and widespread emigration from the Caucasus, which came to a head in the fifteenth to eighteenth centuries, is an interesting question which has not attracted the attention it deserves. The population of the Caucasus in the time of Queen Tamara must have been very great indeed, and the inhabitants per square mile would appear to have been more numerous than in England and Scotland at the same period. England and Scotland were then backward countries in North-Western Europe,[1] whereas the Caucasus was one of the most prosperous regions of the Middle East. The evidence of ruins of castles and monasteries all over Georgia and Armenia tell their story of a numerous and prosperous population, much greater in numbers than during recent generations. The towns of the Mussulman provinces in the eastern Caucasus —Barda'a, Baylakan, Derbend and Shamakha, Ganja and Dabil—were famous throughout the Mussulman countries, which were then the richest regions of the world.

The Mongol census of 1259—after forty years of war— gives figures which are credible for that period, and which can only indicate those of the prosperous days of the Georgian Kingdom and of the Mussulman emirates. The census carried out by the No'in Arghun—an experienced administrator who had as object the levying of troops and the adjust-

---

[1] The passing power of Henry II and of the Angevin dynasty rested mainly on the spreading continental possessions of that house.

ment of taxes—gave the population of Georgia, according to the Annalists, at 4,500,000, and according to Wakhushti at 5,900,000. The different figures are founded on different bases of reckoning, and it is doubtful whether the whole of Georgia or only Kartli and Kakheti were included, although the evidence rather indicates the latter. Brossêt, on the grounds that the population of Kartli and Kakheti in 1836 was, according to the Russian census, only 225,395, cannot bring himself to credit the Mongol census.[1] When we remember, however, that the Black Death and the devastations of Timur followed within 150 years of this census, and that the succeeding 400 years were occupied in almost perpetual warfare, accompanied by such terrible depredations as those of Shah Abbas, Nadir Shah, and Agha-Muhammad-Khan; and when we take into consideration further the evidence of Taymuraz I and of Sir John Chardin, as to the mass annual deportations resulting from the slave-trade, it does not seem difficult to believe that the figures of the Mongol census give no inaccurate indication of the population of Georgia in the thirteenth century.

The results of the dispersal of the Georgians and Circassians over the neighbouring Muhammadan countries were noted by the shrewd Chardin, who coming from Georgia to Persia, was probably observant in this matter.

> "In other parts of the Kingdom", he says, "the Persian blood is now grown clearer by the mixture of the Georgian and Circassian Blood, which is certainly the People of the World, which Nature favours most, both upon the account of the Shape and Complexion, and of the Boldness and Courage; they are likewise Sprightly, Courtly and Amorous. There is scarce a gentleman in Persia whose Mother is not a Georgian or a Circassian Woman; to begin with the King who commonly is a Georgian or a Circassian by the Mother's side; and whereas that Mixture begun about a hundred years ago, the Female kind is grown fairer as well as the other, and the Persian Women are

---

[1] Brosset, *H. de la G.*, I, 550–1, and notes; cf. also Elysée Reclus (*Universal Geography*, VI, 47), who, on slender evidence, estimates the population of the Caucasus in classic and mediæval times at sixteen millions. The population of Daghestan was reckoned by the Russians, at the time of the Murid War at about two millions, of Circassia at a million, even after the plague of the late 'twenties. Both these regions were relatively uncivilized, particularly by comparison with Georgia and the Mussulman parts of Transcaucasia during the Middle Ages. According to Tournefort (*Voyage*, p. 312) the population of Persian Georgia was estimated at 60,000 hearths at the beginning of the eighteenth century. He says (p. 319) that military service was levied as one man to a hearth, a reckoning which corresponds exactly with Krusinski's statement that Wakhtang VI raised an army of 60,000 men in 1719 (*History of the Revolutions of Persia*, I, 266–7). These figures compared with those of the Russian census of 1836, for exactly the same area, indicate a decline in population of at least one-third during the century which saw the invasion of Nadir Shah and Agha-Muhammad-Khan.

now very handsome and very well shap'd, tho' they are still inferior to the Georgians." [1]

And so the wheels of suffering turn. The pious Chardin in his century had not the gift "to see oursels as others see us". The Caucasian trade in kind's flesh was certainly more disgusting than the English and Spanish trade in negroes, which was flourishing during and long after this period, and it was more barbarous than the slave-holding in America which outlived the Turkish Black Sea slaving of the Crimean War days. But while *The Travels of Sir John Chardin into Persia* were going to press, his fellows in France and England were being herded in chains to the West Indian plantations where not even a Janissary's career awaited them. And indeed it may be doubted whether the physical and spiritual miseries of the cargoes of the Turkish ships (where at least their owners, as we read from other works, were accustomed to keep them in good trim with a view to high prices on the domestic market) were worse than the sufferings endured during the last century by the convict transports to the Antipodes or in the abominably squalid emigrant ships which took the victims of the Irish famine across the Atlantic.

The better sort of men in Georgia, even during the flourishing days of the slave-trade in the seventeenth and eighteenth centuries, do not seem to have regarded the evil without serious heart-searching. We have already quoted Taymurazi's denunciation of the Dadiani and the Gurieli. The practice of selling slaves was strongly condemned by the heads of the Church, and severe penalties were threatened —more often than imposed—for the sale of Christian souls to the Muslim. The Laws of the Catholicos, which are included in the *Codex Vakhtangi*, pronounce excommunication on those who sell slaves to the Muslim, and impose hanging as a penalty in the case of failure to repurchase a victim. The canons of the ecclesiastical assemblies ring with denunciations of the practice. In effect, however, the intervention of the Church appears to have taken milder form. There is extant a charter of the seventeenth century in which a Prince Palavandishvili undertakes to the Catholicos Nikolaoz Amilakhori not to sell

---

[1] *Chardin* (Argonaut ed.), pp. 183–4; cf. also *Don Juan of Persia*, who states that Shah Abbas on his accession, "took into his service to form his bodyguard 12,000 Georgian renegades". (*Don Juan of Persia: a Shiah Catholic* (1560–1604), translated and edited by G. Le Strange, London, 1928, p. 209); and Krusinski, who mentions "several great towns inhabited by Georgians of the King's Guard . . . Schah-Abas after having drawn their ancestors from Georgia, plac'd them in this canton, which they began to inhabit one hundred and thirty years before" (*History of the Revolution of Persia*, II, 124, ed. 1728).

THE SLAVE TRADE

any more slaves, and by another, two noble brothers promise the Catholicos Domenti II to repurchase slaves which they had sold at Akhaltzikhé, and also not to divide up families.[1]

Furthermore the practice existed, on the occasion of levies of slaves by Turkish and Persian armies, of buying substitutes from among the mountaineers—Ossetians and Cherkess—in order to avoid surrendering Georgians into slavery. King Wakhtang VI of Kartli is commended for only sending slaves to the Shah when they were actually demanded, and then for buying substitutes instead of sending Georgians.[2] Wakhushti states that, in the reign of King Simon I of Kartli, a special tax of one *marchil* (about two shillings) was levied on each peasant's house in order " to buy Ossetians, Caucasians and Cherkess, which he sent to the Qaen ".[3]

Again there was a special obligation laid on the Tatar nomads of Borchalo to provide for the slaves on their way to the Persian border.

Ground down by an inequitable and tyrannous fiscal system, oppressed by onerous feudal obligations, harassed by the perpetual civil warrings of their masters, harried by continual Mussulman incursions, duped and mulcted by an ignorant and unworthy priesthood, and living under the constant threat of deportation and the break-up of their families, the lot of the Georgian peasants was a miserable one. Nature alone was their friend: their physical needs in a mild and equable climate were insignificant; a rich soil, a warm sun and an adequacy of water could rapidly make good to them their losses and their deprivations; a primitive and all-surrounding forest and mountains difficult of access, which they could know better than their masters and their enemies, offered them a near and friendly refuge in their dangers and their troubles. The Georgian peasantry certainly had more to suffer than any other peasantry during the three centuries following the Division of the Kingdom—whatever may have been their relative situation during earlier periods of history. For neither the Armenians nor the peasantry of the Balkan lands nor of Persia and Turkey—great as were their tribulations—had to endure the existence of a perpetual state of war, and the continuous and virulent driving of the slave-traffic. It is the character of the Georgians—the " æsthetic irresponsibility " of them—that has carried them through their miseries; and it is, perhaps, these miseries,

[1] Brosset, *Introduction*, p. lxxiii.   [2] Brosset, *H. de la G.*, I, 105.
[3] *Idem.*, *Introduction*, p. clxi.

endured under a bright sun among the wild and primitive woodlands that has made their character what it is—which has given them their gay and brave fatality.

"The Poor People", says Chardin, "go almost naked: such is their misery not to be paralell'd; as not having anything to cover their Nakedness but a pitiful sorry Felt like to the Chlamys of the Ancients; into which they thrust their Heads, and turn which way they please as the Wind fits; for it covers but one side of their Bodies, and falls down no lower than their knees. . . .

"He that has a Shirt and a pair of pitiful Drawers thinks himself Rich: for almost all of 'em go Bare-Foot; and such of the Colchians who pretend to Shooes, have nothing but a piece of Buffalo's Hide, and that untann'd too; which piece of raw Hide is lac'd about their Feet with a Thong of the same: so that for all these sort of Sandals, their Feet are as durty, as if they went Bare-foot."

The respectable jeweller cannot understand the ragged gentlemen at all. He mentions:

"another most inhuman Tenent of theirs, that it is a piece of Charity to Murder Infants newly born, when they have not sufficient wherewith to maintain 'em; or such as are sick and past hopes of recovery. And the reason they give is this, that by so doing, they put those Children out of a great deal of misery, which they would undergo in a languishing Distemper, which in the end must of necessity carry 'em off. Such are the Arguments of these Barbarous People that have neither shame nor Humanity."[1]

---
[1] *Chardin* (1686 ed.), pp. 85-6.

BOOK V

THE LIFE OF GEORGIA

"Ministrelry is, first of all, a branch of wisdom; divinely intelligible to the godlike, very wholesome to them that hearken. . . .

"Like a horse running a great race on a long course, like a ball-player in the lists striking the ball fairly, and aiming adroitly at the mark, even so it is with the poet who indites long poems, when utterance is hard and verse fails him. Then indeed behold the poet and his poesy will be manifest. When he is at a loss for Georgian words, and verses begin to fail, he will not weaken Georgian nor will he let it grow poor in words. Let him strike the ball cunningly and he will make his goal.

"He who utters somewhere one or two verses cannot be called a poet; let him not think himself equal to great singers. Even if they compose a few discrepant verses from time to time, yet if they say 'Mine are the best', they are stiff-necked mules."

Shota Rusthaveli.

CHAPTER XXVII

THE ART OF MEDIÆVAL GEORGIA

ART is the tangible indication which we have that man is no mere physical phenomenon. Art is the idealization of the practical in life, the sublimation of the mechanical. Art is essentially a voluntary manifestation, for, while in the practical and mechanical world man reacts to the urge of his economic need, in art he does that which is not necessary—he responds, a volunteer in the æsthetic, to an inner aching to fulfil himself as the complement to beauty.

Beauty cannot be defined, no more than can man's immortal soul nor the Unknown God of our generation and of others. But then all that is sublime is undefinable, as each of us cannot define and analyse the reason of his love, but it is there and submergent of definable and reasonable realities.

The æsthetic sense has its sexual connection. We do not know whether the more intelligent animals have their sense of beauty, but it would seem that their lust is not discriminative. And that which distinguishes man from animals is his discriminative sexuality, sometimes and often not very far developed. Sexual discrimination is, from an animal point of view, an abnormality. And all individuality is abnormal. The roots of æsthetic appreciation lie deep in sex, and the appreciation of the more ethereal forms of beauty is a refining of this primitive " taste ", " the sense " of beasts. " Taste ", the " sensing " or " sensation " which gives pleasure —rightly expressed in these essentially physical words even to-day—found itself first in appreciation of sexual beauty. Sexual discrimination and the desire to attract that discrimination is at the base of all primitive attempts at self-decoration—the earliest form of art; and the theme of all primitive art, of early historic art, and of most modern art, is the idealization of sex. The repressionist Semites—Hebrews and Arabs—perfected the geometric style and they banned representation of the human form; and in sculpture and calligraphy they evolved an art that was geometrically beautiful, calming and sterilizing, like the floating fumes of a drug. But colour, that great inflamer, eluded their high principle, and geometrical design blazed into the colour of draperies, embroideries and rugs before the eyes of always æsthetic man. It was not until the Reformation that colour, as well as form, came beneath the repressing of the pure in mind.

The mediæval Church compromised between the frank representationalism of the pagan world—with its iteration and sublimation of the sexual affinities of the æsthetic—and the lean repressionism of Islam. The Church took colour and representationalism and combined the two in the formalized austerity of ecclesiastical art. The Byzantine painted icons of the eleventh and twelfth centuries were the masterpieces of this coloured and representational severity. But the indecent gargoyles grinning down high from the cornices of Gothic cathedrals gave their warning of the smoothing away of this austerity in the soft and reverent loveliness of the Italian Renaissance, and of what was to come later when æstheticism, so long repressed, sprawled its reaction from the canvasses of Goya to the stone of Epstein.

Art in the Caucasus is never a distinct and regional art. The history of it is part of the history of the art of surrounding lands; yet the history of Caucasian art is important in that it reflects the interplay of artistic motives and developments in the West and East; and it is interesting also of itself. Caucasian art—interpreted varyingly by the Georgians, the Armenians and the Caucasian segment of the Islamic world—was at once adaptation and creation.

The Bronze Age art of the Caucasus has never been adequately studied and its relation to the later national art of Georgia and Armenia is difficult to estimate. The explorations which give us our knowledge of the Caucasian Bronze Age have been haphazard, and whereas important finds have been made in the Kuban country, at Koban in

THE ART OF MEDIÆVAL GEORGIA

Osseti, in the Mtkvari valley and in Armenia, the principal seats of culture during the Bronze Age, particularly in Colchis, have remained unexplored.[1]

The animal style—variations of which are characteristic of the Bronze Age, not only in the Ægean and in Iran, but also over the Russian plains—was developed in the Caucasus to a state of high technical value; and the mind which seems to interpret itself in this style—the free and lustful ingenuous pagan mind—is the mind of the Caucasians in the pages of Xenophon and Strabo. In the Caucasian Bronze Age there also developed a fine geometrical style, in many respects original to the Caucasus, and with characteristics distinct from the geometrical style of Iran and Mesopotamia which reached its apogee in the early centuries of Islam. This geometrical style with the interlaced and vegetable designs, continued to be a motive of Georgian mediæval art, where it is combined with the Byzantine decorative motives in Georgian ecclesiastical architecture.

With the spread of Hellenic, later Roman, and later Byzantine power round the shores of the Black Sea, the art of the great Mediterranean cultures came to have a direct and overwhelming influence on Georgian art. Christian thought and Christian art came to the Georgians through the magnificent and engulfing channel of the East Christian Church.

The Armenians were original and inventive in architecture, and it has been suggested by Strzygowski and others that Armenian architecture—rooted in the traditions of the older cultures of Iran, Syria and Mesopotamia—itself had a fundamental influence on the development of East Christian art. Whatever may have been the interplay of Byzantine, Armenian and Anatolian influences in the evolution of East Christian architecture between the sixth and twelfth centuries, the Georgians themselves contributed little of originality to the development of East Christian—or of their own local— architecture. At the same time they created many fine interpretations of Byzantine and Armenian architectural conceptions; and it is probable that the Georgians themselves had a definite influence on the spread of Byzantine, and more particularly of Armenian artistic ideas to the Russian principalities.[2]

The Caucasus is celebrated for its rug-weaving. The most beautiful rugs come from the Muslim parts of Caucasus —from Daghestan, Shirvan and Karabagh and from the

[1] See Chaps. II and V.   [2] Cf. Dalton, *East Christian Art*, p. 56.

Kazakh district of Georgia. No very ancient examples of Caucasian rug-weaving exist, but it is certain that the industry was developed from remote times. But here again, as Georgian architecture is part of East Christian architecture so is the Caucasian weaver's art an integral part of Islamic art —although the Christian weavers of Armenia, using what has come to be an essentially Islamic medium, have acquired no little renown.

Georgian and Armenian illumination, which achieved a certain degree of quality, cannot compare with the gorgeous workmanship of the Persians, and its technique is an adaptation of the Persian manner—including the aged animal style—and East Christian ecclesiastical formalism. The little that remains of Georgian fresco-painting and mosaic-work is crude copying from the Greek masters, but Georgian carving on wood and stone, although in the Byzantine tradition, is good work and has some originality. It is certainly the equal of the Armenian stone-carving which has attained some celebration in Europe.

In two spheres of art did the mediæval Georgians achieve not only quality equal to the best of Byzantium and Persia, but creative originality. In epic poetry, the Georgians far surpassed the Byzantines; and although comparison is difficult and invidious, it may be claimed that the masterpieces of Shota Rusthaveli and Sargis Tmogveli rival, if they do not surpass, the more celebrated works of their Persian contemporaries. And in the metallurgical arts—particularly in their own speciality, the metal icon—the Georgians produced creations which certainly equalled the products of the Islamic and Mediterranean cities of the time.

The churches of Georgia in their general design and structure may be divided into two principal types, which correspond in character to contemporary monuments through the Byzantine world and Armenia. The more ancient was the *centralized* type—the circular or quadrangular chapel, so constructed as to direct the gaze of the devout upward to the arched dome of the cupola, which with its sacred frescoes was to be identified with the vault of heaven. By the sixth century the majority of churches were being built in this style—which Strzygowski derives from the domed tent of the nomad Sacæ and the fashion of which he attributes to the influence of Iranian and Armenian ideas. The old Roman *basilica*, with its broad nave and impression of deep perspective, was passing. Justinian built his church on the Grave of Our Lord in Jerusalem in the new style. It was followed in the magnificent churches of Syria, at St. Elias of Brusa, at St. George of Salonika and at St. Vitali of Ravenna, at St. Serge and Little Sophia and St. Irene in Byzantium, and it was finally brought to its apogee in St. Sophia.

The *centralized* type owed much to the initiation if not to the invention of the Armenians, and there are many churches built on this design in Armenia. In Georgia the churches of the *centralized* type which survive are few in number; the best examples are the Church of the Holy Cross at Mtzkheta, and the churches of Martvili and Ateni in Mingrelia and Dranda in Abkhazeti. In churches of this type the *cupola* had no *drum*, or the *drum* was only of very stocky dimensions.

Between the tenth and twelfth centuries a more complex structure representing a combination of the *centralized* plan with the older *basilica* had resulted in the development of the *cruciform* conception, in which the intention was to concentrate the gaze of the worshipper round and over the altar. The churches of SS. Andrew and Theotokos in Constantinople, the Catholic and Apostolic Church in Athens and Daphni near Athos, belong to this type. The diameter of the *cupola* was not so great as in the earlier *centralized* style; it had a lesser interlie and for that reason held much more lightly; this latter fact allowed the construction of a taller *drum* which enabled the building to be given a "head". A better proportion was given to the whole *ensemble* and the frontal appearance was greatly improved. In Georgia the majority of churches were built on variations of this latter *cruciform* plan, the most notable examples of which are Kutais Cathedral, and the churches of Mokvi, Bedia, Porta and Pitsunda. The type and plan of these churches belong to the period between the tenth and twelfth centuries, although many of them are of later times, and the reconstruction of some on the ancient model, dates from the seventeenth century. In the churches of the tenth to twelfth centuries, the *ensemble* was more pleasing than in the earlier structures, and the fronts were built higher and were decorated with cornices and carved ornamentations. The whole contrasts in its grace and harmony with the more ancient type, where there is practically no *drum* under the *cupola* or if there is a *drum*, it is of low structure and distinguished by its heaviness and stuntedness.

After the combination of the *centralized* type with the old *basilica* type, the *cupola* was heightened and the *drum* assumed a greater importance. Separated masses came into being, the structural joining of which made it possible to evolve from a formless mixture of outbuildings—as in St. Sophia of Constantinople—the form of integral beauty which is exemplified in St. Sophia of Trebizond and at Gelati in Imereti. The high and graceful *cupola* of the Caucasus covered often with a *tent* or *head* (the ancient symbol of sanctity) perfected the whole conception of composite harmony. Bedia in Abkhazeti—built in the first decade of the eleventh century by King Bagrat III, in honour of Our Lady of Blachernæ—with its finely carved walls covered with the ancient interlaced design, must have been, in its unruined state, one of the finest examples of this Georgian interpretation of Byzantine and Armenian architectural principles.

Abkhazeti and Samtzkhé—the Chorokhi country—were always favoured by the Bagratid kings as their ancient patrimony, and it was in those two regions that the most beautiful churches were built during the vigorous days of the rising monarchy, when Kartli still lay open to Mussulman incursions, and Kakheti was an obscure and independent principality. In the heart of Samtzkhé, along the Chorokhi valley and its tributaries, a number of beautiful churches were built; such are the ruins of Tbeti in Shavsheti, Yeni Rabat (Antonisi) and Opisa, of Khulo in Achara and of Zarzma in the valley of the Jaqis-tsqali.

The churches of Samtzkhé were less influenced by Byzantine conceptions than those of Abkhazeti. The spreading vault of Dranda, Mokvi and Pitsunda in Abkhazeti is met with rarely in other parts of Georgia. The church at Mokvi, which like that at Dranda bears indications of a later reconstruction, had, to begin with, a spreading vault, which indicates undoubtedly the Byzantine origin of its plan and mass. Pitsunda, despite the tradition of its foundation by Justinian, belongs to the same period as Mokvi, and, like Mokvi, it bears a strong resemblance to the contemporary churches of St. Sophia in Kiev and Novgorod.

Other churches—as Bedia in Mingrelia and the Meskhian foundations—although they are in many ways like those of Abkhazeti and are of the same period, have already their own differences both in plan and construction; there are no altar projections and niches appear. The walls are covered with carvings showing local originality, braidings and broad connecting lines of crosses and animal figures, hemming round the windows and doors. Intervals between the lines are filled with ornamentation—interlaced and vegetable designs: the top is cut out like a tent; there are no columns, but lines are already abundant.

Lastly we see the ultimate evolution to which Georgian ecclesiastical architecture attained, where capitals and bases appear and the lines develop into columns of different widths. This type includes the finest of all the ecclesiastical monuments of the Caucasus—Kutais Cathedral—and the Chorokhi churches of Shatberdi (Porta) and Dolisi Khana. The churches from which columnar decoration is absent may be regarded as appertaining to the more local Georgian type, the decorative affinities of which are oriental; those with columnar decoration—although local characteristics are not absent—have definitely the stamp of Byzantine art.

Kutais was the capital of the Bagratids until the first quarter of the twelfth century; under the Mongol hegemony it was a safer seat for the Georgian kings than was Tiflis, and during the Turkish and Persian wars Georgian cultured life was continued here with less interruption than in the eastern country. It is not surprising therefore that the artistic centre of the mediæval Georgian Church is to be found at Kutais and Gelati, rather than at Tiflis and Mtzkheta.

Bagrat III began the construction of Kutais Cathedral as a shrine in honour of his mother, the noble Queen Gurandukhti, in 1003; it was completed by his grandson Bagrat IV, whose first wife, Elena, a niece of the Emperor Romanos Argyros, had brought in her train a number of Byzantine artists and craftsmen. The Cathedral was finally wrecked by the Turks in 1691. The plan of Kutais Cathedral represents a rather late development of the *cruciform* plan, and on the same design several of the finest Georgian monuments which survive have been built—Gelati, Tortomi in Samtzkhé, and the restored Cathedral of Mtzkheta built by King Alexander after the devastations of Timur. It is in its carved stone decorations that the Cathedral of Kutais is most notable and the wealth of carving distinguishes it, with Tortomi and Tbeti, from other contemporary monuments.

The façade of Kutais varies in its decorations; the western side is poorest, probably because it was little seen from the road. The eastern front is richest and it is likely that on this side the Cathedral was most open to the view of believers. Rich cylinders on three ramparts with bases and capitals, indicate the trunks of columns, and in form correspond

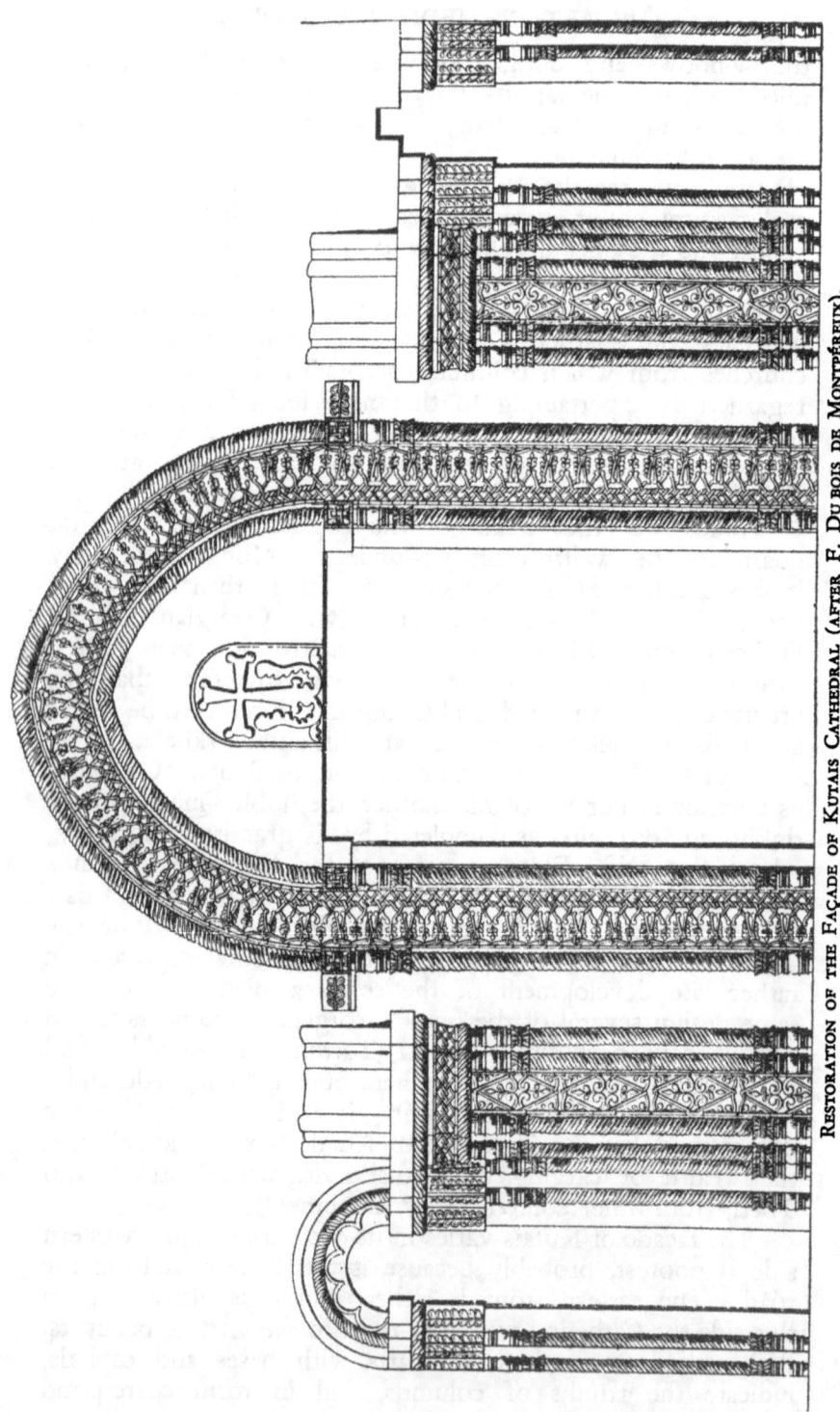

Restoration of the Façade of Kutais Cathedral (after F. Du Bois de Montpéreux).

closely to the decoration of Tbeti and Gelati. This columnar decoration is, of course, essentially Byzantine, but the Cathedral has, nevertheless, its distinct Georgian identity and its characteristic Georgian details, as, for instance, the altar-niche and the interlaced ornamentations.

The great days of Georgian church-building came to an end in the thirteenth century. After the period of the Mongol and Timurid wars, the architectural history of the country is chiefly notable for the ambitious reconstructions of Mtzkheta and Sioni by the Kartlian kings. The ancient churches of Abkhazeti fell into ruins and stand half-buried in the forest, and Mongols and Osmanli wrecked the shrines of Samtzkhé. Only here and there where a rich feudatory had achieved independence and a temporary prosperity did a new foundation rise beside the humbler church of the domain. Thus in the middle of the fifteenth century the Atabegi Manuchar raised the fine Church of Safar over against Akhaltzikhé, seven thousand feet above the sea. An Armenian architect seems to have built for him, and his craftsmen achieved some exquisite stone-carving and some of the best surviving mural frescoes of the Caucasus. About the middle of the sixteenth century the kings of Kakheti embellished and reconstructed Alaverdi as the Metropolitan See of their precarious kingdom; and the Eristavni of the Aragvi raised the large brick pile of Ananuri—with its elaborate and grotesque carvings of trees, and serpents biting their tails, chained lions and hares. But the kings of Georgia were in extremity and the fount of East Christian art—Byzantium—was choked for ever. No trickle of the influence of Renaissance architecture came through into the closed Pontine lands, and the Baroque, spreading with the commercing of the French and the Italians, penetrated into Anatolia only far enough to be remembered in the bastard mosque of Yuzgad.

Separated from the Georgian districts of Lechkhumi and Radsha by passes which are only accessible to the traveller from the last half of June to the end of August, Svaneti, in language, in customs and in art, has always been distinguished from the more open parts of Georgia. The tall and slender stone towers, resembling in character the round towers of Ireland, are an individual feature of Svanian architecture and their origin has never been satisfactorily explained. These towers indeed, together with the ancient interlaced design, and in combination with certain physical, psychological and linguistic affinities, have suggested an intangible and mysterious connection between the Iber-ni of the Black Sea and the Hiberni of the Atlantic island—a remote connection which will probably never be scientifically explained, but which nevertheless exists. The geographical isolation of Svaneti preserved always a conservatism in both linguistic and cultural processes, and here remnants of things most anciently Georgian survive. The ecclesiastical architecture of Svaneti affords an example of this cultural conservatism.

In Svaneti, the *basilica* form of church survived and was developed centuries after the *centralized* and *cruciform* types had become common in Georgia and throughout the East Christian world. The poverty of Svaneti may serve to explain the *basilica* type. The low arched vault employed in the construction of the *basilica* is more simple and easy to build than the *cupola* with its *drum*. Countess Uvarov argues against this explanation on the ground that the frescoes covering the interiors of the Svanian churches and the wealth of icons and sacerdotal plate found therein, the carved doors and iconostases and wrought gates, contradict the assumption of poverty in Svaneti during the great days of the Bagratid Kingdom. But the fact that the frescoes are of later date than the buildings themselves and that they were mostly painted during the days of the Imerian King Giorgi II (1548–85) and his Queen, Tamara Diasamidze, and of their son Alexander, and of King Bagrat IV and his Queen Tamara (1662–80), indicates that Svaneti was specially favoured by royalty during the harryings of Imereti by the Turks, while it is an established fact that much of the wealth in the churches was carried there during troubled times to save it from the sack of the richer churches and monasteries in the south.

The explanation of the striking difference between Georgian and Svanian architecture seems to lie in the poverty and natural conservatism of Svaneti and in the fact that while the *basilicas* of Georgia were destroyed during the Arab wars and later replaced by the newer *centralized* and *cruciform* types, the ancient *basilicas* of Svaneti remained untouched, while the shrines might be repaired but seldom rebuilt.

Again, it is possible that the *basilica* form in Svaneti developed from those pagan sanctuaries *Khati, Nishi, Mairemi,* in which the inhabitants of the mountains first began to learn to sing praises to the Christian God. The Church of Nuzala in Osseti and a multitude of small chapels scattered all along the high passes of the Caucasian Alps represent the first attempt at turning sanctuaries into churches of Our Lord —the first architectural attempts at the reconstruction of *Mairemni* into buildings more suitable for Christian worship. From these crude experiments there grew and developed those Svanian *basilicas*, the best examples of which are the Churches of the Prophet John in Enashi and of the Archangel Michael in Pkhotreri.

The Svanian *basilicas* are not, strictly speaking, very ingenious either in their form or in their detail; even the altar-sections—which together with the south walls are, in Georgian churches, usually most distinguished by luxurious decorations—are unattractive and unassuming. There are exceptions, however, as in the case of the Church of the Virgin at Zhibiani; the Church of Christ near Chubiani; the Church of the Transfiguration at Nemskhvira; the Church of the Archangel Michael at Matskhvarishi and the Church at Pkhotreri.

Ornamentation in Svanian churches generally consists of flat pilasters separated from each other by small and narrow arches as in the Church of the Virgin at Zhibiani. These pilasters have not developed capitals and their decoration is confined to shallow gashes with crude ornamentation carved in zig-zag shape.

Finer and more architecturally artistic are the columned arches which are found on the western and eastern walls of the Church of St. Barbara at Khé, of the Archangels at Matskhvarishi; on the western side of the Enashi Church and of the church at Tenali in Dadianis-Svaneti. This method is, no doubt, copied from Kutais Cathedral and was fashionable in the Byzantine west and in Russian churches of the Vladimir-Suzdal type.

The peculiar genius of the Georgians in the metallurgical arts and in enamel work has already received some recognition in Western Europe. The writings of Kondakov have made known to Western students the treasures of the monasteries and churches of Georgia and Svaneti, and examples of the work of the mediæval Georgian smiths and enamellers have found their way into European and American Museums.[1] The best known examples of the Georgian metal-smith's work are the three principal icons preserved at Gelati; a twelfth-

[1] The gold and enamel reliquary of Queen Katévani described by O. M. Dalton in *Recueil d'études dédiées à la mémoire de P. Kondakov*; the Georgian gold and enamel objects in the Svenigorodskoi Collection in the Metropolitan Museum of New York, including plaques from the twelfth-century icon of Jumati.

century Christ, and a Virgin attributed by Kondakov to the tenth century, at the monastery of Khopi in Mingrelia, and another Virgin dating from the eleventh or twelfth century; a Christ of the twelfth century decorated with contemporary enamels from the Mingrelian monastery at Kezkheri; and the tenth-century Hodigitria at Martvili. The most celebrated of the Gelati icons is the Virgin of Kakhuli, so called since it belonged originally to the monastery of Kakhuli in the Chorokhi country whence it was removed during the Turkish wars of the sixteenth century. The Kakhuli icon is a large gold triptych into which are set no less than ninety-four enamels, of which seventy are of Byzantine and the others of Georgian provenance. The icon itself is attributed to the second quarter of the twelfth century, but many of the enamels are of older date; namely the plaque of Christ crowning the Emperor Michael VII and his wife Maria of Alania,[1] and the two crosses bearing inscriptions in honour of King Kwiriké of Abkhazeti. Diehl compares the Khakhuli icon as a technical masterpiece to the Pala d'Oro of St. Mark's; and Kondakov states that

> "the enamels are notable for precision of design and for the brightness of their colours, in which sky-blue and turquoise blue, tones of violet and purple, and delicate shades of flesh are notable; you see there a self-confidence, a mastery and delicacy in the execution of detail which are only possible when art, having emerged from the period of experiment and uncertainty, has already evolved a set of forms and a perfectly developed ornamentation".[2]

Less known than the Mingrelian icons are those found in Svaneti, many of which have been published by Countess Uvarov.[3] In the Svanian churches are some of the finest survivals of Georgian and Byzantine metallurgical iconography from the eleventh to the fifteenth centuries, such as the Christ of Zhibiani, the Archangel Gabriel of Lagani and the Archangels Gabriel and Michael of Chukhuli, for the earlier period, and the magnificent Christ of Lagani and the Mother of God of Chukhuli for the fifteenth century.

Icons derive from the portraits of mummies of Hellenistic Egypt executed in *tempera* on wooden panels, first coated with *gesso*, which were laid on the coffins. From the fourth century they began to have a great vogue in the Byzantine

---

[1] Maria of Alania—or of Abasgia (Abkhazeti). For the discussion of the identity of the Byzantine Empress Maria of Alania see Brosset, who suggests that she was probably no other than Martha, daughter of Bagrat IV (H. de la G., p. 330, note 2).
[2] Kondakov, *Emaux*, p. 126.   [3] Uvarov, *Mat. Kav.*, Vol. X.

world, and the adoration which the icons aroused among the masses of the population led to the great "iconoclastic" struggle within the Empire. With the triumph of the Iconophils in the ninth century, there was a great revival in the fashion, and icons of every class were produced, from the painted wooden panels of the poor to the exquisite achievements of the jeweller's art which decorated the palaces of the great.

The icon was essentially an artistic medium of the Byzantine mind and the Georgians undoubtedly adopted from the Byzantines the cult and the art of the icon. Georgian painted icons are never of first quality, although they early achieved a certain humanism which is lacking in Byzantine and contemporary painting, and which is exemplified both in some of the Gelati icons and in the frescoes at Nekresi in Kakheti. Georgian goldsmiths work is, however, the equal of any that came from the workshops of Byzantium—where indeed many Georgians were employed—and Georgian enamel work is little, if at all, inferior to Byzantine work. The metallurgical arts—which had such a high development in the Middle Ages—seem to have attracted the genius of the Georgians, and they attained a degree of technical perfection which compares with that of Byzantium and Italy, and elevates them far above the contemporary workers in metallurgy in Eastern Europe, Russia and Armenia. The chief difference between Georgian and Byzantine metallurgical iconography is to be found in the non-representational character of the Georgian work. Byzantine icons generally have a plain background, although they may have an embossed frame-like border; the background of Georgian icons is entirely filled by complicated designs, similar in character to the elaborate sculptured designs of Georgian churches. These backgrounds constitute the very special beauty of Georgian icons, and the combination of this non-representational and geometric art with the essential elements of East Christian artistic technique represents a Georgian synthesis of Western and Eastern conceptions.

Georgian enamels are rather coarse in drawing and less accurate in finish than the Byzantine examples. The *cloisons* are more distinct and less neat, and the colour-schemes are less delicate in tone, although the Georgian enamellers achieved the eight colours of the Byzantines. The Georgians excelled particularly in the manufacture of elaborate geometrical plaques, and here they surpassed the Byzantine workers, the development of whose process was always limited by their tendency to adhere to representational designs.

By the fourteenth century the Georgian icon had already begun to deteriorate, and by the end of the sixteenth century it has lost all artistic value. The influence of Capuchin monks had introduced a certain element of the Italianate, and the icons of this period, as for instance the Virgin of Kavtis-Khevi, were becoming thoroughly bastardized.

The church plate of the time of the mediæval Georgian Kingdom illustrates further both the skill of Georgian craftsmen and the wealth of the Georgian nobles. Byzantine influence was strong, and the finest example of all which survives, the enamelled gold cross in the Svanian church of Matskhvarishi, is attributed by Countess Uvarov to Byzantine workmanship of the twelfth century. Georgian workmanship in reliquaries, cups, plate and crosses was, however, exceedingly fine, and in many pieces, as in the large gold and enamel *hazarpeshni* or drinking spoons (a purely Georgian fashion), the Georgian craftsmen evolved their own interpretation of both Byzantine and Persian decorative motives.

The few of the Georgian bronze church-gates which survive show exquisite workmanship, and like the stone-sculptures and the carved wooden gates which are preserved at Mghvimé Monastery, in the Svanian churches, and in the Tiflis Museum, they are essentially of local inspiration, a Georgian combination of the national decorative designs—such as the interlaced—with Persian and Byzantine elements introduced.

Byzantium, before all, was a civilization; secondly, a political Empire. And until the fifteenth century the civilization of the Near Eastern lands was in essentials Byzantine. East Christian art was the expression of the Byzantine mind—a stone the facets of which reflected different lights according to whether the eyes cast upon it were Bulgarian or Armenian, Rumanian or Georgian, Serbian or Russian.

The Byzantines were the creators of painting as a living art, and their pupils were Italy in great degree, the Russian Masters of the fifteenth and sixteenth centuries, the provincial schools of Greece and Serbia, Bulgaria and Rumania (which though limited in many ways were not without merit), and the Armenians and Georgians. The Balkan schools, in the last decade, have come in for their meed of appreciation from European students, and the material for Greek and Balkan iconography is plentiful. But the Armenian and

THE ART OF MEDIÆVAL GEORGIA

Georgian artists have been ignored; and indeed, wars, anarchy and time have destroyed the most of the material by which their work could have been compared with that of the western schools of East Christian art.

Georgia has preserved few examples of pure Byzantine colour work. The most celebrated is the twelfth-century mosaic of the Church of the Virgin at Gelati; the mosaic was a gift from Alexios Comnenos to David Aghmashenebeli. The Church of Gordi in Mingrelia possesses a Virgin, attributed to the tenth century—and if the attribution is correct it is the oldest known Byzantine painted icon. It was brought to Georgia, according to tradition, by Elena, wife of Bagrat IV—he who completed the building of Kutais Cathedral. In Svaneti, Countess Uvarov noted in different churches eleven Byzantine painted icons, two of which she attributed to the twelfth century. There are also in the shrines of Gelati, Khopi, Mtzkheta, Tsalendjikhi, Alaverdi and Largwisi, a number of attractive painted icons, but these belong to the relatively late period of the seventeenth and eighteenth centuries.[1]

In the manufacture of icons it has been remarked that the Georgian genius and taste developed in the direction of the smith's craft. There are, however, two early painted icons described by Mourier, the character of which indicates that the Georgians had attained merit in this class of painting; one at Gelati showing King Bagrat IV in an attitude of prayer before the Virgin and Child; another at Shemokhmedi of the Virgin and Child. Both these icons are in clear bright colours and the physiognomy of the subjects is typically Georgian.

The churches of Georgia were covered with frescoes and of these some remain, although they are without exception in a badly neglected condition. The native work is, on the whole, of inferior quality. The laws of perspective were not studied, and the colours were applied flat without any shading. A slavish adherence to Greek formulas without the knowledge to interpret them produced an inferior style, which resulted in monotony of design, absence of relief, crudity of execution and lack of *nuances*. Much attention was, however, devoted to accuracy of detail in costume, which gives the work

---

[1] The author had in his possession a Virgin and Child of this class—with a Russian superscription imposed. The type is very distinct from the formalized Greek and Russian styles, and represents in fact the portrait of a Georgian girl and child. The humanistic treatment is remarkable. The icon now belongs to the Church of the Georgian community in Paris.

an historical, if not an artistic, value. Again the frescoes preserve the only authentic memories of the likenesses of historic figures. The eleventh-century church of Sioni at Ateni in Mingrelia has the family of Ashot the Kuropalatês, although in this case the frescoes appear to have been painted two hundred years after the subjects were living. The more famous frescoes at Gelati show the likenesses of Bagrat III, Giorgi I, Bagrat IV and his wife Elena and David Aghmashenebeli and Rusudani. The church of Betani in Kartli, which collapsed half a century ago, contained the portraits of Tamara and her father and her son. The churches of Nikortzminda, Ertatzminda, Safar and Mghvimé contain the remnants of frescoes some of which appear to be by Greek hands; and at Mtzkheta and in the Mingrelian churches there are many portraits of rulers who were living between the fifteenth and seventeenth centuries. An interesting characteristic of the later frescoes is the indications which are patent of the influence of Italian Renaissance and Persian art —both indifferently apprehended.

It was in calligraphy and in the illumination of manuscripts—work giving scope to individual delicacy and skill —that the Georgians excelled. The beautiful Georgian alphabet lent itself to the genius of the calligrapher—work in which the leisurely and child-like mind of the eastern artist delights. From the ninth and tenth centuries the Georgian monks on Mount Athos were engaged with the enthusiasm of the discoverers of a new knowledge in translating the Scriptures and Greek theological and theosophical works into Georgian. Others, returning to Georgia, pursued their work in the Georgian monasteries. The most ancient of the Georgian manuscripts are the Evangel from Adishi in Svaneti —attributed to the end of the ninth century—and the manuscript completed in 940 at the Shatberdi monastery on the Chorokhi and now in the Convent of Djruchi near Sacheri in Mingrelia. The Cathedral of Mtzkheta has a tenth-century manuscript of Gregory the Theologian, and for the eleventh century there are various manuscript Evangels, the principal of which are those at Alaverdi—by the hands of the most famous of Georgian calligraphers, the brothers Dvali—and at Gelati. The churches of Svaneti contain a number of Evangels written during the eleventh and twelfth centuries. In the Gelati Evangel Oriental influences are evident, and various motives from Persian art are introduced. The perspective is bad. There are no less than two hundred and

THE ART OF MEDIÆVAL GEORGIA

forty miniatures. The colours used are blue, red, carmine, green and violet. A fine miniature from Svaneti of the same period illustrated by Uvarov, shows a much more highly developed artistic taste and is in the best Byzantine tradition.

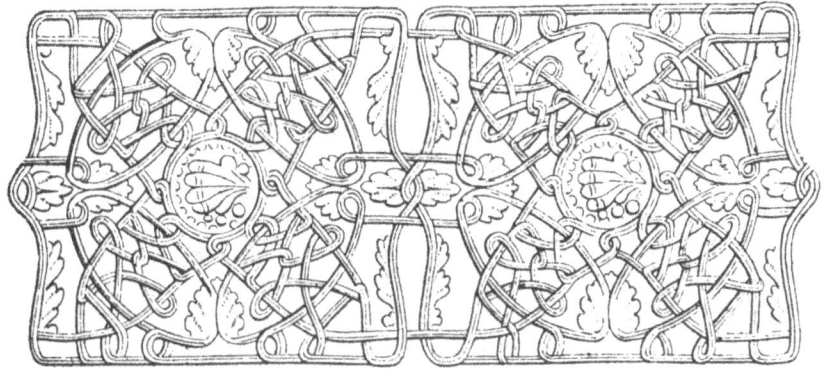

CHAPTER XXVIII

GEORGIAN LITERATURE

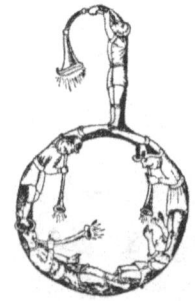

THE literature of mediæval Georgia occupies a significant place in the history of Middle Eastern culture. It enfolds the divergent elements of two distinctive civilizations. The staleing intellectualism of Imperial Christianity was transformed by the Georgians into the simple and ingenuous fidelity of their Church literature. Here was a people to whom the Christian dialectics, already a thousand years old, were interesting and novel, and the monks of Georgia mingle with their translations of Holy Writ and their rehashings of Greek ecclesiastical polemics charming and childish personal biographies of the Fathers of the Georgian Church, whose adventures remain attractive reading, long after their theses and beliefs have turned to dust. At the same time Georgian lay literature—the great poetry of the twelfth century—sparkles with the vibrance of the Persian epics of the time. Nizami was writing in his house in Ganja, when, no more than a hundred miles away, Shota of Rusthavi first saw the light upon the tawny mountains of Samtzkhé. The coincidence has meaning. For if Rusthaveli has been compared to Tasso and Ariosto, if he was the creator, almost, of the Georgian language, and the interpreter of his nation, he was at the same time the pupil and the equal of the Classic Persian thinkers. The first and short-lived Renaissance of the twelfth century, which flowered and faded in the west, found expression in the east through the schools of Rusthaveli and Nizami. It was a brief stirring of the human spirit—a false dawn which faded quickly behind the sombre clouding of perpetual arms and of perpetual creeds.

"No one knows my affairs like myself, what embitters me, what sweetens me. The discourse of idle men greatly grieves me. . . ."

wrote Rusthaveli in a world where thought was to remain, for yet five hundred years, a priestly perquisite. And he quoted Plato and lauded the wisdom of China and Persia, so that an archbishop in the eighteenth century was set upon burning all the manuscript copies of his work which remained in existence.

The early importance of Oriental influence in the development of intellectual life in Georgia is brought out in the study of the origin of the Georgian alphabet. The Georgians, in the Middle Ages, made use of two scripts, the cursive script called *mkhedruli* or "military" and the ecclesiastical script called *khutzuri*. Considerable controversy ranges round the origin and relative antiquity of these two scripts. According to the Georgian Annals, writing was introduced into Georgia, during the reign of King Farnavazi in the fourth century B.C. The Annals do not distinguish between the two scripts, but popular tradition holds that the *mkhedruli* was the older. On the other hand the ecclesiastical tradition, supported by Armenian writers, states that the *khutzuri* script was introduced in the fifth century by Mesrop, the inventor of the Armenian alphabet, and that it was founded on the Armenian.

Now, in the time of Farnavazi, systems of conveying ideas by making signs to represent phonetical sounds were not rare. All the peoples with whom the Georgians were in contact—Persians, Greeks, Syrians and Indians—were becoming accustomed to alphabetical systems of writing. And it seems likely that in introducing writing, Farnavazi would have followed the natural course of borrowing from the Persians, since not only were the Georgians in intimate contact with Persia, but Farnavazi himself was actually representative of Persian influence in the country. The Zend script was in the fourth century B.C. current in Persia; and a comparison of the Zend alphabet with the Georgian *mkhedruli* script makes it possible to recognize the equivalents among Georgian letters of no less than twenty-five out of thirty-five of the letters in the Zend alphabet. Some of the Zend letters have been incorporated into the Georgian alphabet without any real change in form; others, while retaining their shape, have changed their position from horizontal to perpendicular or reverse; others have been changed from right to left, which is explained by the fact that Zend was written from right to left, while Georgian, like the Roman scripts, is written from left to right. Lastly, other letters are recognizable with the addition or subtraction of lines. The resemblance between Zend and the Georgian *mkhedruli* script is, in fact, very strong.[1] And if the derivation of the Georgian

[1] Cf. Khakanov, *Ocherki po ist. gruz. slov.*, Vip. II, pp. 14 *et seq.* For comparisons of certain Georgian letters with Indian alphabets see Brosset, *Eléments de la langue Géorgienne*, pp. 6 *et seq.* The most recent researches, embodied in Prof. Javakhishvili's treatise on Georgian palæography, have not been available to me.

script from Zend is correct, it would appear that the Georgian alphabet was actually introduced about the time of Farnavazi, since the Zend alphabet passed out of use in Persia after the conquest by Alexander of Macedon, and was succeeded by the Pehlevi script of the Arshakids and Sasanids.

That the Georgians had a script of their own before the alleged introduction of the *khutzuri* by Mesrop in the fifth century is borne out by certain references in the Annals. We read, for instance, that King Miriani in the fourth century, before adopting Christianity, endeavoured to inquire into the worth of the new religion, and with this object read many "old and new books—and also the *Book of Nimvrod*". The Annals state also that St. Nino, the Illuminator of Georgia, before her death, related the events of her life, and the Princess Salome wrote all down. Prince Murvano, a son of King Waraz-Bakur, is also recorded to have learnt reading so quickly that he astonished his elders.[1]

The Armenian script has little resemblance to the Georgian *khutzuri* except in the case of two or three letters, while the *khutzuri* resemble the *mkhedruli* if they are compared on the basis that the essential of the ecclesiastical script is the straight line, while that of the "military" script is "pot-hooks" and "hangers". Khakhanov suggests that the *khutzuri* (Church) script came in after the introduction of Christianity, because it was necessary to wean away the priests and the people from the old pagan script, and also possibly because the straight lines of the *khutzuri* were more suitable for the carving of inscriptions in stone. The impetus to the conversion of Georgia came from Armenia, and if the new script was part of ecclesiastical policy, it is very likely that the assistance of a learned Armenian churchman, such as Mesrop, would have been secured.

The Georgian alphabet is a perfect instrument for rendering the wealth of varied sounds in the language; the letters give each different sound with accuracy and clearness, and no other alphabet, including the Armenian, compares with it in efficiency. It would seem that the alphabet had a long and slow evolution to its present state of perfection, rather than that it was invented whole by a foreigner. Even the powerful cultural instrument of the Greek language has only contributed two letters to the Georgian alphabet ($\omega = \omega$, and ϕ) and the words for "pen" and "ink" to the vocabulary of writing.

---

[1] Called Peter the Iberian; was Bishop of Gaza (412–88); his Syriac *Life* is well known to students; the Georgian *Life* was published by Marr in 1896.

GEORGIAN LITERATURE

The Georgian script is, like the Georgian language, ancient and original, and in its perfection to the use for which it is required, it bears the stamp of a venerable individuality.

The first two periods in the history of Georgian literature are that between the sixth and the tenth centuries, which is characterized by the production of works of a spiritual character,[1] translations of Holy Writ and other sacred writings, theses of the Fathers of the Church, edifying compositions and Lives of the Saints; and that between the tenth and twelfth centuries, which saw the development of chronology and history, and the composition of the Georgian epic poems.

Since the sixth century there had taken place a great literary development in the Georgian monasteries which grew up throughout the Byzantine Empire, in Sinai and Palestine and Syria, and on the Mountains of Athos and Olympus. Holy fathers were constantly passing from the hermitages of the just into their native Georgia—not infrequently with the object of raising funds from the devout Bagratid princes. Conversely, serious young men and jaded nobles (how many saints have risen from the beds of the dissipated!) were accustomed to go from Georgia to their national monasteries abroad. The two most remarkable men of this type, towards the latter end of the tenth century, were Torniké,[2] a member of the Meskhian house of Chordvaneli, who was in the Byzantine service and who founded the Iberian monastery on Mount Athos out of the proceeds of a successful military career; and a certain nobleman Ioanné of Ardanuchi who abandoned the service of the Kuropalatês David of Tao to his master's indignation, and became a noted theologian and translator of Greek works into Georgian.

In the monasteries abroad whole families settled and the names of some have survived as copyists and calligraphers; in the ninth century there were the brothers, Zosimé, Ioanné and Kwiriké Sokhastreli on Mount Sinai; and in the eleventh century the numerous family of Dvali at the Monastery of the Holy Cross in Palestine.

On Mount Athos, the leaders of Georgian intellectual life pursued their studies; during the later part of the tenth century, Ioanné of Ardanuchi and his son, Evthimé; and in the eleventh century, Ephrem *Mtsiré* (the Little) and Saba Tukhareli,[3] and

---

[1] The earliest Georgian manuscripts, palimpsests discovered by Javakhishvili, date from sixth to seventh centuries.
[2] For an account of the important part played by Torniké (or Tornigi) in contemporary Byzantine politics, see Schlumberger, *L'Epopée Byzantine*.
[3] Tukhareli—of Tukharisi in the Chorokhi country.

Giorgi Mtatzmindeli ("of Holy Mount"), who, in addition to his numerous writings, had no little influence on the relations of Byzantium and Georgia.

As so often happens in life, the incidental doings of these holy men were far more important than their lives' works in copying and dogmatizing. The Georgian monasteries abroad became universities for the youth of Georgia, and in their travels they absorbed the knowledge of the Classic philosophers who had passing fashions in Byzantium, and they learnt the ways and the practical achievements of the great Mediterranean world. By contrary, the renown of the Georgian monasteries in the orthodox Byzantine Empire impressed the rulers of the West with the signal virtues of the Georgian nation, and the imposing theologians from Athos visited the capital as the diplomatic and, not infrequently, the matrimonial agents of the Georgian kings. Again, the returning studious youth, and the divines who came back to Georgia to forage among the wealthy and uneasy-minded, carried with them admiration for and desire to emulate the magnificent intellectual organization of the Byzantine Church. In Georgia the monastic system had been developing from early times. Grigol Khandzteli, in the ninth century, had founded a group of monasteries along the Chorokhi, and the excellent educational system which he introduced at Khandzti, Shatberdi and Tbeti was copied and encouraged by the Georgian kings, to the extent that in the eleventh century universities were in being at Gelati in Imereti, and at Alaverdi and Gremi in Kakheti.

The vast literary output of the monks, in Georgia and abroad, is of little interest except to the specialist and to the student of illumination and book-making. It is only the "Lives" of Georgian Saints which have a certain historical interest and their own originality, in that the subject-matter is new. These "Lives" include those of Prince Murvano (St. Peter of Iberia); St. Nino, the Illuminator of Georgia; Saints Ioanné and Evthimé; St. Grigol Khandtzeli; St. Abo; and St. Giorgi Mtatzmindeli. Of these, the *Life of St. Abo*, who lived in the eighth century, is by far the most entertaining. St. Abo was originally a perfumer's boy in Baghdad. He met with Nersé, the son of Adarnasé Kuropalatês of Kartli, who was held prisoner in Baghdad, and accompanying the prince back to Georgia, was converted to the Christian faith. Later Nersé was involved in war with the Arabs, and accompanied by Abo, fled to Osseti and then into the land of the Khazars. After many adventures, they found their way to

Abkhazeti and finally returned to Tiflis, where Nersé made his submission to the Arab Emir. Abo lived for three years in peace, but the fact that he was a renegade from Islam finally came to the ears of the Emir, and a painful death removed the poor young perfumer to the calendar of Georgia's Saints.

The pursuit of historical studies was a minor interest of the Georgian monkish class, but with the patronage of the Georgian kings and of the lesser territorial magnates, the writing of chronicles and chronologies and the translation of Byzantine historical works became a favoured occupation.

Wakhtang VI of Kartli, an unfortunate king but an enthusiastic student, caused many of the early chronicles to be collated, and in the first decade of the eighteenth century this work of revision and completion of *Kartlis-Tzkhovreba*, or the *Life of Georgia*, was finally accomplished. *Kartlis-Tzkhovreba* is generally referred to as *The Georgian Annals* and is to be distinguished from the historical work of Wakhtangi's son, Wakhushti, which includes also local histories of the different Georgian principalities down to the middle of the eighteenth century. Again, the so-called *Armenian Chronicle* published by Brosset is a mediæval Armenian translation of a *Georgian Chronicle* which ends with the reign of David II.

The various existing manuscripts of King Wakhtangi's work which were made in the eighteenth century differ in certain details, and there is further an earlier manuscript of the seventeenth century, known as Queen Mary's, which indicates that attempts to co-ordinate the original sources of Georgian history had been made before King Wakhtangi's time.[1]

The earliest source of Georgian written history was a manuscript known as *The Conversion of the Georgians*, which was compiled in part by the disciples of St. Nino and in part at a latter date. A manuscript of the work attributed to the monk Mroveli, who lived at the end of the seventh or beginning of the eighth century, was known. To the ninth century belongs an *Anonymous Chronicle*, with a short *History of the Kings, Gods, Bishops and Catholicoses of Georgia*; and to the tenth century, *The Exaltation of the Living Cross of Mtzkheta* and an account of the *Conversion of the Somekhians* (Armenians). These works are essentially ecclesiastical. In the eighth century, however, Juansher Juansheriani wrote his *Narrative of the House of Wakhtang Gorgasali* (Gurgaslani), and the eleventh century saw *The Chronicles of Sumbat*, in which Sumbat Davitisdze

---

[1] For the sources of the *K.-Tz.*, see the works of Th. Jordania, Javakhishvili, Taqaishvili, Kekelidze and Janashvili.

recounts the deeds of the Bagrationi family; and the *Abkhazta Tzkhovreba* or *Life of Abkhazeti* compiled by King Bagrat III.

An anonymous eyewitness described the life of King Gioagi II and also of his son David Aghmashenebeli. The writer was obviously a contemporary and a familiar of the Court ("*all this we saw with our own eyes*"), and his intimate account of the literary habits of the great Restorer is worth quoting, both as indicating the position of the writer and as an illustration of the studious way of the Georgian Court of the first quarter of the twelfth century.

> "He loved tenderly all that pertained to the Scriptures, ancient and new, translated from other tongues into Georgian. . . .
>
> "Day and night in his comings and his goings, in his ceaseless expeditions, in his work, which was for him, without rest as well as without weariness, books—with which he always loaded several mules and camels—constituted his pleasures, his feasting and his daily exercise. The moment he dismounted from his horse, he armed himself, before all, with a book, and did not quit reading it except from weariness. After the evening meal instead of sleeping or occupying himself in some other way, he began to read again. If his eyes were weary he replaced them with his ears and then as a listener, not distrait, but always extremely attentive, he would analyse, question, or would explain the value and intrinsic meaning of the Texts.
>
> "I will cite another instance of his love of books . . . often he would place before him and read the Apostles; when he had finished he made a mark at the end of the book, and at the end of the year he counted the marks, by which means we found one day that he had read it twenty-four times."

For the reigns of Giorgi III and Queen Tamara there is a further account of an anonymous eyewitness. The style is official and the language is that of the ecclesiastical works of the period. Janashvili suggests that the account of these reigns was probably compiled by the Dchqondideli—the Bishop of Dchqondidi—who was *Mdsignobart-Ukhutsesi*.

The period of the Mongol wars was covered by the writings of one who, from internal evidence, was a native of Samtzkhé. He was of an independent mind, and he does not hesitate to criticize Giorgi Lasha and Rusudani. He was acquainted with the Mongol language, and consulted other chroniclers of the time ("*as the monks of Mghvimé write*"). For the fourteenth century there is also the *Dzegli Eristavta* or *Monument of the Eristavni*—a sort of family history of the Eristavni of the Ksani with some account of the history of the Ossetians.

The fourteenth century is badly documented and "the ancient history" of Georgia is brought to an end by the compilers of *Kartlis-Tzkhovreba* with the death of Giorgi

Brtsqinwalé in 1346. There is some account of the invasions of Timur Leng, but the anonymous author states that "*I have not the strength to describe and praise the heroism of the Georgian braves in the way that the Georgian army has been described in Persian books.*" What these Persian books were is not known, but it is possible that the Georgian writer was referring to the work of the Arab Elkalkashandi, who records the admiration of the Muslims for the Georgians.[1]

For the later period of Georgian history, from the Division of the Kingdom to the Russian conquest, there is a mass of material, which in its detail creates a dire confusion. It is sufficient to mention the provincial histories of Samtzkhé, Imereti and Kakheti and other Georgian districts—all collated by Wakhushti—and the contemporary accounts of events compiled by Farsadan Giorgijanidze (or Janashvili) in the seventeenth century and by Sekhnia Chkheidze and Papuna Orbeliani in the eighteenth century.

The enquiring intellect of the Georgians was not, even in the Middle Ages, circumscribed by devotional interest in religious subjects and the concern of the political mind for history and tradition. Even the ecclesiastical writers could apply themselves to the study of Classical philosophy, and the Georgians as early as the eighth century—maybe as a result of their intimate contact with the Islamic world—were concerning themselves with the exact sciences. The catalogue of the Shatberdi Monastery on the Chorokhi shows that under the early Bagratid dynasts of Tao and Klarjeti, the monks were studying anatomy and medicine, natural history and astrology, and there were manuscript dissertations on such essentially lay subjects as "the Nature of the Universe" and "Why Man was Born Last". There were further, in existence, two essays on the Georgian language and studies on Greek and Hebrew writing. In the eleventh and twelfth centuries men were known by name for their achievements in scientific work. There were Ioanné Petritzi, philosopher, poet and grammarian, who was celebrated also as a rhetorician; Ioanné Tarichisdze (1089–1145), a divine, philosopher and noted translator; Saba Sinieli (about 1150), rhetorician and jurist; Arsen Iqaltoeli, the confessor of David the Restorer, who founded a high school at Iqalto on the model of the Byzantine colleges; and Anton Dchqondideli, who in Tamara's reign wrote on *The Structure and Organization of the Army*.

[1] Cf. *Zap. Vost. Ot. I.R.A.O.*, I, 208–16; V. Tiesenhausen, *Zametka Elkalkashandi o Gruzinakh*.

THE LIFE OF GEORGIA

The Mongol, Turkish and Persian wars seared the vivid intellectual life, as they scarred the valleys of the Georgian Kingdom. The first Renaissance of the twelfth century flowered in Georgia, as in the West—but ruin choked the delicate growth of a splendid and an individual culture. Sargis Tmogveli, poet and philosopher, was the last representative of a school of originality and promise.

In the seventeenth century, Chardin, in his none too friendly appraisal of the Georgians, allows himself to say that they—

> "Are Naturally very Witty, Nor would there be more Learned Men, or more Ingenious Masters in the World, were they best improv'd by the knowledge of Arts and Sciences." [1]

Even when he wrote, a few rare spirits were preparing the meagre Georgian Renaissance which struggled to overcome the political conditions of the early eighteenth century. King Wakhtangi imported the first printing-press from Wallachia and in the midst of invasion and petty revolts inspired the revision of the historical and juridical works which bear his name. His son, Wakhushti, pursued his father's courses. After some soldiering and politics in Georgia, he settled down, an impoverished refugee in Moscow, living with a large family in lodgings in the Presna Street, a neighbourhood which was for generations much favoured by the Georgian community. He interested himself in the production of the beautiful Georgian edition of the Bible, which was published in Moscow in 1742. He dabbled also in religious and philosophical studies, but his real and valuable contribution to the advancement of knowledge was the work which he completed in 1745—*The Geographical Description of Georgia*. The work contained a long introduction on the customs of the Georgians, and a consideration of the country in provinces, with a mass of topographical detail and twenty-two manuscript maps. As a production of the mid-eighteenth century, the whole geographical work of Wakhushti not only represented a great advance on any other material which had been written up to that date, but it may certainly be regarded as among the most competent and scientific productions of the time.

The same period saw the revival of the exact sciences in Georgia. Saba Sulkhan Orbeliani travelled in Europe at the end of the seventeenth century; he composed the first Georgian dictionary and himself illuminated it; and in his *Book of Wisdom*

[1] *Chardin* (1686 ed.), p. 190.

and Lies he showed that the light shrewd wisdom of the old Georgian epics was still a living thing.

In the eighteenth century, the Catholicos Anton I revived the studious traditions of the Church by a series of devotional and educational works; and King Irakli of Kartli, in the third quarter of the century, continued amidst wars and tumults, the enlightened literary patronage of Wakhtang VI.

Some reference has already been made to the great school of epic poets which flourished in Georgia between the tenth and the twelfth centuries. The famous names are associated with the reign of Queen Tamara, but the poetry of the Georgians had a long history before it flowered into the glories of the Tamaran epoch. The earliest of Georgian epics is that known as *The Wisdom of Balavari*. The tale is of a wise hermit, Balavari, who converted to Christianity an Indian prince, Iosapha, in spite of the angry persecutions of his father Aveniri. The tale of *The Wisdom of Balavari* or *Barlaam and Joseph* had widespread fame through Europe in the Middle Ages. Whether the Georgian version was the original, or only one among the many others, remains in doubt. The tale was first carried into Europe through a Latin translation from the Greek made by the monk George of Trebizond, and about 1230 Abbot Guido in turn rendered it into German. French, Italian, Swedish, Czech and Polish versions followed and finally it appeared in Iceland as the *Varlaams-saga*.

The story of *The Wisdom of Balavari* seems to be a monkish interpretation of the life of Buddha. Now Georgian knowledge of India was fairly extensive even at an early date, as a result of the service of Georgian contingents in the armies of the Sasanids. There are frequent references to India in the Georgian Annals and the mediæval poets show a considerable knowledge of Indian life. The tale was popular in Georgia from an early date, and it seems probable that it was originally carried into the country by Georgian monks from Jerusalem some time in the seventh century. There are indications that it was translated from Georgian into Greek by Saint Evthimé in the tenth century.[1] There were doubtless other popular epics in Georgia before the days of the great poets, and they would have been passed from mouth to mouth as is *The Man in the Panther's Skin* among the peasants to this day.[2]

The earliest of the epic poems of the twelfth century was

---

[1] For detailed discussion see Khakhanov, Vip. II, pp. 82–116.
[2] I have met officers, soldiers and peasants who can recite long pieces. It is in many cases their only and a sufficient literary education.

the *Amiran-Darejaniani* of Moses Khoneli (from the village of Khoni in Imereti). The *Amiran-Darejaniani* is a collection of heroic tales centring round the legendary figure of Amiran, and rich in the lore of the peasants. The poem contains many indications of Persian influence and it is imbued with much pre-Christian and pre-Muslim fantasy and tradition. It throws an interesting light on the state of geographical knowledge in Georgia, for it includes characters who come from the Yemen, Egypt, Astarabad, India, Basra, Bahrein, Ghazni, China and Khazaria.

The second of the great poems *Visraminiani* or *Visramiani* (the "Loves of Vis and Ramin") is based on an old Pehlevi tale which was current in contemporary Persia. Wardrop is of opinion that " it may have had a good deal to do with that development of European romanticism which finds utterance in the songs of the Minnesinger, the lays of the Troubadours, and the letters of Heloisa . . ." and he refers to the fact that " a comparison has been drawn between the Persian version and Gottfried von Strassburg's *Tristan and Isolt* ".[1]

Visramiani, like *The Man in the Panther's Skin*, is a tale of fantastic romance, and it is full of the exaggerated metaphor and erotic sentimentality of the great Persian poems. Yet there is a gay and lilting strain throughout which carries the reader easily through the burdened passages. Throughout the poem there is a knowledge of human nature, a joy in the natural beauty of life, a brave and light yet sad philosophy, which is characteristic of all of the great Georgian poets, and which makes the reading of them at once pleasing to the taste and salutary to the spirit.

The poet gives descriptions, which are instinct with knowledge of his fellows:

"Among these was a renowned, generous, wise-minded man, complete in manhood, fearless, prudent, cheerful, faultless in speech, brave and a seeker after wisdom, perfect in all virtues, exquisite; he was right cunning in leechcraft; a lover of all men, a man of God, and he was lord of a great land. Besides all these virtues he was a seeker after strange stories and poetry."[2]

And here is the account of a beautiful lady:

"Now she has grown up with much self-will, and like a falcon's fledgling begins to soar upward. I fear that her flight will be so high that this nest will no longer content her and she will go away somewhere to seek her peers. Peerlessness and solitude go ill together.

---

[1] Wardrop, *Visramiani*, "Introduction," p. 7.
[2] I follow Sir O. Wardrop's excellent version.

I have nurtured her most delicately, and now she is no longer pleased with our raiment, nor our meat and drink, although by God's help we lack not. Our power prevails not against her self-will; however matchless the robes I sew for her, she casts shame on sixty colours. If I give her yellow, she says this is garb for the sick; if I give her red she says that is for harlots; blue is the colour of mourners; white, quoth she, is for monk's gowns, and two-coloured for scribes. When she wakes in the morning, she commands her slaves and handmaidens and demands silk attire; at midday she demands a dress of gold brocade, and in the evening a dress of cloth of gold; every moment she demands another kind."

Shota (Ashot) Rusthaveli, the greatest of the Georgian poets, was a Meskhian, a native of Rusthavi, a small village between Akhaltzikhé and Khertvisi. According to tradition he received his early education from his uncle, a monk, and was later sent to the monastery of Tbeti. From there he went into Kakheti and spent some time in the monastic schools of Gremi and Iqalto. He then visited the Georgian monasteries on Athos and Olympus and, according to some writers, also travelled to Jerusalem. He achieved a fine familiarity with Greek poetry and philosophy and as is patent from his work, had some knowledge of Persian and Arabic. On his return to Georgia, he received an appointment in the royal treasury. In this position he no doubt gained the wide knowledge of the merchant-class which is apparent in his work. During the years at court he composed his famous poem, and popular tradition alleges that he concealed always a hopeless passion for the Queen. He received a fief on the Aragvi and appears to have attained considerable affluence. He died, according to tradition, in the same year as Queen Tamara.

The construction of Shota Rusthaveli's masterpiece *The Man in the Panther's Skin* shows strong Persian influence, and is, in Rusthaveli's words, " A Persian tale, now done into Georgian ". The work is attractive in its philosophy of life, in its rich and vivid descriptions and its knowledge of character, rather than in its incidents, which are amazingly involved. As a document of the mediæval mind, it is a very precious thing. It is a mirror of the soul of the Georgian of the period, who dabbled in Greek philosophy, who was sporadically devout, and who rode in wild cavalry raids across all Northern Persia. It lights for us the cosmopolitan free-thinking mind of the Georgian noble, his easy, sentimental sensualism, his aggressive and gallant sense of his own unique superiority. We can see as vividly as though he rode past us on his " jet-black " charger, clad in " Khwarazmian armour ", the mediæval Georgian paladin, a courageous slayer of the enemy, a daring huntsman, a respecter of the aged, a patron of the poor, chivalrous to women, a loyal friend and a great drinker, but withal, callous, passionate and cruel, ingenuously treacherous. Here is primitive man, with a gay fatalism, a light-hearted wisdom, a smattering of Greek learning, with a craving to assert his manhood in combat and to slake his passions in beauty and barbaric luxury.

Shahrukha or Shahrukhadze (the name is a Persian one) was the other of the great Georgian poets and he like Rusthaveli was a Meskhian. He has left a set of odes, some of which are very interesting, and one, an elegy of the knight-errant, has all the heroic and humanistic spirit of Rusthaveli's masterpiece.[1]

The Classic age of Georgian literature passed with the great Queen Tamara. But the Georgians have always been lovers of books and song, and the tradition was carried on during the troubled centuries by a number of indifferent rhymsters and imitators.

In the Renaissance of the seventeenth and eighteenth centuries, the poets did not parallel the achievements of Wakhushti and Sulkhan Orbeliani in the sphere of historical and literary studies. For the lives of Taymuraz I and of Irakli II, there were two writers, Prince Archili and Guaramashvili, who voiced the deeds of these kings and the aspirations towards a national revival. But it was not until the nineteenth century that writers appeared whose creations in prose and verse could in any way bear comparison with the work of the twelfth-century poets.

[1] See Marr, *Drev. Grug. Odopistzi*, in *Tek. Raz. A-G.*, IV.

CHAPTER XXIX

THE WEALTH AND STATE OF THE MEDIÆVAL KINGDOM

HERE is not the place to consider the vast structure—at once political, social and economic—which was represented by Dar-ul-Islam, the Mussulman world of the Middle Ages. Socially, Dar-ul-Islam was a unity; politically, it was a loose aggregration of spiritually sympathetic states; economically, it was the greatest form in which the human genius had as yet expressed itself in practice. In the four great sciences of mathematics, navigation, medicine and astronomy the Muslims led and taught the mediæval world. In wealth, the Caliphate, the official organism of Islam, equalled the Byzantine Empire; but the whole sum of the wealth of Dar-ul-Islam far exceeded that of Christendom or of the isolated Chinese world. Northward the Caliph's *dirhems* passed as welcome currency in the markets of the rude Baltic tribes [1]; southward Arab vessels were plying to Madagascar and the eastern coast of Africa. And from Timbuktu to Malaya and even to Canton, a good Muslim could still travel and trade with some facility, when the cities of Islam had been long shattered and desolated by Christendom and the Mongols in the dog-days of the fourteenth century.[2]

The Caucasian lands were a valuable appanage of the Arabs, for their varied local products were sought after in the wealthy cities of Iran and Iraq. But the prosperity of the Caucasian lands during this period must be attributed mainly to the development by the Arabs of the trans-Caspian traffic. The Mussulman provinces of the eastern Caucasus—Shirvan, Aran

---

[1] Cf. J. F. Baddeley, *Russia, Mongolia, China*, I, xxiv-xxvi.
[2] Cf. Ibn-Battuta, *Travels in Asia and Africa*, 1325-1354 (translated and selected by H. A. R. Gibb, London, 1929).

and Mughan—throve on the Caspian trade as, during preceding centuries, Colchis had flourished in the heyday of the driving of the Euxine traffic by the Greeks and Romans.

The Arabs never succeeded in establishing themselves as a power in the Black Sea, and the Black Sea commerce, declining as it was, remained the monopoly of Byzantium and the Italian cities until the fifteenth century. A certain amount of Muslim trade filtered through to the Pontine ports; we have already quoted Constantine Porphyrogenitus on the prosperity of the Kuropalatês of Tao in the tenth century as a result of Ardanuchi having become the entrepôt of trade passing by the Chorokhi route between the sea and the Persian and Armenian territories of the interior. And el-Masudi, in the same century, records the attendance of large numbers of Muslim merchants at the annual fairs of Trebizond.[1]

The Arabs failed to overthrow the commercial supremacy of the Greeks in the Black Sea, but, by opening up the Caspian-Volga route, they managed to tap the great markets of the Eurasian plains, which had until the seventh century been the monopoly of the masters of Constantinople.

The military policy of the Arabs in the Caucasus was definitely directed to securing the flank of their great south-to-north trade route. They held Tiflis and the line of the Mountains of Likhi, and on the north they held *Bab-el-Abwab*—Derbend, the " Gate of Gates ".

At the mouth of the Volga and round the north-eastern shore of the Caspian were established the Khazars, a people of mixed stock who spoke a Turkish tongue, and who were in process of passing from the pastoral and predatory habits of a nomad people to the settled way of merchants and carriers. The Khazars had been a sore pest to the Byzantine and Sasanian rulers. It was only in the eighth century that the Arab, Mirvan-ibn-Muhammad, finally established the mastery of the Muslims over the western littoral of the Caspian and put an end to the Khazar raids into Caucasia and north-eastern Persia. Nevertheless, in the following century, the Khazar Khagan was still a potentate of great influence, and it is probable that he was of little less importance in the view of the Byzantine Court than the Emperor Charles the Great and his successors.[2]

---

[1] el-Masudi, I, 402: " On this sea is the town of Trebizond. There is a fair once a year at which merchants assemble from all nations—Moslems, Byzantines, Armenians and others from the country of Kashak." Of the Kashak (Circassians) (p. 347): " I have only to observe that their sea is not far from the country of Trebizond and that a constant navigation and trade are kept up between them and this city."

[2] See Bury, *Eastern Roman Empire*, p. 402.

WEALTH AND STATE

The Khazar capital was Itil—near the site of Astrakhan—straddling three channels of the Volga and controlling all the trade of the great river to the north. Between Itil and the Arab frontier-town of Derbend were a number of Khazar settlements, whose location indicates the exact course and the considerable extent of the trade between the south and the north.[1] The Khazars were, in fact, the commercial heirs of the Aorsi about whom Strabo wrote and they were moreover the progenitors of the Eastern European Jews.[2]

> "The King of the Khazars", says el-Masudi, "has no ships on this sea, for the Khazars are no sailors."[3]

The sea portage of the Caspian was thus in the hands of the Arabs and ibn-Haukal records that "it is much frequented by the ships of the merchants who traffick from one town to another; and it affords much fishing".[4] Later in the tenth century, with the decline in the power of the Caliphs, the Russians who had formerly been accustomed to come as traders into the sea, grew sufficiently daring to undertake piracies, and on one occasion took and sacked the wealthy city of Bardaʿa in Aran.

In the thriving days of the Caspian trade when the peoples of the north, Rus, Bolghars and Khazars rubbed shoulders in the streets of Itil with Arabs, Persians, Jews and Armenians, the towns of the eastern Caucasus grew rich and famous throughout the Muslim world. At Bardaʿa, the capital of Aran, roads converged from Kermanshah by Tabriz and Dabil (Dwin), chief town of Muslim Armenia; from Ray by Ardabil and the towns of the Mughan plain; from Tiflis and the north-western marches; and through Shamakha from Derbend, the gate to the Khazar country. Bardaʿa was the great centre of the north-western provinces of the Caliphate.

> "Bardaʿa", says ibn-Haukal, "is a populous and flourishing city with cultivated lands and much fruit. After Ray and Isfahan there is not in Iraq nor Khurasan, a city more large, more beautiful or pleasant than Bardaʿa ... and for a day's journey the whole country is laid out in gardens and fruits. The fruits are excellent; their filberds are better than those of Samarkand, and their chestnuts superior to the chestnuts of Syria, and the figs of Bardaʿa are more delicious than those of any other place. There are also mulberries; and silk is sent from there to Khuzistan and to Iraq."[5]

---

[1] Cf. article *Khazars* in E.I.
[2] Ripley, *Races of Europe*.
[3] el-Masudi, p. 412.
[4] ibn-Haukal, p. 184.
[5] *Idem*, p. 157.

THE LIFE OF GEORGIA

Two centuries later el-Idrissi found that "*the town covers nearly nine miles*",[1] but in the fourteenth century after the Mongol devastations Abu'l Fida found it mostly in ruins,[2] and Barbaro another hundred years later speaks dolefully of "*a great citie heretofore destroied by Zamberlan*".[3]

Tiflis in the days of the Caliphate had no great consideration. ibn-Haukal says that it is "*a pleasant place and abounds in provisions*",[4] and el-Idrissi commends the low cost of living there.[5] Greater than Tiflis was Baylakan in the Mughan plain, which ibn-Haukal describes as a fine city watered by many streams and canals and plentifully supplied with milk and orchards. It was noted for its syrups.[6]

On the road from the north to Tiflis and Barda'a were Shaberan [7] and Shamakha, which latter place el-Mukadassi in the tenth century remarked as a fine stone-built town, surrounded by gardens and fertile corn-lands.

Derbend was with Barda'a the principal town of the north-western provinces of the Caliphate. ibn-Haukal recalls that "*the sovereigns of Persia have considered the possession of this city as a matter of great importance*" [8] and Idrissi describes it as "*the port for all the traffic of the Khazar Sea*".[9]

The trade over and around the Caspian had a wide expansion in the early centuries of Islam. A regular maritime traffic was carried on between the ports of northern Persia, Baku and Derbend and the Khazar towns, then up the Volga to the Slavonic and Turki principalities and tribes. At the same time ibn-Khurdabdih states that the Rus merchants traded down as far as Baghdad,[10] and el-Masudi says of the Bulgars (Targhiz): "*their caravans go as far as Khowarezm (Khiva) in Khurasan and from Khowarezm caravans go up to them*".[11] He adds that there was also an "active navigation" carried on between the Bulgars and other Turkish tribes and the Khazars.

"From this country come the furs of black and red foxes which are called the Bortasian furs. A black fur of this kind costs one hundred

---

[1] el-Idrissi, p. 321.   [2] Abu'l Fida, p. 154.   [3] Barbaro, p. 85.
[4] ibn-Haukal, p. 160.   [5] el-Idrissi, p. 325.
[6] Cf. Guy Lestrange, *Lands of the Eastern Caliphate*, p. 178.
[7] For Shaberan, see Bartold's article *Shirwan* in E.I. It was in the early Middle Ages the capital of Shirvan and the name of the province is derived from it. Bartold quotes the traveller Gmelin as only finding "miserable ruins" at Shaberan in 1770. As late as the previous century it was noticed by Evliya as still a town, "three journeys east of Baku" (*Travels*, II, 163). ibn-Khurdabdih (p. 200, ed. de Goeje) says that Shaberan was built by Khusraw Anushirwan, at the same time as he fortified Derbend against the Khazars.
[8] ibn-Haukal, pp. 158–9.   [9] el-Idrissi, p. 322.
[10] ibn-Khurdabdih, p. 115.   [11] el-Masudi, I, 414.

dinars and more; but the red are cheaper. Dresses of these furs are worn by the kings of the Arabs and the Barbarians; and they form part of their vanity; for they are considered more valuable than the furs of sable, hermeline and the like. The kings wear tiaras, kaftans and robes of these furs. If kings have their kaftans and robes lined with black Bortasian foxes' fur it is excusable (although it is against the divine laws)." [1]

It would be interesting to follow the influence of the fur trade on the development of industrial civilization. In northern Asia and in North America the little furry beasts have led men on to Empire; and beyond the trappers' gins and the road to world power lies perhaps "part of the vanity" of kings, but more potently the vanity of women in their furs, for in that most primitive manner of clothing, those primitives are themselves most beautiful.

Such barbarous products—furs and wax and honey—were the stable traffic of the northern tribes, and in these prime products the peoples of the Caucasus had their share; [2] but they traded also other articles, at once, of greater value, rarer and more varied.

The peoples of the Caucasus have been noted since Classical times for their skill in the manufacture of textiles. Under the Caliphate, Caucasian textiles had a great reputation. Of all, Circassian stuffs were most sought after, and el-Masudi in his description of the Kashak praises both their persons and their fabrics.

> "They are, among all the nations whom we have mentioned, the cleanest and the most handsome in their appearance, both men and women. They have good persons, are slender round the waist, have well-shaped hips, and are of a comely form. They dress in white, in Greek brocade, in cloth of scarlet colour and other sorts of cloth or gilt brocade. In their country various sorts of cloth are manufactured of hemp and other materials; one sort is called et-Talli cloth; it is finer than damask (silk) and stouter than (our) hemp cloth. One piece of this sort of cloth costs about ten *dinars* and is exported to the neighbouring Muslim countries. The same cloth is exported from other nations who live near the Kashak; but the best comes from them." [3]

Derbend was the distributing centre for the Caucasian textile industry. "*From it*", says ibn-Haukal, "*they send linen clothes to all parts of Aran and Azerbaijan. Here they also weave tapestry and carpets.*" [4]

[1] el-Masudi, I, 412. [2] Cf. Procopius, II, xxviii, 29; el-Idrissi, II, 375.
[3] el-Masudi, I, 437. (For Classical references to the celebrated linen of Colchis, see Strabo, Book XI, Cap. II, 17; cf. also Rawlinson's *History of Herodotus*, II, 148, and note 1).
[4] ibn-Haukal, p. 159.

THE LIFE OF GEORGIA

Marco Polo, writing of Georgia at the beginning of the thirteenth century, observes that

> "silk is produced in great abundance. They also weave cloth of gold and all kinds of very fine silk stuffs. The country . . . has indeed not lack of anything, and the people live by trade and handicrafts." [1]

Again, in the fifteenth century, Josaphat Barbaro, writing of Shirvan and Aran after the troubled days of the Mongol domination, can still note their manufacture of "*fustians, lynen cloths, fryses, many rugges, and a lytel sylke . . . which they conveyed into the Sea Maggiore and to the towns about*" [2]

The mediæval Caucasus was no less important as a centre both of the dyeing industry and of the production of the raw materials of that industry for export. Such necessaries of the dyers' art as acorns, gall-nuts and vine and mulberry leaves, were, of course, to be found in abundance in the forests of Georgia, and in the orchards of Shirvan and Aran. But more valuable than these common products were the insects inhabiting oak-trees from which the mediæval dyers made "the beautiful colour called *kirmiz*",[3] and the madder and saffron which was grown in large quantities in Georgia, Shirvan and Aran. These two vegetable products were of vital importance to the dyeing and weaving industries of the countries of Islam. Madder—and particularly its roots—was one of the plants most necessary to the coloration of rugs. Used alone, it produced many shades of red from a rich scarlet to a gentle shade of pink; and the red most common in Persian rugs was produced by a mixture of alum-water, grape-juice and madder. Applied over indigo, madder effected many shades of brown, while the rich Persian blue was obtained by the reverse process; combined with indigo and other ingredients madder gave many variations of purple; diluted with milk and water and sour grape juice it obtained violet. Again, saffron, with all its variations of yellow and orange, gave, when mixed with indigo, many of the shades of green.

el-Idrissi states that

> "in all the country of Ran, that is to say from Bab-el-Abwab as far as Tiflis, madder grows on the ground, and they collect great quantities of it. This substance is transported by way of the Caspain Sea to Jorjan,[4] and from there on the back (of beasts of burden) into India. It is superior in quality to all other kinds of madder ".[5]

Saffron likewise was exported from Derbend.

---

[1] Polo (Yule, I, p. 50).   [2] Barbaro, p. 86.   [3] ibn-Haukal, pp. 160–1.
[4] Jorjan, ancient Hyrcania, called later Ghilan.   [5] el-Idrissi, II, 330.

WEALTH AND STATE

The eastern Caucasus had been famous at least from Achæmenian times as the land of natural fires, and the neighbouring Persian province had borrowed the fame in its name Azerbaijan—*ader-badagan*, the " garden of fire ". From the early days of the Arab rule in Shirvan extensive industrial use was made of the petroleum of the Apsheron peninsula. el-Masudi speaks of Baku and " the Naptha country ", and Yakuti, himself a native of the place, states that two hundred mule loads a day were, in his time, exported. Marco Polo, who did not himself pass through the Caucasus, had heard tell of Baku oil.

> "On the confines towards Georgiana ", he says, "there is a fountain from which oil springs in great abundance, insomuch that a hundred shiploads might be taken from it at one time. This oil is not good to use with food, but it's good to burn and is also used to anoint camels that have the mange. People come from a vast distance to fetch it, for in all the countries round, they have no other oil." [1]

Barbaro's description is as usual distinguished by a certain crude realism in detail.

> " Upon this side of the sea there is another citie called Bachu, whereof the sea of Bachu taketh name, neere unto which citie, there is a mountaigne that casteth foo'the blacke oyle stynkeng horryblye, which they nevertheless use for furnissheng of their lightes, and for the anoynteng of their camells, twies a yere. For if they were not anoynted they wolde become skabbie." [2]

Among products of a more special character, the people of the Caucasus were noted for their caviar,[3] their armour and their falcons. In parts of Daghestan, according to el-Masudi, "*most of the inhabitants are employed in making coats of mail, stirrups, bridles, swords and similar instruments of iron*".[4] Marco Polo had heard the fame of the bowmen of Georgia, and el-Masudi records that from the district of Shulaveri on the Armenian marches, came the prized battle-axes called " Shulaverdian "—"*which are in use with the Sia'bibah and other Barbarian corps*".[5] Again, Polo says of Georgia, that " *the country produces the best goshawks in the world, which are called Avighé* ",[6] and el-Masudi has a dissertation on the falcons of the Caspian coasts and of Armenia.

---

[1] Polo (Yule), I, 46. [2] Barbaro, 88.
[3] el-Masudi, I, 438. [4] *Idem*, I, 433.
[5] *Idem*, I, 461, see *Encyclopædia of Islam* under Sayabidja, article by G. Ferrand, who states that these people were pre-Islamic emigrants from Sumatra to India, and later to Iraq. They were generally employed by the Arabs as guards and gaolers.
[6] Polo (Yule), I, 50.

THE LIFE OF GEORGIA

"In this sea", he says, "are islands opposite the coast of Jorjan, where a sort of white falcons are caught. These falcons are soon made tame; and one has little to fear that they will associate (with the wild birds); but they are rather weak, for the sportsmen who catch them in these islands feed them with fish; and if any other food is given to them, they become reduced in strength. Men who distinguish themselves by their knowledge of falconry, and of the different sorts of rapacious birds which have been employed for the same purpose, among the Persians, Turks, Byzantines, Hindus and Arabs, say that falcons of a white colour are quickest and handsomest; that they have the best shape and chest; and that they are soonest tamed, and the strongest of all falcons to rise in the air; that they have the longest breath, and fly furthest, for they are very light and spirited, and they have a hotter temper than any other species of falcons. The difference of colour depends upon the difference of climate. Hence they are of pure white in Armenia, in the country of the Khazar, in Jorjan, and the neighbouring countries of the Turks, on account of the great fall of snow in these climates." [1]

The Arab writers pay little attention to the western parts of the Caucasus, since the Euxine trade had little concern for them. They note only the names of the declining ports along the coast from Trebizond to the entry of the Sea of Azov. Phasis and Dioscurias had certainly lost much of their importance. Imier—" that side "—beyond the Mountains of Likhi and the marches of the Muslim—had been desolated in the long wars between the fifth and the eighth centuries; and the life of Georgia was growing young again, in the rockbound fastnesses of Samtzkhé. Yet an extensive find—at the small roadstead of Arkhavé in Lazistan—of gold and silver coins minted in the cities of Islam—tells of the constant come and go of trade between the provinces of the Caliph and the independent parts of Georgia, during the generations when strife was continuing in perpetual iteration.

The coins found at Arkhavé all date to the beginning of the ninth century, and are *dirhems* minted at Baghdad, Muhammadiah, in Armenia, at Kufa, at Basra, in Aran, at Balkh, in Africa, at Harunabad, Ray and Kirman.[2] This was the circulation of trade under the great Caliphs—from Africa and Balkh to Lazica. Sargis Tmogveli, three centuries later, recalls the fame of it when he exclaims:

"*Thou art master of Eran and T'huran; from China to Qirovan, all is thine and under thy command.*"[3]

---

[1] el-Masudi, I, 423.
[2] Pakhomov, p. 53; cf. ibn-Haukal, p. 163; "In Azerbaijan and Aran and Armenia, gold and silver coins are current."
[3] *Visraminiani*, p. 160, Qirovan is Kerouan in Tunisia.

The decline of the Imperial power of the Caliphate at the end of the ninth century marked the beginning of a period of decentric development across the whole stretch of the old world. The revival of Byzantine Imperial power under the Macedonian emperors did not outlast the first quarter of the eleventh century, and so for two full hundred years, until the sudden looming of the First Mongolian Empire, decentric forces were in illimitable play. A time of political inefficiency gave chance to the condottieri of the world. The heirs of the Arab Caliphates—Turks in Iran and Anatolia, Berbers in Africa and Spain—founded their dynasties of embattled parvenus, and over all Roman Europe the pirate Northmen fixed their castles and their kingdoms from Scotland to Tmutarakan. The new political erections were superficial, but the decentric upgrowths all the way from Spain to Georgia were primal. The human spirit sparkled, curious, lively and dynamic; and kingdoms and rich cities, foundings of the new decentric genius, spread themselves and flourished from Granada and Cordoba to Ani, Kiev and Kutais. And they shone in the young centuries before the great empires of iron and stuffing, Hapsburg and Bourbon, Osmanli and Romanov, overlay them.

The Kingdom of the Bagratids took full share in the original and varied splendour of these Middle Ages. The relations of the Georgian kings with the outer world extended from the Mediterranean to Central Asia, and knowledge they had of the lands which lay to the Atlantic on the west and to China on the east.

In the eleventh century, the Georgian St. Ioanné, on a visit to Byzantium, planned to visit Spain in order to study the community of origin of the Iberians of Spain and the Iberians of the Caucasus. Giorgi III according to the Annalists entertained relations with Germany, Byzantium and the Papacy, and with various princes of Russia, India and Arabia.[1] His daughter, Tamara, whose relations with the Russian principalities were close, played an intimate part in Byzantine politics at the time of the Latin Conquest, and she was informed of events at Venice and in Bulgaria.[2] Rusudani and her heirs during the period of the Mongol hegemony had somewhat chequered diplomatic relations with Pope Honorius III and his successors. Tamara, indeed, had been the first to develop these relations, and her endowment of churches in Cyprus and France may have been a diplomatic gesture to the Latin powers.

The Popes pursued with interest the possibility of estab-

[1] Brosset, *H. de la G.*, I, 401.   [2] *Ibid.*, I, 465.

THE LIFE OF GEORGIA

lishing a definite Catholic influence in Georgia, although they were not prepared to give the material assistance in money which the Georgian kings were seeking. Finally, during the reign of Giorgi V, a monk named John of Florence was sent to Georgia by Pope John XXII and became first Roman Catholic Bishop of Tiflis.[1]

Such European products as entered Georgia came in through Byzantium and they are referred to as Greek,[2] for it was not until the period of Mongol hegemony and the political decline of Byzantium, that the Genoese obtained the monopoly of the Black Sea traffic. Trade between Georgia and the west through Byzantium during the eleventh and twelfth centuries must have been considerable, and there was always a numerous Georgian element living in Constantinople.

But trade with the south and east was always more important. In this trade, the Armenians, Jews and Arabs were the principal middlemen. Through Lajazzo and the other Cilician ports, Armenian and Latin merchants brought the products of the Mediterranean and of Africa into the Turkish emirates of Anatolia and up to the Black Sea coast, and through Tabriz came the goods from India and the East. Greek and Chinese and Baghdad brocades and woven stuffs,[3] wool from Alexandria,[4] Tibetan musk,[5] Indian steel[6] and diamonds,[7] and Greek locks[8] were all greatly prized. And Sargis Tmogveli, describing a royal letter, says, " instead of paper was used Chinese vellum, for ink T'humbat'hian (Tibetan) musk, an Egyptian reed, rose-water from Nisibrand, ink-horns of Saman aloe ".[9]

During the heyday of the Bagratid monarchy in the eleventh and twelfth centuries, the wealth and luxury of the Court and aristocracy equalled that of the contemporary kingdoms in Spain and Italy. Gorged with the loot of victorious forays,[10] and masters of a fertile land spread with industrious and thriving towns, the Georgian aristocracy spent their leisure from the wars in hunting, feasting and tournaments. And splendid are the accounts which the Annalists give of great celebrations and tourneys at Tiflis in honour of royal marriages or of visits of foreign princes.[11]

---

[1] For an account of the relations of the Papacy with the Georgian kings see Michel Tamarati, *L'Eglise Géorgienne*, pp. 403 *et sqq.*
[2] Brosset, *H. de la G.*, I, 463. [3] *Visraminiani*, pp. 194, 285, 249, etc.
[4] Brosset, *H. de la G.*, I, 449. [5] *Visraminiani*, p. 225, etc. [6] *Ibid.*, p. 217.
[7] Brosset, *H. de la G.*, I, 463. [8] *Visraminiani*, p. 217. [9] *Ibid.*, p. 284.
[10] Cf. Brosset, *H. de la G.*, I, 366, for a description of loot gained after a victory over the Persians.
[11] See *Ibid.*, pp. 418–19, 422, 438, etc.

WEALTH AND STATE

Since the capture of Tiflis from the Muslims by King David Aghmashenebeli in 1122, the Court of the Bagratids had been removed there from Kutais. But those strong and watchful rulers were always moving. In summer, the half-nomadic Court passed up into the highlands of Samtzkhé, where the King might enjoy an equable climate, while overlooking the most turbulent of his feudatories.[1] During the autumn the Court hunted over the vast preserves of Nadcharmagevi on the marches of Amier and Imier,[2] and in the winter it went sometimes to Geguti or to Tzkhomi (Sukhum) in Abkhazeti.[3]

On great feast-days, the people, as they love, got their sight of the magnificence of royalty and nobility.

"On the first day of January", writes Wakhushti, "before the morning prayer, the Dchqondideli offered the King and Queen a cross, an icon, a robe and some sugared cakes; after mass all the *eristavni*, the officers and persons about the court made gifts of objects relating to their own particular functions. For instance the Chief of the Falconers offered a falcon, a kite and the gilded head of a wild goat; the Master of the Horse, a horse in gilded harness; and the other court officials gifts relating to their employment; for the *eristavni* it was a matter of a horse each. These last and also all the others brought an arrow, meaning that they intended it for the King's enemies, and saying, 'God prolong your reign for many years, and may this arrow reach the heart of your enemy'. After the acclamation of the army, there was a great feast, rejoicings and fêtes. As for the horses presented by the *eristavni*, the Chief of the Falconers had them led into the enclosure of the royal hunt near the palace where he killed them in the evening. During the night the enclosure filled with foxes, jackals and wolves; in the morning a keeper shut the gates and prevented the beasts from getting out. The next day at an early hour the King came there on horseback with all his nobles and the beasts were released and shot down with arrows. After that they returned to the feast.

"Here are the Easter ceremonies. Mass at daybreak; after Mass, the King and the nobles broke the fast with a light meal of meats, then they went to the hippodrome. There they set at the top of a mast the royal cup of gold and silver, which served as a target for the arrows of the young boys; the one who knocked it down received it as a reward. After that the tourney; the victors had the royal box on their side and each received a reward. The same thing was done on the royal marriage-day and other important occasions; later the company was entertained by the King at superb banquets, accompanied by music and other diversions.

"While the Catholicos and bishops were present there was no music but simply chants. When they departed, music, dancing and diversions began."[4]

The culture of mediæval Georgia was in character with the feudal culture of the contemporary Christian world, but it

[1] Cf. Brosset, *H. de la G.*, I, 474.
[2] Wakhushti, *Dés. Géo.*, p. 251.
[3] Brosset, *H. de la G.*, I, 474.
[4] Wakhushti, *Dés. Géo.*, pp. 32-5.

had its very individual aspects. The Georgian feudal monarchy through all its vicissitudes retained the tradition of an antique and continuing civility and something of this continuing civility had come down from the period of the Achæmenians and maybe from the centuries before the Swarming Time from Khaldi and the forgotten Caucasian kingdoms of the Bronze Age.

The habit of a settled life, possession of wealth, no little splendour, the mind of kingship, all were old in Georgia. And of all the antique spontaneities, of all the back-dating, free and individual upgrowths of Western Asia, the Georgian nation had alone contrived continuing survival. For the Armenians in the eleventh century were finished as an independent social body.

Therefore, the Georgians, in tradition, culture, sense of nationhood, were apart from the moving, scarcely conscious mass of the Muslim peoples around them. And they were by far ahead of, different from, the new raw peoples forming into nations, in Russia, Hungary and the Balkans. The Georgians had an aristocracy of their own blood, and kings the same, a political fact not common over all the variegated mosaic of Europe of the twelfth century. But with all the strong marking of their early come-by individual nationhood, the Georgians were in close and running contact with the two living cultures of the mediæval world, Christendom and Islam, and the mind of their rulers—in constant dangerous intimacy with the great Imperial powers in Byzantium and Persia—could never afford to be parochial.

The Georgian nobles were typical of the feudal classes over all the mediæval world—hard-living, turbulent, superstitious and amoral. To them, life was an affair of forays, huntings, joustings, quick come-and-go of looted wealth, abundant wine and easy women. And they cowered before the Church, as even the best of them trembled and marvelled at the tricks and contortions of astrologers, magicians and dervishes.[1]

Yet these truculent soldiers, princes of the mountains, were at the same time wealthy gentlemen and dilettanti, who followed the fashions of Byzantium, not only in dress and ceremonial like the aristocracies of the Balkan and Danubian lands, but in tastes, in art and books. David Soslani, the swashbuckling husband of Tamara who could give a village

---

[1] Cf. Brosset, *H. de la G.*, I, 329 and 460 *et sqq.*, for accounts of sorceries in mediæval Georgia. Even by Tamara, Evlogi, "the madman of Christ", was regarded with respect.

and a castle for the bay charger of the Prince of Khachen—
" a famous animal "[1]—was recognized as the equal of learned
men.[2] And in those days it was not unfitting that a man might
mingle with his love of dogs and falcons, some familiarity
with the Greek philosophers and the Persian poets. To find
a parallel to the enlightened catholicity of the mediæval
Georgian aristocracy, we have to turn to the petty Christian
courts of the Iberian Peninsula and to that fair flower of
twelfth-century culture, the court of the Sicilian Angevins at
Palermo. In Georgia, Spain and Sicily—on the marches of
Christendom and Islam—we find that rich mingling of the
two cultures, that coming together of varied types of man and
mind along a common borderland. And as in Spain were
produced the easy-thinking Mozarabs—men who took a turn
of fortune with facility and were not unfavoured by changing
masters—so in Georgia we find the same phenomenon.
Between the bloody wars of Christian against Muslim were
intervals when the master gave easy toleration to vassals of
another faith, and even Muslim and Christian could combine
against Christian and Muslim. The Georgian kings were
frequently in alliance with the Shirvanshah and other Mussulman princes of the Caucasus, and in spite of the savage warfare,
the Mussulman population of Tiflis and other Georgian towns,
which was always numerous, was generally treated with consideration. The Arab historian al-Aini, in a remarkable
passage, recites the benefits which David Aghmashenebeli
accorded to the Muslims of Tiflis after his capture of the city
in 1121, and he adds that the King showed a greater consideration for the Muslims than had the Mussulman princes themselves.[3] According to al-Aini, David undertook to strike
coins bearing the Arabic superscription on one side, and certainly the coins of his successor Dmitri bear Georgian inscriptions with the Arabic on the reverse.[4]

To the wealth of the Georgian Kingdom, the ruins of
churches, monasteries and castles and the debris of the movable
riches, which has been deposited and remains to this day in
the parish churches of Svaneti, all bear witness. The tradition
of an antique accumulation, of long familiarity with luxury,
runs through the Georgian Annals. The contemporary

[1] Brosset, *H. de la G.*, I, 441.   [2] *Ibid.*, p. 423.
[3] Brosset, *Add. et Eclair.*, pp. 240–1, quoting al-Aini. At the same time, according to the Georgian Annals, a Mussulman invasion of the previous year had been occasioned by an appeal of the merchants of Ganja, Tiflis and Dmanisi to the Seljuk Sultan Mahmud-ibn-Muhammad (cf. Brosset, *H. de la G.*, I, 368).
[4] Pakhomov, I, 83.

writers describe in some detail the treasures of Giorgi III, of Tamara and of Rusudani. The hoards of settled monarchy were scattered, lost or looted during the periods of barbarian devastation. Very curious is the circumstantial account of the hiding of the treasure of the Georgian kings at the time of the Arab invasion. This treasure included:

> "two crowns of emerald and purple rubies brought back from India and from Sind by our ancestor the great King Wakhtangi, and a mass of gold and silver things, the transport of which, together with the archives, required 500 beasts of burden and 2,000 carriers".[1]

Again, during the period of the Mongol hegemony, we read, in connection with the division of the Kingdom between the two Davids, that the royal arsenal was divided between the two kings, but from the treasure hidden in the cave at Khomli, only certain articles were taken, of which the share falling to David, son of Rusudani, comprised

> "the famous chain of diamonds, the superb jewel cut in the form of an anvil and a great pearl, of which the like was never seen".[2]

---

[1] Brosset, *H. de la G.*, I, pp. 240–1, reference is made to "*gujarni* on skin" or parchment charters.

[2] *Ibid.*, I, 560–1; cf. also p. 561, Note 1; see also *Sbor. Mat.*, XXIV, i, 1–72. M. G. Janashvili, *Dragotsennye Kamni, ikh Nazvania i Svoistva; iz gruz.: Sbornika X Veka.* For Khomli, see Wakhushti, pp. 372–3; Brosset (*op. cit.*) states that excavations made there by Prince Dadiani were without result.

CHAPTER XXX

DOG-DAYS OF THE GEORGIANS

IN the thirteenth century something like a revolution was effected in the economic life of the lands of the Near and Middle East. The establishment of Mongol rule resulted in the creation of a single economic unit over all the area from the Black Sea to the Pacific. At the same time the relations between the Kings of Christendom and the Great Khans were far from unfriendly. In spite of the fearful drive of the Mongols to the Adriatic in the second quarter of the century, many of the European courts during the following decades came to regard the Mongol power as holding no real threat to themselves, and as being, furthermore, a formidable counter-weight to the historic enemies of Mediterranean Christendom—the Seljuk Turks of Anatolia and the Mamluks of Egypt. Thus while the Papacy, and the Kings of France, of England, and of Aragon undertook the development of diplomatic relations with the new world-power in Karakorum, the Byzantine dynasts in Constantinople and Trebizond, and the Armenian Kings in Sis, conscious of their own weakness and ready always to assail the hereditary Muslim enemy with the support of such a potent ally, truckled with tributes and contingents to the dreadful conquerors of Asia.

The commercial reactions were considerable. Baghdad was destroyed by the Mongols in 1258, and throughout the latter half of the thirteenth century, Syria was the battleground between Mongols and Mamluks. The great trade route from Asia to the Mediterranean became utterly disorganized. Hence the alternate routes from Asia under full Mongol control were opened up. Tabriz replaced Baghdad as the great entrepôt of international trade, and Trebizond succeeded to the Syrian ports as the sea-gate for this traffic, while the Latin settlements at Caffa and Tana, at the embouchure of the caravan-routes from Central Asia to the Don, rapidly grew to a wealth and importance which they had not enjoyed since the days of the Bosporan Kingdom. The profits of this commercial revolution fell in the main to the Genoese. For if the Venetians had reaped the harvest of the Latin

Empire at Constantinople, and had begun through the Polos to explore the markets of Further Asia, it was to their rivals that the prizes went, when in 1261 the ships, the money and the diplomacy of Genoa furthered Michael Palaiologos to the restoration of the Greek Empire. The clauses of the Treaty of Nymphæum gave to the Genoese the virtual monopoly of foreign trade with the territories of the attenuated Byzantine Empire, but, more important, it gave them control of the Black Sea trade, and the members of their numerous and powerful colony at Pera entered upon a period of great and profitable activity. At Trebizond and Kerasund, at Caffa and Tana and in the Rumanian principalities, they had their depôts and their consuls, and the *Officium Gazariæ* at Genoa was set up to administer a commercial machine which seemed to have many of the potentialities of a political Empire.[1] Far in the wake of the Genoese followed the Venetians, the Pisans and the Florentines, the Catalans and the Provençals. And for the two hundred and fifty years which elapsed between the passing of Byzantium as an Imperial control over the narrow straits, and the setting of the Osmanli at that old seat of power, the Black Sea became an extension merely of the Mediterranean, where the mercantile city-states contended, as in the Mediterranean, for mastery and profit.

The Latin cities, as the Romans in earlier times, were attracted by the trade of the wide Russian steppes and of the caravan routes which debouched at Caffa, Tana and Trebizond, rather than by the local produce of the Caucasian lands. Nevertheless, that the Latins had an intimate knowledge of all the coast of Georgia and Circassia is clear from the Catalan Map and from the Manual of Pegolotti;[2] they drove a thriving trade in boxwood, wine and nuts and in the wool and silk of the interior and the coloured linens of Riza.[3] At the same time, as in the Kingdom of Little Armenia, the Popes proyed as anxious to pursue the political and religious implications of the decline of Byzantine power as their shrewd countrymen were to profit from the commercial situation which had been created. During the whole of the thirteenth century, the Popes solicited the unfortunate Kings of Georgia—harried always by the Mongols—with promises of aid, sympathetic compliments and hints at the desirability of the union

---

[1] For the history of the Genoese in the Black Sea, see G. I. Bratianu, *Recherches sur le Commerce Génois dans la Mer Noire* (Paris, 1929), and W. Heyd, *Histoire du Commerce du Levant* (2 vols., Réimpression, Leipzig, 1923). Gazaria (Khazaria) was the mediæval Latin name for the Crimea.

[2] Heyd, II, 190; cf. also Marco Polo.   [3] *Idem*, p. 110.

"TO THE MOUNTAINS OF TREASURE. A BARQUE OF OUR FATHERS IN THE TOWN OF ARACHEA, BRINGING PROVISIONS FROM CONSTANTINOPLE" (CASTELLI).

of the Georgian Church with Rome. By the end of the thirteenth century Latin influence in Georgia was strong, and growing. As early as the time of Marco Polo, Genoese merchants were navigating and trading across the Caspian,[1] and in the first decade of the fourteenth century the Italian monks William of Chiero and Matthew of Chieti were working in Tiflis.

The Bank of St. George and the Vatican, not always in unison, supplemented each the other's efforts in the furtherance of Latin influence. In 1316, the *Officium Gazariæ* was organizing the administration of Caffa; and two years later the city became the See of a Roman Catholic Archbishop, whose diocese comprised the whole area from Varna to Saray on the Volga, and from the Black Sea to the Russian dukedoms.[2] In 1314, the Genoese obtained their first treaty from Alexios II of Trebizond; in 1321, John XXII addressed a letter to King Giorgi Brtsqinwalé urging the union of the Georgian Church with Rome, and seven years later John of Florence arrived in Tiflis as first Roman Catholic Bishop, and busied himself in translating Latin ecclesiastical texts into Georgian.[3]

During the period between the establishment of Mongol power and the capture of Constantinople by the Turks, the contact between Georgia and the states of Western Christendom must have been continuous. As early as 1330, there was an English Roman Catholic bishop, Peter Gerald, at Sukhum, whom we find lamenting that his flock were being sold as slaves to the Saracens without his being able to check the traffic;[4] and Germans, Italians and Frenchmen succeeded each other in the See of Tiflis. In 1441, a Georgian bishop was in attendance at the Ecumenical Council of Florence; and in 1461, Georgian and Trapezuntine ambassadors, escorted by Ludovico of Bologna, the Papal Legate in the East, were present at the coronation of Louis XI.[5] In 1496, the Borgia Pope Alexander VI was writing to thank Constantine III of Kartli for his congratulations on the capture of Granada from "the Agarians";[6] and there is a letter extant which shows that Constantine sent an ambassador by way of Poland and Lithuania with a gift for Isabella of Castile, of nineteen

---

[1] Polo, Yule's ed., I, 52.
[2] W. Bartold, Article "*Kafa*" in *Encyclopædia of Islam*.
[3] Tamarati, *Histoire de l'Eglise Géorgienne*, pp. 403 et seq.
[4] Heyd, II, 192, quoting Raynaldi, *Ann. eccls. ad. an.* 1330, No. 57.
[5] Tamarati, *seq*.
[6] Ibid.

pieces of embroidered brocades of Yezd, fourteen *mithkals*[1] of large pearls and eighteen panthers' skins.[2]

The writings of Latin travellers and diplomatic agents during the two centuries of Latin activity in the Black Sea reflect the rapid decay of social conditions in Georgia. The earlier travellers write in terms of admiration. Marco Polo's information on Georgia refers to the third quarter of the thirteenth century, to the time of King Dmitri Tavdadébuli. The Georgians in those days held a good name. They were "*very handsome, capital archers, and most valiant soldiers*".[3] Ruy Gonzalez de Clavijo, a little more than a century later, is little less favourable in his brief reference to the Georgians. He regards them as "a fine race of men"; and he speaks with admiration of the King, Giorgi VII, the hero of the Georgian struggle against Timur.

In the last quarter of the fifteenth century the picture is a very different one. Weakened by the ravages of the Black Death and the invasions of Timur, Georgia had, in the middle of the century, been stricken by civil war and by the raids of the Turkoman masters of Iran and Eastern Anatolia. Pontic Christendom was in extremity, and the last ambassadors of Georgia, Trebizond, and Byzantium had made their vain approaches to the courts of Europe. The Turks had Constantinople in 1453, and while Georgian and Trapezuntine ambassadors were attending the levées of the French and the Burgundian monarchs, the Sultan marched to Trebizond. Ludovico of Bologna, that errant, rather sinister Legate in the East, had been entraining many years a plan for uniting the contentious Georgian dynasts with Uzun-Hassan, the Turkoman tyrant in Tabriz, and with the frightened Greeks of Trebizond, against the Ottoman Sultan. Too late, the Venetian Signory made an urgent effort to implement the Legate's plan. Three agents, Josaphat Barbaro, Ambrogio Contarini and Caterino Zeno—the last a relative of Uzun-Hassan's Comnenian wife—were sent to the East, and between the years 1471 and 1474 they were travelling and intriguing in Persia and Georgia. Constantinople and Trebizond were already lost; and while Contarini was waiting in Fassó for a ship to take him to Caffa, he heard that that city had fallen to

---

[1] The *mithkal*, a Persian weight, was equivalent to 10 ounces.
[2] Brosset, H. de la G., I, 409. The difficulty which Brosset found in the synchronization of the date 1465 is removed, in view of the evidence published by Tamarati in the letter of Alexander VI. The date of Constantine's letter to Isabella would be 1495 and not 1465.
[3] Polo (Yule), I, 50.

the Turks (1475).[1] Contarini quarrelled with Ludovico the patron of the Georgian princes, and Barbaro saw the alliance between Uzun-Hassan and these princes—which had been propounded in Venice, Rome and Paris—come to an end with an attack on Tiflis by Uzun-Hassan.[2] The death of Uzun-Hassan in 1478 destroyed all prospect of a grand alliance of the east Pontic potentates and Persia against the new Ottoman power, and the Venetian agents found their perilous way back to Europe, having achieved nothing towards the solution of the contemporary political problem, but with a wide and new knowledge of lands from which their commerce was in future to be excluded.

The Venetians have left a sad picture of the anarchy and social dissolution in the Georgian lands at the end of the fifteenth century. In the politics of the moment the Imerian King, Bagrat II, was in the ascendant; the young Atabegi Bahadur at Akhaltzikhé was deporting himself as an independent[3] sovereign; great Georgian nobles like the Dadian Lipariti were so impoverished and so reckless that they were reduced to waylaying and blackmailing the ambassadors in the manner of common brigands; while after the capture of Tiflis by Uzun-Hassan, King Bagrati and Qwarqwaré of Samtzkhé were unable to find the 16,000 ducats which they had agreed to pay to the Turkoman tyrant, and they sought the favour of Barbaro in the valuation of stuffs which they were offering instead of money. On this occasion 4,000 or more people were carried away as slaves by the Persians.[4] Nevertheless, Barbaro found Kartli

> "a faire countrey, plentyfull of breade, wyne, fleshe, graine, and many other fruietes; the most parts of which wynes growe on trees as that doth in Trabisonda.... It hath a citie called Zifilis, by the which passeth the ryver Tigris, and that is a good towne, well inhabited."[5]

Barbaro gives an interesting description of the Georgians of that time.

> "The men", he says, "are faire and bigge, but they have very fylthie apparill and most vile customes. They go with their heades

---

[1] *Venetians in Persia*, p. 140.
[2] *Ibid.*, p. 91. Cf. Brosset, *H. de la G.*, II, pp. 383–5. Constantine III of Kartli took part with Uzun-Hassan in the attack on Tiflis in order to secure the defeat of his usurping cousin Bagrat II of Imereti, who is the Georgian King Pancratio of the Venetian reports.
[3] Giurgura, mentioned by the Venetians, was Qwarqwaré, a cousin of the reigning Atabegi; he afterwards became Qwarqwaré III, but he had virtually ruled Samtzkhé during the reigns of Bahadur and Manuchar (1466–87), the sons of Qwarqwaré II. He died at the age of eighty-two in 1500.
[4] Barbaro (*V. in P.*), p. 91.   [5] *Idem.*, pp. 35–6.

rounded and shaven, leaving only a little heare,¹ after the manner of our abbotts that have great revenewes, and they suffer their mostacchi to growe a quarter of a yard longer than their beardes. On their heades they weare a litell cáppe, of divers colors, wth a creste on the toppe. On their backes they weare certein garments meetely lenge, but they be straite and open behinde downe to the buttocks; for otherwise they coulde not gett to horsebacke; wherein I do not blame them, for I see the Frenchmen use the like. On their feete and leggs they weare bootes or busgynes, made with their soles of such a sorte that wann they stande the heele and the too too^uche the grounde, but the plante of the foote standeth so high that yo^u may easilie thrust yor fyst undernethe w^thout hurting of it, whereof it foloweth that wann they go afoote, they go wth paine. I wolde in this part blame them, if it were not that I know the Persians use the same. In their feeding (as I have seen the experience in the house of one of the principall of them) they use this maner. They have certain square tables of halfe a yarde brode, with a ledge round about; in the myddest whereof they putt a quantitie of panico sodden, w^thout salte or other fatt; and this they use in steade of podaige. On an other like table they putt the fleshe of a wilde bore, so litell brooyled that wann they cut it the bloudee cometh out, which they eate very willingely. I coulde not awaie w^thall, and therefore drave foo'the the tyme with that podaige. Wyne we had plentie and that trugged about lustilie: but other kinde of vittails we had none." ²

Contarini who appears to have been rather an impatient traveller, of the pompous and indignant kind with which all ages and all " natives " are familiar, had a poor opinion of the people, whom he had come to embroil in a new war. He was, he says, "*much annoyed by the Georgiani, who are as mad as the Mengrelians* ³ . . . *the brutes appeared never to have seen man before*".⁴

Contarini had sailed from Caffa for Atina, but he eventually landed near Fasso, whither he proceeded to Kutais and Gori. He found the Mingrelians in a bad way.

"There are stone quarries in the country, and a little corn and wine is also produced, but of no great value. The men live miserably on millet made hard like polenta, and the women fare more miserably still; and were it not for a little wine and salt fish imported from Trebizond, and salt from Capha, they would be very badly off. They produce canvas and wax, but in small quantities. If they were industrious they might procure as much fish as they required from the rivers." ⁵

Barbaro was a bluff, more genial man than Contarini, and his observations which have come down to us in William Thomas' English of the time of Mary I, have about them

---

[1] Cf. *Chardin*, p. 86.
[2] Barbaro (*V. in P.*), p. 36.
[3] Contarini (*V. in P.*), p. 119.
[4] *Ibid.*, p. 122.
[5] *Ibid.*, p. 118.

certain terse reality. Barbaro's account of Mingrelia is a descriptive masterpiece, in that in one short incident he gives a picture of the political dereliction, the social misery and the economic poverty of the country, and it is an immortal irony —withal unconscious—on the mind of the superior European who pursues his way in foreign parts.

> "The Lorde of the province, named Bendian,[1] hath two walled townes on the foresaid sea, one called Vathi,[2] and an other Souastopoli,[3] and besides that divers other piles and stronge houses. The cuntrie is all stonie and barayn without any kinde of graine, saving panico. Salte is brought into them out of Capha. They make a litell clothe but it is both course and naught; and they are a beastly people. For proof whereof, being in Vathie (where one Azolin Squarciafigo, a Genowaie arryved in companie of a Paranderia of Turks that went thither with us from Constantinople), there was a yonge woman stode in her doore into whom this Genowaie said SURINA PATRO NI COCON? which is 'mistress is the good man within?' meaneng her husbande. She answered ARCHILIMISI that is, to wit, he woll come anon. Whereupon he swapped her on the lippes and shewed her unto me, saieng, behold what faire teeth she hath, and so shewed me her breast and touched her teates, which she suffered without moving. Afterwards we entered into her house, and sate us downe, and this Azolin fayneng to have vermyn about him beckoned on her to search him: which she did verie diligentlie and chastely. This, meane while, the good man came in, and my companion put his hands in his purse and said PATRON TETARI SICA,[4] which is as much to say as, Mr. hast thow any mooney? Whereunto he made a countenance that he had nothe about him: and so he tooke him a fewe aspres, wth the wch he went streight to bye some vittaills. Within a while after we went through the towne to sporte us and this Genowaie did every wheare after the maner of that cuntrey what pleased him w^thout reproche of any man, whereby it may appear weather they be beastly people or no, and therefore the Genowaies that practise in those use for a proverbe to saie, Thou art a Mongrello wann they are disposed to saie, thou art a foole."

With the closing of the Black Sea by the Turks at the end of the fifteenth century the Georgians became isolated from those Greek and Latin influences with which they had been in intimate contact during the Middle Ages. And during the whole of the sixteenth century Georgia and the rest of the Caucasian lands were the battle-ground of the recurrent Turko-Persian wars, which endured, with intermissions, from the defeat of Shah Ismail Safi by Sultan Selim

---

[1] There is a confusion here between the Dadiani of Mingrelia and the Bediani or Bishop of Bedia; Barbaro apparently refers to the Dadiani Lipariti of Wakhushti.
[2] Vathi = Fasso = Poti.
[3] Souastopoli = Iskaur, near the site of Sukhum.
[4] Tetari = *tetri*, in Georgian, "a white" = silver coin and the smallest unit of Georgian currency.

at Chaldiran in 1514 to the long campaigns of Shah Abbas during the first quarter of the seventeenth century. The sources for this period are the provincial chronicles of the Georgian appanages, which are merely a record of incessant conflict, and the few memoirs of foreign travellers. Of these the principal is the description by Don Juan, a Persian soldier and diplomat, who became a Catholic while on a mission to Europe, and who was killed in a brawl at Valladolid on the 15th May 1605.[1] There is too the work of the imaginative and entertaining Turk, Evliya Chelebi, " the globe-trotter ", who in parts II and VII of his stupendous *Traveller's Chronicle* describes parts of Georgia and the Caucasus.[2] But prior to Chardin's great work, the most reliable material for the period comes from Russian sources. The first Georgian embassy, sent to Russia by King Alexander II of Kakheti, was at the court of Tsar Theodore in 1586, and in the following year the mission of Rodion Birkin and Peter Pivov visited Alexander at Zaghani. In Russia " The Times of Troubles ", at the beginning of the seventeenth century, interrupted the process of Imperial expansion by means of war, exploration and diplomacy, which had been initiated by Tsar Ivan IV. Nevertheless, the relations of Moscow with the Caucasian potentates, with both the petty kings of the Georgians and the chieftains of the mountain tribes, were maintained, and numerous Russian missions visited the three Georgian courts.[3] It is in the reports of these missions that we have the first accounts, since the time of the Venetian ambassadors to Uzun-Hassan a century and a half before, of the social and economic state of Georgia. Between the years 1640 and 1643, the Russian emissaries, Prince Euphima Mishetzki, and the Deacon Ivan Kliucharev were in Kakheti, during the eclipse of King Taymuraz I, and after the Persians had established their nominee Rustem Khan as King in Tiflis.[4] The Russians found the whole of Kakheti and Kartli in a state of desolation and the country—after the spoliation by the Persians—lying open

---

[1] His work has recently been published in English under the title *Don Juan of Persia: A Shi'ah Catholic* (1560–1604), translated and edited with an introduction by Guy Le Strange, London, 1928. See my paper " Notes on Don Juan of Persia's Account of Georgia, in *B.S.O.S.*, Sept. 1930.
[2] Evliya Chelebi; only the first three parts of his work have been published in English (von Hammer, *Narrative of Travels in Europe, Asia and Africa by Evliya Effendi*, London, 1846–50); the first six parts are printed in Turkish, see *E.I.* under name).
[3] See S. A. Byelokurov, *Snosheniya Rosii s' Kavkazom*, Part I, 1578–1613, Moscow, 1889.
[4] *Posolstvo Knyazya M. i dyaka K. v' Kakhetiyu* (*The Mission of Prince M. and the Deacon K. into Kakhetia*). Original text with Georgian and Russian introduction by M. Polievktov, Tiflis, 1928.

to the recurrent raids of the Dido and other Mussulman tribes of Daghestan.

"In the parts of his domain bordering on Tefliz, King Teimuraz possesses only two inhabited places, namely Kizik and Martkop. In other parts inhabited places are few. . . . There are no towns now in the Gruzinian land. Towns there may have been many in the Gruzinian land in former years, but the Shah has destroyed them all, and erased them altogether. . . . The arable land is all under forest. . . . In all the villages of his domain there are only about 3,000 peasant hearths and these people are distributed among all ranks, being assigned to the King and the Prince David, to the princes and all the aznaurs. And when the Kumyks invade the country they resist them as best they can by means of guerilla warfare, each prince and aznaur coming out with their peasants and retinues, and watching for the enemy in the mountain passes, in the forests and on the cliffs. They dare not engage in open battle with the Kumyks, for the King no longer possesses a regular army, because of the small number of fit men in his domain. Some villages in the plains at the foot of the mountains have been given to a section of the Kumyks on the understanding that they keep watch on the mountaineer Kumyks and warn King Teimuraz of their advance into his domain and thus avoid a surprise invasion. In the Egorev Monastery of Laverdy,[1] and at Krym,[2] in the Archangel Monastery and in other monasteries and churches of the whole land there is no service conducted; they have been abandoned in fear of the Kumyks whose frequent invasions and cruelty are dreaded by the people. . . . The high personages of the church and monasteries are with the King, around whom is concentrated all the fighting power of harassed Kakhetia. The Shah waged war with the Georgians most ruthlessly. He has literally razed to the ground all the monasteries and churches, towns and villages, houses built of stone or wood, and those, with the palaces, are now all in ruins, and they are impossible to restore. The King Teimuraz does not stay long at one place. He moves from one village to another . . .

. . . Metropolitan Zakhari of Jerusalem came often from Tefliz to see King Teimuraz. He saw frequently the Ambassador, Prince Euphim. And the Ambassador, Prince Euphim, questioned Metropolitan Zakhari as to the present state of affairs in Kartaleya, as to the position of the Christian faith there, whether many churches were destroyed; whether the Cathedral called Skheto[3] still existed and if so whether service was conducted there. According to the answers the Metropolitan gave, the Christian faith was greatly constrained; Skheto still existed and the service was conducted. During the services however, Persians interfering, jeer and insult the Christians ".[4]

In the following decade between 1650 and 1652, another Russian mission, that of Nikiphor Tolochanov and the Deacon Yevlev, was in Imereti,[5] and they found the country beyond

---

[1] The Monastery of St. Giorgi of Alaverdi.   [2] Krym = Gremi.
[3] Mtzkheta.   [4] Polievktov, *Mishetski's Mission*, pp. 158–60.
[5] *Posolstvo Stolnika Tolochanova i Dyaka Ievleva v'Imeretiya 1650–1652* (*Mission of the Stolnik* (literally, a royal table-decker), *Tolochanov and the Deacon Yevlev into Imeretia*, Georgian and Russian introduction and Russian text by M. Polievktov, Tiflis, 1926).

DOG-DAYS OF THE GEORGIANS

the Mountains of Likhi in far better state than were Kartli and Kakheti. Coming from Astrakhan, the mission in company with a Georgian emissary on his way home from Moscow, crossed the mountains through the Balkar country. In Kutais they conducted protracted business with King Alexander III, the patron of the Dominican Castelli, and they followed his court to Skanda; they also saw the exiled King Taymuraz I of Kakheti, whose fortunes had ebbed even lower than when Mishetski saw him, and to whom Alexander had allotted a country estate in Radsha. The Russian mission passed through a prosperous and thriving countryside, and they remarked the numerous castles, fortified manors, the stone and timber churches, and the many villages with their scattered dwellings lying among gardens, orchards and vineyards. Tolochanov gives a long description of Kutais where he greatly admired the palaces and churches; he visited Gelati and noted carefully, with the interest of a reverend Russian, the most famous of the icons which were shown for the edification of the distinguished foreigners. Tolochanov made what was nothing less than a detailed survey of the country, and he reports information supplied to him by Pashenga (Peshangi) the King's secretary, which may indeed have been prepared with the object of creating a favourable impression on him.[1] According to Peshangi, the important *mtavarni* of Imereti numbered over 100, and there were more than 1,100 *aznaurni* subject either to the Crown or to the different *mtavarni*. The figures given by Peshangi indicate that a full levy of the Kingdom would put about 15,000 men into the field,[2] in addition to the royal forces which were permanently maintained and which numbered 3,000 men. The King's personal serfs, including the people of Kutais, Skanda and other smaller towns, were given by Peshangi as 60,000. Tolochanov reports the crops as wheat, barley, spelt, millet, beans, peas, springcorn, hemp and others, and he states that cereals were gathered twice in the summer. Silkworms were cultivated in almost every home; there were iron-mines in the country and some fagotted iron was produced; copper was plentiful and natural saltpetre was found in the mountains. There were cattle and fowl of all kinds in abundance, and among wild animals he noted deer, elk, roebuck, wild pigs and goats, beavers, otters, foxes, lynx, wolves and rabbits.

[1] Polievktov, *Tolochanov*, pp. 186 *et seq.*
[2] Taking an average of more than 10 serfs to each of the *aznaurni*. Peshangi's statement that 40,000 men could be brought out, seems an obvious exaggeration to impress Tolochanov.

There were vineyards in abundance and apricots, quinces, cherries, nuts of all kinds, mulberries, apples, pears, plums, raspberries, currants of all kinds, melons, water-melons, cucumbers both Russian and Crimean, pumpkins both Russian and Persian, onions and most other green vegetables.

Kutais was visited by traders from many countries, from Turkey and Persia, from Azov, from Gurelei (Guria) and from Didian (Mingrelia). The merchants were mostly Armenians, men of Azov, Persians, Turks and Jews, and a great variety of goods was to be found in the markets, including Persian

"AND AMID HIS NOBLE HORSEMEN I WAS TAKEN TO SEE THE CITY OF COTATIS AND THE CASTLE" (CASTELLI).

velours and all kinds of silk pieces. Trading was mostly done in the local currency.[1]

There are iron deposits in Imereti and Abkhazeti and the production reported by Tolochanov appears to have assumed some importance in the following century, for the traveller Tavernier states that "*the greater part of the iron consumed in Turkey comes from Mingrelia*". The export of nuts from the Georgian lands had always been a staple of foreign trade, and the English traveller, Duckett, speaking of the eastern districts, avers that there "*is carried yearly into Persia an incredible quantity of hazel-nuts, all of one sort and good-*

[1] Polievktov, *Tolochanov's Mission*, p. 188.

nesse and as good and thin-shaled as are our filberts. Of these are carried yearly the quantity of 4,000 camells laden".[1]

Tolochanov has some interesting details on the habits and ways of life of the Imerians. They dressed generally in the Turkish or Persian fashion, although they wore their own local costumes which consisted of a sort of long *caftans* with short sleeves. The high-heeled shoes noted by the Venetians were still in use, although Turkish slippers were much worn and the poorer classes favoured sandals. They wore blouses and shirts of all colours except white, and made generally of silk. All classes carried swords and sabres mostly of Persian or German make which they wore even in church. They wore leather belts ornamented with gold and silver, and all carried *kinjals* (the long thin straight Caucasian daggers). For fighting the bow was still in use, but muskets and pistols were common. The most prized horses were the Argamak stallions of Kabardán breed.[2]

The Georgian dynasts even in the dog-days of the Mussulman hegemony maintained a degree of wealth and enjoyed a state of luxury which was in strange contrast to the poverty and misery in which their subjects wallowed all around them. This contrast always has been, and still is, characteristic of Eastern cultures, and for that matter the phenomenon is by no means confined either to the east or to the centuries preceding the Industrial Revolution.

It would be interesting to devote a separate work to the consideration of how the failure to use specie for its proper function of facilitating the circulation of the products of the world has—as a result of the interplay of the instincts for accumulation and ostentation—checked the full use of the natural wealth of the earth by the people living on it. Tolochanov, during his audience of King Taymurazi in his manor in Radsha, and of King Alexander in the palace at Kutais, must have seen before his eyes a very large part of the movable and unusable wealth of Georgia of the seventeenth century. King Taymurazi, although his fortunes had sunk considerably lower than they were when Mishetski visited him ten years before, was living in no little luxury, surrounded by a numerous retinue and making a display of wealth which excited the admiration of an ambassador accustomed to the splendours of the Muscovite court. Taymurazi was a vigorous patriot and one of the most enlightened men of his day. His country was in enemy occupation, desolate and despoiled. And we

[1] *Hakluyt's Voyages*, p. 447.   [2] Polievktov, *Tolochanov*, pp. 110 *et seq.*

are told by Mishetski that "*King Taymurazi and his heir are much loved by the people . . . the princes and the aznaurs guard the King's life zealously. . . . The people in the land are kindhearted*".[1] The human mind works in a mysterious way. It does still.

The Court of Alexander was a more splendid affair than that of his exiled guest. We are fortunate in that Tolochanov had left us an intimate description of it, and Castelli has made two excellent drawings of the King. The Imerian ruler was about forty years of age when Castelli drew his picture, and he had reigned in Kutais for twelve years at the time of the visit of the Russian Mission. His figure had coarsened from heavy living; his expression is arrogant and lecherous, yet not without a certain shrewdness in it. He had been twelve years married to his second wife—Taymurazi's daughter,[2] and he showed himself during his chequered and not unsuccessful reign, a strange mixture of ruthlessness and generosity, of brutality and kindliness.

When Tolochanov saw the King in audience, he wore his state regalia in which he has been depicted by Castelli —a crown " beautifully set with pearls and precious stones " and surmounted by a cross studded with diamonds, rubies and emeralds; in his hand a sceptre inlaid with gold and mounted with precious stones with inset in its apple a stone with the Christ carved thereon. He wore a mantle of sable and velvet embroidered in gold and underneath a caftan of watered silk stitched with gold thread and bordered with gold lace. Castelli's picture, which answers in detail to Tolochanov's description, shows the King with the long locks fashionable in contemporary Christendom, and he has the heavy sweeping moustaches which were the mode in the East right down to the last century. In Castelli's picture he has not shaved for some days. Tolochanov observed that behind and above the King's head triptyches had been placed, and at his right hand was another sceptre, surmounted by a miniature shrine. The shrine was crowned by a cross in gold, inlaid with precious stones which were rather large in size. Yet another sceptre, of similar design, was placed on his left, and against a pillar, in front of the King, was propped one more of exactly the same kind. The Catholicos of Abkhazeti sat on Alexander's right, and next to him was

---

[1] Polievktov, *Mishetski's Mission*, p. 160.

[2] Nestan-Darejani, who, after Alexander's death, caused the new King, Bagrati, her step-son, to be blinded when he was only sixteen years of age. Her intrigues, her amours, and her horrid death are described in detail by Chardin.

the exiled Kartlian Catholicos Zakharia; with them was the Archbishop Simon and nine other personages of the Court. On his left was the Abbot Nikiphori of Golgotha, and next to the Abbot were the Russian ambassadors. Below these sat officers of the army and notables of Kutais. The Russians were shown to their respective seats by the King himself.

> "The table was covered with a fine cloth and laid with taste. In place of bread they served millet-cakes (*gomi*). Mikiphor, the Abbot from the Sacred Mount, pronounced the Prayer of Our Lord. During the Prayer the King sat without his hat. The King took his crown off just before he began to eat. A stand was brought with silver legs covered with black velvet embroidered in gold; on it was placed the crown, while the royal sceptre was placed nearly in front of the King. The King now put on a velvet hat adorned with pearls and precious stones. He partook of his dinner after the Persian manner, that is, without a table, being waited upon by *Tushmali* (meat carvers) on their knees. Food was served by *Safraji*. The latter were dressed in Turkish caftans of velvet and satin embroidered in gold and silver. The *aznaurs* wore dresses of the same kind. The King himself directed as to who should be served first. The food was served on gold and silver plates and the drinks in gold and silver cups. The drinks were brought from the cellars in large gold and silver pitchers and bottles. . . . Half an hour before dark, wax candles in silver candle-sticks were placed in front of the King, and in front of the ambassadors, the princes and the *aznaurs*. And around the buffet-table whence the dishes were served, were iron lights.
>
> "As the ambassadors approached the palace they were welcomed by musketeers about 300 in number, who fired volleys, upon which immediately, guns to the number of thirty thundered from both sections of the town, from Upper Kutais and from Lower Kutais. One either side of the ambassadors while on the way to the palace, rode *aznaurs* on racing stallions in parade dress."[1]

Alexander died in 1662, and when Chardin was in Kutais, twelve years afterwards, he found a very different state of affairs. The country had been desolated by a long period of civil war which was yet continuing. The Turks were masters of the country, and the different Imerian factions, the Dadiani and the Gurieli, were each prostituting themselves for foreign support, Turkish and Persian, trying in turn to overthrow the latest king in Kutais. At the time of Chardin's visit, the Dadiani had looted the royal treasury and had carried off twelve wagon-loads of "Silver, Plates and Moveables".[2]

[1] Polievktov, *Tolochanov's Mission*, pp. 64 *et sqq*. The sequence of the quotation is that of the original text.
[2] Chardin, p. 139; he adds—an interesting commentary on Tolochanov—"For, as it was said, the Kings of Imeretta had heap'd together such a Vast Quantity of Plate that everything within the Palace was of Massie Silver, even to the Steps and Footstools."

"The King invited me several times... now and then he would put some delicacy into my mouth with his own Fingers and offered me Wines from his own Glass" (Castelli).

DOG-DAYS OF THE GEORGIANS

So great was the misery of Alexander's heir, that his Queen was attempting to pawn the crown which "might be worth Four Thousand Pistols" for eight hundred crowns, "yet no body would lend any money upon it".[1] Chardin gives a pathetic picture of the unhappy blinded King, the victim of half a dozen factions.

> "I am sorry for it, reply'd the King, but I cannot help it; for I am a poor Blind Man and they make me do what they please themselves. I dare not discover myself to anyone whatever. I mistrust all the World; and yet I surrender myself to all, not daring to offend any Body, for fear of being Assassinated by every Body. . . . This poor Prince is young,[2] and well shap'd and he always wears a Handkercher over the upper part of his Face, to wipe up the Rhume that distils from the holes of his Eyes, and to hide such a hideous sight from those that come to visit him. He is of a mild Disposition and a great Lover of Jests and Drollery. He told Father Justin, He should do well to Marry in his Country. To which Father Justin made answer, That he could not Marry, as being under the same Vow with the Bishops and Monks of Imeretta. How! said he, interrupting Father Justin, and bursting out with a great laughter, our Bishops and Monks have every one nine apiece, besides those of their neighbours." [3]

By contrast with Mingrelia and Imereti, Kartli and Kakheti towards the last quarter of the seventeenth century were beginning under the Mukhranian viceroys to enter upon a brief period of relative peace and prosperity. During the whole period between 1656 and 1722, Kartli and Kakheti constituted a half-independent vice-royalty of the Persian Empire, which was hereditary in the Mukhranian family, among those members of it who chose to become Muslims: they also appear to have established something like an hereditary claim to preferment to the governorships of Isfahan and Kandahar.[4]

Chardin visited Tiflis at the beginning of the period of the Mukhranian vice-royalty, in 1672, and Pitton de Tournefort towards the end, in 1717, and both writers agree in a picture which indicates a process of gradual restoration and

---
[1] Chardin, p. 180.
[2] Bagrati was twenty-seven years of age at the time of Chardin's visit.
[3] Chardin, p. 181.
[4] For details with regard to this family in other than Georgian sources, see the works of Chardin, Krusinski, Hanway. Of the sons of Wakhtang V, Giorgi was successively "King" of Kartli and after a period of disgrace governor of Kandahar. He is the celebrated Gurgin Khan of Krusinski and Hanway. His brother Alexander (Skander Mirza) was Governor of Isfahan in 1699. The Georgian princes were in high favour with the Shi'ah faction at Isfahan, of which they were virtually the leaders. The Sunni faction, headed by the Afghan, Mir-Wais, and later by his son Mahmud, were their inveterate enemies. The Georgian troops of Gurgin and Kai-Khusraw were regarded as the best in Persia (Hanway, II, 49), "troops better disciplined and more inured to war than his Afghans" . . . p. 50, "their courage was invincible".

growing prosperity since the visit of Mishetski, thirty years before Chardin. Such is the bounteousness of Nature in defiance of man's stupidity, and nowhere is she more bounteous than in the soft and sparkling Georgian land. Chardin could praise it.

> "Georgia", he says, "is as fertile a country as any can be imagin'd, where a man may live both deliciously and very cheap. Their Bread is as good as any in the World; their Fruit is delicious and of all sorts. Neither is there any part of Europe that produces fairer Pears and Apples, or better tasted, nor does any part of Asia bring forth more delicious Pomegranates. Cattel is very plentiful and very good, as well the larger sort as the lesser. Their Fowl of all sorts is incomparable, especially their Wild-Fowl; their Boars-Flesh is as plentiful and as good as any in Colchis. Their Common People live upon nothing else but young Porkers; of which there are abundance in all parts of the country; and there is no better Food in the World than this Meat; beside that the People of the Country assure us that it never offends the Stomach, let 'em eat never so much. Which I believe to be true; for though I ate of it almost every Meal, yet it never did me harm. The Caspian Sea which is next to Georgia and the Kurr, that runs through it, supplies it with all sorts of salt and fresh Fish, so that we may truly say that there is no country where a Man may have an Opportunity to fare better than in this." [1]

In the seventeenth century the economic situation of the Georgian lands had in many respects reverted to that which existed during the days of the Arab domination in the eastern Caucasus. For if Imier—"that side"—depended on the Black Sea and formed part of the commercial and maritime system of the Turks which extended all round the shores of the Sea from Stambul to Caffa and the Crimean and Danubian ports, Amier—"this side"—had reverted to an Iranian control and was attached to the Caspian lands. During the two centuries following the capture of Constantinople by the Turks and the re-establishment of that site as a focus of political and commercial mastery, Turks and Persians had fought six long wars to decide the control of the Ponto-Caspian isthmus, without either the one or the other securing a lasting supremacy. The Safavid dynasty had its origin in Aran; the Turks during the last quarter of the sixteenth century, under the Sultans Sulaiman and Selim II, had occupied Erivan, Shamakha and Derbend, and when Shah Abbas the Great succeeded to the Persian throne, he had undertaken a long war to expel the Osmanli from a country which was at once the seat of his own family and famous for its ancient wealth

[1] Chardin, p. 189.

DOG-DAYS OF THE GEORGIANS

and venerated in Persian traditions far older than the Safavi dynasty.

By the latter half of the seventeenth century, one of those recurrent crises of decay which seem to be endemic in despotic institutions, was already carrying the Safavids to their bloody end: and in Turkey the reforms of the Kuprulu viziers were not going to check that disastrous cracking which before the century was out first heralded the breaking of the Ottoman Empire (Treaty of Carlovich, 1696). In the Caucasian lands there was a stagnation in politics; the conquerors were falling into fattened age, the conquered were still cowed and always quarrelling. And so, in the Caucasus in the last period of Islamic power, we see much the same conditions as in the first period, a thousand years before.

The loose administration of the Persian Empire in the northern provinces constituted three vilayets. The northernmost was Shirvan which included the old cities of Derbend, Baku and Shamakha. The second was Aran, which comprised the country between the southern parts of Shirvan and the Araks. Its capital was Erivan, and it included the Armenian country as far as Bayazid, and such Georgian districts as Dmanisi and Algeti. The Georgian vice-royalty of Kartli and Kakheti formed, nominally, part of Aran. The third of the northern provinces was Azerbaijan with the residence of the governor at Tabriz.[1] The prosperity of the Muslim towns of the eastern Caucasus was still great. Of Aran, the ambassador of Holstein wrote in 1662, that "*it is one of the Noblest and the Richest Provinces of all Persia and in this particularly, that it produces more Silk than any other*".[2] Barda'a, Baylakan and Kabala had not survived the devastations of the Timurid wars; and Areshi, another important centre on the borders of Shirvan and Kakheti, had never recovered from its destruction during the Turkish invasion of the Caspian provinces. But Baku and Derbend, Shamakha and Shaki, Erivan and Ganja, were still great commercial places. Contarini in the fifteenth century had declared Shamakha to be a better city than Tabriz.[3] Olearius describes its bazaar, its schools, its mosques and baths, and says of its production of textiles, that it was so great that "*Women, nay, very Children, make a shift to get their living there by spinning and preparing the silk and cotton for the workmen*".[4] Evliya, who hoped that the Turks might yet recover the city, says that—

[1] Olearius, p. 197. [2] *Idem.* [3] Contarini, *V. in P.*, p. 144. [4] Olearius, p. 222.

"there are forty caravanserai, in each of which many thousand tomans of wares are deposited ... the coffee-houses are meeting-places for wits and learned men; the air is mild and the land fertile; rice, cotton, seven sorts of grapes, pears and water-melons are in great perfection. ...[1] Shamakha is much frequented by Chinese, Tartars, Kalmucks and Russians, who bring different wares in exchange for which they take salt, naptha, safian and silk".[2]

The exploitation of the naptha deposits at Baku were carried out under a royal lease and the oil was sent all over Persia.[3] Ganja was famous for its gardens and its silk "*and the horse-shoes of Genje are not less famous than its silk*".[4]

The Persian provinces of the eastern Caucasus were essentially part of an economic system which centred round the Caspian basin. Until the middle of the eighteenth century the military control of the Caspian, to the extent that any was exercised, was in the hands of the Persians and there was a complete freedom of trade,[5] in contrast to the strict monopoly which was exercised by the Turks in the Black Sea; and this freedom no doubt goes to explain the relative prosperity of the Caspian littoral countries by contrast with the lands draining to the Black Sea.[6]

During the period of Persian hegemony, between the fifteenth and eighteenth centuries, Kartli and Kakheti were drawn into the economic orientation towards the Caspian, and after the closing of the Black Sea to the Latins, the old economic unity of the Georgian Kingdom, with its attraction to the Black Sea littoral, very largely disappeared. Particularly during the period of the Mukhranian vice-royalty, Tiflis became almost a Persian town, like Shamakha and Erivan and the two provinces dependent on it shared in the relative prosperity of the Caspian countries under Safavid rule. Writers like Evliya regarded Tiflis really as a Persian town; the abundance and cheapness of its good things and the health-giving properties of its famous baths became a

---

[1] Evliya, II, 160.   [2] *Idem.*, II, 163.
[3] *Idem.*, II, 163.   [4] *Idem.*, II, 154.
[5] *Idem.*, II, 164, "thousands of boats and vessels carry on trade, but they are all afraid of Russian Chaiks, with whom they fight. The vessels are not large ships like those of the White (Mediterranean), Black and Red Seas, but small boats of reeds, with small guns; There are no men-of-war or great Caravellas like those of the White Sea, which are necessary to meet the vessels of the Franks in the Archipelago ... such great means of defence are not required on the Caspian, as there are only Cossack boats to be met with."
[6] The Russians in the middle of the eighteenth century began to develop a monopolistic policy with serious damage to British trade with Persia which was growing up via the Baltic Ports and Astrakhan. The Russians subsequently pursued their monopolistic theories in the Caucasus, and so considerably retarded economic development in those lands during the nineteenth century.

DOG-DAYS OF THE GEORGIANS

by-word throughout Iran and Iraq; it had become, moreover, a place of Muslim pilgrimage.¹

We have already referred to the export trade in iron and in nuts which formed two of the staple items of Georgian production. The export of wines to Persia and the Armenian towns was also very great, and the vintages of Kakheti were greatly appreciated by the easy-going Shi'ahs of Isfahan.² Evliya, who visited Tiflis not long after the destruction of the Kakhetian mulberry-orchards by Shah Abbas, states that there was no silk produced in Georgia. Chardin, however, says that great quantities of raw silk were exported to Erzerum for the Turkish market,³ and it may be assumed that the production was thus diverted because the Georgians could not compete in the more accessible Persian market against the celebrated centres of silk production in Shirvan and Aran. Considerable quantities of linen clothes were also exported annually to Turkey, and 60,000 ells of linen represented the tribute paid over by the Dadiani of Mingrelia to the Pasha of Akhaltzikhé.⁴ Georgian falcons and other birds of prey, celebrated in the East throughout the centuries, were exported into Persia.⁵ Georgian horses were also in much demand.

The slave trade was, as we have elsewhere considered, the principal object of commerce into Georgia and the mountain districts during these times, and a great part of the maritime traffic on the Black Sea relied primarily on this trade—their outward cargoes being products to trade against flesh and their homeward cargoes slaves. Chardin says that he had heard several old Turkish captains affirm that there were all together about fifteen hundred vessels trading in the Black Sea in that time, of which about a hundred were lost by shipwreck every year.⁶

In Chardin's ship there were about two hundred people; the Commandant of Azac (Azov) and a suite of 20, 100 Janissaries, 50 passengers and a crew of 30. Chardin's ship arrived at Caffa, having made the journey from Stambul in eight days. From Caffa the ship proceeded to trade down the coast along towards Georgia.

"Our Ships Lading consisted in Salt Fish, Caveare, Oyl, Biscuit, Wooll, Iron, Tin, Copper, Copper and Earthen Ware, in all sorts of Harness, Arms, Utensils of Husbandry, Cloth, Linnen of all Colours, Habits for Men and Women, Coverlets, Carpets, Leather, Boots and

---

¹ Evliya, I, 172.   ² Chardin, p. 189.   ³ *Idem.*, p. 190.   ⁴ *Idem.*, p. 107.
⁵ *Idem.*, p. 92.
⁶ *Idem.*, p. 66; Evliya, II, 67–70, gives a dramatic account of a shipwreck in the Black Sea, when nearly all the ship's company, 300 souls, were lost.

Shooes and in a word in all things most necessary for Man's use. There were all sorts of Grocery and Pothecary's Ware, Spices, Perfumes, Drugs and all manner of Oyntments. So that the vessel seemed to be a little Town, where everything was to be had." [1]

Almost all the foreign trade was transacted by barter, and both Chardin and Pitton de Tournefort found that the people preferred to be paid for goods in stuffs and trinkets rather than in currency.

The long period of perpetual contact, both commercial and political, with their powerful Mussulman neighbours had a profound effect on the peoples of the Caucasus. The more highly civilized Georgians and Armenians, strong in the antique traditions of East Christian culture, were outwardly affected in modes and habits and some ways of thought; the peoples of the mountains, who had not by the fifteenth century emerged from the tribal state, forgot their thin Christianity and became Muslim in culture as well as in outward fashion. Not only did Islam penetrate the remoter valleys of Circassia, but it became the religion of the relatively civilized Meskhians and Abkhaz.[2]

The easy religious casuistry of the Georgian princes was natural to them as well as convenient to their political interests. In the seventeenth century the old mediæval culture of Christendom, which had flourished in the Kingdom of Georgia, was half-forgotten, and it was only the more sensitive spirits who were prepared still to make sacrifices in the memory of its tradition. The new architecture of Tiflis, in the Mukhranian days, was altogether in the Muslim style; dress, manners, furnishing, were Persian. The position of women was also affected and Chardin noted a tendency, since the Persian rule began in Tiflis, towards the seclusion of women. They went veiled in the streets, while in the country districts, where there were no Mussulmans, they still adhered to the Christian custom.[3]

The travellers of the seventeenth century are none too generous in their appraisal of the Georgian character. Chardin has a long diatribe on the Georgians, and he condemns their immorality, their drunkenness, their knavery and their arrogance. But even he admits, by contrary, that "*they are Civil and Courteous and more than that, they are Grave and Moderate*".[4]

---

[1] Chardin, p. 75.
[2] For the progress of Islam in Samtzkhé during the seventeenth century, see Wakhushti, *Histoire de Samtzkhé*, in Brosset, H. de la G., II, i, 232–3.
[3] Chardin, p. 226.   [4] *Idem.*, p. 191.

"Georgian Pastimes and Gaieties" (Castelli).

THE LIFE OF GEORGIA

Pitton de Tournefort, in a few words, probably sums up best a traveller's impression of the Georgians, when he compares them with the Turks—

> "C'est un excellent pays que la Géorgie . . . on s'adresse surtout aux Francs avec un visage riant, au lieu qu'en Turquie on ne voit que les gens sérieux qui vous mesurent gravement depuis les pieds jusque a la teste." [1]

Chardin is, further, strongly condemnatory of the women, although he admits their high standard of good looks.[2] The Huguenot jeweller condemns their morals, of which he had no great opportunity of knowing much;[3] he condemns their conversation, of which he can have understood little; and he condemns their habit of painting their faces, which is, after all, a matter of individual taste.[4] It is not difficult to read between his pompous, downright lines, that he was sometimes rebuffed and often teased and always being laughed at. For in the accounts of Chardin and other writers who have described the Georgians, we can often read between the lines the moving of a gentle humour in the spirit of the people in process of description. For to superior ones it is better to apply your humour than your indignation. And the Georgians in all their splendours and their miseries were humorists. That gentle bantering humour is exemplified, indeed, in the Story of King Shah-Nawaz and the Superior's Spinet.[5] It is too long a story to recount here. But the Georgians could always laugh, and laughter, where high principle goes down, can survive terror and it can outlive Empires.

---

[1] Pitton de Tournefort, II, 301.   [2] Chardin, pp. 84, 190.

[3] "They are naturally very subtle and of clear and quick Apprehensions, Extremely Civil, Full of Ceremonies and Complements; but otherwise the Wickedest Women in the World, Haughty, Furious, Perfidious, Deceitful, Cruel and Impudent. So that there is no sort of Wickedness which they will not put in Execution to procure Lovers, preserve their Affection, or else to destroy 'em."

[4] Chardin, pp. 85 and 119; cf. also Sir Robert Ker-Porter, an exceedingly genteel individual who made his way into the ladies' public baths in Tiflis in 1817: "a stone divan spread with carpets and mattresses was placed round the room, and on it lay or sat, women in every attitude and occupation consequent on an Asiatic bath. Some were half-dressed and others hardly had a covering. They were attended by servants employed in rubbing the fair forms of these ladies with dry cloths, or dyeing their hair or eyebrows, or finally painting or rather enamelling their faces. . . ." After further details Sir Robert adds with supreme unction, "They seemed to have as little modest covering on their minds as on their bodies; and the whole scene became so unpleasant, that declining our conductress's offer to show us further, we made good our retreat, fully satisfied with the extent of our gratified curiosity." (*Travels in Georgia, Persia, Armenia, Ancient Babylonia, etc., etc. during the years* 1817, 1818, 1819 and 1820, London, 1821, Vol. I, pp. 120–1.)

[5] Chardin, p. 229.

BIBLIOGRAPHICAL AND SUPPLEMENTARY NOTES

BIBLIOGRAPHIES

MIANSAROV, *Bibliographia Caucasica et Transcaucasica*, Vol. I. Sections 1 and 2, Spb, 1874-6.
  (The standard bibliography for the Caucasus to 1876, since when no work has appeared which can be considered as an adequate supplement to it.)
BROSSET, LAURENT, *Bibliographie Analytique des Ouvrages de Monsieur Marie-Félicité Brosset*, Spb, 1887.
WARDROP, O., *The Kingdom of Georgia*, London, 1888.
  (Contains a valuable list, particularly of European travellers.)
Kavkazskii Kalendar, Vol. XLV, for 1890, pp. 1-48, *Kratkii Spisok knigam, statyam i izdanyam, otnosyashchimsya k Kavkazovedenyu*, published as Prilozheniya to Part I.
  (Contains a fairly comprehensive list of books, articles and periodicals, with competent descriptive notes by an anonymous editor, probably Zagurski.)
Bolshaya Sovyetskaya Entziklopediya (in course of publication; 23 volumes to 1931).
  (Volume including section "Gruziya" contains valuable new bibliographical notes on Georgia.)
EGOROV, *Bibliographia Vostoka*, published by Nauchnaya Ass. Vostokovedov.
Tpilisis Universitetis Gamotsemani: Katalogi No. 1, Tiflis, 1928.
Klassifitzirovannie perechen pechatnikh rabot po Yafetidilogii, izd. Instituta Narodov Vostoka S.S.S.R., Leningrad, 1926.
Yafeticheski Sbornik, Vol. VI, Spisok rabot N. Ya. Marra za 1888-1930.
MS. Catalogue of the Wardrop Collection of Georgian Books and Manuscripts in the Bodleian Library at Oxford.

LIST OF PERIODICAL AND SERIAL PUBLICATIONS

ABBREVIATION

Akti. . . . . *Akti sobrannye Kavkazkoyu Arkheographicheskoyu Kommissieyu, Arkhiv Upravleniya Namestnika Kavkazskago*, 11 vols., izdan pod redaktziei Predsedateliya Kommissii d.s.s. Ad. Berzhé, Tiflis, 1866-88.
  (Contains a mass of original documents, relating particularly to the period of the Russian occupation of Georgia and the Caucasus; some archæological material, and a series of interesting plates of members of the House of Bagrationi.)
Armeniaca. . . . *Armeniaca*, 2 vols. to date, published by K. Roth, Leipzig, 1926-7.

BIBLIOGRAPHIES AND NOTES

ABBREVIATION	
Aziat. Sbor.	*Aziatskii Sbornik iz Izvestii Rossiiskoi Akademii Nauk*, novaya seriya, 1918, 1919.

(A continuation of the old *Mélanges Asiatiques* published by the Imperial Academy of Sciences during the last century; contains a few philological articles relative to the Caucasus.)

Bol. Sov. Entz. . . *Bolshaya Sovyetskaya Entziklopediya*, 23 vols. to date.

(Contains many excellent articles on the Caucasus, including over 100 pages devoted to a survey of Georgian history, etc.)

Bull. Hist.-Phil. . *Bulletin de la classe Historico-Philologique de l'Académie Impériale des Sciences de Saint-Petersbourg*, Spb, 1844–59.

(Contains many papers by Brosset.)

Caucasica . . . *Caucasica*, published by A. Dirr, Leipzig, Verlag der "Asia Major"; 9 fasc. so far issued.

(Contains many valuable papers by A. Dirr, O. G. von Wesendonk, H. Junker, A. Trombetti, Gerhard Deeters, Joseph Markwart, Emil Forrer, etc.)

Dokladi . . . . *Dokladi Rossiiskoi Akademii Nauk.*

(Numerous fascicules appearing at irregular intervals; contains papers, mostly philological, relative to the Caucasus.)

Drev. Vost. . . *Drevnosti Vostochniya, trudi Vostochnoi Kommissii Imperatorskago Moskovskago Arkheologicheskago Obshchvesta* izd. A. E. Krimskago, 3 vols., 1889–1901–1907.

E.I. . . . . . *The Encyclopædia of Islam*, 2 vols. with supplements appearing.

(Contains many valuable articles on the Caucasus by Bartold, Minorski and others.)

E.S.A. . . . . *Eurasia Septentrionalis Antiqua*, edited by A. M. Tallgren and Ilmari Manninen Helsinki, 6 vols. to date, 1927–31.

(Contains papers and notes on Bronze and Early Iron Age cultures in the Caucasus.)

Iz. R.A.N. . . *Izvestiya Rossiiskoi Akademii Nauk* (of the same character as Dokladi.)

Iz. Vost. Ot. *Izvestiya Vostochniya Otdeleniya Imperatorskago Arkheo-*
I.R.A.O. *logicheskago Obshchestva*, Spb, from 1858.

Iz. Kav. Ot. I.R.G.O. *Izvestiya Kavkazskago Otdela Imp. Russkago Geographicheskago Obshchestva*, Tiflis, from 1872.

(Contains valuable papers on natural and political geography and anthropology.)

Iz. Kav. I.-A.I. . *Izvestiya Kavkazskago Istoriko-Arkheologicheskago Instituta v Tiflise*, 4 vols. published to 1930.

(Contains latest contributions on archæology and mediæval history.)

Iz. Abkhaz. N.O. . *Izvestiya Abkhazskago Nauchnogo Obshchestva*, Sukham, 1926 to 1930, 4 vols.

(Contains some suggestive papers, particularly on the Abkhazian Bronze Age.)

BIBLIOGRAPHIES AND NOTES

ABBREVIATION	
Iz. Fak. Az.	*Izvestiya Vostochnogo Fakulteta Azerbaidjanskogo Gosudarstvennogo Universiteta Vostokovedenie*, vols. 1–2, Baku, 1927–8.
Iz. Ob. Az.	*Izvestiya Obshchestva Obsledovaniya i Izucheniya Azerbaidjana*, vols. 1–5, Baku, 1926–8.
Iz. Gos. Ak. I.M.K.	*Izvestiya Gosudarstvennoi Akademii Istorii Materialnoi Kulturi*, 6 vols., published to 1931, the last in 6 separate fasc.
	(Contains many valuable articles on Caucasian archæology and history, particularly the works of Marr, Orbeli and Meshchaninov.)
J.A.	*Journal Asiatique*, published by La Société Asiatique, Paris.
	(This veteran journal, to which several generations of Orientalists owe gratitude, contains numerous important essays and notes relating to the Caucasus.)
Kav. Kal.	*Kavkazskie Kalendar* for the years 1854–1916, published by Kantseliariei Namestnika, Tiflis.
	(Contains a mass of statistical material on the Caucasus.)
Kav. Sbor.	*Kavkazskii Sbornik*, about 13 vols. from 1875.
Khrist. Vos.	*Khristianskii Vostok*, vols. 1–6, Spb, 1912–22.
	(Contains many valuable papers, particularly on mediæval archæology.)
Mat. Kav.	*Materiali po Arkheologii Kavkaza*, 14 vols. complete, published by the Moscow Archæological Society at various dates up to 1913.
	(The fundamental work for all studies of the archæology of the Caucasus.)
Mat. Gruz.	*Materiali po Izucheniya Gruzii*, Tiflis, 1925.
Mat. Yaf.	*Materiali po Yafeticheskomu Yazikoznaniyu*, appearing in St. Petersburg at varying dates after 1909.
	(Includes many volumes relating to the philology and anthropology of the Caucasus.)
Mimo.	*Mimomkhilveli* (*The Reviewer*) published by Sakartvelos Saistorio da Saetnograpio Sazogadoeba, 3 vols. Tiflis, 1926–9.
Novie Vostok	*Novie Vostok, Zhurnal Vserossiiskoi Nauchnoi Associatzii Vostokovedeniya pri Tzik*, S.S.S.R., 28 vols. complete; publication ceased in 1930. Moscow, 1922–30.
	(Contains a few articles on the history and anthropology of the Caucasus and various notes with regard to the activities of local scientific bodies, which are invaluable.)
Oriens Christ.	*Oriens Christianus*, halbjahrshefte für die Kunde der Christlichen Orients. (Band II, Heft II, published in Leipzig, 1928.)
Oriente Mod.	*Oriente Moderno*, published in Rome from 1921–2.
	(Contains a few papers of value on the Caucasus.)

BIBLIOGRAPHIES AND NOTES

ABBREVIATION	
R.E.A.	*Revue des Etudes Arméniennes*, published in Paris from 1920.
R.E.I.	*Revue des Etudes Islamiques*, Vols. I–V, Paris, 1927–31.
R.E.M.	*Revue du Monde Musulman*, Vols. I–LXIV, Paris, 1906–26.
Sbor. Mat.	*Sbornik Materialov dlya Opisaniya Mestnostei i Plemen Kavkaza*, izd. Upravleniya Kavkazskago Uchebnago Okruga, 44 vols., published 1881–1917; publication recently resumed at Buinaksk and Vols. 45 and 46 issued. (Essential with *Mat. Kav.* to any serious study of the Caucasus.)
Sbor. Muz.	*Sbornik Muzeya po Antropologii i Etnografii pri (Imp.) Akademii Nauk* (S.S.S.R.), Vols. I–VI, Spb, 1900, Leningrad, 1927.
Sbor. Sved.	*Sbornik Svedenii o Kavkazskikh Gortzakh*, 10 vols., Tiflis, 1867–76.
Sbor. Kav.	*Sbornik Svedenii o Kavkaze*, izd. pod red. N. Zeidlitza, 9 vols., Tiflis, 1871–85.
S.M.	*Saistorio Moambé*, published by the Historical Society of Tiflis.
S.M.M.	*Sakartvelos Museumis Moambé*, published by the Georgian Museum, Tiflis.
Soob. Gos. Ak. I.M.K.	*Soobshcheniya Gosud. Akademii Istorii Materialnoi Kulturi*, 2 vols. to 1931.
Tek. Raz. A.-G.	*Teksti i Raziskaniya po Armyano-Gruzinskoi Filologi*, numerous volumes published in Spb. between 1890 and 1914.
Tek. Raz. Kav.	*Teksti i Raziskaniya po Kavkazskoi Filologii*, Leningrad from 1925.
Trudi Abkhaz.	*Trudi Abkhazskogo Nauchnogo Obshchestva*, Sukhum, from 1927.
Trudi Vost. Ot. I.R.A.O.	*Trudi Vostochnago Otdeleniya Imp. Russ. Arkheologicheskago Ob.*, 21 vols., Spb, 1863–1909.
Trudi Vost. Laz. I.V. Yaz.	*Trudi po Vostokovedeniyu izdavaemie Lazarevskim Institutom Vostochnikh Yazikov*, about 35 vols., published in Moscow between 1890 and 1917.
T.U.M.	*Tpilisis Universitetis Moambé*, 7 vols., Tiflis, 1919–27. *Trudi Zakavkazkoi Nauchnoi Associatzii*, see *Materiali po Izucheniya Gruzii*.
Viz. Ob.	*Vizantiiskoe Obozrenie*, Vol. II, published in Yuriev, 1916. (This and the following contain scattered articles on Caucasian history.)
Viz. Vrem.	*Vizantiiskii Vremmenik*, Vols. 23, 24, published in Leningrad, 1923.
Vost. Sbor.	*Vostochnii Sbornik*, Leningrad, Vol. I, 1926.
Yaf. Sbor.	*Yafeticheskii Sbornik*, 6 vols. to 1931. Institute Yafetidologicheskikh uziskanii Rossiiskoi Akademii Nauk, Leningrad, 1922–31. (Numerous articles on Caucasian philology by Marr and others.)

BIBLIOGRAPHIES AND NOTES

ABBREVIATION
Yaz. Lit. . . . *Yazik i Literatura*, 5 vols. to 1931, Nauchno-Izsledovatelski Institut, Leningrad, 1926-30.
(A few articles by Marr on Caucasian philology.)

Zap. Vost. Ot. *Zapiski Vostochnago Otdeleniya Imp. Russ. Arkheolo-*
I.R.A.O. *gicheskago Ob.*, 25 vols. Spb, 1887–1921. Edited by Baron R. Rosen.

Zap. Koll. . . . *Zapiski Kollegii Vostokovedov pri Aziatskom Muzee Akademii Nauk S.S.S.R.*, 4 vols. Izdatelstvo Akademii Nauk, S.S.S.R., Leningrad, 1925-30.

Zap. Kav. Ot. *Zapiski Kavkazskago Otdela Imp. Russ. Geographiches-*
I.R.G.O. *kago Ob.*, Vols. I–XVIII, Tiflis, 1872–96. (Further volumes were published after 1896.)

OTHER PUBLICATIONS (TO WHICH REFERENCE HAS BEEN MADE IN THE TEXT)

A.R. . . . . *Asiatic Review.*
B.S.O.S. . . . *Bulletin of the School of Oriental Studies*, Finsbury Circus, London, E.C.2.
C.A.H. . . . . *Cambridge Ancient History.*
C. Med. H. . . *Cambridge Mediæval History.*
J.E.A. . . . . *Journal of Egyptian Archæology.*
J.R.G.S. . . . *Journal of the Royal Geographical Society*, Kensington Gore, London, S.W.7.
J.R.A.S. . . . *Journal of the Royal Asiatic Society*, 74, Grosvenor Street, London, W.1.
R.A. . . . . *Revue Archéologique.*

NOTE.—In the above list of periodical and serial publications, I have limited myself to those whose contents bear directly on some aspect of the history and archæology of Georgia. I have not included the various Georgian and Russian publications devoted primarily to statistical, agronomical and other subjects. References to the earlier of these series, many of which are very rare and unobtainable in West European libraries, will be found in *Kav. Kal.*, Vol. XLV. Nor have I included the publications of the various learned Societies existing at Rostov, Stavropol, Vladikavkaz and elsewhere, both before and since the Revolution (for these see Egorov, *Bibliographia Vostoka*). The wide field of Armenian bibliography, which everywhere overlaps Georgian, I have not attempted to touch, owing to my complete ignorance of the Armenian language, nor have I made any effort to list the many Russian publications containing scattered articles on Georgia and the Caucasus, such as the rare and voluminous *Journal of the Ministry of Public Instruction*, which runs into well over a hundred volumes and contains many papers of great interest.

The numerous articles in *Kavkaz*, *Zakavkazskii Vestnik*, and other journals of the nineteenth century, it has been impossible for me to consult.

The following short-lived publications, which are of bibliographical interest, I have also been unable to come by:

Zapiski Obshchestva Lyubitelei Kavkazskoi Arkheologii, 1 vol., Tiflis, 1875
    (contains Bakradze's *Kavkaz v drevnikh pamyatnikakh Khristianstva*).
Izvestiya, of the same Society, 1 vol., Tiflis, 1877.
Izvestiya Kavkazskago Obshchestva Istorii i Arkheologii, 2 vols., Tiflis, 1882-4.

BIBLIOGRAPHICAL AND SUPPLEMENTARY NOTES TO BOOK I (CHAPTERS I-V)

BIBLIOGRAPHICAL NOTE TO CHAPTER II

The standard reference book on the anthropology and prehistoric archæology of the Caucasus is still the great work of CHANTRE published over forty years ago.

Recherches Anthropologiques dans le Caucase, 2 vols., Paris, 1885-7.
I. Période Prehistorique
II. Période Protohistorique
III. Période Historique
IV. Populations actuelles
V. Atlas des Planches

The following books and papers also deal with the practical archæology of the region, as distinct from the theories advanced by students who have been specializing primarily on other regions, and to whose works reference has been made in the footnotes.

J. DE MORGAN, *Mission Scientifique au Caucase*, 2 vols., Paris, 1889.
    Vol. I. Les Premières Ages des Métaux dans l'Arménie Russe.
    Vol. II. Recherches sur les Origines des Peuples du Caucase.

Katalog Kavkazskago Muzeya, Vol. V, edited by Gustav Radde.
    (Contains many valuable photographs of Bronze Age remains.)

Mat. Kav. Vol. I, (1888), Prehistoric archæology of the Northern Caucasus including Osseti and Kabardá.
    Vol. II, (1889), Prehistoric archæology of the western coast of the Caucasus.
    Vol. V, (1898), Cuneiform inscriptions of Trans-Caucasia.
    Vol. VIII, (1900), Prehistoric archæology of the Northern Caucasus (principally relating to Osseti).

Reference should be made to the excellent bibliographies published in the volumes of the *Cambridge Ancient History*, for most recent researches on the Hittites, Urartians, Assyrians and other peoples bordering on the Caucasus from the south. Archæological research in the Caucasus has been undertaken with some energy by the Soviet authorities, but funds are lacking and results has been meagre.

The following recent papers should be noted:

Iz. Gos. Ak. I.M.K., Vol. I, pp. 51-60, N. MARR, "Fragment Khaldskoi nadpisi iz Alashkerta."
    Vol. II, pp. 287-324, A. A. MILLER, "Izobrazhenia sobaki v drevnostyakh Kavkaza".
    Vol. III, pp. 283-304, N. MARR, "Zametki po Yapheticheskim klinopisyam".
    Vol. IV, pp. 1-42, A. A. MILLER, "Kratki Otchet o Rabotakh Severo-Kavkazskoi Ekspeditzii Akademii v 1923".
    Vol. IV, pp. 43-64, I. I. MESHCHANINOV, "Geographicheskie nazvaniya verkhovyev Araksa po Khaldskim nadpisyam".
    Vol. IV, pp. 97-114, A. A. MILLER, "Novie istochnik k izucheniu svyazi Skifii c Kavkazom".

BIBLIOGRAPHIES AND NOTES

Soob. Gos. Ak. I.M.K., Vol. I, pp. 71–142, A. A. MILLER, "Kratki Otchet o Rabotakh Severo-Kavkazskoi Expeditzii Akademii Istorii Materialnoi Kulturi".

Vol. I, pp. 217–40, I. I. MESHCHANINOV, "Kratkie Svedeniya o Rabotakh Arkheologicheskoi Expeditzii v Karabakh i Nakhichevan v 1926".

Vol. I, pp. 60–122, A. A. MILLER, "Arkheologicheskie Raboti Severo-Kavkazskoi Expeditzii v 1926-7".

Novie Vostok, Vol. V, pp. 239–54, N. YAKOVLEV, "Novoe v izuchenii Severnogo Kavkaza" (Preliminary report on the work of the Daghestan-Chechen expedition of 1923 in Daghestan).

Vol. XVIII, pp. 218–24, A. ALEKPEROV, "Noveishie arkheologicheskie raskopki v Azerbaijane".

Vol. XX–XXI, pp. 309–23, I. BOROZDIN, "V Gornoi Ingushetii".

Zap. Koll. Vol. I, pp. 241–56, I. I. MESHCHANINOV, "Zmeya i Sobaka na veshchevikh pamyatnikakh Kavkaza".

Vol. I, pp. 401–9, *idem.*, "Kamennye statui rib-vishapi na Kavkaze i v Severnoi Mongolii".

Mat. Gruz. Series I, Yugo-Osetia (Southern Osseti), pp. 252–79, L. M. MELIKSET-BEKOV, "K arkheologii i ethnologii Tualskoi Osii".

Series II, pp. 49–57, *Idem.*, "Asiriiskaya votivnaya busina iz Azerbaijana".

Series II, pp. 58–67, T. PASSEK and B. LATININ, "Khojalinski Kurgan", No. 11.

Iz. Ob. Az., Vol. I, pp. 5–15, I. I. MESHCHANINOV, "Do-istoricheski Azerbaijan i Urartskaya Kultura".

Vol. III, pp. 107–11, *idem.*, "K Voprosu ob Asiriiskoi busine iz Khojalinskago Mogilnika".

Vol. III, pp. 112–57, T. PASSEK and B. LATININ, "Ocherk Do-istorii Severnogo Azerbaijana".

Vol. IV, pp. 104–7, I. I. MESHCHANINOV, "Arkhaeologicheskaya Expeditziya v Nagornyi Karabakh i Nakhkrai". (Nakhichevan Territory.)

Vol. IV, pp. 108–25, "Poezdka v Shemakhinski Uezd c arkheologicheskoyu tseliu".

Vol. IV, pp. 210–16, A. ALEKPEROV, "Poezdka v Zangezur i Nakhkrai".

Vol. IV, pp. 217–22, T. PASSEK and B. LATININ, "K voprosu o keramike iz Yaloilu-Tapa".

For the early metal cultures in Trans-Caucasia, see, in addition to the references in the footnotes—Davidov, *L'industrie du cuivre dans le Trans-Caucasie*, Odessa, 1884. See also the important footnote by J. F. Baddeley in *Russia, Mongolia, China*, Vol. I, p. cv. Referring to the Altai he states: *that the bronze was a local production has been hinted at recently by the discovery of old tin-workings in the valley of the Kara-Irtish, with bronze tools in them. We may hope to know more on this fascinating subject some day; meantime it is worth noting that whereas the bronze of Koban has been given a Malay or European origin, it may more easily have come from the Altai.*

SUPPLEMENTARY NOTES TO CHAPTER II

Note A.—On the History of the Euxine in pre-Hellenic Times

An excellent summary of the mythological sources for the history of the navigation of the Black Sea may be found in VIVIEN DE SAINT-MARTIN'S *Histoire de la Géographie* (Paris, 1873).

VICTOR BÉRARD in *Les Phéniciens et l'Odyssée* (2 vols., Paris, 1897), although he confines his studies to the Mediterranean, has much to say that is suggestive for the early history of navigation.

More recently M. AUTRAN, approaching the subject in *Phéniciens* (Paris, 1925), postulates a " Cadmean " or " Ægean " civilization in contact with the peoples of Asia Minor and the Pontic Coast, and in his last work *Introduction à l'Etude Critique du Nom Propre Grec* (Paris, 7 fasc. so far published) he underlines the racial and cultural connections between the Mediterranean and Pontic regions during the pre-Hellenic period.

PROF. A. A. ZAKHAROV in various articles in Russian periodicals has given his attention to the early maritime activities of the peoples of the Caucasus, and suggests that some at least of the " Peoples of the Sea " who invaded Egypt in the thirteenth century B.C. came from the Caucasus. PROF. H. R. HALL has published a summary and commentary of Zakharov's theory in " The Caucasian Relations of the Peoples of the Sea " (*Klio*, Band 22, Heft 3, pp. 335–44). Compare also " Die Seevolker Namen in den Altorientalischen Quellen " by ROBERT EISLER in *Caucasica*, Fasc. V, pp. 73–130, and my observations on the Laz in " The March-Lands of Georgia " (*J.R.G.S.*, July 1929). It may be remarked that Autran's studies, particularly, confirm from an independent angle some of the ideas advanced by Prof. Marr. It must be emphasized, however, that all theories so far advanced, with the exception of those of Zakharov and Hall, are based on inductive argument from mythological and philological sources. Such must be the case until the archæological exploration of the Caucasus and of the southern shores of the Black Sea is undertaken on a serious and comprehensive plan.

Apart from the theories to which reference has been made, an American writer, R. A. FESSENDEN, in *The Deluged Civilization of the Caucasian Isthmus*, has further attempted to combine Greek myths and the Biblical and other Semitic accounts of the Garden of Eden and the Deluge, and to locate the events recorded therein in Trans-Caucasia. He has found support from no less an authority than SIR FLINDERS PETRIE (see *Egypt*, Part IV, 1924), who further finds in Trans-Caucasia the equivalents of many of the mythical places mentioned in the Egyptian *Book of the Dead* (*Egypt*, Part II, 1926). It is noteworthy that the facts of the geological history of the Caucasus, during the late Quaternary Ice Age, so far as they have been elucidated, do not altogether fail to confirm the theories elaborated by Fessenden. (See RECLUS, *Universal Geography*, Vol. VI, pp. 38 *et sqq.*; WRIGHT, *Asiatic Russia*, pp. 506–7; and *Zap. Kav. Ot. I.R.G.O.*, Vol. XV, pp. 189–225, " Usikhanie Ozer na Severnom Sklone Kavkazskago Khrebta ".) In connection with Fessenden's theory, it may be remarked that the traveller

BIBLIOGRAPHIES AND NOTES

Dubois de Montpéreux was the first to suggest that Books X, XI, and XII of the Odyssey related to the Caucasus (*Voyage autour du Caucase*, Vol. II, pp. 1–30), a postulate with which Rostovtseff is now in agreement (*Iranians and Greeks*, p. 62). Uslar in " Drevneishiya Skazaniya o Kavkaze", published as Vol X of *Sbor Šved*, Tiflis, 1881, first attempted to locate the Garden of Eden and the Deluge in the Caucasus, and his arguments might well attract the study of more recent authorities who have given their attention to this theory without being possessed of the Russian's profound knowledge of his subject. For a recent commentary on Fessenden's and Petrie's theories see *Iz. Ob. Az.*, Vol. IV, pp. 34–43, I. I. Meshchaninov, " Egipet i Kavkaz ".

Note B.—On the Significance of the Root M-S

Marr in *Iz. R.A.N.*, Ser. VI, 1917, No. 5, pp. 317–18, suggests an association between the root M-S and the words *maq* in Avar and *maq* in Kazi-Kummukh, signifying " nails " and hence " iron ", and it may well be that the name for the metal was derived from that of the people who were earliest associated with its use. Again, it is noteworthy that Marr (*ibid.*, 332) connects the tribal name AVAR with ALBAN—ALBANIAN. In Turkish the word *avaré* signifies " vagrant " ; wherefore Reclus (*Univ. Geog.*, VI, 83) quotes Komarov as suggesting that it may mean also " fugitive " and be only of recent origin. But the word may well be a deprecatory derivative from the name, as is, for example, French *bougre* from " Bulgare ", an Albigensian or Bogomilian heretic, hence a politically and/or morally offensive person ; also *ickeny* in Norfolk dialect " a donkey " and also a " slow-witted person "—an obvious derivative of the tribal name Iceni, which must have gradually obtained a deprecatory implication during Roman and early Saxon times. In the name Kazi-Ghumukh, *kazi* is, of course, a Turko-Arab apposition, *ghazi* " victorious ". The identical form *Kummukh* appears frequently in Assyrian inscriptions (*C.A.H.*, III, 16 *et sqq.*), and the region once inhabited by the Kummukh still retained in Classic times the name of Commagene. The Kummukh were neighbours of the Tabal and Mushki.

As for the name Mitanni, which Hogarth couples with that of the Mushki, it should be observed that in Georgian *mta* means mountain (plural *mta-ni*). It may be suggested that the tribal place-name Mitanni signified " the mountains " (cf. the modern names Daghestan, " The Highlands " ; Montenegro).

SUPPLEMENTARY NOTES TO CHAPTER III

Note C.—On the Name Tubal

For the anthropology of Western Asia see the excellent work of PROF. J. L. MYRES in *C.A.H.*, Vol. I, Chapters I and II. Myres (pp. 72 *et sqq.*), in discussing the connection of " Alpine " man with the " lake-dwelling " culture of Europe, remarks :

> " ancient descriptions of pile dwellings in water-logged valleys of North Syria and Georgia, unverified as yet by excavation, suggest that our Alpine lake settlements are to be regarded as a western section of a very large region of early and essentially homogeneous culture, adapted to the conditions of a moist forest-clad lake-land, such as Asia Minor, and much of the highland region eastward of it must have constituted during the long ' pluvial ' period which was the counter-part of the Ice-Age in Europe ".

In relation to this lake-dwelling culture, it is of interest to consider the tribal name-form UPLOS-TUBAL. In Georgian the word *tba* means " lake ". This word forms the root of many Georgian geographical names ; e.g. Tbeti (tba + eti = " the lake district " in Shavsheti ; Tibanieri, a village near Kutais ; Tobaqure, a village in Mingrelia ; Diditba (" great lake "), a village in the Tiflis province ; Tobatqe (" forest lake "), a village in the Zakatali district. Many ethnic names have been interpreted as derived from the names for lakes and rivers, and it may be suggested that the root of the ethnic names TUBAL-TOBEL-TIBAR may be derived from the word *tba* = lake. The Mingrelian equivalent of the Georgian *tba* is *toba*, which is also the old Georgian form. The Svanian word *tibar* means both " lake " and " deep defile ". A lake-dweller is in Georgian *tbeli*, in Mingrelian *tobeli*. The Caucasian name-form TUBAL-TIBER-IBER is widespread through the area of the Mediterranean world, as, for example, Italian TIBER, Spanish EBRO, and its recurrence in regions geographically far apart remains a difficult problem of linguistic palæontology. In connection with the Georgian *tba* it is also interesting to compare Irish place-names, e.g. Tobermory, Toberdaly, etc. Cf. MACBAIN, *Etymological Dictionary of the Gaelic Language*, *tobar* = a well. Old Irish *topur*. . . . Some have referred *tobar* to the root *ber* of *inhibir* . . . *abar* (*obair*). *Abar* occurs only in Pictish place-names.

Note D.—On the Georgian Language

For the comparative study of the Georgian language the reader is referred to the following authorities, all of whose works are to be found either at the British Museum or at the London Library.

1. For the " Indo-European " theory, F. BOPP, *Die Kaukasischen glieder des Indoeuropäischen Sprachstamme*, 1847 ; BROSSET, *l'Art Libéral ou Grammaire Géorgienne*, Paris, 1834.

2. For the " Turanian " or " Ural-Altaic " theory, see works and articles of MAX MÜLLER and JACQUES DE MORGAN ; contra, A. TSAGARELI.

3. For the " Semitic " theory see works of A. KALIAN and A. TROMBETTI (particularly his letter to Hugo Schuchart published in *Giornale della*

BIBLIOGRAPHIES AND NOTES

Società Asiatica Italiana, 1902, in which he deals with the inter-relationship of the Semitic, Hamitic and Caucasian families.

4. For the " Isolierte Volker " theory see works of FRED. MÜLLER, POTT, K. R. LEPSIUS, T. H. BENFEY, SPIEGEL and SCHUCHART.

5. For the " Japhetic " theory see MARR's standard work on Georgian, *Osnovnie Tablitzi Grammatiki Drevne-Gruzinskogo Yazika*, Spb, 1908, and his article " Gruzinskie Yazik " in *Bol. Sov. Entz.*, Vol. 19. Reference should also be made to his many articles in *Dokladi, Iz. R.A.N., Iz. Gos. Ak. I.M.K., Mat. Yaf., Novie Vostok, Yaf. Sbor., Yaz. Lit.*, etc. For a summary of the " Japhetic " theory see MARR's *Der Japhetitische Kaukasus und das dritte ethnische Element in Bildungsprozess der Mittelländischen Kultur*, translated from the Russian by F. Braun, Berlin, 1923.

6. For the " Alarodian Theory " based on Sayce's decipherment of the cuneiform, see the works of SAYCE, LENORMANT, HOMMEL, MARR. *Cf.* also WINCKLER, HUISYNG, BORK, etc. For comparison also of Georgian with Sumerian see HOMMEL, and M. TSERETELI, " Sumerian and Georgian : a study in Comparative Philology " in *J.R.A.S.*, 1913–16.

7. For the Kanesian language of Boghaz Keui see works of KNUDTZEN and HROZNY who established the Indo-European character of Kanesian. There are, however, certain elements in Kanesian which according to Georgian scholars have affinity with Georgian, i.e. adjectival and adverbial terminations. The Kanesian instrumental case-ending " *it* " cannot be explained on an Indo-European basis, but it is strikingly similar to the Georgian instrumental case-ending: e.g. Hittite—"water ", Nom. *vadar*, Inst. *vedenit* ; " man ", Nom. *antuhsas*, Inst. *antuhsit* ; Georgian—" water ", Nom. *tsqali*, Inst. *tsqalit* ; " man ", Nom. *katsi*, Inst. *katsit*. Similarly the Kanesian abl. suffix " *az* " may be compared with the Georgian ablative suffix " *ad* ". Three of the lesser-known languages of Boghaz-Keui may also be compared with Georgian—Kharrian, Luvian and Palan. It has been suggested that these were the languages of autochthonous tribes subject to the Hittite kings. It is interesting to compare the name of the Hittite capital, Karchemish, with the Georgian *Kari*, gate, and *Chemis*, 1st pers. pronoun. gen. case, hence = My gate (of the God).

For the most recent studies of Caucasian linguistics, apart from the work of the Japhetic school, see :

A. DIRR, *Einführung in das Studium der Kaukasischen Sprachen*, Leipzig, 1928 (Verlag der Asia Major).

N. TRUBETSKOI, PRINCE, in *Caucasica*, Fasc. III, pp. 7–36, " Studien auf den Gebiete der vergleschenden Lautlehre der Nordkaukasischen Sprachen ".

M. TSERETELI, " Il georgiano e le sue affinità linguistiche ", in *Oriente Moderno*, Anno I, Nos. 7–8.

Note E.—On the use of the name " Georgia ".

The Georgians call themselves Kartvel-i (-ni), and their country Sa-kartvel-o. The name *Georgia*, used in various forms by European writers, first appears in the Persian form *Gurgistan*, and it is used frequently by Arab writers from Masudi onwards in the forms *Djurz* and *Djorzan*. It appears to have no connection with the *Georgi* of Pliny (VII, 14), nor must it be confused with the *Gurjan* of Muslim writers—a name derived from and applied to the Classical *Hyrcania*. Brosset favours the derivation of the name *Georgia* from that of the river *Mtkvari* ⟵⟶ *Kuros* ⟵⟶ *Cyrus* ⟵⟶ *Kura* ⟵⟶ *Djurzon*, rather than from the Greek word *georgos*, or from the name of St. George—the latter is a popular local etymology. (See Brosset, *H. de le G.*, Introduction, p. 5.)

Bibliographical Notes to Chapter IV

For the comparative study of primitive customs and beliefs in the Caucasus, the best summary of the older and more scattered sources is by Maxim Kovalevski, *Zakon i Obichai na Kavkaze*, 2 vols., Moscow, 1890. A survey of Kovalevski and other more recent periodical writers has been published by Joseph Castagné in *R.E.I.*, 1929, Cahier 2, pp. 245-275, "Le Droit Coutumier Familial des Montagnards du Caucase et des Tcherkesses en particulier". Kovalevski seeks rather to emphasize, and Castagné to minimize, the significance of the survival of "matriarchal" practices among the mountain tribes.

For the history of the primitive social and religious state of the Georgians and Armenians, the following books and papers may be consulted:

Ethnograficheski Fond N.O. Emina pri Lazarevskom Institute Vostochnikh Yazikov, 2 vols., Moscow, 1896, 1897, Vol. II, Izsledovaniya i Statie N.O. Emina, pp. 7-60: "Ocherk religii i verovanii yazicheskikh Armyan".

Tek. Raz. A.-G., Vol. VIII, I. Javakhov (or Javakhishvili), "Gosudarstvennii stroi drevnei Gruzii i drevnei Armenii".

Zap. Vos. Ot. I.R.A.O., Vol. XIV, Part 2-3, pp. 1-30, N. Y. Marr, "Bogi yazicheskoi Gruzii po Drevne-Gruzinskim istochnikam".

Yubelinie Sbornik v'chest V.F. Millera, Moscow, 1900, pp. 13-19, A. S. Khakhanov, "Nekotorie cherti stroi i kulturi drevnei Gruzii".

Caucasica, Fasc. I, pp. 1-102 and Fasc. II, pp. 121-130, O. G. von Wesendonck, "Uber Georgisches Heidenthum" (is superior to all works in Russian as a critical essay on Georgian paganism).

D. Guliya, *Istoriya Abkhazii*, Vol. I, Tiflis, 1925 (see particularly pages 181-232).

Sbor. Mat., Vol. XXVI, Division I, Section II, pp. 1-46, M. Sagaradze, "Obichai i verovania v Imeretiyu", and numerous other papers in this collection.

Sbornik Gazeti "Kavkaz", (1847), Vol. II, pp. 51-59, Baratov, "Kratkie otchet religioznoi zhizni narodov Grusino-Mingrelskago plemeni v epokhu mirnoi yazichestva".

(This short essay contains a number of interesting facts from the personal experience of the author—a country squire in Georgia.)

Iz. Kav. Ot. I.R.G.O., Vol. V, p. 153 *et sqq.*, E. G. Veidenbaum, "Svyashchenniya roshchi i derevya sredi Kavkazskikh narodov".

Ibid., Vol. VII, pp. 99-100, *idem.*, "Svyashchennoe derevo *Segut*".

Iz. R.A.N., Series V, 1911, pp. 759-774, N. Y. Marr, "Bog *Sabadios* sredi Armyan".

Ibid., 1912, pp. 827-930, *idem.*, "Frako-Armyanski *Sabadios aswat* i Bog okhoti Svanov".

Khrist. Vos., Vol. IV, pp. 113-140, Janashvili, "O religioznikh verovaniakh Abkhazov".

BIBLIOGRAPHIES AND NOTES

Yaf. Sbor., Vol. IV, pp. 39–71, I. FRANK-KAMENETSKI, "Gruzinskaya parallel k drevne-Egipetskoi povesti 'The two brothers'".

Khrist. Vos., Vol. IV, pp. 310–312, L. MELIKSET-BEKOV, "K voprosu ob ustroistve altarya v drevni Gruzii".

Zap. Vost. Ot. I.R.A.O., Vol. XXV, pp. 229–256, N. Y. MARR, "Astronomicheskiya i etnicheskiya znachenia dvukh plemennikh nazvanii Armyan".

For further materials on the religious and cultural life of the mountain peoples in particular, see:

for the Svans—Marr in *Khrist. Vos.*, II, pp. 1–34; Tenitzov in *Sbor. Mat.*, X, i, pp. 1–68; and Dolgushin, *ibid.*, XXVIII, i, pp. 137–187, and Chimikadze in *Sakartvelos Sidzveleni*, II, 4, pp. 1–35.

for the Abkhaz—Janashvili in *Zap. Kav. Ot. I.R.G.O.*, XVI, pp. 1–64; in *Khrist. Vos.*, V, pp. 157–208; Marr in *Vost. Sbor.*, I, pp. 123–166; in *Caucasica*, fasc. II, pp. 119–120; in *Iz. R.A.N.* (1913), pp. 302–334; and in *Mat. Yaf.*, V. Machabarinani in *Sbor. Mat.*, IV, ii, pp. 40–76; and Charaya in *Mat. Yaf.*, IV.

for the Ossetians—*Yugo-Osetia*, published as *Ser. I, vipusk I* of *Mat. Gruz.*, of which the sections contributed by Chursin and Pchelin should be noted.

Bibliographical Notes to Chapter V

For the historical topography of Georgia, the essential source will always be *Déscription Géographique de la Géorgie, par le Tsarévitch Wakhoucht*, Georgian text with French translation, published by Brosset, St. Petersburg, 1842. Reference should also be made to the following principal works by Brosset, in addition to his numerous articles in French and Russian periodicals:

Histoire de la Géorgie depuis l'Antiquité jusqu'au XIX siècle, traduite du Géorgien, I^{ière} partie, " Histoire ancienne jusqu'en 1469 de J.C.", Spb, 1849.

Histoire de la Géorgie. Introduction et Table des Matières, Spb, 1858. (An introduction to above published nine years later.)

Additions et Eclairissements à l'Histoire de la Géorgie, Spb, 1851, of which the following " Additions " should be noted:

    Add. III. " Sur les rapports des Persans avec la Géorgie dans la seconde moitiè du Ve siècle de l'ère chrétienne."

    Add. IV. " Sur le royaume de Lazique."

    Add. XXVI. " Extraits de l'Histoire des Aghovans, en Arménien par Moise Caghancatovatsi."

Rapports sur un Voyage Archéologique dans la Géorgie et dans l'Arménie, Spb, 1849.

F. Dubois de Montpéreux, *Voyage autour du Caucase chez les Tcherkesses et les Abkhases, en Colchide, en Géorgie, en Arménie, et en Crimée; avec un atlas géographique, pittoresque, archéologique, géologique, etc.*, 6 vols. and 2 vols. Atlas, Paris and Neuchâtel, 1839–1843.

(The first three volumes contain much valuable information on Georgian topography.)

For the classical topography of Georgia and the Caucasus:

V. V. Latishev has published all relevant extracts from major and minor classical authors in a work which is difficult to come by:

Scythica et Caucasica e veteribus scriptoribus Graecis et Latinis; Vol. I, Parts 1 and 2, Scriptores Latini; Vol. 2, Parts 1 and 2, Scriptores Græci, Spb, 1902–1906.

Latishev gives an interleaved Russian translation.

For a general summary of classical notions of the Caucasus see:

Vivien de Saint-Martin (1) *Histoire de la Géographie*, Paris, 1873.

    (2) *Mémoire Historique sur la Géographie Ancienne du Caucase*, Paris, 1847.

    (3) *Recherches sur les Populations Primitives et les plus Anciennes Traditions du Caucase*, Paris, 1847.

Of the earlier classical writers the most interesting accounts of the Georgian lands are to be found in Xenophon and Strabo; of the later, Procopius (*De bello persico* and *De aedificiis*) and Constantine Porphyrogenitus (*De administrando imperio*), are the most reliable and instructive.

I. Pomyalovskii, *Sbornik Grecheskikh i Latinskikh Nadpisei Kavkaza*, Spb, 1881, gives some record of the sparse archæological remains of the

BIBLIOGRAPHIES AND NOTES

Classic period. See also *Iz. Kav. I.-A.I.*, Vol. IV, pp. 71–88, S. TER-AVETISSIAN, " Kurgani Khasan-Kali ".

For a summary of Armenian topographical knowledge of these regions in the post-Classic period see:

M. J. de SAINT-MARTIN, *Mémoires Historiques et Géographiques sur l'Arménie*, 2 vols., Paris, 1818, of which Vol. I contains a valuable " Mémoire sur la Géographie de l'Arménie ".

L. ALISHAN, *Physiographie de l'Arménie*, Venice, 1861.

J. VARD DASHIAN, *La population arménienne de la région comprise entre la Mer Noire et Erzerum, traduit de l'arménien par F. Macler*, Vienna, 1922.

C. F. LEHMANN-HAUPT, *Armenien Einst und Jetzt*, Berlin, Vol. I, 1910, Vol. II, 1926, Vol. III, 1928. The last volume particularly contains much interesting topographical material for the Classic and post-Classic periods.

For the general political topography of Georgia in relation to the Armenian Kingdom reference should be made to:

J. DE MORGAN, *Histoire du Peuple Arménien*, Paris, 1919.

J. KALATYANTZ, *Armyanskie Arshakidi v " Istorii Armenii Moiseya Khorenskago "*, published as Vol. XIV of *Trudi Vost. Ot. I.R.A.O.*, Moscow, 1903.

For the etymology of Caucasian geographical names, the following sources may also be consulted:

L. M. MELIKSET-BEKOV, *Vvedenie v Istoriyu Gosudarstvennikh Obrazovanie Yugo-Kavkaza*, Tiflis, 1924.

Trudi Kommissii po Izucheniya Sostava Plemen Kavkaza, 3, (1920), N. Y. MARR, " Natzionalnii sostav Naseleniya Kavkaza "; 4, (1922), *idem.*, " Talishi " (indicating the " Japhetic " relationship through the evidence of place-names of these Persian-speaking communities of the Caspian littoral); 5, (1922), *idem.*, " Kavkazskiya Plemenniya Nazvaniya ".

Sbor. Mat., Vol. XL (1909), Part III, pp. 1–28, A. M. DIRR, " Sovremenniya Nazvaniya Kavkazskikh Plemen ".

Ibid., Part III (bis), pp. 1–164, K. GAN, " Opit obyasneniya Kavkazskikh Geograficheskikh Nazvanii ".

Ibid., Vol. XX, Part II, pp. 1–38, E. G. VEIDENBAUM, " Materiali dlya Istorico-Geograficheskago Slovarya Kavkaza ".

On cave-dwellings and, in general, peasant-architecture in the Caucasus, the following may be consulted:

PANTYUKHOV, *O Peshchernikh i pozdneishdikh jilishchakh na Kavkaze*, Tiflis, 1896.

Novie Vostok, Vol. XV, pp. 212–221, V. A. GURKO-KRYAJIN, " Tsiklopicheskie sooruzheniya Zakavazya " (contains notes of several interesting articles published on the subject in Tiflis periodicals).

Cf. also *Iz. Kav. I.-A.I.*, Vol. III, pp. 97–108, S. LISITZIAN, " K izucheniu Armyanskikh Krestyanskikh Zhilishch "; *ibid.*, Vol. IV, pp. 55–70, *idem.*, " Krestyanskie Zhilishcha Visokoi Armenii ".

Sbor. Mat., Vol. VII, Part II, pp. 37–50, B. KIKNADZE, " Pamyatniki Drevnosti Telavskago Uezda "; *ibid.*, Vol. XIII, pp. 128–132, T. Sinakoev, " Samsarskiya Peshcheri ".

Armeniaca, Fasc. I, pp. 15–38, STRZYGOWSKI, " Armenien und die vorromanische Holzbaukunst im Europa "; also pp. 39–114, J. SCHWIEGER, " Haus und Holz als Grundlage zur Entwicklung der Grosskunst in die Vorder-Asiatische Hochlandzone ".

BIBLIOGRAPHICAL NOTES TO BOOK II (CHAPTERS VI TO X)

The Georgian sources for the Middle Ages are collated in M. F. Brosset's *Histoire de la Géorgie*, 1ière partie, Spb, 1849.

For a valuable summary of and commentary on Greek, Armenian and Musulman sources, Brosset's volume of *Additions et Eclairissements à l'Histoire de la Géorgie*, Spb, 1851, should also be consulted, notably:

Add. XI. "Histoire des Bagratides, d'après les auteurs arméniens et grecs jusqu'au commencement du XIe siècle."

Add. XI. "Rapports entre la Géorgie et la Grèce sous Bagrat IV."

Add. XVII. "Concernant le règne de Thamar."

Add. XVIII. "Renseignements sur les règnes de Giorgi Lacha et de Rousoudan."

Add. XXII. "Expéditions de Timour en Géorgie."

The Musulman sources are numerous; Yakubi for the ninth century; el-Masudi, el-Istakhri, ibn-Haukal and el-Mukadassi for the tenth century; el-Idrissi and ibn-Alathir for the twelfth century; Yakuti (el-Bakuli) for the thirteenth century; Abu'l Fida and ibn-Batuta for the fourteenth century. There are two useful summaries of Musulman accounts of the Caucasus: (*a*) "Fragments de Géographes et d'Historiens arabes et persans inédits" by Defrémery in the volumes of *J.A.* for the years 1849–1853; (*b*) "Svedeniya arabskikh pisatelei o Kavkaze Armenii i Azerbeidjhane" by N. A. Karaulov in *Sbor. Mat.*, Vols. XXIX, XXXI and XXXII; see also d'Ohsson, *Des Peuples du Caucase au Xme siècle*, Paris, 1828.

Of Byzantine sources the following may be noted: Constantine Porphyrogenitus for the tenth century; Nicephorus Bryennius, Cedrenus and Zonaras for the twelfth century; Pachymeres for the thirteenth century; Nicephorus Gregoras for the fourteenth century; and Chalchodyles for the fifteenth century. Extracts from the principal Byzantine writers may be found in Stritter's *Memoriae populorum olim ad Danubium, Pontum Euxinum, Paludem Maeotidem, Caucasum, Mare Caspium et inde magis ad Septentrionem incolentium e scriptoribus historiae Byzantinae erutae et digestae*, Spb, 1779. *Sbor. Mat.*, Vol. IX, contains extracts from Stritter by K. Hahn (or Gan).

Armenian sources are the most detailed: the principal are:

(1) *Seventh century*, Bishop Sebeos who gives an account of the Arab invasion. (French translation in *J.A.*, VIe Série, Vol. 7).

(2) *Seventh century*, Bishop Ghevond (French translation by Shahnazarian, *Histoire des guerres des arabes en Arménie*, Paris, 1857).

(3) *Tenth century*, Hovhannes Gathoughipos (John Catholicos), *History of Armenia to the year 925* (translated by Saint-Martin, *Histoire d'Arménie par le Patriarche Jean*, Paris, 1841).

(4) *Tenth century*, Toumas (Thomas) Artzruni of the royal house of Van. (French translation by Brosset in *Collection d'Historiens Arméniens*, Vol. I, Spb., 1874.)

BIBLIOGRAPHIES AND NOTES

(5) *Twelfth century*, Mateos Arhaetsi (Matthew of Urfa) wrote an Armenian Chronicle covering the period 963–1129; another author continued it to 1162. Valuable material for the period of the Seljuk invasions and the Crusades. (French translation by ED. DULAURIER in *Bibliothèque historique Arménienne*, Paris, 1858.)

(6) *Twelfth century*, Samuel Anetsi (of Ani) wrote a chronological work of real value to 1179, which is continued by an unknown author to 1358. (French translation by BROSSET, Spb, 1876.)

(7) *Thirteenth century*, Guiragos Kantsaketsi (of Ganja) gives a realistic description of life in the Caucasus under the Mongols (French translation by BROSSET, *Guiragos de Kantzah : Histoire d'Arménie*, Spb, 1870).

(8) *Thirteenth century*. Bartsr-Perttsi (Vardan) called " the Great " on account of his multifarious writings. (For summary of his geographical materials see SAINT-MARTIN, *Mém. sur l'Arménie*, II, 407–71.)

(9) *Thirteenth century*. Mekhitar Airevanetsi wrote at the end of the thirteenth century a chronology of great value to 1289. (French translation by BROSSET, " Hist. Chronologique par Mkhitar d'Airivank " in *Mém. de l'Acad. des Sciences de Spb*, VIIième série., Vols. 13–14–15, 1869.)

(10) *Thirteenth century*. Stepan Orbeliani, Metropolitan of Siuniq (Karabagh) wrote a history of the principality of Siuniq, with many personal details.

(11) *Fifteenth century*. Toumas Medzopetsi, born in the Monastery of Medzop in Arjish, north of Lake Van, early in the fifteenth century, wrote a history of his times, referring chiefly to the struggle between the Timurids and the Turcomans, Kurds and Armenians. (Extract translated into French by FÉLIX NÈVE in *Bulletin de l'Académie Royale de Belgique*, 1867.)

H. F. B. LYNCH's *Armenia : Travels and Studies*, Vol. I, contains the best account in English of the mediæval Armenian kingdoms, and Vol. II contains an excellent bibliography of the subject. In SIR HENRY HOWORTH's *History of the Mongols*, Part III, are buried numerous extracts from Greek, Georgian, Armenian and Musulman sources, on the history of the Caucasus during the Mongol period.

For the relations of the Emperors of Trebizond with Georgia, see KHAKHANOV, A. S., *Trapezundskaya Khronika Mikhaila Panareta, Grecheskii Tekst*, Moscow, 1905. USPENSKI, F. I., *Ocherki iz istorii Trapezuntskoi Imperii*, Leningrad, 1929. Idem., *Seminarium Kondakovanium*, Vol. I, an article on the relations between Trebizond, Byzantium and Georgia, " Videlenie Trapezunta iz sostava Vizantiiskoi Imperii ".

For Georgian Numismatics see :

BARTHOLOMAEI, J. *Lettres Numismatiques et archéologiques relatives à la Transcaucasie*, Spb, 1859.
BARATOV. *Numizmaticheskie fakti Gruzinskago Tsarstva*, Spb, 1844.
BROSSET, M. F. *Rapport sur l'ouvrage intitulé,* " *Num. fakti gruz. Tzar* " ; *et Revue de Numismatique Géorgienne*, Spb, 1847.
LANGLOIS, V. *Numismatique de la Géorgie au Moyen Age*, Paris, 1852.
Essai de Classification des Suites Monétaires de la Géorgie, depuis l'antiquite jusqu'à nos jours, Paris, 1860.
PAKHOMOV. *Moneti Gruzii*, I, *Domongolskii Period*, Spb, 1910. (? later parts not published.)

BIBLIOGRAPHIES AND NOTES

Book II. Note F

PROVISIONAL LIST OF THE GEORGIAN KINGS OF THE FIRST TO FIFTH CENTURY A.D.

Georgian Source	Foreign Source	Recognized by Modern Historians as probably
ARDEKI	?	ARDEKI (?–30)
KARTAMI or KARRAMI	MITHRIDATES	MIHRDAT I (30–35)
FARSMAN I	PARASMAN	FARSMAN I (35–70)
AZORK or ARSOK II	MITHRIDATES	MIHRDAT II (70–96)
AMAZASPI	—	AMAZASP I (96–116)
FARSMAN KWELI "the good"	PARSMAN II	FARSMAN II (116–40)
ROKI	—	ROKI (140–6)
GHADAM or ADAMI	—	ADAMI (146) 20 days only
FARSMAN III	—	FARSMAN III (146–64)
AM(A)ZASP II	—	AMAZASP II (164–82)
REV MARTALI	—	REV MARTALI (182–90), "The Truthful"
VACHÉ	—	VACHÉ (190–208)
BAKUR I	—	BAKUR I (208–16)
MIHRDAT III	—	MIHRDAT III (216–24)
ASPAGURI	—	ASPAGUR I (224–65)
REVI (bis)	—	LEVI (265–300)
MIREANI	MERIBANES MERIHANES	MIRIANI (300–62)
BAKUR II	—	BAKUR II (362–4)
TRDATI	—	TRDATI (364–8)
SAURMAG I	SAUROMACES	SAURMAG I (368)
AS-PAKURI or WARAZ-BAKURI	ASPAKUR	ASPAGUR II (368–393)
—	ASPAKUR and SAUROMACES	Dual kingship ASPAGUR-SAURMAGI (369–90)
BAKUR III	BAKURIOS	BAKUR III (393–401)
FARSMAN IV	PARASMANIOS	FARSMAN IV (402–10)
BUZMIHR	BUSMURIOS	BUZMARI (410–25)
MIHRDAT IV	—	MIHRDAT IV (425–8)
ARCHILI	ARCILIOS	ARCHILI (428–38)
MIHRDAT V	—	MIHRDAT V (438–50)
WAKHTANG I	—	WAKHTANG I (450–503)

N.B.—After the death of Wakhtang, Iberia passed into the hands of the Persians, who, some thirty years later, abolished kingship in Georgia.

The Georgian sources give about the following kings during this period, Daché, Bakur IV, Farsman V, Bakur V. (See "*Moktsevai Kartlisai*" (*The Conversion of Georgia*) in Jordania's *Kronikebi*, I, 55-57.) The last two authentic kings were Gurgeni 518–23 (revolted against the Persians) and Jamanarsé 527.

Kingship was abolished in 527–32.

BIBLIOGRAPHIES AND NOTES
Book II. Note G
ON THE ORIGIN OF THE BAGRATIDS

At the time of the Emperor Justin (518–27) Gurgeni, King of Iberia, rose against the Persians, but after being defeated, fled to Lazica whence he went to Byzantium in 523.

After his flight the Iberians tried to put on the throne a new king by name Jamanarsé, who in 527 went to Byzantium and received assurances of friendship from the Emperor Justinian (527–65). But all such attempts on the part of the Iberians met with vigorous opposition from the Persian Shah who denied the Iberians the right to enthrone their king.

In 532, the Persian Shah Khusraw (Chosroes) I and the Emperor Justinian concluded the so-called " Eternal Treaty ". One of the items of this treaty was that the Iberian refugees were permitted, if they so wished, to return to Iberia. Many returned, but many also, mistrusting the Persians, remained in Byzantium. Among the latter was King Gurgeni, his family and suite.[1]

Thus even after the " Eternal Treaty " Iberia was to be without a king,[2] and it is clear that this treaty contained no clause or even allusion concerning the kingship in Iberia. This must have been passed over in silence by the Byzantine Emperor, for the Persian Shah entrusted the government of Iberia to a *Marzpan* whose seat he placed in Tiflis, no doubt because Mtzkheta, as the centre of Christianity and of Georgian tradition, was regarded as unsuitable.

Marzpan is a Persian word meaning " guardian (= *pan*) of frontiers " (= *marz*), that is a governor of border provinces. There had been previous appointments of *Marzpans* in Iberia by the Persian Shahs, i.e. actually during the period of the native kingship, but then they were only representatives of the Shah at the court of the Iberian kings, whereas since the " Eternal Treaty " they became the effective administrators of Iberia.

The information of Procopius on the abolition of kingship in Iberia is confirmed by *Kartlis Tzkhovreba* who ascribed this event to the time following the death of King Bakur V.

> " Died King Bakuri ", we read in this Chronicle, " leaving young sons who could not retain the royal power. Then the Persian Shah Urmizd gave Ran and Movakan to his son, Kasré Ambarviz, who came and sat at Bardava (Pertav). He entered into negotiations with the Kartlian *eristavni*, promised them great benefits, confirmed on them hereditarily their *saeristaoni*, and thus by flattery won them over. Each of the *eristavni* declared himself independent and paid contribution to Kasré. The sons of Bakuri remained in Mtiuleti and in Kakheti, while the descendants of Mihrdati, son of Wakhtang Gurgaslani who owned Klarjeti and Javakheti, remained in the rocky fastnesses of Klarjeti."
>
> " Some years after this ", we read in Queen Mary's version of the Chronicle, " internal strife broke out in Persia. . . . Then Kasré Ambarviz left Kartli and Ran and went to help his father. When the Persians were thus preoccupied, the Georgian *eristavni* of the upper and lower country, having agreed among themselves, sent an embassy to the Greek Emperor, asking him to appoint over them a king from the descendants of the Georgian kings, leaving however the *eristavni* undisturbed in their *saeristaoni*. The Emperor acceded to their request and appointed as their king the son of the sister of Mihrdati, son of Wakhtang (Gurgaslani) and his Greek queen (Wakhtang's second wife was a Byzantine princess) who was called Guaram. The Emperor conferred upon this Guaram the title of *Kuropalat* and sent him to Mtzkheta. The children of King Bakuri, descendants of Daché, (another) son of Wakhtang, whom Wakhtang had appointed as king, remained in Kakheti, and having taken possession of Kukheti (= Kakheti in *Kartlis Tzkhovreba*) and of Hereti from the

---

[1] See *De bello persico*, I, 22.   [2] *Ibid.*, I, 28.

Yori, settled in Ujarma and ruled under Guaram Kuropalat" (Queen Mary's version, p. 190).

Thus according to the most ancient text of *Kartlis Tzkhovreba*, in so far as it has been preserved in the version of Queen Mary, Guaram is not a Bagratid. *Moktsevai Kartlisai* also does not even so much as hint that Guaram was a Bagratid. In the Armenian translation of *Kartlis Tzkhovreba* this period is omitted and contains no information about Bakuri and Guaram (see Brosset's *Additions*, p. 46). From among the Georgian sources Guaram is made a Bagratid only in the *History* of Sumbat Davitisdze.

The Bagratids claim descent from King David the slayer of Goliath. That is why on their coat-of-arms they have a catapult (with which David killed Goliath), David's harp, scales, and the seamless robe of Christ, which was brought from Jerusalem to Iberia immediately after the Crucifixion. The coat-of-arms bears an inscription taken also from the Psalms of David.

D. Bakradze in his *History of Wakhushti* states:

"For our part we must state here that although we do not deny the relationship of the Armenian Bagratids, we have no unshakeable and conclusive evidence of when and how this relationship began, in the information collected and quoted by Brosset. That the Armenian Bagratids ruled Taos-Kari or the present Chorokhi valley before the tenth century is not only doubtful, but even archæological facts are against it, for by the evidence of these facts no trace whatever of the Armenian Bagratids is found anywhere in the Chorokhi valley either in the tenth century or before."

Some twenty years ago, E. Taqaishvili discovered a collection of manuscripts containing seventy-seven different articles, one of which, entitled "*Brief Information on Georgian History*", is a most important document showing that the Bagratids began to rule Georgia in the eighth century, and that the first Bagratid was Adarnasé who died in 779.

Analysing this MS., Taqaishvili says (see *Sakartvelos Sidzveleni*, Vol. II, p. 57):

"It is a fact that in the *History of Sumbat* and in the Wakhtang version of *Kartlis Tzkhovreba* the Bagratid dynasty is said to have begun with Guaram Kuropalat (575–600), but it is not true. Our most ancient sources, namely, the *Conversion of Georgia* and Queen Mary's *Life of Kartli*, do not know Guaram and succeeding *eristavni* till Adarnasé, father of Ashot Kuropalat, as Bagratids. The historian Sumbat in his *History of the Bagratids* wanted to enhance the prestige of the Bagratids, not only by their long genealogy, but also by their long reign in Georgia. For this reason he connected them with King David the Prophet, and made the first Eristavi-Kuropalat a Bagratid.

"This tendencious account in Sumbat's *History* was introduced into *Kartlis Tzkhovreba* by King Wakhtang VI's reproduction from Sumbat's own *History*. Our source (the above-mentioned article of the collection) clearly shows that the Bagratids began their rule in Georgia from the time of Adarnasé and his son Ashot Kuropalat from the end of the thirteenth Georgian chronicon, that is from 780."—(For document, see *ibid.*, p. 60.)

This document also reveals some unknown kings, as for instance King Zurabi, son of David Aghmashenebeli, and David and Melkisedeki, Kings of Alastani (in Javakheti, north-west of Akhalkalaki). It is evident from this document that Alastani had been formed temporarily into a kingdom during the Mongol invasions in the thirteenth and fourteenth centuries. The Kings of Alastani so far known are:

Giorgi
David } thirteenth century.
Melkisedeki
Adroniké   fourteenth century.

BIBLIOGRAPHICAL NOTES TO BOOK III (CHAPTERS XI TO XVIII)

The principal sources for the history of Georgia between the fifteenth and the beginning of the nineteenth century are published by BROSSET in his *Histoire de la Géorgie*, 2ième partie, Histoire Moderne, 1^{ière} livraison, 1856, 2ième livraison, 1857.

The 1^{ière} livraison contains the important provincial histories of Kartli, Kakheti, Samtzkhé and Imereti, compiled by Prince Wakhushti, and the valuable genealogical tables compiled by Brosset. Extracts are also included from the works of the Armenian Arakel of Tabriz, of the Persian Iskander Munji, and of the Georgian Farsadan Giorgijanidze, for the period sixteenth to seventeenth century.

The 2ième livraison includes the Chronicles of Sekhnia Chkheidze and of Papuna Orbeliani for the eighteenth century, and the Life of King Irakli II by Oman Kherkéulidze.

MIANSAROV, *Bibliographia Caucasica et Transcaucasica*, Vol. I, pp. 561-804, gives a bibliography for the history of Georgia, and particularly for the relations of Russia with the Caucasus down to 1876. His list of articles published in *Gazeta Kavkaz, Zakavkazskie Vestnik, Kavkazskie Kalendar*, and other rare periodicals is very valuable. His Chronological Notes, pp. 588-675, are also important.

The following works should also be consulted:

NOVIKOV. *Drevnaya Rossiiskaya Biblioteka*, Spb, 1788.
(20 volumes containing much original material for the relations of Russia with the Caucasus, Georgia and Persia.)

BROSSET, M. F. *Chronique Géorgienne*, Paris, 1831.
(Includes an interesting account of Shah Abbas' invasion, and the life of Giorgi Saakadze.)

BELOKUROV, S. A. *Snosheniya Rossii s Kavkazom*, I (1578-1613), Moscow, 1889.
(Published valuable documents particularly on relations between Russia and Persia.)

TSAGARELI. *Snosheniya Rossii s Kavkazom v XVI-XVIII stoletiyakh*, Spb, 1891.
(Valuable source materials.)

Idem. Gramoti i drugie istoricheskie dokumenti XVIII stoletya otnosyashchiesya do Gruzii, 3 vols., Spb, 1891, 1898, 1902.

Peripiska na inostrannikh yazikakh gruzinskikh Tzarei s Rossiiskimi Gosudaryami ot 1639 g. do 1770 g. published by R.A.N., Spb, 1861.

IOSSELIAN, PLATON. *Istoricheskii vzglyad na sostoyanie Gruzii pod vlastei Tzarei-Magometan*, Tiflis, 1849. See also *Akti*, II and III, for other material by Iosselian.

AVALOV, Z. (Avalishvili). *Prisoedinenie Gruzii k Rossii*, Spb, 1906.
(A valuable summary of the relations between Georgia and Russia.)

BIBLIOGRAPHIES AND NOTES

BRONEVSKII, S. *Noveishiya geographicheskiya istoricheskiya izvestiya o Kavkaze*, 2 vols., Moscow, 1823.

(Useful information on the state of Georgia at date of Russian Conquest.)

KUCHAEV. *Polozheniya v krestyanakh i poselyanakh Zakavkazya*, 3 vols., Tiflis, 1886.

LISHIN, A. A. *Akti otnoshyashchiesya k istorii Voiska Donskogo*, 4 vols., Novocherkask, 1891, 1894.

BADDELEY, JOHN F. *The Russian Conquest of the Caucasus*, London, 1908.

(The only satisfactory work in English on the subject, based on the *Akti* and other primary sources.)

DUBROVIN. *Istoriya voini i vladichestva Russkikh na Kavkaze*, 3 vols., Spb, 1871.

The following three foreign sources are also useful:

Sixteenth century, *Don Juan of Persia: a Shiah Catholic* (1560–1604), edited with notes by GUY LESTRANGE, London, 1928.

Eighteenth century, KRUSINSKI, *History of the Revolutions of Persia*, 2 vols., published by Pemberton, J., London, 1728.

HANWAY, JONAS. *A Historical Account of the British Trade across the Caspian Sea, with a Journal of Travels*, 4 vols., London, 1753.

(The historical sections of Hanway's work are based largely on Krusinski.)

CHAPTER XIII

Note H.—On the Persian Succession in 1576 [1]

In the account of the intrigues for the Persian Succession which followed the death of Shah Tahmasp in May 1576 I have adhered to the authority of Wakhushti who is, in general, confirmed by other Georgian sources. Although the Georgian sources throw a new light on that confused moment of Persian history, there are certain discrepancies, when comparison is made with Persian and Turkish sources, which are difficult to clarify.

The Turkish sources used by von Hammer and the Persian sources referred to by Malcolm and later historians, including Browne, make it clear that, at the date of Tahmasp's death, the two factions contending for power were a Georgian faction allied with the chief of the Ustajlu (Kizilbash) Turkomans and a " Cherkess " faction which was supported by the Afshar and others of the Kizilbash tribes. Wakhushti states categorically that Muhammad Khuda-banda was the son of Tahmasp by Shaliqashvili's daughter (cf. Brosset, *H. de la G.*, II, i, 217, and note 2; *ibid.*, II, i, 35, and *Suite des Annales*, II, i, 362). Tahmasp married the Meskhian princess in 1548, so that Muhammad Khuda-banda could not have been more than 28 when his father died. On the other hand, Turkish and Persian sources agree that he was the eldest son of Tahmasp, and that he was about 43 at the time of Tahmasp's death (cf. also *Venetians in Persia, Narrative of Vincentio d'Alessandri*, p. 214). A second son, Ismail, according to Vincentio, was two years younger, and a third son, Haydar, the victim of the first palace-revolution, was only eighteen.

Wakhushti ignores the existence of Haydar, allows the prior succession of Ismail, and finally brings in Khuda-banda, whom he does not claim to have been the eldest son.

I think that the varying statements may be reconciled as follows:

(1) Shaliqashvili's daughter married Shah Tahmasp in 1548, and retained a great influence with him, as is exemplified by the Persian support for her relatives in Samtzkhé (Brosset, *H. de la G.*, II, i, 218 *et sqq.*).

(2) She was the mother, not of Khuda-banda, but of Haydar, who, if he were eighteen in 1576, was born in 1558, ten years after the marriage. The existence of Haydar is ignored by Wakhushti, who, however, emphasizes the continuing influence of the dowager at court during the reign of Khuda-banda. Von Hammer, following the Turkish historian, Ali, indicates that Haydar was protected by two Georgian uncles, Ali and Sal (Zaal). Haydar had another brother, Bahram, and two half-brothers, Mustafa and Imam-Quli, sons of Tahmasp by " a Georgian slave " (von Hammer, VII, 72-4). Don Juan says that Mustafa's mother was " a Christian princess from Georgia " (*Don Juan*, p. 129).

(3) Whether Tahmasp died, as is indicated by Don Juan and Wakhushti,

[1] I dealt cursorily with this question in my " Notes on Don Juan of Persia's Account of Georgia " in *B.S.O.S.* (September, 1930), but have here modified some of the views expressed in that paper.

or was murdered, as in von Hammer's and Malcolm's sources, by the mother of Haydar, an attempt was made on the night of his death by the chief of the Ustajlu tribe with the Georgian adventurers who were the blood-relations of the young prince, to make Haydar Shah.

(4) The opposing faction reacted quickly. They had an ally in the harim, Perijan-Khanum ("the little fairy lady"), a daughter of Tahmasp by a "Cherkess" princess. According to Don Juan (p. 130) the Shamkhal was her uncle; von Hammer is in agreement with this, although Malcolm calls him her "brother".

There are several "Shamkhals" referred to by different writers on this period, and they cannot all have been the reigning Shamkhal (of Tarku) in Daghestan. Of this family, the first that we can identify is the Shamkhal Kara-Musal (Brosset's "Genealogical Tree of Kakheti") whose daughter, in 1529, became the unhallowed consort of King Levan II of Kakheti. If Kara-Musal was the reigning Shamkhal in 1576, he would have been between 80 and 90, but he may have been "the old Prince Shamkhal" of Don Juan. At any rate the reigning Shamkhal was in Daghestan during the campaign of Lala Mustafa in Georgia in the summer of 1578, and on October 5 of that year both the Shamkhal and his brother Burhan-Melikeddin made their submission to the Turks (von Hammer, II, 91; cf. also *Don Juan*, p. 148). During the same winter, however, while Uzdemir-Osman Pasha at Derbend was celebrating his marriage with the Shamkhal's daughter, he professed to have discovered that his father-in-law was plotting with the Persians and had the old man executed (von Hammer, VII, 97, and *Don Juan*, p. 153). The Shamkhal's son, Imam-Quli-Khan, who had held a command in the Persian army at Chaldir (Brosset, *H. de la G.*, II, i, 457), then joined Simon of Kartli who was blockading Tiflis (von Hammer, VII, 91 and 97; *Don Juan*, pp. 140, 154–5, note 6, and Brosset, *H. de la G.*, II, i, 415, note 4). It would appear then that the Shamkhal's line was as follows:

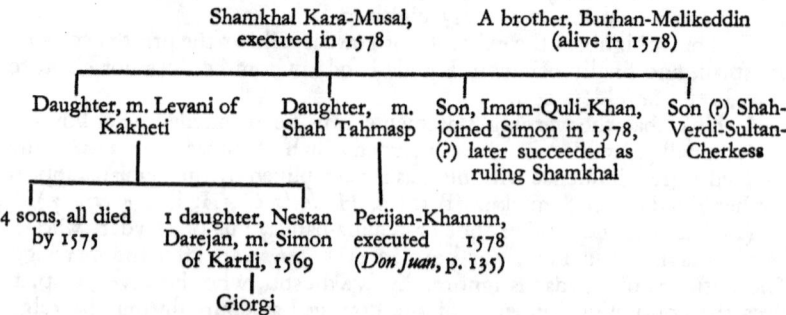

The identity of the Shamkhal who was active in Kazvin on the death of Shah Tahmasp, who was the uncle of Perijan-Khanum, and who, according to Malcolm's sources, was executed with her on the accession of Khuda-banda, is not clear. Don Juan, who persists in calling both "Christians" and "Georgian noblemen", distinguishes between the reigning Shamkhal and the intriguer in Kazvin. Yet the other sources are clear that the latter was a "Cherkess" prince. He cannot have been Burhan-Melikeddin nor Imam-Quli-Khan, who both survived the death of Perijan-Khanum. He can only have been another son of the reigning Shamkhal and a brother of Imam-Quli-Khan. I think that he may be identified as a certain Shah-Verdi-Sultan-Cherkess or Sultan-Shamkhal, who is mentioned only by Iskander Munji, and who as governor of Shaki in 1568 took part in the operations against Simon of Kartli (cf. Brosset, *H. de la G.*, II, i, 454; cf. also p. 33). This Shah-Verdi-Sultan-Cherkess is confused with Shah-Verdi-Sultan-Ziad-oghlu-Kajar, who was *beglar-beg* of Ganja in 1556 (Brosset, *H. de la G.*, II, i, 30–1), was defeated by the Georgians at Garisi in 1558 (*ibid.*, and pp. 349–50), defeated Simon I at Dzegwi in 1561 (*ibid.*, pp. 153 *et sqq.*) and led the expedition in which the other Shah-Verdi took part in 1568. Shah-Verdi, the Kajar, took refuge with Alexander of Kakheti in 1579, during the campaign of Simon in Kartli, and was delivered by Alexander to the Turks (cf. *Chronique Géorgienne*, p. 21). Shah-Verdi-Sultan-Cherkess does not appear again after 1570. I think that he was another son of the old Shamkhal, a brother of Imam-Quli-Khan and the uncle in Kazvin of Perijan-Khanum.

(5) When the "Shamkhal" and Perijan-Khanum murdered Haydar and installed Ismail, the rival faction fled from Kazvin with the two sons of Tahmasp by "a Christian princess of Georgia"—Mustafa and Imam-Quli (von Hammer, VII, 72). Ismail, however, caused the death of all his brothers, with the exception of Muhammad Khuda-banda.

(6) When Ismail died in September–November (?) 1578 and Khuda-banda became Shah, Perijan-Khanum and her uncle "Shamkhal", identifiable with our Shah-Verdi-Sultan-Cherkess or Shamkhal, were executed. The Georgian faction were behind Khuda-banda, and Tahmasp's dowager, the daughter of Shaliqashvili, was in the ascendant. But the former allies of her faction, Da'ud Khan in Kartli and Alexander in Kakheti, were intriguing with the Turks. She therefore turned to Simon, who as an ally of the Shamkhal's party had already been set at liberty by Ismail. Simon had his own interests and willingly accepted her favour.

(7) There is also a certain Isa Khan, whom Don Juan (p. 129) mentions as a supporter of Haydar. Le Strange identifies him with Zaal, the Georgian noble mentioned by von Hammer, the Zalchan of Minadoi and Knolles. But I am inclined to see in Isa, Yésé, a younger son of Levani and full brother of Alexander of Kakheti (Brosset, *H. de la G.*, II, i, 153). According to Iskander Munji, this Isa Khan was imprisoned together with Simon at Alamut, and was liberated with him by Shah Ismail (*ibid.*, p. 455). I think that here he is confusing him with Archili, son of Wakhtangi, Prince of Mukhrani (cf. *ibid.*, p. 34, "Ismail made King Simon come, and brought Archili also from Shiraz").

On the accession of Khuda-banda, Isa Khan was certainly in favour. He was given the daughter of Sam-Mirza, a brother of Tahmasp, in marriage, and was made governor of Shaki (*ibid.*, p. 456), but before very long he had to take flight before the army of Lala Mustafa. He died soon afterwards (Brosset's "Genealogical Tree of Kakheti", *ibid.*).

BIBLIOGRAPHICAL NOTES TO BOOK IV (CHAPTERS XIX TO XXVII)

Javakhishvili, *Sakartvelos Ekonomiuri Istoria*, Vol. I, published by Kartuli Dsigni, Tiflis, 1930.
Idem. *Kartveli Eris Istoria*, 3 vols., Tiflis, 1928, 1929.
Idem. *Kartuli Samartlis Istoria*, 3 vols., published by Tpilisis Universiteti, Tiflis, 1928–1929.
Idem. *Istoriis mizani dsqaroebi da metodebi dsinat da akhla*, Vol. I.
Dzveli Kartuli saistorio Mdserloba (V–XVIII), Tiflis, 1921.
Atonis Iveriis Monastris 1074 dslis Kheltnadseri Aghapebit, published by the Saeklisio Museumi, Tiflis, 1901.
E. Taqaishvili, *Khelmdsipis Karis Garigeba* in *Monumenta Georgica*, Vol. IV, Leges, N. 1, published by Tpilisis Universiteti, Tiflis, 1920.
S. Kakabadze, *Saistorio Dziebani*, Tiflis, 1924.
I. Sabanisdze, *Dsminda Modsame Abo Tpileli*, published by Sakartvelos Saegzarkhos Saeklesio Museumis, N. 3, Tiflis, 1899.
Yakob Khutsesi, *Dsamebai Dsmidisa Shushanikisi*, Kutais, 1917.
Th. Jordania, *Istoriuli Sabutebi Shio-Mghvimis Monastrisa da Dzegli Vahkhanis Kvabta*, Tiflis, 1896.
Idem. *Zaveshchanie Tzaria Davida Vozobnoviteliya dannoe Shio-Mgvimskoi Lavre v 1123*, Tiflis, 1895.
S. Kakabadze, *Saistorio Krebuli*, 5 vols., Tiflis, 1928.
G. M. Sabinini, *Sakartvelos Samotkhé*, Spb, 1882.

Sakartvelos Sidzveleni, 3 vols., published under the editorship of Prof. E. Taqaishvili, by the Georgian Historical and Ethnographic Society, Tiflis, 1899, 1909, 1910.
Dzveli Sakartvelo, 2 vols., published by the above mentioned Society, Tiflis, 1909, 1913.
(These volumes give much valuable material for the social, political and economic history of Georgia. They contain, particularly the former, about a thousand *sigelni, gujarni*, legislative acts, etc., covering a period of over a thousand years.)
Sigel Grusinskago Tsaria Bagrata IV (1027–1072) by E. Taqaishvili, see *Zap. Vost. Ot. I.R.A.O.*, Vol. IX, pp. 56–68.
Gujar Baratovykh iz Betanii, by E. Taqaishvili, *ibid.*, Vol. VIII, pp. 113–128.

For comparison of Armenian with Georgian social conditions, see *Armeniaca*, (im Verlag der Asia Major, Leipzig), Fasc. II, pp. 11–113, A. Sorian, *Die soziale gliederung des Armenischen Volkes im Mittelalter*.

For the history of the Georgian Church the following may be consulted :

Michel Tamarati, *L'Église Géorgienne des Origines jusqu'à nos jours*, Rome, 1910.
K. Tzinadze, *Autokephaliya Tzerkvi Gruzinskoi*, Tiflis, 1905.
N. Pokrovskii, *Kratkii Ocherk tzerkovnoi-istoricheskoi jizni pravoslavnoi Gruzii*, Tiflis, 1905.

BIBLIOGRAPHIES AND NOTES

M. ABDASHKEVICH, *Sv. Nina*, Tiflis, 1912.

DADESH-KELIANI, PRINCE, I. *The Autocephaly of the Georgian Church*, London, 1922.

O. DE LEBEDEV, *Codex 689 du Vatican, histoire de la conversion des Géorgiens au Christianisme par le patriarche Macaire d'Antioche, traduite de l'arabe*, Rome, 1905. (XIVth Congress of Orientalists.)

Iz. R.A.N., Vol. X, 1899, pp. 416 *et sqq.* O. VON LEMM, "Zur Geschichte der Bekehrung der Iberer zur Christentum"; *ibid.*, Séries VI, 1907, pp. 433-46 and 511-36, I. A. JAVAKHOV (Javakhishvili) for the history of the Church schism between Georgia and Armenia at the beginning of the seventh century.

Peradze, G. Die Probleme Der Älteste Kirchengeschichte Georgiens (*to appear in Oriens Christianus.*)

BIBLIOGRAPHICAL NOTES TO BOOK V (CHAPTERS XXVII TO XXX)

Bibliographical Notes to Chapter XXVII

MEDIÆVAL GEORGIAN ART.

(a) *General.*—O. M. DALTON, *Byzantine Art and Archæology*, 1912; *East Christian Art*, 1925. CH. DIEHL, *Manuel d'Art Byzantin*, 2 vols., 1926; J. STRZYGOWSKI, *Die Baukunst der Armenier; Altai-Iran und Volkerwanderung*; *Die Bildende Kunst des Ostens*, and other works. I. TOLSTOI and N. KONDAKOV, *Russkaya Drevnosti*: Part IV, "Khristianskaya Drevnosti Krima, Kavkaza i Kieva", Spb, 1891. KONDAKOV, *Emaux Byzantines*, Frankfort-am-Main, 1892; E. BLOCHET, *Mussulman Painting*, 1930; F. MACLER, *Miniatures Arméniennes*, Paris, 1913; *Documents d'Art Arméniens*, with Atlas, 1924; *L'Enluminure Arménienne aux VIe et VIIe siècles*.

(b) *Georgia.*—*Mat. Kav.*, Vol. III, for churches of Dranda, Mokvi, Ilori, Bedia, Kutais Cathedral, Martvili Monastery, Mamatzminda, Opisa, Porta, Dolis-Khana, Yeni-Rabat and Tbeti; Vol. IV, pp. 1–34, for churches of Abkhazeti; pp. 35–47, for antiquities of Achara, including churches of Khulo and Shkalto; pp. 48–93, for Zarzma and Safar; pp. 104–140, Radsha; pp. 141–148, for churches of Kartli; Vol. VII, pp. 1–65, for churches of Kakheti; pp. 66–111, for antiquities of the valleys of Aragvi, Ksani and Qwirila; Vol. X, antiquities of Pshaveti, Khevsureti and Svaneti. Cf. also DUBOIS DE MONTPÉREUX, *Voyage Archéologique en Transcaucasie*; LYNCH, *Armenia*, Vol. I; MOURIER, *L'Art au Caucase*, Brussels, 1907; *Akti*, Vol. 5, pp. 993–1107: D. BAKRADZE, *Kavkaz v Drevnikh Pamyatnikakh Khristianstva*; KONDAKOV, *Drevnaya Arkhitektura Gruzii*, Moscow, 1876; KONDAKOV and BAKRADZE, *Opis pamyatnikov drevnosti v nekotorikh khramakh i monastiryakh Gruzii*, Spb, 1890.

More recent books and papers are:

E. TAQAISHVILI, *Album d'Architecture Géorgienne* (Georgian and French introduction to an invaluable series of 80 plates), Tiflis, 1924.

J. BALTRUSAITIS, *Etudes sur l'Art Médiéval en Géorgie et en Arménie* (containing 101 beautiful photographic plates), Paris, 1930.

Iz. Kav. I.A.I., I, pp. 1–95, D. P. GORDEEV, "Otchet o Poezdke v Akhaltzikhski Uezd v 1917; Rospisi v Chule, Sapare i Zarzme"; TARANUSHENKO, "Predvoritelnii otchet o komandirovke v Zarzmu, Chule i Saparu", *ibid.*, pp. 96–100; D. A. KIPSHIDZE, O Rospisi bolshogo khramovogo peshchernogo sooruzheniya Vardzii; *ibid.*, Vol. III, pp. 87–96, D. P. GORDEEV, Materiali k izucheniu pamyatnikov Gruzinskogo zodchestva preimushchestvenno po arkhivnim dannim, I, Samtavrisi; also *ibid.*, Vol. IV, pp. 89–122. *Drevnosti Vostochniya*, Vol. I, Part II, pp. 223–81, G. E. TSERETELI, "Polnoe sobranie nadpisei na stenakh i kamniakh i pripisok k rukopisyam Gelatskago Monastiriya". *Khrist: Vost.*, Vol. VI, Part III, pp. 299–302, "Drevnosti Gulekarskoi

BIBLIOGRAPHIES AND NOTES

Tserkvyu ", and other articles in this publication. *Sbor. Mat.*, Vol. XXXV, pp. 1–112, E. TAQAISHVILI, " Zarzmski Monastir, ego restavratzia i freski ", and numerous other articles in this publication.

See also the excellent article " Gruzinskoe Iskusstvo ", *Bol. Sov. Entz.*, Vol. 19, by D. GORDEEV, and *A.R.*, Jan. 1930, TAMARA TALBOT RICE, " The Role of Georgia in Mediæval Art " (containing valuable information on the technical development of the metal icon).

BIBLIOGRAPHICAL NOTES TO CHAPTER XXVIII

MEDIÆVAL GEORGIAN LITERATURE.

A. S. KHAKHANOV, *Ocherki po istorii Gruzinskoi Slovesnosti*, 4 vols., Moscow, 1897 (of which vols. II and III cover period to end of the eighteenth century).

Tek. Raz. A.-G., IV, N. Y. MARR, "Drevnii Gruzinskii Odopistsi", Vol. VII, *idem.*, "Georgie Merchul, Zhitie sv. Grigoriya Khandztiskago, Gruzinski Tekst, Vvedenie, izdanie, perevod N. Y. Marra, s Dnevnikom poezdki v Shavshiu i Klarjiu"; and other publications in this series.

Zap. Vost. Ot. I.R.A.O., Vol. III, pp. 223–306, *idem.*, "Mudrost Balavara, Gruzinskaya Versiya". See also *ibid.*, Vol. IV, pp. 395–397, *idem.*, "Predislovie k jitii Petra Ivera".

Trudi Vost. Laz., I. V. Yaz., Part XIX, A. KHAKHANOV, "Bagrat, Episkop Tavromeniiski, Gruzinski tekst po rukopisyam XI veka"; and other publications in this series.

Oriental Translations Fund, Vol. XXI, by MARJORY WARDROP, "The Man in the Panther's Skin: a Romantic Epic of Shot'ha Rust'haveli"; Vol. XXIII by OLIVER WARDROP, *Visramiani: the Story of the Loves of Vis and Ramin*. Sulkhan Orbeliani's *Book of Wisdom and Lies* was also translated by Marjory Wardrop and published in a limited edition by the Kelmscott Press. A new edition of Sulkhan Orbeliani's *Georgian Dictionary* was edited by KIPSHIDZE and SHANIDZE and was published in Tiflis in 1928.

For Georgian historical literature see: *Sbor. Mat.*, XXVIII, i, 1–216, E. S. TAQAISHVILI, "Sami Istoriuli Kronikebi"; *ibid.*, XXXV, pp. 113–235, M. JANASHVILI, "Kartlis-Tzkhovreba, Obshchiya Svedeniya o K-Tz i eya istochnikakh", etc. See also BROSSET's *Introduction à l'Histoire de la Géorgie*, and other writings. (Ref. *Bibliographie Analytique de M.-F. B.*)

The mediæval literature of Georgia has been the subject of numerous articles in periodical publications by Marr, Taqaishvili, Janashvili, Javakhov (-ishvili), Khakhanov (-ashvili), Kekelidze, Blake and others. KEKELIDZE is the author, in Georgian, of a new *History of Georgian Literature*, Vols. I, II, Tiflis, 1923–4. Other recent materials are: *Caucasica*, Fasc. III, pp. 83–139, H. F. J. JUNKER, "Das Awestaalphabet und der Unsprung der Armenischen und Georgischen Schrift"; *Oriens Christianus*, Serie III, Band II, Heft 3, pp. 1–18, G. PERADZE, "Die Altgeorgische Literatur und Ihre Probleme". Reference should also be made to E. S. TAQAISHVILI's voluminous materials published as "Description of Manuscripts in the Library of the Society for the Propagation of Literacy among the People of Georgia", in *Sbor. Mat.*, Vol. XXXI, pp. 1–102; XXXII, i, 65–238; XXXIII, 1–144; XXXIV, i, 1–162; XXXVII, i, 1–224; XXXIX, i, 1–240; XL, i, 1–64; XLII, i, 1–64 and his "Arkheologicheskiya Poezdki, Razyskaniya i Zametki", *ibid.*, XLIV, 3, 1–146.

BIBLIOGRAPHIES AND NOTES

GEORGIAN LANGUAGE.

BROSSET, *L'Art libéral ou grammaire géorgienne*, Paris, 1830. *Elements de la langue géorgienne*, Paris, 1837.

KLAPROTH, *Vocabulaire (et grammaire) de la langue géorgienne*, Paris, 1827. (Klaproth's grammar was revised and corrected by Brosset and published as *L'Art libéral* in 1830. These works are exceedingly defective and now almost useless.)

Dictionaries are: D. CHUBINOV, *Dictionnaire Géorgien-français-russe avec un abrégé de la grammaire géorgienne de M.-F.B.*, Spb, 1840. *Russko-gruzinskii slovar*, Spb, 1886. (The last is by far the better of the two.)

For Mingrelian there are: *Mat. Yaf. Yaz.*, Vol. VII, 1914, I. KIPSHIDZE, "Grammatika Mingrelskago (Iverskago s khrestomatiki i Slovaryom".

T. KLUGE, *Beitrage zur Mingrelischen Grammatik*, Berlin, 1916.

I am informed that a comprehensive French-Georgian Grammar by Prof. N. Marr is in preparation.

BIBLIOGRAPHICAL NOTES TO CHAPTERS XXIX AND XXX

For Musulman writers on the Caucasus, see references in Bibliographical Note to Book II. For the Arab and Turkish authors referred to in the footnotes to Chapter XXIX the following editions were used:

EL-MASUDI = Maçoudi, *Les Prairies d'Or*, texte et traduction par C. Barbier de Meynard, 8 vols., Paris, 1883.
IBN-HAUKAL, *The Oriental Geography of*, translated by Sir William Gore Ouseley, London, 1800.
IBN-KHURDABDIH = *ibn-Khordabdeh*, *Kitab-el-Masalik wa'l Mamalik. Accedunt Excerpta e Kitab al-Kharadj, auctore Kodamana ibn-Djafar*, in *Biblio. Geo. Arab:*, edited by M. J. de Goeje, Lugd. Batav., 1889.
EL-IDRISSI = *Edrisi, Géographie d'*, traduite par P. A. Jaubert, Paris, 1836.
YAKUTI, IBN-ABD 'ALLAH (el-Bakuli) = Yakout, *Dictionnaire Géographique, Historique et Littéraire de la Perse et des contrées adjacentes du Modjem El-Bouldan*, texte et traduction par C. Barbier de Meynard, Paris, 1861.
ABU'L FIDA = *Abu'l Féda, Géographie d'*, traduite de l'arabe et accompagné de Notes et Eclairissements par M. Reinaud, 2 vols., Paris, 1848.
EVLIYA CHELEBI = *Evliya Effendi, Narrative of Travels in Europe, Asia and Africa in the seventeenth century*, translated from the Turkish by Ritter Joseph von Hammer, 1846.

Other references in the footnotes to Chapter XXIX are to Georgian sources already given in the Bibliography to Chapter XXVIII. For a full bibliography of foreign travellers in Georgia and the Caucasus between the thirteenth and the nineteenth centuries, see MIANSAROV, *Bibliographia Caucasica et Transcaucasica*, Vol. I, pp. 320–388. For a fairly adequate list of European writers, see WARDROP, *The Kingdom of Georgia*, pp. 172–86. Cf. also *Kav. Kal.*, Vol. XLV for 1890, pp. 1–48, "Kratkii Spisok knigam, statyam i izdanyam, otnosyashchimsya k Kavkazovedenyu", published as Prilozheniya to Part I. For the Venetian travellers' references to Georgia, I have used Yule's edition of Marco Polo, and the versions of Josaphat Barbaro and Ambrosio Contarini published in the Hakluyt Society's volume, *The Venetians in Persia*.

The brief references of Marco Polo, Rubruquis, John di Piano Carpini and Ruy Gonzalez de Clavijo are indicative of the little that was known about Georgia by Western writers before the sixteenth century. In the sixteenth and seventeenth centuries relations between the Western nations and Russia and Persia were rapidly developed, and one of the results of this development was that the Caucasian lands became familiar ground to European merchants and travellers. The principal writers up to the early nineteenth century on Georgia and the Caucasus, to many of whom reference has not been made in the text, are:[1]

---

[1] I have not included those travellers, such as Dubois and Chantre, already referred to in other sections of the bibliography, nor does this list in any way pretend to cover the multitude of books published in Europe during the last two centuries.

BIBLIOGRAPHIES AND NOTES

Sixteenth to Eighteenth Centuries—

HAKLUYT, RICHARD, *The Principall Navigations, Voiages, and Discoveries of the English Nation in . . . the Empire of Russia, the Caspian Sea, Georgia. . . .* 3 vols., London, 1589 and 1600.

JENKINSON, ANTHONY, *Early Voyages and Travels to Russia and Persia, by A.J. and others in the reign of Queen Elizabeth*, published by the Hakluyt Society, 2 vols., London, 1886.

ZAMPI, GUISEPPE MARIA, *Relatione della Colchida*, 1620.

LAMBERTI, ARCANGELO, *Relatione della Colchida, hoggi della Mengrellia, nella quale si tratta dell' origine, costumi e cose naturali di quei paesi*, Napoli, 1654.

Recueil des Voyages au Nord, contenant divers mémoires très utiles au commerce et à la navigation, 10 vols., Amsterdam, 1715, includes the works of the above two Italians and also that of the Dominican Giovanni di Lucca. (Chardin drew extensively on the works of Zampi and Lamberti, and Dubois de Montpéreux quotes at length the excellent account of the Circassians given by Giovanni di Lucca.)

VALLE, PIETRO DELLA, *Informazione della Giorgia : datta alla Santita di nostro Segnore papa Urbano VIII da Pietro della Valle Pellerino, L'anno 1614-1627*, 4 vols., Rome, 1650-63.

OLEARIUS, ADAM, *The Voyages and Travels of the Ambassadors sent by Frederick Duke of Holstein to the Great Duke of Muscovy and the king of Persia. Begun in the year 1633 and finisch'd in 1639. . . . Faithfully rendred into Englisch by John Davies*, 2 vols., London, 1662.

DAPPER, OLFERT, *Asia, of Naukeurige Beschrywing van het Rijk des Grooten Mogols . . . Beneffens in Volkome Beschrywing van geheel Persie, Schirwan, Adirbeitzan, Karabach, Sagistan, Dagestan, Georgie, Mingrelie, Imereti, Kacheti, Karduel, Guriel, Avagasie, Cirsassie, Kurdistan en andere Gebuurgewesten*, Amsterdam, 1672; German edition, Nürnberg, 1681.

TAVERNIER, *Six Voyages . . . en Perse* (1663-1669), ed. Rouen, 1724.

CHARDIN, SIR JOHN, *The Travels of, into Persia and the East-Indies*, London, 1686.

TOURNEFORT, JOSEPH PITTON DE, *Relation d'un Voyage du Levant, contenant l'histoire ancienne et moderne de . . . l'Arménie, de la Géorgie*. 2 vols., Paris and Lyon, 1717.

EMIN, JOSEPH, *The Life and Adventures of J.E., an Armenian, written by himself*, London, 1792. (A new edition was published in Bombay, in 2 vols. about 1918.)

REINEGGS, JACOB, *Beschreibung des Kaukasus*, 2 vols., Gotha, 1796-7.

GUELDENSTAEDT, JOHAN, *Reisen durch Russland und im Caucasischen Geburge.* . . . 2 vols., Spb, 1787-91; and other works.

PEYSSONNEL, *Traité sur le Commerce de la Mer Noire*, 2 vols., Paris, 1787.

GAMBA, JACQUES FRANÇOIS, *Voyage dans la Russie méridionale, et particulièrement dans les provinces situées au-delà du Caucase . . .* 2 vols., with Atlas, Paris, 1826.

KLAPROTH, JULIUS, *Voyage au Mont Caucase et en Géorgie*, 2 vols., Paris, 1823.
(Klaproth was the author of other works on the Caucasus, upon which his undeserved reputation as a traveller and Orientalist was partly based. In so far as his Caucasian work is concerned, he borrowed unashamedly and without acknowledgment from previous authors, and is suspect from his text of not having visited places where he claims to have been.)

BIBLIOGRAPHIES AND NOTES

GAGARINE, PRINCE GRÉGOIRE, *Le Caucase pittoresque, dessinée d'après la Nature. Avec une introduction et un texte explicative par le comte Stackelberg*; with 50 lithographed plates, Paris, 1847-9.

For a fine description in English of the mountains of the Central Caucasus, with an account of the geography of Svaneti, see *The Exploration of the Caucasus*, by DOUGLAS FRESHFIELD, the veteran ex-President of the Royal Geographical Society. Among novels and *belles lettres* about the Caucasus the following may be noted: PUSHKIN, *Puteshestvie v Erzerum*; LERMONTOV, *Geroi nashevo vremeni*; TOLSTOI, *Kavkazskie Plennik, Hadji Murad* and *Kazaki*; VERESCHAGUINE, *Voyage dans les provinces du Caucase*; MORIER, *Adventures of Hajji Baba of Isfahan*; DUMAS, *Le Caucase*; KEUHN, *Prince Tariel*.

ADDENDUM

J. MARQUART (MARKWART), Osteuropäische und Ostasiatische Streifzüge: *Ethnologische und historische-topographische Studien zur Geschichte des 9 und 10 Jahrhunderts*, Leipzig, 1903.

Idem in *Caucasica*, Fasc. VI, Teil 1, pp. 25–69, "Waher stammt der Name Kaukasus?"

Idem, ibid., Fasc. VI, Teil 2, pp. 10–77, "Die Genealogie der Bagratiden und das Zeitalter des Mar Abas und Ps. Moses Xorenc'i."

Idem, ibid., Fasc. VII, pp. 111–67, "Die Bekehrung Iberiens und die beiden ältesten Dokumente der Iberischen Kirche."

Idem in *Philologus*, Bande 54 und 55, "Untersuchungen zur Geschichte von Eran."

The late Professor Markwart left some valuable material which he had prepared on the historical topography of Daghestan, but so far as I can ascertain this has not so far been published.

J.A., Vol. CCXVII, No. I, July–Sept., 1930, pp. 42–112, M. V. MINORSKY, Transcaucasica: six valuable studies, including (1) "Le nom de Dvin," (2) "Sogdabil et Ardabil," (3) "Kasaı et Kazah," (4) "La forteresse Alinjak et la Vallée de Hamsa," (5) "Min-Gol et les Expéditions de Timur," (6) "Bab Al-Lal Lalvar."

E.S.A., Vol. VII, pp. 82–97, G. Nioradze, Der Verwahrfund von Kvemo-Sasireth.

Ibid., pp. 98–112, M. M. Ivashchenko, Beitrage zur Vorgeschichte Abchasiens.

Ibid., pp. 113–82, F. Hančar, Die Nadelformen des prähistorischen Kaukasusgebietes.

INDEX

ABAGHA, Il-Khan, 117, 118, 119
Abasgoi, Greek name for the Abkhaz. See Abkhazeti
Abashidze, Katévan, married to Rustem I, 170; Giorgi, a passing King of Imereti, 178 note 1; Simon, supports Wakhtang VI, 186, 187; Kai Khusraw, defeated by Solomon I, 208
Abazadze, Ioanné, *Eristavi* of Kartli, 89
Abbas I, *the Great*, Shah, 150, 157; his policy on his N.W. frontier, 165; conquest of Kartli and Kakheti, 165-7; his methods and cruelty, 168-70; attitude compared with that of Abdul-Hamid, 170; 176, 198, 285, 184 note 1
Abbas II, Shah, 168; his unattractive personality, 173
Abdulla Beg, 197
Abich, explorations of, in Caucasus, 12
Abkhazeti, the Abkhaz (Abkhazia, Abasgia, Apsilia), megaliths in, 13; language, significance of the name-root, 28-9; tree-cult in, 36; type of house in, 54-5; Byzantine missionaries in, 78; Persians invade, *ib.*; Byzantine policy in, 80; rise of the *Eristavni* of, 80-1; political history of, in the 10th c., 83-4; power of Kingdom of, at beginning of 11th c., 85 *et sqq.*; war with Byzantium, 87-8; diplomatic relations with Byzantium, 88-9, 91; expansion in E. Georgia, 89-90; westerly acquisitions, 93; wars with Er-Toghrul and Alp Arslan, 90 *et sqq.*; state of, at beginning of 12th c., 96; supports Bogolyubskoi, 105, 107; supports David IV, 116; Giorgi VII in, 124; Mongols on borders of, 125; Turkish sea-raid on, 135; Sharvashidze established as virtually independent in, 137 and note 1; invaded by Wakhtang V, 177; slave-raids of the A., 178; abortive Turkish invasion of, 189-90; 204, 246, 262, 264, 277, 383 and note 2; ecclesiastical architecture of, 295-6; 299, 302; historical literature of, 313-14; 331, 346, 348, 356
Abkhazta Tzkhovreba, 314
Abo, St., 228; 312-13
Abo, Life of St., quoted, 228 and note 1; 238-9
Abu-Bekr, Atabeg of Azerbaijan, 106
Abulasan, 246-7-8
Abu'l Fida, quoted, 56, 324 *et sqq.*
Abuseridze Tbeli, 231
Achæmenian dynasty in Persian, 40-5, 327

Achara, a district of Samtzkhé between the Black Sea and the Acharis-tsqali, 93, 94, 137, 145, 155, 296
Acorns, 326
Adiabene. See Azerbaijan
Adighé, native name for Circassians, *q.v.*
Adishi, a village in Svaneti not identified on the map, Evangel of, 306
Æa, probable significance of the Kingdom of, 13; identity of, with Nakalakevi suggested, 51
Ælius Spartianus, 75 note 3
Afghanistan, Afghans, Georgian kings in, 176 *et sqq.*, 351 note 4; invasion of Persia by, 181 *et sqq.*; Afghan troops in Tiflis, 192
Agha Kish, 197, 203
Agha-Muhammad-Khan-Kajar, 201 note 10; his rise, 212; his unsavoury character and appearance, *ib.* note 5; his proposals to Irakli II, 213; invades Georgia, 213-14; preparations for second invasion and death, 214; 215, 285
Aghapi, 233-4
Aghmashenebeli, David, The Life of, quoted, 248
Aghmatebit shedsqalebul -i (-ni), 254
Aghovanq. See Albania
Aghsartan I, King of Kakheti, 91, 94
Aghsartan II, King of Kakheti, character of, 98; end of, *ib.*
Aghsartan, Shirvanshah, 106-7
Aghzeebul -i (-ni), 229
Ahmad, (Tekudar), Il-Khan, 119
Ahmad Jalayar, 124
Ahmad Pasha of Baghdad, 190
Ahura Mazda, 42
Aietes, 48, 51
Aini, el-, quoted on character of David II, 97 note 1; 333
Ainina, identified with Anahit-Diana, 39, 42-3
Ain-Jalut, David V present at Battle of, 116
Ajars, migratory habits of, 54. See also Achara
Akhæans, of the W. Caucasus, probably Jikhi. See Circassia, Circassians.
Akhaldaba (*new village*), in Trialeti, Mongols defeated at, 116
Akhalkalaki (*new town*), in Samtzkhé, E. of the Mtkvari, 59, 91, 207, 217, 218
Akhaltzikhé (*new castle*), a town on the Kwablowanis-tsqali, N.N.W. of its junction with the Mtkvari, 9, 57-9, 111, 118, 192 note 8, 207, 217, 218, 262, 282-3, 299, 319

395

INDEX

Akhlat. See Khlat.
Akhmeti, a commune in Kakheti, on the upper Alazani, 218
Akhtala, a village on the Débéda, 19 note 1, 201 and note 4
Akstafa river, an affluent of the Mtkvari, 204
Alaneti. See Osseti.
Alans, 10; origin and early history of, considered, 30–1; axe-cult among, 37; 61. See also Osseti, Ossetians.
Alamut, 116, 153
Ala-ul-din Muhammad Khwarazm-Shah, 110
Alaverdi, town and episcopal see in Kakheti, S. of the Alazani, 63, 167, 173, 272, 299, 305, 312, 344 and note 1.
Alazani, a river of Kakheti, affluent of the Mtkvari, 10, 16, 19, 41, 62 et sqq., 156, 215
Albania, Albanians, in Classical times the country between the Caspian, the Samur and the Mtkvari; Moon-worship among the, 37; Roman victory over the, 43, 47; account of, 63–6; mission to the Huns, 267
Albanian Gates, the. See Derbend.
Alda, reputed wife of Giorgi I, 89
Aleppo, 99, 101
Alexander of Macedon, 52, 310
Alexander VI, Pope, correspondence of, with Constantine III, 338
Alexander I, Emperor of Russia, 215 note 8
Alexander (Alesandré), King of Georgia, defeats the Jaqelis at Kokhta, 126; his devout character, 126–7; his descendants in Kakheti, 138; 297, 300
Alexander, son of David IV, 119
Alexander I, King of Kakheti, recognized, 138; his relations with Russia and Persia, 140
Alexander II, King of Kakheti, fatuous observation of, recorded by Wakhushti, 150; murder of, ib. note 1, 165; disputed succession of, 152; feud of with Simon I, 153; relations with Persians and Turks, 153–55; unchivalrous humour of, 157; relations with Russia, 164–5 and 343; 170
Alexander II, King of Imereti, 138, 145
Alexander III, King of Imereti, 172, 178 note 1; Russian mission at court of, 345 et sqq.; appearance and character of, 348–9
Alexander IV, King of Imereti, 178 note 1
Alexander V, King of Imereti, 178 and note 1; his campaign in Abkhazeti, 188–9; 206
Alexander (Ali Mirza), a son of David III of Kakheti, 191
Alexander (Skander Mirza), a son of Wakhtang V of Kartli, 351 note 4
Alexander, son of Bakari, 203
Alexander, a son of Irakli II, 215, 216 and note 2, 217, 218
Alexandria, in Egypt, 330

Alexandria in Colchis. See Skanda
Alexei Mikhailovich, Tsar, 172 note 1
Algeti, river, an affluent of the Mtkvari, 59, 93, 125, 353
Ali, a town on the borders of Kartli and Imereti, 204
Alinjak, a fortress S.E. of Nakhchevan, 124
Ali-Quli-Khan, 195
Aloni, Plain of, 150, 167
Alp Arslan, Seljuk Sultan, 90; invades Kakheti and Kartli, 91–2; victory at Malaskert, 92; murdered, 93
Alphabet, the Albanian, 65; the Georgian, discussed, 309–10
Alpine physical type, described, extension of, 21–2
Altaic languages in relation to Georgian, 22 et sqq.
Altar-niches, 296, 299
Amazons, 32
America, significance of emergence of, in world history, 161, 208; fur-trade of, referred to, 325
Amida, 83
Amier (*this side*), a term used to describe that part of Georgia E. of the Mountains of Likhi; 7, 8; account of, 9–10; 25, 47; elements of conflict with Imier, 105; 245; dependence of, on economy of Caspian basin, 352 et sqq.
Amilakhori, Bardzim, and Simon I, 153, 157; Tinatin, wife of Alexander II of Kakheti, 153; power of family at beginning of 17th c., 166; at end of 17th c., 178; Giv joins Nadir Shah, 179; arrested, 191 note 4; Otar sent to Persia, 191 note 4; revolts of Giv, 192, 193; plots of family against Irakli II, 203; *tavadi*, 282; the Catholicos Nikolaoz, 286
Amira, 246
Amirakhori, office of, 258, 260; rank and rights of, 261
Amiran, Hill of, near Akhalkalaki, 59; mythical figure of, 318
Amiran-Darejaniani, 318
Amir-Ejibi, office of, 259 and note 1; Ali-Quli-Beg, 191 note 4
Amir-Spasalari, office of, 102, 105, 106, 109, 113, 115, 253; rank and seniority of, 260–61; position of in relation to the King, 264. See also Spasalari, Spaspeti
Ammianus Marcellinus, 30
Amputation, punishment by, 278
Anahit. See Ainina
Anaitis. See Ainina
Anaklia, port and town in Mingrelia, at the mouth of the Enguri; 209
Anakopia, (or Nikopsia), a town and fortress of Abkhazeti; 28, 89, 93, 107
Ananuri, a village in the district of Bazaleti, S. of the Shavi Aragvi, 194, 299
Anapa, a fortress on the Taman Peninsula, 209, 210, 211, 217
Anatolia, 123, 124, 335

INDEX

Anatomy, the study of, 315
Anau, referred to, 12
Anchabadze, family and royal house of Abkhazeti; origin of, 81; policy of, 83-4; extinction of, 84
Andrew, Great Prince of Suzdal, 104
Andreyevo, a Cossack post S. of the Terek, 164
Andronikashvili, family, 108 note 1; Kai Khusraw, Georgian governor of Ganja, 198 note 4; Melkisedek, defeats Russians at Kortokhti, 217
Ani, an Armenian city on the Akhurean river, an affluent of the Araks, in the province of Ararad, 59; capital of the Shirakian Bagratids, 82; a separate Kingdom, 83, 84, 85, 86; pillaged by the Seljuks, 90; taken by David II, 100; restored to banu-Shaddad, 102; 107, 115, 248, 329
Ankarah, 125
Annals, Georgian, traditions in, about early history, 11, 16, 17, 34, 37, 42-3, 51, 52, 71; on the Kingdom of Iberia, 74-9; on character of David II, 97-8; on Kipchaks, 100; on reign of Dmitri I, 100-1; on reign of Tamara, 103 *et sqq.*; on the Mongols and reign of Rusudani, 110 *et sqq.*; on character of Dmitri II, 118; on character of David VI, 120; decay of style of, 121; on the Empire of Trebizond, 122 note 2; 237, 269, 278, 285, 309, 310; composition and sources of, 313-15; 317
Anonymous Chronicle, The, 313
Antioch, 96, 99, 247, 270; Patriarchs of, 269
Antoni, Catholicos, 176, 201, 206, 317
Antonisi, (Yeni Rabat), in the Chorokhi valley, 296
Aorsi, 323
Aphridon, 102, 104
Aphrodite, cult of, in Georgia, 39 and note 3
Appian, 28, 43
Apple, the, grown in Imereti, 7, 346; in W. Caucasus, 26; in Kartli, 352
Apricots, found in Imereti, 346
Apsheron Peninsula, a centre of the fire-cult, 42; 327
Apsilia, (the Apsilai), a Greek form of the native name of the Abkhaz. See Abkhazeti
Apsu, (the Apsua), native name for Abkhazeti, *q.v.*
Aqueduct, provision for the service of an, 234
Arabs, give first reliable information on Daghestan, 32; 51, 61; character of their political development, 69-71; invade Georgia, 79; their policy in Armenia and the Caucasus, 80; collapse of their rule, 81-2; 270, 312, 319; military and commercial policy of, in the Caucasus, 321 *et sqq.*; historical developments following decline of power of, 329

Aragon, relations of Kingdom of, with the Mongols, 335
Aragvi, river, an affluent of the Mtkvari formed by the two streams *Shavi* (black) and *Tetri* (white), 3, 4, 10, 31, 124 note 1; *Eristavni* of, 166; 168, 174, 178; *Eristavni* of, 188; 192, 214, 216, 224, 299, 305
Araks, (Araxes; *Georgian,* Rakhs), river, course of, 9; access by tributaries of, into Georgia, 10; 14, 24, 28, 47; Urartian place-names along, 51; 54, 57, 59, 64, 98, 107, 108, 197, 204
Aran, a province lying between the Mtkvari and the Araks, probably derived from the earlier name-forms *Albania-Aghovanq,* 85, 89, 100, 104, 106, 122, 148, 177; trade of, under Caliphate, 321 *et sqq.*; trade and administration of in 17th c., 352 *et sqq.*
Ararat, Mount, 17, 98, 198
Arbitration, 279
Archæopolis. See Nakalakevi
Archil I, an Iberian king, 76, 229
Archil- (i), an Iberian prince, 79
Archil- (i), (Shah-Nazar-Khan), a son of Wakhtang V, 177-8; his poem, 177 note 4; 180 note 1, 182 note 2, 320
Archil- (i), a brother of Solomon I of Imereti, 213
Architecture, Georgian; contrasted with Byzantine and Armenian, 293 *et sqq.*; *centralized* type, 294-5; *basilica* and *cruciform* types, 295 *et sqq.*; in Abkhazeti, Samtzkhé and Imereti, 296-97 and 299; of Kutais Cathedral, 297-99; of Svaneti, 300-1; Muslim, in Tiflis, 356
Archives, of the Iberian Kings, referred to, 334
Ardabil, sacked by a Georgian army, 108, 323
Ardahani, a town in the district of Poso on the upper Mtkvari, 8, 9, 57-8, 88, 101 note 2, 113, 194
Ardanuchi, a town on the Ardanuchis-tsqali, an affluent of the Mtkvari, 57, 94, 148, 238, 322
Ardon river, an affluent of the Terek, 31
Ares, 39
Areshi, a town on the borders of Kakheti and Shaki, 167, 353
Argamak stallions, 347
Arghun, Il-Khan, 119, 120, 284
Argonauts, significance of the myth concerning, 13; 51
Argueti, a district of Imereti, along the right bank of the river Qwirila, 85; ravaged by the Seljuks, 92, 93
Argutashvili, Mikel, 200, 216
Argyros; Elena, married to Bagrat III, 89; 297, 306; Michael, 89; Romanos, Emperor, 88, 297
Ariosto, 358
Arkhavé, (Archabis), a village of Chaneti, 56, 328
Arkvani, a fortress on the river Khrami, 60

397

INDEX

Armazi, (Armazis-tzikhé, called also Kartli), a city on the Mtkvari, 37, 43, 60-1; separate Kingdom of, 76; decline of, in favour of Mtzkheta, 78
Armazi, (Ormuzd), cult of, in Georgia, 36-42
Armenia, Armenians, of *Alpine* physical type, 21; 22, 26; elements among Ossetians, 31; religious influences of, 39; and Iberians, 42-3; influences of, in Albania, 64-6; national characteristics of, considered, 73; Arab administration of, 79-80; collapse of Arab rule in, 80-81; Kingdom of, in 9th-10th c., 82-4; in 11th c., 85-6; collapse of A. kingdoms, 87 *et sqq.*; Kingdom of Sis and the Crusades, 96, 100; depopulated districts of, settled by Kipchaks, 99; some provinces of, annexed by David II, 100; Georgian reverses in, 102; forays of Bogolyubskoi in, 104; and the Georgian monarchy, 107; A. mercenaries at the Battle of Bolnisi, 111; A. sympathies of Mkhargrdzelis and Orbelianis, 115-6; A. Kingdom in Taurus, 121, 335; A. *meliks* in Karabagh, 185 and note 2, 197, 198, 212; A. renegades among Lazghis, 199-200; A. favourites of Irakli II, 201 *et sqq.*; plans for revolt of, against Turkey, 201 note 8; A. elements in Irakli's Kingdom, 204-5; relations of A. Church with Georgian, 269; 284, 292; influence of A. architecture on Georgian, 293-5; reference to A. iconography, 303-4; influence of, on development of Georgian script considered, 309-10; trade relations of, with Caucasus, under Caliphate, 322 *et sqq.*; falcons of, 327-8; as middlemen, 330; 335, 346, 353, 356
Armenian Chronicle, The, 313
Armenian Language, the, *Japhetic* elements in, 23-4
Armenoid physical type. See *Alpine*
Armenochalybes, 26
Armour, Khwarazmian, 319; manufacture of, in the Caucasus, 327
Army, Georgian, state of in 15th c., 143-4; composition and organization of, 264-5; Imerian, reference to, in 17th c., 345
Arnaud, Vincent, 184 note 5
Arpa-Chai river, an affluent of the Araks, 59
Arrian, 28
Arsakid dynasty, of Armenia, 42-3; of Pontus, 43; of Parthia, 44-5, 310; of Albania, 64-6, 75
Arsianis-mta, a range of mountains in the district of Erusheti in Samtzkhé, called by the Turks Yalanuz-Cham (*lone pine*), 138, 148
Art, significance of, considered, 291-2; Caucasian, in the Bronze Age, 292-3; Georgian, contrasted with Byzantine and Armenian, 293-4; iconography, metallurgy and enamelling, 301-4; fresco-painting, illumination and calligraphy, 305-6
Artagi, (Otokos), an Iberian king, 43
Artisans, 231
Artvini, (Artvaani), a town on the lower Chorokhi, 57, 101 note 2
Artzruni, family and ruling house of Vaspurakan, 80, 82
Aryan languages. See Indo-European
Asad Khan, 197
Ashot, (Artzruni), King of Vaspurakan, 82
Ashot, (Bagrationi), Kuropalatès of Tao, 81, 306
Ashot I, (Bagratuni), King of Kings in Armenia, 82-3
Ashot II, (Bagratuni), King of Armenia, 82
Ashot IV, (Bagratuni), King of Armenia, 87
Ashraf Khan, 188, 189
Aslanduz, a village on the Araks, 218
Aspagur II, an Iberian king, 76
Aspindza, a village in Samtzkhé, victory of Irakli II at, 207
Assyria, (Asshur), Assyrians, 11-12; early contacts of, with Trans-Caucasia doubtful, 15
Astarabad, early art of, 12; death of Taymuraz I at, 173; [Russian flotilla at, 212; 318
Astarte. See Itrujani
Astrakhan, (Hajji-Tarkhan), 123 note 2; conquered by Ivan IV, 162; 164, 172, 184, 192, 323, 345
Astrology, 61 note 2, 315
Atabag-i (-ni), 260; seniority of, 261
Atabagoba, 260
Atasistav-i (-ni), 237
Ateni, a village S. of the Mtkvari, in Kvemo-Kartli, 117, 243, 295; frescoes in Church of Sioni at, 306
Aternerseh, (Adarnasé), *Eristavi-Mtavari* of Kartli, 79, 267, 312
Athens, 295
Athos, Mount, 270, 295, 306, 311, 312, 319
Atina, (*old Greek,* Athenæ), a village on the coast of Chaneti, 56, 341
Atropatene. See Azerbaijan
Atskveri, (Atskhur), a village and fortress on the Mtkvari, above the Tashis-Kari defile; cult of Virgin of, 40; Bishop of, 102, 104; Russo-Georgian allies besiege, 207
Austria, Austrians, and Turkey, 165, 190 and note 3; and Russia, *ib.*; threatened intervention of, 208
Avalishvili, Kai Khusraw, 191 note 4
Avars, a Turkish nomad people, 31
Avars, a tribe of Daghestan occupying the country between the Andi-Koisu and the Kara-Koisu, 184, 198, 211, 215
Aveniri, 317
Avighé, name for Georgian goshawks, 327
Avshandadze, family, a *sigeli* of the, 276; blood-price of a member of the, 277
Axe-cult, referred to, 37
Azalea, profusion of, in Chaneti, 55

398

INDEX

Azerbaijan, (Adiabene, Atropatene), a Persian province extending from the Caspian to the W. of Lake Urmia; 64; Atabegs of, and the Georgian Kings, 102 *et sqq.*; 106, 107, 111, 123 note 2, 124, 156, 185, 187 note 6, 191, 194, 197, 213, 325, 327; administration of, in the 17th c., 353

Aznaur-i (-ni), 41-2, 84, 90, 102, 104, 115; original meaning of word, 225-6; differentiations in the rank of, 226; *did-did-i (-ni), mtsiré (-ni)*, *ib.*; *agbzeebul-i (-ni), mosakargave (-ni), sazuerel-i (-ni), memamule (-ni)*, 229; *mepisai, gwarian-i (-ni)*, 230; *tanamqol-i (-ni)*, 254; *didebul-i (-ni)*, 244, 250; 228, 230, 240, 242, 247-8, 271, 282

Aznaurishvil-i (-ni), 230

Aznauroba, 229; characteristic features of, 244

Azon, a mythical ruler of Iberia, 41

Azov, Sea of, (*Sea of the Az*), 26, 27, 29; Russian policy in, 182

Azov, city, (Azac), 123 note 2, 185, 188, 208, 209, 328; merchants of, in Kutais, 346; description of a cargo consigned to, 355

BAB-AL-ABWAB, (*the Gate of Gates*), Arab name for Derbend, 10

Babarikin, Russian envoy, drowned, 172

Babylon, 12, 14, 15, 17

Bachmeister, taught in Georgia, 201

Bagdati, a town in Imereti, 207

Baghdad, Georgian troops at sack of, 116; Rus merchants trade to, 324; 328, 330, 335

Bagrat III, King of Abkhazeti and Kartli, his succession and reign, 84-5; 229, 239, 276, 296; begins construction of Kutais Cathedral, 297; his likeness at Gelati, 306

Bagrat IV, King of Abkhazeti and Kartli, his character, 88; operations in E. Georgia, 89-90; feud with Liparit Orbeliani, 89 *et sqq.*; his visit to Byzantium, 90; pays *kharaj* to Alp Arslan, 92; death, 93; 247, 250, 297; his likenesses at Gelati, 305-6

Bagrat V, King of Georgia, revolts against, 122-3; taken prisoner by Timur, 123; apostasy and liberation of, *ib.*; 124

Bagrat (Mikelishvili, counted as Bagrat I of Imereti), 122

Bagrat II, King of Imereti, 133; Contarini's account of, 135; in the Wars of the Division, 137-8; 177, 340

Bagrat III, King of Imereti, reputed participation of, in a "crusade", 139 note 1; his wars with the Turks, 145; 148, 159

Bagrat IV, King of Imereti, 178 note 1; a pen-portrait of, by Chardin, 351; his observations on the libidinous character of Imerian priests, *ib.*

Bagrat VI, King of Kartli, 167, 170

Bagrat-i, a pretender to the Imerian throne, 159

Bagrat-i, a son of Constantine III, 174

Bagrat-i, a son of Giorgi XII, 215

Bagrationi, family and royal House of Georgia, 57, 58; rise of, 81 and note 3; dependencies of, *ib.* and 83; history of, in 10th c., 82-4, 101 and note 2, 103, 107, 115; marriages with the Comnenoi and Palaiologoi, 122 and note 2; history of the House considered, 131 *et sqq.*; fecundity and ingenuousness of, 133; extinction of direct line of, 174; the Kakhian and Mukhranian branches, 174 *et sqq.*, 351; capitulation of sovereign rights under Treaty of Georgievsk, 210-11; end of the House of, 215-16; 270, 277, 296, 297, 300; foreign relations of, 329 *et sqq.*; court of, 331. See also Bagratuni

Bagratuni, family and royal House of Armenia, 80 *et sqq.* See also Bagrationi

Bagrevan, a place probably in Somkheti, not identified on the map, massacre at, 81

Bahram Gur, compared with Wakhtang Gurgaslani, 77

Bahr-ul-Khazar (*Sea of the Khazar*), Arab name for the Caspian Sea, 10

Baiburt, (Baiburdi), a town on the upper Chorokhi, doubtfully identified with Gymnias, 56

Baidar, a Tatar commune between the Khrami and the Mtkvari, 197

Bakari, (Shah Nawaz III), a passing King of Kartli, 180; ravages Saguramo, 186; revolts against the Turks, 187; at Astrakhan, 192, 203

Baku, possibly Albanian Pakavan, 66 note 2; captured by Russians, 185, 214, 217; 324; early exploitation of naphtha deposits of, 327, 353

Bakurtzikheli, Egarslan, 115 and note 1

Balkaria, Balkars, 345

Balkh, 328

Bantu languages, referred to, 22

Baratashvili, (Baratiani), *gwari* of, 138, 166, 178, 197, 203

Barbaro, Josaphat, his account of Baku, 327; his adventures in Georgia, 329 *et sqq.*

Barda'a, 80, 82, 98, 284; account of, 323 *et sqq.*, 353. See also Pertav

Barley, rarely sown in Imereti, 7; in ancient Georgia, 53 note 1; wine *ib.*; reported as a crop in Imereti, 345

Basiani, a border district of Samtzkhé between the upper waters of the Oltis-tsqali and the Araks; various forms of the name, 28-9; principality of, 83, 84; Giorgi I defeated in, 88; Turkish encroachments in, 144, 145

Basiani, a district on the borders of Svaneti and Osseti, round the upper waters of the Cherek, 29

Basil II, Emperor, (*Bulgaroktonos*), 84; policy of and campaigns in the Caucasus, 86-8

399

INDEX

Basilica, the Roman, 294, 300-1
Basque language, compared with Georgian, 22
Basra, 318
Baths of bitches' milk, 276
Bathys. See Batum.
Batu, Mongol *no'in*, 113, 114
Batum, (*Georgian*, Batomi; *old Greek*, Bathys), a port and town in the district of Achara, 50, 148
Bayazid, 198, 353
Bayazid I, (Bajazet), Sultan, 124, 125
Bayern, explorations of, in Caucasus, referred to, 12
Baylakan, Arab name for Paidaragan, 125, 284; described, 324, 353
Baziert-Ukhutsesi, 261, 276
Beasts of burden, tax on, 263
Beaver, the, found in Imereti, 345
Bedia, in Mingrelia, between the Egrisis-tsqali and the Kodori, Metropolitan of, 272; Church of, 295-6
Bedshni, a village, probably in Somkheti, not identified on the map, 111
Bee, the, profitable culture of, in Imereti, 8; a goddess protectress of, among Circassians, 40
Begara, 235
Bejan Khan, 183 note 1
Bélad, 198 *et sqq*.
Belakani, a commune of Inner Kakheti, 118
Bendian, 342 and note 1
Beneficiarii, 251
Beneficium, 251
Berduji. See Débéda
Betani, church of, 306
Bibars, Mamluk Sultan of Egypt, 117
Bible, Georgian Edition of the, 316
Bichui, Mongol *no'in*, 113
Bihzad, his paintings of Mongol mountain tactics, 123 note 2
Bintvisi, (? Birtvisi or Kurtin), a fortress on the river Algeti, 125
Birkin, Rodion, 343
Biscuits, imported, 355
Bithynians, reference to invasion of Asia Minor by, 12, 13, 77
Blachernæ, Our Lady of, 296
Black Death, in Georgia, 123, 285, 288, 339
Black Sea (Euxine), early navigation of, 13-15; 27, 31, 48, 49, 71; Sasanian policy in regard to, 77; Georgian policy in, 108; Russian approach to, 164 *et sqq*.; Turkish policy in, 187-8; commerce of, in early Middle Ages, 322, 328, 330; commerce of, under the Mongols, 335-6; the Latins in the, 336-42; commerce of, in the 17th c., 354-5; the navigation of, and frequency of ship-wreck in, 355 and note 6
Blessing, the ceremony of, 212
Blinding, as a penalty, 278
Blood-feud, 275
Blood-price, scale of, 276; punitive character of, 277; of a nobleman, *ib*.

Bodbé, a village in Kakheti, E. of the Alazani, 140
Bodbis-khevi, 218
Bodchorma, (or Déda-tzikhé = "*Mother-Castle*"), an ancient town on the Yori, 52, 63, 85, 215
Bogolyubskoi, George, of Suzdal, marries Tamara, 104; divorce and exile of, *ib.*; first revolt of, 104-5; second revolt of, 106; 246
Bolnisi, Georgians defeated at, 112
Book of Wisdom and Lies, the, 316-17
Borchalo, river. See Débéda
Borchalo, district, along the Débéda river, 202, 211, 213, 287
Borena, wife of Bagrat III, 89
Boris (Godunov), Tsar, 165, 172 note 1, 182
Borjom, (Borjomi), gorge of, 9, 10
Börk, his views noted, 24 note 2
Bosporus, Kingdom of, 13, 47-8, 335
Botinauri, 276; value of, 277
Bow, in use in 18th c. among mountaineers, 204; in Imereti, in 17th c., 347.
Bowmen, of Georgia, fame of, 327, 339
Boxwood, trade in, 336
Bread, quality of Georgian, 352
Brigandage, penalties for, 278
Brockades, 325, 330
Bronze Age, reference to passing of, 12; in the Caucasus, 12 *et sqq.*; in the Kuban, 27, 39, 48, 52, 61; art of, in the Caucasus, 293
Brosset, M. F., his opinion on the identity of Æa with Nakalakevi, 51, 239, 277, 285
Brtsqinwalé, 122
Bryennios, Alexios, 99; Nikephoros, 99
Buddha, 317
Buffaloes, abound in Kakheti, 62; tax on, 187
Bugha-al-Kabir-al-Sharabi, captures Tiflis, 82
Bukai, Mongol *no'in*, 119
Bulachauri, a village in the district of Ertso, E. of the Aragvi, Persians defeated at, 214
Bulgaria, Bulgarians, in Byzantine Army, 70; at Malaskert, 92, 304; Tamara's knowledge of, 329; Bulgars, (Bolghars), on the Volga, 323-4
Bunturki, allusion to by Annalists, explained as "primitive Turks" by Brosset, probably Cimmerians, 52
Burgundy, Georgians at Court of, 339
Byzantium, Byzantine Empire, Byzantines, 45; character of its civilization considered, 70-1, 77; policy in Imereti, 80; Iconoclastic conflict in, 82; weakness of, 83; acquisition of Tao, 84; policy under Basil II, 86-7; invasions of Georgia, 87-8; intrigues in Abkhazeti, 89; in Samtzkhé and Armenia, 89-90; diplomatic relations with Abkhazeti, 88-9, 91; defeat at Malaskert, 92; loss of Georgian territories, 93; relations

400

INDEX

with David II, 99; condition in mid-12th c., 100–1; 104, 105, 108; potentates in Pontus, 121; Black Death in, 123; Catherine the Great's plans for revival of, 209; 242, 264, 275, 283 note 2, 303, 311, 321; and the Black Sea trade, 322, 329; trade with Georgia, 330; fashions of, in Georgia, 332; and the Latins, 336, 339. See also Greeks, Rome, Romans

CAFFA, 335, 336, 339–40, 341
Calligraphy, 306
Cambysene. See Kambechovani
Camel, the, not found in Imereti, 8; treatment of, for mange and scabs, 327; 347
Canvas, production of, 341
Capuchin monks in Georgia, 304
Carians, matriarchy among, 40
Caspian Gates, (probably the Daryal Pass, named from the city of Caspi on the Mtkvari), 64 note 4
Caspian Sea, way along the western shore of, 13; 14, 47, 100, 110, 164; islands of, 167, 172; international trade over, in 18th c., 182 *et sqq.*; policy of Peter the Great in, 183; Russian flotilla in, 184; Turkish policy in, 185–6, 187 note 6; policy of Nadir in, 192; economic dependence of Georgia on, 204–5; Russian policy in, 212–13; Arab trade across, 321 *et sqq.*; falcons of, 327–8; Genoese merchants in, 338; supply of fish from, 352; commerce of, in 17th c., 353 *et sqq.*; shipping on, 354 note 5.
Castelli, his portrait of Taymuraz I, 171, 345; his portrait of Alexander III, 348
Catalan Map, the, 336
Catalans, in the Black Sea, 336
Catherine II, Empress, Eastern policy of, 206–8; at Kherson, 209; policy in Georgia, 210–11; policy in Persia, 212–13; death of, 214
Catholicosate, the Georgian, 270 *et sqq.*
Cattle, kept indoors, 53 note 1; grazed round L. Panavari, 54; tax on, 263; plentiful in Kartli, 352
Caucasian State, in embryo under Tamara, 107–8; development towards, under Mukhranian and Kakhian Bagratids, 170 *et sqq.*, 196, 204–5
Caucasus, mountains, crossed, 3; reflections on passing of history in, 4–5; contrasted with the Eurasian plain, 6; in relation to ancient centres of civilization, *ib.*; in the Bronze Age, 12; cave-cities of, *ib.*; lake-dwellings of, *ib.*; persistence of matriarchal customs among mountain tribes of, 35; human geography of, 47 *et sqq.*; Russian approach in the Northern C., 162–4; development of policy in the Northern C., 182 *et sqq.*; Muslim culture in, 321 *et sqq.*
Cave-cities, cave-dwellings, in Caucasus, 12; some account of, 52–4; 63
Caviar, 327, 355
Census, the Mongol, 284; population of Georgia shown by, 285; the Russian, *ib.*
Centralized, type of church, 294–5, 300
Chakhtauli, 264
Chakobza, a secret language of the Circassian nobles, 30
Chalchedon, Council of, 269
Chaldia, (Khaldia), Byzantine name for the hinterland of Trebizond, 15 note 2
Chaldir, Lake. See Palakatsio, Lake
Chaldiran, (Khaldiran, Childir), Turkish name for the country s. of L. Palakatsio (Chaldir); defeat of Shah Ismail at, 139
Chamois, not found in Imereti, 8
Chaneti (Lazistan), Chans (Channi), significance of name-root, 25, 27–8; account of, 54 *et sqq.*; ceded to the Gurieli, 137; Turkish encroachments in, 138, 144, 145; 275, 328
Chantre, underestimated significance of Bronze Age in Caucasus, 12
Chardin, Sir John, on Persian and Turkish diplomacy in Georgia, 168–70; 178, 262, 273, 283, 285, 316, 348, 349; on the personality of Bagrat IV of Imereti, 351; on the charm of Georgia, 352; on the Black Sea trade, 355–6; on the character of the Georgians, 356; on Georgian women, 358 and note 3
Charmaghan, Mongol No'in, 112, 114
Chavchavadze, Garsevan, signs Treaty of Georgievsk, 210
Chébé, Mongol No'in, 110
Chechens, 62
Cherry, the, flourishes in W. Caucasus, 26, 346
Chesmé, Battle of, 206
Chestnut, the, grows in Imereti, 7; in W. Caucasus, 26; superior quality of, in Barda'a, 323.
Chikhori, a village in the district of Argueti, Giorgi VIII defeated at, 133, 137; victory of Solomon I at, 208
Childir. See Chaldiran
China, Chinese, 110, 123, 125, 162, 308, 318, 328, 330, 354
Chingiz Khan, 112, 113, 114, 120
Chkheidze, Sekhnia, 174 note 1, 178, 186, 315
Choloqashvili, Otar, stratagem of, 153; Nicholas Erbashi, a member of family of, 174 note 4, 178; Kai Khusraw, endorses Treaty of Georgievsk, 211
Chonchol-Musa-Htarisa, Lazghi leader, 199
Chordvaneli, family, 311
Chorokhi river, (Speris-tsqali or ? Boas), 7, 16; erroneously confused with Phasis, 28; 41, 49, 50, 52; description of region of, 53–8; history of region to 10th c., 80–5; 94, 99, 100, 125, 135, 267, 302, 306, 312, 315, 326
Chrapiert'h, an Armenian *melikate* of Karabagh, 185 note 2
Christianity, elements of paganism in Georgian, 38–9; introduction of, into Georgia, 267; and Islam in Georgia, 270

P   401

INDEX

Christie, Major, killed at Aslanduz, 218
Chronicle of Trebizond, the, 122 note 2
Chronicles of Sumbat, the, 238, 313
Chronographer, the Georgian, 245, 247, 248
Chubiani, in Svaneti, not identified on the map; Church of Christ near, 301
Chukhuli, a village in Svaneti, not identified on the map; icon of Archangels Gabriel and Michael of, 302
Chulak-Surkhai-Khan, 184
Chunchirakhi, 262
Church, the Georgian, privileges assailed by David V, 118; favoured by Dmitri II, 118-9; historical sketch of, 269 *et sqq.*; close connection of, with Byzantine, *ib.*; separation of, from Armenian, *ib.*; wealth and privileges of, 270-1; decline of, 272-4; relations of, with the Papacy, 337-9
Cilicia, 330
Cimmerian Bosporus, 48
Cimmerians, said to have passed through Daryal, 3, 11, 17, 24 note 1, 31; probable reference to by Annalists under name Bunturki, 52
Circassia, the Circassians, (*Georgian*, Cherkezeti, the Cherkez; Cherkesses), the mountainous district along the Black Sea Coast, N.N.W of Abkhazeti, called also Jiketi in Georgian sources; megaliths in, 14; different forms of the name, population and language of, 29-30, 31; matriarchal practices in, 35; cult of Merissa in, 40; flight of Mithradates along C. coast, 43; type of house in, 55; Byzantine missionaries in, 78, 80; part of Kingdom of Osseti, 85; Sharvashidzes in, 137 note 1; Russian assumption of suzerainty over, 164; their raids into Mingrelia, 178; abortive Turkish invasion of, 189; employed as mercenaries by Irakli II, 203-4; Turkish policy in, 209 and note 1; slave-trade in, 283, 287; trade with Trebizond, 322 and note 1; description of, by el-Masudi, 325; trade of the Latins with, 336, 356
Clavijo, Ruy Gonzalez de, his reference to the Georgians, 339
Climate, of Imereti, 7; of Amier, 8; of the Western Caucasus, 26
Cloth, 325
Code of Giorgi the Brilliant, 280
Code of Wakhtang VI, 235, 248, 271, 286
Coinage, of David II and Dmitri I, 333
Colchians, Colchis, a name applied to Imereti by classical writers; reputed Egyptian origin of the, 14; 25, 41, 43; description of, 47-51; 74; wars in, 77-8; decline of classical civilization in, 78; 283 note 2; 293, 322. See also Lazica, Imereti
Combat, trial by, 277; process of, 278
Comnenos, family, connections of, with the Bagratids, 108 note 1, 122 note 2, 123, 172 note 1; Alexios, Emperor of Byzantium, 100, 305; John, Emperor of Byzantium, 101; Alexios, Emperor of Trebizond, 108, 138; Andronikos, at court of Giorgi III, 108 note 1; Anna, wife of Bagrat V, 122 note 2, 123
Confiscation of property, 280
Congress, of Bucuresti, 208; of Foksani, 207-8
Conrad, Emperor, 101
Conscription, imposed by Irakli II, 201 and note 3
Conspiracy against Crown, penalty for, 277
Constantine VII (Porphyrogenitos), Emperor, reference to, 51, quoted; 58, 322
Constantine VIII, Emperor, 88
Constantine XIII, Emperor, 120
Constantine III, (Kostantiné), King of Kartli, his correspondence with Isabella of Castille, 132 and 338; his campaigns, 138; recognizes Division of the Kingdom, 138-9; 140, 174; his relations with Pope Alexander VI, 338
Constantine, son of David IV, 119
Constantine, son of David VII, at the camp of Timur, 125; killed by the Turkomans, 126
Constantine, son of Alexander II of Kakheti, a parricide, 165
Constantine, brother of Wakhtang V, 191 note 4
Constantine, (Mahmad-Quli-Khan), of Kakheti, attacks Wakhtang VI, 186-7; a prisoner and fugitive, 187; killed, 188; 191
Constantine, Grand Duke, of Russia, 209
Constantinople. See Byzantium, Stambul
Contarini, Ambrogio, 135; his adventures in Georgia, 339; his account of Mingrelia, 341; his opinion of Shamakha, 353
Conversion of the Georgians, The, 313
Conversion of the Somekhians, The, 313
Conybeare, F. C., quoted on Armenian language, 23
Copper, early mining of, in Caucasus, 12, 18; in the Chorokhi valley, 57; in the Débéda valley, 59; in Imereti, 345, 355
Corn, rarely sown in Imereti, 7
Coronation, royal, ceremony of, 261
Cossack Line, the, 206, 207, 209
Cossacks, as an instrument of conquest, 164-5; invade Daghestan, 184
Costume, adoption of Persian, in Kakheti, deplored by Wakhushti, 150; of merchants, 231; formal, of *eristavni*, 242; attention to details of, in Georgian fresco-painting, 305-6; for a beautiful woman, 309; for the sick, for mourners, monks, harlots, *ib.*; of Georgians in 15th c., 341; of Imerians in 17th c., 347; of Alexander III, 348; imported from Stambul, 355; tendency to adopt Persian, 356; of the women, 358 note 4
Cotton, rarely sown in Imereti, 7; spun in Shamakha in 17th c., 353-4
Court Regulations, the, 260-1
Court, Royal, 255, 257-8, 260, 314, 331; of Justice, 242, 281

INDEX

Crimea, Tatars of, invade Shirvan, 156–7; invade Georgia, 166; Russian policy in, 182 *et sqq.*, 206; Russian annexation of, 209, 210–11; called Gazaria in Middle Ages, 336 note 1
Cruciform, The, plan, in Georgian architecture, 295, 297, 300
Crusades, character of, 95–6; influence of, on rise of the Georgian Mediæval Kingdom, 96, 100–1; failure of Third, 101
Ctesiphon, 45, 47
Cucumbers, found in Imereti, 346
Cupola, the, in Georgian architecture, 294–6, 300
Currants, of all kinds, found in Imereti, 346
Currency, attempt by Irakli II to stabilize, 201; of Imereti, 346
Customs dues, 262
Cyprus, 329

Daba, 240
Dabil. See Dwin
Dachi, a son of Wakhtang Gurgaslani, 79
Dadiani, (territorial patronymic of the ruling princes of Mingrelia, probably deriving from the river Dadi), 104, 107, 120; Tzotné, 112; a D. supports David IV, 116–17; Liparit, becomes virtually independent in Mingrelia, 137; Wamek, rebels against Bagrat II, 138; Mamia, supports pretensions of Rustem to Imerian throne, 159–60; power and unpleasant character of Levan, 166; reference to a D., 178; Otia, and Alexander V, 188–9, 207; Grigol, submits to Russians, 216–17, 218; 271 note 2, 282, 286, 349, 355
Dadianis-Svaneti, that part of S.W. Svaneti owing allegiance to the Dadianis of Mingrelia, 301
Daghestan, 24 note 1, 30, 62, 66, 98; Russian operations in, 164; confederation of tribes of, against Russia, 183–4; previous history of political relations, 184 note 1; state of, note 2; intended invasion of, by Wakhtang VI, 185 and note 4; disasters of Nadir in, 191–2, 193; Safavi pretender in, 193; condition of, in 18th c., 198, 199, 204, 216, 218; 285, 293; manufacture of armour in, 327; 344
Daikh. See Tao
Dakae, probable settlement of Tao by, 24 note 1
Dalakishvili, Wakléman, revolt of, 213
Dalotsva, 252
Damascus, 101
Damat Muhammad Pasha, 194
Damghisi, a village in Hereti, N. of the Mtkvari; defeat of Lazghis at, 199
Danana, identified with Nana, 39 and note 2
Dapanchuli, Gabriel, 244
Daphni, 295
Daraduz, the valley of, in Azerbaijan, 108
Dar-bar, 258; *Darbazi*, 258; *Darbazis Kars Mdgomni*, list of, 258

Dardanians, reference to invasion of Asia Minor by, 12
Dar-ul-Islam, 110, 321 *et sqq.*
Daryal Pass, description of, 3; *dar-i-Alan*, 10; 22, 31, 61; construction of fortress at, 99, 100; 204; passage of, by Gen. Todleben, 207, 211
Dastulamali, 262, 280
Date-palm, found in Imereti, 7
David (Bagrationi), Kuropalatês of Tao, 84, 311
David (Artzruni), defeated by Er-Toghrul, 87
David (Bagratuni), King of Siuniq, 89
David II, (Davit-i), *Aghmashenebeli*, King of Georgia, character of his achievement, 96–7; his personal character, 97; military successes of, 98; diplomacy of, 99; relations with Kipchaks, *ib.*; victories over Seljuks, 99–100; death, achievement considered, 100, 101, 107; his sacred standard, 110; 229, 245, 248, 264, 270, 276; his likeness at Gelati, 305–6; his studious habit, 314; 331, 333
David III, King of Georgia, brief reign of, 101; his son, 102
David IV, *Narin*, King of Georgia, son of Rusudani, 113; at Karakorum, 114; his character, *ib.*; king in Tiflis, *ib.*; proclaimed King of the Imerians, 116; difficulties with David V, 116–17; misfortune and death of, 118–19; 120, 121, 122 and note 2, 135, 334
David V, King of Georgia, bastard son of Giorgi IV, 109; early adventures, 113–14; at Karakorum, 114; his character, *ib.*; king in Tiflis, *ib.*; his service in the Mongol armies, 116; revolt and flight to Kutais, *ib.*; restored, 117; his favourites, *ib.*; death, *ib.*; 118, 334
David VI, King of Georgia, his misfortunes and cynical character, 120, 121
David VII, King of Georgia, 122
David, ("the first", King of Kakheti), 138
David VIII, King of Kartli, his character and undistinguished reign, 139
David III, (Imam-Quli-Khan), King of Kakheti, 180 and note 6
David, (Da'ud Khan), a son of Luarsab I, 152, 153, 155, 167, 170
David, son of Taymuraz I, 344, 348
David, son of Archili of Imereti, assumed the name and style of Solomon II, *q.v.*
David, *Batonishvili*, son of Giorgi XII, 215
Davitisdze, Sumbat, 230, 232, 313; Chronicles of, 238, 313
Daylem, battle of, 189
Dchiaberi, 104–5
Dchqondideli, the Bishop of Dchqondidi, who generally held the post of *Mdsignobart-Ukhutsesi*—Grand Secretary. See under Dchqondidi
Dchqondidi (*great oak*), an episcopal see and village E. of the Tskhenis-tsqali; Bishop Simon of, 100; Bishop Mikel of, 102–4; Bishop Antoni of, 106, 233,

INDEX

315; Bishop Basil of, executed, 117; Bishop Giorgi of, 251; peculiar position of Bishop of, in relation to Army, 264, 331

Débéda, river, (called also Berduji or Borchalo), an affluent of the Mtkvari, reference to, 25, 54; account of, 59–60; 204

Déda, 37

Déda-Tzikhé. See Bodchorma

Deer, as totem, 36; found in Imereti, 345

Delhi, sack of, Irakli II at, 191 note 5

Demna. See Dmitri, son of David III

Derbend, different names of, 10; 61, 64–6, 80, 107, 113, 119, 156, 184, 185–6, 192, 209, 214, 217, 284, 322, 352, 353

Dervish Muhammad, of Shaki, 148

Design, vegetable, 293, 297; interlaced, 297, 299

Dévé-Boyun (*the camel's back*) mountains, form the watershed of the Araks and the W. Euphrates, 9

Diamonds, 330, 334, 348

Diarbekr, 101, 145

Diasamidze, family, plots of, 203; Tamara, 300

Dictionary, Georgian, the, of Saba Sulkhan Orbeliani, 316

Did-didni, 226

Dideba, 244

Didebuleba, characteristic features of, 244

Didebul-i (-ni), 242; explanation of term, 244; in relation to *aznaurni*, 244; position of, 244–5; *tavad-i* (-ni), 249; *aznaur-i* (-ni), 250; *khelisupal-i* (-ni), 251; *koneba*, 253; *kartuelni, sameposani, sakartvelosani*, 244, 246–8, 271

Didgwarian-i (-ni), 255

Did-i (-ni), 258

Didoeti, a mountainous district to the N.E. of Kakheti on the borders of the Avar country; *moʿuravate* of, 140 note 1; 171 note 1, 344

Diehl, Charles, quoted, 302

Dighomi, a village of Shida-Kartli, in the neighbourhood of Mukhrani, not identified on the map, 203

Digori, river, 29, 31

Dio Cassius, quoted, 75 and note 3, 224–5

Diogenes, Romanos, Emperor, defeated at Malaskert, 92

Dioscurias, 50, 262, 308

Djruchi, a village on the Qwirila in Argueti, 306

Dmanisi, (Dbanisi), a village and fortress in Somkheti on the river Machaveri, an affluent of the Khrami; 102, 156–7, 333 note 3, 353

Dmitri, King of Abkhazeti, 246

Dmitri, (Giorgishvili), son of Giorgi I, 89–90, 101, 104

Dmitri I, King of Georgia, anecdote concerning, 97 note 1; reign of, 101–2; coins of, 333

Dmitri, (Demna, son of David III), 101; revolt of, 102–4

Dmitri II, *Tav-dadébuli*, minority of, 118; his character, *ib.*; his morals, 119; his misfortunes and execution, *ib.*; 120, 121, 122 note 2, 267, 270, 279

Dmitri, *Eristavt-Eristavi* of Imereti, 135

Dog, sanctity of, referred to, 36

Dogs, running, 277

Dolis-Khané, in the Chorokhi valley, 297

Domenti II, the Catholicos, 287

Don, river, 335

Donauri, family and ruling house of Kakheti, 81, 83–4, 85–6

Dragon, religious significance of, referred to, 36, 39

Dranda, a village N. of the Kodori in Samurzaqano, 295–6

Drugs, 356

Drum, the, in Georgian architecture, 295–6, 300

Dsarchinebul-i (-ni), definition of term, 245, position of, *ib.*; *sameposani, sakartuelosani, kueqnisani, ib.*

Dshauri, *moʿuravate* of, in Kakheti, 140 note 1

Dsqaleba, 252; manner of, 254. See also *Shedsqaleba*

Dsqalobis dsigni, 254

Dsqalobis qmani, 235

Dsurilni erni, 232

Dubois de Montpéreux, his views on the Circassians, quoted, 29–30; on Vardistzikhé, 50; on Nakalakevi, 51; on Abkhaz and Circassian dwellings, 55

Due(s), the *eristavi's*, 242; *satsikhistao*, 243; *sakhevisupalo, ib.*

Dufréné, erroneous opinion of, 12

Dukas, Constantine X, Emperor, 91; Michael, 91

Dusheti, a town in the district of Bazaleti in Shida-Kartli, 31, 216

Dutch, trade across the Caspian, 182

Dvaleti, a district of Shida-Kartli, 166

Dvali, 306, 311

Dwin, (Dvin, Dovin, *Arab* Dabil, *Greek* Tibion), an Armenian city to the E. of the river Araks, 80, 81, 85–6, 90; captured and lost by Giorgi III, 102; captured by David Soslan, 106; 107, 284, 323

Dyeing industry, importance of in mediæval Caucasus, 326

Dye-houses, tax on, 271

Dzagam, a village of Shamshadilo, between Kazakh and Shamkhor, 106

Dzegli Eristavta, quoted, 240, 314

Dzurdzuks, a Georgian mountain tribe referred to by the Annalists, possibly identifiable with, or occupying neighbouring territory to, the Khevsurs; used as mercenaries by Saurmagi, 41–2

Echmiadzin, a village and Metropolitan See of Armenia, N. of the Araks, 147

Edessa, 96, 101

Education, 269

Egrisi, ancient Georgian name for Imereti, *q.v.*; ancient *Eristavate* of, 238

INDEX

Egros, eponymous hero of the Mingrelians, 16
Egypt, references to raid of Sea Peoples on, 11, 12 ; alleged connection with Colchis, 14 ; 106, 116, 118, 302, 318
Ekaterinograd, a Russian fortified settlement on the Terek, 209
Elam, referred to, 12, 14
Elbruz Mt., 27
Elias, St., cult of, 38
Eliseni (Elisu), *moʻuravate* of, in Kakheti, 140 note 1 ; Sultanate of, 216
Elizabeth, Empress, 192 and note 4
Elk, found in Imereti, 345
Elkalkashandi, 315
Elton, Captain, in service of Nadir, 192
Emeralds, 334, 348
Emin, Joseph, an Armenian traveller, quoted, 196 *et sqq.* ; his friendship with Irakli II, 201-2 ; biography of, 201 note 8
Enamels, 303
Enashi, in Svaneti, not identified on the map, 301
England, English, trade across the Caspian, 182 ; Captain employed by Nadir in, 192 ; officers in Russian fleet, 206 ; policy in Turkey and Persia during Napoleonic Wars, 217-8 ; relations with the Mongols, 335
Enguri river, reference to, 7
Enikolophian, Mirza-Gurgina, favourite of Irakli II, 201 and note 10, 208 ; Karaman, 201 note 10
Ephrem *Mtsiré*, 311
Erbashi, (Isbarghi or Irbakhi), Nicholas, his peregrinations, 171 note 1, 172 ; at court of Alexander III, 349
Eri, 237
Erismtavar-i (-ni), 239. See also *Mtavar-i (-ni)*
Eristav-i (-ni), 41, Thong Yabghu Khakan appointed, 79 ; an Imperial E. in Mingrelia, *ib.* ; of Abkhazeti, 80 ; origin and definition of term, 237 ; introduction of, *ib.* ; position of, 238 ; list of, *ib.* ; office and authority of, 240-1 ; character of the office of, 239 ; struggle for power, 239 ; dress and insignia of, 242 ; 240, 243, 247, 252, 260
Eristavoba, 239
Eristavt-Eristav-i (-ni), 89, 228, 230 ; list of, 238 ; the first mention of title of, 240 ; position of, *ib.* ; authority of, 242 ; power of, *ib.* ; subordinate officials of, *ib.* ; insignia of, 242, 251-2
Eristavt-Mtavari, 78, 79
Erivan, a city of Armenia, on the left bank of the river Hraztan (Zanga), 147, 152, 165, 168, 186, 187 note 6, 190, 194, 197, 198 and note 4, 202, 204, 210, 211, 213, 217, 352-4
Erni, *msoplioni*, 232 ; *dsurilni, ib.* See also *Qma(ni)*
Ertatzminda, a village in Sabaratiano in the valley of the Algeti, 306
Er-Toghrul, 87
Ertso, a district of Kakheti, 167
Erzerum, a name applied since the 11th c. to the Byzanto-Armenian city of Theodosiopolis-Garin. The original Erzerum (arzen-er-Rum = a district or fortress of the Romans) of the Arab writers, probably the Kalikala of Arab travellers, was situated farther to the S., and was sacked by the Seljuks in 1049 ; the surviving inhabitants removing to Garin. Reference to, 54 ; captured by Persians in 502, 77 ; Basil II at, 87 ; Seljuks burn, 90 ; 99, 105, 107, 113 note 1 ; Seraskier of, occupies Samtzkhé, defeats Imerians at Sokhoista, 145-6
Erzinjan, 104, 113 note 1
Etruscan, compared with S. Caucasian languages, 22
Eunuchs, 283 note 2
Euphrates river, 9, 15, 24, 95
Euxine Sea. See Black Sea
Evliya Chelebi, 183 note 2, 343, 353-4
Evlogi, 332
Evthimé, St., 312, 317
Ewstaté, St., Life of, of Mtzkheta, quoted, 78-9, 238
Exaltation of the Living Cross of Mtzkheta, The, 313
Ezekiel, quoted 283, note 2
Ezos-Modzghvari, 262

FACE-CREAMS, 228
Fadlun, Emir of Ganja, 92
Falcons, white, 277 ; stone, *ib.* ; tax on, 263 ; fame of Caucasian and Caspian, 327-8 ; 331, 355
Falkenstein, Count, incognito of the Emperor Joseph II, 209
Farnajomi, King of Iberia, 42
Farnavazi, (Parnabazus), King of Iberia, 40-1, 51, 59, 222, 237-8, 309, 310
Farnavazi, a son of Irakli II, 215
Farsman II, *Kweli*, Iberian king, 75, 224-5
Fartzkhisi, a village on the W. bank of the river Algeti ; Battle of, 93
Fath'Ali Shah, 217
Fealty, oath of, 252
Feast-days, ceremonies on, described, 351
Feodor Ivanovich, Tsar, 164, 343
Feudalism, 250 *et sqq.*
Feudum, 251
Figs, of Barda'a, 323
Finno-Ugrian languages in relation to Georgian, 22 *et sqq.*
Fire-cult, 26-42
Fish, abundance of, in lakes of Samtzkhé, 9 ; cult of, in pagan Georgia, 36 ; unsavoury taste of in L. Panavari, 54 note 1 ; importation of salt, 341 ; abundant supply of, in Kartli, 352, 355
Flax, grown in Colchis, 49 note 1
Flocks, tax on, 263
Florence, Council of, 338
Florentines, in the Black Sea, 336
Foxes, abound in Imereti, 345

INDEX

France, French, ambassador and Russo-Turkish negotiations, 186; diplomat and Russo-Turkish boundary commission, 188 note 2; policy at Stambul, 206; threatened intervention of, 208; policy in Persia during Napoleonic Wars, 217; 299, 329; relations with the Mongols, 335; Georgian envoys in, 339

Franks (Europeans) in Byzantine army at Malaskert, 92

Fraser, Sir James, quoted, 35

Frederick II, Emperor, 111

Frederick the Great, his admiration for Irakli II, 201

Frescoe-painting, 294; frescoes, 294, 300, 303, 305-6

Fruit-trees, tax on, 187, 192, 323, 352

Furnaces, tax on, 263

Furs, fur-trade, across the Caspian, 324-5

GA, a Georgian god, 37 *et sqq.*

Gabriel, a jeweller, 215

Gachiani, a fortress on the Khrami, 60

Gagi, Waraz, lord of, 79; Turks defeated at, 102; Waram, lord of, 109-11

Gagik, King of Kakheti, 89

Galgais (? Ghelæ, Ghlighwis), a sub-tribe of the Chechens, 32, 204 and note 1

Gall-nuts, 326

Gamosavali, Saeristavoi, 242

Gamrekeli, (1) supports Demna, 102; honoured by Tamara, 104; opposes Bogolyubskoi, 105; 107, 253; (2) compounds with the Mongols, 113

Ganja, (Gantzak, Elizavetopol), reference to, 12, 65, 85-6, 90; Kadi, of, his disputations with David II, 97 note 1; 99, 106, 107; revolt of, against Giorgi IV, 109; 111, 113, 139, 153, 166, 186, 187 note 6, 190, 197, 198 and note 4, 202, 204, 211, 213, 214, 217, 284, 308, 333 note 3, 353-4

Ganmgebel-i (-ni) sakmeta, 251

Gardabani, a name for the province between Tiflis and the Berduji, (also Gachiani or Khunani), 79

Garesja, village and hermitage in Kakheti, 119

Garin, an Armenian city by the sources of the Araks, generally identified with Byzantine Theodosiopolis. See Erzerum, Theodosiopolis

Garisi, a village in Somkheti, not identified on map, battle at, 140

Garnhi, in Siuniq, Georgians defeated at, 111

Gatsi, a Georgian god, 37 *et sqq.*

Gazaria, mediæval Latin name for Crimea, 336 note 1

Geese, tax on, 263

Geguti (called also Tzikhé-Darbassé), a village and royal demesne in Imereti, W. of the Rioni, 105, 331

Gelati, in Imereti, S.E. of Kutais, 145, 296-7, 301-3, 305-6, 312, 345

Gelovani, family name of the *Eristavni* of the Svans, 137, 207

Genoa, Genoese, commerce in the Black Sea, 330, 335 *et sqq.*, relations with Byzantium, 336; with Trebizond, Russia and the Caucasus, 336-8; in the Caspian, 338; conduct of, in Mingrelia, 342

Geographical Description of Georgia, 316

George of Trebizond, 317

George, St., Bank of, 338; cult of, 38-9

Georgia, Georgians, character of natural scenery of, 3, 4; natural features of, described, 6 *et sqq.*; Bronze and early Iron Ages in, 9 *et sqq.*; early migrations into, 21 *et sqq.*; languages of, 23 *et sqq.*; geography of mountain districts of, 26 *et sqq.*; matriarchy in, 35-6; pagan cults in, 37-40; Persian influences in, 41-3; Roman conquest of, 43-5; Classical geography of, 46 *et sqq.*; digression on national characteristics of, 71 *et sqq.*; Classical culture of, 74; history to Arab conquest, 74-9; Byzantine policy in 80-1; rise of the Abkhazian Kings, 81-4; state of, at beginning of 11th c., 85-7; Byzantine invasion of, 87-8; baron's wars in, 87 *et sqq.*; Seljuk invasions of, 90 *et sqq.*; influence of Crusades on rise of Bagratid Kingdom at beginning of 12th c., 95 *et sqq.*; establishment of monarchy under David II, 95-100; depopulated districts settled by Kipchaks, 99; character of Kingdom under Tamara, 107; parlous state of, at beginning of 15th c., 125-6; recovery of, under Alexander, 126-7; condition of, in middle of 15th c., 131 *et sqq.*; Georgians in Persia, 152 *et sqq.*; political and economic state of, at end of 17th c., 174-8; state of, in 18th c., 196 *et sqq.*; Georgians among Lazghis, 198-9; character of Irakli's Kingdom, 201-5; Russian intervention in, 206-8; Russian protectorate over, 210-11; Persian invasion of, 212-14; Russian annexation of, 215 *et sqq.*; early social system of, 221-7; the middle and lower classes in mediæval, 228 *et sqq.*; the ruling classes in, 237-49; the institution of feudalism in, 250-6; officials and administration in, 257-62; minting of money in, 262; taxation in, 262-4; organization of the army in, 264-5; religion and the Church in, 266 *et sqq.*; principles and administration of justice in, 275-81; slave-trade in, 282-4, 286-7, 355; estimates of population of, during Middle Ages, 284-5; effects of slave-trade on ethnography of Middle East, 385-6; lot of peasantry in, 286-8; the arts in, 293 *et sqq.*; architecture in, 294-301; metallurgy and enamelling in, 301 *et sqq.*; iconography, 302-5; fresco-painting, 305-6; calligraphy and illumination, 306-7; character of med-

INDEX

iæval literature of, 308 *et sqq.*; origin of alphabet, 309–10; early ecclesiastical literature, 311–12; early mediæval historians of, 312–13; the natural sciences in, 315; mediæval universities in, 315; later writers of, 316–17, 320; the mediæval poets of, 317–19; trade of, under the Arabs, 321 *et sqq.*; prosperity and wealth of, in 11th–12th c., 329–34; trade of Italian cities with, 336; relations of the Papacy with, 329–30, 337–8; relations with Spain, France and Burgundy, 338–9; Barbaro's description of, 340–1; Contarini's description of, 341; Russian relations with, 342 *et sqq.*; Mishetski's description of, 344; economic condition of, in 17th c., 351 *et sqq.*; Chardin's account of the Georgians, 356; of Georgian women, 358. See also Iberia, Kartli, Kakheti, Imereti, Abkhazeti, etc.

Georgian Annals. See Annals, Georgian
Georgian Chronicle, The, 313
Georgian Military Road, made by Russians, 3, 211
Georgievsk, a Russian town in the Northern Caucasus, 209
German language, "*Japhetic*" elements in, 22
Germans, 30
Germany, relations of Giorgi III with, 329
Ghado, name applied by the Annalists to a part of the Likhi Mountains, 52 and note 1
Ghaiath-al-din Kai Khusraw II, Sultan of Konia, 113 and note 1
Ghala, 235
Ghazan, Il-Khan, 119
Ghazi-Ghumukh, a tribe of Daghestan, 184, 192, 344
Ghazni, 318
Ghelæ. See Galgais
Ghilan, Georgian raid into, 108; Georgian troops employed by Mongols in, 116; Wakhtang III in, 120; Kakhians deported to, 167; Russian campaign in, 184–5; 189, 190, 326 note 4
Ghimri, 24 note 1
Ghlighwis. See Galgais
Ghur Turks, 102
Giorgi I, King of Abkhazeti and Kartli, 85; marries Mariam Artzruni, 86; his two campaigns against Basil II, 87–8; his death, 88; 306
Giorgi II, King of Abkhazeti and Kartli, his character, 93; victory at Fartzkhisi, *ib.*; defeat at Kweli, *ib.*; his misfortunes, 94; 250, 314
Giorgi III, King of Georgia, began construction of Vardzia, 53, 101; wars of, 102–3; his character, 102; his domestic policy, 102–3; 104, 105, 229, 238, 245, 255, 314; his foreign relations, 329; his treasure, 334
Giorgi IV, *Lasha*, King of Georgia, 101 note 1, 104, 107; his character, 109; resentment of the nobles, *ib.*; defeat near Khunani, 110; death, *ib.*; 111, 114, 115, 122, 264, 270, 314
Giorgi V, *Brtsqinwalé*, King of Georgia, 120; his vigorous policy and reforms, 121–2, 123; 280, 314–15, 330, 338
Giorgi VI, *Mtsiré*, King of Georgia, 120, 121
Giorgi VII, King of Georgia, revolts against Timur, 123–4, 339
Giorgi VIII, King of Georgia, character of, 133; defeated at Chikhori, 137; further misfortunes of, 137–8
Giorgi IX, King of Kartli, his unimportant reign, 138; reputed "crusade" of, *ib.* note 1
Giorgi X, King of Kartli, 165, 170
Giorgi XI, (Shah Nawaz II or Gurgin Khan), King of Kartli, 176, 178, 180 note 1, 182, 351 note 4
Giorgi XII, King of Kartli and Kakheti, his unattractive appearance and personality, 213 and 215 note 7; his ineptitude, 213–14; reoccupies Tiflis, 214; succession difficulties, 215; his religiosity, *ib.*; death *ib.*; his widow, 216
Giorgi (*Av*—"the Bad", "the first" of Kakheti), 133, 139, 140
Giorgi II, King of Imereti, 159, 300
Giorgi III, King of Imereti, 166, 170
Giorgi V, a passing King of Imereti, 178 note 1
Giorgijanisdze (or Janashvili), Farsadan, 315
Giurgura, (Qwarqwaré III), 340 and note 1
Gizir, 242
Glekh-i (-ni), 232; value of, 282. See also *Qma (-ni)*
Goats, kept underground, 53 note 1; tax on, 137; head of wild g. as ceremonial gift, 331, 345
Gog and Magog, 6
Gogarene. See Samtzkhé
Gold, mines in the Chorokhi valley, 57; along the Débéda, 59; 201; coin, 262, 328 and note 3, 334, 347, 348–9
Golden Fleece, Land of the, possible interpretation of legend about, 4
Golden Horde. See Kipchak
Goldsmiths, 303
Gomi, 349
Gonia, a small port of Guria, 148, 262
Gophanto, a village N. of the river Qwirila in the district of Okriba; victory of Simon I at, 159
Gordedzi, ancient *Eristavate* of, 238
Gordi, a village on the Tskhenis-tsqali in Saliparitiano, Church of, 305
Gori, a town of Kartli, at the junction of the Liakhvi with the Mtkvari, 31, 53 note 1, 60 note 5, 105, 139, 156, 157, 168, 187, 190, 193, 204, 214, 216, 265, 271, 341
Goshawks, fame of Georgian, 327
Grammar, Georgian, 315

INDEX

Granada, 338
Grand Falconer. See *Baziert-Ukhutsesi*
Grand Secretary, office of. See *Mdsignobart-Ukhutsesi*
Grape-vine, the, in Imereti, 7; in W. Caucasus, 26; in Samtzkhé, 54 note 3; tax on, 191; 192, 235, 326, 346, 354
Great Mother, cult of the, 39–40
Greeks, religious influence of, in Georgia, 39–40; use of Greek mercenaries, 41; in the Black Sea, 48 *et sqq.*; in Pontus and Chaneti, 55–6; civilization contrasted with Roman, 69–70; inscription at Mtzkheta, 75. See also Byzantium
Greek miners, employed by Irakli II, 201 and note 4
"Greek" products in Georgia, 330
Gregory, the Illuminator, 65
Gregory, the Theologian, 306
Gremi, a royal town of the Kakhian Bagratids, N.N.E. of the Alazani, 63; *mo'uravate* of, 140 note 1; peacocks at, 150; 312, 319, 344
Guaram (Bagrationi), 78
Guaramisdze, Vaché, 255
Guaramishvili, 320
Gubazes, Colchian leader, 74
Guido, Abbot, 317
Gujarni, 334 note 1
Gulakov, Gen., 215
Gulistan, an Armenian *melikate* of Karabagh (called also Thalish), 185 note 2; Treaty of, 217
Gulnabad, Battle of, 181
Gumri, (Leninakan), reference to, 24 note 1
Gurandukht, (Anchabadze), heiress of Abkhazeti, 84, 297
Gurgen (Bagrationi), Kuropalates of Kartli, 84
Guria, Gurians, a province of Imereti between the Acharis-tsqali and the Black Sea, 50, 78; Wardanisdzes established as virtually independent in, 137; Turkish encroachments in, 148, 204; Turkish disaster in, 208; defeat of Solomon I by, 210; merchants of, 346
Gurieli (territorial patronymic of the Wardanisdze family, princes of Guria), 120, 122; Kakhaber revolts against Giorgi VIII, 137; relations with Bagrat III, 145; loss of Batum and Gonia, 148; and the first Imerian Succession War, 159, 171; Dmitri, Giorgi III and Mamia, passing Kings of Imereti, 178 note 1; 207, 282, 349
Guzani, Lord of Klarjeti, 240
Gwar-i (-*ni*), 34; definition of, 221, 224; size and wealth of, 224; *sameupé*, 222; *samghudelo*, 223; the social status of, 224; social division of, 225; *mamasakhlisi* of, 221; in bondage, 223; *msakhureul-i* (-*ni*), 229; 239, 244, 248–9
Gwarian-i (-*ni*), *gwarishvil-i* (-*ni*), *gwarowan-i* (-*ni*), 225–6, 229, 230, 250, 255. See also *Aznaur-i* (-*ni*)
Gymnias, 56

Gza, 242
Gzir-i (-*ni*), 242

HADRIAN, Emperor, 76, 224
Ha'iq, name of the Armenians, 16, 24
Hajji-Aziz, his offensive conduct, 116; executed, 117
Hajji Da'ud Effendi, 183
Hajji-Chelebi, 197, 203
Halizones, possible connection with Albanians, 19
Hamadan, 110
Hamah, 118
Hanway, Jonas, 178, 182, 183 note 2
Haos, eponymous hero of the Armenians, 16, 24
Harmozika. See Armazi
Harunabad, 328
Harun-al-Rashid, 81
Hasarapat, 237
Hassan Beg, of Shaki, 148
Hassan Pasha, defeated at Tabakhméla, 157
Haukal, ibn-, quoted, 323 *et sqq.*
Haydar, Shah, 155
Hazarpeshni, 304
Hebrew, 315
Hellanicus, 18
Hemp, produced in Colchis, 49 note 1; in Circassia, 325; in Imereti, 345
Heniokhes, 28
Henry II, King of England, 270, 284 note 1
Hephthalites (or White Huns), 77
Heraklius, Emperor, his campaigns in Georgia, 79; 80
Herat, 176
Hereti, the ancient name for a province of Kakheti, occupying the triangle of country above the junction of the rivers Yori and Alazani with the Mtkvari; 62–4, 85, 90, 101 note 2, 102–3, 105, 113, 120, 238, 264. See also Kakheti
Hermann, Gen., 211
Hermonassa, 48
Herodotus, on the Colchians, 14; on Persian rule in Trans-Caucasia, 40; on the Colchian slave-trade, 283 note 2
Hippobotus, (*horse pasture*). See Mughan
History of the Aghovanians, The, 64–6
History of the Kings, Gods, Bishops and Catholicoses of Georgia, 313
Hittites, 11–12; probable contacts with Trans-Caucasia, 15; reference to, 22; gods in the Georgian Pantheon, 36 *et sqq.*
Holders of King's seats, 240
Holsteiners, trade across the Caspian, 182, 353
Holy Land, 271
Honey, abundance of, in Imereti, 8; Colchian h. reported bitter, 49; trade in, 325
Honorius III, Pope, 110, 329
Hormuzd IV, 239
Horse, as totem, 36, 39; breeding in Mughan, 64 note 4; as tribute, 135; tax on, 187; as ceremonial gift, 331; great price paid for, 333; 347, 355

408

INDEX

House, the Royal, limited prerogatives of, 246
Houses, description of, in ancient Iberia, 52; in mediæval Georgia, 53; among the Laz and Abkhaz, 54–5; tax on, 263
Hovannes Smbat, King of Armenia, 87
Huisyng, his views noted, 24 note 2
Hulagu, Il-Khan, 114, 115, 116–17
Huns, 10, 30–31; Albanian missions to, 65
Hussain, Shah, 183, 185 note 4, 186 note 3
Hyena, the, not found in Imereti, 8
Hyperboreans, Land of the, 6
Hyrcania, Classical name for Ghilan, *q.v.*
Hysperitis. See Ispir

IBERIA (Iberians), a name used by the Classical writers to describe Eastern Georgia, 25; paganism in, 37 *et sqq.*; early Kings of, 40–2; Roman conquest of, 43; description of, 47 and 60–2; history of kingdom, 74–9, 224, 270. See also Kartlians, Georgians
Ibrahim, Shaikh, of Shirvan, 125, 126
Ibrahim Khan, 191
Ibrahim, Shah, 282
Iceland, 317
Iconoclastic Emperors, 270
Icons, miracle-working, 234, 280 and note; metal and painted, 294, 296–9, 301–4
Idols, 42; at Baku, 66 note 2
Idrissi, el-, quoted, 323 *et sqq.*
Ildiguz, Atabeg of Azerbaijan, 102, 106
Ilghazi-bn-Ortok, 99
Il-Khans, Mongol dynasty in Persia, 116 *et sqq.*
Illumination, 294, 306
Ilori, village and episcopal see in Mingrelia, 189
Imereti, the country as described by Wakhushti, 7–8; 48 *et sqq.*, 78; Byzantine policy in, 80; acquired by Levan II of Abkhazeti, 81; estates of Orbelianis in, 85; Bagrat III in, 90; ravages by Seljuks, 92, 94; supports Bogolyubskoi, 105; state of, under Rusudani, 112 *et sqq.*; David IV proclaimed King of, 116; internal politics of, 116–17; revolt of Eristavi Kakhaberi, 117–18; succession war in, 119–20; revolts against Bagrat V, 123; line of David IV in, 135; revolt of Bagrat II in, 135; Bagrat crowned King of, 137; Wars of the Division in, 137–9; I. in Gori, 139; wars of Bagrat III with Turks, 147–9; succession war in, 159; invasion by Simon I, 159–60; state of, at beginning of 17th c., 166; Taymuraz I in, 167, 170, 172; civil war in, and state of at end of 17th c., 177–8 and note 1; Turkish occupation of, 187–9; participation of, in abortive Turkish invasion of Circassia, 189, 204; reign of Solomon I in, 206 *et sqq.*; intervention of Irakli II in, 213; I. auxiliaries at Battle of Krtsanisi, 213–14; Russians occupy, 216–17; revolt of, 217–18; 246, 264, 272, 279, 282, 296, 312, 315; Russian account of, 344 *et sqq.*; Anarchy and decline of trade in, 349–52
Imer-Khevi, an affluent of the Chorokhi, 57
Imier ("that side"), a term used to describe the country west of the Mountains of Likhi, 7; a picture of, 7–8; reference to, 25, 47; elements of conflict with Amier, 105; economic and political separation from Amier, 177, 204, 245; state of in early Middle Ages, 328; dependence of, on economy of Black Sea basin, 352 *et sqq.*
India, 110, 123; participation of Georgian princes in Nadir's invasion of, 191 and note 5; I. troops in Tiflis, 192; 212, 309, 318, 326, 327 note 5; Georgian relations with, 329, 330, 334
Indo-European languages, in relation to Georgian, 22 *et sqq.*
Ink, Ink-horns, 330
Insolvency, 235
Investiture, 252
Ioanné, a son of Giorgi XII, 215
Ioanné, St. of Ardanuchi, 311, 329
Ipani, 34 note 1
Iqalto, a place in Kakheti between the upper sources of the Yori and the Alazani, 63, 319
Iqaltoeli, Arsen, 315
Irakli I (Nazar-Ali-Khan), King of Kakheti, King of Kartli, 173, 180; character of, 180 note 2
Irakli II, King of Kakheti and Kartli, in Afghanistan and India, 191 and note 5; character and achievements of, 196–7, 201–2, 204–5; and Russians, 206–7; his operations against the Turks, 207; accepts suzerainty of Russian crown, 210–11; intervenes in Karabagh, 212; in Imereti, 213; relations with Agha-Muhammad-Khan, 213–14; defeated at Krtsanisi, 214; dies at Telavi, *ib.*; 217, 218, 317, 320
Iran, Iranians. See Persia, Persians
Iraq, 95; trade with the Caucasus, 321, 327 note 5
Ireland, Irish, character compared with Georgian, 71–2; round towers and interlaced design referred to, 299–300
Iron, early use of in Caucasus, 18–19; mines in the Chorokhi valley, 57, 327, 345; export of, to Turkey, 346, 355
Isabella, of Castille, receives embassy from Constantine III, 132, 338–9
Isfahan, 94, 168; Rustem as *darugha* of, 170, 176, 178, 188, 190; Barda'a compared with, 323; 351 note 4
Ishak-bn-Ismail, revolt of, 82
Ishak Pasha, 187, 188
Ishtar. See Itrujani
Iskaur, 262. See also Sukhum
Islam, in the Caucasus. See Mussulmans in the Caucasus
Ismail, Shah, defeated at Chaldiran, 139; relations with Kakheti, 140, 144

INDEX

Ismail II, Shah, 155, 156
Ismailis, 106, 116
Ismail-bn-Shuaib, revolt of, 81
Ispir, a town in the middle valley of the Chorokhi, 56–7; captured by David II, 100; Giorgi V at, 122
Italian-Georgian dictionary of Nicholas Erbashi, 171
Italians in the Black Sea, 322; in Asia Minor, 330
Itil, a city at the mouth of the Volga near the site of later Astrakhan, 323
Itrujani, Georgian goddess identified with Ishtar, 39
Ivan III, Tsar, of Russia, relations with Kakheti, 140; reign of, 162
Ivan IV, Tsar, of Russia, conquests of, 162–3

JACKALS, slaughtered on feast-days, 333
Jafar, Emir of Tiflis, 89
Jafar Pasha, 160
Jakobi, Gen., 209
Jalal-ul-din Khwarazm-Shah, defeats Georgians at Garnhi, 111; at Bolnisi, 112, 264
Janashvili, quoted, 228 note 2
Janberdi-Ghazali, reputed participation of Georgian Kings in Turkish war against, 139 note 1
Janisin, 174 note 1
Janissaries, 148, 187, 189, 284, 355
Japhet, reputed progenitor of Kartlos, 12, 16
Japhetic language theory, referred to, 22–5, 30–31
Jaqeli, the ruling family of Samtzkhé, become direct feudatories of the Il-Khans, 118, 120, 121–2; marriages with the Comnenoi, 122 and note 2; their great power in the 15th c., 135–7; their eclipse in the 16th c., 155; Ioanné, compounds with the Mongols, 113; Sargis, supports revolt of David V, 116–17; Béka, father-in-law of Dmitri II, 119, 120, 122; his marriage with a Comnenian princess, 122 note 2; 245; Sargis II, 122; Béka II, revolts against Bagrat V, 123; Ioanné II, 124–5, 126; Qwarqwaré II, 135–7, 138; Bahadur, 138, 144, 340; Manuchar I, 138, 299; Qwarqwaré III, 139 and note 1, 340 and note 1; Mzedchabuki (*the Great*), 144–5; Qwarqwaré IV, 145, 152; Kai Khusraw II, 145, 152–3; Dédis-Imédi, wife of Kai-Khusraw II, 153, 155; Qwarqwaré V, misfortunes of, 155; simplicity of, *ib.*; Manuchar II, early activities of, 155; restored by Simon I, 159
Jaqis-tsqali river, an affluent of the Kwablowani, 93
Jaro, a mountainous district on the borders of Kakheti and Daghestan; Lazghis of, invade Kartli, 186; Persian expedition against, 191; raid Kisiqi, 199; 211, 216

Javakheti, a district of Samtzkhé, E. of the upper Mtkvari, 78, 88; ravaged by Liparit Orbeliani, 90; by Seljuks, 91; 101 note 2, 113; raided by Lazghis, 188, 199; raided by Taymuraz I, 194
Javakhishvili, views quoted, 38; 225, 243, 246
Javakhishvili, Avtandil, 191 note 4
Jerusalem, 95–6, 270, 294, 317, 318
Jews, early settlements of, in Kartli, 60 and note 5; in Kakheti, 64, 323, 330, 346
Jihad, 99
Jikhi, (Jikheti, Jiketi), Georgian name for Circassians, *q.v.*
Jikuri, favourite of David V, 117
John of Florence, Bishop of Tiflis, 330, 338
John the Prophet, Church of, 301
John XXII, Pope, 330, 338
Jonsherisdze, Dadian-Bediani, 247
Jorjan, early mediæval name for Ghilan, *q.v.*
Joseph II, Emperor of Austria, at Kherson, 209
Jotori, a village on the borders of Kakheti and Kartli, defeat of Alexander II at, 157
Juan, Don, of Persia, 343
Juansheriani, Juansher, 228 note 4, 229, 239, 313
Juansheri, last Iberian prince, 81
Juaris Mtwirtveli, 262
Juaris-tzikhé, (*castle of the Cross*), 58
Jujuniashvili, Wakhtang, a passing King of Imereti, 178 note 1
Julfa, 108
Jumati, 301 note 1
Justice, 242; custom of blood-feud, 275; system of blood-price, 276; trial by combat, 277–8; trial by ordeal, 277–8; trial by oath, 278; penal legislation, 278; ordeal of oath, 279; arbitration, 279; local justice, 280
Justinian, Emperor, 242, 294

KABAGHAK, (Kabalaka, Kabala), a town in Albania, 64, 65–6, 353
Kabardá, (Kabards, Kabardans), the country between the rivers Malka and Urukh, occupying the Northern slopes of the Caucasus; K. elements among the Ossetians, 31; Byzantine missionaries in, 78, 80; part of K. of Osseti, 85; Russian assumption of suzerainty over, 164; attack Russians, 199; Russian possession of, confirmed, 208; horses, 347
Kabardá Regiment, 218
Kai Khusraw, a passing King of Kartli, 180 and note 4, 351 note 4
Kaikul, a Tatar commune in S.W. Somkheti, 197
Kaisariah, a city of Anatolia, 113 note 1
Kakabadze, S., quoted, 229 note 1
Kakhaberi, *Eristavi* of Radsha, revolts against David IV, 117–18

410

INDEX

Kakhaberisdze Kakhaberi, 247

Kakheti, Kakhians, that part of Georgia bounded on the west by the Aragvi and the Mtkvari and on the east by the mountains of Daghestan. Until the 15th c. divided into the provinces of Kakheti, Kukheti and Hereti; later Gaghma-Mkhari, Shignit (Inner) Kakheti and Garet (Outer) Kakheti; description of, 62-4, 79; Arab defeats in, 82; Donauri dynasty in, 83, 84, 85-6; participate in campaigns against Tiflis, 89; Bagrat IV in, 90; Seljuks ravage, 91; 93-4; conquered by David II, 98; supports revolt of Demna, 102; nobles of, submit to Mongols, 113; rule of David V in, 116-17; hermitage in, 119; Giorgi V in, 122; Wars of the Division in, 138-9; Alexander I, recognized as independent King of, 138; David VIII in, 139; policy of Av Giorgi I, 139-40; relations of Levan I with Russia and Persia, 140 and 343; character of Levan I, 141; state of, at end of 16th c., 150; succession war in, 152; relations with Kartli, 153; threatened by Tahmasp, 153; and the Turkish War, 155-7; relations with Russia, 164-5; murder of Alexander II, 165; devastations by Shah Abbas, 166-7; reign of Taymuraz I in, 170-3; position of at end of 17th c., 177 *et sqq.*; Lazghi raids into, 183 and note 1; Constantine of, supports Persians, 186; defeated by Turks, 187; Lazghi raids into, 188; K. princes accompany Nadir's Indian expedition, 191 and note 5; Persian rule in, 191-2; Irakli II, crowned in, 193; Persian levy on, 194; preparations for resistance, *ib.*; block-house system established in, by Irakli II, 201; and Treaty of Georgievsk, 210-11; K. troops fail to support Irakli, 214; Alexander opposes Russians in, 215; revolts against the Russians, 218; 229, 238, 264, 272-3, 276 note 1, 279, 282, 285, 296, 299, 303, 312, 315; Russian account of, 344; economic condition of at end of 17th c., 354 *et sqq.*

Kakhuli, a village and fortress between the Chorokhi and the Tortomis-tsqali, 58; monastery and icon of the Virgin of, 302

Kak-i, a small district of S.E. Kakheti, 211

Kalah of Tiflis, 61, 78, 90

Kalb-Ali-Khan, 198, 214

Kaldi-Kara Mountains, in Somkheti, 15 note 2

Kalmakheli, Daniel, 250

Kalmakhi, *Eristavate* of, 238

Kalmucks, in Russian army, 184; employed as mercenaries by Irakli, 204; frequent Shamakha, 354

Kalnis-mta, Georgian name for Sughanlidagh, 15 note 2

Kalukhi, 235

Kambechovani (Cambysene), *the plain of buffaloes*, the district above the junction of the Mtkvari and the Yori, 64, 106

Kanak, river, an affluent of the Alazani, doubtfully identified on the map, 156

Kandahar, 190, 191, 351 and note 4

Kanesian language, reference to, 23

Karabagh (*the black garden*), the mountainous district S.E. of Lake Sevang, 53, 185, 187 note 6, 197, 210 note 10, 212, 213, 214, 215, 217, 293

Karaia, a district of Kakheti along the Mtkvari, 199

Kara-Kaituk, a Tatar-Mussulman principality along the shore of the Caspian, to N.W. of Derbend, 184, 190, 209

Kara-Kalkanlik, probably Georgian mountaineers, 124 note 1

Karakorum, 6, 114, 335

Kara-Koyunlu (*Black Sheep*) dynasty of Tabriz, 126. See also Turkomans

Karchikai Khan, massacres of, in Kakheti, 167 note 2

Karchkhali, *massif*, part of the Pontic Alps, 7, 54

Kardukhoi, connection of name with root Kart, 17 and note 2

Karim-Khan-i-Zand, 197, 198, 212

Karnal, battle of, Irakli II present at, 191 note 5

Kars, reference to, 8, 57, 59, 80; Bagratid Kingdom of, 81-2, 83, 85, 87, 90, 92; Giorgi II seizes, 93; capitulates to Georgians, 107, 118, 124, 152, 186, 194

Kartli, divided historically into three divisions: (1) Zemo-K (upper K. comprising Samtzkhé); (2) Shida-K (middle K. the country N. of the Mtkvari, sometimes referred to also as Shignit or inner K.); (3) Kvemo-K (the country south of the Mtkvari); name-root, 16-17; description of, 58-61; Bagratid principality of, 81, 83, 84, 85; campaigns of Bagrat IV in, 89-90; ravaged by Seljuks, 91-2, 93-4; ravaged by the Khwarazmians, 111-2; ravaged by Mongols, 113; nobles of, submit to Mongols, *ib.*; rule of David V in, 116-17; under Giorgi V, 122; devastations of, by Timur, 123 *et sqq.*; Wars of the Division in, 137-9; conflicts with Persia, 139-40, 148-50; misfortunes of Simon I, 153; occupied by Turks, 155-6; victories of Simon I, 156-7; intervention in Samtzkhé, 159; campaigns of Simon I in Imereti, 159-60; state of at beginning of 17th c., 165-6; conquest of, by Shah Abbas, 166-7; revolt of Saakadze, 167-8; Persian policy in, 168-70; reign of Rustem I, 170-1; intrigues of Taymuraz I in, 171-3; Mukhranian Bagratids in, 174 *et sqq.*; relations with Persia, 185-7; Kakhian invasion of, 186; Turkish invasion and occupation of, 187-8; Persian recon-

411

INDEX

quest of, 190; Persian administration of, 191-3; establishment of the Kakhian Bagratids in, 191-4; raid of Agha Kish into, 197; ravaged by Lazghis, 199-200; Turkish invasion of, defeated, 207; and Treaty of Georgievsk, 210-11; K. troops intervene in Imereti, 213; 238, 246, 249, 262, 264-5, 272, 273, 279, 285, 287, 299, 306, 312-13; Barbaro's description of, 340; Russian reference to, 344; economic situation and administration of, at end of 17th c., 353 *et sqq.*

Kartli, ancient city of. See Armazi

Kartlis-Khevi, 61

Kartlis-Qeli (Turkish Gurgi-Bughaz, *the throat of Georgia*), a pass in Basiani, leading from the Araks into the valleys of Tortomi and Olti, 57, 125, 137

Kartlis-Tzkhovreba (*Life of Kartli*), quoted, 221-2, 237, 313, 314

Kartlos, eponymous hero of the Georgians, 11, 16; worship of, 37 *et sqq.*

Kartvelian language. See Georgia

Kashak, Arab name for Circassians, *q.v.*

Kashmir, 212

Kaspi, ancient city in Iberia, 52, 60

Kassites, 12

Kata, daughter of David II, 99

Katevani, mother of Taymuraz I, her sufferings, 170; 273; her reliquary, 301 note 1

Katis-Sopheli, a village in Kartli, not identified on the map, 157

Kavtis-Khevi, a commune of Sabaratiano, massacre at, 124; 160; icon of, 304

Kazakh, a town in district of Kvemo-Kartli, bounded by the Mtkvari, the Débéda and the Akstafa, 186, 199, 211, 293

Kazan, conquered by Ivan IV, 162, 164, 338

Kazbek Mt. (Mqinvaris-Mta), 12, 27; axe-cult at, 37

Kazvin, the capital of the earlier Safavids, 108, 151 *et sqq.*, 188

Kechek, Arab name for Circassians, *q.v.*

Kerasund, a port and city of Pontus, 55, 336

Kerdzi saeristavoi, 242

Kerketes. See Circassians

Kerkud, battle of, 189

Kermanshah, 323

Kerouan (Qirovan), referred to by Sargis Tmogveli, 328 and note 4

Kertsen Dagh, a "*massif*", part of the Pontic Alps, 7

Kezkheri, monastery of, 302

Khachen, an Armenian *melikate* of Karabagh, 185 note 2, 333

Khakhanov, quoted, 310

Khaldi. See Urartu

Khaldis, god, 15 note 2, 36

Khaldun ibn-, his views on history quoted, 4-5

Khalt language, 15 note 2

Khalybes, possible connection with Albanians, 19; associated with early iron-mining, *ib*

Khandzteli, Grigol, *The Life of*, quoted, 244

Khandzti, monastery of, on the Chorokhi, 58; Grigoli of, 267, 312

Kharaj, 91, 92, 94, 124, 125, 252

Khati, 300

Khatoba, 38

Khazars, 10, 30, 31; capture Tiflis, 79; 80, 81, 312, 318; power and commerce of, in early Middle Ages, 322 *et sqq.*

Khé, in Svaneti, not identified on the map; Church of St. Barbara of, 301

Kheli, 257

Khelisupal-i (-*ni*), 257, 260

Khelisupleba, 257

Khelmdsipé, 257

Khelmdsipis Karis Garigeba, 260

Khéoba, meaning in Georgian *the valley*, a term applied to the middle course of the Mtkvari between Tashis-Kari and Gori, 207

Kherk, in Kakheti, early settlement of Jews at, 64; devastated by Shah Abbas, 167

Kherkéulidze, Oman, 202

Kherson, 71, 81, 209

Khertvisi, a town and fortress in Samtzkhé, at the junction of the Mtkvari and the Akhalkalakis-tsqali, 52, 53, 59, 207, 319

Khevi, meaning in Georgian *the valley*, a name applied to the upper course of the Terek, north of Mtiuleti, 120, 122, 203

Khev-i (-*ni*), 240

Khevisupal-i (-*ni*), 243

Khevsureti, Khevsurs, a district between the Shavi and Tetri Aragvis; mountains of, 3; a monk of, encountered, 4; reference to, 25; tree-cult in, 36; cult of St. George among, 38; 62, 124 note 1, 167, 203, 214, 215

Khlat (Akhlat), a town and territory round the N.W. shores of Lake Van, 112

Khomli, a mountain between the Rioni and the Tskhenis-tsqali, 117, 334

Khoneli, Moses, 318

Khoni, a small town in the district of Vaké in Imereti, 50

Khopa (Apsarus), a port of Chaneti, 56

Khopi, a town and port in Mingrelia, 90; icon of, 302, 305

Khoranta (called also Hereti), an ancient town at the junction of the Yori and the Alazani, 63

Khorepiskoposi, of Kakheti, 81

Khornebuji, *Eristavate* of, 238

Khrami river. See Ktzia

Khresili, a meadow or plain in the district of Okriba in Imereti; victory of Solomon I at, 208

Khuda-Banda, Muhammad, Shah, 156 and note 1, 157, 165

Khulo, a commune in Achara, 296

Khunani, a castle at the confluence of the Débéda with the Mtkvari, 52, 60; taken

412

INDEX

by Dmitri I, 102; Giorgi IV, defeated at, 110; *Eristavate* of, 238
Khurasan, 194–5, 214, 323, 324
Khurdabdih, ibn-, quoted, 66, 324 *et sqq*.
Khusraw Anushirvan, 66, 324
Khusraw II Parwiz, 78
Khusrawids, 75 and note 4
Khusraw Mirza. See Rustem I
Khutsuri script, 309–10
Khuzistan, 323
Khvatov, Russian emissary in Georgia, 171
Khvorostin, Boyar, defeated on the Sulak, 164
Khwarazm, (Khiva), Khwarazm-Shahs, 106, 110, 111, 112, 324
Kiev, Kingdom of, referred to, 83, 95, 296, 329
Kilburun, 208
Kilij-Ali-Khan, (Khanjal), 191
Kingship, origin of, in Georgia, 222; sharers of, 257
Kinjal, 347
Kipchak, a name applied to the Kingdom of the Northern Mongols (Golden Horde); wars of with the Il-Khans, 117 *et sqq*.; wars with Timur, 123 and note 2
Kipchaks, 30, 31; mentioned by Annalists probably meaning Cimmerians, 52; employed as mercenaries by David II, 99; settlements in Georgia, *ib*.; mutiny of K. troops, 100; note 1; 104; in army of David Soslani, 106; settlements along the Mtkvari, 107; crushed by the Mongols, 110; in army of Awag Mkhargrdzeli, 111; 264
Kirman, 328
Kirmiz, 326
Kisiqi, *mo'uravate* of, in Kakheti, 140 note 1; Abel, *mo'uravi* of, 191 note 4; raided by Lazghis, 199, 344
Kislyar, a Cossack settlement on the Terek, 192; taken by the Kists, 206, 210
Kists, a sub-tribe of the Chechens, referred to, 25, note 1; employed as mercenaries by Irakli II, 204 and note 1
Kiz-malik, 110
Klarjeti, a district of Samtzkhé along the middle reaches of the Chorokhi, 56, 78, 79, 80, 81; ravaged by Seljuks, 90, 94; loyal to Giorgi VIII, 137; Turkish encroachments in, 138; *Eristavate* of, 238; 240, 251, 315
Kliucharev, Russian emissary in Georgia, 172, 343 *et sqq*.
Klukhor Pass, 27
Knorring, Gen., 215, 216
Koban, a village in Osseti; antiquities of, 12; axe-cult at, 37; 292
Kobi, a village at the sources of the Shavi-Aragvi; Irakli II joins Todleben at, 207
Kodori river, reference to, 7, 31, 189
Koght, town in Albania, site unidentified, 65
Kokhta, a village and defile N.N.W. of Akhalkalaki, 126
Kokhta, a Lazghi *bélad*, 198

Kola, a district of Samtzkhé, to the east of the Upper Mtkvari, 88
Kondakov, quoted, 302
Koneba, didebuli, 253
Konia, 95, 103 and note 1, 168
Koran, David II's disputations on, 97 note 1
Kortokhti, a village in Imereti, doubtfully identified on the map; Russians defeated at, 217
Kosciusko, Thadeus, 212
Kripuji, a sort of honey found in Imereti, 8
Krtsanisi, a village S.W. of Tiflis; Irakli II defeated at, 214
Krtzkhilvani, a commune N.W. of the Liakhvi; Giorgi Saakadze, *mo'uravi* of, 166; Irakli II at, 199
Krusinski, 178, 185
Ksani, a river and district of Shida-Kartli, 10, 120, 153, 157; Elisbari, *Eristavi* of, 153, 157; power of *Eristavni* of, 166, 178; valley of, devastated, 168; Shanshé, *Eristavi* of, 188, 191, 192; sons of *Eristavi* of, 199–200; revolt of *Eristavi* of, 203; character of population of valley of, 204; Persians defeated on, 214; 224, 240, 314
Ktzia (or Khrami), river, an affluent of the Mtkvari, 15 note 2, 54; account of, 59–60
Kuabulis-dzeni, 247
Kuba, a town in Shirvan, S.E. of the Samur, the capital of a Tatar Khanate of that name, 214, 217
Kuban, river, in the Northern Caucasus; Bronze Age in region of, 12, 13; described, 27; Circassian population in valley of, 29; reference to, 31; snake-belts of, 36; Russian settlements along, 164; colonization of, 209; Turkish invasion of, 211, 292
Kueqana, 240 and note 2, 243
Kueqnisani, 245–6
Kufa, 328
Kuji, legendary ruler of Egrisi, 41, 51
Kujo, ancient *Eristavate* of, 238
Kukar, Armenian name for Samtzkhé, *q.v.*
Kukheti, part of Kakheti, 62–3
Kulp, a village near Akhtala, 19 note 1
Kuprulu viziers, 353; Abdulla] K. defeated near Erivan, 190
Kura river. See Mtkvari
Kurdistan, Kurds, significance of the name-root, 17; 22, 54, 82; K. origin of Mkhargrdzelidzes, 104; emirates in the 14th c., 121; operations of Irakli II against, 198
Kutais, (Kutaisi, classical Cytaia or Kotatissium and Oukhimerion), description of, 49–50; capital of the Abkhazian Bagratids, 85, 89, 90; burnt by the Seljuks, 94; becomes capital of Rusudani, 111, 112, 116, 118; becomes capital of the Imerian Bagratids, 137, 138, 145, 177; Turkish garrison in, 188 and note 1; Russians and Imerians attack, 207,

INDEX

210; Russians blockaded in, 217; 265, 297; Cathedral of, 295, 297, 305; 329, 331, 341; Russian mission in, 345 *et sqq.*
Kuyuk, Great Khan, 114
Kweli, a village in Samtzkhé, N. of the Jaqis-tsqali; Giorgi II defeated at, 93; ancient *Eristavate* of, 238
Kwiriké, King of Abkhazeti, 302
Kwiriké III, King of Kakheti, 89, 276 note 1
Kwiriké IV, King of Kakheti, 98

LAGANI, a village in Svaneti, not identified on the map; icon of Archangel Gabriel of, 302
Lajazzo, an Armenian port on the coast of Cilicia, 330
Lala Mustafa Pasha, defeats Tokmak Khan, 155; campaign in Georgia and Shirvan, 155-6
Languages, of the Caucasus compared, 22 *et sqq.*
Lapis-lazuli, produced in valley of Débéda, 59
Largweli, 240
Largwisi, 305
Lazarev, Gen., 215, 216
Lazghis, 30, 32; as mercenaries in Georgian army, 111, 140; devastated Kakheti, 167; and Russian policy, 172; confederation of, against Russians, 183-4; their views on Muhammad, 183 note 1; relations with Turks, 184 note 1; as auxiliaries in invasion of Kartli, 186-7; ravages of, 188, 191; relations with Russia, 192 and note 4; 193; their raids into Georgia and Shirvan, 198-200; historical significance of raids, 200; establishment of block-houses against, 201; use of mercenaries against, 203-4; mercenaries in Imereti, 207; fight Russians in Kakheti, 215. See also Daghestan
Lazi, Greek name for the inhabitants of Lazistan, 74. See also Chaneti, Channi
Lazica, a name applied generally by the later Classical writers to descrbe the west Georgian lands; Roman-Persian wars in, 77-9. See also Colchis, Imereti
Lazistan, the Turkish name for Chaneti, *q.v.*
Lead, mines in the Chorokhi valley, 57; along the Débéda, 59
Lechkhumi, a district of Mingrelia, occupying the upper valley of the Tskhenistsqali; 207, 216, 299
Legæ. See Lazgis
Leki. See Lazgis
Lemon, the, flourishes in W. Caucasus, 26
Lenormant, erroneous opinion of, 12
Leon, Imperial *Eristavi* in Egrisi, 79
Leonidze, Solomon, 217
Lepanto, defeat of Turks at, 133
Lermontov, poetic licence of, 40 note 2, 103

Levan II, (Anchabadze), King of Abkhazeti, 49 note 2; acquires Imereti, 81; assumes title of king, *ib.*
Levan I, King of Kakheti, his reputed participation in a "crusade", 139 note 1; his character, 140-1; his heirs, 152-3
Levan I, King of Imereti, 159
Levan-i, a son of Irakli II, 207, 210 and note 4
Levan-i, a grandson of Irakli II, 218
Liakhvi river, tributary of the Mtkvari, 10, 31, 120, 192, 193, 204, 218
Likhi, Mountains of (called also Suram or Meskhian mountains), 6, 7, 9, 47 *et sqq.*, 85, 112, 113, 116, 118, 159, 160, 172, 178, 204, 270, 322, 328
Lilo, a small canton on the borders of Kartli and Kakheti, to the S.E. of Tiflis, 186
Linen, 49 note 1, 325 note 3, 326, 336, 355
Literature, Georgian, considered, 294, 308; different periods in, 311; ecclesiastical, to 10th c., 311-13; historical and geographical, 313-16; mediæval scientific, 315; poetic, 317-20
Lithuania, 338
Litvinov, Gen., 217
Locks, 330
Lomsia, 58, 59 note 1
Lori, a town and fortress in the district of Tashiri, N. of the Débéda; principality of, 81, 83, 85-6; suppressed by Bagrat III, 90; captured by David II, 98; captured by Giorgi III, 103; 157, 165, 190; Farsadan, Melik of, 191 note 4, 216, 253
Louis VII, King of France, 101
Louis XI, King of France, Georgian envoys at coronation of, 338
Louis XIV, King of France, 176, 181
Loves of Vis and Ramin, 318
Luarsab I, King of Kartli, character of, 139; loses Tiflis, *ib.*; defeated at Sokhoista, 139, 144; killed at Garisi, 140; 152, 174
Luarsab II, King of Kartli, his character, 165; domestic policy, 166; flight and dethronement, 167; drowned, 170, 174
Ludovico of Bologna, 171, 338-9, 340
Lvov, I. L., his relations with Irakli II, 207
Lydia, Lydians, reference to, 13, 36 note 2; patriarchy in, 40
Lynx, the, found in Imereti, 345

MACEDONIANS, 41, 44
Macedonian dynasty in Byzantium, 86, 329
Machabeli, Taymuraz, 188
Macrones, a tribe in the region of the Chorokhi, 74 note 1
Madder, exported to India, 326
Magians, 42-3, 76, 79
Magistros, 84
Mahmud I, Sultan, 189
Mairemi, 300-1
Maize, abundance of in Imereti, 7
Makeli, ancient *Eristavate* of, 238

INDEX

Makhvilo (*the Pointed One*), highest peak of Likhi Mountains, 9
Makriali (Makryalos), 56, note 4
Malaskert, a town in Armenia, N.W. of Lake Van; battle of, 92, 93
Malatia, Emir of, 82
Malik-Shah, 93-4, 95, 98, 100
Mama, 37
Mamasakhlis-i (*-ni*), 34, 41, 63; definition of, 221; office of, 224; *tomis-, temis-, meupé-*, 221; abolition of, 222; 223-4; *særistavt-eristao*, 242; 243, 260
Mamluks, often of Caucasian origin, 106; of Egypt, 116-17, 118 note 3; corps of, 284; 335
Mamulis Katsni, 254
Mamulobit, 253
Man in the Panther's Skin, The, quoted, 231, 318, 319
Mandaturt-Ukhutsesi, office of, 102, 115; rank and seniority, 252, 261
Manglisi, a village N. of the river Algeti; victory of David II at, 99
Mangu Timur, 118 note 3
Mankaberdeli, Sadun, favourite of David V, 117; his great influence with the Mongols, 118; his wealth, *ib.*; regent for Dmitri II, *ib.*; Kutlu-Shah, betrays Dmitri II, 119
Mansur, Shaikh, in the Northern Caucasus, 210; said to have been a native of Montferrat, *ib.* note 1; 211
Mapavri, a village of Chaneti, 56
Maps, of Svaneti, made for Timur, 124
Maragha, 188
Marand, a town in the province of Azerbaijan, taken by the Georgians, 108
Marchili, 287
Mardin, 101
Mareime. See Merissa
Margueti, ancient *Eristavate* of, possibly identifiable with Argueti, 238
Maria, Queen, dowager of Giorgi XII, 216
Mariam (Artsruni), wife of Giorgi I, 86, 88, 93
Markwart, views quoted, 36 note 1
Marr, Prof. Nikolai, his views referred to, 22, 24, 30, 225
Married men, tax on, 263
Martha of Abkhazeti (? Maria of Alania), 91, 302
Martqopi, *moʿuravate* of, in Kakheti, 140 note 1, 344
Martvili, a village in Mingrelia, between the rivers Tekhuri and Abasha, 295, 302
Marushidze, Eristavi Ioanné, his diplomatic skill, 84; family of, 104
Marzpan, 78
Mashhad, 176, 195
Masis, Armenian name for Mt. Ararat; significance of name-root, 17
Maskrat (Muskur), 66
Masudi, el-, quoted, 322 *et sqq.*
Matiane Kartlisai, quoted, 232, 238, 244, 246-8, 250
Matiushkin, Gen., takes Baku, 185

Matrakhi, 277 note 5
Matriarchy in Georgia, 34-5
Matskhvarishi in Svaneti, not identified on the map; Church of the Archangel Michael of, 301, 304
Matthew of Chieti, 338
Maurice, Emperor, 78
Mawsil, 101
Mazandaran, 153, 156 note 7; Kakhians deported to, 167; 189, 190
Mdabioi, 232. See *Qma* (*-ni*)
Mdgomel-i (*-ni*), the *Mtavris dsinashe*, 228, 243
Mdivan-beg-i (*-ni*), 263, 280
Mdsignobart-Ukhutsesi, Grand Secretary, office of, 102, 234, 242; rank and seniority of, 261; position of in relation to army, 264, 314. See also Dchqondidi, Bishops of
Meabjret-Ukhutsesi, 261
Medchurdchlet-Ukhutsesi, 260; rank and seniority of, 261
Medea, 48
Media, Medians, Medes, reference to, 13, 65
Medicine, 315
Mediterranean physical type, does not thrive in Caucasian mountain zone, 21
Megaliths, existence of in Caucasus, 13-14
Melkisideki, Catholicos, 88, 231-2
Melon, the, grows wild in Imereti, 8, 346, 354
Melossopol, project for foundation of, 212
Mématrakhé, 277 note 5
Merchuli, Grigol, 228 note 3, 230, 232
Merissa, 40
Meshek. See Mushki
Meshkin, 17 note 1
Meskhia, Meskhians. See Samtzkhé
Meskhoi. See Mushki
Mesrop, 65, 309
Meupé or Mépé, 34 and note 1; title assumed by Levan II, 81; origin and definition of term, 222 and note 1; the earliest office and privileges of, 223
Mepisai, 230
Meyer, E., views quoted, 39
Mghvimé, a monastery on the Qwirila in Argueti, 304, 306, 314
Miana, a city of Northern Persia, 108
Michael III, Emperor, 82
Michael VII, Emperor, 95, 302
Michael (Mikel), son of David IV, 119
Midsis patron-i (*-ni*), 250
Mihrdati (Mithradates), Iberian king, 75
Mikel, Catholicos, 254
Miletus, Milesians, in Black Sea, 48
Millet, crop in Imereti, 345
Mills, service of the, 233
Min-Göl, Timur in camp at, 124, 125
Mineral springs, 263
Mingrelia, Mingrelians (Samégrélo, Egrisi or Odishi, *Greek* Colchis, Egeria or Lazika), 16, 107, 116, 117; Dadiani established as virtually independent in, 137; campaign of Simon I in, 159-60; occupied by Wakhtang V, 177; Turkish

415

INDEX

occupation of, 187–9; 204, 208, 262, 264, 272, 273, 282, 295, 302, 305, 306; Contarini's account of, 341; Barbaro's account of, 342; 351, 355
Minns, Ellis, his views on the Alans quoted, 30
Minoans, referred to, 14
Mint, 262
Miran Shah, defeated by Giorgi VII, 124
Miri, an Iberian prince, 79
Miriani, Iberian king, 75 note 4, 76, 310
Mirionisdze, Mikel, Catholicos, 102, 104, 270
Mir-Mahmud, Afghan usurper, 186, 351 note 4
Mir-Wais, 351 note 4
Mirski, D. S., his views on the Mongols, 112
Mirvani, King of Iberia, 42
Mishetski, Russian ambassador in Georgia, 172, 343 *et sqq.*
Mitanni, connection with Mushki, 18 and note 1; language, 24 note 2
Mithkal, 125, 339
Mithra, possibly identified with Zadeni, 37
Mithradates, King of Pontus, his campaigns, 43; reference to, 74
Mkhargrdzeli (-dze), origin of family, 104; Sargis, favourite of Giorgi III, 104; support Tamara, 105; 107, 108, 109, 113 note 1, 115, 116; Shanshé, *Mandaturt Ukhutsesi*, 113, 115; Zakharia, *Amir-Spasalari*, 106, 107, 109, 113, 252; Awag, *Amir-Spasalari*, 111, 114, 115, 118; Ioanné, *Atabegi*, 106, 107, 109, 111; Waram of Gagi, *Msakhurt-Ukhutsesi*, 109, 110, 111, 113, 115. See also Toreli
Mkhedruli script, 309, 310
Mkvidr-i (*-ni*), definition of term, 245; position of, 246; *kueqnisani, sameposani, ib.*; 248
Moaphernes, an uncle of Strabo, 74
Mobidan, name explained, 76 note 3
Mocheris. See Mukherisi
Mokhele (*-ni*), 257; *Darbazis Kars mdgomni*, 258
Mokvi, a village in Mingrelia, W.N.W. of the Egrisis-tsqali; church of, 295–6
Molaret-Ukhutsesi, 242
Momgheralt-Ukhutsesi, 262
Mona-mkhevalni, 227; *Mona*, 232. See also *Qma* (*-ni*)
Money, 262
Mongols, invade Armenia and Georgia, 110–12; their character, 112; and the two Davids, 114; policy in Georgia, 114–16; war between Northern and Western M., 117–20; end of power in Persia, 121; invasions of Georgia, under Timur, 123 *et sqq.*; 279, 299, 329; trade of W. Asia under the, 335 *et sqq.*
Monks, Georgian, in Syria and Greece, 269
Moon-worship, 37 *et sqq.*
Morals, decline of Georgian, under the Mongols, 119; softening of Kakhian, due to Persian influences, 150; of the Georgian aristocracy, 272, 332–3, 356; of the priesthood, 273–4; of Georgian women, 358
Morgan, J. de., views of, on Caucasian Bronze Age, 12; on early use of iron, 18–19
Mosaics, 294, 305
Mosakargave (*-ni*), 229
Moschic territory, reference to, 26, 58
Moscow, 164, 171, 172, 184
Moses of Kaghankaituk, historian of Albania, 64–5
Moses of Khoren, 65, 66 note 2
Mosokh. See Mushki
Mossynoekhoi, a tribe encountered by Xenophon in the Pontic Alps, significance of the name, 28; 58, 267
Motaul-i (*-ni*), 247
Movaleni Sheudzlebelni, 232, 235
Mozarabs, 333
Mozdok, a Russian fortified settlement on the Terek, 199, 211
Mroveli, Leonti, quoted, 238–9, 313
Msajul-i (*-ni*), 280
Msakhureul-i (*-ni*), *gwarni, gwarishvilni*, 230; *sakhl-i* (*-ni*), *ib.*; *qma* (*-ni*), 254; *shedsqalebul-i* (*-ni*), 255. See also *gwar-i* (*-ni*), *aznaur-i* (*-ni*), *sakhl-i* (*-ni*)
Msakhur-i (*-ni*), 227; definition of term, 228; duties of, *ib.*; grades of, *ib.*; promotion of, 229, 242
Msakhurt-Ukhutsesi, office of, 102, 104, 109, 115, 233; rank and seniority of, 261; position of in relation to army, 264
Miatzmindeli, St. Giorgi, 312
Mtatzmindeli, St. Giorgi, *the Life of*, quoted, 247
Mtavar-i (*-ni*), 228; explanation of term, 239; relationship of, to *eristavni*, 239–40; wealth, power, influence of, 242, 244, 245, 247, 271
Mtiuleti, the district round the head-waters of the Shavi (" black ") Aragvi, 107, 120, 122, 168, 214
Mtkvari river (Kura, Cyrus), 4; description of the course of, quoting Wakhushti, 8–10; derivation of the name, *ib.*; early migrations into valley of, 11, 16, 24–6, 31, 41, 42; Pompey on the, 43, 49 *et sqq.*; 90; Seljuks in valley of, 98, 107, 135; Crim Tatars invade, 166; 178, 199, 204, 262, 293, 352
Mtkvaris-tzikhé (*castle of the Mtkvari*). See Khunani
Mtsiré, 120, 121, 226, 227, 258
M'*tvaré*, 37
Mtzkheta, an ancient city at the junction of the Aragvi with the Mtkvari; visited, 4; antiquity of the name, 17; shrine of Zadeni at, 37; shrine of Aphrodite at, 39 note 4; a centre of Magian cult, 42; 52, 60–1, 63; Greek inscription at, 75; temporary Kingdom of, 76 and note 1; Magians in, *ib.*, note 3; decline of, 78; Persian artisans in, 79; 102, 114; Cathedral wrecked by Tatars, 124; 139,

416

INDEX

170, 187, 222, 238, 243, 270, 297, 299; Catholicos of, 262, 270, 272; Cathedral of, 270, 297, 305–6, 344; Church of Holy Cross of, 295; Living Cross of, 313
Mtzkhetos, eponymous hero of the Georgians, identified with Mushki, 12, 16, 24
Mughan, the district S.E. of the Araks between the Caspian and the Andarab-Kara-su; significance of name-root, 17; reference to, 53; probably the Hippobotus of Strabo, 64 note 4; Mongols, in, 110; 187 note 6, 190; commercial prosperity of, under Caliphate, 322 *et sqq.*
Muhammad-bn-Hattab, revolt of, 82
Muhammad-el-Hakemi, on character of David II, 97 note 1
Muhammad-Hassan-Khan-Kajar, 197, 198, 212
Muhammad Sanjar, 100–1, 102
Muhammadiah, 328
Mukherisi, 50
Mukhrani, a small town and district E. of the lower Ksani, Timur in camp at, 124; Wakhtang Bagrationi, Prince of, 153; Turks advance to, 157; the Bagrationi Princes of, 174 *et sqq.*; Mamuka, Prince of, 191, note 4; attempts to restore Bagratids of, 197, 202–3; intrigues in Moscow, 203 note 2; Ioanné, Prince of, 198 and note 4; signs Treaty of Georgievsk, 210, 243
Mulberries, 323, 326, 346, 355
Mules, white, 277
Murad III, Sultan, 151 and note 2
Murid war, 285 note 1
Murjakheti, a place in Samtzkhé, doubtfully identified on the map, fight at, 145
Murvano, Prince (Peter) of Iberia, 310, 312
Mush, a town and district in Armenia, significance of name-root, 17; reference to, 82, 90
Mushki (Meshek, Mosokh, Meskhoi), identified with Mtzkhetos, 12; in early sources, 17–18; migrations, language, 24, 26–8; Procopius' account of, 54 note 3, 61
Mushroom, abundance of, in Imereti, 8; a peculiar kind, *ib.*
Musk, 330
Mussulmans, in the Caucasus, 79 *et sqq.*; 321 *et sqq.*; treatment of by David II, 97 note 1, 333; insurrection of, in Georgia, 197; attitude to Irakli II, *ib.*; policy of Irakli II towards, 202; and a Caucasian state, 204–5; and the sacred oath, 280; and the slave-trade, 282 *et sqq.*; rug-weaving among, 293–4. See also Arabs, Seljuks, Turks, Mongols
Mycenæans, referred to, 14
Myrsilus, a Lydian king, 36 note 2
Mysians, referred to, 12
Mzareult-Ukhutsesi, 262
Mzé, 37

NADCHARMAGEVI, the royal forest in Kartli, E. of the Liakhvi, 105, 331

Nadir (Quli) Shah, 182; his rise to power, 189; first campaign in the Caucasus, 190; relations with Georgian princes during Indian campaign, 190–1; defeated in Daghestan, 191–2; policy in Caucasus during second Turkish war, 192–4; his character and tyranny, 189, 194–5, 196, 198; 212, 213, 263, 283, 285
Nadsqalobev-i (-ni), 232, 235, 253
Nairi. See Urartu
Nakalakevi (Archæopolis), account of, 50–1; 60, 78
Nakharar, 82
Nakhchevan (Naxuana), an Armenian town on the left bank of the Araks, 108, 120, 124, 152, 168, 198, 204, 214, 215
Nakhiduri, a village in Trialeti, S. of the Khrami, Giorgi VII, killed at, 126; Simon I at, 160
Nakulbakevi, 61
Nana. See Danana
Napoleon I, Emperor, 217
Naptha Country, the, 327
Narin, 114
Narrative of the House of Wakhtang Gorgasali, The, 313
Nasawi, quoted, 111
Nasqid-i (-ni), 232
Natural History, the study of, 315
Nawaz I, Shah. See Wakhtang V
Nawruz, Emir, 120
Nebier-i (-ni), 232
Nekresi, in Kakheti, 63, 302
Nemskhvira, in Svaneti, not identified on the map, Church of the Transfiguration of, 301
Neophyte, St., 264
Nersé, 228, 312
Nestan-Darejani (1), wife of Simon I, 152; misfortune of, 153, 155; (2) wife of Alexander III, 348 and note 2
Niakhuri, a village in the Alazani, doubtfully identified on the map, 215
Nikephoros III Botiniates, Emperor, 277
Nikiphori (Mikiphor) Abbot. See Erbashi
Nikopsia. See Anakopia
Nikortzminda, a village in Imereti, S.E. of the Rioni, 306
Nimvrod, Book of, 310
Nineveh, reference to, 12
Nino, St., Life of, quoted, 37, 40, 310, 312–13
Nishapur, province of, 108
Nishi, 300
Nizami, 308
Nogai Tatars, employed as mercenaries by Irakli II, 204; slaughtered by Suvorov, 210
No'in, 110 *et sqq.*
Nordic physical type, scarcity of in the Caucasus, except a proportion among the Ossetians, 21–2
Normans, and the Crusades, 95–6; their principalities in the Levant, 100–1
Novgorod, 296

INDEX

Nukha, a town and khanate of Shirvan, 217. See Shaki
Nur' Ali Khan of the Avars, 198
Nuts, trade in, 336; production of, 346; export of to Persia, 346–7, 355
Nutzal, 198
Nuzala, Church of, 300

OAKS, of Kakheti, 62, 326
Oath, sanctity of, 278; ordeal by, 279–80
Odishi, a local name for Mingrelia, the country between the Tskhenis-tsqali and the Kodori. See Mingrelia
Odzrakhé, ancient fortress in the Likhi Mountains, 52, 58; *Eristavate* of, 238
Officials, list of, 258–60
Officium Gazariæ, 336 and note 1, 338
Ogotai, Great Khan, 113
Oil, mediæval production of, in the Caucasus, 327; in the 17th c., 354; 355
Okona, a village of Shida Kartli, icon of, 89
Oksakov, Russian losses at, 185
Olearius, his description of Shamakha, 353
Olti, town and river of Samtzkhé, 57
Olympus, 171, 312, 319
Omar Khan of the Avars, 184, 198, 199, 211, 215
Onions, in Imereti, 346
Onurgurisi, 50
Opisi, in the Chorokhi valley, 58, 296
Orange, flourishes in W. Caucasus, 26
Orbeliani family, their power and territories, 85; rivalry with the Abkhazian Bagratids, 86; their support of Demna, 102–3; their ruin, 103; revival under the Mongols, 115–16; their rank, 248; Ioanné, ambassador to Alp-Arslan, 92; revolt against Giorgi II, 93; Liparit, the Great, ambitious and early exploits of, 88–9; supports pretender Dmitri, 89–90; in service of Byzantines, 90; of Seljuks, *ib.*; crowns Giorgi II at Ruisi, *ib.*; overthrown, *ib.*; exiled, 98; 245, 247; Niania, revolts against of Giorgi II, 93; Rat, death of, 98, 245; Stephen, Bishop of Siuniq, historian, 103; Smbat, 115; Elikum, 115; Zaal, defender of Bintvisi, 125; Saba Sulkhan, 176, 316, 320; Papuna, 202, 203, 282, 315; David, 211; Governor of Tiflis, 216
Ordeal, trial by, 277; process of, 278
Oriental Project, The, 209 *et sqq.*
Orlov, Alexei, 206
Ormuzd, 36 *et sqq.* See also Armazi
Orochs (European bison), found occasionally in territory of upper Kuban, 27
Oromasheni, 255
Osmanli, Ottomans. See Turks
Osseti, Ossetians (also Alaneti), the country between the Urukh and the Terek, occurrence of "Nordic" type among the, 22; identity of with the Alans and early history of, 30–1; tree-cult among, 36, 62; Byzantine missionaries in, 80; Leo the Isaurian's adventures in, *ib.*

note 1; Kingdom of in 11th c., 85–6; relations with David II, 99; connections with Tamara, 103, 104; raids into Kartli, 120; devastation of, 168; employed as mercenaries by Irakli II, 203–4; peasantry, in Georgia, 204; revolt against the Russians, 218; 262, 264, 287, 293, 300, 312, 314
Otene. See Udi
Otokos. See Artagi
Otter, sanctity of, referred to, 36; found in Imereti, 345
Ouseley, Sir W. Gore, 217
Oxen, tax on, 187
Oxyrhynchus, reference to, 18

PAATA, called Tsutska, favourite of Levan Dadiani, 166
Paata, Prince, conspiracy of, 203 and note 2
Paidaragan, (also Baylakan), *q.v.*, 64 note 4, 65
Painting, 304; in Georgia, 305 *et sqq.*
Pakavan. See Baku
Pala d'Oro, 302
Palaiologos dynasty of Byzantium, marriage with the Bagratids, 119–22 note 2; Sophia, married to Ivan III, 162; Michael, Emperor, 336
Palakatzio, lake (Chaldïr-Göl), battle at, in 1021, 88; battle by, in 1578, 155
Palavandishvili, Peshang, 191 note 4; a Prince, mentioned, 286
Palawani, a horse, 160
Palermo, 333
Palestine, 106, 311
Palus Mæotis. See Sea of Azov
Panaretes, Michael, 122 note 2
Panaskert, a town and fortress of Tao, E. of the Oltis-tsqali, 90
Panaskerteli, Zakharia, 250
Panavaris-Tba (Lake Toporovan) in Samtzkhé, 54; unpleasant savour of fish in, *ib.* note 2; Giorgi VII defeated near, 137
Pancratio (Bagrat II of Imereti), 340 note 1
Pankisi, *mo'uravate* of, in Kakheti, 140 note 1; *Eristavate* of, 238
Panther, as totem, 36; skins as a royal gift, 339
Panticapæum, great antiquity of, 48
Paper, mentioned, 330
Parkhali, a part of the Pontic Alps, 90
Parnajaniani, Sargis, 247
Parthia, Parthians, 43–5, 75
Pasean, Armenian name for Basiani, *q.v.*
Pasin, Turkish name for Basiani, *q.v.*
Passes of the Caucasus, 10; Roman policy in regard to, 77
Patriarchy in Georgia, 34
Patrona, revolt of, 189
Patron-i (-*ni*), origin and definition of term, 250–1; in war-time, 254
Patronqmoba, origin and meaning of term, 250; characteristic features of, 251
Paul, Emperor of Russia, 214, 215 and note 8
Paulicians, the, 82

418

INDEX

Peach, the, grows in Imereti, 8; in W. Caucasus, 26
Peake, views on megaliths, quoted, 14, 18; on Mother-Right, 35
Pear, the, flourishes in W. Caucasus, 26, 346; in Georgia, 352, 354
Pearls, 334, 339, 348
Peasant, conditions of, under *patronqmoba*, 232–5; the lot of, during slave-trade, 287; the monetary value of, 282
Pechenegs, 31
Pechora, river, 162
Pegolotti, The Manual of, 336
Pehlevi, script, 310
Peoples of the Sea, 12
Pera, 336
Perfumes, 356
Perozes (Firuz), 65
Persati mountains, 137
Persia, Persians, 13, 30; predominance and influence in the Caucasus under the Achæmenians, 40–3; relations with Iberia during 5th c., 76–7; wars with Rome in the Caucasus, 77–9; Seljuks of, 95, 98, 100, 101; collapse of Seljuk power in, 102; and revolt of Demna, 103; rise of the Khwarazmian dynasty in, 106; Georgian aggressions in, 108; Mongols in, 110 *et sqq.*; end of Mongol power in, 120–1; anarchy in, 127; in the Caucasus, 132 *et sqq.*; rise of Safavid dynasty in, 139; policy in Kartli and Kakheti, 139–40; relations with Turkey, 143; conquests in the E. Caucasus, 148; succession crisis in, 151 *et sqq.*; Turkish War of 1578–86, 152, 155–7; relations with Kartli and Kakheti, 152–5; suspicion of Russian approach, 164–5; revival of power under Shah Abbas, 165; conquest of Kartli and Kakheti, 166–8; policy in the Georgian provinces, 168–70; relations with Taymuraz I and Russia, 170–2; Mukhranian princes in, 176–80; Afghan invasion of, 181 *et sqq.*; Lazghi raids against, 183; Russian invasion of, 184–5; relations with Kartlian and Kakhian Kings, 185–6; Treaty of Hamadan, 188; rise of Nadir Quli in, 189–90; recovery of Caucasian provinces, 190; Treaty of Erzerum, 190; administration of Georgia, 191–3; Nadir's second Turkish war, 193–4; state of in middle of 18th c., 196–7; Persians among Lazghis, 199; Russian designs on, 212; rise of Agha-Muhammad-Khan in, 212–13; attempts to resume control of Caucasian provinces, 213 *et sqq.*; 237, 239, 263, 279, 282, 283 note 2, 284; Georgian elements in, 285; 308, 309, 310, 319; trade relations with Caucasus under Caliphate, 321 *et sqq.*; and Derbend, 324; P. merchants in Imereti, 346; export of nuts from Imereti to, 346–7; policy in Georgia in 17th c., 349, 352 *et sqq.*

Pertav (Perozabad, later Arab Bardaʿa or Barda, Berdaʿa) a city S.W. of the Mtkvari, successively the capital of the Kingdom of Aghovanq and of the Arab province of Aran, 61, 65
Peshangi, 345
Peter, Gerald, English Bishop of Sukhum, 338
Peter, St., of Iberia. See Murvano, Prince
Peter, the Great, at the Pruth, 181; his policy in the Caucasus and Caspian, 182–3; his campaign in E. Caucasus, 184–5; his relations with Wakhtang VI, 185–7
Petra, 50; fortified by Byzantines, 78
Petritzi, Ioanné, 315
Peyssonnel, 178
Phanagoria, 48
Phasianoi, reference to, 29
Phasis, river. See Rioni
Phasis, town. See Poti
Phaziané, Byzantine name for Basiani, *q.v.*
Pheasants, abundance of, in valley of the Yori, 12
Phkhoel, Georgian name for Pshavs, *q.v.*
Phokas, Nikephoros, revolt of, 88
Phrygians, reference to invasion of Asia Minor by, 12, 13; suggested common origin with the Mushki, 18 note 1; language, 24 note 2; religious influences, 39
Pigs, abound in Kakheti, 62
Pillage, penalties for, 278
Pisa, Pisans, in the Black Sea, 336
Pitch, abundant in Colchis, 49 note 1
Pitiunt. See Pitsunda
Pitsunda (Pitiunt), a headland, village and fortress in Abkhazeti, 26; Byzantine fortress at, 78; 100; Church of, 295–6
Pitt, William, his views on Russian expansion, 208 note 3; 212
Pitton de Tournefort, 178, 351, 356, 358
Pivov, Peter, 343
Pkhotreri, in Svaneti, not identified on the map, 301
Plague, in Tiflis, 203 and note 7
Plate, sacerdotal, 300
Plato, 308
Pliny, quoted, 29, 51, 61, 66
Ploughs, tax on, 263
Plum, the, flourishes in W. Caucasus, 26, 346
Poets, of Tiflis, allowed pensions by David II, 97 note 1; quality of Georgian, 294, 308; works of considered, 317–20
Poland, Kingdom of, 206, 208, 212, 238
Polemon, 47, 49
Poll-tax, 263
Polo, Marco, on Georgian production of textiles, 326; on the oil of Baku, 325; on Georgian bowmen and goshawks, *ib.*; on the Georgians, 339
Polovtzi, 31
Pomegranates, delicious quality of, in Georgia, 352
Pompey, his campaign in Georgia, 43

419

INDEX

Pontic mountains, reference to, 6, 7
Pontus, Parthian dynasty of, 43 ; Roman conquest of, 43–5 ; Byzantines in, 97 ; late Byzantine potentates in, 121 ; Arab trade in, 322, 328. See also Trebizond
Population of Georgia in 12th–13th c., 285 ; decline of in 17th–18th c., *ib.* ; and note 1
Porphyry, produced in valley of Débéda, 59
Porta (Berta or Shatberdi) in the Chorokhi valley, church of, 295–7, 306, 312, 315
Portion, the Eristavi's, 242
Potemkin, Gregory, 210 note 2, 212
Potemkin, Paul, first Viceroy of the Caucasus, 210 ; signs Treaty of Georgievsk, *ib.* ; drives to Tiflis, 211
Poti (*Greek,* Phasis, *Italian* Fasso), a port and town of Mingrelia, at the mouth of the Rioni, 50, 52, 187, 207, 218, 262, 328, 339, 341
Powders, 228
Presna Street, in Moscow, 316
Procopius, quoted, 49, 51, 54 note 3, 74
Protos, 225
Provençals, in the Black Sea, 336
Prussia, Prussians, attitude to Russian expansion, 212
Pshaveti, the district between the upper waters of the Tetri (white) Aragvi and the Yori, occupied by the Pshav tribe, 62, 107, 124 note 1, 167, 203, 214
Ptolemy, quoted, 57
Pugachev, revolt of, its effect on Russian policy in Georgia, 207
Pumpkins, found in Imereti, 346
Pythodoris, 47

QAHQAHAH. See Alamut
Qaitmazian, Ter Philipé, a counsellor of Irakli II, 201
Qaplanishvili, Erast, 188 ; Kai-Khusraw, 191 note 1
Qmad qola, 251
Qma (-*ni*), 227 ; origin of, 232 ; definition and meaning of, 232 and 250–1 ; *si-glosanni, ara-siglosanni, nebieri, nasqidi,* 232 ; *nadsqalobevi* or *dsqalobis,* 235 ; *sheudzlebelni movaleni,* 235 ; *didebulni,* 251 ; 252–3 ; in time of war, 254 ; *shedsqalebulni,* 234 and 254 ; *msakhureulni,* 254
Qmoba, 250
Qubazar, 102, 104, 213
Quinces, grown in Imereti, 346
Qulamani Khan, 210
Qulamanishvili, Aghajan, court musician, 214
Qulevi (Redut-Kalé), fort at the mouth of the Khopis-tsqali in Mingrelia, 216
Qwareli, *mo'uravate* of, in Kakheti, 140 note 1
Qwirila river (*the Bawler*), a tributary of the Rioni, 7, 49, 50

RABBITS, abound in Imereti, 345
Radsha, a district of Imereti, between the upper valleys of the Tskenis-tsqali and the Rioni, 118, 120, 172, 187, 199, 207 ; *Eristavi* Rustem of, *ib.* ; 208, 238, 247, 299 ; Taymuraz I in, 345–6
Rafts on the Mtkvari, 9
Raspberries, found in Imereti, 346
Ray, a city of Northern Persia, 323, 328
Reclus, Elysée, quoted, 31
Redut-Kalé. See Qulevi
Regulations for the Coronations of the Kings, quoted, 260–1
Religious struggle, Armeno-Georgian, 269
Reliquaries, 304
Renegades, Georgian, in Persia, 286 note 1
Reptiles, abundance of, in Imereti, 10
Rev, *Martali,* King of Iberia, 74
Rhododendron, profusion of, in Chaneti, 55
Rhodopolis. See Vardis-Tzikhé
Rice, rarely sown in Imereti, 354
Rioni (Phasis), river, referred to, 4, 7 ; early migrations into valley of, 12, 25, 27 ; called Phasis, 28 ; significance of root, 28–9 ; references to, 49 *et sqq.*
Ritualistic prostituion, 39 and note 4
Riza (Rhizæum), 56, 336
Rodshikashvili, Edisher, 186
Roebuck, found in Imereti, 345
Roger of Antioch, 99
Roman Catholicism, in Georgia, 176, 201. See also Vatican
Rome, Romans, campaigns in Pontus, Iberia and Albania, 43 ; Eastern policy of, 44–5 ; in Colchis and Iberia, 47 *et sqq.,* 224–5 ; civilization contrasted with Greek, 69–70 ; intercourse with the Georgians, 74 ; policy towards the Iberian Kings, 74–6 ; wars with Persia in the Caucasus, 77–9. See also Byzantium
Romgor, a town referred to as in the province of Nishapur (unidentified), 108
Rose, the, abundant in Imereti, 8
Rosen, Gen., 211
Rostovtseff, views of, on Caucasian Bronze Age, 12 ; 13, 14 ; on Panticapæum, 48
Rubies, 125, 334, 348
Rugs, rug-industry, in the Caucasus, 293, 325–6 ; exports of, in Middle Ages, 326 ; imports of, 355
Ruisi, a village in Shida-Kartli, W. of the Liakvi, 124 ; defeat of Yusuf Pasha at, 193
Rukn-ed-Din, Sultan of Erzerum, 107
Rumania, 304
Rusas, King, 34 note 1
Russia, Russians, made the Georgian Military road, 3 ; Black Sea coast-road, 26 ; attack on Byzantium, 82 ; in Byzantine army at Malaskert, 92 ; 110, 123 and note 2 ; relations with Kakheti, 140 ; emergence of as a world-power, 162–4 ; in the Northern Caucasus, 164 ; intrigues in Kartli and Kakheti, 165, 170 ; relations with Taymuraz I, 171–2 ; policy in the Caucasus, 182 *et sqq.* ; campaign in N.E. Caucasus and N. Persia, 184–5 ; army, defects of, 184–5 ; rela-

420

INDEX

tions with Wakhtang VI, 186; Treaty with Persia, 187 note 6; relations with Turkey, 188 note 2; Turko-Persian understanding directed against, 189; attitude to Nadir, 190, 192; Taymuraz II in, 199 and note 1; in N. Caucasus, *ib.*, 201; policy in the Caucasus, 206-8; the *Oriental Project*, 209-10; assumption of suzerainty over Georgia, 210-11; Caucasian and Persian policies of, 211-12; annexation of Georgia, 214-17; wars with Turkey and Persia, 217-18; repress risings in Georgia, *ib.*; 264, 275, 279, 285, 293; early trade of, in the Caspian, 323; relations with the Georgian Kings, 329; trade of the Latin cities with, 336 *et sqq.*; missions in Georgia, 343, *et sqq.*

Rustem I, King of Imereti, 150, 160, 166
Rustem I (Khusraw Mirza), King of Kartli, character and reign of, 170-1, 174, 343
Rustem Khan, Usmi of Kara Kaituk, 184 note 1
Rustem Mirza, plots of, 203
Rusthaveli, Shota, 294, 308, 319
Rusthavi, in Kartli, 52, 63; captured by David II, 98
Rusthavi, a village in Samtzkhé, between Akhaltzikhé and Khertvisi, 308
Rusudani, sister of Giorgi II, 103, 104
Rusudani, Queen of Georgia, her character, 110-11; correspondence with Honorius III, 110, 329; with Frederick II, 111; her armies defeated by the Khwarazmians, 111-12; flies to Kutais, 113; compounds with the Mongols, *ib.*; death, 114; 261, 264, 306, 314, 329; her treasure, 334

SAAKADZE, Giorgi: his character and early career, 166; betrayal of Luarsab II, 166-7; his revolt against Shah Abbas, 167-8; his end, *ib.*, and note 1
Saatabago. See Samtzkhé
Sabaratiano, a district of Kartli between the Mtkvari and the Algeti, the territory of the *gwari* of Baratiani (Baratashvili), 166, 188
Sabegrod Gatsema, 235
Sabinisdze, Ioanné, 228 note 1, 239
Sables, as gift to Taymuraz I, 172; a mantle of, 348
Sachéri, in Mingrelia, 306
Sacrilege, penalty for, 277
Saeristavt-erista(v)o, 240
Saeristo (-ni) = *saerista(v)o (-ni)*, 238
Safar, S. of Akhaltzikhé; Church of, 299, 306
Safavid, dynasty in Persia, 133, 139, 144, 148, 151 *et sqq.*, 176 *et sqq.*, crisis and end of the, 181-9; their policy in E. Caucasus, 352 *et sqq.*
Saffron, 326
Safi II, Shah, 168; his friendship with Rustem I of Kartli, 170
Safi Khan, 191

Safian (Saffian), 354
Safraji, 349
Saghamos-Tba (Tuman-Göl), a lake in Samtzkhé, 54
Saguramo, a canton of Kakheti, to the W. of the Yori, 186
Sagwareulo, system of, 221; definition of, 221-2; administration of, 223; principle of ownership under, 224; position of families under, *ib.*; the changes in the system, 224 *et sqq.*; 230, 239
Sailing-boats, on lower Mtkvari, 9
St. Andrew, Church, in Constantinople, 295
St. Elias of Brusa, Church of, 295
St. George of Salonika, Church of, 295
St. Mark's, in Venice, Pala d'Oro of, 302
St. Petersburg, 199, 206, 215
St. Theotokos, Church of, in Constantinople, 295
St. Vitali of Ravenna, Church of, 295
Sajid, dynasty in Tabriz, 83
Sakæ, probable settlement of in Sakasene, 24 note 1; domed tent of, 294
Sakartvelosani, 244-5, 248
Sakasene, a province of Armenia between the Mtkvari and the Araks, probably settled by the Sakæ, 24 note 1. See also Siuniq
Sakharajo (-ni), 252-3
Sakhevisupalo, 243
Sakhl-i (-ni), 221-4; *msakhureuli, gwariani*, 230. See also *gwar-i (-ni)*
Sakmis Mokmed-i (-ni), 257; grades of, 258
Sakueqnod Gamrige (-ni), 258; list of, 260
Sakutari, 253
Sakutarit, 254
Sakutarni, 243
Saladin, 106
Saldukid, dynasty of Erzerum, 107
Salome, Princess, 310
Salt, early mining of, in Caucasus, 3; scarcity of, in Imereti, 341; traded at Shamakha, 354
Saltpetre, 345
Samamulot, 253, 255
Samarkand, reference to, 6, 125, 323
Sameposani, 244-7
Sameupé or *Samepo*, 222-3. See also *gwar-i (-ni)*
Samghudelo, 223. See also *gwar-i (-ni)*
Samsakhurod, 255
Samshwildé—(*the place of the arrow*)—(called also Orbeti), the stronghold of the Orbelianis on the Ktzia, 52, 60; seized by Malik Shah, 93; 156, 157; *Eristavate* of, 238
Samsun, 55
Samtavro, 240
Samtzkhé, Meskhians, Meskhia (called also Zemo (Upper) Kartli, or Saatabago (*the Atabeg's country*), one of the historic provinces of Georgia, bounded on the N. by the Black Sea, on the E. by Trialeti and Somkheti, on the S. by Armenia, and on the W. by the Pontic Alps: origin of name, 17 and note 3; 28; descrip-

421

INDEX

tion of, 53 et sqq.; 85; Byzantine invasion of, 87-8; rising against Orbelianis, 90; Seljuks ravage, 90-1; Giorgi II defeated in, 93; ravaged by Malek Shah, 94; 98; Bogolyubskoi in, 104-5; revolt of nobles in, 105; crown policy towards, 106; M. forces blockade Kars, 107; ravaged by the Khwarazmians, 111; ravaged by Mongols, 113; unsuccessful revolt of David V in, 116-17; Giorgi V in, 122; Turkish raids into, *ib.*; defection of *Atabegi* of, 123; operation of Mongols in, 124-5; defeat of Giorgi VIII in, 133, 137; Turks threaten, 135; character of *Atabegni* of, 135-6; Wars of the Division in, 137-9; Qwarqwaré III virtually independent in, 139; Luarsab I in, 140; Turkish occupation of, 144-5; War between Imerians and Turks in, 145-7; Turkish occupation of, 148; relations of Meskhian nobles with the Persian court, 152-3; Persian invasion of, 155; influence of Simon I in, 157, 159; 171; Turkish rights in recognized by Persians, 177; 187, 188, 199, 204, 207, 211, 238, 245, 246, 265; the Churches of, 296-7; 308, 314-15, 328, 331, 356

Samurzaqano, a province of Abkhazeti, 78
Sanakhevrot, 252-3
Sanakhshiré, 276-7
Sandon, identified with Zadeni, 37
Saneunos, a Scythian King, 18; possible significance of name, *ib.*, note 2, and cf. p. 29
Sanighes, 28
Sanna. See Anakopia
Saparda, doubtfully identified with Ispir, 56
Sapatio, 252-3
Sarapana. See Shopapani
Saratov, 164
Saray, 113, 123 note 2, 338. See also Kazan
Sardes, reference to, 3
Sarkiné (*the place of iron*), in Kakheti, 52, 63-4
Sarmatians, reference to, 31
Sasanian dynasty in Persia, 45; policy in Albania, 64-6; 74 note 4, 239, 310, 317
Satchinoi Katsi, 230
Satin, 277
Satsikhistao, 243
Saurmag I, King of Iberia, 41-2
Saurmag II, King of Iberia, 76
Saxons, 264
Sayce, Prof., his views referred to, 22-3
Saquerel-i (-ni), 229
Scents, 228
Scylax of Caryander, reference to, 28
Scythians, 10, 11, 17, 18, 27, 31; sword-cult among, 37
Selim I Yavuz, Sultan, 144
Selim II, *the Sot*, Sultan, 151 note 2
Seljuk Turks, 83; rise of, 87; invasion of Vaspurakan, *ib.*; campaigns in Armenia and Georgia, 90; tactics described, 91; ravage Kakheti and Kartli, 91-2; victory at Malaskert, 92; settlements in Asia Minor, 92-3; defeated by Giorgi II at Fartzkhisi, 93; victory at Kweli, *ib.*; ravage all Georgia, 93-4; and the Crusades, 95; wars against David II, 98-100; collapse of S. power in Persia, 102; S. of Konia crushed by the Mongols, 113 and note 1; their relations with Rusudani, 113-14; 121, 333 note 3, 335. See also Turks

Semitic languages in relation to Georgian, 22 et sqq.; religious influences in Georgia, 37-9
Senakerim (Artzruni), King of Vaspurakan, 86, 87
Serbia, 304
Sevan (Sevang, Gök Chai or Gökcheh), Lake, 7, 34 note 1, 81
Seven, significance of the number in Georgia, 38
Seven Towers, the, Simon I imprisoned in, 160
Shabanid dynasty in Amida, 83
Shaberan (called also Shirvan), in Albania, site doubtful, 66 and note 2, 324 and note 7
Shaddad banu-, dynasty of Aran, 89, 102
Shadrin, Andrei, 164
Shahrukha (or Shakhrukhadze), 320
Shahverdi, Khan, 196
Shaki, a Tatar Mussulman Khanate, of which Nukha (sometimes called Shaki) was the capital, 88, 124, 148, 197, 211, 213, 214, 217, 353
Shalikashvili, Otar, 145-7; his daughter married to Shah Tahmasp, 152; her influence at Kazvin, 152-3, 155, 156; Waraza killed, 153, 154; Kokola, revolt of, 155
Shamakha, a city of Shirvan, 64, 66, 80, 99, 183, 184 note 1, 190, 284, 323, 324, 352; great prosperity of in 17th c., 353-4
Shamil, 216 note 2
Shamkhals of Tarku, 140, 150, 152, 153, 155, 164, 184, 203
Shamkhor, 106
Shamshadilo, the district along the right bank of the Mtkvari between the rivers Akstafa and Shamkhor, 211
Sharji-Panah, 197, 203
Sharvashidze, ruling family in Abkhazeti, 107; Dardan, 113 note 1; 122, 137 and note 1, 189, 207
Shatberdi. See Porta
Shavsheti, the mountainous district of Samtzkhé between the rivers Chorokhi, Acharis-tsqali and Imer-Khevi, 49, 54, 58, 88; ravaged by Seljuks, 90, 94; *Eristavate* of, 238; 240, 251, 296
Sheep, not kept in flocks in Imereti, 8; the fat-tailed, found in Imereti, *ib.*; kept underground, 53 note 1; flourish in Kakheti, 62
Shedsqaleba, 235; explanation of term, 251, 253; characteristic features of,

INDEX

252; manner of, 254; advantages and disadvantages of, 255-6
Shedsqalebul-i (-ni), 232, 234, 250, 251; momatebita, 252; aghmatebita, 254; qma, 253; his duties, 254, 255
Shedsirul-i (-ni), 232-3
Sheidsqala, 251
Sheidsqalnes, 252
Shemokhmedi, Bishop of, 272; icon of Virgin and Child of, 305
Shesamqrelo, 276
Shi'ah, faction in Tabriz, allied with Georgians, 155; Georgian princes profess S. faith, 176 et sqq.; 183, 190 note 5, 331 note 4
Shilda, mo'uravate of, in Kakheti, 140 note 1
Shio-Mghvimé, a monastery to the W. of Mtzkheta, 233-4, 257
Shipov, Col., invades Ghilan, 184
Shipbuilding, in Colchis, 48 note 1; among the Laz, 55
Shirak, a district of the Armenian province of Ararad, between the rivers Kars and Akhurean, 82, 83
Shiraz, 153, 156, 197, 212
Shirvan, in Arab times the province bounded by the Caspian, the Samur and the Mtkvari; after the 15th c. a Khanate comprising the country round, and to the W. and S. of Shamakhi, 84; invaded by David II, 98-99, 100, 104; ravaged by Mongols, 110; 111, 117, 122, 124, 125, 126, 148, 155, 156, 168; Russian campaign in, 183-5, 189, 190; Safavi pretender in, 193; hegemony of Irakli II in, 198, 204, 211, 213; 293; trade of under Caliphate, 321 et sqq.; administration and commerce of, at end of 17th c., 353 et sqq.
Shirvanshahs, relations of with David II, 99; and policy of Tamara, 106-7; 250, 333
Shkara, Mt., 27
Shketi, a village and fortress in Mingrelia, N.W. of the river Tekhuri, 159
Shorapani (Sapapana), a town and fortress at the junction of the Qwirila and the Dzirula, 50, 78, 207
Shtori, ancient Eristavate, in Kakheti, 238
Shulaveri, a small district in Somkheti, the axes of, 327
Shusha, a town of Karabagh, 198, 213, 214, 217
Shushaniki, the Queen, The Martyrdom of St., quoted, 225
Sia'bihah (Sayabidja), corps, use Georgian battle-axes, 327 and note 5
Siberia, Russian conquest of, 162, 164
Sidi Ali of Shaki, 124
Sigel-i (-ni), 231-3, 236, 276
Siglosan-i (-ni), 232-3
Signakhi, a town in Kakheti, S.S.W. of the Alazani, 63, 213, 214, 218
Silk, 323, 325, 326, 336, 345, 346, 347, 348, 353, 354, 355

Silver, mines at Akhtala, 201 and note 4, 262; coin in Chaneti, 328; and in other parts, ib.; note 3; 334, 347, 348, 349 and note 2
Simon I (Swimoni), King of Kartli, at battle of Garisi, 140; marries d. of Levan I, 140, 152; outlawed by the Persians, 153; a prisoner at Shiraz, ib.; his enemies, ib.; liberated, 155; his character, 156, 159, 160; his military genius, 157; his victories, 157-9; his disastrous campaign in Mingrelia, 159-60; 167, 174, 177, 287
Simon II, King of Kartli, 170
Simon I, passing King of Imereti, 178 note 1
Simon, Archbishop, 349
Sinai, Mt., 311
Sind, legendary campaigns of Wakhtang I in, 77, 334
Sineli, a tribe in the neighbourhood of Taman, 28
Sineli, Saba, 135
Sinope, 55
Sioni, Cathedral, in Tiflis, 156, 299, 306
Sipahsalar, 237
Sirikhnev, Col., 214
Siskhli, 275
Sis (Cilicia), Kingdom of, 96, 335
Siuniq (ancient Sakasene), Armenian province, 64; principality of, 81, 83, 111, 115
Sivas, 87, 90, 95, 113, 118 note 3, 124, 145
Skanda (Alexandria), 50; destroyed, 78; Taymuraz I at, 172; 345
Slave-Trade, reference to, 52; 192; development of, 282; flourished during the period of Perso-Turkish intervention, 283; its effect on the ethnography of Georgia and Western Asia, 284-6; measures against, by the Kings and the Church, 286, 355
Smbat I, King of Armenia, 82
Snake, sanctity of, 36
Soanes, Greek name for Svans, 28
Sokhastreli, Ioanné, 311; Kwiriké, 311; Zosimé, 311
Sokhoista, a village in Basiani, doubtfully identified on the map, battle of, 133, 140, 145-6
Sökölli, Muhammad, Grand Vizier, 151 and note 2, 152
Solomon I, King of Imereti, 204; his character, 206 and note 1; relations with Turks and Russians, 207; his operations against the Turks, 207; victories of, 208; death of, 210
Solomon II, King of Imereti, his relations with Irakli II, 213; aids Irakli against Persians, 213-14; hostilities against Grigol Dadiani, 216; submits to Russians, 217; imprisonment and flight of, ib.; unsuccessful revolt of, 217-18
Somekhni, Georgian name for the Armenians, 25 and note 1

423

INDEX

Somkheti (Somkhiti), a mountainous district of Kartli between the rivers Ktzia-Khrami and Débéda, 10; significance of the name, 25; population and different names, 26; account of, 59; Seljuks in, 98; 101 note 2, 115, 122, 125, 126; Luarsab I in, 140; 188; Bahadur, Melik of, 191 note 4, 248; Lazghi raid on, 200

Son, tribal name-root, see Chan and Svan

Soothsayers, of Tiflis allowed pensions by David II, 97 note 1

Sopeli, 240 and note 1

Soslani, David, marries Tamara, 104; his victory at Dzagam, 106; paid great price for a bay charger, 332-3

Souastopoli (Sukhum-Iskaur), 342 and note 3

Spahpat, 237

Spain, Spanish, character, compared with Georgian, 71-2; history compared with Georgian, 100, 131-3, 329

Spasalar-i (*-ni*), 237, 245

Spaspet-i (*-ni*), power of, 237

Special messengers, 243

Spelt, grown in Imereti, 345

Spices, 356

Stambul, 145, 151; the Jaqelis in, 155; 156, 160, 171, 177, 185, 186, 201 note 10, 206, 217

Stavropol, a Russian town in the Northern Caucasus, 209

Steel, 330

Stephanos I, *Eristavt-Mtavari* of Kartli, 78; flayed alive, 79

Stephanos II, *Eristavt-Mtavari* of Kartli, 79

Stephanos of Byzantium, quoted, 48, 51

Stone-carving, 294-7

Stork, as totem, 36

Strabo, Greek geographer, 25, 26, 27, 29, 32, 47, 49, 51, 52, 58; his origin, 74; 221; his description of the social system of Georgia; 222-3; 293, 323

Strassburg, Gottfried von, 318

Strategos, 238

Stroganov, family, influence in N.E. Russia, 162

Structure and Organization of the Army, 315

Strzygowski, quoted, 293-4

Sturgeon, fished in the Mtkvari, 9; spawn above Ganja, *ib.*

Style, animal, 293-4; geometrical, *ib.*

Suannokolkhoi, 28

Subutai, 110

Suimonovich, Gen., 217

Sukhotin, Gen., his failure before Poti, 207

Sukhum (Tzkhumi or Tzkhomi, also Sevastopolis) in Abkhazeti, Byzantine fortress at, 78, 238, 277, 331, 338

Sulaiman, Sultan, 139 and note 1, 145, 151

Sulaiman, Pasha, 207, 210 note 4

Sulak, river, 164, 184, 190

Sulkhavi. See Chulak-Surkhai

Sultan-Ahmad-Khan, Usmi of Kara-Kaituk, 184

Sultan-Buda, a village N. of the Araks, locality doubtfully identified on the map; Persian victory at, 218

Sumatra, 327 note 5

Sumer, Sumerians, 12; alleged builders of megaliths, 14

Sunni, faction in Kazvin, 155; influence in Daghestan, 183 *et sqq.*; 190 note 5, 351 note 4

Sun-Worship, 37 *et sqq.*

Surameli, Grigol, 233

Surami, a village and fortress N.W. of the Mtkvari, covering a pass over the Likhismta. A name sometimes applied to those mountains, 6; Persian garrison in, 168; character of population of, 204, 215

Surmena (Susurmena), 55

Susa, referred to, 12, 14

Suvorov, Gen., 209, 210

Suzdal, 104, 301

Svaneti (Svans, Svanni), the district occupying the upper valleys of the Enguri and the Tskhenis-tsqali; significance of name-root, 25 and note 1; discussion of the name, 27-8; description of the country, 27; cult of St. George among the, 38; passes into, 50; operations in, 78; support Bogolyubskoi, 105; S. in Georgian army at Battle of Bolnisi, 111; support David IV, 116; the *Eristavi* of, 120; revolt of, 122; Mongols ravage, 124; Gelovanis established as virtually independent in, 137; take Kutais, 138; 204, 238; ecclesiastical architecture of, 300-2; icons and carving of, 302 *et sqq.*; manuscripts found in, 305-6, 333

Sweden, 181, 192

Sweri, citadel west of the middle Liakhvi, 92

Sweti-Tzkhoveli, Church of, wrecked by Tatars, 124; restored by Alexander, 126

Sword-cult, referred to, 37

Swords, of foreign make, 347

Syria, 38, 58, 95, 96, 118 note 3, 120, 139 note 1, 296, 283 note 2, 295, 309, 311, 323, 335

Syrups, 324

TABAKHMÉLA, a village in Kvemo-Kartli between the Algeti and the Mtkvari, victory of Simon I at, 157

Tabriz (Tauris, Tavrej or Gantsag Shahanzan), capital of the Persian province of Azerbaijan, 80; Sajid dynasty of, 83; *atabegs* of, 102, 108, 110, 112, 120, 123, 124; Karakoyunlu dynasty at, 126, 138; 147, 152, 168, 185, 186, 188, 189, 197, 212, 282, 330, 323, 335, 353

Tacitus, 73 note 3

Tadzreul-i (*-ni*), 228-9

Tahir-Sultan, 124

Tahmasp, Shah, 139, 140, 145, 151 and note 1; domestic affairs of, 152; at Ganja, 153; ravages Samtzkhé, *ib.*; 155, 181

Tahmasp, Shah-zadé, 185-6, 189

INDEX

Taman, peninsula, 27-8
Tamara, Queen of Georgia, 40; reputed to have completed construction of Vardzia, 53; accession of and character, 103; policy towards nobles, 104; marriages, 104; confronted with internal revolts, 104-5; aggressive frontier policy of, 105-8; character of her reign, 107; 109, 122, 238, 240, 244-6, 250-1, 253, 255, 260, 267-8, 270; population of Georgia under, 284; 306, 314-15, 317, 319, 320, 329, 334
Tamara, daughter of David II, 99
Tamara, daughter of Rusudani, 113
Tamara, wife of Taymuraz II, 191
Tana, 334, 336
Tanais, Greek name for the Don river, reference to, 30
Tanaziarni Mepobisa, 257
Tanga, 125
Tao (Armenian Daikh), a district of Samtzkhé, between the rivers Tortomi and Olti, 24 note 1; 57; Byzantine influence in, 80; Bagratid principality of, 81, 83; ceded to Basil II by David *Kuropalatēs*, 84; 85, 87, 88; Seljuks ravage, 90; David II in, 100; repeopled, 101 note 2; loyal to Giorgi VIII, 137; conquered by the Turks, 148; 238, 240, 251, 315; trade of, 322
Tapestry, 325
Taqwaneba, 252
Targamos (Togarmah, Torgom), eponymous hero of the Armenians and Georgians, 16, 25
Tarishidze, Ioanné, 315
Tarku, an Asianic god, 36
Tarku, a Mussulman Tatar principality occupying the territory along the Caspian, south-east of the Sulak, 184
Tashiri, district in Somkheti, 101 note 2
Tashis-Kari (*the rock-gate*), ravine of the Mtkvari, 60, 137, 207
Tasso, 308
Tatars, 30; nomadic habits of, 53-4; settlements in Albania, 65; of the Crimea, invade Shirvan, 156-7; on the Volga, overthrown, 162; of the Crimea, invade Georgia, 166; in Russian army, 184; of Somkheti, 197; of Borchalo, 202; in Georgian Kingdom, 204-5; in Crimea, lose independence, 209; 287, 354
Tatishchev, Russian envoy in Georgia, 165
Tauric Chersonese (Taurida), 48, 209, 212
Tavad-i (-ni), 243; definition of term, 246; position of, 247-8; in relation to *mkvidrni*, 248; *didebulni*, 249; *sameposani, sakartvelosani, kartuelni*, 247-8; *katsni*, 247; 281-2, 286
Tavadoba, characteristic features of, 248-9
Tavi, 237, 336
Tavisupal-i (-ni), 226-7. See also *aznaur-i (-ni)*

Tavoba, 246
Taxes, 187, 191, 192, 242, 262, 263
Taymuraz I, King of Kakheti and of Kartli, 160; his succession, 166; his flight, 167; successes against the Persians, *ib.*; his eclipse and peregrinations, 170-2; his character and appearance, 171; his misfortunes and death, 172-3; 174, 177, 182; and the slave-trade, 282-3, 285-6; 320; his residence in Radsha, 347-8
Taymuraz II, King of Kartli and Kakheti, 174, 178; attacks Wakhtang VI, 186; attends Nadir's Indian expedition, 191; at Derbend, 192; relations with Nadir, 193-5; rule in Kartli, 193-4; policy and later reign, 196-7; in Moscow, 199, 206; 263
Taymuraz-i, a grandson of Irakli II, 216
Tbeli. See Abuserisdze
Tbeti, in Shavsheti, 58, 296-7, 299, 312, 319
Teberdá, lake and river, 27
Tekhuri, river, an affluent of the Rioni, 51
Tekudar. See Ahmad Il-Khan
Telavi, a town in Kakheti, between the Yori and the Alazani, 63, 118; university of, 201; 214, 216, 218
Tem-i (-ni), 34; definition of, 221; *Mamasakhlisi* of, 221, 222
Temis-eristav-i (-ni), 242
Tenali, in Svaneti, not identified on the map, Church of, 301
Tents of Nomads, tax on, 263
Terek, a river of the Northern Caucasus, Toktamish defeated on, 123 note 2; Russian settlements along, 164, 170, 214
Terki, a Cossack settlement at the mouth of the Terek, 164, 171 note 1
Teshub, Hittite god, in Georgia, 36 *et sqq.*
Tetri, 277
Textiles, production of, in Caucasus, in Middle Ages, 325 *et sqq.*; in 17th c., 353 *et sqq.*
Thalish, *Melikate* of. See Gulistan
Thédo-tzminda, a village of Shida-Kartli, W. of the Liakhvi, victory of Giv Amilakhori at, 193
Theft, penalties for, 278
Theodosiopolis, a Byzantine fortress the site of which is generally identified with that of Erzerum. See Garin, Erzerum
Thewdos II (Anchabadze), King of Abkhazeti, 84
Thizak, an Armenian *Melikate* of Karabagh, 185 note 2
Thong Yabghu Khakan, Khazar general, 79
Tianeti, a district in Northern Kakheti between the Tetri Aragvi and the Yori; *mo'uravate* of, 140 note 1; devastated by Shah Abbas, 167

INDEX

Tibarenoi. See Tubal
Tibet, 212; musk from, imported into Georgia, 330
Tiflis (Tpilisi), foundation of, 61; capital of Guaram Bagrationi, 78; Persian *marzpan* in, *ib.*; captured by Heraklius, 79; Arabs in, 80-1; revolt of, and capture by Bugha, 82; Muslim *emirate* of, 83, 85; siege of, by Abkhazian and Kakhian Kings, 89; surrenders to Bagrat III, 89-90; 98, capitulates to David II, 99; 101 note 1, 105, 108, 109; captured by Jalul-ul-din, 111-113; 114, 115, 116, 117, 119, 120, 121; taken by Timur, 123; again taken, 124; Khurasani garrison in, *ib.*; Turkoman attack on, 137, 138; Persians in, 139; 152, 156, 157, 165, 166; Persian garrison in, 168; Mukhranian viceroys in, 174 *et sqq.*; Turkish emissaries in, 186; captured by Turks, 187; in hands of Nadir, 190; administration of, 191; Indian and Afghan troops in, 192; Taymuraz II crowned in, 193; evacuation of civilian population of, 194; restoration of University of, 201; famine in, 203; plague in, 203 note 7; character, of population of, 204-5; Potemkin in, 211; Agha Muhammad Khan takes, 213-14; reoccupied by Giorgi XII, 214; Russians in, 215 *et sqq.*; 246, 264, 273, 297, 313; under the Caliphate, 322, 324; Roman Catholic Bishops of, 330, 331, 338; Muslim population of, 333; 344; 351; accounts of, at end of 17th c.; 354 *et sqq.*
Tihran, 217, 218
Timur, his invasions of Georgia, 123 *et sqq.*; at Mukhrani, 124; at Min-göl, 124-5; withdraws to Baylakan, 125; 285, 297, 315, 339; (Zamberlan), 324
Tin, not found in the Caucasus, 12; 18, 355
Tmogvi, a village and fortress in Javakheti, commandancy of, 102, 253; Sargis of (Tmogveli) at blockade of Kars, 107; and the Mongols, 113, 328; Taqiadin of (Tmogveli), 108
Todleben, Gen., in Georgia, 207, 211
Tokmak Khan, 155
Toktamish, Timur's campaigns against, 123 and note 2
Toll-houses, 271
Tolochanov, Russian ambassador in Georgia, 172
Tom-i (-ni), 34; definition and divisions of, 221; *mamasakhlisi* of, 221, 222
Topal Osman Pasha, 189 and note 1
Tori, a district of Trialeti, E. of the Mtkvari, 91; Shalva Mkhargrdzeli of (Toreli), 107, 111; Liparit of (Toreli), 116; Kakha of (Toreli), *ib.*
Torniké, 311
Tortomi, a river affluent of the Chorokhi, and a town and fortress of the name, 52, 57, 125, 297

Totems, 36 *et sqq.*
Trade-routes, from Colchis to Armenia, 49; from Chaneti to the Araks, 56, 57, 322; Caspian-Volga, 322 *et sqq.*; in the Caucasus under the Caliphate, 323 *et sqq.*; from the Volga to Khiva, 324; across Armenia under the Mongols, 325 *et sqq.*
Trans-Caucasian Trough, a general term applied to the country lying between the main chain of the Caucasian mountains and the *periperal rim* of the Armenian highlands, 7; accessibility of in Bronze Age, 14; 25, 47, 177
Treasure, of the Georgian Kings, 334
Treaties,
 of Belgrad, 190, note 3
 of Bucuresti, 217
 of Carlovich, 353
 of Erzerum, 190
 of Georgievsk, 210-11
 of Gulistan, 217
 of Jassy, 212
 of Kuchuk-Kainarji, 208, 209 note 1
 of Nymphæum, 336
 of Passarovich, 190, note 3
 Perso-Turkish of 1612, 184 note 1
 Perso-Turkish, of, 1636, 177
Trebizond, 52, 54, 55; Abu'l Fida's reference to, 56; Georgian troops in, 108; 122; fall of Comnenian Empire of, 135; Turkish occupation of, 138, 144; 166, 282-3; St. Sophia of, 296; trade of, during early Middle Ages, 322 and note 1; relations with the Mongols, 335; with Genoa, 336-8; with France and Burgundy, 339
Trees, tax on, 191, 263
Trialeti (Triare), a district of Kartli between the rivers Mtkvari and Ktzia, 9, 10, 54; described, 59; estates of Orbelianis in, 85; Giorgi I in, 88; Seljuks ravage, 91; Giorgi II's victory in, 93; invaded, 99; 102, 105, 143, 155
Tripoli, in Syria, 96
Tristan and Isolt compared with *Visramiani*, 318
Troy, referred to, 6, 12
Tsalendjikhi, a village in Mingrelia, N.W. of the Chanis-tsqali, 305
Tsanichites, a Laz patronymic, 56 note 2
Tsaritsin, 187
Tsereteli, family, 207; Rustem, defeats Russians at Kortokhti, 217
Tsereteli, M., quoted, 37
Tskhenis-tsqali, river (*horse's water*), a tributary of the Rioni, 7, 27, 50, 51
Tsuketi, *mo'uravate* of, in Kakheti, 140 note 1
Tsunda, ancient fortress in Trialeti, 52, 59; *Eristavate* of, 238
Tuapse, a village on the Circassian coast, 31
Tubal (Tabal, Tibal or Tobel), identified with Uplos, 12; in early sources, 17-18, 24-5, 61, 283 note 2

INDEX

Tukhareli, Saba, 311
Tukharisi, ancient fortress in the Chorokhi valley, 52, *Eristavate* of, 238
Tuman, 263; value of, 282 note 1
Turkistan, 89, 110
Turkomans, Georgians defeated by, 126; raids of, into Samtzkhé, *ib.*; intervention of, in Georgia, 133 *et sqq.*; Jevanshir, 197. See also Kara-Koyunlu
Turks, *Alpine* physical type among Anatolian, 21–2; T. peoples in N. Caucasus, 30–1; wolf-totem among, 36 note 2; early settlement of, in Kakheti, 63; 106; rise of Seljuk, 87 *et sqq.*; rise of Osmanli, 121; raids of, into Samtzkhé, 122; wars with Timur, 124–5; relations with Giorgi VII, 124–5; in the Caucasus, 132 *et sqq.*; rise of Ottoman power, 142 *et sqq.*; relations with Persia, 143–4; Persian war of 1578–86, 151–2, 155–7; suspicion of Russia, 164; expelled from Caucasian provinces by Persians, 165; tactics in Georgian politics, 168; relations with Taymuraz I, 171; policy in Georgia at end of 17th c., 177–8; agents in the N. Caucasus, 183–4 and note 1; Russian policy of, 185–6; invasion and occupation of Georgia, 186–8; Treaty of Hamadan, 188; unsuccessful invasion of Abkhazeti, 188–9; expulsion from Georgian provinces, 189–90; Treaty of Erzerum, 190; second war with Nadir, 193–4; War with Russia, 206; intervention in Imereti, 207; operations in Georgia, 207–8; operations in the Kuban, 209, 211; policy during Napoleonic wars, 217–18; 263, 275, 279, 282, 284, 296, 297; on the Volga, 324 *et sqq.*; in Anatolia, 330; T. merchants in Imereti, 346; exports of Imerian iron to, 346; policy in Georgia, 349, 352–3; and Black Sea trade, 355–6; unfavourable comparison of with Georgians, 358
Tusheti, Tushes, the country round the head-waters of the Alazani, occupied by the Tush tribe, 62, 107, 124 and note 1, 167, 173, 203, 215
Tushmali, 349
Tzikhé-Darbassé, 105
Tzikhé-Didi (*castle-great*) in Iberia, 52, 61
Tzikhis-patroni, 250
Tzikhistav-i (-ni), 243
Tzitzianov, Paul Dmitriivich, Viceroy of the Caucasus, his character and methods, 216; his death, 217
Tzitzishvili, *gwari* of, 178, 248; Bagrat, 188; Archbishop Kirilé, 191 note 4; Zakharia, 199–200; plots of family against Irakli II, 203; 216
Tzivi, a mountain and commune of Kakheti between the Yori and the Alazani, massacre of nobles at, 122
Tzkhumuri, 277
Tzulukidze, family, 207

Uazno (-ni), definition of term, 225; social position of, 225–6; division of, 226–7; promotion of, 229; 255
Udi (Otene), Armenian province, 64
Ugwaro (-ni), 225, 255. Also see *Uazno (-ni)*
Ujarma, in Kakheti, 63
Ukhutsesi, 258 note 1
Uljaitu, Il-Khan, 120, 121
Ulu, 114
Ummayyads, 260
Upali, 226
Upleba, 34 note 1, 222 note 1
Uplistzikhé (*the castle of Uplos*), an ancient city of Iberia, on the middle Mtkvari, antiquity of the name, 17; described, 52–3, 60 and note 5; capital of Kartlian Bagratids, 81; reference to 85; victory of Irakli II at, 207
Uplos, eponymous hero of the Georgians, identified with Tubal, 12, 16, 24; reference to, 41
Urartu, Urartians (Kingdom of, called also Nairi, Khaldi or Van), influence of, as far north as the Araks valley, 15; language of, *ib.* and note 1; importance of cultural influence of, 16; 23, 34 note 1, 36, 51, 57
Urban II, Pope, 95
Urbnissi (*Uriat-Ubani = the Jew's town*), an ancient town of Iberia, on the middle Mtkvari, 52, 60 and note 5, 267
Urdubad, 108
Urumia (Urmia), lake and city, 7
Usbeg, *Atabeg* of Azerbaijan, 106, 110
Usbegs, of Turkistan, relations of the Ottoman Sultans with, 184 note 1
Utavisuplo (-ni), 227
Utemish, a village of Kara-Kaituk, 184
Uvarov, Countess, 300, 302, 304–5, 307
Uzun-Hassan, of the Kara-Koyunlu, 133, 138, 339, 340

Vadchar-i (-ni), first mention made of, in Georgian documents, 231; division of, *ib.*; *Did-Vadchar-i (-ni)*, *ib.*; their participation in the state affairs, *ib.*; distinctive dress of, *ib.*
Vadchart-Ukhutsesi, 231
Van (Biana or Tospis), the capital of the Kingdom of Urartu, 15; later of the Kingdom of Vaspurakan, 81, 82
Van, Lake, 7, 15
Vandals, 30
Varangians (Warangs, Warings) in Kiev, 83; in army of Basil II, 88; in army of Bagrat III, 90, 264
Vardis-Tzikhé (Rhodopolis) described, 50; destroyed, 78
Vardzia, in Samtzkhé, account of, 53
Varg, 230
Vargi da satsnauri, 230
Varlaam's Saga, 317
Varna, 338
Varranda, an Armenian *melikate* of Karabagh, 185 note 2

INDEX

Vaspurakan, an Armenian kingdom composed of the districts round Lake Van, 81, 82, 86; ravaged by Seljuks and ceded to Basil II, 87

Vathi (Vathie). See Poti

Vatican, policy of, in Georgia, 171-2, 329-30, 335-9; relations with the Mongols, 335

Vazir-i (*-ni*), definition of term, 260; grades and seniority of, 261

Vaziroba, 261

Vaz-irum, 260

Vegetables, tax on, 187; abundance of, in Imereti, 346

Vegetation, sanctity of, 35 *et sqq.*

Vellum, 330

Velours, 346, 348

Vengeance, principle of, 275

Venice, contact of Tamara with, 329; relations with Byzantium, 335-6; in the Black Sea, 336; diplomacy of, in Georgia, 339 *et sqq.*

Vezhini, ancient *Eristavate* of, 238

Virgin Mary, cult of, 40

Visramiani (*Visraminiani*), 318; quoted 328 note 4

Vladikavkaz—*Ruler of the Caucasus*, 3, 211

Volga, 113, 162, 207; trade up, 322 *et sqq.*; 338

Volkonski, Russian ambassador in Georgia, 171-2

WAKHTANG I, Gurgaslani, Iberian King, legendary character of his exploits, 76-7; his seed, 78-9; sacred standard of, 110; treasure of, 334

Wakhtang II, King of Georgia, 119

Wakhtang III, King of Georgia, 120

Wakhtang V (Shah Nawaz I), King of Kartli, 170, 173, 174; his character and reign, 176 *et sqq.*; 191 note 4, 351 note 4, 358

Wakhtang VI (Hussain-Quli-Khan), 176; policy in Persian crisis, 185; relations with Russia and Turkey, 185-6; character of, 186; misfortunes of, 186-7; at Derbend, 190; 197, 203, 216, 271, 273, 313; his literary activities, 316-17

Wakhtangi, a son of Irakli II, 215

Wakhushti, his account of Imereti, 7-8; his description of the Mtkvari, 8-9; quoted 50 *et sqq.*; his account of Kakheti under Alexander II, 150; 178, 184, 203, 261, 277, 287, 313; his work and life, 315-16; his account of feast-days, 331

Wakil, 192, 212

Wallachia, first printing-press imported into Georgia from, 316

Wardani, *Eristavi* of the Svans, revolt of, 93

Wardanisdze, family, 104, 105, 107; Kakhaberi becomes virtually independent in Guria, 137. See also Gurieli

Water, significance of names for, in formation of Caucasian tribal names, 29; sanctity of, discussed, 36

Wax, abundance of, in Imereti, 8; Colchian production of, 49 note 1; trade in, 325; 341, 349

Wesendonk, views on Georgian paganism, quoted, 36 *et sqq.*

Wheat, 53 note 1, 345

Wild-fowl, reaches of the Mtkvari, abound in, 12; considered incomparable, 352

Wild pig, in Imereti, 345, 352

William of Chiero, 338

Wine, trade in, 263, 336, 341, 355

Wisdom of Balavari, the (or *Barlaam and Joseph*), 317

Wolf, cult of, referred to, 36 and note 2; found in Imereti, 345

Women, industrial employment of, at Shamakha in 17th c., 353; condition of, at end of 17th c., 356; character and toilet of, 358 and notes 3 and 4

Wood-carving, 294

Wool, 330, 336, 355

XENOPHON, 17, 29; on troglodytic dwellings, 53 note 1; 55, 74 note 1, 267, 293

YAKUB KHAN, of the Kara Koyunlu, 138

Yalanuz-Cham-Dagh. See Arsianis-Mta

Yazdagird I, of Persia, 65, 66, 76

Yazdagird II, of Persia, 76

Yeletz, river, 123 note 2

Yemen, 318

Yeni Rabat (Antonisi), 296

Yermak, 164

Yésé (? Isa Khan) of Kakheti, 140, 152, 153

Yésé (Ali-Quli-Khan, or Mustafa Pasha), a passing King of Kartli, 180 and note 5; disreputable character of, 187, 188; 197

Yevlev, Russian emissary in Georgia, 172, 344 *et sqq.*

Yori, river, an affluent of the Mtkvari, 10, 16, 62 *et sqq.*, 98

Yuloni, a son of Irakli II, 215, 218

Yusuf Pasha, 193

Yusuf and Zuleika, a Georgian translation of, 171

Yuzgad, 299

ZADENI, a Georgian god, 37 *et sqq.*, 63

Zaghani (or Zagem), a royal town of the Kakhian Bagratids, N.E. of the Alazani, doubtfully identified on the map, 63, 171 note 1

Zakharia, Metropolitan, 344, 349

Zampi, Brother, Théatin of Mantua, 273

Zanar, Svan name for Mingrelians, *q.v.*

Zanavi, ancient town on the Mtkvari, 52, 60

Zarzma, on the Jaqis-tsqali, 296

Zarzmeli, Basil, 232

Zarzmeli, Serapion, the Life of, quoted, 228, 240

Zedamkhedvel-i (*-ni*) *sakmeta*, 257

Zedazadeni, a place on the left bank of the Aragvi, 42, 63; captured by David II, 98

Zekhi, Byzantine name for Circassians, *q.v.*

INDEX

Zend, script, 309, 310
Zeno, Caterino, 339
Zghvis-Kari (*the sea-gate*), Georgian name for Derbend, 10
Zhibiani, in Svaneti; Church of the Virgin of, 301–2
Zichi, Venetian name for Circassians, *q.v.*
Zifilis, a mediæval Italian name for Tiflis, 340
Zinjan, the town of, in Northern Persia, 108
Ziphias, revolt of, 88
Zorobabeli, Zankan, 246
Zubov, Platon, 212
Zubov, Valerian, 214

(NOTE.—It has not been possible to include in the Index the names occurring in the Supplementary Notes at the end of the Volume.)

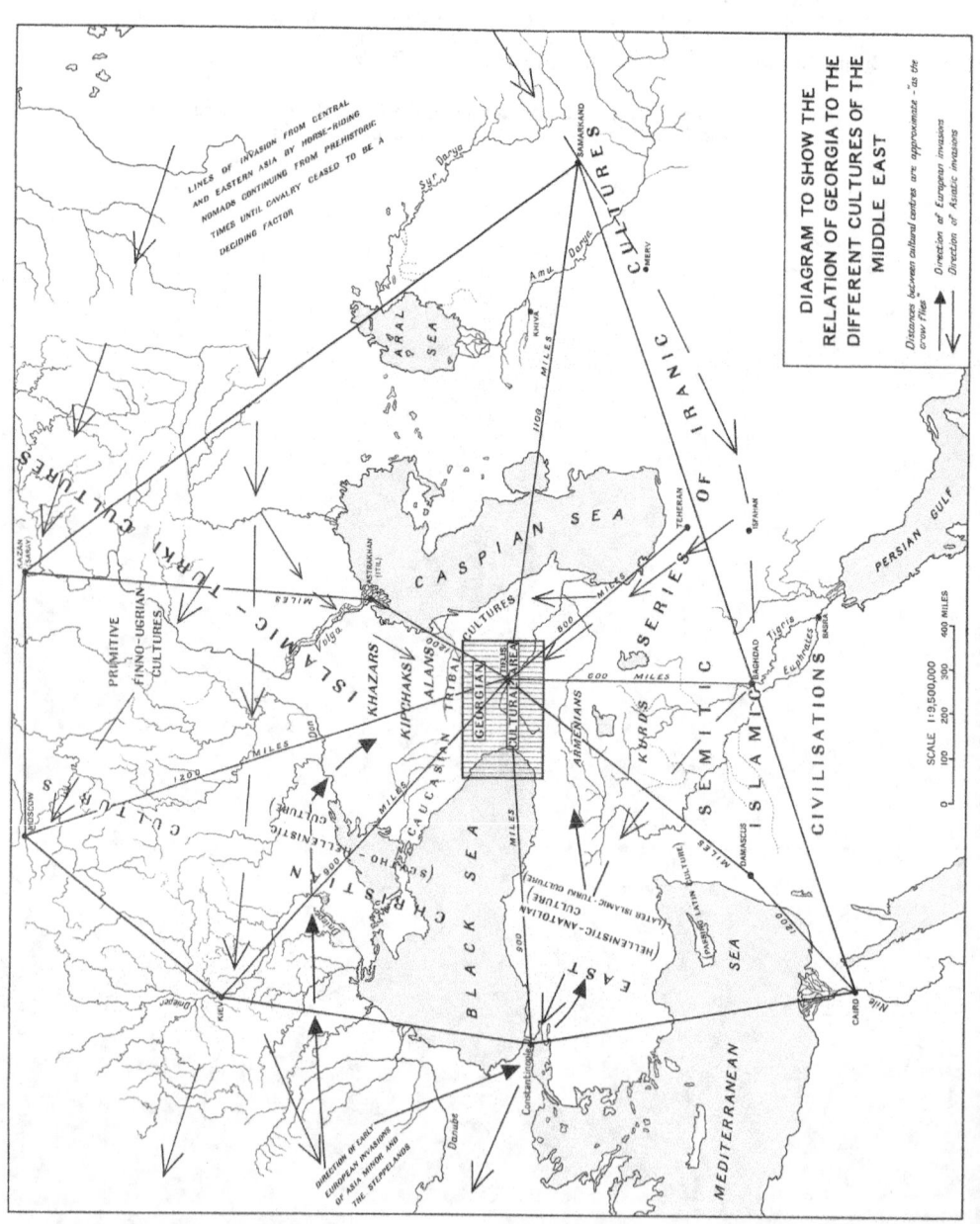

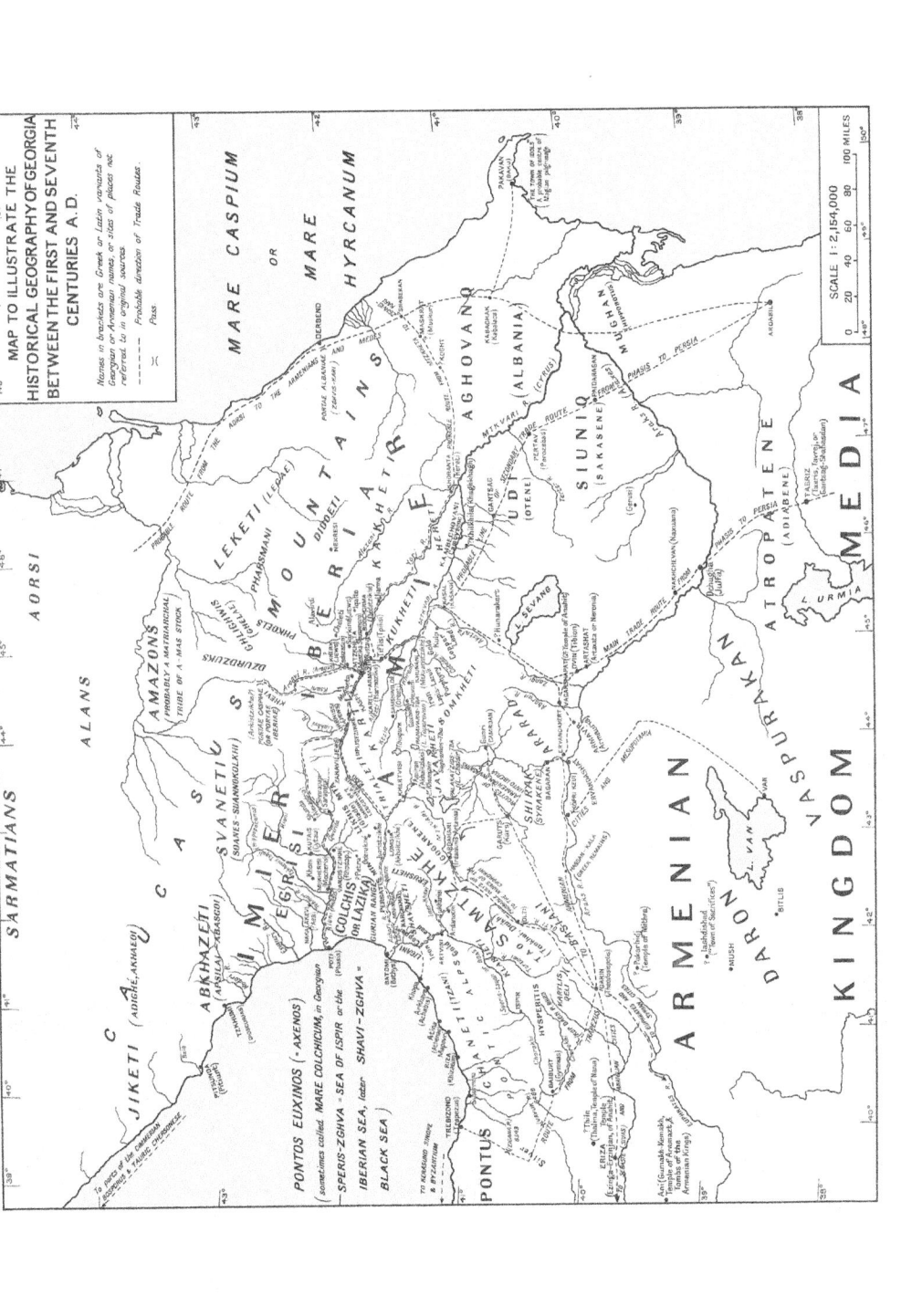

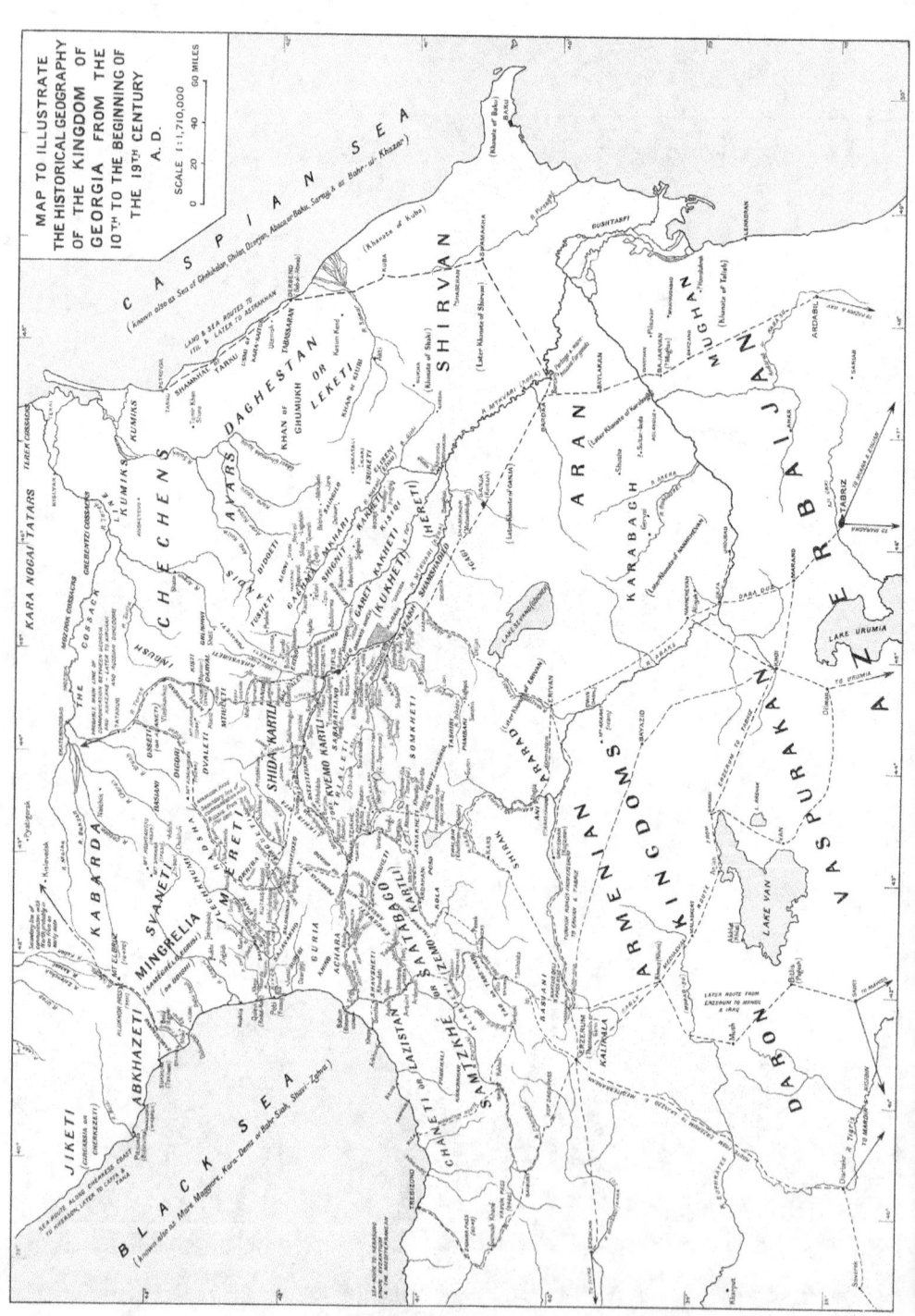

For Product Safety Concerns and Information please contact our EU representative GPSR@taylorandfrancis.com
Taylor & Francis Verlag GmbH, Kaufingerstraße 24, 80331 München, Germany

www.ingramcontent.com/pod-product-compliance
Lightning Source LLC
Chambersburg PA
CBHW052136300426
44115CB00011B/1408